Congress and Public Policy

A Source Book of Documents and Readings

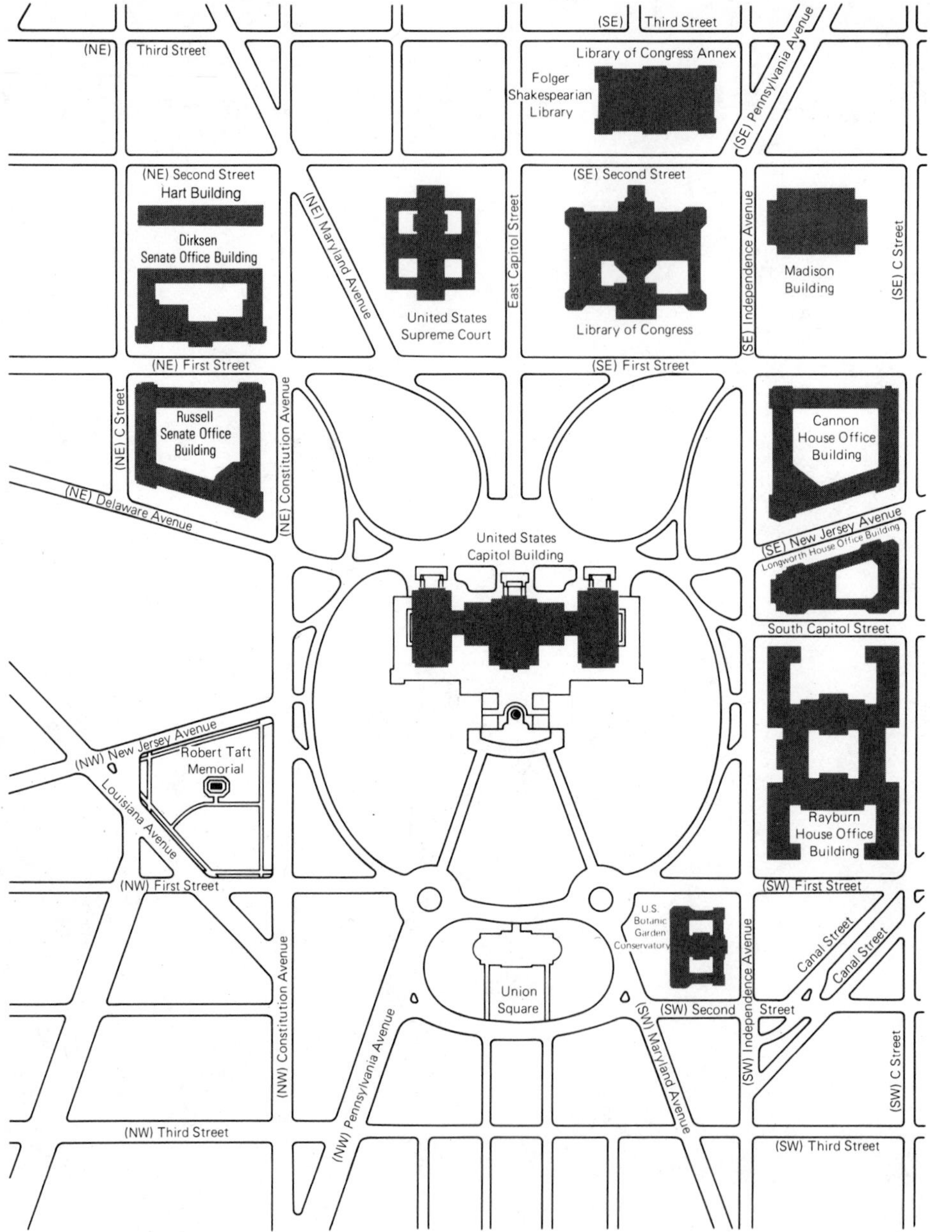

(SE)
Third Street
(NE)
Third Street
Library of Congress Annex
Folger
Shakespearian
Library
(SE) Pennsylvania Avenue
(NE) Second Street
Hart Building
Dirksen
Senate Office Building
(NE) Maryland Avenue
United States
Supreme Court
East Capitol Street
(SE) Second Street
Library of Congress
(SE) Independence Avenue
Madison
Building
(SE) C Street
(NE) First Street
(SE) First Street
(NE) C Street
Russell
Senate Office
Building
(NE) Constitution Avenue
(NE) Delaware Avenue
Cannon
House Office
Building
(SE) New Jersey Avenue
Longworth House Office Building
United States
Capitol Building
South Capitol Street
(NW) New Jersey Avenue
Robert Taft
Memorial
Louisiana Avenue
Rayburn
House Office
Building
(NW) First Street
(SW) First Street
U.S.
Botanic
Garden
Conservatory
Canal Street
Canal Street
(NW) Constitution Avenue
Union
Square
(SW) Second
Street
(SW) Independence Avenue
(NW) Pennsylvania Avenue
(SW) Maryland Avenue
(SW) C Street
(NW) Third Street
(SW) Third Street

CONGRESS AND PUBLIC POLICY

A Source Book of Documents and Readings

Second Edition

Edited by
David C. Kozak, Ph.D.
The National War College
John D. Macartney, Ph.D.
Defense Intelligence College

The Dorsey Press
Chicago, Illinois 60604

To our children
Steve Macartney
Jeffrey, Timothy, and Jacqueline Kozak

ISBN 0-256-05600-5

Library of Congress Catalog Card No. 86–50820

Printed in the United States of America

1 2 3 4 5 6 7 8 9 0 K 4 3 2 1 0 9 8 7

Foreword

Americans who work on Capitol Hill probably see Congress differently from the way this institution is viewed by their fellow Americans. Those of us who have the privilege of working in the Congress as members and staffers are likely to have greater detailed knowledge of its norms, structures, and processes, but that knowledge can suffer from a lack of objectivity.

News people regularly assigned to cover federal lawmaking, while generally objective, often tend to see and report the shape of the trees rather than the wider view of the forest.

It seems to me that the best place for a thoughtful citizen to seek a balanced understanding of Congress is academia. There it is that the most objective and panoramic, which is to say scientific, view of this turbulent bastion of liberty can be found.

Still, there is much to be learned from those who have been in the arena, the political practitioners. In this volume, masterfully edited by Professors Kozak and Macartney, one finds a satisfying blend of both academic and applied perspectives.

Former U.S. Representative Jim Lloyd and former U.S. Senator Fred Harris will take you behind the scenes and tell you a story so vivid that you can almost hear the sound of wood striking against wood as the gavel falls. The precise examples of bills, rules, committee reports, information sources, including the Congressional Record, found in this book are more educational than a thousand descriptive newspaper articles could ever be.

The discussions of Congress—history, elections, committee procedures, party organizations, floor rules, decision making, policy relationships, and perhaps most of all, change—provide a political science course most universities cannot match.

The editors cover ground heretofore unreported. Macartney's study of staff and home districts is illuminating, as is Kozak's huge study of congressional decision making. And, what is more, Dear Student, both studies are interesting, even, you might say, fun.

Not many students of government get the privilege of serving three-month internships on Capitol Hill. This book is the next best thing to being there.

*Honorable Andy Jacobs, Jr. (D-Ind.)**

*Editors' Note: Andy Jacobs represents the 10th District of Indiana. First elected to Congress in 1964, he served on the Select Committee on the Adam Clayton Powell case, writing a very favorably received book on this experience. Defeated in 1972, he was reelected in 1974, serving on the Ways and Means Committee and chairing its Health Subcommittee. A recent article in *Notre Dame Alumni Magazine* described him as "the best U.S. Congressman."

Preface

This is a unique academic reader, as well as a collection of data and documents about the Congress of the United States. While many selections here will be familiar to those who keep up with the literature, much of the material—more than half—comes from a different and heretofore untapped source: congressional documents. That source is a gold mine!

We know of no other institution that has committed so much effort to self-analysis, nor produced so many high-quality, readable studies of itself. Over the past decade, Capitol Hill has convened a number of special committees and commissions, each given the task of analyzing the legislative branch and producing reform proposals. After the Bolling Committee came the Obey and Patterson Commissions. Meanwhile, over in the Senate, there were the Stevenson Committee and the Hughes Commission, and last year, the Quayle Committee.[1]

Congressional scholars know only too well how meager were the outcomes of those reform efforts, but of more lasting value are the analytical outputs, the by-products. Although many of the specific reform recommendations came to naught, their legacy is volume upon volume of high-quality data and analysis written by both reputable scholars and staff members of the Congressional Research Service. Selections from these documents appear in this book.

In assembling this reader, we found that the reports of those prominent reform commissions were really only the tip of a documentary iceberg. To begin with, many working papers and preliminary studies did not make it into the final reports. We've included some of those. Beyond that, we discovered an incredible array of useful material in such miscellaneous Hill products as a Senate history by Senator Robert Byrd (D-W. Va.) printed in the *Congressional Record*, a handbook for newly hired congressional employees, glossy public information handouts, detailed synopses of legislative procedures, histories provided by various leadership offices, internal publications such as *Staff* magazine and *Roll Call*, and research products, as well as bylaws from various caucuses and releases from lobbying groups. Generally speaking, this material is well-written and very informative.

In addition to the analytical materials described above, we've included a number of exhibit documents as examples of everyday items on the

[1]The formal titles of these bodies are: Bolling (House Select Committee on Committees, 1973–1974); Obey (Commission on Administrative Review, 1976–1977); Hughes (Commission on the Operation of the Senate, 1976–1976); Stevenson (Senate Select Committee on Committees, 1976–1977); Patterson (House Select Committee on Committees, 1979–1980) and Quayle (Temporary Select Committee to Study the Senate Committee System, 1983–1984). The reform efforts are named after their chairmen: Representative Richard Bolling (D-Mo.), Representative David Obey III (D-Wis.), Senator Harold Hughes (D-Iowa), Senator Adlai Stevenson III (D-Ill.), Representative Jerry M. Patterson (D-Calif.), and Senator Dan Quayle (R-Ind.).

Hill—a bill, a rule, a Whip Notice, a few pages from a calendar, a Dear Colleague letter, and such. The idea here is to give readers, especially undergraduate students, a source book that features an insider's experiential "feel" for the legislative milieu and "blood" of Congress.

The book is not only made up of congressional documents and exhibits, of course. We've supplemented that material with a number of excellent excerpts and articles from academic books and journals, together with original essays by leading authorities. The original essays in this second edition are particularly noteworthy. Alan Abramowitz, a leading authority on congressional elections, provides a basic statement on those phenomena together with predictions for the watershed 1986 elections. Staffers John Oberg and Lee Godown write about service in the Senate and the House, respectively. Larry Burton, a former aide to Senate Republican leadership, discusses this unique vantage point. A professional lobbyist, Rich Roberts, gives an overview of his craft. Noted budget expert Howard Shuman writes about the Gramm-Rudman Act. Roger Davidson gives an up-to-date perspective on the "two Congresses."

In this second edition, we excerpted from some of the major works that have appeared since the first edition in 1981: Gary Jacobsen on congressional elections, Smith and Deering on subcommittees, Barbara Sinclair on party leadership, Norm Ornstein on the President and Congress, and John Johannes on legislative casework. Also, for the first time since its appearance in 1977, we offer a reproduction of Fenno's important "Congressmen in Their Constituencies." The resulting volume, we believe, will be useful to graduate scholars as well as new staffers and interested observers of Congress and public policy. We expect it to be particularly valuable for undergraduate courses focused on the Hill. Our intention is to provide a collection that advances an understanding of basic concepts and fundamental points.

The substance and organization reflects the two editors' very different approaches to matters congressional. Both teach and write about Congress, but David Kozak is more apt to focus on the legislative process and the floor votes of members, while John Macartney is fascinated by the organizational/bureaucratic dynamics and the contributions of staff. Those orientations are evident in the table of contents, which also reveals selections on the history of Congress, elective politics, the membership, the committee system, partisan leadership, legislative rules and procedures, and public policy. We believe we are presenting a most comprehensive collection, containing an unparalleled variety of materials.

As is the case in all major endeavors, this project was not completed alone. The editors received much advice, encouragement, and assistance. Professor Samuel C. Patterson, former editorial adviser for the Dorsey series in political science, provided the initial impulse. Walter Oleszek and Roger Davidson of the Congressional Research Service were instrumental in pointing the way to a wealth of documents. Indeed, Oleszek's bookshelves at CRS were an absolutely indispensable source, especially for working papers from now-disbanded committees and commissions. Additionally, Roger Davidson, now serving as the current Dorsey editorial adviser, gave thoughtful advice and helpful encouragement for this second edition. We wish to acknowledge the helpful suggestions provided by the following colleagues: Sandy Maisel, Colby College; Glenn R. Parker, Florida State University; and William M. Lunch, Oregon State University.

Two former members of Congress, Representative Jim Lloyd and Senator Fred Harris (both political scientists) were especially helpful. Along with encouragement and sage advice came original pieces from each. Also, Jim Lloyd made his Hill office available to us as a base while we were chasing down all those documents in the fall of 1980. In addition, he gave a great deal of useful advice that has found its way into these pages. Many thanks also go to Congressman Andy Jacobs (D-Ind.) and his staff, David Bryant, Phyllis Coehlo, Cathy Noe, Tricia Roberson, and David Wildes, for sponsoring the second edition; to Lee Godown and Dan McGinn of Congressman Bob Wise's (D-W. Va.) office; and to Greg Pallas and Edna Ravnholt of Senator Jim Exon's (D-Neb.) office.

Overall, the lion's share of kudos and thanks are due to Maryanne M. Kozak. Nominally a part-time secretarial assistant for this project, her contributions greatly exceeded her status. Along with her own busy life as a wife, mother, and English instructor at Northern Virginia Community College, she did everything from typing to proofreading, correspondence, and editing. We simply could not have made it without her.

A final word on our numbering system for tables and figures within individual selections: They are numbered sequentially throughout the book, with each chapter and essay number in the collection preceding the table number. Thus, the second table in the third article in Chapter 4 becomes Table 4.3.2.

It goes without saying that we remain fully responsible for the contents, although we'll always be tempted to claim that the inevitable minor discrepancies or omissions were probably the faults of our employer, our publisher, the individual contributors, the other co-editor, or mischievous gremlins.

David C. Kozak
John D. Macartney

List of Contributors

Abramowitz, Alan I. Professor of Political Science, State University of New York at Stony Brook

Bibby, John F. Professor of Political Science, University of Wisconsin, Milwaukee

Blakely, Steve. Correspondent, *Congressional Quarterly*

Bullock, Charles S., III. Richard Russell Professor of Political Science, University of Georgia

Burton, Larry. Legislative Liaison Specialist, Office of Management and Budget, former Legislative Assistant to the Republican Majority Leadership of the Senate

Carroll, Holbert N. Professor of Political Science, University of Pittsburgh

Cigler, Allan J. Political Science Professor, University of Kansas

Davidson, Roger H. Senior Specialist in American Government and Public Administration, The Congressional Research Service, Library of Congress, and Professor of Political Science, Georgetown University

Deering, Christopher J. Associate Professor of Political Science at The George Washington University

Dove, Robert B. Parliamentarian of the U.S. Senate

Fenno, Richard F., Jr. Kenan Professor of Political Science at the University of Rochester

Fisher, Louis. Specialist in American National Government at the Congressional Research Service, Library of Congress

Franklin, Grace A. Senior Research Associate at the Mershon Center at the Ohio State University

Godown, Lee. Legislative Assistant to Congressman Bob Wise (D-Va.)

Harris, Fred R. Professor of Political Science, the University of New Mexico, and a former United States Senator, presidential candidate, and Chairman of the National Democratic Committee

Hero, Rodney. Associate Professor, Graduate School of Public Affairs, and Department of Political Science, University of Colorado, Colorado Springs

Hildenbrand, William F. Secretary of the U.S. Senate

Jacobson, Gary C. Professor of Political Science, University of California, San Diego

Johannes, John R. Professor, Department of Political Science, Marquette University, Milwaukee, Wisconsin

Jones, Charles O. Robert Kent Gooch Professor of Government and Foreign Affairs at the University of Virginia

Keefe, William J. Professor of Political Science at the University of Pittsburgh

Lanoue, David. Ph.D. Candidate in the Department of Political Science, State University of New York at Stony Brook

Lloyd, Jim. Member of Congress (D-Calif.), 1974–1980, and a college teacher

Loomis, Burdett A. Political Science Professor, University of Kansas

Malbin, Michael J. Resident Fellow, American Enterprise Institute for Public Policy Research

Mann, Thomas E. Executive Director, the American Political Science Association

Mayhew, David R. Professor of Political Science, Yale University

Oberg, John H. President, Association of Independent Colleges and Universities of Nebraska, formerly Chief Legislative Assistant to Senator James Exon (D-Neb.)

Ogul, Morris S. Professor of Political Science, University of Pittsburgh

Oleszek, Walter J. Specialist on Congress, Congressional Research Service, Library of Congress

Ornstein, Norman J. Resident Fellow, American Enterprise Institute, adjunct professor, Johns Hopkins University, formerly Political Editor for "The Lawmakers," a weekly TV series on PBS

Patterson, Samuel C. Professor of Political Science at the Ohio State University, Managing Editor, *The American Political Science Review*

Ripley, Randall B. Professor and Chairperson in the Department of Political Science at the Ohio State University

Roberts, Rich. Former college professor, now President and Director of Roberts and Co., a lobbying firm representing outdoor and roadside advertising

Shuman, Howard E. Professor of Public Policy, The National War College, and former Chief Administrative Assistant to Senators William Proxmire and Paul Douglas

Sinclair, Barbara. Professor of Political Science, University of California, Riverside

Smith, Hedrick L. Chief Washington Correspondent, *New York Times*, and Fellow, American Enterprise Institute

Smith, Steven S. Senior Fellow, The Brookings Institution, and Associate Professor of Political Science, Northwestern University

About the Editors

Kozak, David C. BA, Gannon College; MA, Kent State University; advanced work Wichita State University; Ph.D., University of Pittsburgh. Formerly: Associate Professor, U.S. Air Force Academy; Adjunct Professor, Graduate School of Public Affairs, University of Colorado; 1981-82 American Political Science Association Congressional Fellow, serving on the staffs of Congressmen Jim Lloyd and Andy Jacobs and Senator Exon. Currently Professor of Public Policy, The National War College. Author of *Contexts of Congressional Decision Behavior* (1984) and *Doing The Business of Congress* (forthcoming) and co-editor and contributor to *Readings on the American Presidency* (1984) and *Bureaucratic Politics and National Security* (forthcoming).

Macartney, John D. BS. USAF Academy: MA. Ph.D., University of California, Los Angeles. Career Air Force officer and fighter pilot, currently serving as the Commandant, Defense Intelligence College, in Washington D.C. Former Associate Professor at both the U.S. Air Force Academy and The National War College.

Brief Contents

Contents

Chapter One

The Historical Context

As with any institution, Congress must be viewed in historical context in order to be understood.

A historical review of Congress is most revealing. It shows over time different organizations, different relationships with Presidents, different public expectations and demands. The Congress of the 20th century is a very different animal from the Congresses of the 18th and 19th centuries, and there is every reason to believe that the Congress of the 21st century will be strikingly different from its 20th-century predecessor.

The selections in this section will address the historical context of Congress by illustrating different normative perspectives that have evolved over time and by examining recent changes in the modern Congress.

Reading 1.1

Historical Perspectives on Congress

Charles O. Jones

Over time, the U.S. Congress has evolved through a number of stages: incipient institutionalization, strong party government, committee government, subcommittee government, and individualism (or member-oriented government). Although this development has been somewhat chronological, it has also been somewhat cyclical inasmuch as each generation has experienced traces of each of these forms.

Relations with the President comprise a most important facet of congressional development. The following excerpt is the introduction to a major text in the field. It gives an overview of different historical perspectives on Congress, with emphasis on the different interpretations of the proper congressional relationship with the Presidency: legislative primacy, presidential primacy, cooperative government, and adversarial government. In reading this, one should ask which interpretation best describes congressional relations with the Reagan administration and which is likely to dominate the 1990s and beyond?

The Continental Congress met in York, Pennsylvania, in the fall of 1777 to establish a confederation. It began work in Lancaster but only held one session there. "It was deemed the part of wisdom to put a good-sized river [the Susquehanna], in addition to the many miles, between them and the British army" (Burnett, 1964: 248). And so the delegates moved across the river to York. The issue of voting in the new Congress came up immediately and was resolved in favor of one vote for each state. On October 14 the issues of the size of state delegations and length of terms for delegates were resolved. The results are contained in Article V of the Articles of Confederation—our first national constitution.

> Article V. For the more convenient management of the general interests of the united states, delegates shall be annually appointed in such manner as the legislature of each state shall direct. . . .
>
> No state shall be represented in Congress by less than two, nor by more than seven Members; and no person shall be capable of being a delegate for more than three years in any term of six years. . . .
>
> In determining questions in the united states in Congress assembled, each state shall have one vote.

In commenting on these provisions, Edmund Cody Burnett declared that "Congress effectively inoculated itself with the germ of pernicious anemia" (1964: 250). A British observer, James Bryce, wrote that: "This Confederation, which was not ratified by all the States till 1781, was rather a league than a national government" (Bryce, 1915: 20). The Articles themselves declared as much in Article III: "The said states hereby severally enter into a firm league of friendship with each other." The league was not to last. In a sequence of actions familiar to all, a group met in Annapolis, Maryland, to discuss trade problems; this group recommended that Congress authorize "a future Convention, with more enlarged powers;" and the Congress did, on February 21, 1787, pass a resolution authorizing the Constitutional Convention (Tansill, 1927: 46).

> Resolved that in the opinion of Congress it is expedient that on the second Monday in

Source: Charles O. Jones, *The United States Congress: People, Peace, and Policy* (Chicago, Ill.: Dorsey Press, 1982), pp. 1–9.

> May next a Convention of delegates who shall have been appointed by the several states be held at Philadelphia for the sole and express purpose of revising the Articles of Confederation and reporting to Congress and the several legislatures such alterations and provisions therein as shall when agreed to in Congress and confirmed by the states render the federal constitution adequate to the exigencies of Government and the preservation of the Union.

Shortly after the delegates finally assembled in late May 1787, Edmund Randolph of Virginia introduced a bold plan for a new government. On the very next day, Randolph went even further by introducing a resolution "that a Union of the States merely federal will not accomplish the objects proposed by the articles of Confederation" and "that a *national* Government ought to be established consisting of a *supreme* Legislative, Executive and Judiciary."[1] The resolution was adopted and, according to Alfred H. Kelly and Winfred A. Harbison (1948: 124)

> The Convention had thus committed itself to a serious breach of its authority. Called to amend the Articles, a majority of the delegates had boldly decided to disregard their instructions and instead to create an entirely new frame of government.

Had the Convention decided to stay within its charge, it probably would have adopted the features of the so-called New Jersey plan, introduced by William Paterson on June 15. Significantly this plan did not change the unicameral legislature of the Articles, but it did give it more authority. Had it been accepted we may well have developed a parliamentary system since Congress was "authorized to elect a federal Executive" (Tansill, 1927: 205). But the New Jersey plan was not adopted.

The Randolph or Virginia plan provided for a two-house legislature. The pertinent provisions were as follows (Tansill, 1927: 116–17):

> 3. Resolved that the National Legislature ought to consist of two branches.
> 4. Resolved that the members of the first branch of the National Legislature ought to be elected by the people of the several States. . . .
> 5. Resolved that the members of the second branch of the National Legislature ought to be elected by those of the first, out of a proper number of persons nominated by the individual Legislatures.

Having agreed on two houses, the Convention then determined the basis of representation for each. The conflicts between the large and small states need not be reviewed here. Suffice it to say that they occupied a great deal of time and debate in Philadelphia. The final results are contained in Article 1 of the Constitution—a House of Representatives "composed of Members chosen every second year by the People of the several States" and a Senate "composed of two Senators from each State, chosen by the Legislature thereof, for six years."

So the United States Congress was born. There had never been any institution quite like it for governing a nation. It remains an extraordinary legislature in the world today. And it is constantly undergoing change. As William J. Keefe rightly observes (1980: 143): "No new Congress is the same as the previous one. Congresses differ from one session to the next and in some respects even from one month to the next." What an exciting if complex institution to explain.

HISTORICAL PERSPECTIVES ON CONGRESS

What did the founding fathers think they had created in Article I? And what functions have been attributed to Congress through time? Sampling various perspectives on the role of Congress serves the useful purpose of illustrating the adaptability of this institution to the dynamics of national politics. Not only does its role shift with the political context, but it may even appear to serve different functions for different people at any one time. This adaptability should not surprise us. It is well suited to the interdependency of institutions so carefully devised by the framers. So let's turn first to the creation.

In their analysis of political bargaining in the United States, Robert A. Dahl and Charles E. Lindblom observe that "no unified, cohesive, acknowledged, and legitimate representative-leaders of the 'national majority' exist in the United States" (1953: 336). Other political systems are designed to facilitate the development and expression of national majorities. In our case, however (Dahl and Lindblom, 1953: 336):

> The convention did its work so well that even when a Congressional majority is nominally of the same party as the president, ordinarily they do not speak with the same voice.
>
> On a great many questions the "preferences of the greater number" or "the majority" is a fiction. But even if there were a national majority in the United States, it could not rule unless it were so overwhelmingly large as to include within its massive range the diverse "majorities" for which different elements in the bureaucracy, the president, and congressmen all claim to speak.

What Dahl and Lindblom have described sounds like a football team unable to score even when the opposing players leave the field! What possible rationale could there be for devising a system with so many internal checks? The answer to this question is found in *The Federalist*, that remarkable set of essays by Alexander Hamilton, John Jay, and James Madison, written in support of ratification of the Constitution. The argument, greatly simplified, goes something like this.[2]

> ***Republicanism***
>
> It is essential to such a government that it be derived from the great body of the society, not from an inconsiderable proportion, or a favored class of it; otherwise a handful of tyrannical nobles . . . might aspire to the rank of republicans (Number 39).
>
> ***Separation of powers***
>
> The accumulation of all powers, legislative, executive, and judiciary, in the same hands, whether of one, a few, or many, and whether hereditary, self-appointed, or elective, may justly be pronounced the very definition of tyranny (Number 47).
>
> ***Legislative primacy***
>
> In republican government, the legislative authority necessarily predominates (Number 51). Its constitutional powers being at once more extensive, and less susceptible of precise limits, it can, with the greater facility, mask, under complicated and indirect measures, the encroachments which it makes on the coordinate departments (Number 48).
>
> ***Legislative expansion***
>
> We have seen that the tendency of republican governments is to an aggrandizement of the legislative at the expense of the other departments (Number 49).
>
> ***Bicameralism***
>
> The remedy for this inconveniency [natural legislative primacy and expansion] is to divide the legislature into different branches; and to render them, by different modes of election and different principles of action, as little connected with each other as the nature of their common functions and their common dependence on the society will admit (Number 51).
>
> ***Checks and balances***
>
> It may even be necessary to guard against dangerous encroachments by still further precautions (Number 51). Ambition must be made to counteract ambition (Number 51).

As collected, these pronouncements add up to an extraordinarily cautious approach to government making. The people must be represented in government, but not all in one place. Given the power of the idea of popular representation, the legislature is bound to dominate and one simply cannot permit that to happen. Therefore it is necessary to divide the legislature and, as well, give the other branches some authority to override its judgments. This remarkable balancing act between institutional independence and dependence produced an ambiguity in the political and policy functions to be performed by each branch. This ambiguity, in turn, has led to widely varying interpretations regarding the proper role of Congress in the national policy process. Among the more prominent interpretations are those promoting legislative primacy, presidential primacy, and mixed government (either cooperative or adversarial).[3]

Legislative Primacy

The inevitability of legislative primacy led James Madison and his coessayists in *The Federalist* to justify the need for checks and balances. Their statement on the subject (see above) provides the rationale of those supporting legislative superiority—legislators come from the people. But it was left to John C. Calhoun in 1817 to provide the most eloquent statement on the subject. Then serving in the House of Representatives from South Carolina, Calhoun articulated the view that the separation of powers by no means implied equality of power among the branches. Congress was unquestionably supreme because of its close connections to the people.

> The prevailing principle [for our structure of government] is not so much a balance of power as *a well-connected chain of responsibility*. That responsibility commenced here, and this House is the centre of its operation. The members are elected for two years only; and at the end of that period are responsible to their constituents for the faithful discharge of their public duties. . . .
>
> If we turn our attention to what are called the co-ordinate branches of our Government, we find them very differently constructed. The Judiciary is in no degree responsible to the people immediately. To Congress, to this body, is the whole of their responsibility. Such, too, in a great measure is the theory of our Government as applied to the Executive branch. It is true the President is elected for a term of years, but that term is twice the length of ours [in the House]; and, besides, his election is in point of fact removed in all of the States three degrees from the people; the Electors in many of the States are chosen by the State Legislatures. . . .
>
> This, then, is the essence of our liberty; Congress is responsible to the people immediately, and the other branches of Government are responsible to it (Hyneman and Carey, 1967: 150–51; emphasis added).

The chain of responsibility theory was certainly forceful before the popular election of presidential electors. By 1836, however, in only one state, Calhoun's own South Carolina, were electors still chosen by the state legislature. All other states held popular elections, thus permitting the president to claim legitimacy by reason of direct public approval. Still many members of Congress and others continue to rationalize legislative superiority within the national political system.

Presidential Primacy

On March 15, 1789, Thomas Jefferson wrote to James Madison expressing concerns about the new government:

> The tyranny of the legislature is really the danger most to be feared, and will continue to be so for many years to come. The tyranny of the executive power will come in its turn, but at a more distant period.[4]

The dominance of the executive over Congress may be said to have developed as a consequence of the growing complexity of issues facing the national government. Though these forces were understood by Woodrow Wilson, it was not until the Franklin D. Roosevelt administrations that developments shaped the modern presidency and encouraged its imperial quality. Certainly by the end of the 19th century, Congress was the premier institution in Washington. In his classic work, *Congressional Government*, Woodrow Wilson confirmed

Madison's fears about the legislature. (1913: 43, 45, 57).

> . . . the power of Congress has become predominant . . . Accordingly it has entered more and more into the details of administration, until it has virtually taken into its own hands all the substantial powers of government. . . . Anyone who is unfamiliar with what Congress actually does and how it does it . . . is very far from a knowledge of the constitutional system under which we live.[5]

Two world wars and a great depression contributed a vastly strengthened presidency to national politics. Dubbed the imperial presidency by Arthur Schlesinger, Jr., the White House came to be the center of decisionmaking. Fred I. Greenstein concludes that with the Franklin Roosevelt administrations "the presidency began to undergo not a shift but rather a metamorphosis" (in King, 1978: 45). The justification for expansion of executive authority was manifold. Among the more important reasons cited were the priority of international politics, the growing complexity of domestic issues, and the national constituency represented by the president. Schlesinger believes that the Nixon presidency brought matters to a head by forcing public realization of the extraordinary growth of power in the executive branch (1973: 377).

> The imperial presidency, created by wars abroad, was making a bold bid for power at home. The belief of the Nixon administration in its own mandate and in its own virtue, compounded by its conviction that the republic was in mortal danger from internal enemies, had produced an unprecedented attempt to transform the presidency of the Constitution into a plebiscitary presidency. If this transformation were carried through, the president, instead of being accountable every day to Congress and public opinion, would be accountable every four years to the electorate. Between elections, the president would be accountable only through impeachment and would govern, as much as he could, by decree.

Those promoting presidential primacy are not typically endorsing executive imperialism. They believe that the president alone can initiate large-scale integrated policy proposals to treat the complex issues of the modern era. Congress has a role in modifying these proposals and has a responsibility to check excesses of presidential power. This group remains steadfast, however, in the belief that the presidency has become the primary institution in the national policy process.

Mixed Government—Cooperative Mode

Another view is that neither branch works for the other. Both are viewed as contributing within their spheres of authority, knowledge, and expertise. It may be that this cooperation is what the framers intended. Unfortunately, however, they created many impediments to its realization. The separation of the election bases for the two institutions, as well as for the two houses of Congress, plus the checks each can impose on the actions of the other virtually make cooperation an unnatural act. Theoretically, political parties provide a means for joining the two institutions in a common cause and many persons have recommended as much. The Committee on Political Parties of the American Political Science Association described the potential role for parties as follows (1950: 89):

> The president could gain much when party leaders in and out of Congress are working together with him closely in matters concerning the party program. As party head, the president could then expect more widespread and more consistent support from the congressional leaders of his party. These, in turn, would present a more united front. As a result, on issues where the party as a party could be expected to have a program, the program of the party, of the party leaders in each house of Congress, and of the president would be the same program, not four different programs.

The committee also envisaged a rational division of responsibility emerging from a strengthened party system. The president would initiate proposals for congressional consideration, depending on political parties to provide support. Congress benefits from "prior effort and concrete recommendations." The president gains "dependable political support" (1950: 94).

This solution may sound attractive, but the separation of election base can result in insuperable obstacles to cooperation. Thus, for example, the cooperative mode as worked through the party system breaks down when a president of one party faces congressional majority leaders of the other party.[6] Even when the same party controls both, however, major differences may develop with few effective means for their resolution.

Mixed Government—Adversarial Mode

By this view, Congress and the presidency are coequal and competitive. The separation is accepted as is the improbability of strengthened political parties acting to promote cooperation. Each branch may be expected to encroach on the other with the court enforcing the separation where constitutional bounds are violated. I know of no one who publicly advocates this particular pattern of institutional behavior. But it has been characteristic of interbranch relations during periods in which different parties control the White House and Congress (*e.g.*, Truman and the 80th Congress, Nixon and the 93d Congress). Thus it results from each branch accepting its *own* primacy and refusing to yield to the other.

STUDYING THE MODERN CONGRESS

Note that the interpretations above are more than mental images of what should be. They also are useful descriptions of particular presidential-congressional relations, even in the 20th century. For example:

- Congressional primacy: The Cannon era (1902–1910, when Joseph G. Cannon was Speaker of the House), the weak president era (1920s—Harding, Coolidge, Hoover).
- Presidential primacy: The Roosevelt era (1933–1945), variable in the post–World War II era.
- Cooperative mode: The early Wilson and Johnson administrations (1913–1917, 1964–1966).
- Adversarial mode: The several administrations with split-party control (Wilson, 1919–1920; Truman, 1947–1948; Eisenhower, particularly 1959–1960; Nixon-Ford, 1973–1976), but also characterizing some relationships in Kennedy, 1961–1963; Johnson 1966–1968; and Carter, 1977–1981 despite Democratic control of both branches.

This review of historical perspectives as descriptions of reality tells us something else of profound importance about the Congress. Given the emergence of complex foreign and domestic issues in the 20th century, one might have expected Congress to suffer steady decline in influence. After all, how can a two-house legislature hope to grapple with the social, economic, and political issues of a technocratic society? It is true that Congress has had to accept a lesser role at various times since the 1930s, but the graph of legislative power is one of peaks and valleys not one of straight linear decline. And as of this writing Congress is definitely on one of the peaks.

Remarkable as it may seem, then, this awkwardly structured policy institution continues to position itself at the very center of national decisionmaking. In an era that invites the creation of efficient hierarchies, one is faced with having to explain the important political and policy functions performed by an inefficient and nonhierarchical Congress. How can this body even presume to participate actively in the development of programs to resolve such issues as energy supply and use, deterioration of the environment, redistribution of resources, complex questions associated with human relations? And how do the members justify getting involved in foreign policy issues—including going to war?

In large part Congress can justify its influential participation in the national policy process because of the persistent devotion in the country at large to the idea of political representation. The republican principles espoused by Madison remain strong today as does the practical expression of these principles by a legislature. In fact, Congress comes under particularly heavy criticism if it appears not to represent dominant opinions in the society. The point is that Congress continues to have power in the political system because most people want it that way. At the same time, however, it is as predictable as night following day that a representative body will be subject to constant criticism. Why? Simply because support for representation as an abstract principle by no means guarantees support for specific representative acts in regard to resolving public problems. In fact, almost any decision by a representative produces some winners and some losers. The losers may criticize the act, however, without abandoning their faith in representation as a way of doing business. The trick for Congress is to prevent the losers from drawing this second conclusion—that the whole system has gone wrong. The importance of events in the 1960s and 1970s (Vietnam, civil rights, the women's rights movement, environmental concerns) was precisely because they resulted in challenges to the current structure for realizing republican principles. It was not altogether surprising, therefore, that Congress sought to alter that structure—enacting more reforms in the 1970s than in any other period in its history.

Studying the modern Congress is an uncommonly challenging endeavor. I have always believed that, but I am even more persuaded after having written this book. The task would be greatly simplified if there were just one commonly accepted perspective on its role, or if it had less authority to get involved in all phases of all public issues, or if it would just stay in one place. But there are many perspectives on its role, it does have great power, and it is a moving target. This variability itself tells us something important about the institution—that it adapts to the changing national political environment, suggesting again how important it is since lesser structures resist change and suffer accordingly.

Reading 1.2

Theories of Congress

Roger H. Davidson,
David M. Kovenok,
and Michael K. O'Leary

Throughout American history several contending theories have emerged concerning the role of Congress in the American polity. In the following selection, Davidson, Kovenok, and O'Leary argue that the three major theories of Congress differ in terms of the functions of the legislature they choose to emphasize. This piece is especially useful for its enumeration of the major functions of Congress.

The Congress that emerged from the Philadelphia Convention of 1787 was the outgrowth of a prolonged institutional struggle, which affected both sides of the Atlantic and which produced a rather explicit theory of legislative functions. Though scholars often correctly observe that the Founding Fathers were pragmatic politicians who were loath to bind succeeding generations to excessively rigid formulations, they tend to neglect the fact that the pragmatism of the Framers was conditioned by an accepted body of political thought—a set of explicit beliefs about the nature of man and his institutions that were assumed to be valid. The Framers were not always able to see what they had done, but a serious study of their debates and commentaries indicates that they were intensely aware of what it was they *intended* to do.

Nothing less should be asked of contemporary students of legislative institutions. The advice which Harold D. Smith, then director of the Budget Bureau, gave to the LaFollette–Monroney Committee in 1945 is so relevant that it deserves repeating:

> This is a different sort of world from that which existed when the Constitutional Convention devised the framework of our government. Yet we still lack a penetrating and practical restatement of the role of representative assemblies in light of the changing problems under which they operate. . . . Your own talents and the keenest minds you can command could very well be devoted to rethinking the functions of the Congress under present conditions. A sound reformulation of the role of the representative body is basic to all the work of your committee.[1]

This was and is sound intellectual procedure, quite apart from the question of whether the constitutional formula demands radical revision. More important, Smith's injunction has not always been heeded by the proponents of congressional reform, including the LaFollette–Monroney Committee itself.

In recent years, a number of students have devoted explicit attention to the functions that the contemporary Congress performs in the political system.[2] Sometimes their conclusions have led them to propose or to evaluate remedial steps that would alter the roles of Congress or would assist it in performing its present roles more effectively. But it is fair to conclude that, by and large, students of Congress have not been sufficiently attentive to the theory of

Source: From *Congress in Crisis*, by Roger H. Davidson, David M. Kovenok, and Michael K. O'Leary, pp. 15–16, 35–36.

Congress. Ralph K. Huitt observed that "there is no 'model' of a proper legislature to which men of good intention can repair."[3]

What should be included in a theory of the legislature? Such a theory would begin with a series of factual generalizations specifying those functions that the legislature does in fact perform in a political system. Within this framework, specific traditions and practices may be accounted for and their consequences (intended or not) for the system may be spelled out. The analyst who chooses not to lay down his tools at this point would then set forth his view of an ideal legislature in an ideal system. He would specify the point of disharmony between this ideal world and the real world. Finally he would propose specific innovations that would bring the ideal world into being.

Hopefully, the theorist would be attentive to the probable and the unintended consequences of these innovations. More attention to objectives and possible consequences would make the proposal of reforms more meaningful than it has been in the past.[4]

Implicit in most of the recent writing on congressional reform are concepts that can be categorized into reasonably distinct theories of the proper functions of a legislative body. These theories are three in number: the "literary" theory, based primarily on a literal reading of the Constitution; the "executive-force" theory, which stresses policy leadership emanating from the President and the bureaucracy; and the "party-government" theory, which emphasizes the legislature's responsibility to the national party constituency. In terms of the weight given Congress in relation to the executive, the literary theory comes closest to legislative supremacy, the executive-force theory stands at the opposite pole, and the party-government theory stands somewhere in between. The overall weight that each theory gives to Congress is less important, however, than the kinds of functions which each assigns to Congress and to the other branches of government.

Divergent theories of the congressional function are the outgrowth of a complex, contentious society marked by numerous and often conflicting demands upon the institutions of government. Those citizens who urge upon the federal government an interventionist, problem-solving role will conceive of a legislature far differently than will those who see the government's role as a passive consensus-building one. The rules of the political game, as defined by the structure of institutions, cannot be divorced from the stakes for which the game is played. Moreover, these differing stakes are related to divergent intellectual interpretations of the role of institutions in a democratic polity. The theories of Congress should not be characterized merely as rationalizations for one's substantive positions; yet the two levels of debate are closely related. The struggle being waged over the character of Congress is indeed a part of the "war over America's future."

When the three theories are compared, a composite picture of the American Congress emerges—a picture with important convergences and deep differences. In this chapter's discussion, formal "powers" of the legislature were consciously played down, in favor of the broader and more fundamental concept of "function"—those things of major consequence that an institution (in this case, Congress) does for the political system as a whole. Figure 1.2.1 presents a rough comparison of the functions specified for Congress by the three theories discussed in this chapter, and the following paragraph defines these functions as they have emerged from the discussion.

Lawmaking is the traditional task of deliberating, often at a technical level, the actual content of policies. *Representation* is the process of articulating the demands or interests of geographic, economic, religious, ethnic, and professional constituencies. The legislator may accomplish this through actual contact (residence in a district, membership in a pressure group) or through "virtual" means ("taking into account" a

Figure 1.2.1.
Three theories of congressional functions.

	Literary Theory	Executive-Force Theory	Party-Government Theory
Primary Functions	Lawmaking Representation Consensus building Oversight	Legitimizing Oversight Representation	Policy clarification Representation
Secondary Functions	Policy clarification Legitimizing	Consensus building Policy clarification Lawmaking	Lawmaking Legitimizing Consensus building

viewpoint, perhaps by anticipating constituent response). *Consensus building* is the traditional bargaining function through which these various constituency demands are combined (or aggregated) in such a way that no significant constituency is severely or permanently disadvantaged. *Legitimizing* is the ratification of a measure or policy in such a way that it seems appropriate, acceptable, and authoritative. The legislature promotes *policy clarification* by providing a public platform where issues may be identified and publicized. *Legislative oversight* is the review of the implementation of policy in order to either alter the fundamental policy or introduce equity into the application of laws. Other functions—for example, *constituent service* and *recruitment of political leadership*—might also be explored, but are omitted here because they are not fundamental to the current debate over Congress.

The functions that theorists choose to emphasize have a profound impact upon the nature of the "model" Congress, not to mention the relationship of Congress with other elements in the political system. The most ambitious mandate is offered by the literary theory, which would involve the legislature at almost every step in the policymaking process—from initial conception to detailed review of implementation. In addition, this theory views the legislature as the prime representational and consensus-building institution in the political system. The executive-force theory, on the other hand, sees the legislature as ancillary to the executive establishment, which by the nature of things must assume the lead in both policy initiation and implementation. Like the board of directors of a corporation, Congress would have certain review powers but few operating powers; the legislature would find itself in most cases ratifying decisions of the executive "managers." According to the party-government conception, Congress (as well as the executive) would be set in motion by a strong and lucid party structure, serving chiefly as a forum for the staged confrontation of party ideologies.

No matter how far-reaching the consequences of accepting one theory over another, the differences in the concepts of the normative functions of Congress are differences of emphasis. Few observers would deny that Congress should, at one time or another, perform all the roles that have been discussed. Even the most dedicated advocate of executive dominance, for example, would undoubtedly concede that certain occasions may demand legislative initiative in policymaking. Most theories of congressional functioning therefore admit to what might be called the "multifunctionality" of the institution. The priority assigned to these various functions then becomes the all-important question.

Illustration 1.A.
The multiple thrusts of congressional reforms in the 1970s.

It has been argued that the 20th century Congress is strikingly different from the Congresses of the 18th and 19th centuries. The differences are said to lie in increased institutionalization: careerism, seniority, membership stability, leadership by inside party stalwarts, developed committee and party infrastructure, provincialism, differentiation from the executive branch, coherent norms, and professional staff.

These differences stem not only from changes in American society and politics in general, but from a spate of both leadership excesses and reactions to them in the period surrounding the turn of the century.

In the 1970s, a number of major changes and reforms occurred that significantly altered the 20th century Congress. A 1980 report by a U.S. House select committee on committees pinpointed and summarized these changes in the form of ten major developments:

1. More openness.
2. The expanding work load of Congress.
3. Growth in the number of ad hoc groups.
4. Larger membership turnover.
5. Greater dispersal of power of subcommittees.
6. Some steps toward a stronger speakership.
7. New multiple referral process.
8. Increase in staff.
9. Resurgence of the party caucus.
10. Decline of informal membership norms.

The report went on to argue that these changes had the following six effects: (1) shift from committee government to subcommittee government, (2) more difficulty in formulating coherent public policies given so many participants in policymaking, (3) numerous committee scheduling conflicts, (4) jurisdictional overlaps, (5) concern about committee capacity to conduct oversight, and (6) leadership having a harder time governing. The following illustration displays the specific twists and thrusts of congressional reforms in the 1970s.

Illustration 1.A. (concluded)

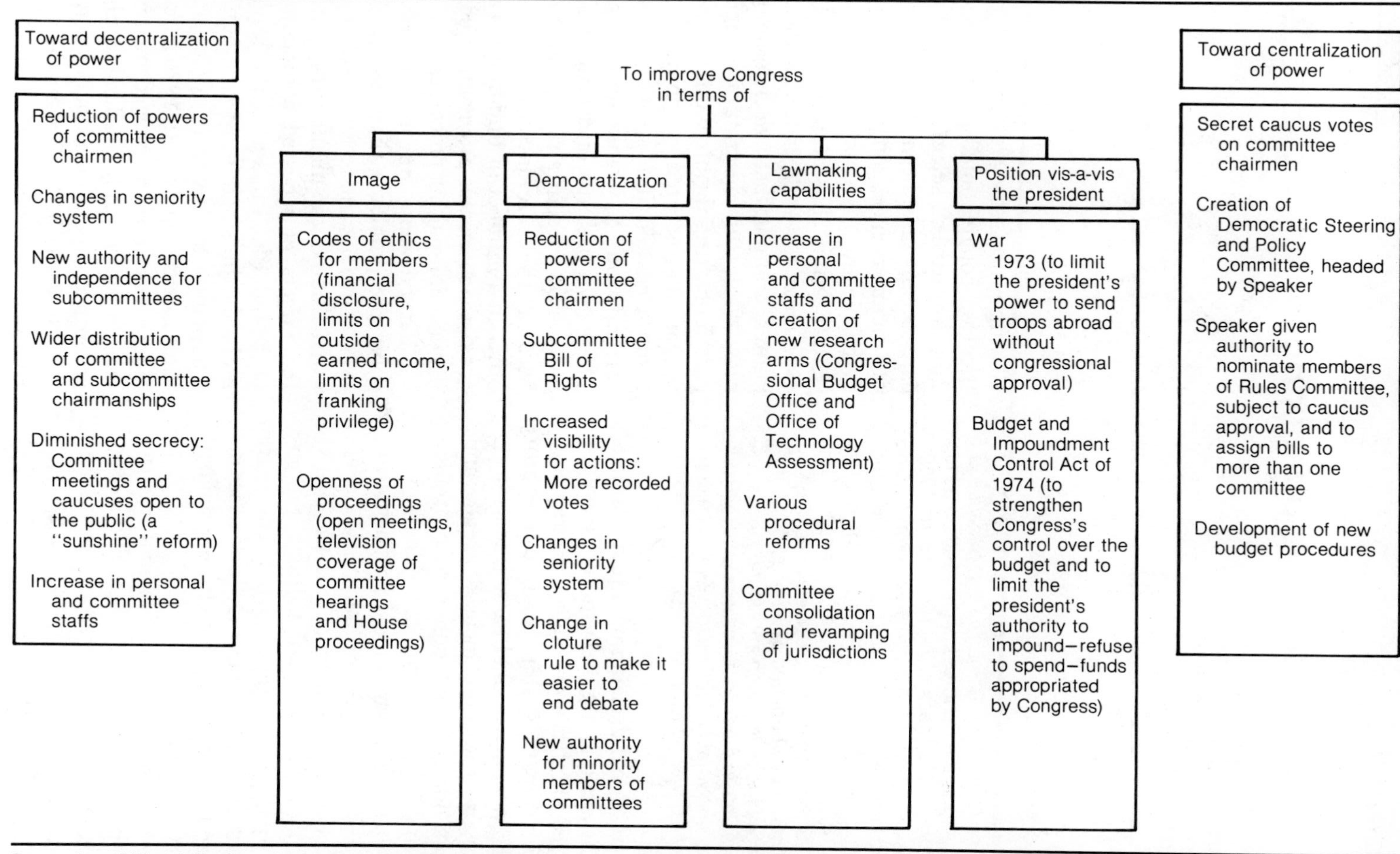

Source: from William J. Keefe et al., *American Democracy: Institutions, Politics, and Policies* 2d ed., (Chicago, Ill.: Dorsey Press, 1986), p. 336.

Reading 1.3

New Patterns of Decisionmaking in Congress

Steven S. Smith

The decade of the 1970s was one of immense change on Capitol Hill. Some say that because of those changes, the Congress of the 1980s is as different from the Congress of the 1960s as the 1960s Congress was from its 19th-century forerunner. The following important essay addresses the new structures of power yielded by the legacy of the reforms of the 1970s and the political circumstances of the 1980s. In reflecting on this piece we should ask: Are the newer power patterns identified by Smith likely to change or to continue? What changes or developments in the broader political environment are likely and what impact will these have on congressional power structures?

Is congressional decisionmaking fundamentally different in the Reagan era? Have an increased emphasis on budget politics and heightened partisanship changed the process? Have congressional party leaders been able to use the more focused agenda and demands for coherent policy to centralize policymaking and control individualism? In short, has the congressional fragmentation of the 1970s, criticized by journalists and academics alike, been overcome in the 1980s? If one looks behind the headlines, the answer to these questions is no. There are changes taking place, but they have other origins and are operating largely independent of these influences.

Two trends in congressional politics —an increase in the number of decisionmaking units and a wider access to decisionmaking processes—are having a pervasive effect on congressional policymaking. New subcommittees, select committees, and party organs have been created as rank-and-file members have sought ways to increase their role in policymaking. The term "decentralization" has been used to label this movement toward a more fragmented, disjointed, and pluralistic decisionmaking process. While this description is accurate in part, it obscures the distinction between participation structured by committees or subcommittees and more open opportunities for participation by rank-and-file members. These two patterns of decisionmaking can be labeled "decentralized" and "collegial." Because they are inconsistent with each other in a number of important ways, their coexistence creates a tension in congressional decisionmaking processes.

Party leaders are often called upon to solve the problems that are created; however, they lack the resources to do so to the satisfaction of the membership, and become the targets of repeated complaints of the rank and file. In fact, party leadership is probably the single most common target of complaints by members of Congress about their institution. In both 1976 and 1980, the House class of 1974 reported greater dissatisfaction with party leadership than with committee operations, caucus activities, or staff support. In 1975 a majority of House Democrats, junior and senior members alike, expressed dissatisfaction with Speaker

Source: From *The New Direction in American Politics*, ed. by John E. Chubb and Paul E. Peterson, pp. 203–33.

Carl Albert's leadership. Many House members have been disappointed that Speaker Thomas P. O'Neill's leadership has not lived up to its original billing. Robert Byrd was roundly criticized for lack of policy direction in his first two years as Senate majority leader, and he received an unprecedented challenge to his reelection as minority leader in 1984 on the grounds that he offered weak leadership. Without exception, leaders respond that the nature of Congress now precludes the kind of leadership offered by Lyndon Johnson and Sam Rayburn in the 1950s.[1]

In the 1980s the tension between decentralized and collegial decisionmaking patterns has increased in several ways, making the job of party leadership even more difficult. This essay puts these developments into the larger context of congressional decisionmaking processes and evaluates recent developments in party and committee operations. It does so by defining the alternative decisionmaking patterns, examining the changes of the 1970s in the context of these alternatives, outlining the consequences of the tension between decentralized and collegial patterns for congressional party leadership, and detailing recent congressional developments and likely new directions.

PARTICIPATION AND STRUCTURE

Most treatments of Congress characterize decisionmaking processes, usually implicitly, as a continuum running from very centralized to very decentralized. At the centralized end, a single leader, or perhaps a tightly knit group of members, makes the important policy decisions for the institution. The number of members and organizational units with an effective role in decisionmaking is very limited. At the decentralized end, members share decisionmaking responsibilities through a division of labor, with successive decisions made by separate individuals or small groups of members. There are many effective participants, all working within the limited jurisdiction of the units to which they are assigned.

The centralization-decentralization continuum has been useful in past analyses of House decisionmaking processes, but is inadequate for analyzing the Senate and many recent developments in the House. For example, the continuum does not capture collegial patterns of decisionmaking. In pure form, the collegial pattern involves a single unit, such as a committee of the whole, that gives all members an opportunity to participate in deliberations over all issues the chamber considers. (This would be labeled pure democracy in other settings.) Neither centralized nor decentralized patterns would allow collegial decisionmaking. Centralization limits the number of organizational units involved in effective decisionmaking, but also radically limits participation. Decentralization requires a division of labor that limits members' participation to the issues falling under the jurisdiction of their subunits.

Four Patterns of Decisionmaking

Figure 1.3.1 shows four pure patterns of decisionmaking, each of which has important advantages. The collegial pattern comes closest to the pattern intended by members of the first Congresses.[2] In the collegial pattern, the absence of structural barriers to broad participation facilitates a free exchange of ideas and, ideally, produces a process of mutual enlightenment that takes full advantage of all members' talents and knowledge. Such a process, it is often hoped, encourages members to rise above their parochial concerns and discover the larger common good.[3] While this pattern risks atomized individualism, its egalitarianism enables members to broaden their interests and collaborate with colleagues to solve policy problems, unlike a fully decentralized pattern.

The decentralized pattern is consistent

Figure 1.3.1.
Four decisionmaking patterns.

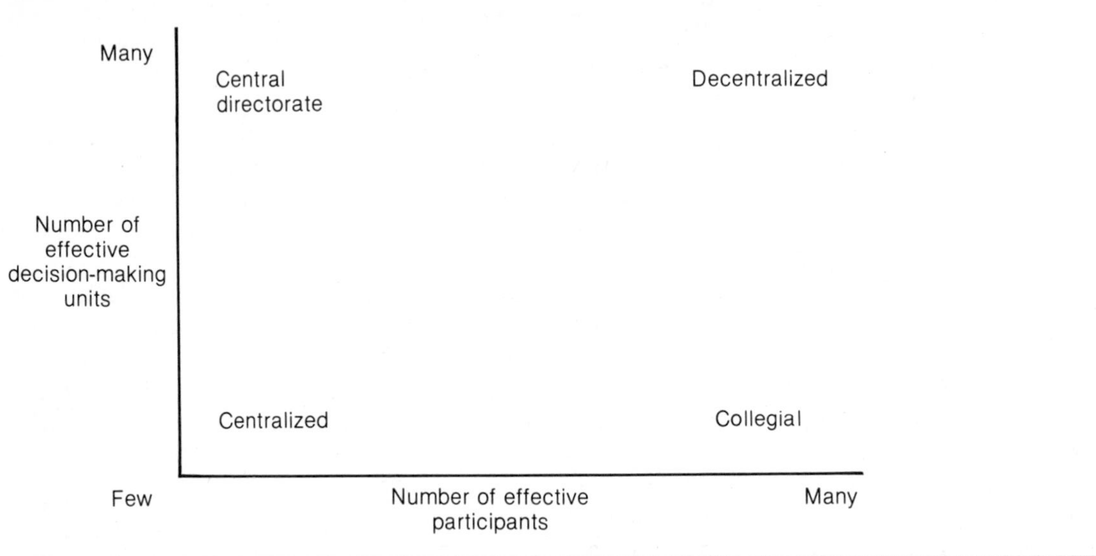

with the informal norms of apprenticeship, specialization, and committee reciprocity that governed members' behavior during most of the post–World War II period.[4] A division of labor gives Congress the means to manage a large and diverse work load, allows members to specialize in a limited number of policy areas and develop expertise, and provides specialized units (committees, subcommittees) through which the institution may interact with the executive branch and organized interests. Complex, divisive issues can be partitioned into manageable segments, and conflict can be resolved more readily by the members and outsiders most concerned about the issues. In some policy areas, the fragmentation of jurisdiction facilitates the development of norms of universalism, in which policy benefits are distributed widely among the active participants.

The centralized pattern increases the likelihood that Congress will produce well-integrated, coherent policy. A central actor is in a position to set policy and coordinate the construction of legislation. This is especially important for complex problems because the various aspects of policy must be carefully balanced. This pattern permits central decisionmakers to focus institutional resources and makes clear who is responsible for the policy product.

The fourth pattern, with a few effective participants directing the activities of a large number of subunits, perhaps through a central directorate of committee chairmen, is difficult to imagine in Congress. The conditions that limit participation are also likely to limit the number of effective decisionmaking units. But this approach has some of the advantages of the decentralized pattern, such as multiple points of access and the partitioning of policy problems. And it has some of the advantages of the centralized pattern; indeed, rank-and-file members themselves may serve largely as staff to a few core decisionmakers. This combination puts this pattern as close to a hierarchical form as is possible in Congress. Efficiency in decisionmaking in an institution with many members, each of whom must have some organizational assignment, may be an advantage of this pattern. The Senate of the late

1800s came close to this pattern, when a few senior Republican committee chairmen ran the chamber.[5]

The Tendency toward Decentralization

It is well understood that powerful forces propel Congress toward a decentralized pattern of decisionmaking. The members' ties with geographical constituencies and the frequency of elections encourage individualism and parochialism. Constituency differences push members in a variety of directions, and the political parties do not provide substitute ties to bind legislators together for more than very short periods. Members enjoy a fragmented structure in which they can freely pursue policies meeting their individual political needs. In contrast, the centralized and central-directorate forms limit participation and impose roles on members that may not be consistent with their individually defined political needs. Collegial decisionmaking may undermine the control over policy exercised by subunit members and their political clienteles by risking the interference of other members.

It is not only the reelection imperative that encourages decentralization. Rank-and-file members pursuing strongly held policy objectives or simply an interest in challenging policy problems prefer the opportunities to participate in significant policy deliberations offered by the decentralized pattern. Decentralization, with its multiplicity of effective decisionmaking units, also gives many members a piece of the institution's power. In sum, decentralization meets well the needs of members with a variety of political objectives, constituency demands, and policy concerns while providing a division of labor required for managing a massive work load.

The important differences between the chambers that continue to shape their decisionmaking processes should not be forgotten, of course. Senators' larger constituencies give them incentives to concern themselves with a broader range of policy problems; there is some breathing room at the beginning of senators' six-year terms that can be used to pursue personal policy interests; and the Senate's smaller size permits the average senator to take a more active role in chamber decisionmaking than is possible in the House. All of these factors, each a product of constitutional design, lead the Senate closer to the collegial form than the House.[6] Self-imposed rules and informal practices sometimes reinforce House-Senate differences and sometimes narrow them, but the difference in central tendency has existed since the early Congresses.[7] Consequently, the centralization-decentralization continuum has been more useful in describing change in House decisionmaking processes, where participation and structure have been related more closely.

Preferences for Decentralized or Collegial Patterns

The trade-off between decentralized and collegial patterns is a difficult one for the typical member. Decentralization constitutes a fragmentation of legislative power, with each subunit autonomous within its jurisdiction. Collegial processes do not fragment legislative power; all power is shared equally by all members. So the trade-off is dominance over a small fragment of jurisdiction versus a little influence over the total jurisdiction of Congress. Several observers claim that members favor fragmented power, and the record for most of this century supports that view.[8] But the record of the last two decades is not so clear.

What would lead members to prefer one pattern over the other? One reasonable speculation is that members' personal political goals shape their attitudes about decisionmaking processes.[9] Those pursuing narrow interests or concentrating on reelection favor a decentralized institution with committee self-selection. Those seeking personal control over policy and staff also have to settle for decentralization. Members with broad policy interests, on the other hand, feel too constrained in a highly structured, decentralized institution. Collegial processes are much more compatible. And members seeking higher office find that the collegial pattern offers opportunities to increase their visibility to new and larger constituencies. Changing admixtures of member goals over time can be expected to produce shifts in aggregate preferences for the two patterns.

A common observation about members is that a "new breed" has arrived since the late 1950s. The first members to be so labeled were the liberals elected to the Senate between 1958 and 1964.[10] With their wide-ranging policy interests, many of them felt constrained by the decentralized system under the domination of conservative chairmen with the aid of Majority Leader Lyndon Johnson. Many also had presidential ambitions. The Senate, in fact, has since "become a vertiable breeding ground for presidential candidates," recent observers comment. As a result, "more and more senators are involved in a wide spectrum of policy areas extending beyond their committee assignments and often well beyond their Senate work."[11] Many House Democrats elected since the early 1970s also have been identified as a new breed, described as "young, activist, nationally oriented and interested in a variety of issues."[12] Similar tendencies have been noted for House and Senate Republicans elected in 1978 and thereafter. A commentator summarized the characteristics of the "new-style" member: "His absorbing interest is governmental policy. He came to Congress with a sense of mission, even a mandate, to have an impact on the legislative process. He is impatient . . . [and] has no habit of being deferential to the established and the powerful, and he will not be so in the Congress, either in committee or on the floor."[13]

The implication is clear. Those members who can be labeled a new breed should favor collegial processes over decentralized ones. Of course, not all members, even among those elected in the last decade, are a part of the new breed and not all new-breed members have consistent views—after all, the trade-off is difficult. The result is a tension between preferences for the two patterns.

Several related aspects of Congress's environment also shape attitudes toward decisionmaking processes. Members who perceive that their institution's or party's collective image greatly affects their own political fortunes are more likely to seek influence over the relevant issues and thus seek to remove structural barriers to participation. Such a perception may be the product of an out-party's grappling with a popular President or the presence of an unusually salient issue that divides the parties or the branches of government. Members may recognize that their pet legislative causes will be better served, at least in the short term, by expanding the number of members involved and overwhelming those in positions of committee or subcommittee authority. They may find that their political interests are disadvantaged by a particular division of jurisdiction between committees. Or Congress's agenda may be so highly focused, perhaps because of a crisis or an unusual presidential effort, that participation limited to one's committees or subcommittees is meaningless. And finally, shifts in the policy agenda may produce changes in members' preferences for decisionmaking processes. For example, a shift from distributive issues to regulatory or redistributive issues is likely to expand the number of members demanding the right to participate.[14] Such circumstances would reinforce the interest of members with broad policy or higher office concerns in collegial processes and may convince others that a more collective process is desirable. Unlike members' political motivations, however, these conditions are likely to be quite transitory.

Over the last two decades several developments have stimulated interest in overcoming the obstacles of decentralized decisionmaking. New regulatory issues in areas such as the environment, energy, consumer protection, and civil rights have attracted the interest of a wide range of members and have not fallen neatly within the division of committee jurisdictions. Sharp institutional conflicts between Congress and Presidents have arisen, as have related divisions between the parties, especially between congressional Democrats and White House Republicans. And the domination of television as a medium of political communication has increased the visibility of and the interest in these issues and conflicts.

THE 1970s IN PERSPECTIVE

Both chambers of Congress undertook major reappraisals of their decisionmaking processes during the 1970s.[15] Although the mix differed, both chambers considered structural changes and ways to improve opportunities for effective participation of rank-and-file members. The search for structural reforms was motivated by a number of concerns: poor alignment of committee jurisdictions with policy problems, unevenly distributed work loads among committees, and severe scheduling problems caused by multiple committee and subcommittee assignments. The drive to increase avenues of participation was aimed primarily at powerful committee chairmen who maintained firm control of committee agendas, staff, and policy development. Both structural and participatory concerns, then, stemmed from the manner in which the chambers had decentralized their decisionmaking processes. The resulting reforms do not fall neatly into categories, but in most cases their basic thrust is readily discernible.

The House of Representatives

House Democrats moved to consider wide-ranging reforms after reactivating their caucus in 1969. Between 1971 and 1974, changes in House and Democratic caucus rules limited committee chairmen to one subcommittee chairmanship, stripped chairmen of their ability to authorize and appoint subcommittees, forced the creation of subcommittees on most committees, granted subcommittees staffs and jurisdictional identities, and guaranteed the minority party significant staff assistance. This set of reforms had a decentralizing effect on House decisionmaking processes and closely tied participation to structure: more subcommittees and more members gained an effective role in decisionmaking. Despite repeated attempts, no significant jurisdictional realignment was adopted in the House, in part because strengthened subcommittee chairmen now had a greater stake in the old jurisdictional arrangement.[16] As a result, the fragmented, overlapping jurisdictions of House standing committees remain, along with the attendant problems of managing complex policy and scheduling problems.[17]

A few House reformers, led by Richard Bolling, Democrat of Missouri, sought to improve policy coordination capability and increase accountability by strengthening centralizing forces. After proposals to add to the functions of the Rules Committee were dropped, the speakership was given new political tools by House Democrats. The Speaker was made chairman of the revitalized Steering and Policy Committee (which was given committee assignment authority) and gained new powers to refer legislation to multiple committees or to ad hoc committees (with House approval) and the authority to make the nominations of all Democrats on the Rules Committee. The Democratic party leadership also gained additional assistant whips and staff. The clear intent was to counter decentralization by increasing the authority of the Speaker, although the focus on the "service industry" of the committee system (committee assignments, bill referral, floor scheduling, and rules) did not directly reduce the autonomy of the standing committees.[18]

Increased decentralization, qualified by limited centralizing reforms, is only part of the story in the House. The major thrust of the reforms in rules and practices was a shift toward more collegial decisionmaking processes.[19] Collegial reforms came in two forms. One was to create additional opportunities for rank-and-file participation at nearly every stage and level in the decisionmaking process. The most important was the reactivation of the Democratic caucus.[20] While the caucus was not as active as it could have been during the 1970s, it occasionally provided a forum for the expression of views that would not otherwise be heard by committee members. In addition, twelve elected members were placed on the revitalized Steering and Policy Committee to represent geographic regions in its deliberations on committee assignments and policy matters. Caucus rules were changed to require rotation of the elected and appointed members of Steering and Policy and replacement of senior members by junior members. The reform enabled the Speaker to place representatives of junior and minority members on the committee. The reforms of standing committee procedures not only guaranteed subcommittees independence from full committee chairmen but also democratized committee operations by providing for subcommittee self-selection, giving a majority of members the power to call meetings, restricting abusive uses of proxy voting, and forcing full committee chairmen to promptly report legislation approved by their committees. And Democratic party leaders have created numerous informal opportunities for rank-and-file members to influence chamber and party decisionmaking: lengthy whip meetings, Speaker's task forces, and caucus committees.

The other type of collegial reform was to make members with special sources of influence accountable to rank-and-file members. Caucus and whip meetings created situations in which top party leaders were obliged to explain their agendas and strategies. The Democratic caucus assumed the power to require the Rules Committee to issue special orders permitting amendments in floor debate. Full committee chairmen were required to face election by the caucus every two years and subcommittee chairmen to be elected by their committee caucuses. During the 1970s, three full committee chairmen and one Appropriations subcommittee chairman were denied election by the Democratic caucus; at least six members in line for subcommittee chairmanships by virtue of seniority were denied election by their committee caucuses; and many others faced substantial opposition.[21]

House Republicans played an important role in shaping many important reforms of chamber rules in the 1970s, but were excluded in other areas where Democratic reformers sought the shelter of the majority party caucus to impose reforms on the committees. The Republicans themselves had already increased the number of opportunities for junior members to participate by the late 1960s. New and more active party committees and a more active party caucus had given rank-and-file Republicans a greater voice in party affairs by the time Democratic reformers moved their caucus to action in the 1970s. However, House Republicans lack the formal strictures limiting the power of ranking committee Republicans over the use of staff and other resources. As a result, Republican activities on several House committees remain far more centralized than those of the majority party Democrats.[22]

The net effect of the 1970s was to increase opportunities for Democratic rank-and-file members to participate actively in party and chamber decisionmaking. Change took both decentralized and collegial forms, reflecting the multifaceted nature of the attack on the power of full committee chairmen. And as attacks on the same targets, the two approaches appeared consistent; together, they represented a rightward shift in the patterns shown in Figure 1.3.1 on p. 16.

Most visible conflicts between the two models during the 1970s, such as committee chairmen's resistance to Democratic caucus discussion of issues under their committees' jurisdictions, could be explained away as "sour grapes" on the part of the older generation of losers in the reforms.[23] More serious conflict between decentralization and collegial patterns generally was avoided because the collegial opportunities were not fully exploited in the 1970s. While the Democratic caucus played a role in Vietnam War and tax issues for limited periods, the use of the caucus late in the decade was limited to organizational matters.[24] Very few meetings of the Steering and Policy Committee were devoted to specific legislation. Both Speakers Albert and O'Neill attempted to avoid meetings in which intraparty factionalism would surface. O'Neill flatly disliked having the caucus or Steering and Policy dictate policy or strategy to standing committees or party leaders.[25] House Democratic leaders repeatedly found themselves as the defenders of decentralized decisionmaking. In any case, there was less demand for caucus involvement than there might have been because of the policy direction offered by a president of the same party. Overall, then, the House became more decentralized, although important collegial processes were put in place as well.

The Senate

Although Senate Democratic leader Robert Byrd asserted greater control over the staff of his party's Policy and Steering committees and assumed more responsibility in managing legislation on the floor, no significant centralizing changes occurred in the Senate.[26]

The major structural change was the 1977 consolidation of committees and subcommittees. The Senate eliminated two standing committees and several special and select committees; rearranged committee jurisdictions in areas such as energy, the environment, science and technology, and foreign commerce; and, as a by-product of new limits on senators' committee and subcommittee assignments, abolished over thirty subcommittees. These consolidating changes did not reduce opportunities for participation significantly, however, because ninety subcommittees remained and other reforms had spread subcommittee chairmanships to nearly all majority party members. In 1970 the Senate had limited senators to no more than one subcommittee chairmanship on the same committee. And at the time of the 1977 consolidation, full committee chairmen were restricted to two subcommittee chairmanships. As a result, Senate decisionmaking was slightly more decentralized by the end of the 1970s as fewer full committee chairmen held multiple subcommittee chairmanships.

The more overwhelming direction of change in the Senate, however, was toward more collegial decisionmaking. In the 1960s Democratic liberals had asserted their independence of the conservative committee chairmen, using the floor to challenge committee recommendations and raise issues blocked in committee. The liberals were tolerated and sometimes encouraged by Majority Leader Mike Mansfield, who opened more and more avenues for rank-and-file members to participate effectively, including expansion of the Democratic Policy and Steering committees and floor scheduling more in accordance with individual members' needs.[27] By the early 1970s the committee-centered norms of apprenticeship and specialization, at least in the sense that involvement in noncommittee matters was proscribed, were no longer operative in the Senate.[28] The committee and subcommittee structure retained great significance in Senate decisionmaking, but no longer posed insuperable obstacles to senators seeking to influence policy outside the jurisdiction of their own committees. As one observer noted in 1973, the Senate combined "high participation and low specialization."[29]

In the 1970s additional changes institutionalized the power of rank-and-file members. In 1970 rules were instituted formalizing each senator's right to a seat on one of the top four committees and permitting committee majorities to call meetings.[30] A Mansfield-initiated practice of submitting Democratic committee assignments to his party's conference for approval began in 1971, and a 1972 rule required that Senate delegations to conference committees represent the Senate's majority view. In 1973 the Republicans provided for the election of ranking committee members by the committee caucuses, and in 1975 Democrats decided to permit secret ballot votes on committee chairmen at the request of one-fifth of the conference. Democratic Majority Leader Byrd began in 1977 to submit the Steering Committee's committee assignment nominations to the party conference for approval. And in 1977 rules were adopted giving each senator additional staff for committee duties and urging committees to give all senators their first subcommittee choice before any are given two subcommittee assignments. By the end of the 1970s rank-and-file senators had gained a formal voice in nearly all aspects of party, committee, and floor decisionmaking processes.

The conflict between decentralized and collegial decisionmaking was pervasive in the Senate of the 1960s and 1970s but, in contrast to the House, majority party leaders did not offer a strong defense of decentralization. Indeed, Mansfield, who served as floor leader from 1961 to 1976, has been cited frequently as having stimulated the breakdown of the apprenticeship and specialization norms and the associated increase in the willingness of senators to challenge committees on the floor. Mansfield believed that even the decision about how to make a decision was best left to the Senate as a whole.[31] "Coequal" was the codeword often used by Mansfield to describe senators' roles, a word that captures the essence of collegial decisionmaking.

The Budget Process

The new congressional budget process created by the Congressional Budget and Impoundment Control Act of 1974 offered the potential of radically altering the decentralized fiscal policymaking process in Congress. The process was designed to coordinate, but not undermine, the decentralized process by which Congress had made budget decisions. Budget resolutions provided a legislative vehicle through which Congress could set broad budget policy objectives and guide or direct the separate appropriations, tax, and authorizations committees to develop specific legislation consistent with the broad policy. As a result, budget resolutions provide a means for centralized decisionmakers to shape a wide range of policies. But the budget act of 1974 did not guarantee that the vehicle would or could be exploited in this manner. New House and Senate Budget committees were assigned the responsibility to write and report the budget resolutions, but they could not impose their will without the endorsement of their chambers, which were stacked with defenders of the role of the old committees. Nor did party leaders automatically acquire the power to see that coherent policy was enacted through the new process.

The record of the 1970s shows mixed results. The occasional success of both Budget committees in overcoming major challenges by other committees often has been interpreted as a victory for a newly centralized decisionmaking process over the "evil" centrifugal forces of Congress. This interpretation misses an important distinction. In the first place, the budget resolutions were constructed with an eye to what would pass the chamber. This required Budget members, and especially their chairmen, to anticipate the preferences of their colleagues. Moreover, the contests between the Budget committees and challenging tax or authorization committees were decided on the floor of the two houses, usually after lengthy debate and the active participation of a cross section of members. The membership of the two houses played a genuine, significant role in setting broad policy that had previously not received formal legislative attention.

THE CONSEQUENCES OF COLLEGIAL DECISIONMAKING

In the abstract, there are several significant implications of a shift from a decentralized pattern toward a more collegial policymaking process. The most obvious is that it greatly increases the "scope of conflict" by expanding the number of members and the size of the constituency involved in a policy debate.[32] Because more interests are involved, the definition of the issue debated, the salient political divisions, and the balance of power are all likely to be different from those in committees and subcommittees. Setting the agenda is likely to be a more difficult task in the collegial pattern as members with a variety of interests seek meaningful participation. As a result, predicting which issues and political divisions will surface is more difficult.

When compared with the decentralized pattern, in which issues are often partitioned and decided in a piecemeal fashion, the collegial pattern provides opportunities for members to connect parts of policies. Such opportunities make it more difficult to suppress deeply or widely held attitudes. This may mean that underlying ideological or regional divisions will surface more frequently, increasing the intensity of divisions and, ironically, undermining norms of collegiality.

Building coalitions is difficult enough in a large institution where majorities must be re-created frequently. With a larger number of effective participants, however, coalition building is even more difficult, time consuming, and expensive. Efficient means of communication and persuasion are sought by members seeking to shape policy. In fact, coalition building may look like mass marketing. Mass mailings, such as "Dear Colleague" letters, are employed frequently. Members use the media to sell legislation to colleagues. The line between legislative assistant and press secretary becomes blurred. Indirect persuasion—through outside groups—is routine as coalition builders seek to influence members with whom they have little familiarity.

In a collegial setting, rank-and-file members recognize that their political reputations can be molded by their activity on the floor, in party caucus, in the mass media, or wherever policy debates take place. Committee and subcommittee assignments no longer constrain individuals' choices of issues on which to focus or commit staff resources. In the absence of a formal structure that effectively limits interaction between members and funnels individuals' efforts, ad hoc groups may proliferate as members coalesce in multiple combinations to pursue common interests, share resources, and create opportunities to publicize their causes and themselves.

Finally, the less structured participation of the collegial pattern poses the risk that the institution will eventually disintegrate into atomized individualism. In contrast to the decentralized pattern, no member or group of members is in a position to enforce norms of collegiality and courtesy. Committee chairmen are not in a position to provide sanctions against violators of institutional norms, and members are reluctant to infringe upon the liberties of colleagues. The collegial pattern entails greater risks because it depends more completely on the cooperation and good will of the membership.

This description captures a great deal of the change that has accompanied the move to more collegial patterns. Other observers have noted an increased number of challenges to committee recommendations on both the House floor and Senate floor, national visibility for more House members, increased salience of ideological divisions within the Democratic party, the spread of ad hoc caucuses, and a breakdown in the observance of the norm of courtesy.[33] But the picture is even more complicated because of the continuing power of the forces of decentralization in both chambers.

An Uncomfortable Mix

The mix of decentralized and collegial patterns creates serious problems for Congress. Most concretely, the combination makes members' relative status more ambiguous. The egalitarianism of collegialism is not consistent with the special status granted to chairmen in a decentralized committee system. To take a current example, how should Republican members of Ways and Means treat Representative Jack Kemp when the committee considers tax simplification? Are they to defer to his expertise even though he has never been a member of the committee? The budget process has posed similar problems repeatedly as Budget Committee members and others shape reconciliation instructions. Chairmen and committee members believe they do not get the credit and deference they deserve, while other members are still careful not to alienate chairmen and committees responsible for acting on their pet legislation. Members complain when a chairman, such as Senator Jesse Helms, Republican of North Carolina, ignores committee duties to pursue interests on the floor, but they demand the right to participate themselves on any issue coming before the chamber.

The combination also enhances the chances that norms of collegiality and courtesy will weaken. The independence granted committee or subcommittee chairmen in a decentralized institution breeds an individualism that is not always well suited to a collegial process in which it is hoped that participants will share ideas and talents, welcome differing views, and seek common ground to resolve conflict. This problem can be expected to be especially acute when the number of chairmen is numerous, as it is in the House and Senate today.

A combination of decentralized and collegial patterns also multiplies the number of decision points at which legislation can be blocked and coalitions must be built.[34] Both committees and subcommittees retain great independence in initiative and resources, but they lack the autonomy that a truly decentralized system would provide.[35] The scope of conflict changes continually, usually expanding, as legislation passes from one stage to the next. Deals and accommodations devised at one stage cannot be adhered to later because negotiations must be reopened at each stage. Norms of mutual accommodation or logrolling, which made decisionmaking more efficient in many policy areas, are weaker as a result. Legislative outcomes are uncertain until the very end. Consequently, planning for the effective use of legislative talent and political resources is very difficult and fraught with error. The legislative process may be more exciting and challenging as a result, but it also is more frustrating and exhausting.

Problems for Leadership

These problems affect party leaders as much as other members, if not more so. James Sundquist offers this interpretation:

> The headlong trend toward democracy, and dispersal of power, in the Senate and the House has changed the task of leadership. Whereas the problem of Lyndon Johnson and Sam Rayburn, in the 1950s, was to wheedle and plead with committee chairmen who held the keys to legislative action, the problem of Robert Byrd and Tip O'Neill, in the 1970s, was to organize the new individualism—or new fragmentation—into some kind of working whole. And the leaders must do that without seeming to grasp for power, because the resistance of the rank and file of the new-style congressman to any hint of bossism would be instant. In their ambivalence, junior members will accept leadership only on their own terms, and subject to their continuous control. They insist on the right to decide day by day and case by case, without coercion, when they will be followers and when they will assert their right of independence.[36]

The tension is no longer one of centralization versus decentralization, leaders versus committee chairmen, sometimes a tug-of-war and sometimes cooperation.

Increasingly, the tension is between decentralization and collegialism, with party leaders serving as referees, traffic cops, or fire fighters. As one sports fan in the Senate Republican leadership suggested to me, there is a sense that the party leaders are always playing away games on the home turf of the committees or of the rank and file on the floor and in caucus.

Not surprisingly, this situation yields ambiguities about leaders' roles as well. Leaders are frequently called upon to resolve conflicts between committees and other party members—that is, to resolve the disputes that arise between decentralized and collegial patterns. In a genuinely decentralized system, leaders would feel compelled to protect the prerogatives of committees; in a purely collegial setting, committee recommendations would have no special preference. In a mixed situation, there is no obvious solution. Developing a consensus about the decisionmaking process, let alone meeting the varied policy demands of members, is nearly impossible.[37]

As noted, House leaders have more frequently defended the more entrenched role of committees than have their Senate counterparts. Senate leaders have devised a more comfortable accommodation of the two sets of demands. Senate leaders of both parties have held regularly scheduled meetings with all committee chairmen, for example. These meetings give leaders opportunities to press for committee action at crucial times in a setting that does not single out particular committees. In the House, majority party leaders have felt that chairmen would resent regular leadership supervision. Even House leadership staff have been hesitant to organize meetings of top committee aides, and, when they have attempted to do so, senior committee aides often have been conspicuously uncooperative. But in neither chamber has the pattern been consistent as leaders have attempted to meet the inconsistent demands of their members.

Leaders often are forced to devise ad hoc mechanisms to create policy and build coalitions in this context. Formal and informal task forces of members may be created to devise policy proposals and push others; committees and their staffs may be asked to contribute to packages of party proposals; or temporary committees may be established to write legislation. All of these measures, and others, were tried in some form during the late 1970s. These innovations reflect attempts to overcome the continuing deficiencies of decentralization while being sensitive to the political egos of committee members. They also reflect a desire to accommodate the demands of those who are not members of a particular committee while recognizing that not all members can sit around the same table to write legislation and devise strategy. None is completely satisfactory and none can be applied to each major policy problem Congress faces.

Ironically, the expectations for party leadership are higher in this context than they are in the more clearly decentralized situation. Where legislative responsibilities are clearly defined, as they are in a purely decentralized institution, the role of leadership is more narrowly limited to building coalitions at the floor stage on a few major pieces of legislation. In the present context, however, leaders must regularly handle decisions about how decisions are going to be made. Deciding who is going to take the lead, write working drafts, offer alternatives, and set legislative strategy are problems party leaders frequently are called upon to solve. But leaders do not have recipes for solving these problems and they are unlikely to have them in the future. It is hardly surprising that leaders must suffer frequent criticism in this environment.

INTO THE 1980s

The new decade witnessed an even more rampant individualism in the Senate and further moves toward more collegial processes in the House. The changes, reflecting the trends established in the previous two decades, were colored by the dominating items on the agenda of the new Republican administration, budgets and deficits.

Budget Politics

The 1980s have been dominated by budget politics, beginning in 1980 when the reconciliation procedures of the 1974 budget act were first used successfully to package deep spending cuts. In 1981 the Reagan administration's supporters in Congress used the reconciliation procedure after the first budget resolution to prevent committees from pigeonholing administration proposals. Republican leaders in Congress served as "point men" for the president, and much of the administration's success was due to their efforts.[38] Budgetary stalemate prevailed in 1982 as President Reagan and members of Congress looked toward the midterm elections. Few appropriations bills were passed, and the major struggles were over supplemental appropriations bills and a continuing resolution. Most appropriations bills were passed in 1983 and 1984, although executive-legislative branch confrontation and stalemate ruled most of both years. By 1983 congressional budget making had again become dominated by the centrifugal forces in the committee system.

The record teaches several lessons about the evolution of congressional decisionmaking. The experience of the House in 1981 demonstrated the inherent weaknesses of party leaders in Congress when they are not reinforced by a president of their party. House Democratic leaders and weakened committee chairmen were in no position to insulate their members from the president and had no resources that could counter his. The "open" Congress was vulnerable to a popular president with a well-focused program.[39]

The subsequent years also demonstrate that 1981 was very unusual and that the centrifugal forces in Congress are still powerful. Both House and Senate committees exercised great independence from Reagan and party leaders after 1981. And many members, including Senate majority party Republicans, expressed concern that congressional decisionmaking processes not be "subverted" in the fashion of 1981 again.[40] In the House, the experience stimulated interest in formal reforms to ensure that the role of standing committees was not undermined again. No action was taken because House Democrats did not want reform to interfere with ongoing developments in budget politics.

The experience also stimulated other innovations. In 1981, for example, Representative Toby Moffett, Democrat of Connecticut, attempted to organize House subcommittee chairmen to write an alternative to the Republican budget plan. Few subcommittee chairmen took much interest and the effort was dropped. Before the Ninety-ninth Congress, Democrat Anthony Beilenson of California proposed that the Speaker be given the authority to appoint the Budget Committee chairman, thereby inserting the leadership more directly into the process of devising budget resolutions. The proposal was set aside by a committee of the Democratic caucus after Speaker O'Neill turned down the offer, indicating, according to a staff member, that "the caucus deserves to select its own Budget chairman."[41] In the absence of clear lines of authority and assignment of responsibility, there is a constant search for new organizational forms in the House.

The House of Representatives

The House majority party Democrats continued the movement toward more collegial decisionmaking that had begun in the 1970s but was now also entwined with the budget politics of the 1980s. The most conspicuous developments occurred in the Democratic caucus. Much of the interest in the caucus was stimulated by the desire of many

Democrats to participate in constructing alternatives to Reagan administration proposals. Both new caucus chairmen—Gillis Long of Louisiana, who served as chairman in the Ninety-seventh and Ninety-eighth Congresses, and Richard Gephardt of Missouri, who was elected at the start of the Ninety-ninth—promised and delivered frequent meetings of the caucus, which had not been active in the Ninety-fifth or Ninety-sixth Congresses. Under Long, the caucus met about once a month while Congress was in session, and Gephardt promised meetings every other week. Long moved to close the meetings to the public so that members would feel free to participate. Among other things, this meant that party members were more willing to question party and committee leaders. In fact, Gephardt has commented that a major purpose of more frequent meetings is to "allow the leadership to talk to us and us to talk to the leadership."[42]

Gephardt's proposal for biweekly meetings faced vigorous opposition from several committee chairmen. The chairmen objected to Gephardt's suggestion that committees be barred from meeting at the same time as the caucus. And the more telling complaint concerned Gephardt's plan to use frequent caucus meetings to discuss specific policy proposals, many of which would be pending in committee. The chairmen, believing that the caucus activity would undermine their committees' roles, asked rhetorically, "Why don't we just dismantle the committees?"[43] When the strong objections were voiced in a late January caucus meeting, Gephardt's formal proposal was referred to the caucus's Committee on Organization, Study, and Review and, as of late March, no action had been taken on it. Nevertheless, Gephardt is free to call frequent caucus meetings.

The caucus has created special forums for discussion and for the creation of party policy documents. The most prominent of these is the Committee on Party Effectiveness created by Long in 1981. The committee, which had forty-three members in the Ninety-eighth Congress, has attracted the active participation of many new-breed members, most notably Richard Gephardt and Leon Panetta, Democrat of California. The committee has an explicitly collegial purpose. Its members comment that "it's one of the few places where a broad cross section of Democrats can sit down and get to know each other" and "the truth is scattered and the caucus committee is a place for an exchange of disparate views."[44] The committee produced lengthy statements on economic policy in the Ninety-seventh and Ninety-eighth Congresses that were endorsed by the caucus and helped shape the 1984 Democratic platform.

The caucus was also the site of the first successful effort since 1975 to unseat an incumbent committee chairman. Les Aspin, Democrat of Wisconsin, campaigned against eighty-year-old Melvin Price of Illinois, chairman of the Armed Services Committee, on the grounds that Price's physical infirmities impaired his ability to lead the Democrats on vital defense issues and that his support of the defense establishment was out of step with the views of most House Democrats. Aspin's effort, in contrast with the rejection of three chairmen in 1975, represented a personal campaign by a challenger to unseat the incumbent. In 1975 the new chairmen played no significant role in deposing the incumbents. Aspin also was the seventh-ranking Democrat on Armed Services, leap-frogging over five other Democrats to the chairmanship; in 1975 the second-ranking Democrat was elected chairman in all three cases. And, finally, Aspin succeeded in the face of active opposition from Speaker O'Neill. Aspin appealed directly to the caucus, overcoming both the dictates of the seniority system, which insulated chairmen before the reforms of the 1970s, and the defensive maneuvers of the Speaker.

The Democrats have moved in yet other

ways to increase avenues of participation for rank-and-file members and hold leaders accountable. In 1982 Democrats decided to require appointed Steering and Policy Committee members to rotate every two years instead of four, thus providing an opportunity for more members to serve on the committee that makes committee assignments and occasionally endorses legislation. At the start of the Ninety-ninth Congress, reformers succeeded in making the majority whip's position elective and convinced the Speaker to hold more frequent Steering and Policy Committee meetings to discuss policy. Democratic leaders also expanded the number of deputy whips from four to seven and the number of at-large whips from twenty-one to thirty-one. This increased the leadership's resources but also enlarged the size of whip meetings at which party strategy is discussed. Several task forces were created within the whip organization in the Ninety-eighth and early Ninety-ninth Congresses to give whips additional opportunities to shape party strategy. An innovative change was the creation of a "speaker's cabinet" composed of top party leaders, top committee chairmen, and at-large members. The group is designed to expand the range of members with regular contact with party leaders on party strategy and scheduling. These changes, Gephardt explains, are designed to "include people, to practice participatory democracy, so the actions of the leadership, Steering and Policy and the caucus come with a lot of sharing of information and consensus."[45] Democratic leaders expressed reservations about many of these developments, but they offered no significant opposition to them.

Thus the 1980s have seen even more efforts by House Democrats to broaden participation through the party caucus and to make the party leadership a more collective enterprise. The caucus is meeting more often, members have more opportunities to express themselves, there is less deference to committee chairmen, the leadership is expected to explain itself to the membership more frequently, and the caucus is seen increasingly as the vehicle for tapping the talent and stimulating the creativity of the membership. Whether these recent efforts reflect the tribulations of the out-party or represent a more permanent transformation is difficult to say. What is clear is that the gains toward more collegial processes will be difficult to reverse and that the likelihood for tension between decentralized and collegial processes is even greater.

The Senate

The recent record in the Senate is very different. Members of the new Republican majority, especially the newly elected senators, sought to take full advantage of their new status. In the view of many observers, the result was even further abuses of the committee system and floor procedures. The extreme individualism that followed in the aftermath of the 1981 budget battles stimulated a reform effort in 1984 and led to the adoption of some committee assignment reforms in February 1985. Efforts to reform floor procedures received greater opposition, indicating the determination of senators to protect their individual rights to participate actively and fully on the Senate floor.

The Senate reforms of 1977 had placed new limits on the number of committee and subcommittee assignments senators could hold. They were permitted three full committee assignments and eight subcommittee assignments, although some were granted exemptions. Because senators had to accept fewer subcommittee assignments, the total number of Senate subcommittees was cut by thirty-two. The number of exemptions has grown in each Congress since then, however, and several committees have added subcommittees since the Republicans assumed control in 1981. By the end of the Ninety-eighth Congress (1983–84), nearly one-third of the senators had more than three full committee assignments and well over a third had more than eight subcommittee assignments. Scheduling committee meetings and gaining a quorum became nearly impossible in many cases, and senators themselves had become weary of conflicting committee schedules and overextended commitments.

In February 1985 the Senate adopted a reform resolution reestablishing the 1977 limit of three full committee assignments per senator, thus cutting the number of slots available on "major" committees from 231 to 214.[46] However, the number of slots on minor committees was later increased by 9, in part to compensate senators for lost major committee assignments, producing a very small net decrease of 8 committee seats. Reformers failed to get the Senate or majority party caucus to impose a strict limit on the number of subcommittees that could be created by standing committees, but a number of committees complied with the Republican conference request to reduce the number of subcommittees. The Banking Committee, for example, abolished four subcommittees at the price of taking a subcommittee chairmanship away from one senator. These voluntary committee actions reflected the widespread recognition that the proliferation of subcommittees had become a major problem. Nevertheless, the Senate still lacks a formal cap on subcommittees similar to the one imposed by the House Democratic caucus in 1981.[47]

Reform of floor procedures proved more difficult to achieve. Three aspects of floor procedure had come to be especially troublesome. First, despite the 1975 reform that made it easier to invoke cloture against a filibuster, filibusters and postcloture filibusters continued to be a major obstacle to orderly floor proceedings in the late 1970s and 1980s. Filibusters and threat of filibusters stimulated cloture motions more than five times as often in the 1970s as in the 1960s.[48] A 1979 rule limiting consideration of amendments after cloture to one hundred hours has been invoked, but has not been effective, as senators have devised means to circumvent it.[49] Second, the Senate never has had a broad germaneness rule for amendments to legislation offered on the floor. As a result, committees have been bypassed on the floor through amendments to unrelated legislation, and a great deal of floor debate is devoted to issues extraneous to the legislation on the table. Finally, the informal practice of permitting senators to place "holds" on legislation they object to blocked committee access to the floor and made floor scheduling very difficult for the majority leader. Majority Leader Howard Baker's 1982 announcement that he would no longer honor holds has not yielded a significant change in practice.[50]

These problems have created great frustration for nearly all senators at one time or another as they have sought to pass legislation from their committees—and party leaders have become increasingly frustrated in their efforts to correct the problems by informal means. Senator Sam Nunn, Democrat of Georgia, argued that the Senate was "choking on its own processes," and the chairman of the Senate reform committee, Senator Dan Quayle, Republican of Indiana, stated that there was a "growing consensus that we ought to do something."[51] Senator John Stennis, Democrat of Mississippi and the dean of the Senate, complained that the Senate "has lost much in the way of ability to debate and be heard, transmit ideas to other leaders and thereby produce conclusions."[52] The collegial processes simply have been abused by the strong individualists of the Senate. As of mid-March, the outcome of the reform effort on floor procedures was uncertain, although some action seemed likely on a limit on debate over motions to proceed with the consideration of legislation and on germaneness.

The continuing weakness of Senate party leaders in their collegial yet decentralized chamber was evident in Majority Leader Robert Dole's effort to create a Republican budget package at the start of the

Ninety-ninth Congress. On January 4, 1985, Dole announced that, with the help of committee chairmen and their staff, he would produce a Republican budget plan by February 1. Dole failed to do so, as some committee chairmen refused to support deep cuts in programs under their jurisdiction and a few simply did not recommend anything to Dole. Most chairmen did report to Dole, however, although several indicated that they felt that cuts in programs under their jurisdiction were contingent on the willingness of other committees to cut spending for other programs. Dole failed to attract a quorum of Republicans to a party caucus meeting to discuss the package just before the self-imposed deadline arrived. Dole seemed helpless in the face of delay and outright obstructionism from committee members and staff.

PROSPECTS FOR THE NEAR FUTURE

The defense of collegial decisionmaking in the Senate and the search for more ways to improve participation for rank-and-file members in the House are unlikely to weaken in the forseeable future. There is no sign that a membership with a substantially different mix of personal political objectives will be elected to Congress. Weak local parties and independent campaigns will continue to produce a Congress whose members have weak ties to one another. And there is no reason to believe that members of Congress will become any more tolerant of organizational structures that limit their ability to participate in debates over major issues. No reversion to insulated committees or dominating party leaders can be expected. As a result, the near future offers a continuation of a mix of decentralized and collegial decisionmaking processes. Committees and their subcommittees will continue to have the dominant role in shaping policy, but their relation to party leaders, caucuses, ad hoc groups, and the floor will vary greatly. Because the two patterns are not fully consistent, party leaders will continue to be called upon to mold different decisionmaking processes for each major issue before Congress. Rank-and-file members will have very inconsistent views over time about the best combination of decisionmaking processes as their political interests vary. To the public, Congress will appear even more chaotic and confusing.

In this context, leadership in Congress will come from even more numerous and less predictable sources. Nonelected leaders will lead partisan efforts and noncommittee members will author major policy innovations. Successful party leaders will be those who recognize these new conditions, adapt to them, and take advantage of them. Party leaders will have to take advantage of collegial processes to direct their parties and of the mass media as an element of legislative coalition-building strategies.

Much of the change has made Congress appear more party-oriented and will continue to do so, but this is misleading. Many of the new opportunities for collegial activity have been created within the parties, especially in the House. To a limited degree, the collegial opportunities offered by party caucuses and committees will stimulate more party-centered policy debate and encourage standing committee members to think about policy questions in party terms. Yet much of the use of party mechanisms will continue to derive from the nonpartisan motivations of individuals or groups to influence policy through any process that works to their advantage. Because party mechanisms provide more flexible procedural settings, members seeking ways to participate in debate over important policy questions will use them frequently.

A reasonable question is whether the Republicans would retain the same mixture of decentralized and collegial practices if they should gain control of the House. Many of the reforms took the form of changes in the rules of the House, but others were the product of actions by the majority party caucus. Key rules guaranteeing independence of subcommittees—bill referral to subcommittees, management of legislation on the floor by subcommittee chairmen, written subcommittee jurisdictions—are a part of Democratic caucus rules. And many of the new avenues of participation for junior members have been created within organs of the House Democratic party.

While the political circumstances under which Republicans might organize the House cannot be foreseen, a few reasonable speculations can be made. The Senate's experience after the 1980 elections suggests that a new House Republican majority would temporarily bypass normal decentralized processes to respond to the perceived mandate that carried them into office. However, it is unlikely that Republicans would permanently reverse the thrust of the Democratic reforms. New cohorts of Republicans during the last decade have been noted for their activism and independence of elected party leaders, and there is no foreseeable shift away from issues that attract the widespread interest of the membership. Republicans occasionally have complained about the inefficiencies in House decisionmaking created by the reforms of the 1970s, but it is difficult to separate the partisan from the nonpartisan in their criticism.

Will policy produced in this mixed system be less consistent or coherent than before? There is little reason to think so. It has been argued persuasively that a more complex process, one that has more stages and makes coalition building more difficult, reduces Congress's capacity to enact coherent policy and to do so expeditiously. But the more singularly decentralized system of the 1950s and 1960s, with its jurisdictional jealousies, awkward jurisdictional divisions, an autonomous committee chairmen, was hardly more capable of producing coherent policy. A more collegial process does not solve the problem as a more centralized one might, but it does offer opportunities to overcome some of the obstacles of decentralization and it does so in a manner far more consistent with congressional egalitarianism.

Chapter Two

The Congressional Election Process and Representation

Congress is a representative assembly. As such, congressional elections are an important topic of study. Congressional elections provide a major link between governed and governors. The electoral process strongly affects what happens in the Congress by channeling mass demands and opinion and ultimately by deciding who will serve as members and, thus, who will make decisions and whose views and preferences will prevail.

The congressional election process is a long gauntlet, invoking in all districts and states the drama of high theater. The writings offered in this chapter address the major aspects of elections and how the ensuing incentive system affects member behavior.

Political scientists have developed three different theories of congressional elections. One theory is a "surge and decline" interpretation that emphasizes straight-ticket voting and coattail effects during congressional elections coinciding with presidential elections (or in what are referred to as "in" years). According to this theory, the historic pattern of losses during the midterm or "off-year" elections for the party controlling the Presidency can be explained by a surge of support by marginal voters for the winning presidential candidate's party during the in year and then an eventual decline of support during the "off" year. In other words, in-year and off-year congressional elections reflect very different electoral dynamics. The in-year elections are heavily influenced by short-term factors, such as issues and presidential candidate appeal. An expanded, surging electorate of both marginal voters and strong partisans carry the day in marginal or competitive districts in what is generally a "high-stimulus," politically charged atmosphere. In contrast, in off years, politics return to normal; strong partisans and a sense of partisanship are the determining factors; and coattail-related gains of the President's party are pruned by the normal vote.

A second theory that has emerged is one of "incumbency retention." Congressional elections are viewed as heavily determined by incumbency. Attention is called to a high rate of careerism in Congress among many members and, the 1980 elections aside, their relatively high survival rate when challenged. An election is conceptualized as a ratification of an incumbent member's district-serving ability. Incumbency survival is tied to incumbent savvy in the performance of casework and errand-boy functions and the adroit political use of the resources of incumbency.

The third theory might best be called "presidential referendum." Many now view congressional elections, especially the midterm ones, as a referendum on the Presi-

dent's leadership accomplishments and programs. From this perspective, it is argued that congressional elections are influenced strongly by presidential popularity and the state of the economy, with the President's party doing well when things are good and doing poorly when things are perceived to be less good.

In concluding a consideration of congressional elections, three thoughts should be kept in mind. First, the electoral process involves more than just nomination, campaign, and general election melodrama. It also includes debates and decisions concerning reapportionment, districting, and gerrymandering that occur in state capitals at the outset of each decade following the federal census. Decisions concerning the configuration, contours, and character of House districts strongly color election outcomes in these districts.

Second, congressional nominations are an important but not well-studied aspect of congressional recruitment. Through an infinite variety of different nominating systems, prospective legislative elites are winnowed in and out of the election contest.

Third, elections are not the only mechanism of leader/follower linkages in Congress. There are other avenues—group lobbying, parochial contracts (one-on-one lobbying), media crusades—through which popular demands can be forwarded to legislative elites. These channels differ in terms of the pressure they exert, the specifics of their communications, and their representativeness. Elections are the most representative but exert only diffuse pressure and communicate only the most general preferences.

Reading 2.1

Congressional Elections and American Politics

Alan I. Abramowitz
and David J. Lanoue

In the following essay, original to this collection, leading authorities on congressional elections detail the major facets, stages, and aspects of the congressional election process: reapportionment and redistricting, turnout in congressional elections, party alignment, candidate choice, incumbency, campaigns, presidential roles and influences, and predicting and interpreting election results. This essay proffers a major maxim that congressional elections are best understood in terms of distinctions. A comprehensive and sophisticated understanding of congressional elections requires us to differentiate between in- and off-year (midterm) elections, filled and unfilled (vacant, no incumbent) seats, new and established districts, and, most important, between House and Senate elections.

The election of Ronald Reagan as President in 1980 has been described as a turning point in American political history. During his first four years in the White House, the most conservative President since Herbert Hoover was able to achieve many of his policy objectives—cutbacks in domestic social programs, a sharp rise in defense spending, and a substantial reduction in tax rates for individuals and corporations. Reagan's success in achieving his major economic policy objectives during his first term has been attributed to a variety of factors, including the President's personal popularity, his charm and skill in cultivating members of Congress, and a conservative mood in the country.

All of these may have contributed to President Reagan's legislative success, but without one other result of the 1980 election, it is doubtful that they would have been sufficient. Along with the election of Ronald Reagan to the Presidency, the 1980 election also resulted in dramatic Republican gains in the U.S. Senate and the House of Representatives. In the Senate, the GOP gained 12 seats to become the majority party for the first time since 1955. In the House, the Republican gain of 33 seats was not enough to produce a GOP majority, but these additional Republican votes made it possible to forge an effective legislative coalition with conservative southern Democrats to enact the President's economic program. The results of the 1980 Congressional elections may, therefore, have been just as significant for American politics and public policy as the results of the 1980 presidential election.

It is important to understand why some elections produce changes in the fabric of political life, and political scientists have proposed and tested several explanations for such elections. However, most congressional elections do not have such dramatic policy consequences; stability, rather than change, is the rule. Even in 1980, over 90 percent of all House incumbents seeking reelection were successful; the average for all House elections since World War II is close to 95 percent. Although incumbents have been somewhat less successful in Senate elections, an average of about 85 percent

Source: An original essay commissioned for this collection, written in the fall of 1985.

have been re-elected. Stability of membership is one of the most important consequences of modern congressional elections. It is the fondation of a legislative process based on specialization, seniority, and mutual deference (Polsby, 1968). To understand congressional elections, we must explain stability as well as change.

One of the most important sources of stability in congressional elections has been the allegiance of most voters in the United States to one of the two major political parties. Since 1952, the proportion of American adults who identify with the Democratic Party has ranged between 40 and 50 percent, while the proportion of Republican identifiers has ranged between 20 and 30 percent. The proportion of self-identified independents has increased from about 25 percent in the early 1950s to about 40 percent in recent years (Miller et al., 1980). In many House districts, supporters of one party greatly outnumber supporters of the other party. In the central cities, and in some parts of the South, Democrats greatly outnumber Republicans; in some suburban and rural districts in the Northeast and Midwest, Republicans greatly outnumber Democrats. The districts can usually be considered "safe" for the candidate of the majority party.

Although most Americans continue to identify with one of the two major parties, there is a great deal of evidence that party loyalties have declined in importance since the 1960s. The proportion of self-identified independents in the electorate has increased, and young voters are much more likely to call themselves independents than are older voters. Moreover, voters who do identify with a party have more willingly crossed party lines in recent years (Mann and Wolfinger, 1980). As a result, many House districts that were once considered safe for one party are no longer as predictable in their party preference—Democrats have been elected from rural districts in the Midwest, and Republicans have been elected from districts in the deep South. In Senate elections, no state can be considered absolutely safe for either party.

Despite the spread of two-party competition to parts of the United States that were once dominated by a single party, congressional elections have not become more competitive in recent years. This is because of the second important stabilizing factor in congressional elections: the advantage of incumbency. Incumbent members of Congress are generally better known and more positively evaluated than their challengers. This is especially true in House elections. As a result, most incumbents receive a larger share of the vote than what would be expected based on the strength of their party. This incumbency effect varies considerably depending on the reputation of the incumbent and the strength of the challenger (Abramowitz, 1975; Mann, 1978). However, by measuring the average increase in the share of the vote received by House incumbents in their first bid for re-election (the "sophomore surge") as well as the average decrease in the share of the vote received by a party with a retiring incumbent (the "retirement slump"), we can estimate that the average incumbency "bonus" has increased from two to three percentage points in the 1950s to six to ten percentage points in recent elections (Cover and Mayhew, 1981). Some of the reasons for this increase will be discussed below.

The advantage of incumbency does not mean that representatives or senators can relax once they get to Washington and assume that their constituents will re-elect them every two or six years. With fewer districts that can be considered safe for one party, most members of Congress have to work hard to keep their constituents happy and to ward off particularly strong challengers. Even if a Representative or senator works tirelessly to cultivate constituents, a strong national tide, as in 1980, can turn what looked like a safe seat into a precarious one.

Where do these national tides come from? One source can be presidential coattails.

When a party's presidential candidate wins by a decisive margin, some of that party's candidates for the House and Senate may ride into office on the presidential candidate's coattails. Even in midterm elections, national tides are sometimes evident. The party controlling the White House almost always loses seats in Congress in a midterm election. The size of this loss, however, seems to depend on the state of the economy and the popularity of the incumbent President at the time of the election (Tufte, 1975).

Just as there are important differences between the rules and decision-making processes of the House of Representatives and the Senate, there are also important differences between House and Senate elections (Fenno, 1982). Although the Senate was designed by the nation's founders to be more insulated from shifts in public sentiment than the House, Senate elections in recent years have actually displayed greater volatility than House elections. In the three elections held from 1976 through 1980, just over one-third of incumbent Senators seeking reelection were defeated (24 of 71). As a result, the Senate actually had about the same rate of turnover in its membership as the House during these years, even though only one-third of Senate seats (as opposed to all House seats) are contested every two years. The rate of incumbent eviction in the 1976, 1978, and 1980 Senate elections may have been unusually high. In 1982, only two incumbent senators were defeated, and in 1984 only three senators lost their jobs. Nevertheless, over the last 30 years, the average success rate of Senate incumbents has been substantially lower than that of House incumbents. Some of the reason for this difference will be examined later.

REAPPORTIONMENT AND REDISTRICTING

One potentially important source of change affects only House elections: reapportionment and redistricting. Every 10 years, following the national census, House seats are reallocated among the states based on changes in population. In addition, state legislatures must redraw the boundaries of House districts within each state to reflect shifts in population. Since the Supreme Court's one-person/one-vote ruling (*Wesberry* v. *Sanders* in 1964), the federal judiciary has played a major role in overseeing the process of redistricting. In some cases, redistricting plans proposed by state legislatures have been rejected and replaced by plans devised by the courts.

As a result of population movement, congressional seats have shifted strongly away from the urban-industrial states of the Northeast and Midwest and toward the Southeast and Southwest. New York, Pennsylvania, and Illinois, which had 104 seats in the House of Representatives in 1950, had only 79 seats in 1985; California, Texas, and Florida, which had only 50 seats in 1950, had 91 seats in 1985. There has been a good deal of speculation about the political consequences of this shift of seats from the "frost belt" to the "sun belt." Many of the states that have lost seats are heavily unionized and have tended to send liberal representatives to the House; many of the states that have gained seats have weak union movements and have tended to send conservative representatives to the House. However, not all of the areas of population growth have conservative political tendencies. Texas, Arizona, and southern California, for example, have large Hispanic populations. Moderate-to-liberal Democrats have had some success in recent years in mobilizing these voters.

While the effects of reapportionment have received relatively little attention from political scientists, some research has studied congressional redistricting. As a result of court decisions limiting the discretion of state legislatures in drawing district boundaries, the blatant gerrymandering that legislatures practiced in the past has been limited. House districts must now have almost identical populations, and their boundaries must be contiguous and relatively compact.

Nevertheless, it is still possible to draw boundaries in such a way as to maximize partisan strength or protect the seats of incumbents (Cain, 1985). In drawing House district boundaries for the 1982 election, some Democratic legislatures apparently sought to increase the number of Democrats elected to the House by shifting Democratic voters from relatively safe Democratic districts to more marginal districts (Gopoian and West, 1984). This strategy was most successful in states where Democrats controlled the governorship and both chambers of the legislature (Abramowitz, 1983). This manipulation achieved its most dramatic results in California, where a plan devised by Congressman Phil Burton helped the Democrats to gain several seats in 1982, despite only a small increase in their share of the statewide popular vote (Cain, 1985).

While redistricting can benefit the party that draws the new boundaries, its partisan consequences are probably limited. For one thing, incumbents whose seats are threatened by changes in the boundaries of their districts can use perquisites such as the franking privilege to cultivate their new constituents. Population shifts and the unpredictability of voters mean that the results of redistricting are not always what those drawing the boundaries expected (Born, 1985; Squire, 1985).

The most important long-term consequence of redistricting has probably been a shift in congressional seats from the inner cities to the suburbs. Superficially, this shift would appear to benefit the GOP—suburban areas have traditionally supported Republican candidates, while the inner cities have traditionally elected Democrats. However, with an influx of migrants from the cities, many suburbs have experienced an increase in two-party competition. The suburbs can no longer be regarded as safe Republican territory. At the same time, the departure of many middle-class whites from the cities has left inner city districts more solidly Democratic than before. One result of this has been the election of more black and Hispanic representatives from inner city districts.

TURNOUT IN CONGRESSIONAL ELECTIONS

Figure 2.1.1 plots voter turnout in congressional elections since the beginning of the New Deal realignment in 1932. Two features of the plot should be immediately apparent. First, the sawtooth pattern over the entire period indicates that turnout has been consistently higher during years in which presidential elections are held than during midterm election years. Clearly, highly publicized presidential elections provide stronger incentives for voters to go to the polls than do off-year congressional elections. Second, we can note that after reaching a peak in the early 1960s, turnout has declined. Jacobson (1983a:76) argues that this decline "is surely linked in some way to the growing cynicism and distrust of political institutions" generated by the Vietnam War and the Watergate scandal.

The information presented in Figure 2.1.1 raises some interesting questions about the nature of voter turnout in congressional elections, and its consequences for policy making in the United States. American voters turn out in far fewer numbers than their counterparts in Western Europe and Canada, where voting rates of over 75 percent are the rule. By contrast, in this country, the highest postwar turnout in a congressional election has been 58.5 percent in the presidential year of 1960. The highest off-year turnout occurred in 1962 and 1966, when 45.4 percent of eligible voters cast ballots. On average, then, roughly half of all qualified citizens fail to take part in electing representatives to Congress. The votes of those who do, therefore, determine which people and parties pass the laws that govern all of us. If the half that votes is

Figure 2.1.1.
Voter turnout in congressional elections since 1932.

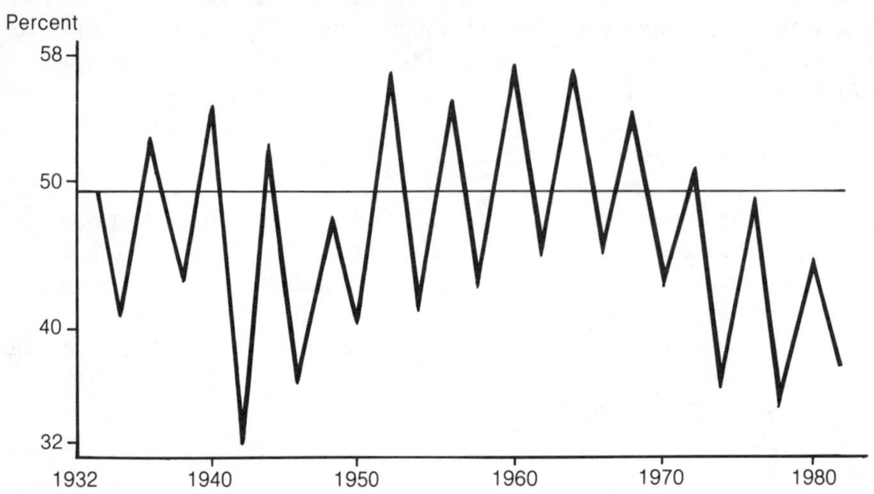

Source: B. Hinckley *Congressional Elections* (Washington, D.C.: Congressional Quarterly Press, 1981), and *The Statistical Abstract of the United States* (Washington, D.C.: U. S. Government Printing Office, 1985).

unrepresentative of the electorate as a whole, this unrepresentativeness could greatly influence which interests and ideologies receive the strongest support in Washington.

A number of explanations of turnout have been advanced over the years, emphasizing political efficacy and partisanship, the restrictiveness of voter registration laws, and socioeconomic factors such as income, sex, and education (Caldeira, et al., 1985: 492). Perhaps the most exhaustive study of turnout was conducted by Wolfinger and Rosenstone (1980), using census data from 1972 and 1974. Their major finding was that education is the most important predictor of voter turnout, even after controlling for related variables such as income. "Education," they argue (p. 102), "increases one's capacity for understanding complex and intangible issues such as politics, as well as encouraging the ethic of civic responsibility." They found that age was a lesser, but still important, predictor of electoral participation. Turnout rates increase as age rises, not dropping off after middle age (as some have argued), but continuing "through the seventies" (p. 47). Age, the authors say (p. 102), "is a measure of individual experience" with the electoral system. The more accustomed one is to the rules and procedures of elections, the less costly the voting act becomes, and hence, the more likely that one will choose to vote.

What difference does it make that voters are unrepresentative of the general public in terms of education and income? Are older voters more conservative? Are educated voters more liberal? Surprisingly, and (for those who believe in the virtues of pluralism) fortunately, Wolfinger and Rosenstone report that the effect is slight. The older and more educated electorate is a fairly accurate mirror of the political preferences of the population as a whole. Demographic unrepresentativeness does not, in this case, translate into ideological unrepresentativeness. The authors warn that if future issues are split along educational or generational lines, this situation could change. Nevertheless, for now we apparently need not fear that the 50 percent who vote are giving us a different kind of government than we would receive were we all to vote.

It should be noted that although age and education are good predictors of voter turnout in congressional elections, participation is not totally deterministic. Caldeira et al. (1985) look at various models of turnout, and agree that the legal, demographic, and sociopsychological variables that dominate the literature do matter. However, they argue that the degree of turnout in a given election is strongly influenced by the efforts of the political parties and candidates in the race. Where vigorous parties and ambitious candidates work hard at getting out the vote, the results can be most rewarding. There is no reason, the authors say, why parties and politicians must be satisfied with a "merely emergent electorate." Rather, they argue, "political mobilization can enlarge and enhance participation in elections" (p. 507).

We should not conclude from this section that turnout is unimportant in determining who wins elections and what the winners do in office. Jacobson (1983a:81) points out that low turnout increases the prospects that incumbents will be reelected. Thus, turnout rates may still have a significant effect on who wins elections to Congress. Jacobson also suggests (p. 79) that some recent congressional actions may have been influenced by the unrepresentativeness of the electorate demonstrated by Wolfinger and Rosenstone. Congress's unwillingness to cut social security, he says, indicates members' "respect for the clout of older voters"; social welfare cuts, on the other hand, may owe their enactment to the knowledge that so few of the uneducated poor vote. Finally, some scholars have argued that the difference in turnout between presidential-year and midterm congressional elections has important electoral consequences. This will be discussed in greater detail below. Even if voter turnout rates are not as important as we might have thought, it would be unwise to discount them altogether.

CANDIDATE CHOICE IN CONGRESSIONAL ELECTIONS

Political scientists have tried to explain voting decisions on the basis of voters' attitudes toward the political parties, the candidates themselves, and the issues in the campaigns. Of these three factors, the political parties were regarded until recently as the most important in congressional elections. Studies of voting in congressional elections during the 1950s indicated that most voters knew little or nothing about the congressional candidates or about the issues dividing the two parties. As a result, the large majority of voters made their choice for Congress on the basis of their traditional party affiliations. The relatively small number of voters who crossed party lines seemed to be influenced by simple name recognition: most of these defectors voted for the incumbent, since incumbents were better known than their challengers (Miller and Stokes, 1963). In short, since more voters identified themselves as Democrats than as Republicans, the Democratic share of the two-party vote should usually be the highest. Figure 2.1.2, which displays the partisan division of the vote in congressional elections since 1932, seems to bear out this argument. The Democratic vote exceeds the Republican vote during almost the entire period.

Recent research, however, has modified our understanding of voter decisionmaking in congressional elections. Voters appear to be more knowledgeable about congressional candidates, especially incumbents, than earlier studies led us to believe. The large majority of voters are able to recognize and evaluate their representative and the senators from their state. Most can recognize and evaluate challengers in Senate elections. Still, only a minority of voters can recognize and evaluate challengers in House elections (Mann and Wolfinger, 1980; Abramowitz, 1980; Hinckley, 1980).

Voters' impressions of congressional candidates appear to consist largely of personal qualities and characteristics. Knowledge of specific issue positions is unusual. Voters are most likely to be aware of candidates' issue positions when candidates take relatively extreme positions (Hurley and Hill, 1980). In addition, issues and ideology

Figure 2.1.2.
Democratic share of major party vote for U.S. House of Representatives, 1932–1982

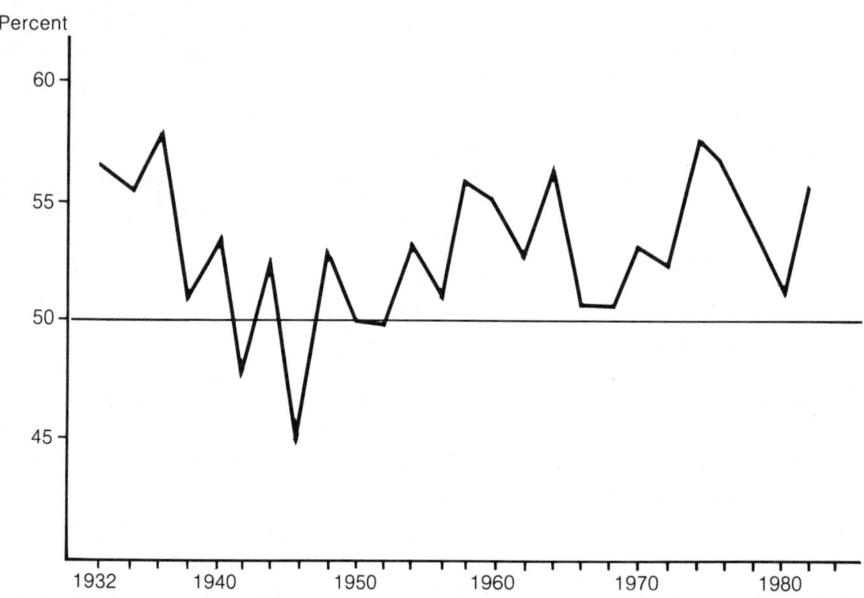

Sources: Norman J. Ornstein et al., *Vital Statistics on Congress* (Washington, D.C.: American Enterprise Institute, 1984), and United States Census Bureau, *Historical Abstract of the United States* (Washington, D.C.: U.S. Government Printing Office, 1985).

appear to have a greater impact on evaluations of Senate candidates than on evaluations of House candidates (Abramowitz, 1980).

Candidate evaluations are the most important factor influencing voting decisions in congressional elections. The reason most voters favor incumbents is not just that incumbents are better known than challengers, but that incumbents are evaluated more favorably than challengers (Mann and Wolfinger, 1980). The fact that most voters cannot recognize the name of the House challenger in their district gives incumbents an added advantage. Even if voters think the incumbent is doing a mediocre job, they tend to favor a known quantity (the incumbent) over an unknown quantity (the challenger).

The increased importance of candidate evaluations in voting for Congress has been paralleled by a decrease in party-line voting. In 1958, for example, about 85 percent of all votes cast for the House of Representatives were party-line votes; in 1978, only 69 percent of the votes for the House were cast along party lines (Mann and Wolfinger, 1980:620). Although party identification still plays an important role in shaping evaluations of congressional candidates, the rate of partisan defection has increased substantially in House elections. In addition, the proportion of defections favoring the incumbent has increased significantly since 1970 (Cover, 1977). It is not clear whether this increase in the proportion of pro-incumbent defections reflects an increase in the popularity of incumbents, a decrease in party loyalty among voters, or both. Whatever its cause, the result of this phenomenon has been larger margins of victory for House incumbents.

THE ADVANTAGES OF INCUMBENCY

What explains the increased advantage enjoyed by incumbents in elections for the House of Representatives? In the first place, members of Congress enjoy many perquisites that can be used to cultivate constituents, including the franking privilege, stationery allowances, staff and district office allowances, subsidized television studios, and paid trips to the district. These perquisites allow members of Congress to continue campaigning between elections, and Congress has increased the value of several of these perquisites in recent years (Cover, 1977).

In addition to their perquisites, which are provided to all members of Congress, the congressional committee system also helps representatives and senators to cultivate constituents (Mayhew, 1974). By serving on committees and subcommittees that specialize in issues of particular concern to their states or districts, members of Congress can claim credit for government programs or projects that benefit constituents.

The increased role of the federal government and expansion of the federal bureaucracy since the end of World War II has provided members of Congress with increased opportunities for credit-claiming of a different sort (Fiorina, 1977). Citizens who experience problems dealing with bureaucratic agencies often turn to their senators or representatives for help. Members of Congress, and especially members of the House, often act as ombudsmen, providing citizens with information and assistance in dealing with the bureaucracy. Many members of Congress have staff in their district or Washington offices who work primarily on constituent "casework," and some members make casework the major focus of their activity.

What impact does all of this advertising and credit claiming have on the voters? In most cases, it means that the incumbent has a huge advantage over the challenger in recognition and favorability before the campaign begins. Voters' opinions of congressional candidates appear to be based largely on direct or indirect contacts with the candidates. For House incumbents, mailings appear to be one of the most effective means of cultivating constituents. Most voters remember receiving newsletters or questionnaires from their representatives, and these mailings appear to have a positive impact on evaluations of the incumbent (Abramowitz, 1980).

Other items that members of Congress send to selected constituents, such as baby books to families of newborn children, also appear to have a positive influence on evaluations of incumbents (Cover and Brumberg, 1982). Personal visits to the district, while they reach a smaller proportion of voters, can be effective, as well. Voter-initiated contacts also provide incumbents with opportunities to win over constituents. A large proportion of voters report contacting their representative for information or assistance with a problem, and even more voters have heard of a friend or relative who has sought such assistance. The large majority of voters appear to be satisfied with the results of these contacts (Abramowitz, 1980; Parker, 1980; Yiannakis, 1981).

While Senate incumbents, like their House counterparts, use newsletters and questionnaires to project a positive image among constituents, voters' impressions of sentators appear to depend more on information received through the mass media, and particularly television. Senators receive much greater news coverage on television and in newspapers than House members. As well, Senate campaigns rely much more on television than House campaigns do. Since most House districts encompass only a small fraction of the population receiving a television station's signal, TV is usually a very ineffective and prohibitively expensive medium for House candidates.

Television news and advertising allow senators to reach large numbers of constituents more effectively than they could through mailings or personal visits. However, television news and advertising also allow Senate challengers to reach the voters with their message. As a result, Senate incumbents enjoy a much smaller advantage over their challengers in recognition and favorability than House incumbents enjoy. In addition, senators appear to have less control than House members over the information voters receive about their performance on the job (Abramowitz, 1980). Since newspapers and television news programs devote very little coverage to House members, most of the information voters do receive is supplied by the incumbent, either directly in the form of newsletters or indirectly in the form of news stories inspired by the incumbent's press releases. It is hardly surprising, therefore, that voters' images of their own representatives are overwhelmingly positive (Parker, 1980).

CONGRESSIONAL CAMPAIGNS: CANDIDATES, RESOURCES, AND STRATEGIES

The advantage incumbents enjoy as a result of their activities in office is usually compounded by the election campaign. The most important factor determining the degree of competition in congressional elections is the quality and effort of the candidates. When there is no incumbent running, both major parties usually nominate capable candidates who raise substantial amounts of money and wage active campaigns. When an incumbent is running for re-election, the degree of competition depends largely on the quality and effort of the challenger. The lack of real competition in most House contests, in both the primary and general elections, is due to the inexperience of most House challengers and their inability to obtain the resources needed to wage effective campaigns. The fate of most House challengers is to go, in the words of one unsuccessful candidate and political scientist, "from obscurity to oblivion" (Maisel, 1982).

In a typical election, less than one-third of House races are seriously contested—open seats with two viable candidates or seats held by incumbents with active challengers. Almost all of the net change in party strength is produced in these races. One of the most important questions in explaining the extent of competition and turnover in elections for the House of Representatives, therefore, is why viable challengers run or (more often) fail to run. Several factors seem to be involved in these decisions, including the strength of the parties in a district, the incumbent's margin of victory in the last election, and national tides expected to favor one party or the other. The greater the strength of the opposition party in a district, the smaller the incumbent's margin of victory in the last election, and the more the national tide is expected to favor the opposition party, the greater the likelihood that a viable challenger will emerge (Bond et al., 1985).

Congressional campaigns vary considerably in terms of the strategies employed by the candidates, the resources available to implement these strategies, and the impacts of the campaigns on the electorates. Party, incumbency, and expectations about the candidates' chances of winning seem to be the most important factors influencing campaigns. Democratic candidates in predominantly Democratic districts concentrate on mobilizing their party's supporters. Republican candidates, even in districts that normally vote Republican, are more concerned about appealing to independents and Democrats. Incumbents emphasize their experience and defend their records; challengers try to exploit perceived weaknesses and vulnerabilities in the incumbent's record. Candidates in competitive races tend to take more similar positions on issues than candidates in noncompetitive races do (Goldenberg and Traugott, 1984).

Incumbents enjoy a substantial advantage over challengers in acquiring campaign resources such as volunteer workers, endorsements, information, and money. Of these resources, money is the most important because it can be used to acquire other resources (Fishet, 1973). The cost of congressional campaigns has increased dramatically in recent years: in constant (1982) dollars, spending by incumbents increased from an average of about $120,000 in 1972 to an average of about $260,000 in 1982. Spending by challengers increased from an average of about $70,000 in 1972 to an average of about $130,000 in 1982 (Jacobson, 1983b). Increased use of television advertising, paid consultants, and public opinion polling in House campaigns has contributed to rising campaign expenditures.

One of the most important reasons for increased spending in congressional campaigns in recent years has been increased availability of contributions by Political Action Committees (PACs). With public financing of presidential campaigns since 1972, PAC funds have been channeled into congressional races. Total PAC contributions to House and Senate campaigns increased from about $35 million during 1977–1978 to about $83 million during 1981–1982 (Goldenberg and Traugott, 1984:68).

Although business PACs contribute far more money to congressional candidates than labor PACs, Democratic candidates have received more than half of all PAC contributions in recent elections. This reflects the fact that most PACs concentrate their contributions on incumbents, and most incumbents (at least in House races) are Democrats. Republican candidates, however, do receive more financial assistance from their party than their Democratic counterparts. The Republican National Committee has provided much more support for Republican congressional candidates in recent years than the Democratic National Committee has provided for Democratic candidates (Goldenberg and Traugott, 1984).

Although incumbents have maintained a two-to-one advantage over challengers in campaign expenditures, the most important factor limiting competition in congressional elections is not excessive spending by incumbents, but inadequate spending by challengers. In fact, spending by incumbents appears to have very little impact on the outcomes of congressional races.

Spending by challengers, on the other hand, does have a strong impact on election outcomes. The more money the challenger raises and spends, the more money the incumbent raises and spends, and the larger the challenger's share of the vote (Glantz et al., 1976; Jacobson, 1978). Heavy spending by the challenger does not guarantee success. One House challenger in 1982 spent almost $2 million and received only 43 percent of the vote. Still, a large campaign budget is usually necessary for a challenger to have any chance of defeating an incumbent.

The incumbent has a huge head start in most campaigns. He or she is usually widely recognized and well-regarded as a result of activities in office. There is usually little that an incumbent can do during the brief campaign to drastically alter his or her reputation. The challenger, by contrast, is usually almost unknown at the beginning of the campaign. The campaign is the only opportunity for the challenger to make an impression on the voters. That is why the challenger's expenditures are much more important than the incumbent's expenditures.

THE PRESIDENTIAL ROLE IN CONGRESSIONAL VOTING

Ronald Reagan was not on anyone's ballot in November 1982; his term would not expire for two more years. Nevertheless, his Presidency (especially his handling of the economy) was the major issue of that "off-year" Congressional election (Tidmarch et al., 1984). Republican advertisements urged voters to "stay the course," to give Reaganomics a chance to prove whether or not it could bring prosperity. The Democrats, citing high unemployment and cuts in social spending, gave the voters a different assessment of the Reagan program: "It isn't fair, it's Republican." In the end, the Republicans lost 26 seats in the House of Representatives, while their Senate margin remained unchanged. The result was perceived as a show of dissatisfaction with the 1982 recession, but an unwillingness to totally reject Reagan's policies after only two years. *Time* magazine assessed the voters' message in terms of the GOP's campaign slogan: "Stay the course, but trim the sails" (Mann and Ornstein, 1983:137).

The interesting point here is that 1982 was not an unusual case. Congressional elections (particularly midterm elections) are largely seen to be an opportunity for voters to cast an early verdict on the President's term in office. Thus, major Republican losses in 1974 can be interpreted as the electorate punishing the party for Nixon's Watergate scandal and an ongoing economic recession (Uslaner and Conway, 1985). Likewise, Democratic losses in 1966 are viewed as evidence of the falling popularity of President Johnson and public misgivings over the course of the Vietnam War (Jacobson, 1983a:126). Indeed, it has become almost an article of faith among scholars and journalists that presidential popularity is a major factor in determining the outcomes of congressional races.

This view of congressional elections as presidential referenda is, however, a fairly recent one. Until the 1970s, the prevailing belief among political scientists was in a theory known as "surge and decline" (Campbell, 1966). This theory looks at voter turnout in an attempt to explain why the President's party has lost seats in every midterm congressional election in the 20th century except the one in 1934. According to this theory, midterm elections rarely provide much stimulus to voters. They are not very well publicized and candidates and issues are often unknown. Those who vote in such elections are usually people who require little incentive, the more politically interested and aware segments of the population, and those with the greatest attachment or loyalty to their party. Such people are called "core voters."

In presidential elections, by contrast, heavy turnout is motivated by the publicity and excitement that could only be generated by a race for the nation's highest office. Candidates and their issue positions are well-covered in the popular press, enhancing the seeming importance of the election. The result, of course, is that many citizens with little political sophistication or party allegiance are drawn into the ranks of the voting public. Such people are called "peripheral voters."

The actual process of surge and decline is quite simple. During a presidential year, many peripheral voters, attracted by a popular candidate (but not very knowledgeable about politics), will vote for that candidate's party in other races on the same ballot. Further, some core voters may become sufficiently driven by the short-term issues and personalities of the presidential campaign to temporarily abandon their party loyalties and vote for their favored candidate's entire ticket. Two years later, without the excitement of the presidential race, the peripheral voters sit out the midterm election. Moreover, the core voters who rejected their party in the previous election, rejoin the fold and once again vote for their party's congressional candidates. Consequently, the sources of extra support (the surge) enjoyed by the President's party when he is on the ballot dry up (decline) when he is no longer there. The midterm losses almost always suffered by the party in control of the White House are thus explained.

Surge and decline, while apparently a useful and reasonable theory, has two major flaws. First, it does not do a very good job of explaining variations in seat loss over a number of midterm elections. Eisenhower's Republicans, for example, lost 48 seats in 1958, while Kennedy's Democrats lost only 3 in 1962 (Kernell, 1977:45–46).[1]

Second, the theory is flawed in its analysis of who does and doesn't vote in midterm elections. While we would expect voters with strong party attachments to make up a larger share of the midterm electorate (when less partisan peripheral voters drop out) than they do during presidential years, evidence from the 1950s and 1960s reveals no such pattern (Kernell, 1977:46). Moreover, those demographic characteristics we normally associate with political interest and activity (education, income, occupation) have been found in roughly equal proportions in both the midterm and presidential electorates (Wolfinger et al., 1981).

An alternate view of congressional fortunes, and particularly midterm outcomes, states that House elections are largely reflections of how the public evaluates the President's handling of his job (particularly with respect to the economy). A number of studies have demonstrated a link between fluctuations in economic indicators and the share of the vote won by the President's party in House elections (Kramer, 1971; Bloom and Price, 1975; Hibbing and Alford, 1981). It was this kind of "economic voting" that, many argue, took place in the 1982 midterm election. According to this model, the President's role in congressional elections goes beyond simply supplying coattails to fortunate candidates. Voters respond to more than short-term campaign issues and party identification: They evaluate the economic conditions delivered by the party in power, and cast their ballots accordingly.

This much more informed, rational voting has been used to explain the midterm losses usually suffered by the President's party. Edward Tufte (1975, 1978) has developed a model in which midterm voting is based on two factors: annual change in real income levels and the President's level of popularity in the Gallup Poll. A prosperous economy (with rising income levels) will benefit the incumbent party, while declining income levels will help the opposition. Likewise, a popular President's party will suffer fewer midterm losses than will that of an unpopular one. The inclusion of presidential popularity in Tufte's model permits him to take into account many noneconomic factors, such as wars and scandals, for which the President and his party may be punished, but which are not measured by income changes. Tufte's work has also been applied with success to the electoral fortunes of U. S. senators (Abramowitz and Segal, 1985).

Tufte's model has two important features. First, it allows us to explain variations in midterm losses suffered by Presidents. Second, it suggests the beginnings of an explanation as to why the President's party almost always loses seats. Mueller (1970, 1973) has indicated that Presidents begin their terms with a great deal of support, only to see it slip away as time passes. This steady decline in presidential popularity seems to occur even after economic fluctuations, wars, and scandals are accounted for (Norpoth, 1984; Lanoue, 1985). Mueller has argued that the decline represents an erosion in the "coalition of minorities" that elected the President in the first place. Every action a President takes will offend some segment of the population, and so, the argument goes, his group of supporters will inevitably shrink as his term progresses. Tufte also notes that income levels are usually lower in off-years than in presidential years, which means that the President's party is often facing voter dissatisfaction with the economy during midterm campaigns. In either case, the position of the "in-party" in off-years is rarely an enviable one.

This problem becomes even greater when we consider the findings of Samuel Kernell (1977). Kernell discovered that not only did people's evaluations of presidential performance influence their congressional vote, but that negative evaluations have a greater effect than positive ones. He found that those who disapprove of the President's handling of his job are more likely to vote in midterm elections than those who approve. Further, partisan defections (votes against one's party identification) are more likely to come from followers of the President's party unhappy with their leader than from those identifying with the opposition, who approve of the President's performance. Finally, negative voting is also more prevalent than positive voting among those with weak party identification (such as registered independents, who make up a sizable portion of the electorate). In short, an asymmetry exists in midterm congressional voting, and it works against the party in power.[2] Negative voting, says Kernell, accounts for most of the President's midterm woes.

This recently accepted view of congressional elections as presidential referenda is not without its controversy. Most studies that demonstrate that economic fluctuations affect the fortunes of the President's party have used aggregate data. That is, they have analyzed the relationship between overall levels of economic change and the nationwide vote for Congress in a given year. It is assumed, but not proven, that the individuals who have suffered economically are the ones who are punishing the President's party.

Such a relationship, however, has not been found in survey research. Various studies using individual voters' responses to survey questions have been unable to detect a strong, consistent link between changes in personal economic fortunes and one's vote choice (Fiorina, 1978; Kinder and Kiewiet, 1979). Further, Owens and Olson (1980) have indicated that local economic conditions, which should have a greater impact on the individual than do national conditions, are not a major factor in explaining the vote in individual congressional districts. These negative findings have called into question the conclusions reached by scholars using aggregate data.

One answer to this discrepancy between aggregate and individual-level findings may be that one's vote does not depend strictly on personal economic plight. Indeed, it has been argued, Americans' "belief in economic individualism leads people to accept personal responsibility for their economic condition, which in turn eliminates any connection between personal well-being and political evaluations" (Feldman, 1982:446). What aggregate studies may be showing, according to Kinder and Kiewiet (1979), is that people reward or punish the President's party not on the basis of personal economics, but rather, on the basis of the economic health of the entire nation. Thus, national economic hard times might even influence the votes of people unhurt by them. By this reasoning, it is the individual's job to keep his or her own economic house in order; it is the President's job to do the same for the country as a whole.

Clearly, the consensus in political science is that congressional elections are, at least in part, presidential events. (Support for this view is far from unanimous. See, for example, Ragsdale, 1980.) The sins of Presidents are apparently visited upon their congressional allies, and this explains much of the variation in election outcomes not already explained by factors such as incumbency.

We might conclude this section by reconsidering whether or not the old, popular notion of presidential coattails has any role to play once incumbency and negative voting are taken into account. The conventional wisdom of the last decade has been that coattails aren't what they used to be. During the New Deal, an increase of 1 percent in the vote for the Democratic presidential nominee resulted in a pickup of 11 additional Democratic House seats. From 1968 to 1976, however a 1 percent gain in the presidential vote increased the Democrats' tally by only two seats (Calvert and Ferejohn, 1983). The newfound importance of incumbency, it was argued, may have relegated presidential coattails to the pages of history.

The huge Republican congressional gains coinciding with Ronald Reagan's 1980 election have given researchers cause to reexamine coattails, and the results have been mixed. Coattails still matter, says Born (1984), and they might not even be weaker than they were in the past.[3] Calvert and Ferejohn (1983) argue that despite the decline in coattails, a strong presidential candidate can still turn some 20 to 30 races in his favor, a fairly substantial number since it implies a 40 to 60 vote shift in the partisan makeup of the House. Coattails, whether or not they have lost some of their value, apparently still represent a meaningful factor in explaining and predicting presidential-year congressional voting.

CONGRESSIONAL ELECTIONS: THE BIG PICTURE AND THE SMALL PICTURE

There are two ways of analyzing congressional elections. One approach emphasizes the big picture: a congressional election is a national contest between two parties in which the outcome depends on national issues such as the state of the economy and the popularity of the President. The other approach, which has been more common in recent years in political science, emphasizes the small picture: a congressional election is really 435 separate House races and 33 or 34 separate Senate races. Their outcomes depend mainly on the characteristics, resources, and strategies of the candidates in each district or state. These two approaches have yielded two seemingly contradictory conclusions about congressional elections. In the big picture, the makeup of Congress and public policy seem to respond to the changing preferences of the electorate. In the small picture, incumbency is the dominant force, and stability is the normal result.

How can we reconcile these two approaches? Both are correct. In fact, the big picture and the small picture are connected. In the first place, national conditions and issues affect the resources and strategies of candidates for the House and Senate. When national conditions seem to favor one party, that party is able to recruit stronger challengers and raise more money than the opposing party (Jacobson and Kernell, 1981). Thus, its candidates are doubly advantaged. In addition, national issues can become local issues. The extent to which an issue such as the state of the economy affects the outcome of a congressional election may depend on the extent to which House and Senate candidates emphasize this issue in their own contests. Thus, in both 1974 and 1982, the performance of the incumbent President had a much greater impact in House races with a Republican incumbent than in other types of races (Abramowitz, 1985). It appears that the issue of presidential performance was more likely to be emphasized by candidates in House contests involving a GOP incumbent who had served under the Republican chief executive.

The salience of national issues varies considerably from one election to another. In 1974, the economy and the Watergate scandal were the major issues in the campaign, and these issues did affect the outcomes of many House and Senate races (Uslaner and Conway, 1985). In 1978, neither the economy nor the performance of the incumbent President were salient issues in congressional campaigns, and the outcome was very close to a normal vote. In 1982, however, the issue of Reaganomics was emphasized by the national parties and many of the candidates running for the House and Senate (Hunt, 1983). Once again, a national issue had a substantial impact on the outcomes of many House and Senate contests.

Similarly, in some presidential election years, such as 1980, we observe a strong coattail effect, while in others, such as 1984, the President's coattails are very short. It is not entirely clear why national issues and conditions have much greater effects on some congressional elections than on others. It is clear that congressional elections, like presidential elections, are not all cut from the same cloth. Looking ahead to 1986, one of the most interesting and important questions to be answered is whether national or local concerns will be dominant in the midterm election.

CONCLUSION: IMPLICATIONS FOR 1986 AND BEYOND

The 1986 congressional elections represent perhaps our best chance to guage the success of the "Reagan revolution." As in any midterm election, the President's party should be expected to suffer substantial losses in the House of Representatives. In the Senate, 22 Republican seats will be contested, the largest number of GOP senators to stand for re-election in decades. The results of these races may determine which party will control the upper house well into the 1990s. If the Republican resurgence is to continue past Ronald Reagan's Presidency, it will be necessary for the party to buck the trend of midterm House losses, and to lose no more than two or three Senate seats. In any event, talk about political realignment will be a great deal more informed after the 1986 outcome is known.

What can we predict about the outcome of the 1986 midterm House elections? First, if recent history is any guide, an overwhelming majority of incumbents will win reelection. Second, the Republicans, as noted above, should lose seats in typical midterm fashion. The GOP's prospects, however, might be even worse than the usual midterm drop would lead us to expect. Abramowitz, Cover, and Norpoth (1985) find evidence of what might be called a "six-year itch" phenomenon. Voters, it appears, are much harder on the President's party at the second midterm (the sixth year of the party's term in office) than they are in the first one. The 1958, 1966, and 1974 contests, each representing the in-party's second midterm race, saw huge losses, in the range of 35–50 seats. By contrast, in 1982 (Reagan's first midterm election), even with the economy suffering from a deep recession and record postwar unemployment, the Republicans lost only 26 seats. This suggests that any problems Reagan has between now and election day may be magnified by an electorate whose attitude is that it's time for a change.

In the Senate, Republican chances appear similarly discouraging. Abramowitz and Segal (1985), in applying Tufte's model of House seat-loss to the Senate, find that real income, presidential popularity, and the number of seats a party has to defend strongly influence the in-party's prospects. The latter variable distinguishes this model from Tufte's, with important consequences. The more seats a party has at risk in an election, the more they can expect to lose, even after the economy and presidential popularity are taken into account. This is particularly relevant now, since about two-thirds of the seats up in 1986 are Republican. This imbalance increases the GOP's odds of losing seats. In fact, according to Abramowitz and Segal, even if the economy is booming and Reagan's popularity is extremely high, the Republicans can still expect to lose one seat. Clearly, adverse changes in either income or the President's approval rating will only make the situation worse. Democratic takeover of the Senate is thus a real possibility.

If we want to know want to expect in 1986, we should probably start by looking at the economy and presidential popularity. The economy has been very strong since 1983. If it once again turns sour, Reaganomics might be the major issue in the coming midterm election, just as it was in 1982. This time, appeals to "stay the course" may fall on less sympathetic ears. President Reagan spent most of 1985 with his popularity over the 60 percent mark, helped there by public satisfaction over the conclusion of the Beirut hostage crisis, and relief over the President's apparently successful fight against cancer. Nevertheless, those who refer to Reagan as the "Teflon President" (meaning that his personal popularity overcomes his political problems) have forgotten the period between late 1982 and early 1983, when economic recession caused the President's approval rating to dip below 40 percent (Lanoue, 1985). A similar drop in Reagan's popularity in 1986 could have disastrous consequences for his party.

It should be pointed out that predicting election outcomes is far from an exact science. The fact that we can use past elections to help us forecast later results must not blind us to the fact that every election is unique. Congressional elections are, after all, won and lost on the state and local level, and local issues and personalities often make a difference. Further, it is difficult to know what national issues will matter, or how the economy will fare as election day approaches. We ordinarily expect, for instance, that a President's popularity will decline as time passes. Who would have predicted that Reagan's would be so high five years into his term? Who would have predicted the effects of Watergate, presidential resignation, and presidential pardon on the 1974 midterm election results? Who could anticipate the Cuban Missile Crisis occurring less than a month prior to the 1962 midterm election (in which the President's party lost only three seats)? We can say, judging by the past, that 1986 looks like it could be a good year for the Democrats. Whether or not we are right, however, will depend on economic conditions and President Reagan's popularity during 1986.

Reading 2.2

The Electoral Incentive

David R. Mayhew

In a classic statement, Congress: The Electoral Connection, *David R. Mayhew argues that members of Congress are driven by a desire to be re-elected. As such there is a sense of "shared fates" among incumbents and an effort by them collectively to enhance the prospects for their return. We include two excerpts from Mayhew's work. One, addressing the characteristics of policymaking, is presented in Chapter Nine. The selection at hand emphasizes the behavior of legislators as they vie for re-election. Here, Mayhew's argument is that, because of the "electoral incentive," Congressmen behave in a certain way in dealing with their constituents.*

Source: From David R. Mayhew, *Congress: The Electoral Connection* (New Haven, Conn.: Yale University Press, 1974), pp. 49–77.

Whether they are safe or marginal, cautious or audacious, Congressmen must constantly engage in activities related to reelection. There will be differences in emphasis, but all members share the root need to do things —indeed, to do things day in and day out during their terms. The next step here is to present a typology, a short list of the *kinds* of activities Congressmen find it electorally useful to engage in. The case will be that there are three basic kinds of activities.

One activity is *advertising,* defined here as any effort to disseminate one's name among constituents in such a fashion as to create a favorable image but in messages having little or no issue content. A successful Congressman builds what amounts to a brand name, which may have a generalized electoral value for other politicians in the same family. The personal qualities to emphasize are experience, knowledge, responsiveness, concern, sincerity, independence, and the like. Just getting one's name across is difficult enough; only about half the electorate, if asked, can supply their House members' names. It helps a Congressman to be known. "In the main, recognition carries a positive valence; to be perceived at all is to be perceived favorably."[1] A vital advantage enjoyed by House incumbents is that they are much better known among voters than their November challengers.[2] They are better known because they spend a great deal of time, energy, and money trying to make themselves better known.[3] There are standard routines—frequent visits to the constituency, nonpolitical speeches to home audiences,[4] the sending out of infant-care booklets and letters of condolence and congratulation. Of 158 House members questioned in the mid-1960s, 121 said that they regularly sent newsletters to their constituents,[5] 48 wrote seperate news or opinion columns for newspapers; 82 regularly reported to their constituencies by radio or television,[6] 89 regularly sent out mail questionnaires.[7] Some routines are less standard. Congressman George E. Shipley (D–Ill.) claims to have met personally about half his constituents (i.e., some 200,000 people).[8] For over 20 years Congressman Charles C. Diggs, Jr. (D–Mich.) has run a radio program featuring himself as a "combination disc jockey–commentator and minister."[9] Congressman Daniel J. Flood (D–Pa.) is "famous for appearing unannounced and often uninvited at wedding anniversaries and other events."[10]

Anniversaries and other events aside, congressional advertising is done largely at public expense. Use of the franking privilege has mushroomed in recent years; in early 1973 one estimate predicted that House and Senate members would send out about 476 million pieces of mail in the year 1974, at a public cost of $38.1 million—or about 900,000 pieces per member with a subsidy of $70,000 per member.[11] By far the heaviest mailroom traffic comes in Octobers of even-numbered years.[12] There are some differences between House and Senate members in the ways they go about getting their names across. House members are free to blanket their constituencies with mailings for all boxholders; Senators are not. But Senators find it easier to appear on national television—for example, in short reaction statements on the nightly news shows. Advertising is a staple congressional activity, and there is no end to it. For each member there are always new voters to be apprised of his worthiness and old voters to be reminded of it.[13]

A second activity may be called *credit claiming*, defined here as acting so as to generate a belief in a relevant political actor (or actors) that one is personally responsible for causing the government, or some unit thereof, to do something that the actor (or actors) considers desirable. The political logic of this, from the Congressman's point of view, is that an actor who believes that a member can make pleasing things happen will no doubt wish to keep him in office so that he can make pleasing things happen in the future. The emphasis here is on individual accomplishment (rather than, say, party or governmental accomplishment) and on the Congressman as doer (rather than as, say, expounder of constituency views). Credit claiming is highly important to Congressmen, with the consequence that much of congressional life is a relentless search for opportunities to engage in it.

Where can credit be found? If there were only one Congressman rather than 535, the answer would in principle be simple enough.[14] Credit (or blame) would attach in Downsian fashion to the doings of the government as a whole. But there are 535. Hence it becomes necessary for each Congressman to try to peel off pieces of governmental accomplishment for which he can believably generate a sense of responsibility. For the average Congressman the staple way of doing this is to traffic in what may be called "particularized benefits."[15] Particularized governmental benefits, as the term will be used here, have two properties: (1) each benefit is given out to a specific individual, group, or geographical constituency, the recipient unit being of a scale that allows a single Congressman to be recognized (by relevant political actors and other Congressmen) as the claimant for the benefit (other Congressmen being perceived as indifferent or hostile); (2) each benefit is given out in apparently ad hoc fashion (unlike, say, social security checks) with a Congressman apparently having a hand in the allocation. A particularized benefit can normally be regarded as a member of a class. That is, a benefit given out to an individual, group, or constituency can normally be looked upon by Congressmen as one of a class of similar benefits given out to sizable numbers of individuals, groups, or constituencies. Hence the impression can arise that a Congressman is getting "his share" of whatever it is the government is offering. (The classes may be vaguely defined. Some state legislatures deal in what their members call "local legislation.")

In sheer volume the bulk of particularized benefits come under the heading of "casework"—the thousands of favors congressional offices perform for supplicants in ways that normally do not require legislative action. High school students ask for essay materials, soldiers for emergency leaves, pensioners for location of missing checks, local governments for grant information, and on and on. Each office has skilled professionals who can play the bureaucracy like an organ—pushing the right pedals to produce the desired effects.[16] But many benefits require new legislation, or at least they require important allocative decisions on matters covered by existent legislation. Here the Congressman fills the traditional role of supplier of goods to the home district. It is a believable role; when a member claims credit for a benefit on the order of a dam, he may well receive it.[17] Shiny construction projects seem especially useful.[18] In the decades before 1934, tariff duties for local industries were a major commodity.[19] In recent years awards given under grant-in-aid programs have become more useful as they have become more numerous. Some quests for credit are ingenious; in 1971 the story broke that Congressmen had been earmarking foreign aid money for specific projects in Israel in order to win favor with home constituents.[20] It should be said of constituency benefits that Congressmen are quite capable of taking the initiative in drumming them up; that is, there can be no automatic assumption that a Congressman's activity is the result of pressures brought to bear by organized interests. Fenno shows the importance of member initiative in his discussion of the House Interior Committee.[21]

A final point here has to do with geography. The examples given so far are all of benefits conferred upon home constituencies or recipients therein (the latter including the home residents who applauded the Israeli projects). But the properties of particularized benefits were carefully specified so as not to exclude the possibility that some benefits may be given to recipients outside the home constituencies. Some probably are. Narrowly drawn tax loopholes qualify as particularized benefits, and some of them are probably conferred upon recipients outside the home districts.[22] (It is difficult to find solid evidence on the point.) Campaign contributions flow into districts from the outside, so it would not be surprising to find that benefits go where the resources are.[23]

How much particularized benefits count for at the polls is extraordinarily difficult to say. But it would be hard to find a congressman who thinks he can afford to wait around until precise information is available. The lore is that they count—furthermore, given home expectations, that they must be supplied in regular quantities for a member to stay electorally even with the board. Awareness of favors may spread beyond their recipients,[24] building for a member a general reputation as a good provider. "Rivers Delivers." "He Can Do More For Massachusetts."[25] A good example of Capitol Hill lore on electoral impact is given in this account of the activities of Congressman Frank Thompson, Jr. (D–N.J., 4th district):

> In 1966, the fourth was altered drastically by redistricting; it lost Burlington County and gained Hunterdon, Warren, and Sussex. Thompson's performance at the polls since 1966 is a case study of how an incumbent Congressman, out of line with his district's ideological persuasions, can become unbeatable. In 1966, Thompson carried Mercer by 23,000 votes and lost the three new counties by 4,600, winning reelection with 56 percent of the votes. He then survived a districtwide drop in his vote two years later. In 1970, the Congressman carried Mercer County by 20,000 votes and the rest of the district by 6,000, finishing with 58 percent. The drop in Mercer resulted from the attempt of his hard-line conservative opponent to exploit the racial unrest which had developed in Trenton. But for four years Thompson had been making friends in Hunterdon, Warren, and Sussex, busy doing the kind of chores that Congressmen do. In this case, Thompson concerned himself with the interests of dairy farmers at the Department of Agriculture. The results of his efforts were clear when the results came in from the fourth's northern counties.[26]

So much for particularized benefits. But is credit available elsewhere? For government accomplishments beyond the scale of those already discussed? The general answer is that the prime mover role is a hard one to play on larger matters—at least before broad electorates. A claim, after all, has to be credible. If a Congressman goes before an audience and says, "I am responsible for passing a bill to curb inflation," or "I am responsible for the highway program," hardly anyone will believe him. There are two reasons why people may be skeptical of such claims. First, there is a numbers problem. On an accomplishment of a sort that probably engaged the supportive interest of more than one member it is reasonable to suppose that credit should be apportioned among them. But second, there is an overwhelming problem of information costs. For typical voters Capitol Hill is a distant and mysterious place; few have anything like a working knowledge of its maneuverings. Hence there is no easy way of knowing whether a Congressman is staking a valid claim or not. The odds are that the information problem cuts in different ways on different kinds of issues. On particularized benefits it may work in a Congressman's favor; he may get credit for the dam he had nothing to do with building. Sprinkling a district with dams, after all, is something a Congressman is supposed to be able to do. But on larger matters it may work against him. For a voter lacking an easy way to sort out valid from invalid claims the sensible recourse is skepticism. Hence it is unlikely that Congressmen get much mileage out of credit claiming on larger matters before broad electorates.[27]

Yet there is an obvious and important qualification here. For many Congressmen credit claiming on nonparticularized matters is possible in specialized subject areas because of the congressional division of labor. The term *governmental unit* in the original definition of credit claiming is broad enough to include committees, subcommittees, and the two houses of Congress itself. Thus many Congressmen can believably claim credit for blocking bills in subcommittee, adding on amendments in committee, and so on. The audience for transactions of this sort is usually small. But it may include important political actors (e.g., an interest group, the President, The *New York Times,* Ralph Nader) who are capable of both paying Capitol Hill information costs and deploying electoral resources. There is a well-documented example of this in Fenno's treatment of Post Office politics in the 1960s. The postal employee unions used to watch very closely the activities of the

House and Senate Post Office Committees and supply valuable electoral resources (money, volunteer work) to members who did their bidding on salary bills.[28]

The third activity Congressmen engage in may be called *position taking,* defined here as the public enunciation of a judgmental statement on anything likely to be of interest to political actors. The statement may take the form of a roll-call vote. The most important classes of judgmental statements are those prescribing American governmental ends (a vote cast against the war; a statement that "the war should be ended immediately") or governmental means (a statement that "the way to end the war is to take it to the United Nations"). The judgments may be implicit rather than explicit, as in: "I will support the President on this matter." But judgments may range far beyond these classes to take in implicit or explicit statements on what almost anybody should do or how he should do it: "The great Polish scientist Copernicus has been unjustly neglected"; "The way for Israel to achieve peace is to give up the Sinai."[29] The Congressman as position taker is a speaker rather than a doer. The electoral requirement is not that he make pleasing things happen but that he make pleasing judgmental statements. The position itself is the political commodity. Especially on matters where governmental responsibility is widely diffused, it is not surprising that political actors should fall back on positions as tests of incumbent virtue. For voters ignorant of congressional processes the recourse is an easy one. The following comment by one of Clapp's House interviewees is highly revealing: "Recently, I went home and began to talk about the ——— Act. I was pleased to have sponsored that bill, but it soon dawned on me that the point wasn't getting through at all. What was getting through was that the act might be a help to people. I changed the emphasis: I didn't mention my role particularly, but stressed my support of the legislation."[30]

The ways in which positions can be registered are numerous and often imaginative. There are floor addresses ranging from weighty orations to mass-produced "nationality day statements."[31] There are speeches before home groups, television appearances, letters, newsletters, press releases, ghostwritten books, *Playboy* articles, even interviews with political scientists. On occasion Congressmen generate what amount to petitions; whether or not to sign the 1956 Southern Manifesto defying school desegregation rulings was an important decision for southern members.[32] Outside the roll-call process the Congressman is usually able to tailor his positions to suit his audiences. A solid consensus in the constituency calls for ringing declarations; for years the late Senator James K. Vardaman (D–Miss.) campaigned on a proposal to repeal the 15th Amendment.[33] Division or uncertainty in the constituency calls for waffling; in the late 1960s a Congressman had to be a poor politician indeed not to be able to come up with an inoffensive statement on Vietnam. ("We must have peace with honor at the earliest possible moment consistent with the national interest.") On a controversial issue a Capitol Hill office normally prepares two form letters to send out to constituent letter writers—one for the pros and one (not directly contradictory) for the antis.[34] Handling discrete audiences in person requires simple agility, a talent well demonstrated in this selection from a Nader profile:

> "You may find this difficult to understand," said Democrat Edward R. Roybal, the Mexican-American representative from California's 30th district, "but sometimes I wind up making a patriotic speech one afternoon and later on that same day an antiwar speech. In the patriotic speech I speak of past wars but I also speak of the need to prevent more wars. My positions are not inconsistent; I just approach different people differently." Roybal went on to depict the diversity of crowds he speaks to: One afternoon he is surrounded by balding men wearing Veterans' caps and holding American flags; a

> few hours later he speaks to a crowd of Chicano youths, angry over American involvement in Vietnam. Such a diverse constituency, Roybal believes, calls for different methods of expressing one's convictions.[35]

Indeed it does. Versatility of this sort is occasionally possible in roll-call voting. For example, a Congressman may vote one way on recommittal and the other on final passage, leaving it unclear just how he stands on a bill.[36] Members who cast identical votes on a measure may give different reasons for having done so. Yet it is on roll calls that the crunch comes; there is no way for a member to avoid making a record on hundreds of issues, some of which are controversial in the home constituencies. Of course, most roll-call positions considered in isolation are not likely to cause much of a ripple at home. But broad voting patterns can and do; member "ratings" calculated by the Americans for Democratic Action, Americans for Constitutional Action, and other outfits are used as guidelines in the deploying of electoral resources. And particular issues often have their alert publics. Some national interest groups watch the votes of all Congressmen on single issues and ostentatiously try to reward or punish members for their positions; over the years some notable examples of such interest groups have been the Anti-Saloon League,[37] the early Farm Bureau,[38] The American Legion,[39] the American Medical Association,[40] and the National Rifle Association.[41] On rare occasions single roll calls achieve a rather high salience among the public generally. This seems especially true of the Senate, which every now and then winds up for what might be called a "showdown vote," with pressures on all sides, presidential involvement, media attention given to individual Senators' positions, and suspense about the outcome. Examples are the votes on the nuclear test-ban treaty in 1963, civil rights cloture in 1964, civil rights cloture again in 1965, the Haynsworth appointment in 1969, the Carswell appointment in 1970, and the ABM in 1970. Controversies on roll calls like these are often relived in subsequent campaigns, the southern Senate elections of 1970 with their Haynsworth and Carswell issues being cases in point.

Probably the best position-taking strategy for most Congressmen at most times is to be conservative—to cling to their own positions of the past where possible and to reach for new ones with great caution where necessary. Yet in an earlier discussion of strategy the suggestion was made that it might be rational for members in electoral danger to resort to innovation. The form of innovation available is entrepreneurial position taking, its logic being that for a member facing defeat with his old array of positions it makes good sense to gamble on some new ones. It may be that congressional marginals fulfill an important function here as issue pioneers—experimenters who test out new issues and thereby show other politicians which ones are usable.[42] An example of such a pioneer is Senator Warren Magnuson (D–Wash.), who responded to a surprisingly narrow victory in 1962 by reaching for a reputation in the area of consumer affairs.[43] Another example is Senator Ernest Hollings (D–S.C.), a servant of a shaky and racially heterogeneous southern constituency who launched "hunger" as an issue in 1969—at once pointing to a problem and giving it a useful nonracial definition.[44] One of the most successful issue entrepreneurs of recent decades was the late Senator Joseph McCarthy (R–Wis.); it was all there—the close primary in 1946, the fear of defeat in 1952, the desperate casting about for an issue, the famous 1950 dinner at the Colony Restaurant where suggestions were tendered, the decision that "communism" might just do the trick.[45]

The effect of position taking on electoral behavior is about as hard to measure as the effect of credit claiming. Once again there is a variance problem; Congressmen do not differ very much among themselves in the methods they use or the skills they display in attuning themselves to their diverse constituencies. All of them, after all, are professional politicians.

There is intriguing hard evidence on some matters where variance can be captured. Schoenberger has found that House Republicans who signed an early pro-Goldwater petition plummeted significantly farther in their 1964 percentages than their colleagues who did not sign.[46] (The signers appeared genuinely to believe that identification with Goldwater was an electoral plus.) Erikson has found that roll-call records are interestingly related to election percentages: "[A] reasonable estimate is that an unusually liberal Republican Representative gets at least 6 percent more of the two-party vote . . . than his extreme conservative counterpart would in the same district."[47] In other words, taking some roll-call positions that please voters of the opposite party can be electorally helpful. (More specifically, it can help in November; some primary electorates will be more tolerant of it than others.)

Sometimes an inspection of deviant cases offers clues. There is the ideological odyssey of former Congressman Walter Baring (D–Nev.), who entered Congress as a more or less regular Democrat in the mid-1950s but who moved over to a point where he was the most conservative House Democrat outside the South by the late 1960s. The Nevada electorate reacted predictably; Baring's November percentages rose astoundingly high (82.5 percent in 1970), but he encountered guerrilla warfare in the primaries which finally cost him his nomination in 1972—whereupon the seat turned Republican.

There can be no doubt that Congressmen believe positions make a difference. An important consequence of this belief is their custom of watching each other's elections to try to figure out what positions are salable. Nothing is more important in Capitol Hill politics than the shared conviction that election returns have proven a point. Thus the 1950 returns were read not only as a rejection of health insurance but as a ratification of McCarthyism.[48] When two North Carolina nonsigners of the 1956 Southern Manifesto immediately lost their primaries, the message was clear to southern members that there could be no straying from a hard line on the school desegregation issue. Any breath of life left in the cause of school busing was squeezed out by House returns from the Detroit area in 1972. Senator Douglas gives an interesting report on the passage on the first minimum wage bill in the 75th Congress. In 1937 the bill was tied up in the House Rules Committee, and there was an effort to get it to the floor through use of a discharge petition. Then two primary elections broke the jam. Claude Pepper (D–Fla.) and Lister Hill (D–Ala.) won nominations to fill vacant Senate seats. "Both campaigned on behalf of the Wages and Hours bill, and both won smashing victories. . . . Immediately after the results of the Florida and Alabama primaries became known, there was a stampede to sign the petition, and the necessary 218 signatures were quickly obtained."[49] The bill later passed. It may be useful to close this section on position taking with a piece of political lore on electoral impact that can stand beside the piece on the impact of credit claiming offered earlier. The discussion is of the pre-1972 sixth California House district:

> Since 1952 the district's Congressman has been Republican William S. Mailliard, a wealthy member of an old California family. For many years Mailliard had a generally liberal voting record. He had no trouble at the polls, winning elections by large majorities in what is, by a small margin at least, a Democratic district. More recently, Mailliard seems caught between the increasing conservatism of the state's Republican party and the increasing liberalism of his constituency.
>
> After [Governor Ronald] Reagan's victory [in 1966], Mailliard's voting record became noticeably more conservative.

> Because of this, he has been spared the tough conservative primary opposition that Paul McCloskey has confronted in the 11th. But Mailliard's move to the right has not gone unnoticed in the sixth district. In 1968 he received 73 percent of the vote, but in 1970 he won only 53 percent—a highly unusual drop for an incumbent of such long standing. Much of the difference must be attributed to the war issue. San Francisco and Marin are both antiwar strongholds; but Mailliard, who is the ranking Republican on the House Foreign Affairs Committee, has supported the Nixon Administration's war policy. In the sixth district, at least, that position is a sure vote-loser.[50]

These, then are the three kinds of electorally oriented activities congressmen engage in—advertising, credit claiming, and position taking. It remains only to offer some brief comments on the emphases different members give to the different activities. No deterministic statements can be made; within limits each member has freedom to build his own electoral coalition and hence freedom to choose the means of doing it.[51] Yet there are broad patterns. For one thing Senators, with their access to the media, seem to put more emphasis on position taking than House members; probably House members rely more heavily on particularized benefits. But there are important differences among House members. Congressmen from the traditional parts of old machine cities rarely advertise and seldom take positions on anything (except on roll calls), but devote a great deal of time and energy to the distribution of benefits. In fact, they use their office resources to plug themselves into their local party organizations. Congressman William A. Barrett (D–downtown Philadelphia), chairman of the Housing Subcommittee of the House Banking and Currency Committee, claimed in 1971 to have spent only three nights in Washington in the preceding six years. He meets constituents each night from 9:00 P.M. to 1:00 A.M. in the home district: "Folks line up to tell Bill Barrett their problems."[52] On the other hand Congressmen with upper-middle-class bases (suburban, city reform, or academic) tend to deal in positions. In New York City the switch from regular to reform Democrats is a switch from members who emphasize benefits to members who emphasize positions; it reflects a shift in consumer taste.[53] The same difference appears geographically rather than temporally as one goes from the inner wards to the outer suburbs of Chicago.[54]

Another kind of difference appears if the initial assumption of a reelection quest is relaxed to take into account the "progressive" ambitions of some members—the aspirations of some to move up to higher electoral offices rather than keep the ones they have.[55] There are two important subsets of climbers in the Congress—House members who would like to be senators (over the years about a quarter of the senators have come up directly from the House),[56] and Senators who would like to be Presidents or Vice Presidents (in the 93d Congress about a quarter of the Senators had at one time or another run for these offices or been seriously "mentioned" for them). In both cases higher aspirations seem to produce the same distinctive mix of activities. For one thing credit claiming is all but useless. It does little good to talk about the bacon you have brought back to a district you are trying to abandon. And, as Lyndon Johnson found in 1960, claiming credit on legislative maneuvers is no way to reach a new mass audience; it baffles rather than persuades. Office advancement seems to require a judicious mixture of advertising and position taking. Thus a House member aiming for the Senate heralds his quest with press releases; there must be a new "image," sometimes an ideological overhaul to make ready for the new constituency.[57] Senators aiming for the White House do more or less the same thing—advertising to get the name across, position taking ("We can do better"). In recent years presidential aspirants have sought Foreign Relations Committee membership as a platform for making statements on foreign policy.[58]

There are these distinctions, but it would be a mistake to elevate them over the commonalities. For most Congressmen most of the time all three activities are essential. This closing vignette of Senator Strom Thurmond (R–S.C.) making his peace with universal suffrage is a good picture of what the electoral side of American legislative politics is all about. The Senator was reacting in 1971 to a 1970 Democratic gubernatorial victory in his state in which black turnout was high:

> Since then, the Republican Senator has done the following things:
>
> - Hired Thomas Moss, a black political organizer who directed Negro voter registration efforts for the South Carolina Voter Education Project, for his staff in South Carolina, and a black secretary for his Washington office.
> - Announced federal grants for projects in black areas, including at least one occasion when he addressed a predominantly black audience to announce a rural water project and remained afterwards to shake hands.
> - Issued moderate statements on racial issues.
>
> In a statement to *Ebony* magazine that aides say Thurmond wrote himself, he said, "In most instances I am confident that we have more in common as southerners than we have reason to oppose each other because of race. Equality of opportunity for all is a goal upon which blacks and southern whites can agree."[59]

Illustration 2.A.
Congressional districts.

Congressional districting is an important component of the congressional election process, for how and where district boundary lines are drawn will affect significantly election returns and outcomes. Excessive manipulation of district lines is called "gerrymandering." Although not as egregious as the infamous "rotten boroughs" of 17th and 18th century Great Britain, the following map of U.S. House districts in California shows the work of political cartographers: drawing district lines for political advantage.

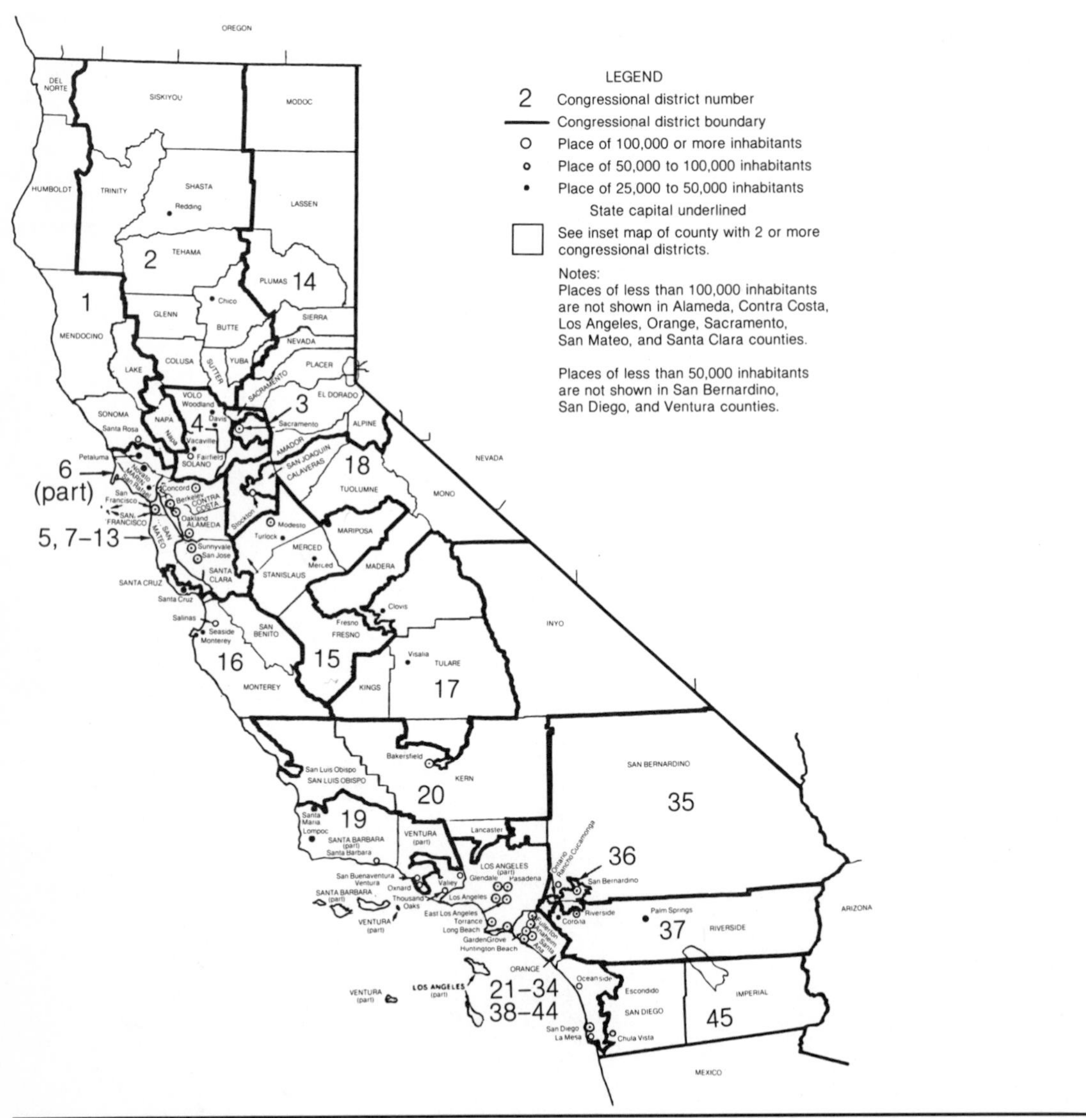

Source: "Districts of the 99th Congress," Congressional District Atlas.

Illustration 2.B.
Excerpts from federal campaign and election law.

Congressional campaigns and elections are conducted under myriad federal statutes and regulations concerning sources of contributions, recording and disclosure of contributions, and expenditures of funds. The following brief excerpts reveal the nature of these laws.

CONTENTS

UNITED STATES CODE

TITLE 2. THE CONGRESS

Illustration 2.B. *(continued)*

Illustration 2.B. *(concluded)*

Reading 2.3

Representation, Responsibility, and the Future of Congressional Elections

Gary C. Jacobson

Representation of political interests is a major function of a legislature. Representation is also a major issue with regard to congressional elections, for it has been argued that through the current scheme of congressional elections, segmental or district interests rather than unitarian or national interests are served and advanced. To many, the result is the absence of collective will and accountability in the U.S. Congress and the making of highly particularistic and parochial policy. The following excerpt from the concluding chapter of a major text on congressional elections emphasizes the problem of "representation without responsibility."

Concluding questions to be asked with regard

Source: From *The Politics of Congressional Elections*, by Gary C. Jacobson, pp. 184–91. © by Little, Brown 1983. Reprinted with permission.

to representation are: Do particularistic and parochial interests get balanced out in the give and take and push and shove of brokerage politics in the legislature? Under what conditions are public opinion and mass sentiment represented fairly accurately in the legislature? When are special interests likely to prevail? Does a legislature have to reflect the demographic or opinion universe to be representative? Is responsiveness to organized and intense groups unrepresentative if the public is not mobilized? Should the legislature reflect member, district, or national considerations? Which of these usually prevails and when?

These are classical issues of representation that must be grappled with in any survey of congressional elections. Conventional notions of pluralism stress the integrating and conflict resolving nature of the legislature, and especially its ability to deal with the classical problem of intensely held segmental or minority preferences. Revisionists, on the other hand, stress the deficiencies of pluralistic democracy, emphasizing the costs to and short-changing of national priorities and the public interest of group politics.

Congress is a representative assembly. Put most simply,[1] it is a representative assembly because its members are chosen in competitive popular elections, and if voters do not like what they are doing, they can vote them out of office. Voters can hold congressmen accountable for their actions as long as members care about reelection. Nearly everyone does. Representation is an effect of electoral politics; the electoral system structures the kind of representation Congress provides. What kind of representation is that?

REPRESENTATION

Political scientists have customarily paid the most attention to one aspect of representation: policy congruence. The central question is the extent to which the policy views of people in a state or district are reflected in the policy stances (usually measured by roll-call votes) of the people they elect to Congress. This has never been an easy question to answer. Information on constituency opinion is scarce and often unreliable, and it is frequently doubtful that there is any "constituency opinion" on a given issue. Measuring constituency attitudes has challenged the ingenuity of a generation of scholars, since the one unquestioned solution—adequate sample surveys of a large number of states and districts—is simply too expensive.

Demographic indicators, simulations, referenda voting, and aggregated national survey data have all been used to estimate state and district attitudes.[2] Each of these approaches has its drawbacks, and there is the additional problem of establishing some kind of comparability between any of these measures and measures of congressional behavior.[3] Still, a number of general conclusions can be drawn from this work. Most research suggests that congressional roll-call votes are indeed related to estimated district opinion, although the strength of the connection varies across issue dimensions and is never overwhelmingly large. The relationships are strongest when votes and attitudes are combined and reduced to a few general dimensions—for example, domestic welfare policy or civil rights for minorities—and weaker for specific votes on single pieces of legislation.[4] The connection is also stronger if the constituency is defined as the member's supporters (defined by voting or partisanship).[5]

All of these findings make sense. Members of Congress develop highly differentiated images of their constituencies and have a fair notion of who keeps them in office. It is no surprise that they are more responsive to some groups than to others. There is not a great deal of pressure to vote district (or supporting constituency) preferences on every vote, especially since on many specific votes constituency preferences are unknown or unformed. Members need only take care to cast "explainable" votes. On the other hand, anyone who consistently votes contrary to the wishes of his or her constituents is likely to run into trouble; a string of bad votes will attract serious opponents and give them ammunition.

Congress is broadly representative on another dimension. Aggregate election results are responsive to national political and economic conditions. When things are going badly, the administration's party suffers the consequences. The opposing party picks up more seats, and even those who remain in Congress get the message that they had better watch their step. Reagan was able to win budget victories not only because more Republicans sit in the 97th Congress, but also because the remaining Democrats read the election results as a demand that something drastic be done about taxes and inflation. The issue in 1980 was not whether the budget and taxes would be cut , but which package of cuts—the administration's or the House Democrats'—would be adopted.

Aggregate representation of this kind is necessarily crude and rests on somewhat shaky foundations, depending, as it now does, on the self-reinforcing prophecies of congressional elites. And it can only operate when there is some public consensus on the general direction of policy. The energy crisis, designated by Carter as the "moral equivalent of war," was certainly the dominant national issue when gas lines developed and energy prices skyrocketed. But Congress could not produce any systematic plan to cope with it because all of the proposed solutions would impose major costs on politically powerful groups.

The scholarly interest in measuring degrees of policy congruence to assess congressional representation is in itself a consequence of congressional election politics. The question would scarcely arise in a system built around strong programmatic parties. If voters merely expressed a preference for a party's proposals in their vote and the winning party carried out its promised policies, policy representation would be automatic. Weak parties, the diversity of states and districts, pervasive electoral individualism, and the host of electoral activities that have nothing to do with national policy are what raise the issue in the first place. What kind of representation is provided by independent political entrepreneurs who stay in office by emphasizing constituent services and their own personal honesty, sincerity, and availability rather than policies or partisanship?

One of Fenno's important insights is that much of what goes on in the pursuit of congressional office is in fact essential to meaningful representation in a system without strong, programmatic parties.

> There is no way that the act of representing can be separated from the act of getting elected. If the congressman cannot win and hold the votes of some people, he cannot represent any people. Further, he cannot represent any people unless he knows, or makes an effort to know, who they are, what they think, and what they want; and it is by campaigning for electoral support among them that he finds out such things. During the expansionist stage of his constituency career, particularly, he probably knows his various constituencies as well as it is possible to know them. It is, indeed, by such campaigning, by going home a great deal, that a congressman develops a complex and discriminating set of perceptions about his constituents.[6]

This knowledge is the basis for making judgments about what constituents want or need from politics. Two-way communication is essential to representation. The stress members of Congress put on their accessibility invites communication from constituents at the same time it attracts their support. The knowledge and work it takes to win and hold a district not only establish the basis for policy congruence, but also let the members know when it is irrelevant or unnecessary.

There is much more to representation than policy congruence, of course. The work of Fenno and others has made that clear. Members certainly "represent" their constituents in important ways by helping them cope with the federal bureaucracy, by bringing in public works projects, by helping local governments and other groups to take advantage of federal programs, or by helping an overseas relative get permanent resident status. Particularized benefits are still benefits, and an important part of representation evidently involves making sure one's state or district gets its share.

Representation of still another kind is provided by members who take it on themselves to become spokesmen for interests and groups not confined to their constituencies. Black congressmen, for example, often present themselves as representatives of all black Americans. Senator Jesse Helms takes it upon himself to represent the preferences of the ultraconservatives of the "New Right." Representative Henry Hyde leads the legislative fight against abortion and has become a major figure on the "Right-to-Life" speaking circuit. Opposition to the Vietnam War absorbed the energies of more than a few members some years back. Most members are not so careless that their commitment to a group or cause upsets their supporting constituency; more often it becomes a way of pleasing constituents (especially their core supporters) and so coincides nicely with electoral necessities. But not always. A few members invite consistently strong opposition and regularly court defeat in representing their vision of the national interest. The electoral system, however, tends to weed them out.

On a somewhat more mundane level, the current electoral process gives representation of a sort to any group that can mobilize people or money to help in campaigns. The corporate PACs, trade associations, labor unions, and ideological groups that provide campaign resources help to elect congenial candidates and gain, at least, access to them; both provide these groups with representation. It is a matter of debate whether this is a benign or pernicious phenomenon, and the controversy is not likely to die down as long as PAC contributions continue to grow. But it would be hard to argue that some mechanism for representing the enormous variety of economic and political interests that cannot be encompassed within the framework of single-member districts is not essential. With the decline of political parties, no obvious alternatives exist.

In one way Congress does not represent the American public well at all: demographically. It contains a much greater proportion of white, male, college-educated, professional, higher-income people than the population as a whole. Almost half of its present members are lawyers; a blue-collar background is rare. Yet it is probably quite representative of the kinds of people who achieve positions of leadership in the great majority of American institutions. It would be unlikely in the extreme for an electoral system like the American to produce a Congress looking anything like a random sample of the voting age population. What it does produce is a sample of local elites from an incredibly diverse, heterogeneous society. And from this perspective, a basic problem may be that the electoral politics of Congress generates legislative bodies that are *too* representative of the myriad divisions in American society.

American citizens are seriously divided themselves on most important political issues. But their divisions do not form coherent patterns. No clear political battle lines have developed across the range of contemporary issues. Most of the time there is little consensus on what issues are important, let alone what alternative solutions are preferable. Mayhew argues that "half the adverse criticism of Congress . . . is an indirect criticism of the public itself."[7] Like the members of Congress whom they elect, Americans have wanted to have it both ways. We have enjoyed the programs and benefits that the federal government provides, but we dislike paying the price in the form of higher taxes, more inflation, and greater government regulation. Public opinion polls have found, in recent years, solid majorities for national health insurance, wage and price controls, government guarantees of jobs, and current or greater levels of spending on the environment, education, the cities, and health care. They have found equally solid majorities believing that the federal government is too large, spends too much money, and is too intrusive in peoples' lives.[8] As Senator Lowell Weicker once put it, "everybody wants to go to Heaven, but nobody wants to die."[9]

RESPONSIVENESS WITHOUT RESPONSIBILITY

The dilemmas this creates for Congress reinforce the fundamental flaw in the kind of representation produced by electoral politics: great individual *responsiveness*, equally great collective *irresponsibility*. Emphasis on constituency services becomes more attractive as policy matters become more divisive and threatening. Beyond that, the safest way to cope with contradictory policy demands is to be acutely sensitive to what constituent and other politically important groups want in taking positions but to avoid responsibility for the costs they would impose. Voting for all your favorite programs and then against the deficit total is the paradigmatic strategy. The pervasive temptation to engage in symbolic position taking rather than working to find real solutions to national problems is harder to resist when every solution is likely to anger one politically important group or another. It does not help matters that members are rewarded individually for taking pleasing positions but are not punished for failing to turn them into national policy or, when they do become policy, for seeing that they work.

As long as members are not held individually responsible for Congress' performance as an institution, a crucial form of representation is missing. Responsiveness is insufficient without responsibility. Political parties are the only instruments we have managed to develop for imposing collective responsibility on legislators. There is nothing original about this observation; it is a home truth to which students of congressional politics are inevitably drawn.[10] Morris Fiorina has recently put the case cogently:

> A strong political party can generate collective responsibility by creating incentives for leaders, followers, and popular supporters to think and act in collective terms. First, by providing party leaders with the capability (*e.g.*, control of institutional patronage, nominations, etc.) to discipline party members, genuine leadership becomes possible. Legislative output is less likely to be a least common denominator—a residue of myriad conflicting proposals—and more likely to consist of a program actually intended to solve a problem or move the nation in a particular direction. Second, the subordination of individual officeholders to the party lessens their ability to separate themselves from party actions. Like it or not their performance becomes identified with the performance of the collectivity to which they belong. Third, with individual candidate variation greatly reduced, voters have less incentive to support individuals and more to support or oppose the party as a whole. And fourth, the circle closes as party line voting in the electorate provides party leaders with the incentive to propose policies which will earn the support of a national majority, and party backbenchers with the personal incentive to cooperate with leaders in the attempt to compile a good record for the party as a whole.[11]

Pristine party government has never been characteristic of American politics, to be sure. But any reader who has made it this far will recognize that all its necessary elements have been eroded alarmingly over the past several decades. This has surely contributed to political drift, immobilism in the face of tough, divisive problems like energy and inflation, shrill single-issue politics disdaining compromise, enfeebled leadership, and growing public cynicism and distrust of politicians and political institutions.[12] Responsiveness is insufficient without responsibility. The politics of congressional elections, and the structural characteristics of Congress, which they have done much to shape, produce the former but not the latter, and we are all the worse for it.

Chapter Three

The Congress: Who Is It?

In addition to being a political institution and instrument of government, Congress is a human organization, replete with its interpersonal relations, cliques, norms and folkways, and dynamics of power, authority, and formal and informal leadership.

The readings in this section aim to define Congress as a human organization. To do this, selections are included on the legislator as actor, the House versus the Senate, staff growth, staff in the district, office dynamics, and congressional agencies, together with the views of two former, prominent insiders concerning the sociology of Congress.

A major issue to be aware of concerning the social and human side of Congress pertains to the enormous proliferation of congressional staff. According to some, burgeoning staffs have led to a system of "unelected representatives" that pose the danger of overwhelming members with analytical studies and self-serving and self-justifying make-work. For others less concerned, staff recruitment places boundaries on staff behavior, requiring staffers to anticipate member positions and to work within "parameters" of acceptability established by members. From this perspective, staff growth is a boon, not a bane, assisting Congress in its oversight responsibilities and strengthening the Congress's hand vis-à-vis the executive branch.

Illustration 3.A.
Origanizational charts of House and Senate.

The following are organizational schematics of both houses of Congress. These charts graphically illustrate that the Congress is more than just 435 House members, 100 senators, and their staffs. Congress is comprised of numerous support organizations and offices. These charts show the many offices established to support each house.

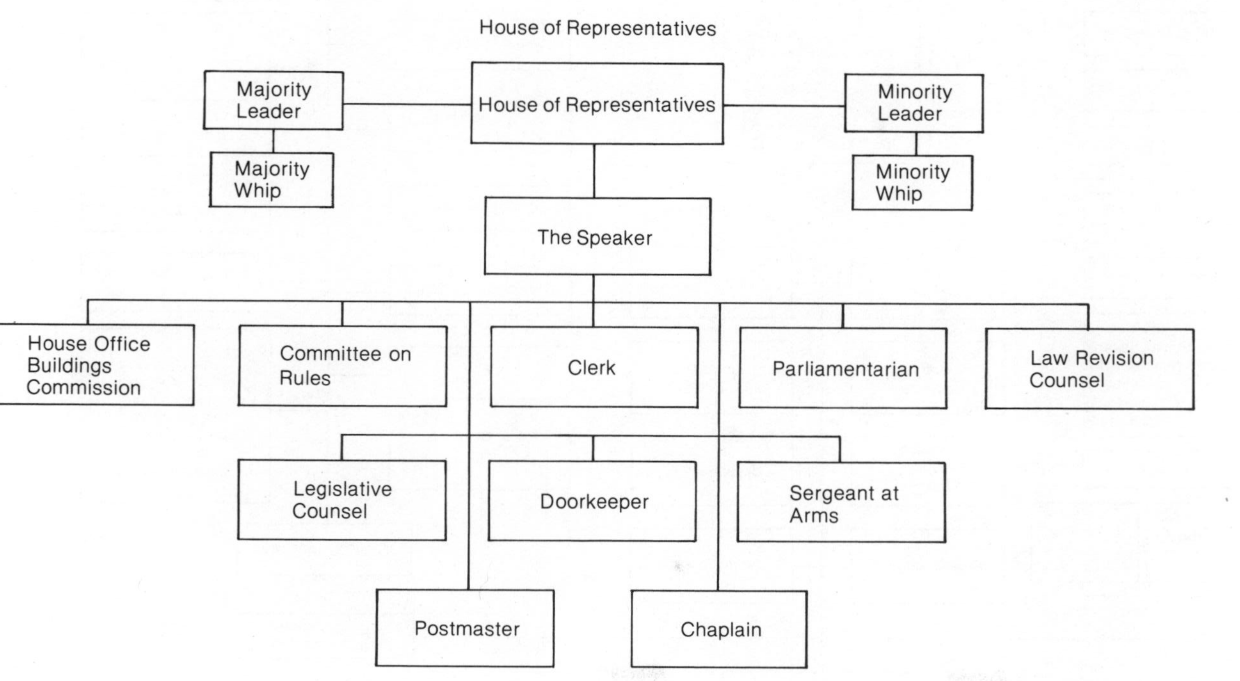

Source: From United States Government Manual, 1985–86, pp. 829–30. Reprinted from the public domain.

Illustration 3.A. (concluded)

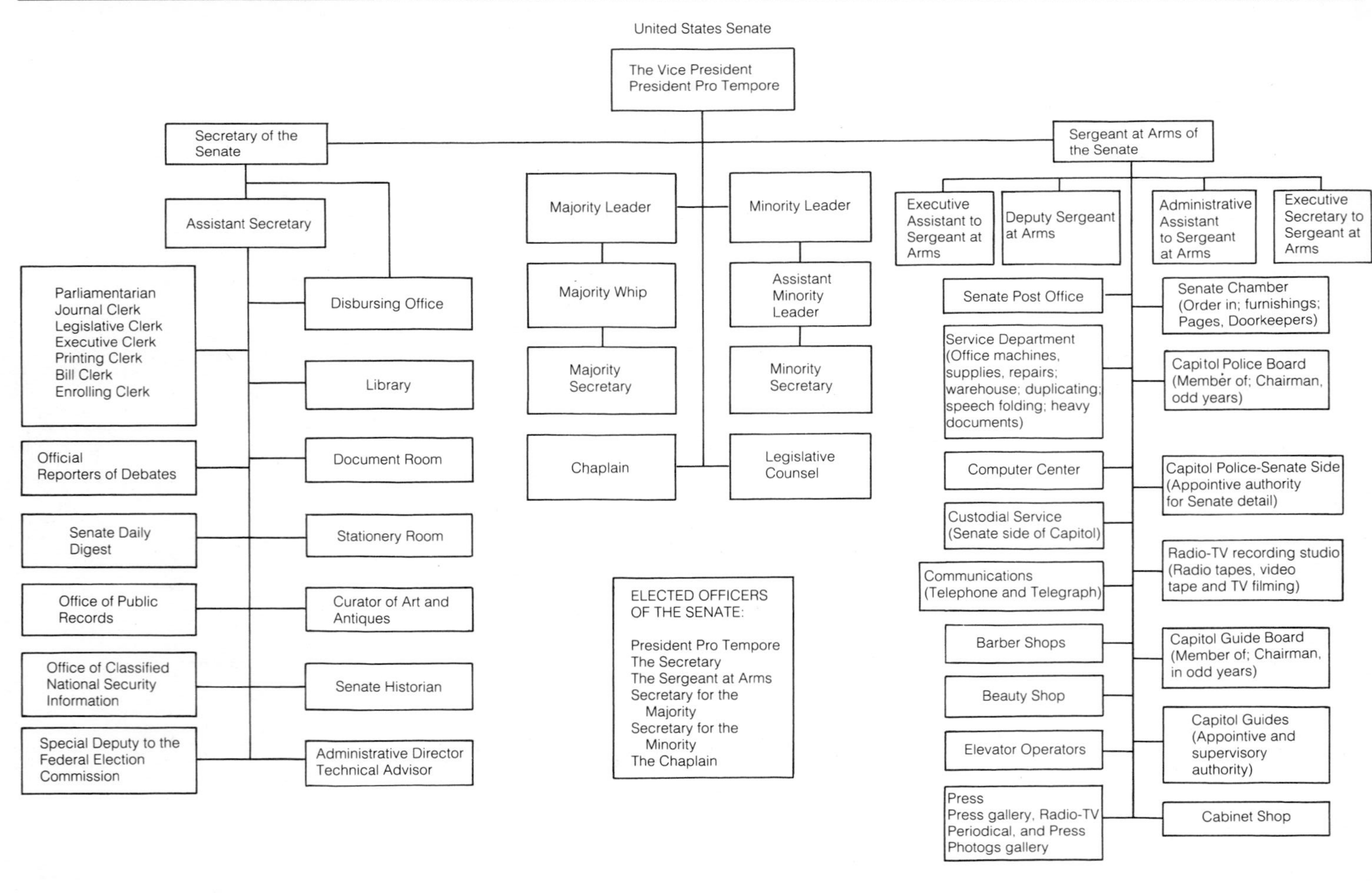

Reading 3.1

Congressional versus Bureaucratic Policy Actors

Randall B. Ripley
and Grace A. Franklin

Congressmen and their staffs are major actors in policymaking. The following selection from a widely used text illustrates the distinctive personal and institutional characteristics of members of Congress and congressional staffers in comparison to political executives and bureaucrats.

Table 3.1.1 summarizes the personal characteristics of major congressional and bureaucratic policy actors. When added to the information in the following section, a composite picture of the various groups of policy actors begins to emerge that shows that these characteristics can have some impact on the nature of relations between the groups as they labor on public policy.

THE INSTITUTIONAL SETTING

The institutional setting in which congressional and bureaucratic actors function is simply the general work environment that serves as a framework for any person in a particular job. A member of Congress operates in a different job environment from an agency head, as does a staff member for a congressional committee from a secretary of a department. The literature suggests a number of factors important in the institutional setting or job environment for each of the four groups of actors being examined. These include method of selection, job tenure and orientation, principal loyalties and representativeness, substantive specialization, professionalism, political expertise, and anonymity. In general, these factors are relatively unchanging over time, regardless of the individuals holding the positions.

Method of selection means simply how actors achieve the positions they hold. The principal options are election, political appointment, or merit advancement. *Job tenure and orientation* are related to the means of selection and involve the length of service and careerist aspirations associated with different actors. *Principal loyalties* involve the actors' perceptions of the entity to which they feel they owe primary allegiance. *Representativeness* of various actors varies both according to the geographic area represented (national versus local) and the breadth of interests represented (broad-gauged interests versus narrow, special interests). Do actors tend to become experts in a few issues (specialists) or do they tend to have a general understanding of many issues (generalists)? The notion of *degree of substantive specialization* addresses these questions. An actor's identification with a profession, in addition to identification as a government employee, is the focus of the discussion of *degree of professionalism.* The *degree of political expertise* inherent in different actors' jobs involves how political those jobs are and how much political skill is necessary for successfully holding them—skill in bargaining,

Source: From Randall B. Ripley and Grace A. Franklin, *Congress, the Bureaucracy, and Public Policy,* 3d ed. (Homewood, Ill: Dorsey Press, 1984).

Table 3.1.1.
Personal characteristics of major congressional and bureaucratic policy actors.

Characteristics	Senators and Representatives	Professional Congressional Staff Members	Higher Career Civil Servants	Federal Political Executives
Geographical representativeness	Broadly representative geographically; overrepresentative of small towns	Broadly representative geographically	Overrepresentative of east and urban areas	Broadly representative geographically; overrepresentative of large cities (especially New York and Washington)
Education	Highly educated	Highly educated	Highly educated	Highly educated
Occupation	Heavily in law and business; some educators; many professional politicians	Occupational specialty tied to job; many professional public servants; some generalists	Occupational specialty tied to job; many professional public servants; many with business background; some educators	Heavily in business and law; some educators
Age	Median: late 40s (senators slightly older)	Median: about 40	Median: late 40s	Median: late 40s
Sex and race	Mostly white males	Mostly white males	Mostly white males	Mostly white males
Previous governmental and political experience	High experience in both government and politics	Considerable Hill and political experience; limited executive branch experience	High government experience through civil service career	Moderately high experience in federal service
Beliefs	Believe in subgovernments and interest group access; ideology shifts with election results	Believe in subgovernments and interest group access; ideology reflects that of congressional employer	Believe in subgovernments and interest-group access; ideology reflects that of agency	Usually believe in subgovernments and interest-group access, with limits; ideology reflects that of agency and/or President

negotiations, and competing for limited amounts of power and resources. The final factor presented to describe the institutional setting is the *degree of visibility* (or conversely, *anonymity*) associated with the actors—how publicly visible are different groups as they perform their daily routines?

Method of Selection

Of the four groups, only one—members of the House and Senate—is elected. This simple fact makes an enormous difference in the kinds of considerations that are most salient to members as they deal with policy.

Concern for job security nurtures a predisposition for members of Congress to provide the voters back home with sufficient tangible benefits that they will reelect the providers. Legislators usually evaluate their behavior, either consciously or unconsciously, in terms of the impact it will have on the electoral constituency and the constituency's reaction to it (Mayhew, 1974).

Once in Congress, members seek appointment to specific committees and subcommittees for a variety of reasons (see Fenno, 1973). A number of members consciously seek a certain position because of the electoral advantage it can bring them. Even those who pursue memberships primarily because of their policy interests and because of their interest in increasing their influence within their chamber are mindful of opportunities a given assignment might afford them to serve their constituents. As members become more senior, they are generally less vulnerable at election time and can afford to pursue policy views that are particularly congenial to them as they work in committee and subcommittee settings.

The congressional staff is appointed by members of Congress and so reflects some of the members' concern with reelection and constituents. But, given the fact that an experienced staff member with an individual senator or representative can probably find another such job with a different member if the first employer should lose an election, the employee's personal stake is not nearly as strong as the member's own stake.

Political appointments in the executive branch are made by the President. At least in theory, he is responsible for selecting the appointees, but in practice many appointees are chosen by other high-ranking officials in the administration, either because they know and want a particular individual or because that person comes highly recommended by an important party figure—such as a major contributor of funds or an important senator or representative. Financial disclosure required by the 1978 Ethics in Government Act has made some potential political appointees reluctant to accept appointments.

Civil servants and their military and foreign-service equivalents are appointed on the basis of competitive examinations in the first instance, and they advance on the basis of merit after that. In the upper levels of the civil service, some political considerations are also used in filling selected top positions.

Job Tenure and Orientation

Not surprisingly, job tenure and orientation are related to the way an actor acquires office. Personnel turnover in positions dependent on electoral results is greater than in nonelective positions among civil servants. The shortest length of service occurs among political appointees in the executive branch. Median tenure in the mid-1960s was only 28 months in a position and 31 months in an agency (Stanley, Mann, and Doig, 1967: 57; see also Heclo, 1977: 104). Because of their short tenure, political appointees generally have their careers in some field other than government service.

Tenure for individual legislators will always be uncertain because of the vagaries of elective office, but overall length of service in Congress has increased over time (not always steadily, depending on election results). The average number of years of service for members of both houses has dropped a bit in the late 1970s but is still high: in 1981 it stood at almost eight years in both houses. Careerist aspirations are now well entrenched among most members of Congress. (See Huntington, 1973; Polsby, 1968; Price, 1971; and Witmer, 1964 on the development of a congressional career.)

Although data are relatively scarce, it seems that many congressional staff members have become oriented toward a career in legislative staff work and are able to realize their ambitions, in many cases, for two reasons: First, the long service of the members (the appointing authorities) helps them stay in their positions for a long time. Second, even if their original patron is unseated, they are often sought out by new members of the House and Senate and offered jobs because of the high value placed on their experience. (On the development of a congressional staff career, see Fox and Hammond, 1977: 62–65.)

Data from 1977 on tenure in current jobs in the House—both committee staff and personal staff—show that tenure in specific positions was relatively short. But this fact was offset by the additional fact, documented in the same study, that over half the top positions on both personal and committee staffs were taken by individuals with experience on the Hill. Thus even those who have worked in a specific top job for a short time are likely to have been a staff member in Congress for a much longer time (Brady, 1981).

The numbers of congressional staff have expanded dramatically in recent years. Between 1967 and 1980, for example, House personal staff increased by 114 percent, Senate personal staff increased by 145 percent, House committee staff increased by 226 percent, and Senate committee staff increased by 78 percent. This growth has helped make overall staff appear to be relatively young and relatively junior in service. If growth stops, the existence or nonexistence of a career for Hill staff will be easier to demonstrate.

Careerism among bureaucrats at the policymaking levels is characterized by long service but low mobility in terms of shifting occupational specialties, shifting between agencies, and shifting between Washington and federal field installations (see Corson and Paul, 1966: 22, 175, 176, and Stanley, 1964: 27, 32–34, 102–3). In the early 1960s, for example, the higher civil servants had an average length of service of 23 years. Almost three quarters of these individuals had served for more than 20 years. Over 86 percent of them had spent their entire careers in no more than two departments (almost 56 percent had been in only one department), and over 68 percent had served in no more than two bureaus (over 37 percent had only been in one bureau). Movement between Washington headquarters and field offices was very low (almost 90 percent had never left headquarters to go into the field). Recent figures published by the U.S. Civil Service Commission (1976) show the same lack of mobility in the 1970s.

Corson and Paul's (1966) figures on supergrade civil-service employees in 1963 show the same pattern: two thirds had worked in no more than two bureaus and about 40 percent in only one. About half had worked in the same agency or department for their entire careers. Only 15 percent had ever worked outside the federal government once they had begun service and over three fourths had held all of their federal jobs in the same occupational field.

The civil servants are the most career oriented of all the four groups and are also most likely to serve a full career wholly within a single institutional location. For example, a sample of federal civil servants interviewed in 1960 and 1961 showed that most were highly intent on staying in federal service; 88 percent of the general employees were very sure or fairly sure they wanted to stay in federal service, and only 7 percent planned to leave. Among executives in the civil service, 94 percent were very sure or fairly sure they wanted to stay and only 3 percent planned to leave. Even among professionals (natural scientists, social scientists, and engineers whose major loyalties might have been to their professions and not to the government organization with which they were employed), there was a high propensity to stay with federal service. Between 69 and 82 percent of these three professional groups were either sure or fairly sure they wanted to stay in federal service, and only between 10 and 18 percent planned to leave (Kilpatrick, Cummings, and Jennings, 1963:

188). Predictably, civil servants who were older and had more service were the most wedded to remaining.

Principal Loyalties and Representativeness

The principal loyalties of members of the House and Senate are generally split between loyalty to their constituencies (or, more accurately, to their perceptions of various constituencies—see Fenno, 1978) and loyalty to their congressional parties. In general, congressional life is structured so that the two loyalties do not compete in head-on fashion a great deal of the time. When they do compete directly, a member will ordinarily stick with his perceptions of the constituency's interest.

Congressional staff members are primarily loyal to their appointing authority—that is, to the individual senator or representative responsible for having put them in their present jobs. Thus if a staff member's "sponsor" is highly oriented toward constituency interests, the staff member is also likely to reflect that concern. If a sponsor is more oriented toward maintaining a given programmatic or ideological stance, then the staff member is more likely to take that tack too.

In theory, executive political appointees are primarily loyal to the president, the president's program, and the administration as a collectivity. In practice, political appointees are also at least partially loyal to the organization to which they are appointed. Thus a secretary of agriculture will try to be responsible to the president who made the appointment, but if career bureaucrats within the department perceive their interests to be at odds with the president's policy initiatives, the secretary will encounter cross-pressures. Ordinarily the secretary will try to find some compromise that will avoid direct disagreement with the president, at least publicly, while still not "selling out" the department. Even in the Reagan administration, unusual in part for its greater-than-normal reliance on ideological criteria for making presidential appointments to the agencies and departments, some of those same ideologues turned out to defend agency budgets against severe cuts proposed by the Office of Management and Budget (the president's budget arm).

Civil servants are primarily loyal to the organizations in which they work and in which they are likely to make their career. They are perhaps less cross-pressured than the other major actors. Those in agencies who are also professionals (lawyers, engineers, scientists, etc.) may also feel considerable loyalty to the standards of their profession and may be cross-pressured by the perceived competing demands of profession and agency at times (see Wilensky, 1967). The Reagan administration was also unusual in terms of the ideological demands made on top civil servants. These demands, coupled with staff reductions and reassignments, helped render many of the domestic agencies inefficient and demoralized. How permanent this effect will be of course remains to be seen.

Members of the House and Senate are concerned with representing their geographical areas—their districts or states—and are usually also concerned with representing a variety of interests they perceive to be important. While the notion of representation may be interpreted differently by different senators and representatives, they are virtually all genuinely concerned with being representative. For some, this may mean focusing mostly on tangible benefits for the district and for the most important organized groups in the district. For others, this may mean thinking about the broader needs of the district and of national interests and groups—both organized and unorganized. For most members, representation probably involves a range of activities—from seeking a new post office for some town in the district or state to worrying about the welfare of all poor people or all cotton farmers or all black people or whatever group seems to the member to be important.

Congressional staff members are also interested in representation in the same several senses in which members are interested. Their interest is largely a reflection of the interests of their sponsors, although some individuals personally may also feel strongly about their representative capacities serving in a staff role.

Executive branch officials are also concerned with representation, but they are not concerned with a specific constituency in the same sense as individuals on Capitol Hill. The geographical ties to a local constituency of both political appointees and civil servants stationed in Washington are weaker than those of members of Congress and usually weaker than those of congressional staff members. They may retain some ties to the region in which they grew up, or, more likely, their program may have a particular regional focus (an Agriculture Department official working with cotton price supports is, of course, going to be concerned mostly with the cotton-growing regions of the South, and an official in the Bureau of Reclamation is going to be concerned mainly with the arid lands of the West). But many Washington officials are involved with programs that have a national scope, and they are therefore likely to think about the program in national terms.

But seven eighths of federal bureaucrats in the United States are not located in the metropolitan Washington, D.C., area. These individuals are scattered throughout the country in a variety of federal field installations such as state, regional, and local offices. The bureaucrats who populate these field installations outside Washington have regional and local geographic loyalties tied to their agencies' programs, and they undertake their work in such a way as to maximize the size of their particular operation in their region, state, or locality.

In addition to geographic interests, bureaucrats—both political appointees and civil servants—are also typically concerned with representing interests they perceive to be important to their programs and worthy of their attention. In general, political appointees are expected to be supportive of and sympathetic to the programmatic interests of the president and to represent these interests to Congress. They also may be concerned with representing the interests thought to be important to their political party, and thus their concern with specific representation may not be very well developed, although it seems reasonable to argue that a Republican secretary of labor, for example, will be concerned with representing managerial interests at least some of the time and that a Democratic secretary of labor will be concerned with representing organized labor's interests most of the time. To survive politically, appointees in departments and agencies are most likely to be representative of many interests involved with their agencies rather than representing only one or two interests. An appointee who principally advocates a single, narrow interest is apt to be a controversial figure and a political liability for the president's program and in the national electorate.

Political appointees can be representative in the critical sense of allowing competing points of view to be heard in the executive branch on controversial matters before final action is taken. Sometimes policy debates take place almost wholly within the executive branch, and the major decisions are made and the major compromises are struck before the matter even becomes an important item on the congressional agenda. This was the case, for example, with the bargaining and arguments that led up to the passage of the Communications Satellite Act of 1962 and the Economic Opportunity Act of 1964 (Davidson, 1967: 390–93).

Civil servants often become very concerned with representing interests and organized groups they conceive to be important in the substantive fields in which they are working. Sometimes this representational activity simply takes the form of advocacy by strategically placed civil servants on behalf of interests and groups. In other cases the advocacy of specific interests by a bureaucracy becomes more institutionalized. For example, some agencies use a variety of advisory committees to make and enforce decisions at the local level. These committees operate in several policy areas, including agriculture and land use (see Foss, 1960, Lowi, 1973). A potential problem with advisory committees is that they may become captives of some segment of the served clientele, and bureaucrats, in heeding their advice, are thus responding to only a narrow interest group. This was the case with federal lands grazing policy (see Foss, 1960: chapter 6).

Degree of Substantive Specialization

Members of the House and Senate are both subject-matter specialists and generalists. They are generalists because they are given the constitutional power—which they exercise with considerable, even if uneven, vigor—to oversee the entire range of federal governmental activities. They must consider and vote on literally everything the federal government does, at least in broad outline. Naturally, any individual is going to have a number of substantive areas in which his or her knowledge is minimal, but most senators and representatives who serve for more than a short time begin to develop familiarity with and some competence in a wide variety of subject-matter areas.

At the same time members have also become specialists through their service on the standing committees and subcommittees of the two chambers. The committee system emerged in large part as the congressional response to a bureaucracy constantly growing in size, specialization, and expertise. Especially in the House—where in the 97th Congress (1981–1982) the average member had assignments to only 1.7 standing committees and 4.0 subcommittees—members who serve for more than a short period of time become genuine experts in some piece of the policy world. In the Senate the members are spread more thinly because each Senator has more assignments—an average of 2.5 standing committees and 6.7 subcommittees in 1981–1982 (Ornstein et al., 1982: 100).

The congressional urge to specialize in order to compete with the bureaucrats is reinforced by the staff on the Hill. In both houses, staff members have become genuinely expert in some bounded portion of the policy universe, although staff members working in the offices of individual senators and representatives have much less time for work on substantive legislative matters than staff working for committees. Senate staff members—both those on committees and a few working in individual senators' offices—are particularly important as specialists because of the limited time and attention the typical senator can give to committee and subcommittee assignments. Senators often rely principally on a staff member to do most of the substantive work in some subcommittees to which the senator is formally assigned (Ripley, 1969; chapter 8). Many staff members, including those on committees, are also expected to attend to political matters and to deal with constituents in a variety of ways.

In the bureaucracy the degree of substantive specialization in the civil service is very high. The main reason for the emergence of a large bureaucracy is, after all, to facilitate dealing with technical and complex topics. On the other hand, the degree of specialization among political appointees is typically very low. Commonly, political appointees in the executive branch have little experience in the subject matter with which they are expected to deal and usually do not stay in office long enough to develop much expertise through on-the-job training.

Degree of Professionalism

Professionalism is used to denote allegiance on the part of individuals to a profession other than that of government employee. For example, chemists employed by the Food and Drug Administration may well remain loyal to the norms of the chemistry profession, attend meetings of the American Chemical Society, and subscribe to a variety of professional journals. Such individuals are likely to be equally concerned with national professional standards and judgments as with the narrower interests of the Food and Drug Administration as an agency.

Most professionalism in this sense resides in the civil service. Scattered throughout the bureaucracy are social scientists, natural scientists, engineers, dentists, physicians, and others whose professional identification is very high.

In the rest of the government—the appointed parts of the executive branch and both the elected and appointed parts of the legislative branch—the degree of professionalism is much lower. There are many lawyers, particularly in Congress, but they seem to retain little identification with abstract norms of the profession. For many, law was both a form of academic training and a natural entry into public service, but not a profession actively practiced, at least for very long.

Degree of Political Expertise

By definition, senators and representatives are and must be politicians. A few may not be, but they are likely to be very transient residents of the congressional institution. Members need the political skill of assessing the mood of their constituency and the amount of latitude they have within that mood. They also are likely to develop considerable bargaining skills as they pursue their daily tasks in Congress. Staff members typically possess a number of the same kinds of political skills. Some are hired expressly for their political skills that can be used to help the member gain reelection and/or have the maximum impact on substantive policy questions.

In the executive branch, political appointees presumably possess considerable political skills—both in advancing the interests of the administration and the party of the president and in bargaining. Some political appointees are very adroit politically. In fact, some are so skillful that they develop their own constituency and support apart from the president who is presumably their sponsor. A classic case is that of Jesse Jones, secretary of commerce under President Franklin Roosevelt (Fenno, 1959: 234–47). His ties with powerful business interests and his excellent relations with Congress allowed him to take policy stands contrary to those desired by Roosevelt. Yet the president tolerated his behavior for over four years because, on balance, he thought his independent strength helped the administration more than it hurt it.

Some political appointees turn out to be quite inept politically. President Eisenhower's secretary of defense, Charles Wilson of General Motors, was usually in hot water with some congressional committee for his seemingly thoughtless remarks ("What's good for the country is good for General Motors, and vice versa.") and behavior. Reagan's secretary of the interior, James Watt, also drew constant fire from environmentalist groups and congressional committees but received continued backing from the president anyway. In speaking of the cabinet specifically, Fenno (1959: 207–8) concluded that politically a skillful secretary "maintains legislative-executive relations in an equilibrium and prevents them from deteriorating to the point where they hurt the President. What the ordinary Cabinet member supplies is a kind of *preventive assistance. . . .* The best that he can ordinarily do is to help the President in small amounts—probably disproportionate to the time he consumes doing it." The same generalization probably applies to the whole range of political appointees in the executive branch.

In theory, civil servants are supposed to

be apolitical. They are barred from overt partisan activity by federal statute. The textbooks proclaim them to be "above politics" and concerned only with rational, economical, and efficient implementation of public-policy objectives determined by their political superiors.

In the United States, however, the textbook model does not apply in large part. Senior civil servants are fully political actors, and in many respects the governmental system in which they work expects that they will be if they are to be successful (see Heclo, 1977; Kaufman, 1981; Aberbach, Putnam, and Rockman, 1981; and Yates, 1982).

The political stance of the bureaucracy is the result of several factors—grants of administrative discretion, congressional reliance on the bureaucracy, and competition in advancing the agencies' perceived interests. Broad administrative discretion to fill in the gaps of basic legislation does not promote "neutral" administration. Bureaucrats' decisions have political impact and repercussions, and bureaucrats experience pressure for and against their administrative decisions. Congress relies on the bureaucracy as a primary source of policy ideas and initiatives, and policy is rarely neutral—it almost always conveys benefits to some and deprives others. Who wins and who loses is, after all, what politics is all about. The continuous maneuvering by senior agency officials to maximize the interests of their agencies and programs, especially at budget time, but also throughout daily routines, requires a high degree of political skill. Agency officials cannot afford to be neutral if their agency's interests are to be advanced.

Richard Neustadt has convincingly explained the basic reason for the political nature of our top civil servants: the governmental system puts them in direct competition with other actors and thereby breeds the necessity of developing political skills in order to gain or preserve the resources to perform programmatic tasks effectively. The following excerpt elaborates the idea (Neustadt, 1973: 132):

> We maximize the insecurities of men and agencies alike. Careerists jostle in-and-outers (from the law firms, business, academic life) for the positions of effective influence; their agencies contend with the committees on the Hill, the Office of Management and Budget, other agencies for the prerequisites of institutional survival, *year by year*. Pursuit of programs authorized in law can be a constant struggle to maintain and hold support of influential clients, or the press. And seeking new authority to innovate a program can be very much like coalition warfare. Accordingly, most agencies have need for men of passion and conviction—or at least enormous powers of resistance—near the top. American officialdom may generate no more of these than other systems do, but it rewards them well: they rise toward the top.

Degree of Visibility

Visibility is, of course, relative, and it may vary from observer to observer. To even an interested part of the general public, for example, virtually all of the actors being discussed here except some senators and representatives are anonymous. To most journalists covering Washington, only senators and representatives and a few political appointees in the executive branch are consistently visible. A really skillful reporter will also come to know important congressional staff members and, occasionally, even a civil servant or two. Skillful lobbyists will tend to know individuals in all of the major clusters of actors. In general it would be most accurate to say that senators and representatives and the major political appointees in the executive branch, such as the president's cabinet, tend to be the most visible to most observers. Congressional staff members and civil servants tend to be relatively unknown to a large number of observers.

Table 3.1.2 summarizes the discussion of the institutional work setting for the four major clusters of actors.

Table 3.1.2.
The general institutional setting for congressional and bureaucratic policy actors.

Characteristic	Members of House and Senate	Congressional Staff Members	Executive Branch Political Appointees	Civil Servants and Equivalents
Method of selection	Election	Appointment by Senators and Representatives	Appointment by President	Competition and merit
Job tenure and orientation	Relatively long service; careerist orientation	Relatively long service; relatively careerist orientation	Short service; noncareer orientation	Long service; career orientation
Principal loyalties	Constituencies and congressional parties	Sponsors (appointing members)	President and agency to which appointed	Agency
Degree of concern with representation	High for geographical constituencies and special interests	Moderately high for geographical constituencies and interests	Low for geographical units; moderately low for special interests	High for special interests; moderate for geographical units among non-Washington-based civil servants; low for geographical units among Washington-based civil servants
Degree of substantive specialization	Moderately high (especially in House)	Moderately high	Low	High
Degree of professionalism	Low	Generally low	Low	High for major subgroups of employees
Degree of political expertise	High	Moderately high	Moderately high	Moderately high (for highest grades)
Degree of anonymity	Low	High	Moderately low	High

Reading 3.2

House-Senate Differences: A Test among Interview Data (or 16 U.S. Senators with House Experience Talk about the Differences)

David C. Kozak

Firsthand experience on Capitol Hill quickly teaches that there is not a "Congress" per se. Congress as an institution more often than not is a media fixation. In reality, there are two separate legislative institutions: House and Senate. It has been said—not with tongue in cheek—that the two houses have only three things in common: their members are elected, they both pass legislation, and they share the same building. Each has a distinctive time frame, constituency, structure, way of doing business, and policy role. The House, because it is larger, is more formal, rigid, and hierarchical. The Senate, because it is smaller, is more informal, flexible, and nonhierarchical. Moreover, the House is a nuts and bolts institution while the Senate is a forum for high debate.

ABSTRACT

A bicameral perspective is one of the major concepts used by political scientists to explain how Congress works. Many important distinctions have been emphasized in the literature, but many of these have been called into question recently by Norman Ornstein, who detects a recent blurring of House-Senate roles and behavior. This paper seeks to explore House-Senate differences through interviews with members who have served in both houses—a previously untapped data source relevant to this general topic. Also investigated are members' perceptions of the validity of the Ornstein thesis.

Among the major differences not stressed in the literature that emerge from the interviews are different social settings, work environments, campaign dynamics, and degrees of partisanship inherent in the two houses. Interviews reveal concurrence with Ornstein, with many senators elaborating on his thesis. The paper concludes with a discussion of the cause and effect relationship of major and minor differences and the policy consequences of the contemporary U.S. bicameral legislature.

Source: This essay was written originally for this volume. See reference section (p. 527) for disclaimer, acknowledgments, and list of interviewed senators.

INTRODUCTION

"The House and Senate are naturally unlike."

Woodrow Wilson

In teaching a college course on the U.S. Congress or when giving a lecture or public address on the national legislative process, we all feel obliged to make a few basic but essential points:

- Congress's job is to make laws, represent constituents, and oversee the executive.
- Congress is a credit-claiming institution driven by an electoral connection.
- Congress is an internally fragmented, nonhiearchical institution.
- Most of Congress's work is done in its committees.
- Many actors and groups try to influence what Congress does.
- The legislative process is a labyrinthian one involving multiple, successive decision points.

- Congressional leadership, using limited and constrained resources, is the force that brings the fragmented Congress together.
- Many actors and factors influence congressional outcomes.
- Congressional policy output reflects the unique, peculiar, and changing character of Congress.

Perhaps the most basic of all points to be made, however, is that Congress is a bicameral legislative body, that is, it is comprised of two houses.

All political scientists have the same standard lecture on bicameralism. We start by emphasizing that to use the term "Congress" to refer to the national legislative body is an oversimplification. The national legislative process is best understood in terms of two different legislative bodies: the House and the Senate. We conclude that the differences between them thoroughly overshadow their similarities. While the House and Senate have in common the same building, and despite the fact that members of both bodies are elected, make laws, and work within a very decentralized structure, comparisons are best made by discussing differences.

Congressional literature usually points us in the direction of what Fenno calls "a bicameral perspective" (Fenno, 1981). For example, most of the main texts emphasize the importance of distinguishing between House and Senate. Davidson and Oleszek (1981: 28–29) write:

> In the smaller and more intimate Senate, vigorous leadership has been the exception rather than the rule. The relative informality of Senate procedures, not to mention the long-cherished right of unlimited debate, testify to the loose reins of leadership. Compared with the House's elaborate system of rules and its voluminous precedents, the Senate's rules are relatively brief and simple. Informal negotiations among senators interested in a given measure prevail, and debate is typically regulated by unanimous consent agreements engineered by the parties' floor leaders. Although too large for its members to draw their chairs around the fireplace on a chilly winter morning—as they used to do in the early years—the Senate today retains a clubby atmosphere that the House lacks.

For Jewell and Patterson (1977: 28), the differences are expressed as follows:

> The casual visitor to Capitol Hill cannot help noticing one of the most important differences between the House and the Senate: the House is a much larger body. One consequence of this is that the House follows more rigid rules regarding debate and the conduct of business. It is too large to be a deliberative body, to give any substantial proportion of the members a chance to speak on issues; as a result, the House does not try to be a deliberative body, seldom devotes itself seriously to debate, and rarely tries to rewrite the committee's version of a bill on the floor of the House. Sometimes there are drastic limits on the amendments that can be considered on the floor. Much of its decision making with regard to amendments is carried on in the committee of the whole, where the quorum requirement is small (100 members, instead of a majority), with the result that important decisions are often made by a small minority of representatives.

Jones (1981: 132) emphasizes electoral and organizational dissimilarities. He writes, "Representing something called states, senators experience much greater variation in representing constituents than do representatives." Moreover,

> In general, it is fair to say that the debating function remains today as central to Senate operations. If the House functions particularly well as a chamber of representation, the Senate at least has the potential for serving well as a chamber of integrated review and analysis. Open debate is a method for discovering connections between issues. It is in this sense that I made the point earlier that the Senate is more oriented toward the institutional functions of debating issues and discovering the basis for compromise across issues (Jones, 1981: 266).

Keefe's writing best illustrates the treatment of bicameralism by standard texts.

> The House and the Senate are not peas in the same pod. The differences define the character of both houses, the way each goes about its legislative tasks, and how each thinks about itself (not to mention how each thinks about the other) (Keefe, 1980: 16).

More specialized works by Froman (1967), Jones (1977), Oleszek (1978, 1984), and Polsby (1970) have been helpful in pinpointing more specific differences in membership, constituency, time perspective, structure, process, policy functions, and organizational properties. An integration of their insights in terms of these seven broad categories is presented in Table 3.2.1 following a format for comparing differences used by Froman (1967: 7). These comparisons are most useful for emphasizing that Congress is comprised of two very different legislative bodies.

Table 3.2.1.
The House and Senate compared: A perspective from literature.

Basis of Comparison	House	Senate
1. Membership	Larger (435)	Smaller (100)
	Less prestigious	More prestigious
	More incumbency	Less incumbency
2. Constituency	More homogeneous, narrower	More heterogeneous, broader
3. Time perspective	Shorter (elected every two years)	Longer (elected every six years)
	Noncontinuous body (two-year cycle)	Continuing body (staggered terms of office)
4. Structure	More hierarchical; less equitable	Less hierarchical; more equitable
	Speaker is power broker	Majority leader is power broker
	Fusion in speaker's office of presiding powers and head of majority party	Separation of presiding officer and majority party head
	Committees more important	Committees less important
	Members serve on fewer committees	Members serve on more committees
	Less staff reliance	More staff per member
5. Process	More formal, rigid	Informal, flexible (much business done through unanimous consent)
	Less comity	More comity
	Rules Committee structures debate	Rules Committee does not structure debate
	Most floor work done in "committee of the whole"	No counterpart to "committee of the whole"
	More complex: five calendars	Less complex: two calendars

(Table continued on next page)

Table 3.2.1. (concluded)

Basis of Comparison	House	Senate
	Limited debate (five-minute rule)	Unlimited debate until cloture invoked or unless a unanimous consent limitation
	Nongermane amendments (riders) not allowed	Nongermane amendments (riders) allowed
	Acts more quickly	Acts more slowly
	Electronic voting	No electronic voting
	TV coverage	No TV coverage (1985)
6. Policy functions	Originates revenue measures	Executive counsel (appointments and treaties), debate, deliberation, discussion of national priorities
	Expertise, specialization	
7. As an organization	Representative assembly	Forum of functional self-indulgence; Breeding grounds for presidential candidates
	Less visibility/media coverage	More visibility/media coverage

Sources: Froman, 1967; Jones, 1977; Oleszek, 1984; Polsby, 1970.

Recently, Norman Ornstein has challenged the validity of many of these differences. In his "The House and the Senate in a New Congress," he argues that the House and the Senate are increasingly behaving like one another. In his words:

> Since Froman wrote, the House has become less formal and impersonal, less hierarchically organized and with more fluid rules and procedures. The House has also become less able to act—much less act quickly—on policy matters. . . . the Senate has changed too—becoming in several respects more like the House. Since Froman wrote, the Senate has become much less leisurely (Ornstein, 1981: 367).

Ornstein emphasizes that, "The Senate and House are not now identical by any means . . ." (p. 368), but he concludes that:

> Thus, the House has become less identified with legislative carpentry and more noted for grappling with the larger issues in policy debates. The Senate has moved away from its focus on debate and deliberation, and toward a preoccupation with the legislative nitty-gritty (p. 371).

The purpose of this research at hand is to generally explore House-Senate differences, investigating the validity of the Ornstein thesis in this era of changing internal and external congressional environments.

METHODOLOGY

Little empirical work has been done on the institutional differences between House and Senate. Some work on the conference committee process has examined behavioral and policy differences between House and Senate by studying roll-call data (see Vogler, 1981). Fenno compared House and Senate committee behavior (1973) and examined different campaign contexts (1981). Except for Fenno and an occasional interview with, or published reflection by, a newly elected senator with prior House experience (for the best recent such reflection, see Senator Cohen, 1981), members who have served in both bodies have not been systematically interviewed concerning House-Senate differences.

In the spring of 1982 and again in the spring/summer of 1984, I collected interview data with a total of 16 Senators who had experience in the House, including U.S. Representative Claude Pepper, who had previously served in the U.S. Senate.

In the summer of 1984, approximately 23 senators had had prior House experience. Using the auspices of a congressional fellowship assignment in the Senate, I contacted all 23 and asked for an interview concerning House-Senate differences. Fifteen, plus Congressman Pepper, granted the request.

The party affiliations of the sample of participating senators were evenly mixed: nine Republicans and seven Democrats. Helpfully, most were elected within the previous four years, and thus were still new enough in the senate to make first-impression comparisons. Several middle- and long-seniority senators were able to provide historical perspective.

The time of the interviews averaged about 20 minutes, with two lasting only five minutes (and one of these through an intermediary). Four lasted longer than half an hour. Questions were asked concerning general House-Senate differences, the Ornstein thesis, the role of leadership, keeping informed on floor votes, and (of middle- and long-seniority Senators) changes resulting from Republican control of the Senate since 1980. The specific line of inquiry employed appears in Table 3.2.2.

Table 3.2.2.
Line of inquiry used in interviews with senators.

1. Senator, I'm writing a paper on House-Senate differences. Given your service in both, what do you think are the most important differences? Is there anything else you think I ought to emphasize?
2. Senator, a prominent student of the legislative process has argued that recently the House and Senate are behaving more alike, with the House engaging more in grand debate and the Senate more involved in the nuts and bolts of legislation. Do you think this is an accurate assessment? (If yes, why?)
3. How does the role of party leadership differ from House to Senate?
4. Is it harder to keep up with floor votes here? How do you do it?
5. (To those elected before 1980 only) Have there been any major changes in the workings of the Senate with Republican control?

The remainder of this paper will analyze data yielded from these interviews. It should be emphasized that these data are offered with full appreciation of the limitations of interview studies: skewed or unrepresentative sampling, unequivalent responses, self-serving reconstructions, and unreproducible results. Regardless, it seems that the importance of the data more than outweighs the limitations imposed by these necessary caveats, if for no other reason than the data tap what James S. Young calls the "inner life of Washington."

> —a special culture which carries with it prescriptions and cues for behavior that may be far more explicit than those originating outside the group, and no less consequential for the conduct of government (Young, 1966: 151).

RESULTS

The results of the research will be reported under the following headings: general differences, specific differences, miscellaneous differences, the Ornstein thesis, and causal relationships between major and minor differences.

1. GENERAL DIFFERENCES

When asked about House-Senate differences, all spoke eloquently of the importance of differentiating between the bodies in order to fully understand and appreciate the Congress. Although several stressed housekeeping procedures with statements such as "the major difference is that the computer system here stinks" or "they won't let pages deliver mail within the same building" and although almost all recently elected Republicans talked about how nice it is to be in the majority party after years of frustration in the House minority, all at one time or another discussed major constitutional and institutional differences and saw the importance of them. Several were emphatic in discussing the two houses as "worlds apart."

In pointing out general differences, several senators were most helpful. One stated that, "Although you would think you could run a Senate office like your House office, you can't. It's the same zoo, but they are very different cages."

Another emphasized the different political norm served by each house, "The House is set up to expedite majority rule. A determined majority can pull if off there. In the Senate we are set up to protect the rights of minority opinion. That's the major difference."

Still others talked of "genuine bicameralism," of a "different character" in each house, of the two houses being "the antitheses" of each other, and of the Senate's role as "a second look." Perhaps the most definitive statement on general differences came from a more senior senator who stated that to understand Congress you must concentrate on House-Senate differences:

> The founding fathers intended the two to be unlike, and their intentions have been very influential to this very day. Although we are physically close together, the House and Senate are far apart in reality. Any understanding of how things are done here must give this attention.

2. SPECIFIC DIFFERENCES

In response to the question on most important differences (Question 1), senators mentioned many different bases of comparison, some of which previously have not been highlighted in the literature. Table 3.2.3 lists the differences mentioned by senators in the interviews. Each senator seemed to offer a personal perspective by identifying a pet difference. Consequently, no single difference was mentioned by all senators, and most of the identified differences were mentioned by four or fewer of the sample ($n = 16$). Only four differences were mentioned by more than half or near-half of the sample. Combining these various personal perspectives yields a very detailed portrait of two very different legislative institutions.

The most frequently mentioned differences are those pertaining to a different social setting, a busier work environment, less partisanship, and unlimited debate.

a. A Different Social Setting

Senators depict a Senate *social setting* most different not only from the House, but from a Senate popularly portrayed as a club. Three-fourths of the 16 member sample point to different social settings as the most important difference. The social setting of the Senate is characterized as wider, more formal, less personal, and more isolated than that of the House. Many senators emphasized that while in the House it is impossible to get to know all 435 colleagues, especially with large biennial turnovers. You can get to know all of the other 99 senators. As one senator noted,

> You have more chance to get acquainted over here. In the House, you don't get to know everyone. You don't see people unless it's on

Table 3.2.3.
Differences between House and Senate as identified by senators: Percent of mention by interviewees.

The Senate Is/Has	*n* Mentioning	Percent Mentioning
A different social setting.	12	75
Busier.	10	66
Not as partisan.	7	44
Unlimited debate.	7	44
More committee assignments.	5	31
Six-year term.	5	31
Statewide responsibilities.	5	31
More staff/more staff dependency.	5	31
A consequential minority.	5	31
Agenda uncertainty.	5	31
More direct interaction with leaders.	5	31
Less self-discipline.	4	25
Strict seniority.	4	25
More diverse expertise.	4	25
Different campaign dynamics.	3	19
The representation of states.	3	19
Member individualism.	3	19
More diverse districts.	3	19
A fairer committee staff quota.	2	13
Less of a common bind.	2	13
More remote from constituents.	2	13
More mail/intense lobbying.	2	13
Less turnover.	2	13
Staff on the floor.	2	13
No TV coverage.	2	13
More prestige.	2	13
Fewer members to go around.	2	13
More important responsibilities.	2	13
Access to the floor.	2	13
Greater visibility.	2	13
Different skill requirements.	2	13
More in-depth study of issues.	2	13

n = 16; multiple responses included

> committee, in state delegation meetings, or unless they are in your election class.

Another noted,

> More senators know more senators. There are more interpersonal relations among senators because of the environment. There are fewer people here and it's just easier to get to know everyone when you have less than a fourth of what you have on the House side.

But the opportunity for wider interaction does not mean the Senate is friendlier. All of the 12 who emphasized different social settings made the point that although senators get acquainted more with their colleagues, they get to know them less well. One senator expressed well what several others alluded to, "In the House you develop closer friendships. In fact my closest friends are still in the House. In the House people are more informal and friendlier on the floor and off."

In several interviews, senators portrayed a Senate that is less warm, less friendly, and less personal than the House. One called attention to the different social atmospheres found on the floors of the two chambers, saying, "In the House, by the time you leave the cloakroom you can say hello to many. In the Senate, colleagues are not so friendly. Only a few are there at any one time and they are too busy for chit chat."

Another said the Senate is less collegial than the House. It is best thought of as 100 individual fiefdoms because of large staffs and pressures of statewide office. In his words, "You just don't get to see other senators that much. We are more isolated from our colleagues." A final quote comes from a senator who was emphatic in calling attention to the more impersonal, formal relations that now prevail in the Senate:

> There is not much time for small talk here, unfortunately. On the House side, you had more time to speak with members. In both committee and on the floor, you don't have personal staff. In the Senate I talk more with my staff than with other senators. In the Senate, conversations are polite, but very formal and usually quite serious. You always feel pressured to return to your office, and while there you are quite isolated.

b. A Busier Work Environment

Ten of those interviewed stressed a busier and more demanding work load in the Senate. One senator noted that, "In the House you have time to play—not so in the Senate. The schedule really keeps you hopping." Another emphasized that, "Senators are more busy. There are more challenges because there are fewer of us to go around." Two senators detailed the challenges in terms of a senator's committee and office work. One stated:

> You have to work harder because there are fewer of us to work on legislation. I'm on 12 committees and subcommittees. There is no way you can get in all the meetings. You are constantly making adjustments and trade-offs.

Another stated:

> The demands on your time are simply greater. Work mounts up here more than it ever did on the other side. Everyone wants to see you; there is more competition for your time. Those from relatively close states are even more busy.

c. Less Partisanship

Seven senators mentioned that the Senate is not as partisan as the House. Said one, "It really hits you between the eyes here. Things just aren't as partisan. You work more as a whole in the Senate."

Another said that the first thing that struck him in the Senate was that, "the Senate is less likely to get derogatory along party lines. In the House, people are quicker to attack. You have people being obstructionalistic, trying to tie things up. You don't have that here that much."

Several senators amplified the nature of less Senate partisanship and the reasons for it. Said one senator, "You must understand that the House divides along party lines on everything. In the Senate only procedural votes are truly partisan." Another said that the Senate is an institution that "goes out of the way to be accommodating. Breaches of this accommodative spirit—especially along party lines—are unusual." A more senior member emphasized the necessity for such bipartisanship, saying, "Because the Senate is almost evenly divided, you get to work both sides of the aisle to accomplish legislative goals. You can't burn bridges. You have to keep all your options open. This is very much unlike the House."

d. Unlimited Debate

Rule 22 gives senators the right of unlimited debate unless cloture is invoked. Although most debate is in fact limited through the adoption of unanimous consent agreements, the potential for unlimited debate was mentioned as a major difference by seven senators. Said one, "You've got to keep in mind that old saying of Daniel Webster's—'Once a senator takes the floor, only God can take him off'—that's the essence of the Senate."

One senator saw this difference as a positive force, saying that, "It ensures that you will have your say—that you will be able to get people's attention." Several others saw it as a black mark, "one of those things that makes us look ridiculous" or "because of the long-winded speeches, we can never go to televised debate. We are just too undisciplined a body."

e. Less Frequently Cited Differences

In Table 3.2.3, after unlimited debate, a number of less frequently cited differences appear, several of which should be elaborated upon because of the insights they afford. Some are self-explanatory. Others need amplification.

The *role of staff* in the Senate as opposed to that in the House was addressed by several senators. One stated, "In the Senate you have more staff. All senators—especially the ones from larger states—must manage extensive bureaucracies." Another talked of being both "blessed and cursed with more staff. You have more, but you are far more dependent on them." Two distinctive senatorial uses of staff emerged from the interviews. One use is as policy experts, as one senator elaborated:

> Staff in the Senate is more professional and less personal. In the House, you could staff primarily with people loyal to you from back home who are good for the district. In the Senate, the major committee assignments require that you have a substantive expert.

Another use of senatorial staff is as intermediaries between senators. As one senator pointed out, "In the Senate you instruct staff to deal with another senator's staff. If there is an impasse, then and only then do you work it out at the senatorial level."

A *consequential minority* was mentioned by several senators, especially Democrats who have recently become a minority. One senator addressed the differences as follows, "In the House, being in the minority is frustrating. There is only so much you can do. In the Senate, the minority has a say."

One senator noted the ways in which the Senate's minority can have a say:

> The House is the house of the people. You must get a majority of the representatives to pass a bill. Most of the hot votes are party ones. In contrast, the Senate is a body that represents individuals (states). When it comes to unanimous consent resolutions, any individual senator has a veto. Any minority senator can gum up the works. He's got to be accommodated.

Agenda uncertainty was stressed in several interviews. Senators spoke of "things being able to pop up without much notice" and "more fluidity in the schedule." Senators talk of the difficulty in obtaining committee reports, the "hopping around back and forth from bill to bill," and "the general unpredictability of the Senate's schedule in comparison to the House where you knew the order of bills, their numbers and titles, and had the report from committee."

Stricter seniority was mentioned by four of the senators, surprisingly since many commentators have observed the weakening of the seniority norm, especially given recent high turnover in the Senate. Two senators mentioned seniority as a strict criterion for committee assignment, something not found on the House side where, as one senator said, "It depends on who you know." Two other senators mentioned the need to be deferential. "There is an institutional thing in the Senate; you've got to wait your turn and try to develop good working relations with the leaders and the chairman."

Different campaign dynamics were mentioned and stressed in several interviews. Echoing Fenno's (1981) findings, senatorial campaigns were seen as more expensive, less partisan ("Most senators of the other party won't come in and campaign against you."), harder ("You don't have an organization together as you do in the House with elections every two years."), and more competitive ("You are more vulnerable in the Senate—you aren't seen back home as much and you are held to blame for the economy."). Several senators mentioned that although senatorial campaigns are tougher and more expensive, it is easier to raise money than on the House side.

Member individualism was mentioned by three senators as the hallmark of the Senate. Each pointed out that the Senate affords the opportunity for each to go at it alone and in his or her way. "There are a lot of solo acts up here," one senator stated, "and everyone's got their agenda." *Less of a common bind* was eloquently mentioned by two senators who pointed out that staggered six-year terms diminish the "sense of shared-fates" you have in the House. "With retirements, less than one-third of us are up, so the institution is not as affected by an election as the House."

Different skill requirements were mentioned. As one senator put it,

> In the House, you "mass market" your success. You go and get 15–20 cosponsors and, if you choose the right 20, you can have legislative success. Not so in the Senate. The Senate is much less susceptible to that approach. Debate and "personal selling" make the difference in the Senate.

Several senators pointed to *more in-depth study of issues*, acknowledging that Senate floor debate and the amendment process "made you get into it more, to think through the various facets in anticipation of 10 or so amendments."

3. MISCELLANEOUS DIFFERENCES

In addition to the differences listed in Table 3.2.3, other differences were brought to light, but only by the mention of one interviewee. Table 3.2.4 lists these miscellaneous differences. Although they are very idiosyncratic, they offer important insights into the functioning of the House and Senate. Although most are self-explanatory, an elaboration of a few enumerates some important differences. One senator emphatically stated that in the Senate a member is *more able to be a "Burkean" legislator* than in the House. As he stated, "in the Senate you have more freedom to play it the way Edmund Burke wanted it. You are less encumbered by narrow parochial interests and can better serve the public interest and your own conscience." *Less substantive impact* was mentioned by one senator who noted the superior expertise of House members:

Table 3.2.4.
Miscellaneous differences (mentioned by only one interviewee).

The Senate is/has:

- More chance to be Burkean.
- Less substantive impact.
- More member isolation.
- A more leisurely pace.
- Presiding responsibilities.
- Committees not meeting during floor debate.
- More member say in the schedule.
- Within-state bipartisan coordination.
- Committees that are less influential.
- Presidential fever.
- Fewer informal groups.
- Generally older members.
- National constituency.
- To vote on treaties and presidential appointees.
- Scheduling by consent rather than calendars.
- Lobbied member-by-member rather than by voting blocs.
- A role in selecting federal judges.

> When I was in the House and we went to conferences, we always felt that the senators were too superficial, and now that I'm here, I see it for sure. That gives the House an edge not only on conference committee, but also in legislating. Most legislation originates and goes through the House first. That's where the fine-tuning is done.

A more leisurely pace was emphasized by one senator who argued that you have more time to prepare for votes in the Senate with the "dead quorum calls." *Presiding responsibilities* were mentioned by a junior Republican who stated that "nothing can make or break your image quicker in your first year." *More say in the schedule* was highlighted by a senator's comments that, "The unanimous consent process of bringing legislation up with a chance for any senator to put a 'hold' on it confers on the individual senator a say in the schedule not even members of the House Rules Committee have."

Committees that are less influential were accentuated in one interview during which a senator noted that, frequently, committees are by-passed or over-ruled in the Senate process, unlike the House where committees usually prevail. *Presidential fever* was seen as a major difference. "I counted more than half of the Senate who would like to be President or Vice President. That has an impact around here." *Fewer informal groups* was mentioned by one who felt the absence of election class, ideological, or regional groupings in the Senate made a difference. Finally, one mentioned the Constitutional requirements of *age*, noting that "in the Senate, you find few under age 45."

4. THE ORNSTEIN THESIS OF HOUSE-SENATE CONVERGENCE

In response to Question 2, 14 of the 16 Senators agreed that the House and Senate are behaving more alike. The two who responded in the negative took what they thought was a broader historical view. In the words of one, "I don't see any change along those lines. The overall and the specific have always been debated and dealt with in both. This is nothing new."

The other Senator stated:

> There are other instances in history where convergence has occurred, instances where House members have made bold and vast statements and where senators have expertise. You can find people who have done both in either house.

Most senators (14) expressed agreement with the Ornstein thesis and they saw the fusion or consequence as affecting both houses and moving both together. Examples of general responses are:

> The Senate used to be a lot different from the House, but it's not the same now. The House and Senate *are* behaving like each other.

> That concept is more right than wrong. This converging is occurring. It's a natural development. That notion is absolutely true.

> I agree with that proposition. The process that exists in the Senate now looks a lot like the House.

Moreover, a few added that changes in policy roles are not the only changes to overtake the House and Senate. Several pointed to recent changes in the Senate's social setting, work load, and campaign dynamics as part and parcel of changes in policy focus. As one senator said, "When you stress nuts and bolts, you'll be busier, more impersonal, and targeted." Others pointed to changes resulting from Republican control: a more predictable schedule, Howard Baker's attempt to cope with postcloture filibusters, and more general concern for order and procedure.

In discussing converging behavior, six possible explanations were offered in the courses of the interviews: (1) less institutional loyalty and self-discipline, (2) the advent of the new congressional budget process, (3) the recent transplantation of many former House members to the Senate, (4) the re-election strategies of incumbent senators, (5) the advent of TV coverage in the House, and (6) the emerging inflated egos of more senior House members.

Less institutional loyalty is pointed to by two senators, one of whom stated that, "There are fewer senators who are loyal to the Senate as a collegial institution that works through compromise—when this breaks down, we will resemble the House."

The advent of *the new congressional budget process* (1974) with the creation of budget committees in both houses was seen as a force promoting convergence. In one senator's words,

> The budget process makes us both go through the same damn three-ring circus: budget, authorization, and appropriations. That's what forces us to treat legislation the same. It causes a fusion of responsibility in both houses. We do the same thing in a smaller world with the deferral and recision roles pertaining to impoundments. We have to get into mechanics.

In discussing a *transplantation interpretation*, one senator stated that he and other senators believe that the Senate is behaving more like the House because of high turnover, with so many new senators coming from the House recently. As he stated,

> Many members are looking into nuts and bolts more because so many of the new senators have come from the House where they do that. They bring it here with them and there aren't enough "Senate types" to set them straight.

The *re-election strategies* of incumbent, recent-vintage senators was pointed to by one senator in a particularly persuasive way as a cause of House-Senate blurring. He felt the area where we see convergence most is an emphasis in the Senate on "constituency-services." He stated that:

> Younger senators are more constituency-oriented for reasons of self-preservation. Older senators look down on this "as not the appropriate role of a senator." They think you should deal only with monumental policy questions. But House members are seen more back home. Senators don't see that many folks, can't press the flesh. Thus, constituency casework allows you to keep in touch. If you can't attend a ball game back home like the House members, at least you can claim credit for getting the lights added to the park.

The advent of TV coverage in the House was seen by several more senior senators as the reason why the House gets into broader questions more. "They now have a grandstand. It gives many of them more visibility than us. We better go too or risk getting knocked off by some House member who is getting a national following."

Finally, one senator in discussing ego in the House said:

> Some of those more senior guys in the House like to throw their weight around. They want to be big shots, so they take positions on a lot of issues outside their range of expertise. Some of them want to run for the presidency. Super-egos in the House are causing them to change.

5. MAJOR AND MINOR DIFFERENCES AND CAUSE AND EFFECT RELATIONSHIPS

Froman (1967) calls our attention to the importance of distinguishing between major and minor differences between House and Senate. As he states:

> Probably the two most important differences between the House and the Senate, and the two from which most of the others are derived, are that the House is more than four times as large as the Senate, and that senators represent sovereign states in a federal system, whereas most congressmen represent smaller and sometimes shifting parts of the states (Froman, 1967: 7).

In other words, certain major differences (such as the size differential and differences in constituency) act as independent variables that account for and explain certain minor differences (committee system, work load, proclivity to generalism), which serve as dependent variables.

This kind of cause-and-effect reasoning from major to minor differences was evident in the interviews. Examples are the following propositions posited by senators during the interviews:

> Because there are fewer of us to go around, we are busier, and more dependent on staff, and less rigid in procedure.

> Because of the fact we represent states, there is more individualism. You can only run the Senate as an institution highly responsive to the individual senators.

> Because of the six-year staggered term of office, there is less of a common bind holding us together.

Table 3.2.5.
Causal flow of differences as relayed by interviewed senators.

Major Institutional Differences	→	Minor Institutional Differences	→	Policy Process Implications
"Upper house"		More prestigious		Macro policy views
		Individualism		Particularistic policy
Representation of states		More informal, flexible, looser busier		Decisionmakers more isolated
				Different skills required
Fewer members to go around		More staff		More staff dependence
		Less partisan		
Treaty and advice and consent responsibilities		Less of a common bind		
		Formal social environment		
		More emphasis on seniority		
Six-year staggered terms		Different campaign dynamics than the House		

> Because we have more staff, we are more isolated.
>
> Because we handle foreign policy matters, we are less partisan than the House.

Table 3.2.5 presents a summary of such causal statements offered in the interviews. In summary, senators imply that major institutional differences lead to minor institutional differences, which, in turn and together, lead to differences in the character of the policy process. An important conclusion developed by senators is that in the Senate, because of major and minor institutional differences, the policy process will be more macro-oriented, but particularistic in terms of serving both states and the wishes of the individual senators. Decisionmakers are more isolated, more dependent on staff, and require different skills when engaging in the process.

SUMMARY AND CONCLUSIONS

This research has provided insights into House-Senate differences from the perspectives of and in the words of 16 senators who have experience in both bodies. It offers four major conclusions. First, different senators stress different differences. No one difference was mentioned by all 16.

Second, senators mentioned differences in social setting, work environment, and campaign dynamics that have not been previously emphasized in the literature of bicameralism (see Table 3.2.1). In fact, the interviews lead to a necessary amending of the traditional treatment of bicameralism as presented in Table 3.2.1. Table 3.2.6 presents such an addendum to Table 3.2.1, integrating differences identified in interviews with differences identified in the literature.

Third, an overwhelming majority of interviewed senators subscribe to the Ornstein thesis of contemporary House-Senate convergence. They explain these tendencies toward blurring in terms of the advent of a new congressional budget process, televising of House floor proceedings, the recent influx of senators with prior House experience, the casework orientation of new senators, the emergence of inflated egos in the House, and the breakdown of senatorial self-discipline. Fourth, senators make causal links between major and minor institutional differences and the policy process.

The founding framers of the U.S. Constitution intended that the legislative body would function through meaningful bicameralism. In Madison's words,

> The remedy for this inconvenience [legislative supremacy] is to divide the

Table 3.2.6.
The House and Senate compared: A perspective from interviews.

Basis of Comparison	House	Senate
1. Membership	Larger (435)*	Smaller (100)*
	Less prestigious*	More prestigious*
	More incumbency*	Less incumbency*
	Less visible*	More visible*
2. Constituency	More homogeneous, narrower*	More heterogeneous, broader*
	Represents people*†	Represents states*†
	Closer to constituents*†	More removed from constituents*†
3. Time perspective	Shorter (elected every two years)	Longer (elected every six years)
	Noncontinuous body (two-year cycle)	Continuing body (staggered terms of office)
4. Structure	More hierarchical;* less equitable*	Less hierarchical;* more equitable*
	Less seniority*†	More seniority*†
	Speaker is power broker‡	Majority leader is power broker‡
	Fusion in speaker's office of presiding powers and head of majority party‡	Separation of presiding officer and majority party head‡
	Committees more important‡	Committees less important‡
	Members serve on fewer committees	Members serve on more committees
	Less staff per member†	More staff per member†
	Less staff reliance	More staff reliance
5. Process	More formal, rigid	Informal, flexible (much business done through unanimous consent)
	Less comity*	More comity*
	Rules Committee structures debate	Rules Committee does not structure debate
	Most floor work done in "committee of the whole"	No counterpart to "committee of the whole"
	More complex: five calendars‡	Less complex: two calendars‡
	Less access to the floor*†	More access to the floor*†
	Less emphasis on debate*†	More emphasis on debate*†
	Limited debate (five-minute rule)	Unlimited debate until cloture invoked or unless a unanimous consent limitation
	Nongermane amendments (riders) not allowed	Nongermane amendments (riders) allowed
	Acts more quickly‡	Acts more slowly‡
	Electronic voting‡	No electronic voting‡
	TV coverage	No TV coverage (1985)

Table 3.2.6. (concluded)

Basis of Comparison	House	Senate
6. Policy functions	Originates revenue measures* Expertise, specialization	Executive counsel* (appointments and treaties) debate, deliberation, discussion of national priorities
7. As an organization	Representative assembly	Forum of functional self-indulgence;* Breeding ground for presidential candidates*
	Less visibility/media coverage	More visibility/media coverage
	Facilitates majority rule†	Facilitates minority rule †
8. As a work environment	Friendlier†§	Less friendly†§
	More personal†§	More impersonal†§
	Less mail/lobbying*†	More mail/lobbying*†
	Less busy†§	Busier†§
	Less emphasis on debating skills†	More emphasis on debating skills†
	More partisan†	Less partisan†
	Less individualism*†	more individualism*†
	Less institution-oriented*†	More institution-oriented *†
	More of a common bond*†	Less of a common bond*†
	More informal groups*†	Less informal groups*†
9. Different campaign dynamics	Continuing campaign structure*†	New structure each election*†
	Less expensive*†	More expensive*†
	Most incumbents less vulnerable*†	Most incumbents more vulnerable*†
	Harder to raise money*†	Easier to raise money*†

* = mentioned by 3 or fewer senators
† = added by interviewed senator
‡ = not mentioned by any senator
§ = mentioned by 10 or more senators
No annotation = mentioned by between four and nine senators
n = 16

> legislature into different branches; and to render them, by different modes of election and different principles of action, as little connected with each other as the nature of their common function and their common dependence on the society will admit (*Federalist Papers*, No. 51: 322).

To the federalists, the American polity would be best served by a lower house that reflected the popular will and an upper house that provided stability, continuity, and policy deliberation. What emerges from this research is that members who have served in both bodies feel that the Congress is indeed comprised of two fundamentally different institutions with "different principles of action." Although the 17th amendment providing for the direct election of senators changed the mode of election as envisioned by the federalists, the two houses still do their business differently. This research, however, shows that many senators feel the differences are starting to blur due to a number of factors.

Of course, the next question is, "how far have they blurred, i.e., to what extent?" If the convergence in policy focus and social and working environments reflects in the prose of *The Federalist*, "the nature of common function" and "common dependence on the society," then there really is no reason for concern. But if the convergence of policy roles goes to the heart of the differences, if because of the blurring of responsibility and behavior, the Senate will provide less policy deliberation and less cross-issue comparison, and if we expect this trend to continue, then we indeed should be concerned.

Having the House and Senate performing different functions and doing business differently, though frequently resulting in stalemate, provides many benefits for policymaking. All of us need to think through exactly what it is we want the modern Senate to do and to be. Each proposal for change and each recent trend should then be evaluated in terms of how it affects and serves our preferences. Quite clearly, nuts and bolts micro legislating, impossible work loads, more emphasis on casework and constituency service, and increasingly rancorous partisanship and obstructionalism do not enhance the role of the Senate as policy deliberator and generalist. The impact of an increasingly more formal, more isolated social environment in the Senate is not clear.

Reading 3.3

The Growth of Staff

Norman J. Ornstein,
Thomas E. Mann,
Michael J. Malbin
and John F. Bibby

The fastest-growing bureaucracy in Washington, D.C. is not, as some would think, the institutionalized Presidency in the Executive Office of the President; it is congressional staffs. The following excerpt from a congressional data book details the expansion of staff at both the personal-office and committee levels.

Congress is made up of a great deal more than elected senators and representatives. With more than 31,000 employees in 1983, (Figure 3.1.1) the legislative branch is larger than the Department of State, Labor, or Housing and Urban Development. In comparison, the second most heavily staffed legislative branch in the world is the Canadian Parliament, which gets by with a staff of fewer than 3,500.[1]

Of course, Congress's employees include more than the personal and committee staffs of congressmen and senators. Also included are major research agencies, such as the Congressional Research Service (CRS) of the Library of Congress, and support personnel, such as mail carriers, police officers, barbers, hairdressers, television technicians, computer specialists, printers, carpenters, parking attendants, photographers, and laborers.

The development of this large congressional establishment is a twentieth-century

Source: From *Vital Statistics on Congress*, 1984–1985 by Norman J. Ornstein, Thomas E. Mann, Michael J. Malbin, Allen Schick, and John F. Bibby, pp. 116–127.

Figure 3.3.1.
Staff of members and of committees in Congress, 1891–1983.

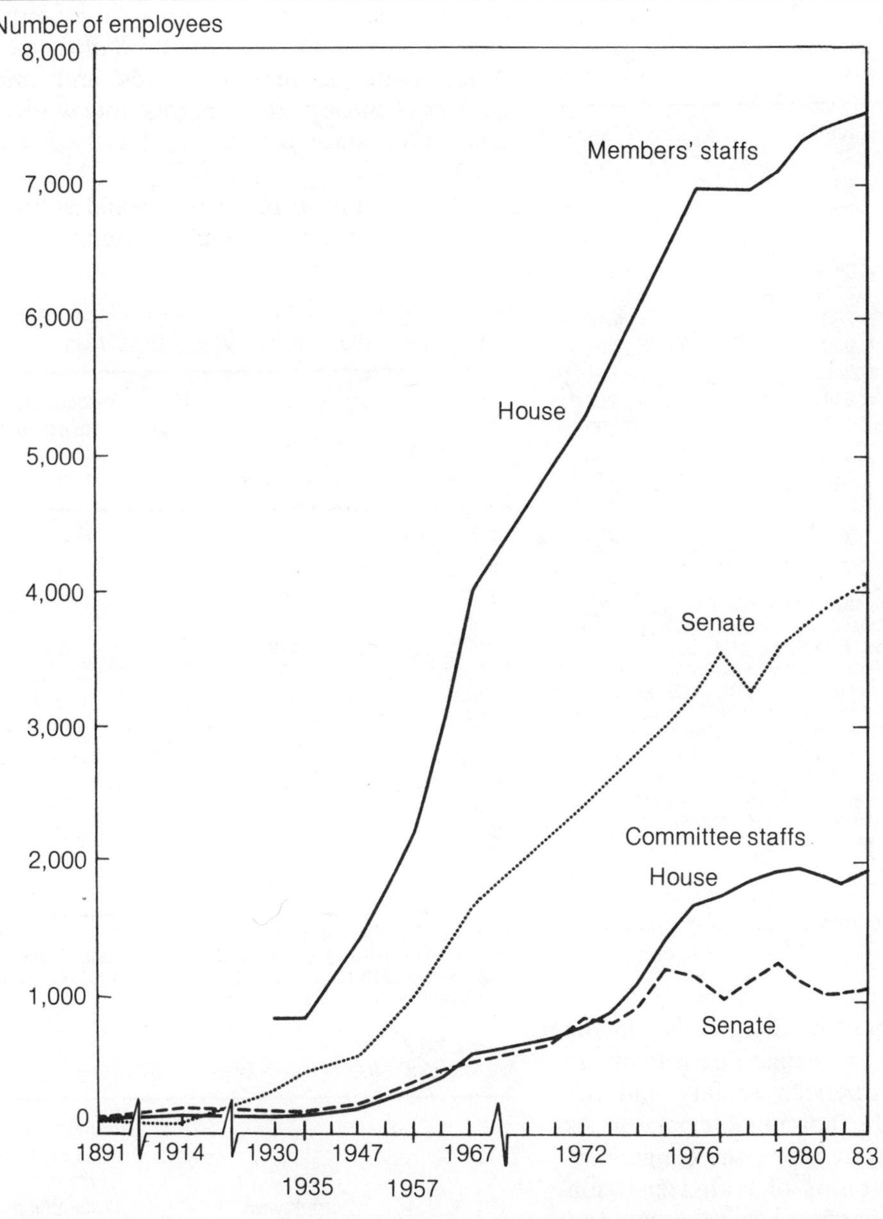

Source: Tables 5–2 and 5–5, Ornstein et al., *Vital Statistics on Congress* (Washington, D.C.: American Enterprise Institute, 1984).

phenomenon. At the turn of the century, representatives had no personal staff, and senators had a total of only thirty-nine personal assistants (Table 3.3.1 and Figure 3.3.1). Committee staffs consisted of a few clerks (Table 3.3.4). By contrast, 11,665 persons served on the personal staffs of representatives and senators in 1983, and over 3,000 people were employed by congressional committees.

Table 3.3.1.
Personal staffs of members of the House and the Senate, 1891–1983.

Year	Employees in House	Employees in Senate
1891	n.a.	39
1914	n.a.	72
1930	870	280
1935	870	424
1947	1,440	590
1957	2,441	1,115
1967	4,055	1,749
1972	5,280	2,426
1976	6,939	3,251
1977	6,942	3,554
1978	6,944	3,268
1979	7,067	3,593
1980	7,371	3,746
1981	7,487	3,945
1982	7,511	4,041
1983	7,606	4,059

Note: n.a. = not available.
Sources: For 1891 through 1976: Harrison W. Fox, Jr., and Susan W. Hammond, *Congressional Staffs: The Invisible Force in American Lawmaking* (New York: Free Press, 1977), p. 171. For 1977 and 1978: Judy Schneider, "Congressional Staffing, 1947-78," Congressional Research Service, August 24, 1979, reprinted in U.S. Congress, House, Select Committee on Committees, *Final Report*, April 1, 1980, p. 540. For 1977, 1978, and 1979 House: *Report of the Clerk of the House*. For 1979 Senate: *Report of the Secretary of the Senate*. For 1980: *House LBA Hearings for 1982*, pt. 1, p. 25; and *Senate LBA hearings for 1981*, pt. 1, p. 26. For 1981: *House LBA Hearings for 1983* pt. 1, pp. 24-28; and *Report of the Secretary of the Senate*, October 1, 1981-March 31, 1982. For 1982: *House LBA Hearings for 1984*, pt. 1, p. 25; and *Report of the Secretary of the Senate*, October 1, 1982-March 31, 1983. For 1983: *House LBA Hearings for 1985*, pt. 1, p. 24; and *Report of the Secretary of the Senate*, October 1, 1983-March 31, 1984.

The enlargement of Congress's support staff reflects both the expanding role of the government in American society and the changing role of the individual legislator. As government has done more, the congressional workload, in terms of both legislation and constituency service, has increased, and the staffing needs of Congress have expanded accordingly. The most dramatic staff growth has taken place since World War II, the personal staffs of the House and Senate having increased more than fivefold and sixfold, respectively, since 1947. One reflection of the increased demands on legislators for constituency services and the members' encouragement of those demands for reelection purposes is the dramatic expansion of congressional staff working in constituency offices. More than one-third of the personal staffs of representatives and one-quarter of those of the senators now work in district or state offices (Tables 3.3.2 and 3.3.3).

The explosion in congressional staffing is also evident on the standing committees:

Table 3.3.2.
House staff based in district offices, 1970–1983.

Year	Employees	Percentage of Total Personal Staffs in District Offices
1970	1,035	n.a.
1971	1,121	n.a.
1972	1,189	22.5
1973	1,347	n.a.
1974	1,519	n.a.
1975	1,732	n.a.
1976	1,943	28.0
1977	2,058	29.6
1978	2,317	33.4
1979	2,445	34.6
1980	2,534	34.4
1981	2,702	36.1
1982	2,694	35.8
1983	2,785	36.6

Note: n.a. = not available.
Sources: For 1970-1978: Schneider, "Congressional Staffing, 1947-78." For 1979-1983: Charles B. Brownson, ed. *Congressional Staff Directory*, Washington, D.C., annual editions.

Table 3.3.3.
Senate staff based in state offices, 1972–1983.

Year	Employees	Percentage of Total Personal Staffs in State Offices
1972	303	12.5
1978	816	25.0
1979	879	24.3
1980	953	25.4
1981	937	25.8
1982	1,053	26.1
1983	1,132	27.9

Source: Brownson, *Congressional Staff Directory*, annual editions.

House committee staffs increased twelvefold and Senate committee staffs more than fourfold between 1947 and 1983 (Table 3.3.4). Committee staffing has grown steadily since the turn of the century, but the most dramatic increases occurred in the 1970s. House committee staffs were two and three-quarters times as large as in 1979 as they were in 1970, and Senate committee staffs doubled over the same period.

This enlargement of House committee staffs after 1970 is to a significant degree a result of the reform movement that swept the chamber. The sentiment for diluting the powers of committee chairmen extended to their nearly exclusive authority to hire and fire staff. Reforms allowed a much larger number of subcommittee chairmen and ranking members to hire their own staffs. The 1975 surge in committee staffing in the Senate reflects the passage of Senate Resolution 60, which authorized each senator to have a personal legislative assistant for each committee assignment. The modest reductions in Senate committee staffs in 1977 were caused by the committee reorganization that went into effect that year, which among other things reduced the number of Senate subcommittees and shifted people hired under Senate Resolution 60 to personal staff payrolls.

The 1980s have not, so far, been a repeat of the 1970s. Personal staffs have continued to grow, but committee staff numbers have leveled off somewhat. Senate committee staffs underwent a one-shot 19 percent cut after the Republicans gained control in 1981 and promised to reverse the previous decade's trends. Note, however, that more than one-third of the cuts came from one committee, Judiciary (Table 3.3.6). As significant as the cuts may be, they left the Senate with almost 70 percent more committee staff in 1983 than in 1970.

Tables 3.3.5 and 3.3.6 rank the standing committees according to staff size. Each committee except the Senate Judiciary Committee had a significantly larger staff in 1983 than it had in 1960. Most committees employ well over fifty persons, a far cry from the post–World War II era of small, intimate, informal committee staffs. The size of a committee staff does not appear to be related uniformly to the reported power or desirability of an assignment to a particular committee. The powerful Senate Finance Committee, for example, is modestly staffed compared with the less influential Labor and Human Resources and Governmental Affairs committees. Of course, some

Table 3.3.4.
Staffs of House and Senate standing committees, 1891–1983.

Year	Employees in House	Employees in Senate
1891	62	41
1914	105	198
1930	112	163
1935	122	172
1947	167	232
1950	246	300
1955	329	386
1960	440	470
1965	571	509
1970	702	635
1971	729	711
1972	817	844
1973	878	873
1974	1,107	948
1975	1,460	1,277
1976	1,680	1,201
1977	1,776	1,028
1978	1,844	1,151
1979	1,909	1,269
1980	1,917	1,191
1981	1,843	1,022
1982	1,839	1,047
1983	1,970	1,075

Note: Figures for 1947-1983 are for the statutory and investigative staffs of standing committees. They do not include select committee staffs, which varied between 31 and 238 in the House and between 62 and 172 in the Senate during the 1970s. For this reason, the numbers do not agree with those in Table 3.3.1.
Sources: For 1891-1935: Fox and Hammond, *Congressional Staffs*, p. 171. For 1947-1978: Schneider, "Congressional Staffing, 1947-78." For 1979-1980 Senate: U.S. Congress, Senate, Committee on Rules and Administration, *Senate Inquiries and Investigations*, 96th Congress, 2d session, Committee Print No. 2, March 5, 1980. For 1981-1983 Senate: Committee on Rules and Administration, *Senate Committee Funding*. (annual committee prints). For 1981 House: *House LBA Hearings for 1983*, pt. 2, p. 107. For 1982 House: *House LBA Hearings for 1984*, pt. 2, p. 77. For 1983 House: Office of the Clerk of the House (unpublished document).

Table 3.3.5.
Staff size of House standing committees, 1947–1983.

Committee	1947	1960	1970	1975	1979	1981	1983
House Administration*	7	4	25	217	273	252	267
Appropriations	29	59	71	98	129	127	160
Energy and Commerce	10	45	42	112	160	151	158
Education and Labor	10	25	77	114	121	121	121
Budget	†	†	†	67	86	93	97
Ways and Means	12	22	24	63	99	91	94
Banking	4	14	50	85	97	87	93
Government Operations	9	54	60	68	85	84	87
Post Office and Civil Service	6	9	46	61	66	74	87
Foreign Affairs	10	14	21	54	82	84	85
Public Works	6	32	40	88	81	86	84
Judiciary	7	27	35	69	80	75	82
Merchant Marine and Fisheries	6	9	21	28	91	82	81
Science and Technology	†	17	26	47	87	74	78
Interior	4	10	14	57	75	70	73
Agriculture	9	10	17	48	66	62	70
Armed Services	10	15	37	38	48	49	56
Small Business	†	†	†	27	46	54	53
Rules	4	2	7	18	47	43	47
District of Columbia	7	8	15	43	41	41	46
Veterans' Affairs	7	18	18	26	34	34	32
Standards of Official Conduct	†	†	5	5	15	9	19
Internal Security	10	46	51	27	†	†	†

Note: Committees are ranked in order of their staff size in 1983.
*After 1972, figures include employees of House Informations Systems, the House of Representatives' central computer facility.
†Not a standing committee.
Sources: For 1947-1975: Schneider, "Congressional Staffing, 1947-78." For 1979: *House LBA Hearings for 1981*, pt. 2, p. 136. For 1981: *House LBA Hearings for 1983*, pt. 2, p. 107. For 1983: Office of the Clerk of the House (unpublished document).

Table 3.3.6.
Staff size of Senate standing committees, 1947–1983.

Committee	1947	1960	1970	1975	1979	1981	1983
Judiciary	19	137	190	251	223	134	141
Governmental Affairs	29	47	55	144	179	153	138
Labor and Human Resources	9	28	69	150	155	119	125
Commerce, Science, and Transportation	8	52	53	111	96	78	90
Appropriations	23	31	42	72	80	79	82
Budget	*	*	*	90	91	82	79
Foreign Relations	8	25	31	62	75	59	63
Environment and Public Works	10	11	34	70	74	56	56
Energy and Natural Resources (Interior)	7	26	22	53	55	50	56
Finance	6	6	16	26	67	50	53
Armed Services	10	23	19	30	31	36	41

Table 3.3.6. (concluded)

Committee	1947	1960	1970	1975	1979	1981	1983
Banking, Housing, and Urban Affairs	9	22	23	55	48	39	39
Agriculture	3	10	7	22	34	34	34
Rules and Administration	41	15	13	29	37	31	30
Veterans' Affairs	*	*	*	32	24	22	22
Aeronautics and Space Sciences	*	10	12	22	*	*	*
District of Columbia	4	7	18	33	*	*	*
Post Office and Civil Service	46	20	31	25	*	*	*

Note: Committees are ranked in order of their staff size in 1983.
*Committee not in existence.
Sources: For 1947-1975: Schneider, "Congressional Staffing, 1947-78." For 1979-1983: Senate Committee on Rules and Administration, *Senate Committee Funding*, This annual committee print lists the number of positions authorized for each committee; the number actually employed at any one time may be less.

Table 3.3.7.
Staffs of congressional support agencies, 1946–1983.

Year	Library of Congress	Congressional Research Service Only*	General Accounting Office†	Congressional Budget Office	Office of Technology Assessment
1946			14,219		
1947	1,898	160	10,695		
1950	1,973	161	7,876		
1955	2,459	166	5,776		
1960	2,779	183	5,074		
1965	3,390	231	4,278		
1970	3,848	332	4,704		
1971	3,963	386	4,718		
1972	4,135	479	4,742		
1973	4,375	596	4,908		
1974	4,504	687	5,270		10
1975	4,649	741	4,905	193	54
1976	4,880	806	5,391	203	103
1977	5,075	789	5,315	201	139
1978	5,231	818	5,476	203	164
1979	5,390	847	5,303	207	145
1980	5,047	868	5,196	218	122
1981	4,799	849	5,182	218	130
1982	4,803	849	5,027	218	130
1983	4,815	853	4,960	211	130

*Legislative Reference Service through 1970.
†Before 1950 the GAO was responsible for auditing all individual federal transactions and keeping a record of them. Legislation in 1950 transferred these responsibilities to the executive branch. The staff reductions through 1965 result from this 1950 change. See Frederich C. Mosher, *The GAO: The Quest for Accountability in American Government* (Boulder, Colo.: Westview Press, 1979), p. 124.
Sources: Library of Congress: *Annual Reports of the Librarian of Congress*. GAO (1946-1965): *Annual Reports of the Comptroller General of the United States*. OTA (1974-1976): *Appendixes of the Budget of the United States* for fiscal 1976 (p. 18), 1977 (p. 18), and 1978 (p. 40). CBO (1975): Joel Havemann, *Congress and the Budget* (Bloomington: Indiana University Press, 1978), p. 109. Data are as of October 1975. The CBO's director took office on February 24, 1975. GAO (1970-1978), CBO (1976-1978), and OTA (1977-1978): Schneider, "Congressional Staffing, 1947-78." For 1979-1983: same as Table 3.3.1.

committees that are generally considered less desirable assignments may well have expanded their staffs to attract new members.

A significant part of the congressional staff works for Congress's four major research agencies (Table 3.3.7). Two of these, the Congressional Budget Office (CBO) and the Office of Technology Assessment (OTA), were created in the mid-1970s, their creation reflecting a basic factor underlying the growth of congressional staff. The expanded role of the government in domestic and international affairs had made Congress increasingly dependent on the executive branch for information. A growing distrust of the executive, festering during the Johnson and Nixon administrations, convinced Congress of the necessity for congressionally controlled sources of information. Congress thus authorized these new agencies and simultaneously expanded the roles of the Congressional Research Service and the General Accounting Office (GAO). The GAO has multiple functions, including audit responsibilities with limited relevance to its role as a congressional agency. The same is true of the Library of Congress.

Reading 3.4

Congressional Staff: The View from the District

John Macartney

Congressional staffs on Capitol Hill are only part of the picture. Huge congressional bureaucracies have been established "back home" in states and congressional districts to assist members in the performance of congressional functions. This original essay by John Macartney presents data on the operation of district staff offices. These data are based on the author's extensive field study of legislative offices, federal, state and local, in southern California.[1]

The theme of this article is simple: Only part of the U.S. Congress is to be found on Capitol Hill. Much of it is located in storefront offices, professional, and federal buildings across America.[2] A look at the phone book—any American phone book—tells the tale. Virtually everyone in this country resides within 25 miles of Congress.

Civics texts and news accounts notwithstanding, most "lawmakers," especially their staffs, spend the lion's share of their time and effort on a variety of nonlawmaking functions, most of which relate to the constituents back home. Increasingly, the bulk of those operations are being carried out from district offices, and that is the stuff of this essay. What is Congress accomplishing? Only part of the answer is recorded in roll-call votes, committee hearings, and legislation, while much of the remainder concerns what's going on back in 435 districts and 50 states. In many respects, the district is where Congress is at.

Consider the case of an imaginary but typical office of a member of the House of

Source: Prepared especially for the first edition of this volume.

Representatives. It is divided into two distinct operations—one on Capitol Hill and another back in the district. Both offices—the one in Washington and the one in the district—share the member's various tasks, but legislation receives much more attention in Washington, while constituents and local matters dominate the district office. The congressman shuttles between the two offices, spending almost two-thirds of his or her time at the capitol. The Washington office, of course, deals with the more weighty, national issues, while the district office concerns itself with minor, local matters. But four things stand out: (1) The congressman does not share influence with so many powerful rivals at home; the district is a smaller pond. (2) The kinds of tasks and projects undertaken at the district office are such that they usually are pursued to completion instead of dying in the hopper—the fate of 96 percent of the proposed legislation with which Washington busies itself. (3) The staff at the district office enjoy more autonomy than their counterparts in Washington simply because the boss is away. Most of the time the top field aide is the acting congressman. (4) Issues and projects that may seem minor on the national scale are crucial on individual and local scales.

The variety of issues and projects undertaken at the field office is endless. For example, there is the widow who gets a bureaucratic run-around instead of a social security check; a call from the district office cuts red tape. There is also the businessman looking for a government contract, the school district that wants a federal grant, and the GI seeking an early discharge. Multiply those cases by 6,653* and it adds up to "who gets what, when, and how" in our imaginary district. And there are a great many undertakings that seemingly have nothing at all to do with Congress or the federal government. Some are private matters; others involve state or local government. Maybe the issue is a municipal park—or parking lot—putting the schools on double sessions, a local election, attracting industry and jobs to the community, promoting a charity drive, organizing a Little League program, encouraging local merchants to hire teenagers, or changing zoning laws. Whatever the issue, if it is important to the community, the congressional district office is likely to become involved.

Additionally, there often is the direct delivery of public services. Consider, for example, just one project undertaken over the last several years by the district office of Los Angeles Congressman Barry Goldwater, Jr. Goldwater's constituency is predominately suburban and is located about 20 miles from the coast, across the Santa Monica mountains. The problem was finding transportation to the beach—primarily for youngsters, but also to reduce fuel consumption, pollution, and parking problems. (Los Angeles has no public mass transit worthy of the name.) Goldwater's field representative organized the Recreation Transit System (RTS), a massive program involving hundreds of leased school buses, a nonprofit corporation, and a huge fund-raising and publicity campaign. Result: Several hundred thousand San Fernando Valley residents, mostly young people, have been transported to the beach over the past few summers.

No legislation and no federal funds are involved in this operation, yet it is part of what the Congress is doing (a part not acknowledged in lists of congressional functions found in political science texts). For many youngsters and their grateful parents in California's 27th District, the RTS is probably more important and certainly more visible than all the committee work, all the bills introduced, and all the floor votes cast by Mr. Goldwater (of which they know little). And Goldwater's direct delivery of

*The average number of constituent cases handled by each House district office in Los Angeles County during the 1973–1974 congressional term. Another 2,851 cases, on the average, were handled at the respective Washington offices. The volumes would be considerably higher today. Success rate—resolving a case in the constituent's favor—is better than 80 percent.

public services is not at all unique. To cite one more example, Denver Congresswoman Pat Schroeder's large district operation (a three-story suburban house with 10 employees plus 20 eager volunteers) sponsors a low-income housing project, plus a grocery store on wheels for shut-ins, among other direct services.

Today, virtually every senator and representative maintains one or more full-time offices back in his/her state or district. That is a relatively new development in the 200-year history of the U.S. Congress. Little is recorded about the development of district offices.[3] However, one woman interviewed for this study had been working in Chet Holifield's California district office since it was established in 1942, when, she believes, it was the only one in the country. Decentralization, the deployment of office resources to states and districts, accelerated during the 1960s, and by the late 70s no member was without such an operation.

Decentralization has several roots. An obvious one is the electoral advantage of a strong district office. Another is simply staff growth. Until staffs were large enough to have two complete operations, there was an either-or dilemma. Today, the average House member uses about one-third to one-half of 22 staff positions (18 full-time, 4 part-time) to operate one or more offices back home. Senators usually keep a fifth to a third of their much larger staffs in the state.

Since each member decides for him- or herself how office resources will be deployed, the variations are great. Such decisions depend upon what Dick Fenno calls "home style," but by and large, the more extensive field operations can be expected in urban areas, particularly if the incumbent is recently elected or anticipates stiff electoral competition. Many southern and most rural legislators maintain relatively small field offices.

Decentralization is also encouraged by the lack of office space in Washington and the avalanche of constituent business that threatens to overwhelm lawmaking efforts. Deploying part of the congressional office organization to the district serves both purposes. Hundreds of square feet of additional space becomes available, while the efforts of staffers remaining on the Hill can be focused on legislation.

DISTRICT OFFICE FUNCTIONS

What do district offices do? What goes on there? The short answer would be constituent service and promotion. In order to tell the story in more detail, this paper will discuss 13 separate functions carried out by congressional field offices.

1. Office management.
2. Communications and public relations.
3. Casework.
4. Political organizing.
5. Surveillance.
6. Alter ego.
7. Group liaison.
8. Representation.
9. Scheduling and advancing.
10. Community organizer/direct action.
11. Oversight.
12. Legislative support.
13. Personal errands.

1. Office and Staff Management

Although the incumbent is ultimately the director of his own staff, the burdens of that task usually fall on a chief of staff. The job includes training and supervision of other staff employees and volunteers and, in 71 percent of these offices, the hiring and firing of other staffers. There are funds and budgets to handle, as well. This can be a major task because of the separate office accounts, private funds, campaign contributions, and (sometimes) the incumbent's personal accounts. The practice in some offices of switching staffers on and off the payroll (in order to circumvent the maximum employee limit) further complicates the manager's task.[4] Many offices have bookkeepers who handle office accounts as well as campaign finances.

2. Communications and Public Relations

Words and symbols are the ammunition of politics; no politician can endure without attending to his public image. In many respects the incumbent's staff is a communications machine, a public relations organization.

The communications effort generally has two goals: *promotion* of the incumbent's political fortunes, and *education* of the citizenry—to inform and persuade about policy alternatives. These two goals are difficult to separate; all communications, simply by naming the incumbent, result in promotion. Most communications involve education, as well. Research on Congress has indicated promotion, rather than education, is usually the central concern.[5]

That conclusion seems to hold for most of the offices studied in Los Angeles, but there were exceptions. A few offices devoted their communications efforts primarily to education on specific issues or causes. Some legislators, just like some candidates, use the bulk of their office resources not for the apparent purpose but to espouse some cherished cause or idea. The prestige and office resources of an individual legislator, especially a congressman (because of the frank) can be an excellent vehicle for advocacy that goes far beyond district boundaries. In practice, such educational efforts take the form of nationally syndicated newspaper columns and broadcast messages, pamphlets, books and articles, and statewide or national mailings (to selected subscribers) of ideological newsletters—all prepared and distributed, at least in part, by staff. Four of the 19 Representatives' offices were engaging in major educational efforts on a statewide or national basis, as were four offices of state legislators. In these cases the incumbent was either a doctrinaire conservative with an ideological message or a spokesman for some minority group.

In order to communicate, staffs make use of five basic mediums: direct mail, telephone, face-to-face, news media, and publications. Communications are received and sent from both central and district offices. Generally speaking, the Washington office communicates with constituents by mail while the district office relies on the telephone. Constituents, as will be shown, prefer the phone—at least in Los Angeles.

Mail

The mails carry the bulk of the outgoing (office-to-constituent) messages. Although district offices handle considerable mail, the Washington offices are likely to handle even more.

Mass Mailings Nearly all of the offices in this study send out *newsletters* on a regular basis. Most include *questionnaires* that poll constituents about various issue questions and legislative proposals. Table 3.4.1 indicates newsletter and poll use. The average number of newsletters per year is fairly representative, but there are offices that send many more. One L. A. congressman has sent as many as 24 newsletters in a single year; one assemblyman sends 15. Such efforts, of course, depend upon private contributions.*

Newsletters keep the incumbent's name, picture,** and accomplishments before his constituents. Questionnaires are primarily a promotional device, "a placebo for constituents," as one aide put it. When sent in bulk mailings, addressed to "occupant," the questionnaire's purpose is to stimulate contacts and supplement mailing lists. Questionnaires tend to flatter voters because they indicate the incumbent's concern for their opinions. Results are tabulated (a time-

*At the time this research was conducted, congressmen received no funds for the printing and preparation of newsletters and all congressional newsletters were dependent upon "slush funds." At present, allowances are provided, numbers of mailings are limited, and slush funds are prohibited.

**The California Legislature allows only two photographs of the incumbent per newsletter. Most newsletters have a sketch of the incumbent on the masthead—to squeeze in a third picture.

Table 3.4.1.
Newsletter and questionnaire use by Los Angeles-based political offices.

	Percent Sending Newsletters	Opinion Polls	Average Number of Newsletter Issues per Year/per Office
U. S. senator	100%	50%	Unknown
Representative	94	83	4.4
State senator	93	89	2.8
Assemblyman	100	87	3.6
Supervisor	20	60	3.0
City councilman	87	60	2.2

Note: In most cases the newsletters/polls emanate from the central offices. The U. S. senators do not send a statewide newsletter, but they do send newsletters periodically to selected sub-areas (usually congressional districts). The senator's goal is to have covered most of the state, at least the more politically crucial districts, once per six-year term.

consuming staff chore) and reflected in subsequent newsletters. Sometimes congressional staffs will insert the results into the *Congressional Record* and then mass mail reprints of the *Record* back to the district.

Most offices break down mailing lists into categories of constituents to allow for *specialized mass mail appeals* to, for example, newspaper editors, union members, businessmen, policemen, teachers, physicians, etc. These mailing lists are computerized, and a few offices go to the trouble and expense to prepare their newsletter in multiple editions, specialized for different categories or neighborhoods of constituents.

Congratulations and Condolences A member of thc PR staff (often an intern or volunteer) usually monitors newspapers and other sources to find names for "congrat" and condolence mailings. Major accomplishments —election to the school board, winning a special honor—rate a personal letter, a phone call, or a presentation. More mundane achievements—graduating from high school, Eagle Scout awards, bar mitzvahs, marriages, anniversaries, births, business promotions, even birthdays—result in cards. Similarly, deaths or illnesses are occasions for condolence cards, telegrams, or flowers. Congressmen are provided with materials besides greeting cards—baby books (2,500 per year), bride kits, flags, etc.—that they can send. Names may be gathered from institutional sources—schools, churches, hospitals, marriage license offices, or wherever—as well as from local newspapers.

Some offices send congratulatory mailings to as many constituents as possible, while other offices honor only those who are identified supporters or limit their effort to really significant achievements. The volume of this activity is related to security and seniority in office as well as higher ambitions.

Table 3.4.2.
Specialized mail appeals—Percentage of L.A.-based offices that send specialized mass mailings to subgroups of constituents.

U.S. senators	50%
Representatives	65
State senators	62
Assemblymen	93
Supervisors	100
City councilmen	87

> We did more of those PR-type things years ago, but it's not necessary anymore.
>
> Congressional Aide

> We used to do that, but casework takes all our time these days. A new congressman should do it. Once you're entrenched, you can let it go.
>
> Congressional Aide

Table 3.4.3.
Volume of congrat activity by office type.

	Average Volume per Year	Top Volume	Lowest Volume
Representatives	5,877	30,000	0
State senators	1,220	5,300	48
Assemblymen	2,326	7,500	140
Supervisors	5,588	7,900	2,000
City councilmen	1,908	13,000	40

Note: Includes all types—letters, plaques, telegrams, flowers, etc. Based on estimates supplied by top aides. A very few offices had actual counts: these tended to be higher than the estimates received elsewhere. Both U.S. Senators perform this function, but from Washington; no estimates on volume were available.

The volume can be substantial—running to 30,000 honored constituents per year. Usually there is a choice of honors, ranging from a greeting card through letters and wall plaques or mention in the *Congressional Record*, plus flags or legislative resolutions. The more substantial honors are usually presented rather than mailed.

During one interview, a State Assemblyman's administrative aide received a call from a city recreation department requesting a legislative resolution for a winning Little League coach. Negotiations ensued. Resolutions cost the state $600 each, the administrative aide explained, and frankly, his boss wanted to maximize their political effect. If the recipient coach was going to keep the award at home, he'd have to settle for a letter of congratulations, but if, on the other hand, the award could be permanently displayed in a public place, perhaps at the recreation department, a resolution would be possible. (A resolution was the final decision.)

A related activity is the sending of Christmas and Hanukkah cards to favored constituents. These mailings may go just to close friends and supporters or to all constituents who have ever come into contact with the office. One congressional aide said that volunteers begin in July of each year to prepare their Christmas card mailing of 10,000.

General Correspondence Political staffs, of course, handle a great deal of general correspondence. Letters from constituents are answered promptly. If a great many are received on the same issue, a form response is prepared for the robo-typewriters. Inquiries usually result in copies of bills or committee reports along with letters. This is one reason such an incredible number of bills with absolutely no hope of passage are introduced each year—members can demonstrate their concern for the issue raised by the constituent by sending along a bill they have introduced, no matter what the issue. While district offices send and receive large volumes of such correspondence, much more is handled in Washington.

Telephone

Frustrated citizens are advised to write their congressman, and studies of legislative bodies never fail to mention the large and increasing volumes of incoming mail. The importance of Alexander Graham Bell's invention should not be overlooked. While Washington offices rely primarily on the mails, the field office communicates by phone. The recent growth of field office operations is changing the means of communication between constituents and Congress;

Table 3.4.4.
Medium of communication—Percentage of constituent-initiated communications by medium of communication (Los Angeles-based).

	Mail	Phone	Drop-in Visitors	*n* =
U. S. senators	80%	19%	1%	2
Representatives	52	39	9	18
State senators	41	49	10	13
Assemblymen	39	51	10	31
Supervisors	50	46	4	4
City councilmen	38	50	12	14

Note: Estimates by top aides. Covers communications received by entire office organization—field *and central*. One council office maintained actual records on this: 16 percent by mail; 65 percent by phone; and 20 percent drop-ins.

Table 3.4.5.
Constituent-initiated communications—Percentage of offices reporting half or more of communications.

	By Phone	Through Field Office
U.S. senators	0%	0%
Representatives	31	63
State senators	62	85
Assemblymen	69	79
Supervisors	50	25
City councilmen	80	29

Note: Number of cases (*n*) same as for Table 3.4.4.

more and more southern California citizens telephone the local number rather than write to the Washington address.

Although conventional wisdom holds that letters are *the* means of citizen-legislator communication, that is reasonably valid only for the two U.S. Senators among Los Angeles-based officials. Generally speaking, the Washington office takes in most of the mail while the field office gets some mail plus most of the calls and visits. For Los Angeles-based congressmen it is actually the field office that is the primary point of incoming contacts. Less than two decades ago, field offices were rare; now they are common. One result is that citizens are dropping by or telephoning more often than they write those letters so prominent in the literature.

Face-to-Face Communications

District offices receive a steady stream of drop-in visitors, while field aides spend much of their time (about 25 percent) out in the community meeting with constituents. This takes the form of attendance by staffers at countless local meetings and what aides refer to as "town halls." Town halls are previously announced open-house meetings where the incumbent and his staff meet with all comers at the district office, a school, or other convenient location. Use of this technique, incidentally, has increased dramatically since data for this study were gathered in 1974. Even President Carter did it.

More and more incumbents have "mobile field offices" in vans or campers that crisscross the district to take advantage of large public gatherings such as athletic events, street fairs, carnivals, etc. Colorado Senator Gary Hart keeps a large van crisscrossing his state.

While the vast majority of communications are handled by mail or phone, face-to-face contacts are important, especially from a political standpoint. Political aides are personable people; when they can talk to a constituent they usually secure a friend, and a voter, for their patron.

> I tell each of my staff that they are responsible for making five friends a day —friends for me, for the office. If they do that we don't have to worry very much about re-election.
>
> Southern California Congressman

News Media: The Press Aide's Bailiwick

Press aides usually have been working journalists or public relations specialists.

> First I was a newspaper reporter, then a TV newsman. Then I was editor of a magazine line. After that I worked in public relations for an aerospace corporation, and next I opened my own PR firm. This job is part of the same line.
>
> Supervisor's Deputy

They are responsible for preparing press releases, organizing news conferences, monitoring the local media, and, usually, overseeing the other communications/PR activities discussed here. They are often recruited from the ranks of local media people, and their friendships and contacts with their former colleagues constitute one of the office's more valuable resources. Part of the job is media liaison—keeping on good terms with the local newspapers and TV/radio stations. Whenever possible, the press aide seeks to maximize favorable media coverage and minimize unfavorable exposure—old friends help. One state legislator's administrative aide (known as an AA) told of using news tips to cultivate reporters. She kept a record of "scoops" handed out—to insure the largess was evenly distributed—and and she attempted to reward more favorable coverage with better tips.

Writing

A major staff activity in all offices is writing—speeches, press releases, newsletters, legislation, correspondence, and so on. Usually it is the press aide who doubles as a professional writer and whose products may include ghostwritten articles and books published under the incumbent's name.

3. CASEWORK

The core of constituent service is casework —the troubleshooting of constituent requests for assistance. Case variations are infinite. They include requests for jobs, government publications, expediting or overturning bureaucratic decisions, helping constituents to get out of the Army or to secure a better assignment, sightseeing tours around the Capitol, etc. The matters may seem trivial, except to aggrieved or hopeful citizens and their families.

In theory (and in the literature) casework means assistance in dealings with *government* agencies applicable to the incumbent's *level* of government. Practice does not follow theory in Los Angeles. Casework problems, as often as not, cross jurisdictional lines, while a large number of cases do not involve government at all.

Consider the following case handled by a Los Angeles congressional office. A shipyard worker had been severely crippled in an on-the-job accident. Because of technicalities in his former employment status, he had been three times ruled ineligible for disability compensation. A "catch-22" interpretation also made welfare unavailable. By the time the constituent sought help at his congressman's field office, the situation was desperate. He had been unable to work for several years, medical and other bills had piled up, the family budget was in shambles, home utilities were about to be cut off, the family car had been repossessed, and a bank was about to foreclose on the home mortgage.

Resolving this one case required several months and more than a hundred caseworker hours. Eventually the shipyard (federal agency) was persuaded to reclassify the former employee. That enabled the constituent to qualify (following more appeals by the caseworker) for disability compensation (state agency) as well as for welfare (county agency—more appeals). Meanwhile, the caseworker and the AA used their patron's good offices to persuade the constituent's banker (private), automobile credit agency (private), hospital (county), and utility company (city) to accept delayed debt-repayment schedules. Finally, the caseworker went to the constituent's home to give advice and instruction on home economics and family budgeting.

While this case is unusual in its complexity, cases similar to this are taken on every day in Los Angeles. Note that this case involved several different agencies at three levels of government as well as the private sector and the family unit itself. The constituent received no more than his legal due—but would in all likelihood have received nothing without the intervention of this congressman's staff.

> He was merely a statistic in some bureaucrat's in-basket without our help. Once we started making inquiries he became a "problem" for the agencies. By the time we were through he had become an individual person—instead of a statistic or problem.
>
> Congressional Aide

Although cases come in all varieties, most offices—at all levels—report that miscellaneous welfare and income maintenance cases are the largest category. These include county welfare, social security, unemployment, disability, Medicare and medical, and old-age security. While the most frequent case types handled by any given office usually fall within their own government jurisdiction, the host of other miscellaneous cases they also handle may well constitute the bulk of their work load and may often take them across jurisdictional boundaries. Furthermore, many cases, like the one with the shipyard worker, involve multiple problems, agencies, and government levels. Political offices tend to categorize such cases according to their own levels of government. Thus, that particular case was regarded as a shipyard (federal) case by the congressional office involved; a state legislator's aide, had he handled it, would probably have considered it a workers' disability (state) problem.

Different offices define casework differently. In some offices it is a "case" only if correspondence and/or fieldwork are involved; problems handled by a phone call or two aren't counted. But other offices handle everything by phone. Sometimes, especially in congressional offices, a distinction is made between "projects" and casework. Projects (or "major casework") involve institutional clients, such as labor unions, corporations, school districts, or city governments seeking assistance, usually with government contracts or grants. But many offices recognize no such distinctions; they count almost all constituent contacts as casework, whether the constituent is Widow Jones asking for the dogcatcher's phone number or the University of California seeking a multimillion-dollar grant.

Attempts to tally the volume of casework have foundered on thesc definitional problems and on the fact that most studies have excluded field offices—and hence the major portion of the casework load. Data on volume for this study are derived from staff estimates—aides were asked to count only those cases that resulted in an entry in their files (thus excluding requests for phone numbers, routine advice, and information).

As Table 3.4.6 reveals, a great many Los Angeles citizens receive "service," and the bulk of the casework load is handled by the field staff rather than Washington employees. Some offices handle casework at the point of contact—and keep caseworkers busy in both Washington and field offices. More typical in Los Angeles is the practice of concentrating most of the work load in the field office—cases received in Washington are passed on to the district.

Some well-managed field offices are organized and deployed to dispense constituent favors on an assembly-line bases. Some-

Table 3.4.6.
Casework volume (per office).

	Average Annual Volume	Average Percent Handled by Field Office	Lowest Volume Reported	Highest Volume Reported	*n* =
U.S. senators	29,520	73%	14,400	42,640	2
Representatives	4,752	70	650	10,500	17
State senators	1,775	78	120	4,500	13
Assemblymen	1,623	89	180	7,800	29
Supervisors	4,800	n.a.	3,600	5,200	3
City councilmen	6,025	36	2,000	12,000	13

Note: Includes "projects" as well as casework. Based primarily on aides' estimates, but in a few offices actual counts rather than estimates were available. All U. S. Senate data above are from 1973 records. One representative *counted* 1,040 cases in 1969 (volume much higher now). One assembly aide estimated 20,000 annually (this was discounted as too high); two assembly offices had *counted* 800 and 6,000 cases, respectively. A supervisor's office *counted* 3,600 cases (1972), and three council offices had counts of 2,800, 4,000, and 5,000.

body handles correspondence on the matter, others specialize in certain types of cases—military personnel problems, social security, veterans' benefits, and immigration are the big four at the federal level. When a particularly touching case is favorably resolved, it is turned over to the press aide for media exposure (which stimulates still more requests).

Saloma's data on House offices show that the staff is the principal instrument for casework,[6] while this study reveals (see Table 3.4.6) that it is the field staff that handles three-fourths of the work load. And they handle a great deal. The offices of the 85 Los Angeles federal, state, and local legislators, taken together, were working some 340,641 cases in 1974, and the volume has been rising. Since most cases involve a family unit and some involve groups of constituents, a significant portion of the southern California citizenry receive annual "service" from their representatives.

What all this casework activity means for public policy—who gets what—is a matter that needs investigation. Essentially two things can happen when a political office goes to bat for a constituent: The issue can be resolved in the constituent's favor (about 80 percent); or the constituent can "lose" anyway. If the constituent does "win," several explanations are possible:

- The constituent gets exactly what he or she would have gotten anyway. The representative's intervention has no real effect, except to bring credit upon the incumbent.
- The constituent gets what he or she would have eventually gotten without the intercession of the representative, but gets it sooner. Thus the incumbent gets credit, while citizens who are competing for the agency's attention (without political benefactors) are elbowed to the rear of the line or bottom of the in-basket.
- The constituent gets what he or she deserves, but would not have gotten at all (because of red-tape snarls) without the intercession of the political representative. (This is how casework is supposed to function.)
- The constituent gets something he or she would not normally qualify for, but the representative's clout tips the scales in the constituent's favor. (The system is subverted.)

Judging from information gleaned during this study, plus conversations with bureaucrats who handle "congressionals" for Social Security and for the Veterans Administration, as well as my own experience in handling congressional inquiries for the Air Force Office of Legislative Liaison, it would seem that the second option is most frequent.[7] Since public resources—time, money, food stamps, government contracts, etc.—are always limited, the growing volume of political casework efforts may have important ramifications. Citizens who take advantage of these "services" get more of what there is to get, and get it sooner, than citizens who do not. Thus these extensive service operations by political staffs increase political representation for some constituents at the expense of others.

4. POLITICAL ORGANIZING

Political offices are just that—political; staffers are, for the most part, political animals. Scratch an incumbent's top aide, especially his top field aide, and you'll often find his campaign manager.

Campaign management is only one political activity at the field office. Another is the continuous care and upkeep of political supporter lists. Names are added daily, 10 or 20 or more per week, and the lists are kept for campaign purposes—to mobilize volunteers, solicit funds, turn out voters.[8]

> Your list is one of your main assets. Politics is people—without a list you can't even get started. You don't just appear on a street corner and start campaigning, you know.
>
> Assemblyman's Aide (former party professional, candidate for Congress)

Besides management and the building of lists—both of which go on year in and year out—there is also staff participation in the actual campaign effort. This is a sensitive subject because so many challengers try to make a campaign issue of it. Some aides were more frank than others in discussing this subject, but most denied any staff campaign work whatsoever on government time.* Denials to the contrary, campaign activities were actually observed in 54 percent of the offices visited during this study. While all types of activity were in evidence at one office or another, the most common (and the hardest to conceal from an interviewer) were interrupting phone calls concerning fund raisers, campaign strategy, rallies, volunteers, and endorsements.

Political fund raising was not a subject many aides were willing to discuss. That some government-paid staffers work as fund raisers is certain—two aides were especially frank.

> You might say that I'm a professional fund raiser—that's where my expertise lies, that's why I'm here. I've been running charity drives in [the Los Angeles area] for over 20 years. I do all of [the incumbent's] fund raising.
>
> Congressman's Field Representative

> My biggest job is fund raising. And I'm damn good at it. I've raised almost $200,000 this year for our office. And that doesn't count money I've raised for other candidates—here in California, in Michigan, in New Mexico, Arizona, all over. We're not going to be an assemblyman forever.
>
> Aide

One final point about political activity should be stressed. Political staffs are politically active, but not only and not necessarily in their patrons' behalfs. Many aides run for office themselves, and many participate in campaigns other than those of their employer, including issue campaigns (ballot propositions, stop oil drilling, outlaw abortion, etc.).

> You can bet your ass I'm working on the campaign—about 15 hours a day worth. But I'm not working for [aide's employer], he's a shoo-in; we don't need to campaign. I'm working for Jerry Brown.
>
> Assembly Aide

Many of the observed incidents of outright campaigning took place in offices where the incumbent was not running in 1974 and/or involved candidates other than the boss.

5. SURVEILLANCE

The surveillance function is often overlooked. The national media, for example, made a great to-do of congressmen using the 1981 July 4 recess to personally "take the pulse" of their constituents on the economy issue. But pulse taking is continuous and institutionalized; the field staff is always performing this function. The field staff are political antennae—monitoring local newspapers and broadcast media, listening to talk shows, conversing with newsmen, citizens, community leaders, and activists, attending countless meetings and functions, cross-checking findings with other aides, and relaying all this information to the incumbent. When elected officials return to their districts (as in the 1981 recess) their time is carefully programmed by field aides who squire them about, partly to hear opinions, but primarily to maximize media exposure—hence those stories about "pulse taking."

Some offices systematize their surveillance efforts. Staff members are actually assigned to read certain newspapers and journals, monitor designated news broadcasts, and keep track of what goes on in specific organizations, businesses, and institutions. Efforts are also made to cultivate contacts throughout the district.

> I've developed a network of neighborhood contacts—friends of the office. They keep me posted. So I always know who is supporting whom, and who is doing what to whom, politically. I also hear who has lost their job, gone to the hospital, been arrested, opened a business, had a baby, or whatever.
>
> Assembly Aide

*After-hours campaigning is perfectly legal. Political aides—at all levels of government—are specifically exempted from Hatch Act provisions.

Table 3.4.7.
Staff political activities (percentage of occurrences by office type).

	Top Aide Active in Patron's Campaign	Political Lists Maintained by Staff	Staff Member Had Run for Office*	Staff Campaigning Observed
U.S. senator	100%	100%	50%	100%
Representative	90	100	61	53
State senator	86	100	43	50
Assemblyman	94	100	42	68
Supervisor	100	100	90	20
City councilmen	100	100	33	33
All offices	93%	100%	47%	54%
Number of Offices	79	78	40	46

*Percentage of offices where a member or former member of the staff had ever run for public office. Five aides interviewed were candidates in 1974.

6. ALTER EGO

In many respects, top aides are assistant incumbents, not merely assistants *to* the incumbent. They share their patron's office. In his absence, they speak for him, deal with lobbyists and other legislators, make decisions—the line between top aide and employer can be a hazy one.

Four out of five top aides interviewed for this study used a collective "we" when discussing the incumbent: "We decided to duck that whole issue"; "We hope to be a senator, someday"; "We got our committee chairmanship because we backed the right guy for speaker." In a very few cases the operative pronoun was "I": "I decided against [his] running for the Senate this year."

7. GROUP LIAISON

Some offices assign staffers to join certain community organizations. Others seek to develop a contact—a friend of the office—who is already a group member. The number of group contacts a new employee can bring into the office is sometimes a criterion for hiring new staffers. Group leaders are cultivated with care by aggressive offices. This is one place the letters and resolutions of congratulations come in.

> We have a part-time college student—the guy who stepped in a minute ago. He's been politically active since he was about 12, and he runs errands and does legwork for us. He's just compiled dossiers on all the community and organization leaders in our new district. We're using them to cultivate those people and groups.
>
> Congressman's Field Representative

What groups? The list is endless and depends on the district and the incumbent. Frequently mentioned in Los Angeles:

Chamber of Commerce
Service clubs
Senior citizens groups
Student groups
Political party clubs
League of Women Voters
School teachers
Public employees
Labor unions
City governments

8. REPRESENTING THE INCUMBENT

Incumbents are deluged with invitations to be at ceremonies, give speeches, and attend luncheons and dinners. More invitations are received than the incumbent himself can possibly fulfill. When possible, the congressman attends, but more often he sends one of his assistants. As a group, district political aides must attend more retirement ceremonies, award presentations, ribbon cuttings, luncheons, meetings, etc., than any other group alive. And they actually deliver more formal speeches than their patrons do—before district audiences.* Representing the incumbent takes a great deal of field staff time—including evenings and weekends. This function, more than any other, made interview appointments for this research difficult.

9. SCHEDULING AND ADVANCING

While staffers attend many meetings and functions, the incumbent is busy, too, especially on his visits back to the district. Seeing to the incumbent's public appearances is essentially the same function described by Bruno and Greenfield in their book, *The Advance Man* (Bantam, 1971).

Scheduling is a major task. It is also a professional one involving decisions—how many appearances, where and where not. The object is to maximize the incumbent's time and exposure.

> When there is a choice—and there usually is—I always schedule him to meet with groups that don't agree with him—businessmen, conservatives, you know. They need to listen to what he's got to say, and he ought to hear them, too. His supporters all agree with him, and they'll vote for him anyway. It's the others that count. He gets pretty tired of it [unfriendly audiences], but he goes where I tell him.
>
> Congressman's Aide

The scheduler (usually the top aide, assisted by the incumbent's private secretary) decides which invitations are answered with regrets, with an aide representative, or by the incumbent. In most offices, scheduling goes beyond deciding where to go—it becomes advancing.

> Let me tell you something about advancing. I try to have ______ make two or three functions per evening when he's in town. That means he'll pop in and out—arriving late and leaving early. The trick is to get the group to appreciate his being there without being "pissed off" because he ducks out before the chicken is served. The MC has to handle this just right, and one of my biggest jobs is seeing to it that he does.
>
> Congressman's Field Representative

Staffers sometimes arrange their employer's public appearance with meticulous detail. The schedule becomes an operations plan that may include recommendations for attire (incumbent and wife), transportation arrangements, information on podium lighting, a pocket diagram of seating arrangements with names, recommendations on whom to talk to and whom to avoid, what to say and not say, entrance and exit plans, and so on.

10. COMMUNITY ORGANIZER/DIRECT ACTION

In some respects political field offices are like agencies. They go beyond the legislative function and do things directly. Often they are the organizational catalyst behind local movements ("save the pier," "stop oil drilling," "stop the freeway").

When such issues develop, local activists will take their case to the nearest political field office. The object, of course, is to get the incumbent's endorsement for "their side." But another goal is to enlist the office's resources—staff, expertise, mailing lists, contacts, prestige, duplicating machines, telephones—into the battle.

The direct delivery of services by congressional district offices is not unusual. Congressman Goldwater's operation of a mass transit system was mentioned earlier, as were the housing project and the grocery store on wheels operated by Pat Schroeder's

*One state senator does not make speeches at all. His speaking engagements (even when he is in attendance himself) are all handled by aides.

office. Congressman Hawkins' top field aide is president of the South Central Improvement Action Council and also director of Ujima Village. The former has secured $10 million in SBA loans for minority businessmen and has a $275,000-a-year operating budget; the latter is a subsidized, 300-unit, low-income housing project and shopping center. Another office was using volunteer law professors to operate a public service law office.

11. OVERSIGHT[9]

While oversight is a traditional legislative role, it does not concern many field staffers. Washington aides are much more likely to be involved in this.

Nevertheless, because casework inquiries serve to keep agencies and bureaucrats on their toes, oversight is a by-product, albeit a generally unintended one, of the massive constituent service load carried by Los Angeles field offices. Occasionally a local issue campaign will also involve field staffers in oversight.

12. LEGISLATIVE SUPPORT

Field staffs, for the most part, play a minor role in legislation; it's not within their task environment. District offices relay ideas from constituents and local groups, act as "thermometers"—gauging the temperature of the district in regard to major vote decisions—and are sometimes the focus of lobbying efforts. Thus the field staff normally enters the lawmaking process only as a communications relay.

Legislative committee hearings held back in the home state or district are becoming commonplace. The responsibility for arranging such hearings often falls on personal field staff. Indeed, for some Los Angeles aides this is their principal function. Whether or not this is a legislative support function is another matter. In most cases the goal is local media exposure—promotion of the incumbent or of an idea. During interviews, several congressional aides cited these hearings as examples of how they carried out their PR responsibilities. Not one mentioned them as part of the legislative process.

13. PERSONAL ERRANDS

Personal assistants are often "coat holders"; they are frequently called upon to perform private and personal chores for their employers. Tasks such as looking after the incumbent's house or aging mother while he is away in Washington, delivering clothes to the cleaner, and driving the incumbent or a member of his family to or from the airport are not uncommon. While many observers criticize such use of government-paid staff, staffers see this as a legitimate function.

> We think of his time as a valuable commodity, something to be protected. He only gets to spend a few days here a month, and they should be spent seeing people and doing useful things—not running little errands or waiting for taxis.
>
> Congressman's Aide

Many aides pointed out that their performance of personal favors stemmed more from their private relationship with their boss than their employee–employer relationship.

> We're like a family. When he's here for a visit, I pick him up at the airport, he uses my car and stays at my house. When I go to Washington, he meets me and I stay at his house.
>
> Congressman's Field Representative

SUMMARY: PUBLIC SERVICE AND PROMOTION

Thirteen distinct functions were discussed. These include some functions traditionally associated with Congress—citizen education and communication, legislative support, casework information gathering, representation, oversight. Also included were functions not usually acknowledged as things the Congress does: surveillance, group liaison, community organizing, direct action, nongovernment projects.

Fundamental to office functions is the combination of public service and political promotion. Good deeds are done, but each one has the incumbent's label firmly attached. Several offices in Los Angeles, for example, have mass mailed telephone adhesives to their constituents. These stickers are to be placed on the citizen's phone where they conveniently display emergency fire and police numbers (a public service) along with the incumbent's name and local phone number (promotion). Similarly, there are field offices that regularly hold showings for local artists. Every month or so a different artist is invited to show his work at the field office; the artist's friends are invited to an opening reception, as are friends of the office and the general public. Result: The arts and aspiring artists are encouraged (public service); the artist and his friends are grateful (promotion); the incumbent increases his visibility and public contact (promotion); and office decor is enhanced.

THE ELECTORAL CONNECTION

A simple yet profound approach to understanding Congress is set forth by David Mayhew. In Mayhew's scheme, electioneering and legislative behavior emerge as one and the same. He offers "a vision of United States congressmen as single-minded seekers of reelection."[10] Although conceding the simplicity of this unidimensional viewpoint, he goes on to argue rather convincingly that virtually all aspects of legislative behavior can be usefully explained or predicted from that one premise.

Mayhew also notes that personal organizations, rather than political parties, are the key to the re-election goal and that incumbency is the foundation of the personal followings. He finds that all congressmen feel politically insecure, all of the time, even those who in reality are quite safe. He goes on to show that campaigning is endless, and that besides keeping supporters in line and insuring that necessary contributions and other vote-getting resources will accrue to him, an incumbent seeks to minimize the probability he will face a serious, well-financed challenger.

Once the "electoral connection" is perceived, according to Mayhew, it is also easy to see why the chief activities of "lawmakers" consist of "advertising," "credit claiming," and "position taking." Mayhew's work is especially relevant to this study. While Mayhew barely mentions staff, much if not most of the activity he attributes to congressmen (casework, newsletters, public relations, etc.) are actually staff functions. Furthermore, the single-minded devotion to reelection Mayhew attributes to incumbents extends to their aides as well. The Mayhew approach, in short, can be used to explain why staffs, especially field staffs, do what they do.

DOES CONSTITUENT SERVICE PAY OFF?

The late Vice President Alben Barkley's favorite story was about Farmer Jones. Over a period of 33 years Barkley had done favors for Mr. Jones—visited him at an Army hospital in France, interceded with General Pershing to get him shipped home early, got the VA to speed up his disability compensation, assisted in getting federal loans to start his farm and later to rebuild it after a flood. On top of all this, he got Mrs. Jones an appointment as postmistress. Then, in 1938, Barkley was flabbergasted to learn Mr. Jones was supporting his opponent in a close primary battle. "Surely," Barkley said, "you remember all these things I have done for you?" "Yeah," said Farmer Jones sullenly, "but what in hell have you done for me lately?"

The moral of the story is clear, and politicians are fond of repeating it. Nevertheless, there is ample evidence to show they don't accept its message. Incumbents seem to believe the key to re-election lies in what they do for their constituents.[11]

> The best way to get reelected is to spend a great majority of your time on casework.
>
> Representative Ken Hechler[12]

> You take care of your constituents and they'll take care of you.
>
> President Gerald Ford

> The goodwill from casework comes back in a thousand ways—in the voting booth, volunteer workers, good publicity, useful contacts, even campaign contributions.
>
> Congressman's Aide

Ninety-eight percent of the Los Angeles aides agreed that casework is an important electoral asset; one out of five believe it is *the* most effective electioneering technique of all. Satisfied constituents, it is hoped, will not only vote for their benefactor themselves, but will also influence their families and friends to do the same. A number of the Los Angeles aides mentioned a rule-of-thumb figure of six to eight votes influenced by every well-handled case. Morris Fiorina argues that constituency service is the key to re-election. Furthermore, he implies that Congress creates, or at least acquiesces to, red tape because of the credit incumbents can reap from cutting through it for their constituents.[13]

Over 90 percent reported that they had received campaign contributions or volunteer help from persons who had been "serviced." In some offices this source of contributions or workers was substantial. One aide told how a single afternoon he'd spent on a case years ago—steering a business license application through the bureaucratic maze—continued to pay off. The grateful businessman had afterwards volunteered to help raise funds and to have his employees design, prepare, and install all the signs and posters for the upcoming campaign—services he has continued to supply for every subsequent election, for the city council, later the state senate and, recently, the U.S. Congress.

While most aides spoke of generating goodwill and influencing votes through casework, there was a different and perhaps more insightful view expressed by some. These aides saw the re-election problem primarily as a matter of avoiding strong challengers rather than of securing votes.

CONCLUSION

A congressman is a "big man" among the people who elected him, and his district office can become a real force in the community—directly involving itself in anything that concerns the constituency. Besides significantly altering the distribution of public goods through their casework efforts, field staffs were found to be organizing charity drives, managing nonprofit corporations, campaigning for or against ballot propositions and local candidates, running public service law firms, changing the routes of planned freeways, mounting state- and even nationwide propaganda campaigns in behalf of some cherished idea, lobbying other levels of government, creating and running mass transit systems, producing regular radio programs and ghostwriting syndicated newspaper columns, establishing bird sanctuaries and parks, and so on. Many of the constituent service cases, as well as a number of the direct-action efforts, exceed the jurisdictional boundaries of the applicable government. Congressional offices lead campaign efforts for or against state ballot propositions, state legislative offices lobby local city councils, and all offices seem to be in continuous contact with the county welfare department. Such nongovernment matters as attracting industry to the community, finding jobs for teenagers, organizing senior citizen activities, planning civic celebrations, sponsoring art shows, and promoting home vegetable gardens are commonplace in all types of "legislative" district offices. In short, much of Congress' impact on "who gets what" takes place far from Washington and bears little resemblance to what we read in the papers and are taught in civics courses.

Reading 3.5

Legislative Support Agencies

In addition to staff in personal offices, district offices, and committees, congressional bureaucracy extends to major congressional support agencies: CRS, GAO, OTA, and CBO. The following excerpt from a congressional manual, intended for staff, specifies the roles of each of these support agencies and the kinds of services they offer.

LIBRARY OF CONGRESS

The Library of Congress is an aggregate of many libraries. Its Law Library, for instance, is among the finest in the United States. Much of its usefulness stems from the fact that new legislation grows from records of the past. This was recognized early in the library's history when, in 1832, Congress established the law collection. Other notable collections include those of Japanese, Chinese, and Russian materials, the largest outside the Orient and the Soviet Union, respectively.

Daniel J. Boorstin, a distinguished American historian, educator and prize-winning author, presides over this unique combination of facilities and services as The Librarian of Congress. Nominated by President Ford and confirmed by the Senate on September 26, 1975, Dr. Boorstin is the 12th Librarian of Congress in the institution's history.

The Congressional Research Service

The Congressional Research Service, a separate department within the Library, serves as one of the research arms of the Congress. The Service was first established in 1914 for the periods during which Congress was in session. As the complexities and the burden of the problems before Congress increased, its staff and functions were enlarged accordingly, comprising today a staff of more than 800 persons, including selected experts in such fields as law, economics, political science, international relations, natural sciences, and history. Senior specialists on the staff are frequently called upon to serve as consultants to Congressional committees. The Director of the Service, Gilbert Gude, is a former Maryland Congressman whose 10 years of congressional service place him in a unique position to anticipate and serve the needs of Congress.

Formerly called the Legislative Reference Service, the Congressional Research Service received its new name and greatly expanded responsibilities under legislation passed by Congress in 1970. The Service, at the beginning of each Congress, prepares and presents to each Congressional committee a list of subjects and policy areas related to its concerns and also a list of programs and activities scheduled to expire during that Congress. Upon request the Service prepares legislative histories on measures to be considered in hearings; supplies committees with experts to prepare objective, nonpartisan analyses of legislative proposals that include evaluations of whether enactment of these or alternative proposals is advisable and the probable results of each; and gathers, analyzes and makes available to Members and committees other information needed

Source: *The Capitol: A Pictorial History of the Capitol and of the Congress*, 8th ed. Washington, D.C.; U.S. Government Printing Office, 1981, pp. 172–85.

in the performance of their duties. Also prepared regularly is a comprehensive digest of bills and resolutions of a public general nature introduced in either House.

CONGRESSIONAL BUDGET OFFICE

In a major effort to reassert its constitutional authority over the Federal budget, the Congress, in 1974, enacted a comprehensive budget reform measure, the Congressional Budget and Impoundment Control Act of 1974. The Budget Act established a process whereby each year the Congress determines the appropriate level of federal revenues, spending and debt, and the size of the deficit or surplus, through the passage of two concurrent resolutions on the budget.

Each spring the Congress formulates and adopts a concurrent resolution setting budget targets for the fiscal year to begin on the coming October 1st. In September the Congress reviews the detailed spending and revenue decisions it has made since the first resolution in the form of individual bills. It then debates and adopts a second concurrent resolution, confirming or changing the totals in the spring resolution. While the first resolution sets targets, the second establishes an actual ceiling on spending and a floor for revenues. If changing circumstances require subsequent adjustments, the Congress can enact additional concurrent resolutions.

To implement this process the Budget Act created three new Congressional institutions: a Committee on the Budget in both the House and the Senate and the Congressional Budget Office (CBO). CBO is a nonpartisan organization mandated to provide the Congress with budget-related information and with analyses of alternative fiscal and programmatic policies. The office does not make recommendations on matters of policy. Its principal tasks are to present the Congress with options for consideration and to study the possible budgetary ramifications of those options.

The organization is headed by a director who is appointed to a four-year term by the Speaker of the House and the President Pro Tempore of the Senate, after considering the recommendations of the Budget Committees.

The Budget Act requires CBO to provide cost estimates on proposed legislation. CBO prepares, to the extent practicable, a five-year estimate of what it would cost the Federal Government to carry out any public bill or resolution reported by a Congressional committee. These estimates include projections of new or increased tax expenditures and new budget authority when applicable. CBO compares its cost estimates with any estimates available from Congressional committees or Federal agencies.

As soon as practicable after the beginning of each fiscal year, CBO prepares a report that projects Federal revenues and spending for the next five years, if current laws and policies were to continue unchanged. The purpose of these projections is to provide a neutral baseline against which the Congress can consider potential changes as it examines the budget for the upcoming fiscal years.

CBO keeps track, or score, of Congressional action on individual appropriation and revenue bills against the targets or ceilings in the concurrent resolutions. The office issues periodic reports showing the status of Congressional action.

Since the Federal budget both affects and is affected by the national economy, the Congress must consider the budget in the context of the current and projected state of the economy. To provide a framework for such considerations, CBO prepares periodic analyses and forecasts of economic trends. The office also prepares analyses of alternative fiscal policies.

CBO undertakes analyses of programmatic or policy issues that affect the Federal budget. These reports include an examination of alternative approaches to current policy. All reports are nonpartisan in nature.

Major studies have been completed in such diverse areas as agriculture, energy, housing, hospital and medical costs, defense, state and local government, employment programs, transportation, education, budget procedures, international economic policy, taxation, child nutrition and ways to cut government spending.

CBO prepares estimates of the inflationary effect of major legislative proposals. More generally, the office is charged with identifying and analyzing the causes of inflation.

By April 1 of each year, CBO furnishes a report to the House and Senate Committees on the Budget that combines many aspects of the functions outlined above.

CBO prepares its studies and cost estimates at the request of the chairman or ranking minority member of a full committee of jurisdiction or the chairman of a subcommittee of jurisdiction. The Budget Act establishes the following priority for these services: first, the Senate and House Budget Committees; second, the Senate and House Appropriations Committees, the Senate Finance Committee, and the House Ways and Means Committee; finally, all other Congressional committees.

CBO's published reports are distributed to all Members of Congress.

GENERAL ACCOUNTING OFFICE

Finding ways to run the Federal Government—a $900 billion enterprise—more efficiently, effectively and economically is the task of the U.S. General Accounting Office.

The General Accounting Office came into existence as an independent, nonpolitical arm of the Congress in 1921 when the Budget and Accounting Act was enacted.

GAO's basic purposes are:

- To assist the Congress, its committees, and its Members as much as possible in carrying out their legislative and oversight responsibilities, consistent with the agency's role as an independent, nonpolitical agency.
- To audit and evaluate the programs, activities and financial operations of Federal departments and agencies and make recommendations toward more efficient and effective operations.
- To carry out financial control and other functions with respect to Federal government programs and operations including accounting, legal and claims settlement work.

GAO's primary internal objective is to perform all of its functions as effectively, efficiently, economically and promptly as possible.

Government has become much more complex since the Congress established GAO 60 years ago. The needs of the Congress for help have grown and will continue to grow.

This agency's greatest contribution is to provide answers to questions such as:

- Where are there opportunities to eliminate fraud, waste and abuse in government?
- Are Federal programs, whether administered directly by the Federal Government or through other organizations, such as the United Nations, or through state and local governments, achieving their objectives?
- Are there other ways of accomplishing the objectives of these programs at lower costs?
- Are funds being spent legally and is the accounting for them adequate?

Using such information, Members of Congress are in a better position to make decisions concerning Government programs—whether the issue is continuing an innovative education program, acquiring a major weapons system for the Defense Department or providing development assistance for a foreign country.

Concerns are being voiced in the Congress and elsewhere about the apparent decrease of confidence in the Government, particularly in the Government's ability to make programs effective and to serve well those individuals and groups for whom public funds are spent. Greater attention is also being focused on the accountability of Government officials to taxpayers. Thus it is more important than ever that the public be aware of the work of GAO as an organization with principal concern for fiscal integrity and the economical and effective management of Government programs.

Another concern frequently expressed in the Congress is that the executive branch has increased its power in relationship to the legislative branch for the simple reason that the executive branch has most of the experts and information on such complex subjects as major weapons systems, energy, space exploration, health care, and pollution control.

Many of these experts and much of the information from the executive branch are made available to the Congress through hearings and reports, or by less formal means. However, inevitable questions remain.

- Were the proper alternatives to proposed programs fully considered and set forth objectively to the Congress?
- Does the executive branch keep the Congress adequately advised on progress and on problems which develop as programs are carried out?
- Does the information provided facilitate, rather than frustrate, legislative oversight?

Accordingly, one of GAO's objectives is to strengthen the processes through which the Congress can obtain reliable information.

Public Responsibility

In a broad context, the agency is responsible to the public. GAO reports to the Congress, if not classified for national security reasons, are public reports. Although GAO has no official ombudsman responsibility, it tries at all times to be sensitive to responsible criticisms of Federal programs and to take these criticisms into account in planning its work.

GAO does not seek publicity for its reports. But it is important that the public have full access to its findings and conclusions.

The agency recognizes that certain information must be classified in the interest of national security. The legal authority to classify information rests with the operating agencies. GAO has as one of its objectives, however, the questioning of security classifications which seem unnecessary for the purposes of security legislation and regulations.

The organization's role will continue to change as the needs of the Congress respond to the increasing size and complexity of our Nation and its Government.

GAO performs much of its work with the objective of improving Government operations. As a result of its recommendations, Federal agencies take many actions to make their programs and services more economical and effective.

It is not possible to determine the full effect of GAO activities in terms of financial savings, improvements in Government operations, and increased effectiveness of Government programs and activities. However, GAO attempts to record actions attributable to its work which result in dollar savings or other benefits to the Federal Government, contractors, grantees and the general public. These actions may be taken directly by the agency, as in the case of claims collections. Usually, however, they are taken by the Congress, Federal agencies and others, in response to suggestions and recommendations.

For fiscal year 1980, GAO identified estimated savings of $3.7 billion attributable to its work. At the same time, it should be remembered that many accomplishments cannot always be stated in precise dollar terms. Savings resulting from management improvements often cannot be measured accurately, nor can improvements which make programs work better but not cheaper. Such improvements are often more important than simple financial savings.

Early in its history, most GAO employees were accountants or auditors who spent long hours poring over vouchers and other financial records of Government agencies.

However, in the 1950s, the organization extended the scope of its reviews to include:

- checking for compliance with applicable laws and regulations,
- examining the efficiency and economy of operations, and
- reviewing the results of operations of evaluating whether desired results, including legislatively prescribed objectives, have been effectively achieved.

In the past years, GAO's professional staff—numbering 4,200—has been expanded to include engineers, mathematicians, statisticians, computer specialists, economists, business and public administrators, and even a medical doctor.

During fiscal year 1980, the agency issued 935 audit reports and special studies, addressed to the Congress, its committees or Members, or to heads of departments and agencies.

GAO provides information to the Congress by testifying before Congressional committees; holding informal briefings on agency problems for committees, Members and staffs; assigning staff members to work on Congressional committees; and providing legal opinions and comments on pending legislation.

In addition, the Office undertakes reviews of major Government programs on its own initiative. Although GAO is authorized to investigate all matters relating to the receipt, disbursement, and application of public funds (with some exceptions), the policy is to review programs, activities, or functions of direct interest to the Congress and the public.

Other GAO Responsibilities

GAO prescribes principles and standards for accounting in executive branch agencies, and cooperates with the agencies in developing and improving their accounting and financial management systems.

The office settles legal questions concerning the legality of planned expenditures of Federal funds.

Questions over the award of Government contracts may prompt requests for a Comptroller General ruling on the bid protest. GAO decisions on questions about the award of Government contracts are binding on the executive branch, but may be overturned by the Congress or the courts.

The agency also settles claims for or against the Government. Claims which involve no doubtful questions of law are paid or collected by the agency involved, subject to GAO audit.

Some Further Facts about GAO

The Comptroller General of the United States is the head of GAO. The Comptroller General is appointed by the President, with the advice and consent of the Senate, to a 15-year term—the longest set term in the Federal Government. He cannot be removed except for cause. These provisions guarantee his independence from political influence.

The Comptroller General heads an operation that includes the headquarters office and 83 audit sites, 15 regional offices in the continental United States and branch offices in Bangkok, Frankfurt, Honolulu, and Panama City.

OFFICE OF TECHNOLOGY ASSESSMENT

The Office of Technology Assessment (OTA) is a nonpartisan analytical support agency created in 1972 to serve the Congress. OTA's job is to analyze complex issues involving science and technology for both the Senate and House committees. It clarifies the range of policy options on a given issue and the potential physical, biological, economic, social and political impacts of adopting each of these options. OTA does not advocate particular policies or actions.

A 12-member bipartisan Congressional Board—six Senators and six Representatives—governs OTA. These posts alternate between the Senate and House with each Congress.

The Board appoints the OTA Director, who is chief executive officer and a nonvoting Board member. The Congressional Board is assisted by an Advisory Council comprised of 10 citizens from the private sector and, ex officio, the Comptroller General of the United States and the Director of the Congressional Research Service of the Library of Congress.

OTA has three assessment divisions, each headed by an Assistant Director: Energy, Materials and International Security; Health and Life Sciences; and Science, Information and Natural Resources. Within these divisions are nine general program areas: energy, international security and commerce, materials, food and renewable resources, health, human resources, communication and information technologies, oceans and environment, and space technology.

OTA has a relatively small in-house staff of 80 to 90 professionals whose skills span the range of physical, life and social sciences; engineering; law; and medicine. Throughout each project OTA uses advisory panels of experts and representatives of major parties-at-interest as a way of ensuring that reports are nonduplicative, objective, fair and authoritative. OTA draws extensively on the broad spectrum of resources throughout the private sector.

Last year the agency completed studies on a number of issues, including: impact of advanced group rapid transit technology; alternative energy futures, part 1—the future of liquefied natural gas imports; impact of advanced air transport technology, part 1—advanced high-speed aircraft; recent developments in ocean thermal energy; taggants in explosives; forecasts of physician supply and requirements; ocean margin drilling; oil shale technologies; a critique on conservation and solar energy programs of the Department of Energy; technology and steel industry competitiveness; energy from biological processes; the implications of cost-effectiveness analysis of medical technology; and world petroleum availability, 1980–2000.

Reading 3.6

Senators' Staffs: A Reflective View

Jon H. Oberg

In this essay, the author describes senators' staffs: their jobs, their power, and their shortcomings. It is the view of a former chief state planning and fiscal officer who spent five years in the Senate as a senator's legislative director and administrative assistant.

United States Senate staff positions are coveted. Ph.D.s will volunteer to do clerical work to get a foothold in a senator's or a committee's office. Many political campaign workers in Senate races are motivated by the potential Senate staff job that lies ahead. Temporary interns and even Congressional Fellows, already secure in other professions, will scout offices daily for future openings. To be a Senate staffer is to be close to the heart of one of the world's most powerful institutions. The work is hard, the pay—psychic as well as monetary—is good, the challenges supreme.

Source: Specifically written for this volume.

Who gets these jobs? What are the different types of jobs? What does a person actually do once he or she has one? What marks the person who becomes, for better or for worse (staff can become *too* powerful), a Senate mover and shaper?

A walk down the corridors of the Russell, Dirksen, or Hart Senate Office Buildings (where senators' personal offices and committee staffs are located) will reveal youth: bustling, serious, energetic youth. That well-dressed young lady bursting from a committee hearing is just as likely to be a lawyer and staff director of a Senate subcommittee as she is a clerk typist. Or she could be a senator's legislative assistant, newly credentialed by a prestigious university, or hired simply as a favor to a campaign supporter.

Therein lies a problem: uneven job preparation, and a lack of experience in even the most talented. Since senators seldom fully read the legislation they enact, or get personally involved in casework for their constituents, the work of the Senate is often the work of the staff, and reflective of the staff's ability or lack thereof.

Senate staff hold job assignments from the sublime to the mundane. There is, however, a consistent pattern of organization and job titles among senators' personal offices and committee staffs, although each senator and each committee chairman runs his or her staff operation differently. In a senator's personal office, one will find from a dozen to several dozen aides, the number roughly dependent upon the population of the state represented. Commonly at the top is the administrative assistant, whom the senator holds responsible for the entire staff operation, including offices in the home state. The "A. A." is expected, above all, to know politics and run an office with, usually, the goal of the re-election foremost; if the A. A. knows legislative policy matters and is a good manager of people, so much the better.

The chief legislative assistant ("Chief L. A.") focuses on legislation and often directs several subject area experts. An office manager is expected to handle the logistics of an office and supervise the secretaries, caseworkers, and the handling of constituent mail. The jobs often overlap and intertwine. Caseworkers will work with legislative assistants on solving constituents' problems; mail on a particular subject may be handled first by a legislative assistant, who drafts a universal letter (with room for computer-generated variations to make it look personal to each recipient), and all the answers that follow will be handled by a computer operator.

The workload is formidable: thousands of bills and amendments to read and follow, scores of constituents' problems, and a volume of mail that can be in the thousands weekly, often in the tens of thousands. Senators typically get involved only when there are major policy decisions to be made or to try to solve intractable problems. The job of senator is too big not to delegate considerable authority to staff.

Committee staffs are headed by two people: the majority staff director and the minority staff director. They are chosen by the committee chairman and the ranking minority member, respectively. Most of the staff positions (with the exception of a few special positions created to help individual committee members) are filled by appointment by the chairman and ranking minority member, with the staff directors doing the balance of the hiring. Some committees have subcommittees with separate subcommittee staffs, whose operations are guided by the subcommittee chairman and the ranking minority member. Among many Senate committee and subcommittee staffs there is more age and experience than among personal staffs, and that is good, for most of the products of the Senate are the work of its committees and subcommittees.

Senators have the most contact with their A.A.s, their Chief L.A.s, their press aides, and their personal secretaries. Add the respective staff directors in the case of committee chairmen and ranking members.

These individuals have the power of access, of disclosing or withholding information, of working to shape agendas, of being go-betweens, of making deals, of writing legislation. They are subject to control only by senators themselves, and that control varies greatly among the 100 elected senators. The mark of a good staffer is the careful exercise of that power, the realization that he or she is acting on behalf of an elected senator, not as a separate entity or as the representative of an outside interest group with whom he or she may have close ties. The good staffer will also know when and how to use power when necessary: to make the bureaucracy bend for a constituent, to make a commitment on a bill on a senator's behalf, or to initiate a compromise on the floor of the Senate with other senators' staffs to resolve impasses.

Listen to one end of a hypothetical telephone conversation to get a feel for the job, the responsibility, the power, and the potential of a senator's staff; in this case, the job of a legislative assistant:

> Senator: "I'm in the cloakroom. I missed the debate on this amendment—I was at Armed Services Committee. Fill me in . . . Who spoke? . . . Didn't we vote on that last year? How did I vote? . . . Have we had any mail on it? . . . How did my colleague vote, did you hear? . . . I saw the governor back home last week, and he said this was important to him. . . . What do you recommend? . . . Can I still put my amendment on if this passes? . . . How soon can you have it ready? . . . Let the cloakroom know I want to offer it, I'll try to stall while you get here. . . . Now, how should I vote on this one? . . . I don't know, I'll talk to some of the people in the "well." Get down here as soon as you can.

As the legislative assistant hurries to the floor of the Senate, he learns that his senator has voted opposite his recommendation. He suspects he could have influenced the vote the other way, but is secure in the knowledge that the senator, not he, is the elected official. On the way to pick up a floor pass, the L. A. sees a friend from another senator's staff. "Good luck on your amendment," he says, "but we'll have to vote the other way." The L. A. grimaces at the use of the word "we." It is, in his office, *verboten*, because of all that it symbolizes.

Senators' staffs are a lot of what makes the Senate the institution it is; their hiring and control is an important aspect of representative democracy. Those who know the Senate know that staffs often make a difference—for good or ill—in the conduct of the nation's government.

Reading 3.7

Staff in the House: The View from the Hill

Lee Godown

For 38,000 individuals, Congress is a place of employment. Most of the 38,000 work in support and auxilliary capacities, such as for the Library of Congress, Capitol Hill police, or food services. But, many work directly for members (both in Washington and 'back home') or for their work groups (committees, subcommittees, group caucuses). Working in Congress inevitably leads to an insider's perspective. The following essay, written by a professional personal staffer on the House side, provides an astute statement of such an insider's viewpoint.

Source: Specifically written for this volume.

Washington, D.C. is a city of vistas. Its architect, Pierre L'Enfant, it is said, designed it to confuse the British sufficiently to keep them from successfully capturing the city. For example, while one can stand on the west front of the Capitol Building and look toward the Lincoln Memorial with an unobstructed view, the route one must take to travel between those two points is almost maze-like. Never mind the British, it confuses everyone.

Understandably, there are many places in and around Washington that have truly extraordinary views. One of them is Jenkin's Hill, more commonly known as "Capitol Hill." From the top of it, one can see almost all of Washington.

As a legislative assistant to two congressmen, and a legislative director to one, I have had the opportunity to view the rest of the nation from the Hill for the better part of seven years. During that time I have learned an incredible amount about how the American government works, does not work, and functions under a variety of stresses, quirks, and applications of power. Washington, I think, is capable of changing more dramatically in a short period of time than is any other place I know. Having experienced the brutal reality of the will of the electorate on a couple of occasions (that is, working for a congressman/candidate who lost) I know how fast circumstances can change in politics. In power, everybody is your friend—out of power and you have trouble getting a telephone call returned. Without a word having been spoken, everyone here knows. The Washington establishment is very practical—and fluid.

Like a spider in the center of a web, Washington (and the Hill in particular) senses the slightest movement through the thin strands that connect it with the fringes of the nation it governs. Washington is a focal point, a microcosm, if you will, of the nation as a whole. There is virtually nothing that happens during any given day anywhere in America that someone in Washington doesn't become aware of in some manner. Surprisingly, however, even though that is the case, it is very hard for one who lives here to keep his or her perspective on just what life is really like on the other side of the Potomac. The view from the Hill can become distorted by any number of erroneous and false perceptions. People here speak of becoming jaded by the Washington milieu. Washington may know all, but seldom is it the authoritative source. This is an important difference.

On Capitol Hill, then, the rule of thumb is never to forget that the main reason you are here is to help represent the people who put you here—your congressional district. No matter what the reality in Washington is, as a member of Congress (or a staffer of one) the reality for you is what is in the hearts and minds of the 650,000 plus constituents that you represent. Most of the time, that is an easy thing to gauge. With the flood of mail that each congressman's office receives, the phone calls and other forms of communication from the district, a member is more than well-equipped to vote the way that a majority of his or her constituency wishes. It simply becomes a matter of statistics. You might ask, why then do congressmen get defeated, or why don't they always do what it is obvious the electorate wants? Why not just have two buttons in everyone's home labeled "yes" and "no" to enable them to vote the way they wish on national issues personally?

As the man who taught me the art of politics often says, "politics is bringing home the bacon, without spilling the beans." I don't think I realized how true this saying is until I started working on the Hill. No matter how well-informed voters are, they are not prepared to make the decisions, react to the politics involved, or participate in attitude changing debate like a single legislative representative is. That is, as my professor used to say, "the beauty of a democracy."

Yes, the majority of Americans are

aware of what the issues of the day are. Yes, the majority of Americans are capable of voting for a President or congressman intelligently. But do they know what is contained in Section 6, Paragraph 2 of the Gramm/Rudman Deficit Reduction Bill, and how it affects them directly?

There needs to be a clearinghouse of ideas, someplace for men and women whose job it is to make the educated, intelligent decisions required to make the path of America a safe and profitable one. Members of Congress and their staffs have literally every conceivable source of information on any given subject at their fingertips. There needs to be a Congress, but there is a built-in problem: The constituent at home is often frustrated by the seeming lack of knowledge that a representative has on a given issue, but the representative himself is probably over-educated on the matter, and is struggling mightily to retain his grip on the real pulse of the body politic. Who is more correct? I think it is a tie.

When I return to the district that my employer represents, I often am disheartened by some of the things that I hear people say. Some often-heard remarks are: "those politicians sit there in Washington and impose restrictions on our lives as though they were God," or "why are the staffs of Congressmen so large; can't they cut down like they are asking the rest of us to do?" Almost invariably, the attitude of the average "guy on the street" is one of disdain for politicians. They are held in low regard by many, but at the same time are respected by some curious twist of emotion that people designate "being an American." It is one of the great ironies, I think, that Americans can be so critical of their government, but at the same time cannot think of any other country in the world they would rather call home.

It may surprise many voters to learn that the majority of staffers on the Hill (including this one) work, on average, 11–12 hours per day as a matter of practice. Congressional staff often are seen at their desks on weekends, catching up on the work that they literally did not have the time to do during the regular week. I wonder how many individuals in private industry would be willing to do this for the low scale of pay that, believe it or not, is the rule rather than the exception on the Hill? An entry-level legislative assistant can expect only $12,000 per year, after having studied for over four years at a college or university. Sure, the psychic income is considerable, but it doesn't pay the rent.

In defense, then, of a Congress and government that many think has grown too large to be effective, I must say that my view from the top of Jenkin's Hill is quite different. There are useless government agencies and regulations, to be sure, but that doesn't mean we should eliminate all of them. There are crooks here, but the Congress as a whole should not be thought of as such. There are political deals made on the Hill everyday (I know, because I engineer a few myself) but we should not think of them as being harmful.

Does the system work? Using my experience as a guide, I answer a confident "yes." It is precisely because the American electorate doesn't have all the facts that individual Congressmen are constantly trying to let them know what is going on in those "Congressman So-And-So Reports from Washington" pieces that arrive with unnerving frequency in our mailboxes.

Unfortunately, an ignorant public cuts both ways. While public ignorance may prompt many congressmen to try to educate their constituents, it prompts others to "tell them what they want to hear." The challenge democracy poses for you and I as citizens is to make sure that we express our views to our respective congressmen in a fair and equitable way. We must realize that our congressman is not going to vote the way we would like 100 percent of the time, for he/she has other constituents to represent, too.

We must also realize that a congressman

could have more information available to make a decision than we do. Sometimes, for that reason, a decision may look wrong to us.

Finally, unless we are willing to be fair to the person we elected to represent us in the Congress, we can't expect him or her to return the favor. The congressman/constituent relationship is a symbiotic one. One cannot live without the other very well or long.

The view from the Hill is spectacular and detailed. The Hill is literally a microcosm of the whole country. It is a mirror of what the country collectively thinks, feels and wishes, and it reflects these emotions and beliefs back at America.

Illustration 3.B.
A representative's workday.

A major development in the modern Congress is the increased busyness of the institutions and its members. The heavy work loads of members are best dramatized by these two illustrations. The table shows the portrait of an average day as revealed by a survey and statistical study of House members. The example of Congressman Wise's day is a fairly typical one faced by most members.

A representative's "average day."

Activity	Average Time	
In the House chamber		2:53 hours
In committee/subcommittee work		1:24 hours
Hearings	26 minutes	
Business	9 minutes	
Markups	42 minutes	
Other	5 minutes	
In his/her office		3:19 hours
With constituents	17 minutes	
With organized groups	9 minutes	
With others	20 minutes	
With staff aides	53 minutes	
With other representatives	5 minutes	
Answering mail	46 minutes	
Preparing legislation, speeches	12 minutes	
Reading	11 minutes	
On telephone	26 minutes	
In other Washington locations		2:02 hours
With constituents at Capitol	9 minutes	
At events	33 minutes	
With leadership	3 minutes	
With other representatives	11 minutes	
With informal groups	8 minutes	
In party meetings	5 minutes	
Personal time	28 minutes	
Other	25 minutes	
Other		1:40 hours
Total average representative's day		11:18 hours

Source: From Samuel C. Patterson and Roger H. Davidson, *A More Perfect Union* (Homewood, Ill.: Dorsey Press, 1979), p. 453.

Illustration 3.C.
Actual daily schedule of Congressman Bob Wise (D—W. Va.), Wednesday, June 19, 1985.

8:00	Weekly staff meeting: 1508 Longworth House Office Bldg.
9:00	Meet with Congressman Marty Sabo regarding leadership race.
10:00	House meets.
11:00	Public Works and Transportation Committee meeting and markup of hazardous waste legislation.
12:00	Dunbar Ladies Garden Club to visit: 1508 Longworth.
1:15	Meeting with John Hoving regarding fundraising: Bullfeathers Restaurant. Lunch.
3:00	98th Democratic Caucus members meeting on budget.
3:30	Meeting with Marilyn Harris of U.S. Steel: 1508 Longworth.
4:00	Legislative meeting with legislative staff: 1508 Longworth.
5:30	Reception: Dennis Hertel fundraiser, Democratic National Committee.
6:00	Reception: Robin Tallon, Reserve Officers Association.
7:00	Reception: J. C. Penney, Hyatt Regency Gold Room.

Reading 3.8

So You Want to Go to Congress: A Political Scientist Looks Back on the House

Honorable Jim Lloyd, Former U.S. Representative (D–Calif.)

In the following essay, written especially for this volume, Jim Lloyd gives some insights and impressions gleaned from six years of service in the U.S. House of Representatives.

There is an all-American myth harbored in the heart of every mother that her son or daughter may some day go to Congress. In the history of our nation, some 11,509 sons and 100 daughters have fulfilled this great hope. Some bright offspring have gone even further and proved they can become President of the United States. However, Congress is the subject of this book, so let's take a look at what it takes to become a part of this incredible American institution.

Obviously, the first thing that needs to be done to achieve in this arena is to be successful in running for congressional office. The variables that have propelled, shoved, provided an opportunity, or whatever might be the methodology of winning an election are the subject of another discussion. Suffice it to say, you have obtained more votes than your opponent and have been declared the official winner of the congressional seat in the ______ district of the great state of ______ (you fill in the blanks).

Having won the election, you are now ready to make your triumphant entry into the mecca of democracy—namely, Washington, D.C.—and the hallowed halls of the House of Representatives. The first glimpse of the Capitol after you have been elected takes on a new euphoric meaning; the perspective you now have is entirely different

Source: Prepared especially for this volume.

from that which is projected in the average political science textbook. You arrive in Camelot . . . the Capitol dome shining in the bright blue sky and the whiteness of that awesome great building beckoning you as no powerful magnet ever attracted a metal object. As you walk up the steps of the Capitol and inform the doorman or policeman that you are the new Congressman/woman from whatever that district of that great state is, the magic occurs. Recognizing you immediately, the policeman or doorman is all too eager to help. You must remember, however, that he has a list indicating who all the new members of Congress are, and he will immediately check out who you are and from where as he welcomes you to the environs of this historical legislative body—so don't fake it! You will find that your wish is his command, because, in the final analysis, the business of the Capitol is indeed you, the representative. Everything turns on what you will do in the ensuing two years—longer if you are lucky enough, agile enough, quick enough, smart enough, and there are even those who say dumb enough, to be re-elected.

The first thing you must do is establish yourself with the Clerk of the House, and probably more important, the Sergeant at Arms (which in reality is a complete misnomer because he is your banker). It is always good to remember that the Clerk of the House, the Sergeant at Arms, the Postmaster, the Doorkeeper, the Chaplain, and a lot of other folks who are there to do your bidding are functionaries of the party of the majority. Simply stated, if the House is Democratic, then all of these jobs will be filled with those who are Democrats; and if the House is Republican, the job holders will be, too. It makes no difference whether you are with the majority or the minority party insofar as your pay, selection of an office, acquisiton of staff, or the normal operations of the day are concerned. It does make a difference, however, when it comes to getting on the committee of your choice, having access to your chairman, or scheduling legislation (remember those political promises). The majority party, indeed a majority of its members, governs; while it can be a benevolent ruler, the majority party, nonetheless, is in the driver's seat and very conscious of its position. Fortunately, the "ins" realize they can be the "outs" in the next term, and conduct themselves accordingly.

Having basked in the reflections of your newfound glory (even though there was no brass band waiting to meet you, the President of the United States did not instantly call you to the White House for consultation, and sadly enough not even the Speaker of the House or the Majority or Minority Leader immediately called you into session to seek your sage political advice), you are there, and you are one of 535 people in the nation's Capital who will vote on the critical (and not-so-critical) issues that will affect our nation for the next two years.

One of the most important facts that suddenly will dawn on you is that having won an election does not necessarily prepare you for putting together the administrative forces that will turn your election victory into substantial performance. Simply stated, now that you have won, you must get to work, and with very little fanfare at that. And you thought *campaigning* was stressful!

We shall now test your mettle in ability to do administratively, legislatively, and politically what you promised all those good folks back home you would do.

Let's take a look at your task of selecting a staff. Surely you were careful not to make any commitments to hire anyone if you won, because if you did, you have violated the law, and you wouldn't want to break those laws before you start making them, would you? In all probability you have at least "thought" about bringing some of the campaign staff along with you; if so, you are in good company. There probably isn't a congressman who, upon arrival in Washington, hasn't had strong feelings about wanting his dedicated and loyal workers to continue right along with him.

But first things first. You can hire 18 full-time and 4 part-time workers. You must pay a minimum of $100 and no more than $52,000. Now comes the kicker—you are restricted to a total of $300,000. It won't take you very long to figure out that $52,000 goes into $300,000 less than six times. And since it seems easier to ask all those good friends who worked so hard to get you elected (and who worked for little or nothing) to continue their loyalty, it's difficult not to try to hire them. They, too, know how much you can pay. Will the new member of Congress from (that state and district again) show proper gratitude?

You will probably decide that you want a Washington/Capitol Hill pro to head up the staff. He or she will henceforward be known as "my AA" (administrative aide). This is a very "in" term; it shows you to be a real member of "The Hill." And as you already know, "The Hill" is Capitol Hill. (And yes, its altitude, low though it may be, does qualify it to be a hill!)

By this time you have hired legislative aides, clerks, et al. for Washington, and have selected a "field rep" (representative), caseworkers, secretaries, etc., in the home district.

Now you discover you don't yet have an office in either Washington or the district. If there is a federal office building in your district, you will automatically get an office there. If not, you've got to come up with one in a hurry, and that means locate it, contract for it, and equip it, but probably not before you are sworn in office in January. And by the way, from the moment you were elected in November, many of the folks assume you are already the congressman/woman, and as such you are ready to handle casework, get flags, respond to their various requests, arrange White House tours, etc.

However, the person you defeated or otherwise succeeded is still in the seat until early January. You guessed it—this is a transition period where he holds all the cards. The smoothness and efficiency with which you take over depends on the rapport you can establish with the outgoing member. Oh my! Remember all those cute little zingers in the campaign? Fortunately, it is at least the Christmas and New Year's season with joyful tidings and goodwill to all (you hope)!

January swearing-in day arrives, and you say "I do." And if you had any doubts about it, you now find you really *do* work a 15-hour day every day.

By now you have acquired your new office in Washington through the perilous process of a drawing. If you are lucky, great! If not, it will be a miserable two years with regard to space, because obviously the least desirable offices are left for the new members. The rooms you draw may not even be together and possibly may be on different floors. Incidentally, if you split a full staff of 18 with half in the district and half in Washington, you will have at least 10 people (counting yourself and probably an intern) in an incredibly small (just over 1000-square-foot) Washington office. OSHA would not tolerate industry having the same space on a per-person basis.

Congress has convened and is sorting out what it wants to do for the coming two years. If the Senate is of one party and the House another (as in 1981-1982), you will find some heavy pushing and shoving, both politically and legislatively—and you, dear new congressman/woman, are caught in the middle. Also, just before all of this is underway, you will have been subjected already to some personal pushing and shoving as your own political party is "getting organized." *Getting organized* is a term meaning political mayhem wherein the decisions as to who is going to be boss take place.

Remember that $1,000 that showed up for the last mailer from good ol' (Congressman) Harry, who was sure you'd win and wanted to help? Well, good ol' Harry is a candidate for the Majority Leader race; he's now ready to collect some of his political IOUs (from you). And you were going to rise above such questionable political dealings. But this push and shove goes all the way to who serves on what committee and can greatly affect your future in the House for years to come. Your desire to be on Appropriations or Ways and Means may now go down the drain as you find senior members have first choice on these committees. You do remember that seniority system you were going to change, don't you? You, sir or madam, will have to wait your turn. You might jump the traces if you have the votes on the Committee on Committees, but review that decision carefully because, even if you win (few rarely do), you still have to negotiate your legislative and committee access with your leadership, which tends to tenaciously support the system that brought it to power. This is a very difficult position, if not impossible, and not easily handled. No, you will fall into line with the rest.

The month of January is now well underway. If it is a presidential election year, you will of course have invited some of your good supporters to attend inauguration festivities. Even if you are not a member of the President's party, still you will have had supporters who were willing to cross the party lines to help you. They expect (sometimes demand) that you deliver the appropriate tickets to the presidential balls, and of course you will take care of Mr. and Mrs. Smith, who expect to have good seats at the swearing-in. If the President is of your party, the requests are tenfold—and I would remind you, no matter how it works, you only get so many tickets. Remember that letter the new President, who was then a candidate, sent to all the constituents in your district saying that he could not go to Washington without you and urging them to vote for you? Now you find that the help he was talking about was more legislative than political. As such, you may have slipped his mind a bit during this crucial period while you are trying to get hotel reservations, tickets, and maybe even enough money to take everybody out to dinner.

You are in what can be referred to as the social phase, not only because of the inauguration, but also because of all of the other routine invitations that deluge your office for this organization's party or that group's soiree. All of them just can't have a successful event without your presence, even if there are 382 people in a room big enough for 200. At first you will try to do it all. But as time goes by, you will begin to be more selective, simply because you do not have adequate time to meet all the requests. The fact remains, however, that it is all very heady wine to be in social demand in Washington, D.C.

Social involvement notwithstanding, you are now shifting gears to get on with the legislative program. You do want to make a favorable impression on the media, your friends at home, and certainly the leadership with your legislative prowess, don't you? The committee chairmen begin the organization of the legislative committees. In all probability you will be on two committees, one major and one minor. You will find your major committee will have anywhere from 35 to 47 members, depending on the percentages agreed to by the leadership. You personally will be number 30 or above; if luck is really against you, you could be number 47 on your major committee. This means that during the questioning period (which allows each member five minutes) you will have to wait for your chance to ask those brilliant questions that will so impress the media and the folks at home. But don't be undaunted; you will have an opportunity to ask your questions and to participate at the subcommittee level. But it doesn't take long for you to realize that there is no possible way to meet the demands of both full committees, your subcommittees, and the action of the floor, all of which are going on simultaneously.

Another problem that will present itself is that the full committee staff and the subcommittee staff serve at the pleasure of the chairmen of those bodies. I need not remind you that you are not the chairman. Therefore the legislative direction will be somewhat dependent upon the chairman's desires, not yours. Don't despair, however, for you do have a say. First of all, your subcommittee chairman wants your goodwill and, more important, your vote, in order to accomplish the programs he wishes. The same is true of the chairman of the full committee; if it ever comes down to it, and it often does, your vote could be the decisive one. The chairman will also need your vote and support for the committee's bills as they go to the House floor. I would remind you, too, that, as a member of the committee, your right to speak on the floor takes precedence over the right of other members of other committees, including those who are in the leadership. In addition, at every level (subcommittee, committee, and committee of the whole) you have the right, and I might point out sometimes the obligation, to submit or support amendments to which your committee chairman does not necessarily agree. Through this process, for all of the frustrations, you will be able to exert a little bit of your will on the legislative action.

In order to make your legislative will more effective, it is imperative that you select those staff members who are legislative pros, who not only agree with you philosophically, but who can also help you project that philosophy effectively in your role as a member of Congress. These selections must be made giving full consideration to all of the variables that present themselves administratively, legislatively, and politically.

Another facet that is like a mantle over all of the areas of your congressional involvement is your political posture vis-à-vis the leadership, your staff, friends, etc. Your participation in this highly structured but not-so-visible arena is very important for you as a member of your party, with its goals and aspirations.

It is possible that, as a new member, you may be elected to the Steering and Policy Committee, or you could serve as a member of the Whip's organization. You might even be asked to serve on an ad hoc committee by your state or regional party organization in some specific area, such as the steel caucus, the women's caucus, the black caucus, or many other involvements. As with all decision-making processes, you must weigh these commitments against what you are already doing, comparing them to the goals that you either articulated in the campaign or have now defined for yourself. Time is of the essence, and you can't do everything.

I have saved what I consider the most difficult task of all for last—that is, your ethical involvement, both in your district and in Washington, D.C. In the light of the Watergate era, which initiated investigative reporting, and the scandals that have beset Congress à la Elizabeth Ray, Fanny Fox, Rita Jenrette, and Paula Parkinson, not to mention Koreagate and Abscam, you and you alone will have to determine whether you possess the necessary moral fiber and personal integrity, based on all the religious, educational, and moral training you bring with you, to negotiate these political jungles.

As you move further into your congressional career and correspondingly rise in importance and visibility, you can rest assured there will be somebody who is willing to misuse your position of power for his or her own gain. You must also remember that there are misguided members of the press, who will be unscrupulous enough, through innuendo and omission in the text of their stories, to taint your personal integrity. Along with this fact of life, a genuine antagonism exists in the political arena because some candidate in the other party can't wait to whisper out-and-out lies about you in order to weaken your political position and thereby eventually defeat you.

Perceived power, or better yet the image of power, brings forth those misguided and foolish people who will encourage you in acts of moral indiscretion. It's not because they wish to damage you personally (although there are those who have that clearly in mind—remember Abscam). It's because they wish only to be on the inner circle of power, with you as their vehicle.

Remember, you have the ability to affect literally billions of the taxpayers' dollars, to say nothing of the direction and thrust of the United States for the next 5, 10, or 20 years.

Those "single issues" that were so important while you were running can clearly come back to haunt you, whether they be handguns, food stamps, abortion, or what-have-you. Such issues can greatly cloud an infinitely more important issue, whether it be national defense, foreign policy, or domestic policy. In the final analysis, while there is no question that you must answer to your constituency, you must answer to your own conscience. This, my new congressional friend, can be an awesome responsibility.

This paper has in no way presented all the problems of administering to the needs of your staff, constituents, and family. (We haven't even touched upon the aspects of congressional family life.) Nor has it addressed how to respond to the political realities commensurate with the desired legislative goals. But it is hoped that this paper has shed some light on what it is to be a congressman in this day and age, with all the problems that beset "your" district, state, nation, and, finally, the world itself. You are, indeed, as a member of Congress, a very important person. Good luck and God bless you!

Reading 3.9

An Insider's Impressions of the U.S. Senate

Honorable Fred Harris, Former U.S. Senator (D–Okla.)

In this essay, original to this collection, Fred Harris gives his perspectives on the U.S. Senate, comparing his service there with his experience in the Oklahoma State Senate.

I used to say that I came to the U.S. Senate (in 1964) with all the expertise in national and international affairs that eight years in the Oklahoma State Senate affords. I was not entirely joking. One thing I thought I did know from my previous experience, though, was how a legislative body functions. But the U.S. Senate was (and is) unlike the Oklahoma State Senate in a number of ways.

Source: Prepared especially for this volume.

I already knew from an earlier visit to Washington that few members were ever on the floor of the U.S. Senate while it was in session, except when it came time to vote; Oklahoma's State Senators *were* on the floor during sessions. Debate counts for little in the national body; only once during my eight years there did it make a major difference on a measure—the final speech of Edmund Muskie (D-Maine) in favor of model cities legislation.

What I did not know at first was that, besides these facts, there were some others that also made the U.S. Senate different from the Oklahoma Senate. First, the U.S.

Senate is not only a deliberative body but a deliberate one as well. Major issues that come to floor vote have generally been around awhile; most senators already know how they are going to vote on them, without waiting for the debate. Second, the committees (and subcommittees) of the U.S. Senate are almost always allowed to meet during the Senate session—causing senators to spend most afternoons hurrying back and forth between a meeting of their committee (and, often, more than one) and a roll call on the floor. Third, U.S. senators lead harried lives, a typical day beginning with a breakfast with constituents and ending with a dinner with interest-group representatives. Sandwiched in between are interviews, committee meetings, votes, staff meetings, mail, phone calls, working lunches, and "walking" conferences. Senators feel that they cannot afford the time to sit and listen to floor debate.

The U.S. Senate was different from the Oklahoma Senate in other ways. Since committee assignments are relatively permanent in the national body, the norm of "specialization" is stronger in the U.S. Senate (although not as strong as in the U.S. House, where members have fewer assignments and less power to amend on the floor). Nevertheless, it is expected of both Oklahoma senators and U.S. senators that they will not "dance every set" (speak out on every issue); those who do are generally less influential than those who do not.

The number of staff members who assist U.S. senators is lavish compared to the staff available to Oklahoma State Senators. A member of the British House of Commons once asked me, "Whatever do they all do?" I answered that they handled constituent casework and other matters, did research, typed, filed, and wrote speeches. "Write speeches?" he questioned, incredulously. "In the Commons, it is assumed that members can rise and make their own speeches." Some U.S. senators do worry that having so many staff members insulates them somewhat from the real work, the issues, and the real world. But still, no senator ever feels that he or she has enough staff. That is one of the several reasons senators desire to become chairpersons of committees and subcommittees. (Added visibility, prestige, and ability to affect policy are among the other reasons.)

It is harder for U.S. senators to stay in touch with their constituents than it is for Oklahoma state senators. Of course, there is the problem of the great diversity in the numbers of people involved. Distances are not so great at the state level, either, and state legislators can go home every weekend. Also, state legislative sessions are usually much shorter. Then, it's home for the rest of the year. More than that, for a state senator, "home" really is home, where the senator actually lives. Not so for U.S. senators. For them, "home" is where they are *from.* Washington or one of its suburbs is where they live. In this regard, senators sometimes envy governors (and a number are former governors). Governors stay in their home states to do their jobs. Senators must leave their home states to do theirs. Senators, then, must work at staying in touch. And they must work, too, at *appearing* to stay in touch. Nothing is worse politically for a U.S. senator than a growing feeling among the people of the home state that the senator has "gone Washington" and has "forgotten us."

The importance of *appearing* to stay in touch with the home folks is illustrated by the home-state images of two U.S. senators from Oklahoma—the late Robert S. Kerr, my predecessor, and A. S. Mike Monroney, with whom I served. Kerr, who was recognized at his death as the "uncrowned king of the Senate," never spoke on a national issue without tying it into Oklahoma's interests. He took President Truman's side, for example, when the Missourian fired General Douglas MacArthur during the Korean War. But Kerr emphasized that a principal reason for his doing so was that the members of

Oklahoma's 45th Division of the National Guard would have been put in greater jeopardy by MacArthur's policies, which might have brought the Chinese into the war. Also, when Kerr went back to Oklahoma, he made a special point with his appearances. For example, I remember a headline about his commencement speech at a little Oklahoma school that only had *seven* graduating seniors.

Monroney, on the other hand, did not always try to find an Oklahoma "angle" for his actions. He was a noted liberal leader on national and international matters. He authored legislation that created an international development bank. He co-authored major congressional reform. I am confident that Monroney spent *more* time in Oklahoma than Kerr did, but Monroney's home-state appearances did not especially call attention to the fact that he was still "one of us." The result was, as one of Kerr's sons once told me, "My dad could spend all of his time in Washington, and people would think he was in Oklahoma, while Mike could spend all his time in Oklahoma, and people would think he was in Washington." Staying in touch requires more than appearances, of course, but an image of *not* staying in touch was one factor that eventually defeated Monroney. It was a big problem for me, too, when I simultaneously served in the Senate and as Chairman of the Democratic National Committee (1969, 1970), even though during that time I purposely went home more often than before.

In both the Oklahoma State Senate and the U.S. Senate, a number of the norms are much alike. In both there is a weak norm of "apprenticeship." (In earlier times in the U.S. Senate, first-year members were expected to be "seen and not heard," and there was a lot of fanfare at the time of a senator's first major speech on the floor.) Other norms are stronger in both bodies. A member's word must be good. The norm of "courtesy" —being "able to disagree without being disagreeable"—is also valued. So is "institutional loyalty." Former U.S. Senator Joseph Clark (D-Pa.) found this out when he ran for, and lost, a Senate leadership post after having written *The Sapless Branch*, a book critical of the Congress and the U.S. Senate.

The "legislative work" norm is important in both bodies. To have influence, members must be earnest about the body's work. It is still true, as in Lyndon Johnson's Senate time, that U.S. senators are graded somewhat by their colleagues on the basis of whether they are "show horses" or "work horses." Those elevated to internal, legislative office are generally of the show-horse, inward-looking variety—one reason chief executives are better at affecting public opinion than are legislative leaders. Still, a number of the members of both the Oklahoma State Senate and the U.S. Senate at any one time entertain thoughts of running for higher office. They may seek notice outside the legislative body (and outside their constituency) for this reason. They may seek wider notice, too, because they feel, as the late Hubert H. Humphrey told me he did (and as I did): If a senator is to be effective in the Senate, he or she must not only work earnestly in that body, but must also seek to influence public opinion generally and to bring it to bear on the Senate.

In neither the Oklahoma State Senate nor the U.S. Senate can a member know all there is to know about any one issue. When it comes time to vote, then, members often rely on "cues"—most of all cues from trusted fellow members. As U.S. senators rush to the floor for a roll call, they often ask other Senators, "Whose amendment is this?" An answer such as "It's Miller's education amendment" may be about all a senator needs to know in order to decide to vote for or against the amendment. On the floor, senators may ask a seatmate, a senator who usually votes the way they do, the manager of the bill, or some other member they respect or trust, "What are *you* going to do on this?" The answer can be influential.

Most of the time, U.S. senators (as well

as Oklahoma state senators) are "delegates"—doing what they think a majority of their constituents want. This usually causes no strain, because most senators probably agree on most matters with their constituents, at least the active ones. Sometimes, senators act as "trustees"—knowingly taking a different view from their constituents, perhaps hoping to change public opinion. As one Oklahoma state senator once jokingly put it to me (when he decided to reverse a long-standing position and vote to repeal prohibition, despite the trouble that his vote would cause him back home), "Every now and then, you have to rise above principle and do what's right." Hubert Humphrey told me that a senator should be willing to compromise on nonfundamental matters, but should be willing to die politically on issues of basic importance (such as civil rights). But he said the trouble is that "you may like it here so much that you begin to decide which is which on that basis."

Whether a senator acts like a delegate or a trustee may depend upon how long it is until he or she must face re-election. The late Senator Richard Russell (D-Ga.) told me that he could watch a senator walk down the hall and tell what period of the six-year senatorial term the senator was in. Those with six years ahead of them walk along looking up and thinking lofty thoughts. Those in the middle of their terms walk along looking straight ahead. But those who are nearing re-election time, he said, walk along looking down, watching where they step. There is something to that.

Service in the U.S. Senate can be frustrating. It often seems impossible to move things very much at any one time. Former Senator Edmund Muskie (D-Maine) once told me that after a year of hard senatorial work, he often looked back and felt that, during the year, he had only been able to do something like "change Section 22(*d*) slightly." For many senators, certain issues may be uncompromisable. (I felt this way about civil rights issues and, later on, about ending the Vietnam War.) That makes legislative work—where often the essence of the job is compromise—difficult, to say the least. But the U.S. Senate is a great platform. It is probably still the "world's greatest deliberative body," as senators like to call it. For a time at least, it is a great place for those who want to serve the country—and speak to it.

Illustration 3.D.
A rough idea of congressional allowances, 1984.

There are two conclusions about allowances: (1) they have risen greatly in recent years, and (2) the exact figures are hard to obtain.

Following is a list of available figures for House and Senate allowances in 1984. In some Cases, no dollar value is given because it is hard to determine the range of reimbursed costs—for example, in travel or telephone reimbursements. Most of the 1984 allowances can be transferred from one account to another.

	House	Senate
Salary	$72,600*	$72,600*
Washington office		$668,504–$1,343,218†
Staff	$379,480	
Committee legislative assistants	‡	$207,342
Interns	$1,840	
General office expenses	$47,300	$36,000–$156,000†
Telephone/telegraph	15,000 minutes long-distance §	
Stationery	Two 3-room suites	1.4–25 million pieces
Office space		
		Five 8-room suites
Furnishings	§	§
Equipment	Provided	Provided
District/state offices		
Rental	2,500 sq. ft.	4,800–8,000 sq. ft.
Furnishings/equipment	$35,000	$22,500–$31,350
Mobile office		One
Communications		Provided by Senate
Automated correspondence	§	Computer Center
Audio/video recordings; photography	§	§
Travel	Formula (min. $6,200; max. approx. $67,200)	§

*Salary established January 1, 1984; leaders' salaries are higher.
†Senators are allowed expenses based on a sliding scale linked to the state's population.
‡Provided for members of Appropriations, Budget, and Rules committees.
§Expenses are covered through the general office expenses line item. In most cases supplies and equipment are charged at rates well below retail levels.
Source: Committee on House Administration; Senate Committee on Rules and Administration.

Chapter Four

Structural Characteristics I: The Committee System

In this and the next two chapters, selections will be presented concerning the structural characteristics of Congress: committees, political party organizations, and legislative procedures. As is the case with any organization, structural aspects strongly affect the way business is done and the nature of decision outcomes. This is especially true with regard to Congress. Although elections, politics, bargaining, debate, and floor voting are intrinsically more glamorous and interesting than structural characteristics, an appreciation of organizational structure is vital for an understanding of Congress. One cannot overemphasize the importance of the organizational features of Congress in explaining congressional output. Quite simply, our argument is that the decentralization of the committee system, the nonhierarchical and undisciplined nature of the congressional party system, and the multiple decision points and stages of the legislative process make inevitable particularized and incremental policy that usually involves a compromise among contending interests.

Committees are the "work horses" of Congress. As political scientist Woodrow Wilson argued at the turn of the century, prior to his debut in politics, congressional government is committee government. Most of the important decisions of government are thrashed out in these "little legislatures."

Committees decide which of the many proposed bills will be seriously considered. It is in those panels that proposed legislation is studied and scrutinized. For bills under consideration, committees hold hearings and call various witnesses to give testimony. Before a bill goes to the floor of the House or Senate, its exact wording is hammered out in a "markup" session of the committee, and the committee issues a report on the legislation to its parent house.

Readings in this chapter address the different kinds of committees, committee jurisdictions, committee assignments and leadership selection, and committee decision making. An actual committee report is also presented.

It should be emphasized that the major trends in committee government over the past decade have been (1) the proliferation of subcommittees and, especially in the House, their growing autonomy, and (2) the curtailment of the autocratic powers of committee chairmen, making their accession to power less dependent on automatic seniority and more dependent upon party caucus approval. A major issue pertaining to congressional committees is their lack of representativeness. Some contend that, because of the committee appointment process, committees are less microcosms of their parent houses and more re-election vehicles for members with constituencies affected by a committee's jurisdiction.

Illustration 4.A.

Four different kinds of committees.
A variety of committees are used in congressional work. The following excerpt from a government publication details the four types of committees and their major purposes.

Congress in its committee rooms is Congress at work, wrote Woodrow Wilson. It is in the committees of Congress that bills undergo their closest scrutiny, that investigations—including oversight of the Executive Branch—are conducted, and that the differences in bills passed by each House are reconciled into one version acceptable to both.

Congress uses four different types of committees to perform these different functions: standing committees, select or special committees, joint committees, and conference committees.

Committees that continue from Congress to Congress are called *standing committees*. The subject jurisdictions of these permanent committees are set forth in the rules of each house, and virtually every introduced bill is referred to one or more of them according to the subjects involved. These are the committees that actually review proposed legislation and determine which bills shall be reported to each house.

In the 96th Congress, there are 22 standing committees in the House and 15 in the Senate. Most have several subcommittees with specific jurisdictions. Usually a standing committee sends a bill to one of its subcommittees for hearings, review, and recommendations. The bill is then reported to the full committee for consideration. Finally, if approved by the full committee, the bill is reported to the full House or Senate.

Standing committees are also responsible for overseeing the operations of the Executive Branch departments and agencies under their respective jurisdictions. They usually perform this function by studies which provide Congress with the facts necessary to determine whether the agencies are administering legislation as intended. Congressional studies also help committees identify areas in which legislative action might be needed and the form that action might take.

Other congressional studies are performed by *select* or *special committees*. Usually established for a limited period of time, these groups ordinarily deal with more specific subjects and issues than do the standing committees. For example, in recent years each house has established a select committee on aging to study the multitude of problems that affect senior citizens. Select committees in one house or the other have also studied population problems, narcotics, and Indian affairs. During the past decade, each house has used a select committee to study its own committee system and to recommend improvements. Most select committees may investigate, study, and make recommendations but may not report legislation. But both houses have created a few permanent select committees in recent years and authorized them to report legislation.

Congress uses *joint committees* for investigatory and housekeeping purposes. These are usually permanent bodies composed of an equal number of House and Senate members. Although in the past certain joint committees had the authority to consider and report legislation, no joint committee had that power in the 96th Congress. Usually joint committees are used to study broad and complex areas over a long period of time, an example being the Joint Economic Committee. Other joint committees, such as the Joint Committee on Printing, oversee functions connected with the operation of the Legislative Branch.

The last category of committee is the *conference committee*. These are formed to reconcile the differences between the House and Senate when each passes a different version of the same bill. Conference committees are ad hoc joint committees, temporary panels appointed to deal with a single piece of legislation, dissolving upon the completion of that task. Members of both Houses serve on each conference committee, and the number of members from each house may be the same. This is not as inequitable as it might seem because the voting in conference committees is by house; its decisions must be approved by a majority of the Representatives and a majority of the Senators on the committee.

Every member of the House must serve on at least one standing committee except the Speaker and Minority Leader, who, by tradition, serve on none. Senators *must* serve on at least two standing committees. Counting standing, select, and joint committee assignments, some Senators sit on as many as five or six. In the House approximately

Illustration 4.A. (concluded)

90 Representatives have only one committee assignment, usually because they sit on a particularly busy panel, such as Appropriations. All other House members sit on two or three committees. In one way or another, both houses limit the number of chairmanships any single member may hold.

Committee sizes vary considerably and sometimes change from Congress to Congress. Because the House has more than four times as many members as the Senate, its committees are generally larger. In the 96th Congress, the largest House committee—Appropriations—had 54 members; the largest Senate committee—also Appropriations—had 28. Most Senate standing committees have from 14 to 20 members; most House committees have from 30 to 45. Traditionally, party ratios on committees correspond roughly to the party ratio in the full chamber.

Committee and subcommittee service encourages members to specialize in the subject areas of the panels on which they sit. Thus, the committee system continually builds up a reservoir of expertise to guide Congress as it attempts to deal with the nation's problems.

Source: From *The Capitol: A Pictorial History of the Capitol and of the Congress*, 8th ed. (Washington, D.C.: U.S. Government Printing Office, 1981), pp. 136–39. Reprinted from the public domain.

Illustration 4.B.
Jurisdictions of House and Senate standing committees.

The areas of responsibility for each of the standing committees is most complex and far-reaching. In the following abbreviated description of jurisdiction, it should be noted that Senate and House committees are not always coterminous. For example, although the House and Senate Armed Services Committees have roughly identical jurisdictional concerns, space exploration is handled in the House by Science and Technology and in the Senate by Commerce, Science, and Transportation, two very different committees with very different considerations and internal dynamics. It should also be emphasized that each house has a scheme for classifying its standing committees. For example, the Senate distinguishes between "major" and "minor" committees, the importance being that all Senators serve on at least one major committee. The House classifies its standing committees as exclusive, semiexclusive, and nonexclusive. Members on exclusive committees—Appropriations, Rules, and Ways and Means—may serve only on that committee.

House Committee	Responsibility
Agriculture	Agriculture and forestry in general; farms credit and security, crop insurance, soil conservation, rural electrification, and rural development.
Appropriations	Appropriations of government revenues.
Armed Services	All matters related to the national military establishment; conservation, development, and use of naval petroleum and oil shale reserves; strategic and critical materials; scientific research and development in support of the armed services.
Banking, Finance, and Urban Affairs	Banks and banking, including deposit insurance and federal monetary policy; money and credit, including currency; gold and silver, including coinage; valuation and revaluation of the dollar; urban development; housing, generally economic stabilization; control of prices; international finance; financial aid to commerce and industry.
Budget	Federal budget generally; Congressional Budget Office.
District of Columbia	All measures relating to municipal affairs of the District of Columbia except its appropriations.
Education and Labor	Education, labor, and welfare matters.
Foreign Affairs	Relations of the United States with other nations and international organizations and movements.
Government Operations	Budget and accounting measures; overall economy and efficiency of government, including federal procurement; reorganization in the Executive Branch; intergovernmental relations; general revenue sharing; National Archives.

Illustration 4.B. (continued)

House Committee	Responsibility
House Administration	House administration generally; printing and correction of the *Congressional Record;* federal elections generally; management of the Library of Congress; supervision of the Smithsonian Institution.
Interior and Insular Affairs	Public lands, parks, natural resources, territorial possession of the United States, Indian affairs.
Interstate and Foreign Commerce	Regulation of interstate and foreign commerce and communications; regulation of interstate transmission of power (except between government projects); inland waterways; railroads, railroad labor; securities and exchanges; interstate oil compacts; natural gas; health matters generally (except health care supported by payroll deductions); consumer affairs and consumer protection; travel and tourism; biomedical research and development.
Judiciary	Courts and judicial proceedings generally; constitutional amendments; civil rights; civil liberties; interstate compacts; immigration and naturalization; apportionment of representatives; meetings of Congress and attendance of members; presidential succession; national penitentiaries; patents; copyrights; trademarks; protection of trade and commerce against unlawful restraints and monopolies.
Merchant Marine and Fisheries	Merchant marine generally; Coast Guard; oceanography and marine affairs; maintenance and operation of the Panama Canal and administration of the Canal Zone; fisheries and wildlife.
Post Office	Postal and federal civil services; census and the collection of statistics generally; Hatch Act; holidays and celebrations.
Public Works and Transportation	Public buildings and roads; flood control; improvement of rivers and harbors; water power; pollution of navigable waters; transportation (except railroads).
Rules	Rules and orders of business of the House.
Science and Technology	Scientific and astronautical research and development generally; National Aeronautics and Space Administration; National Aeronautics and Space Council; National Science Foundation; outer space; science scholarships; Bureau of Standards; National Weather Service; civil aviation research and development; environmental research and development; energy research and development (except nuclear research and development).
Small Business	Assistance to and protection of small business, including financial aid; participation of small business enterprises in federal procurement and government contracts.
Standards of Official Conduct	Studies and investigates standards of conduct of House members and employees and may recommend remedial action.
Veterans' Affairs	Veterans' measures generally; pensions; armed forces insurance; rehabilitation, education, medical care, and treatment of veterans; veterans' hospitals and housing.
Ways and Means	Revenue measures generally; tariffs and trade agreements; social security.

Illustration 4.B. (concluded)

Senate Committee	Responsibility
Agriculture, Nutrition, and Forestry	Agriculture in general, including farm credit and security, crop insurance, soil conservation, and rural electrification; forestry in general; human nutrition; school nutrition programs; and matters relating to food, nutrition, and hunger.
Appropriations	Appropriations of government revenues.
Armed Services	Military affairs; Panama Canal and Canal Zone; strategic and critical materials; aeronautical and space activities peculiar to or primarily associated with development of weapons systems or military operations.
Banking, Housing, and Urban Affairs	Banking and currency generally; financial matters other than taxes and appropriations; public and private housing; economic controls; urban affairs.
Budget	Federal budget generally; Congressional Budget Office.
Commerce, Science, and Transportation	Interstate commerce in general; transportation; merchant marine and navigation; safety and transportation; Coast Guard; inland waterways except construction; communications; regulation of consumer products and services; standards and measurement; highway safety; science, engineering, and technology research, development, and policy; nonmilitary aeronautical and space sciences; marine fisheries; coastal zone management; oceans; weather and atmospheric activities.
Energy and Natural Resources	Energy policy generally; energy regulation and conservation; research and development; solar energy systems; naval petroleum; oil and gas; hydroelectric power; coal; mining; public parks and recreation areas.
Environment and Public Works	Environmental policy, research, and development; ocean dumping; fisheries and wildlife; outer Continental Shelf; solid-waste disposal and recycling; toxic substances and other pesticides; public works, bridges, and dams; water, air, and noise pollution; federal buildings and grounds.
Finance	Taxes, tariffs, foreign trade, import quotas, social security.
Foreign Relations	Relations of the United States with foreign nations generally; treaties; International Red Cross; diplomatic service; United Nations; foreign loans.
Governmental Affairs	Budget and accounting measures; reorganization of the Executive Branch; general government and administrative problems; intergovernmental relationship between the federal government and the states and municipalities, and between the United States and international organizations of which the United States is a member.
Judiciary	Federal courts and judges; penitentiaries; civil rights; civil liberties; constitutional amendments; monopolies and unlawful restraints of trade; interstate compacts; immigration and naturalization; apportionment of representatives; meetings of Congress and attendance of members; claims against the United States.
Labor and Human Resources	Education; labor; health and public welfare generally.
Rules and Administration	Senate administration generally; contested elections; presidential succession; management of the Library of Congress and the Smithsonian Institution.
Veterans' Affairs	Veterans' measures generally; pensions; armed forces life insurance; rehabilitation, education, medical treatment of veterans; veterans' hospitals.

Source: Summarized from Rules of the House and Rules of the Senate. Reprinted from the public domain.

Reading 4.1

The Selection of Committee Members and Leaders

Charles S. Bullock III

In the following article, written expressly for this work, Charles Bullock, a noted authority on the assignment of members to committees, gives an overview of the selection of both committee members and leaders. This piece emphasizes the distinctive machinery used by each congressional party organization (House Democrats and Republicans; Senate Democrats and Republicans) for selecting members for committee service and leadership. The work also emphasizes the declining importance of seniority in committee leadership selection.

The most important event of most freshman legislators' first term occurs before they have been sworn in as members. Success in the committee assignment process, which is completed a month before a new Congress convenes, may determine the substantive orientation of a legislator's career, the legislator's job satisfaction, and conceivably even the newcomer's electoral success. Nonfreshmen can seek to improve their assignments when committee rosters are filled out before each Congress.

Each party in each chamber determines which of its members will serve on the 22 standing committees in the House and the 16 in the Senate. The first step in the assignment process is to determine the distribution of committee seats between parties. This is done through negotiations between party leaders. On most committees the distribution of Democrats to Republicans approximates the partisan composition of the chamber. Thus, during the 94th and 95th Congresses, when House Democrats outnumbered Republicans by two to one, Democrats held just over two-thirds of the seats on each committee. In the 99th Congress, in which Democrats constitute 58 percent of the House, their share of the seats on 17 committees is between 57 and 62 percent. The primary exceptions to the norm of proportionate representation are the House's most powerful and prestigious committees, on which the majority party traditionally has held an extraordinary majority regardless of the partisan division in the House,[1] and the ethics committee, on which the parties have equal representation. Little variation exists in Senate committee party ratios, with all committees in the 99th Senate having a one- or two-vote Republican majority.

Source: Prepared especially for this volume, and updated for the second edition. The author wishes to express his appreciation of the helpful comments of James Campbell and Loch Johnson on an earlier draft of this paper.

ASSIGNMENT MACHINERY

House Democrats have given their Steering and Policy Committee responsibility for making committee assignments.[2] The makeup of the Steering Committee insures that all major groups can participate in filling committee vacancies. The committee is chaired by the party's leader (the Speaker when Democrats control the House, the Minority Leader if they are the minority party). Also on the committee are the Majority Leader (unless Democrats are in the minority), the chief party whip and the chair of the Democratic Caucus. Speaker Tip O'Neill (D-Mass.) has also included a Representative from the Black Caucus, the Women's Caucus, the freshman class, and several deputy Whips. In 1980, the chair of Rules and the chairs of the three committees having the greatest impact on the budget were added to the Steering Committee. States having a Democratic representative are divided into 12 regions, and each region selects a Representative to the Steering Committee. After the 1980 election, the Steering Committee was enlarged from 24 to 30; in 1985 there were 31 members. Eleven members belonged to the party leadership.

Committee assignments for *House Republicans* are handled by a separate Committee on Committees, which consists of one person from each state having a Republican in the House. The real decision making is done, however, by a subgroup known as the Executive Committee. The representatives of the states with the largest Republican delegations serve on the Executive Committee. The party leader, who chairs the committee, also appoints a representative for the freshman and sophomore classes as well as one person to represent the delegations of sets of states with fewer Republicans—i.e., states with one, two, and three Republicans in the House.

Senate Democrats use the Steering Committee, chaired by the party leader, to make assignments. *Republican Senators* receive their assignments from their Committee on Committees.

PROCEDURES

The seniority norm assures that incumbents can retain their previous assignments. While there are always some members who wish to transfer from one committee to another or to add an assignment to what they already hold, the bulk of the work of those responsible for making assignments involves placing freshmen in committee vacancies.

Freshmen are invited to submit their preferences. House Democrats have classified committees as major and nonmajor; they ask newcomers for their preferences in each group. Some freshmen submit a single request, a few voice none, and occasionally someone will give as many as 10 preferences. The most common practice, however, is to give three top preferences.

Applicants for appointments to popular committees may follow up their written requests with personal appeals to party leaders, members of the Committee on Committees, and the chair of the committee they seek. The dean of their delegation may endorse their request in a letter to the Committee on Committee members.

Candidates for each committee's vacancies are voted on separately. House Republicans conduct this process using a unique weighted voting procedure. Members on the Executive Committee have as many votes as there are Republicans in their state party delegation or the delegations they represent. Thus, in the 97th Congress, the vote of New York's Frank Horton was worth 15, that of Michigan's William Broomfield was worth 7. On the other committees responsible for making committee assignments, each member casts a single vote.

Applicants for seats on many committees outnumber the available slots; for a few committees, volunteers are rare. A generation ago senior members cornered the desirable positions, while the newly elected were often relegated to the committees that no one wanted. Now there is greater equity in the distribution of seats. No member gets seats on two highly desirable committees until every member of the party has at least one good assignment. The major exceptions are the Budget Committees which include several members from other money committees.

When matching applicants with vacancies, a number of factors are considered. Foremost are the preferences expressed by committee applicants. Most House freshmen are now appointed to one of the committees they have requested (Bullock, 1973; Shepsle, 1978).* This has been made easier by a gradual enlargement of the more desirable committees. Those who are disappointed and do not receive their first choice initially are frequently allowed to transfer to a more desirable committee within a few years (Shepsle, 1978). In addition to considering member preferences, those responsible for making assignments also attempt to (1) promote regional representation on most committees, (2) match up applicants' occupational backgrounds with vacancies, (3) accord an advantage to seniority when filling slots on the most prestigious committees, (4) see that women and blacks are distributed across a wide range of committees, (5) allow state party delegations to maintain seats on committees whose responsibilities are of great concern to the state, and (6) reward party loyalists. (Bullock, 1979, Smith and Deering, 1984, 240–43)

The committee rosters developed by a party's Committee on Committees are presented to the full membership of the party.[3] Occasionally, a disgruntled member will mount a successful challenge and get the party to award him the slot he wanted and overturn the Committee on Committees.

House members are generally limited to two standing committee assignments, of which one can be a major committee. Members of Appropriations, Rules, and Ways and Means usually have a single assignment. Those who are tapped to serve on the Standards of Official Conduct (Ethics) Committee or to take a rotating seat on the Budget Committee hold these seats in addition to their other assignments. In recent years Democrats have had to temporarily relax the two-assignment rule in order to find takers for seats on Judiciary. Senators are limited to three committees and eight subcommittees.

*Reference list in Endnotes.

COMMITTEE LEADERSHIP

The seniority norm, which protects the right of members to retain committee seats, is also the single most important determinant for leadership selection. Beginning with the Wilson Presidency and continuing until the mid-1970s, the member of the majority party who had the longest continuous tenure on a committee chaired it. The only exception was that no one could chair more than one committee. Therefore, if an individual was the most senior member of more than one committee, the second most senior member chaired the committee not preferred by the most senior member.

The selection of committee chairs has become less automatic. House and Senate Democrats now provide that each person nominated by the Steering Committee to chair a committee or serve as ranking minority member be approved by secret ballot. Except in 1974, when the chairmen of Armed Services, Banking, and Agriculture were defeated and in 1983, when the chair of Armed Services was again dethroned, the seniority norm has continued to guide the selection of House chairs. Senate Democrats and Republicans in both houses have never rejected the person in line, based on seniority, to chair a committee or serve as its ranking minority member. Nonetheless, the recent defeats have promoted greater responsiveness to party leaders and to rank-and-file committee members by other chairs.

Seniority has also played a large role in the choice of subcommittee chairs, at least since World War II (Wolanin, 1974). Subcommittee leaders used to be named by the chair of the full committee, but beginning in the 1970s, House Democrats authorized committee members to elect the chairs of their subcommittees.[4] While House subcommittee chairs are now elected, a constraint limits individual Democrats to chairing one subcommittee. Since there are approximately 140 subcommittees, more than half the members of the majority party chair a committee or subcommittee. Because of this limitation, it is often necessary to go far down a committee's seniority roster to find a subcommittee chair.

Reliance on seniority has been rejected several times in recent years. In 1979, three aspirants for subcommittee chairmanships were defeated by more liberal, less senior opponents. Two years earlier, the caucus stripped Bob Sikes (D-Fla.) of his long-held chairmanship of the Appropriations Military Construction Subcommittee following his reprimand for conflict of interest. In 1981 a subcommittee chair was replaced when his colleagues became critical of his performance.

In the House, seniority, although not inviolable, plays a major role in the choice of committee and subcommittee leaders. It is even more important in the Senate, where no chair has been rejected by the rank and file and where an individual can chair a full committee and up to two subcommittees.

Illustration 4.C.
Assignment of members to committee and procedures for electing committee chairman: The applicability of party rules.

As Charles Bullock emphasized, party rules govern the assignment of members to committees and the selection of committee leaders. The following excerpts from House Democratic and Republican rules detail the mechanics.

HOUSE DEMOCRATS

Committee Membership

Rule 11. Committee Ratios

Committee Ratio 3-2

Committee ratios should be established to create firm working majorities on each committee. In determining the ratio on the respective standing committees, the Speaker should provide for a minimum of three Democrats for each two Republicans.

Rule 12. Standing Committees—Membership Nominations

Steering and Policy Committee Nominates

A. The Steering and Policy Committee shall recommend to the Caucus nominees for membership to committees, one committee at a time, other than the Committee on Rules for which the Democratic nominee for Speaker, (or Speaker, as the case may be) shall have exclusive nominating authority.

Nomination by State Delegations

B. Upon a letter from a Member, signed by 50 percent or more of said Member's State Democratic Delegation, including said Member, said Member shall automatically be considered for nomination by the Steering and Policy Committee for the committee membership position to which said Member aspires. The Chairman of the Steering and Policy Committee shall see that such Member's name is placed in nomination. This provision shall not apply to nominations for the Committee on Rules.

Seniority Not Mandatory

C. Recommendations for committee posts need not necessarily follow seniority.

Non-Discrimination

D. In making nominations for committee assignments the Steering and Policy Committee shall not discriminate on the basis of prior occupation or profession.

Illustration 4.C. (continued)

Rule 13. Procedure for Electing Committee Members

Voting

A. Once recommendations are received from the Steering and Policy Committee, the Caucus shall vote, one committee at a time, on memberships, except as provided in the following section B.

Debate

B. Upon a demand supported by 10 or more Members, a separate vote, by secret ballot, shall be had on any member of a committee. If any such vote prevails, the Committee list of that particular committee shall be considered recommitted to the Steering and Policy Committee for the sole purpose of implementing the direction of the Caucus. Such demand, if made and properly supported, shall be debated for no more than 30 minutes with the time equally divided between proponents and opponents. If the Caucus and the Steering and Policy Committee are in disagreement after completion of the procedure herein provided, the Caucus may make final and complete disposition of the matter.

Timing

C. The Caucus shall take no action with respect to any committee nominations made by the Steering and Policy Committee at the start of a Congress until after the House has elected the Speaker and approved House Rules for such Congress.

Rule 14. Procedure for Electing Rules Committee Members

The Democratic nominee for Speaker (or Speaker, as the case may be) shall recommend to the Caucus nominees for membership to the committee on Rules. Debate and balloting on any such nomination shall be subject to the same provisions as apply to the nominations of Members of other committees, as set forth in Caucus Rule 13. If a majority of those present and voting reject any nominee for membership to the Committee on Rules, the Democratic nominee for Speaker (or Speaker, as the case may be) shall be entitled to submit new nominations until any such positions are filled.

Committee Chairmanships

Rule 20. Nomination and Election of Committee Chairmen

Nominations by Steering and Policy Committee

A. The Steering and Policy Committee shall nominate one Member of each standing committee, other than the Committee on Rules and the Budget Committee, for the position of chairman and such nominations need not necessarily follow seniority.

Additional Nominations

B. If the Member nominated by the Steering and Policy Committee is other than the immediately preceding chairman, or the ranking majority member, additional nominations shall be in order from the floor of the Caucus and election shall be in accord with the provisions of Caucus Rule 3A3. If a nominee was chairman of the Committee in question at the close of the preceding Congress, no other nominations shall be allowed and the Caucus shall vote by secret ballot to approve or disapprove that nominee alone. No debate shall be allowed unless requested by the nominee or a Member who wishes to speak in opposition to a nomination provided that the request to speak in opposition is supported by three or more Members. Debate on any nomination shall be limited to 30 minutes equally divided between proponents and opponents of that nominee, such time to be further extended only by a majority vote of the Caucus.

Illustration 4.C. (concluded)

Rejection and New Nominations	C. If a majority of those present and voting reject its nominee for chairman, the Steering and Policy Committee shall make a new nomination within 5 days. Five to ten days after the Steering and Policy Committee reports such new nominations, the Caucus shall meet to consider the new nominee of the Steering and Policy Committee and any additional nominations offered from the floor. With the exception of the Budget Committee, only Members who have been recommended for membership on the committee shall be eligible for nomination as chairman. Should additional nominations be made from the floor, the election shall be conducted in accord with Caucus Rule 3.

Source: Preamble and Rules of the House Democratic Caucus, 98th Congress, January 1983.

HOUSE REPUBLICAN COMMITTEE ON COMMITTEES

99th Congress

The Republican Committee on Committees, established by the Conference, consists of one Republican Member from each state having Republican representation in the House, one member elected by the 98th Class, and two Members elected by the 99th Class. The Republican leader serves as Chairman of the Committee, and the Republican Whip serves as ex officio Member of the Committee and its Executive Committee. Each Member of the Committee is empowered to cast the same number of votes as there are Republican representatives from the Member's state.

For the 99th Congress, the Conference authorized the Committee on Committees to:

- Recommend assignments of Republican Members to the Standing Committee of the House.
- Recommend Republican Members to serve as the ranking Members of the Standing Committees of the House. The Member so recommended by the Committee on Committees need not be the Member with the longest consecutive service on the Committee. The Conference votes on each recommendation separately by secret ballot.
- Recommend to the House of Representatives the Republican Members to fill any vacancies on the Standing Committees which occur during the 99th Congress.

Every state which has at least five elected Republican members will have one member representative on the Executive Committee on Committees. The voting strength of each Member of the Executive Committee is equal to the total number of Republican Members that Member represents on the Executive Committee, excluding the class representatives who have one vote each. Members who represent multi-state delegations are chosen by a caucus of each respective group whose delegation numbers are identical. In those instances where a given multi-state delegation has more than one representative on the Executive Committee, the voting strength of these Members is equally divided.

Source: Republican Conference Directory, U.S. House of Representatives.

Reading 4.2

The Anatomy of a Committee

Holbert N. Carroll

Each congressional committee, like its parent house, is a little society. In this selection, Carroll stresses this point and illustrates the divisions of labor and specialization that exist within congressional committees.

FORMAL AND EFFICIENT PARTS

Writers of books on American government generally appreciate the role of committees in the legislative process. The half dozen or so committee decisions required, the resulting decentralization and, in many instances, disintegration of leadership and power, the curious but often tragic consequences of the seniority system, the powerful influence of the committee chairmen, government by a multitude of little governments as Wilson so interestingly described it in 1885—all of these features have been properly stressed.

The tendency in following this textbook analysis, however, is to look upon committees primarily as institutions, as monolithic bodies of 30 or so men, bodies roughly equal in power and respect in the eyes of the House and men equally attentive to their duties. A committee, to use a distinction made famous by Bagehot in another situation, has its dignified, ornamental, or formal parts and its efficient parts.[1] An appreciation of this distinction, as well as certain other features of congressional committees, is essential for an understanding of the role of these little legislatures in foreign affairs.

Source: From Holbert N. Carroll, *The House of Representatives and Foreign Affairs*, rev. ed. (Boston: Little, Brown, 1966), pp. 27–28, 36–37.

The formal part of a committee consists of the chairman and the party majority, a part of the committee which usually sticks together on procedural matters. In short, the formal part of a committee consists of those who in theory supply the initiative and leadership. They may formally approve legislation in the committee and support it with their votes on the floor, but they do little of the real work. On occasion, though, the formal part of a committee may be the efficient part.

The efficient part of a committee consists of a core of members, usually only a handful of men representing both political parties. These men actively participate in the hearings, propose the amendments that are accepted, and shape the legislation. They write parts of the committee's report, or at least take the time to slant it to their satisfaction. The efficient element then takes the bill to the floor and fights for it. Their knowledge of the subjects within the committee's jurisdiction may be more specialized than that of the witnesses from the Executive Branch who appear before them. Department and agency heads and their top assistants are viewed as mere transitory figures by Representatives whose service extends over more than one Administration. More than one witness has been confounded by questions and observations drawn from the vast reservoir of knowledge gained by individual Congressmen over decades.

The efficient element of a committee is rarely composed of a majority of the members even though it must carry a majority with it. Probably less than 10 members of the 32-member Committee on Foreign Affairs, for example, persistently and actively participate in the deliberations of the group. Indeed, in some instances the efficient element may be just one person. This monologic situation is not unknown in subcommittees of the Appropriations Committee, where occasionally just one member has been present to take important testimony to overwhelm his less attentive colleagues.

The efficient part of a committee, moreover, may change from one piece of legislation to another as the interests of the members wax and wane. Each piece of legislation is in a class by itself. The efficient part of a committee, in sum, is the part which wields influence and power. The fruit of its efforts is embodied in statutes and not merely in bills. The men who compose it are the leaders who determine whether the House will play a responsible role in foreign affairs in its committee rooms, on the floor, and in conference committees.

SUMMARY

Ordinarily, a committee is regarded as an institution, as a corporate body with a unitary voice or, at most, majority and minority voices. A committee is in a sense an institution. The continuity provided by senior members who pass the biennial political tests, staff people who survive periodic turnovers of personnel, committee tradition, history, and prerogative—all these serve to bind human beings into a collective body. But beneath the surface, a committee is but a few men who make decisions, men who are blessed with no unique capacities beyond those given to other mortals, who deliberate in a very human, but intensely political environment, and who, like other men, are sometimes lazy and indifferent, overwhelmed with other business, or devoted to duty.

These committees work in jealous isolation from one another and compete for the foreign policy business of the House. Commonly, the scheme of the separation of powers maintained by checks and balances is discussed in terms of the judiciary, the President, and the Senate and the House. But the House of Representatives is afraid of its own power. A scheme of checks and balances has evolved throughout the House, and especially at the committee level. This scheme is not embodied in a clear theory but is nevertheless part of the fabric of the lower chamber. It aims at preventing the massive accumulation of power and decision anywhere in the House. Facets of the scheme include the weak position of party leaders in dealing with committees, the allotment of business among several committees, many of which work simultaneously and at cross-purposes in the same general area of foreign affairs, and the inheritance of committee leadership according to seniority.

Many other facets mark the scheme. Its ramifications penetrate to the Executive Branch. It is not uncommon for a congressional committee to develop intimate relations with leading pressure groups and with the agencies of the Executive Branch in which it has a special interest. The attachment may be sufficiently powerful to defy the best efforts of the President to coordinate and control the Executive Branch. The Committee on Foreign Affairs, for instance, enjoys a clientele relationship with the Department of State, but the foreign policy viewpoint they support may vary quite sharply from that emerging from another committee in deliberations with its clientele. The combination in foreign affairs may be quite weak in bucking the combination of the Department of Agriculture, farm groups, and the Committee on Agriculture or the combination of the shipping interests, the Maritime Administration, and the Committee on Merchant Marine and Fisheries.

Reading 4.3

Committee Decision-Making Processes

Richard F. Fenno, Jr.

Each congressional committee is a unique organism. This has been emphasized by Richard Fenno in Congressmen in Committees. *The following excerpts from that book capsulize Fenno's listing of variables that affect committee decision making and present his argument that different configurations of these variables lend to very different committee decision processes.*

Generalizations about congressional committees are numerous and familiar. The oldest and most familiar is Woodrow Wilson's book-length assertion that committees dominate congressional decision making. A corollary states that committees are autonomous units, which operate quite independently of such external influences as legislative party leaders, chamber majorities, and the President of the United States. Other staples of committee commentary hold: that members specialize in their committee's subject matter, and hence that each committee is the repository of legislative expertise within its jurisdiction; that committee decisions are usually accepted and ratified by the other members of the chamber; that committee chairmen can (and usually do) wield a great deal of influence over their committees. A broader generalization holds that Congress, and by extension its committees, is gradually losing policymaking influence to the Executive Branch.

Most of our empirical generalizations are of the same order. Each one is uttered as if it were equally applicable to all committees. And taken together, they convey the message that committees are similar. Our recent studies of individual committees have taught us, to the contrary, however, that committees are markedly different from one another. Indeed, as we shall show, committees differ in all the respects previously mentioned—their influence in congressional decision making, their autonomy, their success on the chamber floor, their expertise, the control exercised by their chairmen, and their domination by the Executive Branch. If such is—even partially—the case, the need for a new set of generalizations is obvious.

One immediate temptation, of course, is to scrap all our familiar generalizations in favor of a single statement asserting the uniqueness of each committee. But that is a counsel of despair; political scientists ought not to eschew the possibility of making limited comparisons before they have tried. This book should be read as one such effort—to describe and generalize about committee similarities and differences at a level somewhere between that which assumes committee uniformity and that which assumes committee uniqueness.

The need for a middle range of generalizations is not purely academic. Reform-minded members of Congress and citizen groups have also viewed committee operations from the perspectives of uniformity and/or uniqueness, and they have been as ill served by this outlook as the scholar. Every Congressman knows that committees are

Source: From Richard F. Fenno, Jr., *Congressmen in Committees* (Boston: Little, Brown, 1973), pp. xiii–xv, 1, 2, 15, 46, 47, 81.

dissimilar. Assertions to that effect are hard currency on Capitol Hill. "Committee behavior all depends on the chairman and every chairman, of course, is different." Or, "Committee behavior all depends on the subject matter, and every committee, of course, handles a different policy area." Why, then, when they prescribe committee reform, do Congressmen abandon their own wisdom and insist on applying every reform in equal dosages to every committee?

The answer may be partly intellectual in nature—that they cannot conceive of committee similarities and differences in such a way as to formulate a mixed strategy of reform. It is as if the practitioner were waiting for the student to equip him with a middle range of categories in which to think and make his prescriptions. Thus, the political scientist's search for explanation may be related to the reformer's search for change.

Our theme is, then, that committees differ from one another. And, we shall argue, they differ systematically. We shall examine their similarities and differences with respect to five variables—*member goals, environmental constraints, strategic premises, decision-making processes,* and *decisions.* We shall pursue the following line of argument. The members of each congressional committee have certain goals that they want to achieve through membership on a committee. If there is a high level of consensus on goals, they will organize their committee internally in ways that seem likely to aid them in achieving these individual goals.

However, each committee operates within a distinctive set of environmental constraints—most particularly the expectations of influential external groups. Committee members will, therefore, also organize their committee internally in ways that seem likely to satisfy the expectations of these groups that make up their environment. The members of each committee will develop strategies for accommodating the achievement of their individual goals to the satisfaction of key environmental expectations.

These strategies become the proximate premises on which each committee's internal decision-making processes are based.

Figure 4.3.1.
Analytic scheme for comparing committees.

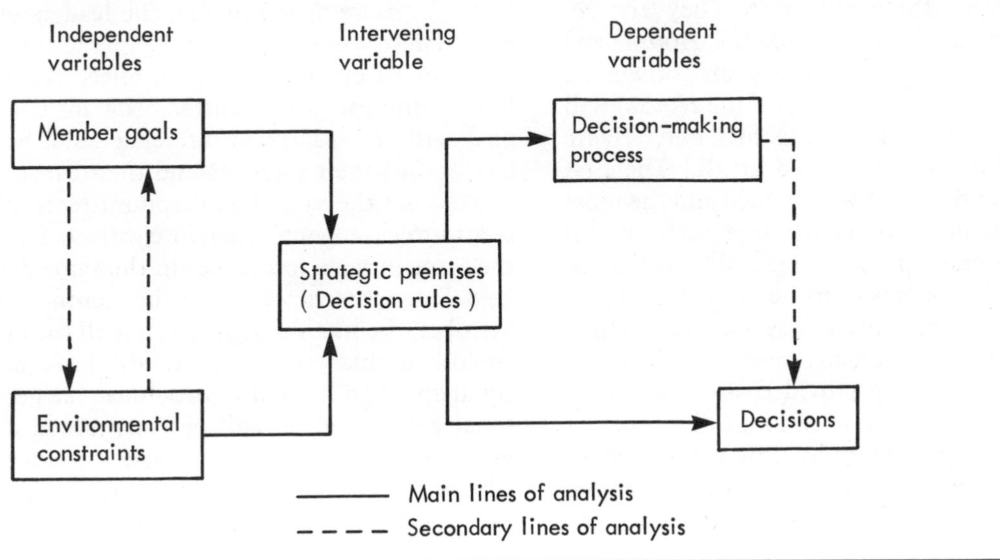

From these strategies, operationalized as decision rules, flow committee decisions. In our explanatory scheme, then, member goals and environmental constraints are the independent variables; strategic premises (or, decision rules) are an intervening variable; and decision-making processes and decisions are dependent variables.

MEMBER GOALS

A member of the House is a Congressman first and a committee member second. As a Congressman he holds certain personal political goals. As a committee member he will work to further these same goals through committee activity. Committee membership, in other words, is not an end in itself for the individuals. Each member of each committee wants his committee service to bring him some benefit in terms of goals he holds as an individual Congressman. And he will act on his committee in ways calculated to achieve such goals. We think it useful to begin our comparative analysis of committees here, by asking each member of each committee what it is he wants committee activity to do for him as a Congressman.

Of all the goals espoused by members of the House, three are basic. They are: *re-election, influence within the House,* and *good public policy.* There are others. A fourth one, *a career beyond the House*, will be treated peripherally. (A fifth one, *private gain*, will not be treated at all.) The first three are the most widely held and the most consequential for committee activity. All Congressmen probably hold all three goals. But each Congressman has his own mix of priorities and intensities—a mix which may, of course, change over time. If every House committee provided an equal opportunity to pursue re-election, influence, and policy, Congressmen holding various mixes would appear randomly distributed across all committees. Such is definitely not the case. The opportunity to achieve the three goals varies widely among committees. House members, therefore, match their individual patterns of aspiration to the diverse patterns of opportunity presented by House committees.

The matching process usually takes place as a Congressman seeks an original assignment or a transfer to a committee he believes well suited to his goals. But it may occur when a Congressman adjusts his personal aspirations, temporarily or permanently, to fit the opportunities offered by the committee where he happens to be. By a combination of processes, then, House committees come to be characterized, at any point in time, by distinctive, nonrandom distributions of individual member goals.

ENVIRONMENTAL CONSTRAINTS

Every House committee inhabits an environment in which committee nonmembers seek to persuade committee members to act in ways the nonmembers deem necessary or desirable. Of the various clusters of outsiders, the four most prominent are: members of the *parent House,* members of the *Executive Branch*, members of *clientele groups*, and members of the two major *political parties*—or, more operationally, the leaders of each. These four elements make up the environment of every House committee. Each has an interest in committee behavior coupled with a capacity to influence such behavior. But their interests and their capacities are not the same for all committees; all committees are not, therefore, affected by the same outside influences in the same degree. From this viewpoint of the committee member, the likelihood is that not all the elements of his environment will have an equal effect on his ability to achieve his personal goals. And he will be constrained to take into greater account those outsiders who are more likely to affect his goals than those who are less likely to do so.

STRATEGIC PREMISES

Once we know something about committee members' aspirations and something about the environment in which they must pursue these aspirations, we are almost ready to describe committee decision making. Almost, but not quite. It will help, we think, to understand the processes of decision making and the decisions themselves if we take an intermediary step and ask whether the members of each committee share any underlying guidelines for their decision making. Are there, in each committee, any agreed prescriptions for decision making—particularly any substantive decision rules—which might help us as we move to view the committee less as an aggregate of individuals and more as a working group?

Each member of each committee faces this strategic problem: How shall I proceed in the committee to achieve my personal goals, given the environmental context in which my committee operates? It is a problem very difficult to solve on a individualistic, every-man-for-himself basis. For the solution, we can now see, necessitates some fairly complicated accommodations between the desires of individual committee members on the one hand and the desires of the interested and influential groups that comprise the environment on the other. These accommodations require a degree of collective action, action which takes the form, mainly, of committee decision making. Our concern is to describe members' agreements on strategy that help to promote collective action and that, therefore, underlie the pattern of committee decisions. We call these agreements—designed to implement, through committee action, a given set of member goals in a given context of environmental constraints—the *strategic premises* of decision making.

Agreements on strategic premises take operational form as agreements on rules for making substantive decisions. In this chapter, we shall try to explicate these *decision rules* for each committee. The evidence may not always be persuasive. Committee members do not readily or easily articulate such agreements. They come closest when they discuss "the job of the committee," but Congressmen are notoriously formalistic and tongue-tied on that topic. Some decision rules are easier to discover than others; the wider the agreement and the more operationalized the rule, the easier to find. Every committee formulates—explicitly or implicitly—a few such rules. Indeed, it must. If a committee is to make hundreds of substantive decisions, it will need to simplify the task by developing standardized decision contexts and standardized responses to them.[1] As simplifying devices, a committee's decision rules will obviously influence its decision-making processes and its substantive decisions. Precisely what that influence will be depends on the strategic context in which a committee's rules get formulated.

DECISION-MAKING PROCESSES

Within certain constraining norms established by the House—norms which act as homogenizing influences—the members of each committee are free to devise whatever internal structure they wish. Accordingly they search for a structure that will help them implement their decision rules—especially as those rules reflect a strategy for achieving their personal goals. A committee will alter its internal structure when a solid majority of members feel that it no longer serves their objectives, provided only that they can agree on an alternative. No decision-making structure will completely satisfy all interested parties. At any point in time, therefore, a committee's structure is only an approximation of an arrangement that would give everyone everything he wants. So long as the members regard it as "good enough" or "satisfactory" or "better than any other practicable possibility," the internal structure displays a certain degree of stability. While the structure is stabilized, we can generalize about it and describe the committee's *normal decision-making process.* We can also describe incremental changes in that process. That is what we shall be doing in this chapter. Our description will focus on three important aspects of committee decision making. They are: *partisanship, participation-specialization,* and *leadership.*

As a prefatory note, however, we should remember that every committee's internal structure is bounded by certain formal and informal norms of the parent chamber. One homogenizing constraint comes indirectly from the congressional electorate, which decides at the polls which party shall control all House committees. Other constraints come directly from House rules. Some internal committee procedures—concerning meeting days, parliamentary practice, record keeping, and reporting, for example—are fixed by the House. Committee size and party ratios are set by the House and altered through time by amicable bargaining among the leaders of the two parties.

Illustration 4.D.
Factors related to policy decisions for six House committees.

In this table, Randall B. Ripley, utilizing the preceding Fenno framework, attempts to summarize the operation of six committees.

	Appropriations	Ways and Means	Foreign Affairs	Education and Labor	Post Office and Civil Service	Interior and Insular Affairs
Members' goals	Maximize influence in the House.	Maximize influence in the House.	Maximize influence in a given policy area.	Maximize influence in a given policy area.	Maximize chances of reelection to the House.	Maximize chances of reelection to the House.
Environmental constraints	Parent chamber coalitions led by executive branch agencies.	Parent chamber coalitions led by partisan clusters in the House and by executive branch agencies.	Coalitions led by Executive Branch agencies (mainly State Department and AID).	Coalitions led by partisan groups in and out of the House.	Coalitions led by clients (civil service unions; and 2d and 3d class mailers).	Coalitions led by clients (many and diverse).
Basic decision rules	1. Reduce executive budget requests. 2. Provide adequate funding for executive programs.	1. Write bills that will pass the House. 2. Allocate credit to majority party for policies adopted.	1. Approve and help pass the foreign aid bill.	1. Allocate credit to parties for policies adopted. 2. Pursue individual policy preferences regardless of partisan implications.	1. Support maximum pay increases and benefits for civil servants; and oppose all postal rate increases. 2. Accede to Executive Branch wishes if necessary to assure some pay and benefits increases.	1. Secure House passage of all constituency-supported, member-sponsored bills. 2. Balance the competing demands of conservationists and private users of land and water resources so as to give special benefits to users.

Source: Randall B. Ripley, *Congress: Process and Policy* (New York: W. W. Norton, 1978), p. 187. © 1978, W.W. Norton. Reprinted by permission. Adapted from Richard F. Fenno, Jr., *Congressmen in Committees* (Boston: Little, Brown, 1973).

Illustration 4.E.
A committee report.

Reprinted here from public domain are excerpts from a report to accompany S. 109, requiring reinstitution of registration for certain persons under the military Selective Services Act, and for other purposes. They illustrate the form and content of a committee report. Pages 157-158 contain a summary of the committee's recommendation and action, together with a precis of the bill; pp. 159-164 contain testimony and hearings; pp. 165-166 present the required information on budgetary impact; pp. 167-168 are the minority, dissenting views of a committee member; and p. 169 discusses changes in existing law.

Calendar No. 240

96TH CONGRESS } SENATE { REPORT
1st Session } { No. 96–226

REQUIRING REINSTITUTION OF REGISTRATION FOR CERTAIN PERSONS UNDER THE MILITARY SELECTIVE SERVICE ACT, AND FOR OTHER PURPOSES

JUNE 19 (legislative day, MAY 21), 1979.—Ordered to be printed

Mr. NUNN, from the Committee on Armed Services, submitted the following

REPORT

together with

ADDITIONAL AND MINORITY VIEWS

[To accompany S. 109]

The Committee on Armed Services, to which was referred the bill (S. 109) to require the reinstitution of procedures for the registration of certain persons under the Military Selective Service Act, and for other purposes, having considered the same, reports favorably thereon with an amendment in the nature of a substitute to the text of the bill and an amendment to the title of the bill and recommends that the bill as amended do pass.

COMMITTEE AMENDMENT IN THE FORM OF A SUBSTITUTE

The committee amended S. 109 by striking all after the enacting clause and substituting a new bill reflecting changes as recommended by the committee.

PURPOSE OF THE BILL

The bill reported by the committee would require the President to commence registration of male persons by January 2, 1980. After registration procedures have been reinstituted the President may suspend registration for the purpose of revising existing procedures or instituting new procedures, but only for a period of 90 days or less and no more than once in any one-year period.

The bill provides only for simple registration. All classification procedures would be suspended until January 1, 1981, unless the Pres-

Illustration 4.E. (continued)

ident determines it is in the national interest to conduct classification before that date.

The bill also requires the President to report, by July 1, 1980, to the Congress on categories for deferment and exemption, procedures to be followed for registration and classification, and any other proposed changes in the act. This report is to contain a certification that the Selective Service Act, including any proposed changes, is equitable and can meet military manpower needs.

The bill would also assign the supervision of manpower mobilization planning in the Department of Defense to the Undersecretary of Defense for Policy and require an assessment of manpower mobilization capabilities in the annual Manpower Requirements Report.

Committee Consideration

The Subcommittee on Manpower and Personnel held specific hearings on S. 109 and a similar bill (S. 226) on March 13 and May 21, 1979 and included testimony on the need for registration during hearings on overall manpower requirements on February 22, March 20 and 27, April 4, 9 and 10, 1979. It heard from a variety of witnesses representing the military and civilian leadership of the Armed Forces, a cross-section of representatives of military associations and from other individuals and organizations. In addition, the subcommittee as well as the full Armed Services Committee, has reviewed the issue of registration in other hearings this year and in the past. A summary of this testimony appears later in this report.

Basis for Committee Action

MOBILIZATION PROBLEMS

Testimony presented to the committee indicates that manpower problems in the event of mobilization are so severe that the Military Services are not now capable of meeting our national emergency requirements in terms of manpower. The Military Services are encountering increasing difficulty in recruiting sufficient manpower to meet active duty levels. The Selective Reserve—the units that would augment active military forces in a mobilization—are over 30,000 below authorized strength. According to testimony, the Individual Ready Reserve, the primary force of trained individuals for replacement and augmentation in emergencies, is 500,000 below mobilization levels for the Army alone. There are critical shortages of doctors and certain other skilled personnel in both active and reserve components.

If an emergency occurred, the Army indicates it would not have sufficient combat manpower in combat units. It would pull people out of units scheduled to deploy at later dates and use those people for individual augmentation and replacement earlier. Even so, according to Army Chief of Staff General Rogers: "We only have sufficient in there for a very small percentage of combat arms requirement. They would only last for "X" days but "X" is not a very large number of days." The Army would also plan to use personnel who were in inactive status but who had not yet completed their 6 years military obligation.

Illustration 4.E. (continued)

is certainly not required and, indeed, would be quite counterproductive. On the other hand, to be reasonably prepared and to have an adequate assessment of the availability of people, if indeed an emergency situation were to arise, it seems to me that a limited registration would be in order so that the availability of people would be in front of us. Time could be saved and it would not be necessary to find out while the emergency was going on, what the availability of the people that you wanted would be.

So it is my personal assessment that it would be sensible for us to consider and discuss a limited registration, not classification, but limited to registration only.

Asked to define what he meant by "limited registration", Secretary Alexander responded:

It would specifically mean accumulating information without a mass of details and without any significant inconvenience to the individuals who would be providing the information.

In answer to a question supplied for the record, Secretary Alexander explained why he felt registration is necessary:

Peacetime registration will permit the Army to meet its wartime manpower requirements much sooner than is possible with the current capability of the Selective Service System. The inadequate enlisted strength of the Individual Ready Reserve (IRR) places increased importance on the responsiveness of Selective Service to meet Army wartime manpower needs. The Selective Service System was phased to its current "deep standby" mode in FY 1977 and has the ability of delivering the first registrants for induction at M+110 days and 100,000 by M+150. The DOD stated requirement for all Services is delivery of the first inductees at M+30, 100,000 by M+60 and 650,000 by M+180. Recent analyses of the Army training establishment indicates that under future emergency conditions the Army could be able to accept 184,000 new trainees by M+60 and 568,000 by M+180. Peacetime registration will assume the availability of the first inductees by M+15, more than 100,000 by M+60 and 650,000 before M+180 days. Although establishing peacetime Selective Service registration will not eliminate the Army's total mobilization manpower deficit or even influence the manpower shortfall in the first 90 days, it will shorten the time of availability to the deployed units of the first newly trained inductees from M+210 to M+110 days.

General Alexander M. Haig, Jr., Supreme Allied Commander, Europe, Commander-in-Chief, U.S. European Command

General Haig, in testimony before the Manpower and Personnel Subcommittee on February 22, 1979, expressed his concerns with the current All-Volunteer Force and possible remedies and stated,

Illustration 4.E. (continued)

> Today I think we need a system of registration, and I would support also, given what we know already, a classification system. Beyond that, we have to look immediately to what is necessary to remedy our shortfalls in the Reserve structure, especially in the Individual Ready Reserve.
>
> As we proceed along those lines, we will require additional empirical data, which should be shared with the American people and the American Congress. If that data shows, as I suspect it will, that early in the eighties we will have to go beyond reserve remedies and into actual structure itself, we will have already developed the consensus that can be supported enthusiastically by the American people or at least without active opposition.

Addressing the subject of national service, General Haig said, his personal feeling is,

> * * * that a young citizen of our Nation should be raised and nurtured in the context of some obligation of service to his Nation in either the military service or some form of Federal service for a brief period of time. It would be hard to judge what impact the all volunteer structure has had on our citizens' sense of obligation, but I think it could be ascertained there must be some.

Admiral Harry D. Train, Commander-in-Chief, Atlantic

Admiral Train, appearing before the Manpower and Personnel Subcommittee on February 22, 1979, was asked whether registration and classification would have an impact on the Navy's manpower problems. He responded:

> I agree with General Haig that it is important that, if we have to resort to this device to man our ships, to fill out our fighting structure, that we at least know where the people are that we would call into the service.
>
> In the past, the impact of the draft, as people were being drafted into the Army, had a beneficial impact on the Navy, people would enlist in the Navy rather than be drafted into the Army. Whether that would prevail today or not, I don't know.

General Bernard W. Rogers, Chief of Staff, U.S. Army
Admiral Thomas B. Hayward, Chief of Naval Operations
General Lew Allen, Jr., Chief of Staff, U.S. Air Force
General Louis H. Wilson, Commandant, U.S. Marine Corps

The four chiefs of the military Services appeared together at a hearing of the Manpower and Personnel Subcommittee on March 13, 1979, and testified on the need for the reinstitution of registration procedures.

The witnesses all acknowledged that the Nifty Nugget mobilization exercise indicated that the Services are not now capable of meeting U.S. national emergency requirements.

Illustration 4.E. (continued)

Asked if it is now necessary to reinstitute registration the replies were as follows:

> General ROGERS. As a minimum, we should to go registration just as soon as we can.
>
> General ALLEN. Yes sir . . . the act of registration, while not needed for us in the same way that it is for the Army, would doubtless benefit the ability to recruit. I support registration and limited classification.
>
> Admiral HAYWARD. I am convinced that registration is a logical and sensible thing to do.
>
> General WILSON. I believe that registration is absolutely necessary.

Generals Wilson and Allen and Admiral Hayward were also asked whether they favored classification. Their responses were as follows:

> General WILSON. Yes, sir. I think classification is a follow-on to registration, and should also include examination. I think examination should probably come first—medical examination, and full classification in that order. Registration, examination, and classification in that order, depending again on the administrative difficulties involved. It is going to be difficult to start up again.
>
> General ALLEN. There are certain steps of classification that can be done with very little cost or administrative difficulty associated with registration. The first big charge, as I understand it, comes up with respect to physical examination. I believe that limited classification should certainly be done as part of registration. And I am, frankly, unsure in the matter of weighing expense against benefit as we get into the physical examination question.
>
> Admiral HAYWARD. I believe that if your legislation were to call for registration that the time required to get the mechanism moving and to be effective in registering would allow us more time in determining whether the next step ought to be medical and classification. There is a cost to that and one ought to do it, in my opinion, in conjunction with a decision to go to the draft for the IRR. If a decision is not to go in that direction, then I am not so sure that I can say now that we ought to make that investment in classification.

Asked if reinstitution of registration should include women, the witnesses stated:

> General ROGERS. Women should be required to register in order for us to have an inventory of what the available strength is within the military qualified pool in this country.
>
> General ALLEN. My personal opinion is yes, sir. I think that the importance, with regard to the inventory, is not nearly the same for women as it is for men. Therefore, I would not believe that registration for women is essential. However, if there were feelings of equal treatment that would make the act of registration more acceptable, if it were done the same for men and women, then I would have no objection to the registration of women.

Illustration 4.E. (continued)

Admiral HAYWARD. I concur almost exactly with what General Allen has said. In my judgment, the requirement for large numbers of women for mobilization purposes, hence registration, is not there. If it were intended to accelerate our ability to mobilize, I would not support a requirement for registration of women nearly to the degree that I could male registration. It seems to me the issue really is a political decision more than a military requirement decision.

General WILSON. Yes. I believe they should be registered. I think from a pure equitable point of view, women in the Marine Corps are doing very well.

Asked whether the witnesses would be in favor of women being drafted for the purposes for which women are used today, they responded:

General ROGERS. I am not prepared to agree that they should be drafted as of today, even for those skills for which they are today being utilized. But if they are to be drafted, they should only be drafted for those skills for which they are being utilized today.

General ALLEN. As far as the Air Force is concerned, the argument as to whether women should or should not be included in the draft is a deferral to the Army, which has a different kind of problem, or is a question of equity, on which I am really not prepared to voice an opinion. It would not have any unfavorable effect on the Air Force. We would have no objection to such a draft.

Admiral HAYWARD. From a military point of view, there is no need for drafting women into the U.S. Navy. From the standpoint of equity, it seems to me as though that really is a political decision rather than a military decision.

General WILSON. I believe that we can meet our goal satisfactorily. From an equitable point of view, or perhaps as a result of the inevitable court contest which will come up if, in fact, men and not women are drafted, we would be perfectly happy to have women drafted. That is, up to the 5 percent goal which I believe we can handle in the Marine Corps.

The witnesses were asked if they would be in favor of this session of Congress reinstituting the draft and they replied:

General WILSON. I believe the draft is necessary. I believe it will be necessary in the decade of the 1980's. At the moment I believe registration should come first.

Admiral HAYWARD. I am not in favor of this session of Congress reinstituting the draft.

General ALLEN. I am not in favor of this session of Congress reinstituting the draft.

General ROGERS. If this session of Congress could reinstitute the draft, I would be in favor of it. I believe that we already are behind the timetable that I would like to have seen to reinstitute registration. I personally believe, that there is nothing that we have underway now or anything on the horizon which will solve the problem of the Individual Ready Reserve, ex-

Illustration 4.E. (continued)

Asked if the ACLU would endorse the computerization and use of Internal Revenue Service and Social Security names in order to avoid going to a registration, Mr. Landau answered:

> If we are in an emergency, if we were in a declared war situation like World War II, we would not object to the use of data matching IRS and Social Security files. We do object to the use of it in peacetime. We think that would be a gross abuse of personal privacy.

Reverend Milton Zimmerman, Hutterian Society of Brothers

> The Hutterian Society of Brothers requests that any change to the Military Selective Service Act provide for continuation of the conscientious objector status, reviewed by civilian authorities, in return for civilian service, and exclude registration and drafting of women.

Ms. Melva Mueller, Executive Director,
Women's International League for Peace and Freedom

The Women's International League for Peace and Freedom objects to registration or conscription of either men or women. They see conscription "as incompatible with fundamental American values negating as it does freedom of choice for the draftees, interrupting his or her work, education or family life." They believe peacetime conscription is unconstitutional and object to the use of Social Security, school records and Internal Revenue Service records to facilitate registration on the grounds it threatens the right of privacy. They advocate a full examination of our military manpower requirements before any action on registration or conscription takes place.

C. A. (Mack) McKinney, Staff
Director, Non-Commissioned Officers Association

"The Non-Commissioned Officers Association believes there is a necessity not only to register our young men, but to induct them into the reserve and guard in order that this Nation, as well as they, are prepared for any wartime emergency." They suggest that women not be included in a draft proposal because of the need for trained combat soldiers.

James E. Bristol, Staff Member,
Friends Committee on National Legislation

The Friends Committee on National Legislation "opposes draft registration as unnecessary and as a first step toward reactivation of the military draft in the United States." They oppose conscription "because it is an integral part of the war system, whose ultimate intent is the destruction of human life. This is deeply abhorrent to our religious values."

Illustration 4.E. (continued)

Lieutenant General Edward C. Meyer, Nominated to be Chief of Staff of the Army

Lieutenant General Meyer, during his nomination hearing to be Chief of Staff of the Army on June 7, 1979, expressed his views on registration as follows:

> I support registration and believe there is some work that has to be done on the Selective Service Act to insure that when we register young people we know what we are registering them for.

Asked how long it would take today, in the event of a national emergency, to process personnel and provide people in new units to bolster our forces, General Meyer responded:

> It would take a minimum of 210 days to get manned, started and turning out the first trained draftees with the current system.

Asked whether he believed there was any military or national security reason to register women General Meyer said:

> It would seem to me that from a purely military point of view, a cataloguing of assets, which is what registration is, is helpful, and therefore, a cataloguing of male and female assets, with a clear understanding that they need never be called, would be useful.

General Meyer was then asked his feelings on calling women in a draft situation and he replied:

> I think that would be a last resort issue involving the survival of this Nation. As you are focusing on the survival of the Nation, knowing where all the available assets are and having them registered makes sense. But calling them up is something that I think you would have to have a national consensus on. That is beyond my military ken.

General Meyer next was asked if he could foresee any scenario under which women would need to be called in a draft situation. He responded, "I cannot, sir.". He was then asked if that were the case, if he did not consider it to be a waste to go through the process of registering and classifying women if there is no intention to use them in a draft situation. He responded, "There is some waste. You said, can I visualize a reasonable scenario? No! Are there scenarios that are unreasonable, but possible? Perhaps—if you had an all-out nuclear exchange, where you really had to know, as best you could, what was left and where people were."

COMMITTEE ACTION

In accordance with the Legislative Reorganization Act of 1946, as amended by the Legislative Reorganization Act of 1970, there is set forth below the committee vote to favorably report this bill, S. 109, as amended.

In favor: Senators Stennis, Jackson, Cannon, Byrd of Virginia, Nunn, Morgan, Tower, Thurmond, Goldwater, Warner, Humphrey, and Jepsen.

Opposed: Senators Culver, Hart, Exon, Levin and Cohen.

Vote: 12–5.

Illustration 4.E. (continued)

Regulatory Impact

Paragraph 5 of rule XXIX of the Standing Rules of the Senate requires that a report on the regulatory impact of a bill be included in the report on such bill. S. 109 as amended requires the registration of 18–26 year old men commencing January 2, 1980, in the manner prescribed by the President. Evaluation of the regulatory impact of the bill is not possible at this time, since the bill requires a complete reexamination of classification and examination, as well as other procedures under the Military Selective Service Act.

Congressional Budget Office Cost Estimate

Congressional Budget Office,
U.S. Congress,
Washington, D.C., June 14, 1979.

Hon. John C. Stennis,
Chairman, Committee on Armed Services,
U.S. Senate, Washington, D.C.

Dear Mr. Chairman: Pursuant to section 403 of the Congressional Budget Act of 1974, the Congressional Budget Office has prepared the attached cost estimate for S. 109, a bill to require the reinstitution of registration of certain persons under the Military Selective Service Act.

Should the committee so desire, we would be pleased to provide further details on this cost estimate.

Sincerely,

James Blum
(For Alice M. Rivlin, Director).

Congressional Budget Office Cost Estimate

1. Bill number: S. 109.
2. Bill title: A bill to require the reinstitution of registration of certain persons under the Military Selective Service Act, and for other purposes.
3. Bill status: As ordered reported by the Senate Committee on Armed Services on June 11, 1979.
4. Bill purpose: The bill requires the President to commence registration of citizens and other persons in accordance with the provisions of the Military Selective Service Act on January 2, 1980. It limits the authority of the President to suspend registration and prohibits, prior to January 1, 1981, the classification and examination of persons pursuant to the Act. The bill has other provisions that do not have a cost impact.
5. Cost estimate:

Estimated authorization amounts and estimated outlays:

Fiscal year:	*Millions*
1980	$6
1981	7
1982	7
1983	8
1984	8

Illustration 4.E. (continued)

The costs of this bill fall within function 050.

6. Basis of estimate: The estimate is based on implementation plans of the administration and assumes that it registers individuals as required by the bill but does not conduct classification or examination procedures even after the date permitted in the bill. This assumption is made because it is neither the intent of the bill nor the policy of the administration to classify or examine individuals under the act.

7. Estimate comparison: The administration has estimated the costs of "nonemergency" registration to be $6 to $8 million annually for ongoing operations but not including start-up costs.

8. Previous CBO estimate: The cost of this bill could be about $4 million in 1980 increasing to about $5 million in 1984 if another implementation plan were used. For example, the bill could be implemented using existing field structures such as the Federal Postal System and computerized files of the Internal Revenue Service or Social Security Administration instead of expanding or creating new structures to gather data and administer the program. The CBO budget issue paper entitled "The Selective Service System: Mobilization Capabilities and Options for Improvement" contains further discussion of this issue.

9. Estimate prepared by: Michael A. Miller (225–4844).

10. Estimate approved by:

James Blum,
Assistant Director for Budget Analysis.

Illustration 4.E. (continued)

MINORITY VIEWS OF MR. LEVIN

I oppose the bill to re-institute registration under the Military Selective Service Act because the measure is unnecessary, premature and inequitable to both men and women. It also rests on insufficient examination of our mobilization and Selective Service requirements.

While many people, including myself, believe that we would have a mobilization problem in an emergency, the case has not been made out for *registration* as the only or best way of solving that problem.

For instance, the Secretary of Defense has written in a letter dated June 8, 1979, to Senator Cohen that "We are concerned that the Selective Service System cannot now meet the thirty-day requirement."

But that same Secretary of Defense, in that same letter, clearly opposes registration in the following words: "That circumstance does not, however, lead to the conclusion that peacetime registration is necessary. In the near term, we think that the proper course of action is to enhance the standby ability of the Selective Service System, including its computer resources, its staffing and its planning."

The Secretary of Defense noted in that same letter that Acting Selective Service Director Robert E. Shuck "is confident that, if adequate funds are provided by the Congress, the Selective Service System will be able to develop the capability to meet our requirements."

While the Armed Services Committee and its Manpower and Personnel Subcommittee, in split votes, voted for registration, their actions were flawed by a failure to call as witnesses Secretary Brown or Acting Director Shuck to testify relative to the Administration's conclusion that our mobilization problem can be solved by enhanced computer capability.

Nor did the Manpower and Personnel Subcommittee or the Armed Services Committee make a specific analysis of the costs of enhanced computer capability, staffing and planning, as compared to the costs of a registration system. It is also significant that the Committee failed to make a specific analysis of the relative advantages and disadvantages of the different mobilization times under the two approaches. In this regard, the Secretary of Defense said in that same letter that the need is to "begin receiving inductees . . . beginning thirty days after a decision to mobilize" and that "the Selective Service System will be able to develop the capability to meet our requirements" according to Acting Director Shuck "if adequate funds are provided by the Congress."

The registration bill would remove from the President the option and the power he now has to institute registration. This bill would, instead, mandate the President to do so.

Thus the bill would undertake the major step of mandatory registration, without giving the President the chance to prove that his alternative approach would work.

Illustration 4.E. (continued)

The President has asked for this chance in the Fiscal 1979 and 1980 budgets. To require registration before giving the President the tools which he believes would work adequately to avoid it is a mistake this Senate need not, and should not, make.

Congress should promptly provide the funding needed by the President so that he can fully explore the alternative which the Secretary of Defense and the Acting Director of Selective Service say will work to avoid a registration system.

Also, before considering the reinstitution of registration under a standby draft system characterized by unfairness to the less-affluent and less educated segments of our citizenry, we should close the "loopholes" in the system which have permitted these inequities.

We should no longer allow a standby draft system which permits the rich and well-educated of our country to avoid military service through deferments and exemptions and which forces, thereby, the brunt of the nation's defense to be borne by the disadvantaged.

The Committee, in its own report on this legislation, recognizes the problems of unfairness inherent in the present law by stating:

"However, the committee believes that the categories and standards for exemption and deferment and the procedures under current law must be completely reviewed. The Selective Service System should be equitable and fair and the committee feels that deferment and exemption categories should be limited to conscientious objectors, those morally, mentally and physically unfit and only such other categories that the President believes are necessary in the national interest."

Indeed, this is why, in part, the Committee bill suspends classification for one year after registration is re-instituted and requires the President to recommend any changes to the registration/classification procedures and to certify that the act is equitable by July 1, 1980.

The Selective Service System should be revamped during which time the enhanced data processing option can be fully tested. In the meantime, we should avoid the spectre of the outdated and unfair draft system which is one reason registration is so disturbing to people across this land.

Finally, in focusing their attention on the mobilization dilemma, and in suggesting registration as the solution to it, the Committee has attempted to address certain manpower problems which affect our armed forces, such as the shortages in selected critical skills areas and shortfalls in the reserves.

Yet even proponents of the bill concede that there is no factual basis for a claim that re-instituting registration will help eliminate these shortages and shortfalls.

Thus, the Committee's recommendation to re-institute registration is inappropriate on these grounds, also.

CARL LEVIN.

Illustration 4.E. (concluded)

CHANGES IN EXISTING LAW

In compliance with paragraph 4 of rule XXIX of the Standing Rules of the Senate, changes in existing law proposed to be made by the bill are shown as follows: Existing law to be omitted is enclosed in black brackets, new matter is printed in italic, and existing law in which no change is proposed is shown in roman.

TITLE 10, UNITED STATES CODE—ARMED SERVICES

* * * * * * *

Subtitle A—General Military Law

* * * * * * *

CHAPTER 4.—DEPARTMENT OF DEFENSE

* * * * * * *

§ 135. Under Secretaries of Defense: appointment; powers and duties; precedence

(a) There are two Under Secretaries of Defense, one of whom shall be the Under Secretary of Defense for Policy and one of whom shall be the Under Secretary of Defense for Research and Engineering. The Under Secretaries of Defense shall be appointed from civilian life by the President, by and with the advice and consent of the Senate. A person may not be appointed Under Secretary of Defense for Policy within ten years after relief from active duty as a commissioned officer of a regular component of an armed force.

(b) [The Under Secretary of Defense for Policy shall perform such duties and exercise such powers as the Secretary of Defense may prescribe.] *The Under Secretary of Defense for Policy shall supervise manpower mobilization planning in the Department of Defense and shall perform such other duties and exercise such other powers as the Secretary of Defense may prescribe.* The Under Secretary of Defense for Research and Engineering shall perform such duties relating to research and engineering as the Secretary of Defense may prescribe, including—

(1) being the principal adviser to the Secretary on scientific and technical matters;

(2) supervising all research and engineering activities in the Department of Defense; and

(3) directing, controlling, assigning, and reassigning research and engineering activities that the Secretary considers need centralized management.

(c) The Under Secretary of Defense for Policy takes precedence in the Department of Defense after the Secretary of Defense, the Deputy Secretary of Defense, and the Secretaries of the military departments. The Under Secretary of Defense for Research and Engineering takes precedence in the Department of Defense immediately after the Under Secretary of Defense for Policy.

* * * * * * *

Reading 4.4

Subcommittees and Committee Decision making

Steven S. Smith and Christopher J. Deering

Subcommittee government is a major characteristic of the contemporary Congress. There are more and more such work groups in the Congress, doing more and more legislating and other legislative work. The following selected extract from a recent, authoritative statement on the congressional committee system documents this recent proliferation of subcommittees, specifying the forces and factors that have stimulated their growth. In other sections of their book, Smith and Deering present two other important points to be kept in mind about subcommittee government. First, subcommittee decision process and influence varies by both House and Senate and by the power structure of the parent committee. Second, how subcommittees make policy also reflects the nature of the issues and policies they deal with.

Despite the variety of decision-making patterns in congressional committees, "subcommittee government" has replaced "committee government" as the term most frequently used to characterize the nature of congressional decision making.[1] Subcommittee government is said to exist, according to one definition,

> when the basic responsibility for the bulk of legislative activity (hearings, debates, legislative markups, that is, the basic writing of a bill) occurs, not at a meeting of an entire standing committee, but at a meeting of a smaller subcommittee of the standing committee. The decisions of the subcommittee are then viewed as the authoritative decisions—decisions that are altered by the standing committee only when the subcommittee is seriously divided or when it is viewed as highly unrepresentative of the full committee.[2]

The term subcommittee government has been applied broadly—to both chambers and to most committees.[3] In this and the following two chapters, committee structure, activities, leadership, and staff are examined to determine the degree to which committee decision-making processes approximate subcommittee government. The argument is that, while generalizations about subcommittee government capture the direction of change in congressional decision making, they tend to oversimplify patterns of committee behavior and to overstate the degree to which many committees have changed during the past 15 years. Even House committees, which experienced externally imposed procedural reforms, reacted in a number of ways, and Senate committees retained the great variety that was present in the late 1960s.

Modal decision-making patterns of the House and the Senate were reflected in the manner in which the House Energy and Commerce Committee and the Senate Energy and Natural Resources Committee handled legislation in 1983 to decontrol natural gas prices. In the House, Energy and Commerce's Subcommittee on Fossil and Synthetic Fuels held a lengthy series of hearings and markup sessions before sending the legislation to the full committee. Thus two battlefields existed for this highly divisive legislation because losers in the subcommit-

Source: From Steven S. Smith and Christopher J. Deering, *Committees in Congress*, pp. 125–34.

tee would wage another battle at the full committee level. The split-level nature of participants' strategies in the House was reflected in an exchange between two staff assistants about a proposal offered by the subcommittee chairman, Democrat Philip R. Sharp of Indiana.

> As Nancy Williams of Sharp's staff began explaining the proposal section by section, she was questioned by Roy Willis, legislative assistant to Democrat W. J. "Billy" Tauzin of Louisiana, the No. 1 gas-producing state in the country.
>
> "You call this a compromise?" asked Willis, whose boss had co-sponsored the Reagan administration's bill to decontrol all natural gas prices by 1986, a concept that was not part of Sharp's committee draft. "There is nothing in it for us at all. But that's all right; we'll deal with *you* in the subcommittee."
>
> "Well, Roy," responded Williams, according to the recollections of others in the room that day, "we'll handle *you* in the full committee."[4]

In contrast, the Senate committee held all of its hearings and markups in full committee, a practice far different from what was typical in the same committee in the late 1960s.

THE STRUCTURE OF CONGRESSIONAL COMMITTEES

Both the nature of committee structure and the location of effective member participation in decisionmaking are essential ingredients of subcommittee government. In this case, structure refers to the number and composition of subcommittees, and the location of effective participation concerns full committee versus subcommittee activity. As Chapter 2 outlined, House reforms directly affected both structure and participation by forcing the creation of at least four subcommittees on most committees and giving those subcommittees the authority and resources to conduct investigations and to write legislation. Senate reforms did neither directly. Indeed, by limiting subcommittee memberships the 1977 reforms indirectly reduced the number of Senate subcommittees.[5]

SUBCOMMITTEE GROWTH

As noted in Chapters 1 and 2, the number of subcommittees in both chambers increased dramatically during the 1950s and 1960s. Subcommittees were almost as difficult to eliminate as committees had been in the nineteenth century. When subcommittees were challenged—a rare occurrence—their defenders often devised ingenious responses to protect positions they found to be valuable. One such instance stands out. In 1967 Republican Sen. Everett M. Dirksen of Illinois, one of the few minority party members permitted to chair a subcommittee after the 1946 reorganization, sought a $7,500 authorization from the Senate for his subcommittee's only employee. He was challenged by conservative Democrat Allen J. Ellender of Louisiana, who took the opportunity to question the need for the subcommittee itself:

> As I recall, that committee has 16 subcommittees, almost one for each member of the committee. I cannot for the life of me understand why legislation pertaining to Federal charters, holidays and celebrations could not be handled by the full Committee on the Judiciary.[6]

Senator Dirksen, who was known for his sharp wit and his deliberate, mellifluous speech, defended his subcommittee and its activities:

> Mr. President, in the first place, I am against disposing of this subcommittee, and the most important reason that I can assign is that I am the chairman. I want no legislative throatcutting here. . . . I have been the chairman or a member of this subcommittee for so long that the memory of man runneth not to the contrary. You are not going to do this to me, are you, and destroy my one and only chairmanship? Why, that is discrimination. . . .
>
> The second reason, Mr. President, is that I am a stickler for tradition. . . . I have to let the Senate in on a little secret. Once upon a time there was a distinguished member of

> this body by the name of William Langer, from North Dakota, and at the time he was ranking Republican member on the Committee on the Judiciary. The distinguished chairman was the Honorable Pat McCarran of Nevada. I recall the day when Senator Langer went to Senator McCarran and said: "There is no justice. There ought to be at least one Republican chairman of one subcommittee on Judiciary." And Senator McCarran, with all the grace and all the generosity in his soul, said: "You are on and you are it. You name the subcommittee that you want." And Senator Langer said: "I'll take Charters, Holidays, and Celebrations."
>
> That is how that subcommittee came into being. It was an absolute, unadulterated, unmitigated, unrefined, unconfined deal. But I did not make the deal. I am only the inheritor of the deal. And I do not want my inheritance destroyed since I came by it very honestly. So you see, this is in the great tradition.
>
> The third reason I assign is that I think this is probably the most important subcommittee in the Senate of the United States. Just think of the question of charters that we have to pass on . . . in due course there may be organizations like the Sons of Rest or the Association of Indigent Senators, or what have you, and maybe they want a federal charter, and if they do, they march up to my subcommittee door and they get good attention. So you see, this is an important subcommittee, because it involves a lot of people. . . .
>
> So, do not destroy this little subcommittee of two men and do not destroy this responsibility of the chairman of this little subcommittee. . . . I stand here today to protect this little subcommittee, and lay no profane hand on it because it will be a charge on your conscience.[7]

Dirksen's position was supported by a voice vote.

The House nevertheless has managed to halt the proliferation of subcommittees in recent Congresses and, in the case of three committees, to trim the number of subcommittees. Once we exclude Ways and Means' subcommittees, which were not created until after the 1974 reforms, and the two new standing committees, the number of standing subcommittees in the House actually fell from 120 to 118 between 1973 and 1983. This is partly the result of the cap on subcommittees adopted by House Democrats in 1981. The caucus rule provides that, except for Appropriations, standing committees are limited to eight subcommittees; committees with more than 35 members and fewer than six subcommittees may increase the number to six or, with Steering and Policy Committee approval, may have seven subcommittees. Agriculture and Banking reduced the number of their subcommittees in order to meet the eight-subcommittee limit. Education and Labor was forced to disband its Task Force on Welfare and Pension Plans to comply with the limit because the rule explicitly counted task forces and other special subunits as subcommittees. No incumbent subcommittee chair was forced to give up a chair, although three members in line for a chair could not assume one. The effect of the cap was that no House committee increased its number of subcommittees at the start of the 97th or 98th Congresses, the first Congresses in which that had happened since 1947. And the average number of subcommittee assignments per member dropped back to about 3.5 after exceeding 4 subcommittees per member in 1975–1976. The House, then, has an effective floor under the number of subcommittees set by chamber rules and a ceiling on the number of subcommittees set by majority party caucus rules. This has homogenized House committee structure: nearly 70 percent of standing committees had between six and eight subcommittees in 1983.

Despite its 1977 attempt at control, the Senate may be repeating its pattern of incrementally adding subcommittees. The number of Senate subcommittees on standing committees fell from 127 to 90 between 1973 and 1979, a result of the 1977 limits on the number of subcommittee assignments and chairs senators could hold. The mean number of subcommittee assignments per senator also dropped from nearly 10 to just under 7. But when the Republicans gained control of the Senate in 1981, they increased

Figure 4.4.1.
Distribution of subcommittee assignments on standing committees among senators, 1977 and 1983

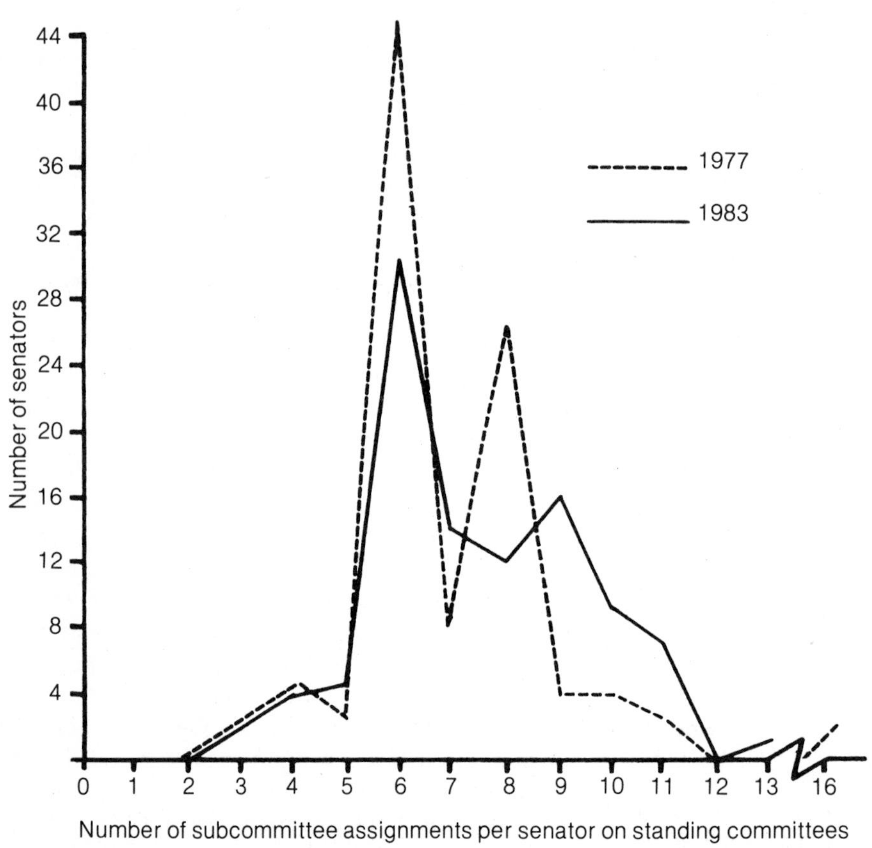

Source: *Congressional Staff Directory* (Mount Vernon, Va.: Congressional Staff Directory, Ltd., 1977, 1983).

the number of subcommittees by two on Judiciary and by one on Commerce. Commerce and Small Business each added a subcommittee two years later when Banking also added two subcommittees—giving Banking more subcommittees than it has had at any time since 1949. The average number of subcommittees per member also began to creep back up, increasing by nearly half-a-seat per member between 1977 and 1983. The change is seen in Figure 4.4.1. In 1977 nearly 80 percent of senators had between six and eight subcommittee assignments on standing committees. The distribution reflects that year's reforms, which limited most senators to three subcommittees on each of two major committees and to two subcommittees on the minor committee on which they served. By 1983 senators regularly were ignoring the 1977 limits; in fact, the number of senators serving on more than eight subcommittees nearly tripled to 32 by 1983.

The Senate retains far greater variation in committee structure than does the House because of the absence of an explicit floor or ceiling for the number of Senate subcommittees. The Senate has had more committees with a large number of subcommittees and more committees with few subcommittees than has the House. In the 98th Congress, for example, the average number of subcommittees per committee was nearly identical for the two chambers, but the

Senate had five committees with nine or more subcommittees and three with no subcommittees. The House had only one committee with more than nine subcommittees and one with no subcommittees, despite having more committees than the Senate.

Stimulants of Subcommittee Growth

Committees of all types, large and small, policy- and constituency-oriented, and active and less active, have faced internal or external circumstances that prompted them to create more subcommittees. In fact, 65 percent of current standing committees that have existed for more than a decade experienced net increases in the number of subcommittees during the past 30 years. This may indicate that there is an underlying motivation, common to members of nearly all committees, that stimulates subcommittee proliferation. Lawrence Dodd, for example, has argued that

> each member wants to exercise power—to make the key policy decisions. This motive places every member in a personal conflict with every other member: to the extent that one member realizes her or his goal personally to control all key decisions, all others must lose. Given this widespread power motive, an obvious way to resolve the conflict is to disperse power—or at least power positions—as widely as possible.[8]

In Dodd's view, subcommittee chairs have been the primary goal of members seeking more positions of power since the 1946 consolidation of standing committees. Unfortunately, no definitive evidence on members' ultimate objectives exists to test Dodd's thesis, but there is little doubt that subcommittee growth represents an effort by members to control those factors that affect their ability to achieve their personal goals, whatever they may be. Nonetheless, our discussions with committee members and staff strongly suggest that there are multiple motivations and circumstances that produce subcommittee growth. Subcommittees, like committees themselves, serve a variety of purposes for members and, as will be seen later in this chapter, the role of subcommittees varies widely among committees. Power is no more an end in itself than is reelection for members. Creating new, well-staffed subcommittees gives their chairs more independence and thus adds to their influence over policy decisions. But it also provides new opportunities to pursue policy interests and to gain publicity vital to reelection. Indeed, any quick review of congressional observers' explanations for the number of subcommittees will demonstrate that there are many sufficient causes for subcommittee growth, but few necessary ones.[9]

Nevertheless, committees with large jurisdictions have had the most opportunities and experienced the greatest pressure to create new subcommittees. There is a distinct tendency for committees of high jurisdictional fragmentation to have more subcommittees than other committees. This is most obvious at the extremes. The Appropriations committees have the most fragmented jurisdictions and the most subcommittees, while the rules, administration, and veterans committees are low in both jurisdictional fragmentation and subcommittees. Overall, the correlation between jurisdictional fragmentation and subcommittees has been positive and moderately strong in recent Congresses (the cross-sectional rank-order correlation has been more than .60 for the House and more than .36 in the Senate in each of the last six Congresses—93d to 98th.)[10]

Other factors, such as member goals and workload, probably reinforce the effects of jurisdictional fragmentation, but do not have a measurable effect on the number of subcommittees independent of jurisdictional fragmentation. In 1969 House policy and constituency committees averaged 6.2 and 6.0 subcommittees, respectively, but their averages increased to 7.8 and 6.7 by 1977. Personal policy interests clearly were important in the subcommittee expansions in Banking, Commerce, Education and Labor, and Judiciary. These committees' large, multifaceted jurisdictions, of course, provided ready-made foundations upon which new subcommittees could be created. In the 98th Congress, policy committees averaged more than one subcommittee more than constituency committees in both the House and Senate.[11]

AGGREGATE PATTERNS OF ACTIVITY

The presence of numerous subcommittees, even when bolstered by rules that grant subcommittees some independence from parent committees, does not guarantee a decision-making pattern properly labelled subcommittee government. Independent activity does not necessarily entail autonomy in decision making, although independence is probably a precondition for autonomy. The simple fact is that subcommittees remain creatures of parent committees that may ignore or emasculate subcommittee recommendations. The question is how much legislation is written in subcommittee and how much of it survives the parliamentary hurdle presented by the full committee.[12]

The percentage of legislation referred to House subcommittees more than doubled between the 91st Congress (before the reforms) and the 96th Congress at the end of the 1970s (Table 4.4.1). Until the 1970s, many full committee chairs did not bother to refer to a subcommittee legislation that was not likely to be taken up by the full committee. This meant, of course, that full committee chairs could retain control of legislation they did not support. But since 1975, when the 1973 Subcommittee Bill of Rights was implemented in most House committees, subcommittees have become the dungeons of Congress in which most legislation dies.[13] Much less change occurred in the path of legislation eventually reported to the House floor. Even in the late 1960s, most legislation brought to the floor had been referred to a subcommittee at some point in committee deliberations. But since the reforms, several House committees have adopted rules to keep certain types of legislation at the full committee level. And several hold Senate bills at the full committee, especially late in a congressional session when there is no chance of further action or when similar legislation already has been reported to the floor. Thus not all referred or reported legislation is sent to subcommittee.

Table 4.4.1.
Percentage of legislation referred to and reported from standing committees that was referred to subcommittee or was the subject of a subcommittee hearing.

		91st Congress	96th Congress
House:	Referred	35.7	79.8
	Reported	75.4	80.0
Senate:	Referred	41.5	41.1
	Reported	40.0	44.8

Note: Excludes House and Senate Appropriations and House Rules committees because they do not produce comparable committee calendars. Excludes matters related to nominations.
Source: Committee Calendars.

In contrast, the aggregate Senate pattern has remained unchanged. Most referred and reported legislation is not sent to subcommittee. The Senate is far more full committee-oriented, and senators can participate more fully in shaping major legislation there than in the House.

The pattern of committee and subcommittee meetings and hearings confirms these chamber differences. The percentage of House meetings and hearings held by subcommittees increased greatly during the 1970s, as Table 4.4.2 indicates. Nearly all House hearings now are held by subcommittees. Subcommittee chairs control the timing and content of their hearings and full committee chairs usually pursue their own interests through subcommittees they chair rather than through the full committee. But the key change in the House is that a majority of the meetings at which substantive policy decisions are made also now are held in subcommittee. The reforms had a clear effect, as is suggested by the presence of

Table 4.4.2.
Percentage of all standing committee meetings and hearings held by subcommittees.

		86th Congress	91st Congress	96th Congress
House:	Meetings	45.6	47.9	56.1
	Hearings	72.3	77.0	90.7
Senate:	Meetings	27.1	30.6	19.1
	Hearings	77.7	79.6	65.2

Note: House Appropriations excluded because it does not report its meetings in the Daily Digest. Excludes meetings and hearings on nominations.
Source: Daily Digest of the *Congressional Record*.

greater change in the number of subcommittee meetings in the 1970s than in the 1960s. Subcommittees gained the authority and resources with which to make substantive policy decisions. And yet the figures also demonstrate that full committee meetings still are not greatly outnumbered by subcommittee meetings, even though subcommittees outnumber House full committees by more than six to one. The pattern of meetings indicates, therefore, that while the House clearly has moved toward subcommittee government, existing committee activities represent a mixed pattern of subcommittee and full committee involvement.

The continuing significance of full committee activity in House members' daily routines after the reforms was demonstrated in a 1977 study of their allocation of time. Based on daily logs of members' activities, the study showed that about 53 percent of time spent on committee activities by House Democrats was spent in full committee. While only 37 percent of the time spent in hearings was in full committee hearings, 64 percent was spent by Democrats in markups at the full committee level. Similar allocations of representatives' time were found for Republicans.[14] A survey conducted a year earlier disclosed that 82 percent of responding House members rated their work "in subcommittees to develop legislation" as "very important," while 71 percent considered their full committee work in developing legislation very important.[15] Again, the appropriate interpretation is that the most frequent House decision-making pattern is one of mixed full committee and subcommittee participation.

The Senate retains its longstanding modal pattern of subcommittee hearings and full committee markup (Table 4.4.2). Most Senate committees operate on the assumption that subcommittee markups are an inefficient use of senators' limited time and that their efforts often will be repeated at the full committee level. As one Senate committee staff director explained:

> We tried a subcommittee markup a couple of years ago, but we could only get two senators to show. They just decided to get together over lunch and make some recommendations to the committee without taking formal action. We haven't tried it since.

Despite the Senate's propensity to create new subcommittees regularly, subcommittee government is not widely institutionalized in that chamber, and there has not been any general movement toward it, at least as is discernible in the pattern of meetings and hearings. Indeed, the percentage of Senate meetings held in subcommittee in recent Congresses is lower than the House percentage of more than 20 years ago.

Chapter Five

Structural Characteristics II: Political Party Leadership and Party Organizations

Party organizations are vital to Congress. In fact, several political scientists, representing a "strong parties" school of thought, have contended that "Congress is as parties are," meaning that healthy, dynamic parties tend to invigorate the Congress, while weak parties lead to an atrophied Congress.

The importance of congressional political parties stems from their being the one, true centripetal force in congressional organization. The four congressional parties —House Democrats, House Republicans, Senate Democrats, and Senate Republicans—are the only real forums in the Congress with the potential to prioritize and coordinate among individual and committee actors.

The centralizing potential of the political parties is seriously circumscribed, however, by their patently nonhierarchical structure. Unlike the organizations with which we are most familiar—businesses, universities, military units—Congress lacks a hierarchy. Those at the top of the congressional pyramid—the congressional party leaders—lack the authority to control member entrance to and exit from the institution. Moreover, the norms of Congress place a premium not on party loyalty but on constituency representation. Thus, deviations from party positions for reasons of constituency are not only tolerated but frequently encouraged by Congress' unwritten rules. Filling the void are a plethora of ad hoc group caucuses that have sprung up in the last several decades, providing competing pressures for members' loyalty.

Despite the weak, fragmented, and undisciplined nature of the congressional parties, the talk of party decline, disaggregation, and deterioration, and the relatively small percentage of party votes (i.e., votes where 90 percent unanimity in one party votes in opposition to 90 percent in the other party), party leaders perform important functions in Congress. The writings in this chapter detail these functions. Essays also discuss leadership positions, roles, constraints, relationships, and change.

In addressing political parties in Congress, one should be alert to the fact that each of the four parties is a unique organization. Each has its own distinctive structure and information apparatus.

Reading 5.1

The Speaker of the House/House Leadership

This selection gives an overview of party leaders in the House with emphasis on the House's most powerful figure, the Speaker.

THE SPEAKER

It would do no violence to the truth to call the Speaker of the House the second most powerful office holder in the U. S. government, surpassed only by the President. In fact, the Presidential Succession Act of 1947 places the Speaker second in line in succession to the Presidency, behind only the Vice President, whose assumption to that office is required by the Constitution.

Selecting a Speaker

In the early days the Speaker was elected by ballot, but since 1839 all have been chosen by roll call or voice vote. The election of the Speaker is traditionally the first order of business upon the convening of a new Congress.

The choosing of the Speaker has undergone a few significant changes over the past 190 years. Only relatively senior members with 20-plus years of experience have been elected Speaker in this century. From 1789 to 1896, each new Speaker averaged only seven years of experience in Congress. Once elected, a Speaker is customarily re-elected as long as his party remains in the majority and he retains his congressional seat.

Although the election officially occurs on the floor of the House, modern-day Speakers are actually decided upon when the majority party meets in caucus on the eve of a new Congress. Despite the foregone conclusion of the contest, the minority party also nominates its candidate, who, upon losing, becomes Minority Leader. Since the 1930s, service in the lesser party leadership posts, such as Majority and Minority Whip, Majority and Minority Leader, have become stepping stones to the Speakership.

The stability of the two-party system in the modern era has led to a period of unbroken lines of succession in the leadership tracks of both parties. This has not always been the case, however. In 1855, more than 130 separate votes were required over a period of two months before a Speaker was finally chosen. In 1859, only four years later, the House balloted 44 times before choosing a first-term New Jersey Congressman for the Speakership—and he was defeated for re-election *to the House* after that one term!

Powers and Duties

The Constitution makes but scant reference to the office, prescribing in Article I, Section 2 that "the House of Representatives shall chuse [sic] their speaker." While the powers and duties of the Speaker are spelled out to some degree in the Rules of the House, the effectiveness of any particular Speaker has depended upon a great many intangibles: the Speaker's own personal dynamism, the size of his majority in the House, his relationship with the Executive Branch, his ability to "get things done." Men of greatly

Source: From *The Capitol: A Pictorial History of the Capitol and of the Congress*, 8th ed. 1981, pp. 78–79, 90–91. Reprinted from the public domain.

differing styles and temperaments have served as Speaker. Freshmen, septuagenarians, dictators, tyrants, moderates, southerners, northerners, former Presidents, Vice Presidents (and would-be Presidents) have all, at one time or another, served in the Speaker's chair.

In the modern era, the many duties of the Speaker include presiding at the sessions of the House, announcing the order of business, putting questions to a vote, reporting the vote, and deciding points of order. He appoints the chairmen of the Committee of the Whole and members of select and conference committees. He chooses Speakers pro tem and refers bills and reports to the appropriate committees and calendars. Although he is not constitutionally required to be an elected member of the House, this *de facto* requirement assures that the Speaker also enjoys the privileges of ordinary House members. He may, therefore, after stepping down from the chair, vote and participate in debate on the floor.

Perhaps the duties of the Speaker were put most idealistically by the first "great" Speaker, Henry Clay, back in 1823. It was up to the Speaker to be prompt and impartial in deciding questions of order, to display "patience, good temper, and courtesy" to every member, and to make "the best arrangement and distribution of the talent of the House," in carrying out the country's business. Finally, Clay noted, the Speaker must "remain cool and unshaken amidst all the storms of debate, carefully guarding the preservation of the permanent laws and rules of the House from being sacrificed to temporary passions, prejudices or interests." But in fact the Speakership today is a partisan office. As Floyd Riddick, parliamentarian emeritus of the U.S. Senate, has commented, "tradition and unwritten law require that the Speaker apply the rules of the House consistently, yet in the twilight zone a large area exists where he may exercise great discrimination and where he has many opportunities to apply the rules to his party's advantage."

Triple Personality

The Speaker of the House is a triple personality, being a member of the House, its presiding officer, and leader of the majority party in the chamber. As a member of the House he has the right to cast his vote on all questions, unlike the President of the Senate (the Vice President of the United States), who has no vote except in the case of a tie. Usually, however, the Speaker does not exercise his right to vote except to break a tie or when he desires to make his position known on a measure before the House. As a member, he also has the right to leave the chair and participate in debate on the House floor as the elected Representative of his district.

As presiding officer of the House, the Speaker interprets the rules that the House has adopted for guidance. In this matter he is customarily bound by precedents, created by prior decisions of the chair. Appeals are usually in order from decisions of the chair, but seldom occur. When they are taken, the chair is usually sustained. The Speaker's power of recognition is partially limited by House rules and conventions that fix the time for considerations of various classes of bills.

He has discretion in choosing the members he will recognize to make motions to suspend the rules on days when such motions are in order. The rules of the House may be suspended by two-thirds vote on the first and third Mondays of the month, the Tuesdays immediately following those days, and the last six days of the session.

As a party leader, the Speaker had certain additional powers prior to 1910: to appoint all standing committees and to name their chairmen; to select members of the Rules Committee; and from 1858 to serve as its chairman. His political power evolved gradually during the 19th century and peaked under the leadership of former Speaker Joseph Cannon.

In 1910, the House cut back some of the

Speaker's power. They removed him from the Rules committee, stripped him of his power to appoint the standing House committees and their chairmen, and restricted his former right of recognition. These actions were not directed so much against the principle of leadership as against the concentration of power in the hands of a single individual.

HOUSE LEADERSHIP

At the beginning of each Congress, the leadership of the House of Representatives is elected. The Constitution authorizes the House to elect a Speaker. Each party caucus also elects its party leader. Under the tradition of the two-party system in this country, the leader of the party with the largest number of members becomes the Majority Leader. The Minority Leader is invariably the member nominated by the minority party for the Speakership.

The Majority Leader works very closely with the Speaker in developing the party's position on major policy issues. He almost always has represented a different geographic area of the country from the Speaker. He consults with committee chairmen and urges them to move legislation which the party considers important.

Each party also appoints a Whip and assistant whips to assist the floor leader in execution of the party's legislative program. The main job of the Whips is to canvas party members on a pending issue and give the floor leader an accurate estimate of the suport or opposition expected on a bill. The term *Whip* refers to the responsibility of these members to pressure the other members of their party to the floor for key votes.

In recent years the majority party has revitalized the caucus of its members and the chairman of the caucus, elected by his party colleagues, has become an important part of the leadership structure.

Usually considered as part of the "leadership" are the chairmen of the 22 committees of the House. Until the congressional reforms in 1975, the chairmen achieved their status solely by virtue of their seniority. Currently, chairmen are elected by the majority party caucus, by secret ballot. Committee chairmen are nominated by the Steering and Policy Committee, composed of House leaders, their nominees, and members elected by the caucus on a regional basis.

Reading 5.2

The House Majority Whip

One of the first things an observer in Congress learns is that "party whips don't whip." Rather than being the control mechanisms of leadership, whips serve as an information conduit, forwarding communications from leaders to members, and vice versa. The following details this information system as it exists in the House when the Democrats are in the majority.

Source: From "The House Majority Whip," *The History and Operation of the House Majority Whip Organization* (Washington, D.C.: U.S. Government Printing Office, 1973, House Document No. 94–162), pp. 1–3. Reprinted from the public domain.

The House Majority Whip has served as an arm of the leadership for more than 70 years. Defined by precedent, modified by practice and varying with the business at hand, the job of the Whip remains essentially unchanged—to assist the Speaker and Majority Leader who appoint him. The Whip organization, therefore, is at the core of Democratic Party unity in the House of Representatives.

It is the Majority Whip, the Chief Deputy Whip, three Deputy Whips, and 24 Assistant or Zone Whips—bridging the gap between the Speaker and the membership at large—who are charged by the leadership with the twofold task of informing the majority party members of the program of the Speaker and the Majority Leader, and, at the same time, keeping the leadership apprised of the views and attitudes of the members. The Whip and his organization accomplish this goal by publishing and making available to the membership much informational material, and always maintaining close personal ties with the majority members of the House.

The function of "whip" dates to 1769, when the great British Parliamentarian Edmund Burke during a historic debate in the House of Commons, used the term *whip* to describe the ministers who had sent for their friends as "whipping them in," derived from the term *whipper-in*, the man who kept the hounds from leaving the pack. The document "whip" or notice of legislative activity, was in use as early as 1621 in the House of Commons. In this tradition, the functions of the Majority Whip are to advise party members of legislative activities, and to encourage them to vote the leadership position.

HISTORY OF THE HOUSE MAJORITY WHIP

The position of Majority Whip in the House of Representatives was not established until the end of the 19th century. Prior to that time, individual members occasionally acted as unofficial Whips on specific issues, but because of the smaller size of the House (186 members in 1810, 391 in 1900, 435 today) and the absence of highly organized parties, a formal Whip's office was not needed.

In 1897, Speaker Thomas B. Reed appointed Rep. James A. Tawney (R–Minn.) as the first Majority Whip, and in the early years of the office, the Majority Whip was very often a confidant of the speaker, appointed by him and acting primarily as an assistant to him.

The first Majority Whip to appoint other Congressmen as his assistants was Rep. John W. Dwight (R–N.Y.) in 1909. Dwight, an appointee of Speaker Joseph Cannon, was also the first Whip to poll members prior to an important vote.

The office of Whip was upgraded and enlarged in 1933, as then Whip Rep. Arthur H. Greenwood (D–Ind.) established a system of 15 Assistant Whips, each representing a specific geographic zone, this being the forerunner of the present organizational structure, which has been expanded to 20 zones. The Zone Whips were then, and still are, either elected by the members in their region or selected by the most senior member of the geographic area they represent.

The House Majority Whip himself and his four deputies are chosen by the Speaker and Majority Leader when the Democrats control the House and by the Republican Caucus when the GOP is the majority party. [Editor's Note: Commencing in 1986, the House Democratic Caucus will also elect its Whip. See Illustration 5.H.]

In 1955, when Rep. Carl Albert (D–Okla.) was Majority Whip, the leadership appointed a Deputy Whip to assist the Whip in his duties; in 1971, during the tenure of Rep. Thomas P. O'Neill (D–Mass.) as Whip, a second Deputy Whip was added. The substructure of the Whip's office was reorganized further in 1973, as Rep. John J. McFall (D–Calif.) assumed the Whip's position with the assignment of a Chief Deputy Whip and three Deputy Whips, in addition to the 20 Zone Whips. In 1975 three at-large Whips were named—representing women, black, and freshman members of the House.

SERVICES AND RESPONSIBILITIES OF THE WHIP

One of the Whip organization's key functions is to poll his party's members prior to consideration of important legislative matters. These polls, or "Whip counts," are undertaken at the request of the Speaker or Majority Leader and include specific questions on the bill or bills to be considered on the floor. These "Whip counts" provide a picture of the attendance and probable outcome of an upcoming vote. Obviously, this information is valuable to the leadership. If party members seem dissatisfied, or if attendance will be low, the party leaders can reschedule or delay consideration of a particular measure or send it back to its sponsoring committee for rewriting. These polls also identify for the Whips members who are uncertain about the legislation in question. Whips can then attempt to persuade the undecided to vote with the leadership.

Another important function of the Whip's office is the distribution at the end of every legislative week of the "Whip Notice," listing all bills to be considered on the floor the following week, and the "Whip Pack," containing a copy of all bills and reports on the Whip Notice. The Speaker may make changes in the legislative program based on a poll of the membership, action by the Rules Committee in clearing a measure for consideration, or for other valid reasons.

The Majority Whip initiated an expanded informational role for the Whip's office in the 93d Congress. "Whip Advisories," a memorandum summarizing the major provisions of a bill and possible amendments to be offered on the floor, are now distributed to all members of the majority party a few days before the legislation is considered by the House. The Advisories, which strive for objectivity rather than espousing a party position, are prepared by the Whip organization with the assistance of the committee which handled the legislation.

With the added resources of a Chief Deputy Whip—who in the 93d Congress for the first time had an office in the Capitol and a staff allowance—the Whip's office now prepares and distributes much additional information for the use of the membership: speeches, testimony for committee hearings, and, perhaps most important, periodic reviews of the legislation passed by the House. These are issued to the members in the form of "speech cards."

The Whip also initiated an improved telephone system in the 93d Congress, which allows the Whip to transmit the schedule for the House to the offices of majority party members on a daily basis shortly after noon, as soon as the Speaker has confirmed the afternoon schedule. The offices are also alerted of important impending votes and other legislative changes via this telephone operation. In addition, members of Congress and their staffs call the Whip's office for information about scheduling and other matters.

THE OPERATION OF THE WHIP'S OFFICE

Because the Whips serve as a conduit of information between the leadership and the members of the majority party, he and his Assistant Whips must spend much more time on the floor than the average Congressman. Moreover, although the Speaker and Majority Leader are relieved of any committee assignments, the Whip and his assistants continue to sit on their regular committees.

The Majority Whip, therefore, serves not only his congressional district and in committee, but also the leadership and all members of his party. He joins the Speaker for a daily strategy session and press conference, and he and all Deputy Whips serve on the

Democratic Steering and Policy Committee. In addition, the Whip accompanies the leadership to the White House for meetings with the President and joins the leadership for meetings with their Senate counterparts.

A weekly meeting of the Speaker, Majority Leader, caucus chairman, and all whips is held each Thursday morning in the Whip's office. It is in these sessions that the legislative program for the following week is discussed and eventually decided upon. These sessions are noted for their free-flow, frank discussions about programs and policies.

During the week, it is the job of the Whip and his deputies to see that his party's members are informed of the leadership's program. In doing so, it is also his role to help implement the plans of the Speaker and Majority Leader, and together with his assistants, the Whip is continually contacting members of the party to acquaint them with the wishes of the leadership. The Deputy and Zone Whips work the floor during debate and often play a pivotal role on closely contested legislation.

These contacts are also the source of much of the Whip's contribution to the formulation of party policy and strategy, as he, his assistants, and the Zone Whips represent each of the 42 states with a Democratic member. The Zone Whips especially must bring the views of all party members to the attention of the leadership.

In addition, the Whip acts as Speaker or floor leader when the Speaker or Majority Leader is absent.

Illustration 5.A.
Whip advisory.

This advisory shows the form of Whip communications to members. They are usually in the form of basic summaries of the proposed legislation. Notice the lack of endorsement and pressure. Explicit party endorsement is usually conveyed in a communique from party policy committees.

WHIP ADVISORY

THOMAS S. FOLEY
MAJORITY WHIP
The Capitol
225-5604

Number Two hundred sixty-nine

December 9, 1985

UNIFORM POLL CLOSING TIMES FOR PRESIDENTIAL ELECTIONS
(H.R. 3525)

The House on Tuesday, December 10, is scheduled to consider a bill to establish a single poll closing time in the continental United States for presidential general elections.

ACTION BY THE 99TH CONGRESS
-Ordered reported by the Committee on House Administration October 23 (voice)
-Reported October 30 (H. Rpt. 99-348)
-Rules Committee December 3 granted open rule, one hour of debate
Floor Manager: Congressman Swift

BILL SUMMARY

H.R. 3525 would establish a single poll closing time in the continental United States for Presidential general elections. On the day of presidential elections, polls will close at 9:00 p.m., Eastern Standard Time (EST), in all states in the continental United States (other than Alaska and Hawaii) and the District of Columbia. This would be 8:00 p.m. Central Standard Time (CST) and 7:00 p.m. Mountain Standard Time (MST).

The bill also provides that in presidential election years only, Daylight Saving Time would be extended in the Pacific time zone for a maximum of two weeks, until the first Sunday after the presidential election, in order to permit a 7:00 p.m. Pacific Daylight Saving Time poll closing which is the same as a 9:00 p.m. EST poll closing time. The Pacific States involved would be Washington, Oregon, California, Nevada and the Idaho panhandle.

The bill takes effect in the presidential general election year of 1988.

BACKGROUND

The committee says that the bill is the culmination of work begun after the 1980 election when the outcome of the presidential race was announced on network television, based on exit interviews, while polls were still open in approximately half of the states. The committee says that concern was expressed that early projections of winners of presidential elections while polls are still open discourage voters from turning out, foster the belief that some votes count less than others and may even affect the outcomes of close state and local elections. The committee says that a major breakthrough was achieved this year when the three major networks, joined by Turner Broadcasting and Westinghouse Broadcasting agreed not to use exit polling data to project, characterize or in any other way suggest the probable winner of an election in a state until polls in that state are closed. While this solves part of the problem, the committee says that it would still be possible for actual vote totals from closed polls to reveal the outcome of an election while polls elsewhere are still open, and that only a nationwide uniform poll closing time as contained in H.R. 3525 can prevent that from happening.

COST: CBO estimates no cost to the federal government.

Illustration 5.A. (continued)

THOMAS S. FOLEY
WASHINGTON
MAJORITY WHIP

Congress of the United States
House of Representatives
Office of the Majority Whip
Washington, D.C. 20515

WHIP NOTICE INFORMATION
Legislative Program — 51600
Floor Information — 57400
Whip Information — 55604

My dear Colleague:

The program for the House of Representatives for the Week of July 30, 1984, is as follows:

MONDAY

July 30

HOUSE MEETS AT NOON
Special District Day
(2 Bills)

RECORDED VOTES ON DISTRICT BILLS AND ON SUSPENSIONS WILL BE POSTPONED UNTIL THE LAST ITEM OF LEGISLATIVE BUSINESS ON TUESDAY

1. H.R. 6007 — Establish Procedures for Judicial Services of Retired Judges
2. H.R. 5951 — Judicial Appointment Authority Act

Suspensions (9 Bills)

1. H.R. 5946 — Conservation Service Reform Act of 1984
2. H. Res. 555 — Sense of House Disapproving Appointment of Ms. Burford as Chairperson of NOAA
3. H.R. 6013 — Small Business Act Amendments
4. H.R. 5799 — Employment Security for Veterans in Certain Civil Service Positions
5. H.R. 5846 — Crime Fine Enforcement Act of 1984
6. H.R. 5910 — Amend Title 18 U.S.C. re Contraband in Prisons
7. H.R. 5872 — Financial Bribery and Fraud Act of 1984
8. H.R. 5526 — Amend Title 18 U.S.C. re Escape from Custody Resulting from Civil Commitment
9. H.R. 5919 — Foreign Evidence Rules Amendment Act of 1984

H.R. 3987 — Improve the Preservation and Management of Federal Records
(OPEN RULE, ONE HOUR)
(GENERAL DEBATE ONLY)
(RULE ALREADY ADOPTED)

Illustration 5.A. (concluded)

TUESDAY
July 31

HOUSE MEETS AT NOON
Suspensions (No Bills)

H.R. 5983 — Interior Appropriations, FY'85
H.R. 5151 — Hunger Relief Act
(COMPLETE CONSIDERATION)
H.R. 5290 — Compassionate Pain Relief Act
(OPEN RULE, ONE HOUR)

RECORDED VOTES ON SUSPENSIONS DEBATED ON MONDAY, JULY 30

WEDNESDAY
August 1

HOUSE MEETS AT 10 a.m.

H.R. ___ — Labor-HHS Appropriations, FY'85
H.R. ___ — Supplemental Appropriations
H.R. 3987 — Improve the Preservation and Management of Federal Records
(COMPLETE CONSIDERATION)

THURSDAY and the
BALANCE of the WEEK
August 2, 3

HOUSE MEETS AT 10 a.m.

H.R. 5399 — Intelligence Authorizations
(MODIFIED OPEN RULE, ONE HOUR)
H.R. 5921 — Transportation Appropriations, FY'85
H.R. 5244 — D.O. Energy Civilian Research Authorizations, FY'85, '86, '87
(OPEN RULE, ONE HOUR)
(RULE ALREADY ADOPTED)
H.R. 5602 — Health Professions and Services Amendments
(OPEN RULE, ONE HOUR)
H.R. 5585 — Railroad Safety Act
(SUBJECT TO A RULE BEING GRANTED)

* * * * * * * * * * * * *

THE HOUSE WILL ADJOURN BY 3 p.m. ON FRIDAY. CONFERENCE REPORTS MAY BE BROUGHT UP AT ANY TIME, AND ANY FURTHER PROGRAM WILL BE ANNOUNCED LATER.

Sincerely,

Thomas S. Foley

Thomas S. Foley
Majority Whip

Illustration 5.B.
Legislative Digest.

House Republicans convey information through their Conference rather than the Whip network. The following is an example of their format.

JACK KEMP, M.C.
CHAIRMAN

DAVE HOPPE
EXECUTIVE DIRECTOR

TERRI HAUSER
PUBLICATIONS DIRECTOR

Vol. XIV, #15
June 14, 1985

WEEK OF JUNE 17, 1985

MONDAY — 9 SUSPENSIONS

TUESDAY AND BALANCE

502 HOUSE OFFICE BUILDING ANNEX #1, WASHINGTON, D.C. 20515 (202) 226-2302

SUMMARIES OF PREVIOUS WEEK'S LEGISLATION

Illustration 5.B. (continued)

H.R. 2378--AMENDMENTS TO U.S. CODE TITLE 5, SECTION 504

Committee on the Judiciary, H.Rept. 99-120
Introduced by Mr. Kastenmeier et al. on May 7, 1985

HIGHLIGHTS

H.R. 2378 permanently extends certain provisions of the Equal Access to Justice Act (EAJA), which expired on September 30, 1984.

The bill clarifies the circumstances under which the federal government is liable for attorneys' fees in administrative actions, limits discovery in EAJA fee proceedings, expands eligibility of individuals and organizations seeking relief under the act, allows a federal agency (rather than an adjudicative officer) to make the final decision on fee awards, defines final judgment under EAJA, clarifies that an EAJA award is not precluded by the Social Security Act (but prohibits double collection), and brings certain cases heard prior to enactment within the purview of the act.

BACKGROUND

EAJA expanded the liability of the U.S. government for attorneys' fees and other expenses in certain administrative proceedings and civil actions. EAJA required the U.S. to reimburse prevailing parties for attorneys' fees and other expenses unless (1) the U.S. could show its position was substantially justified, or (2) special circumstances made an award unjust. The act's primary purpose was to make it more economically feasible for eligible individuals and organizations to seek review of, or defend against, unjustified government actions. The act reduces the disparity in resources between individuals, small businesses, and other organizations with limited resources and the federal government.

EAJA was passed during the 96th Congress and became effective on October 1, 1981, for three years. During that period, Congress conducted oversight hearings which led to House consideration and passage of a bill similar to H.R. 2378 (H.R. 5479) to permanently extend the act. The President vetoed that bill, objecting to an overly broad definition of the position of the United States and to the interest provision. On drafting H.R. 2378, the committee has attempted to address those concerns.

PROVISIONS

Administrative Proceedings

Position of the Agency--H.R. 2378 amends EAJA to clarify congressional intent that the "position of the agency" which must be "substantially justified" is much broader than the litigation position and includes agency actions or omissions which led to the adversary adjudication. This amendment prevents agencies who have acted unjustifiably (thus forcing litigation) from avoiding liability by taking a reasonable

Illustration 5.B. (continued)

position during the adjudicative or civil proceedings.

Limiting Discovery--The bill limits the determination of whether or not an agency's position is "substantially justified" to the court or administrative record of the case (the record is made during the court or administrative proceeding, or in situations when the case is settled or otherwise disposed of without full trial, by affidavits, pleadings, and other documents filed by the parties). The "substantially justified determination" will therefore not involve additional evidentiary proceedings or additional discovery of agency records.

Eligibility

H.R. 2378 provides that eligibility requirements for the act are the same for both court actions and agency proceedings and expands eligibility under the act to include:

* local units of government (cities, counties, villages, parishes, Indian tribes, towns, townships, and special purpose districts),

* individuals (natural persons) whose net worth does not exceed $2.0 million, and

* an owner of an unincorporated business, partnership, corporation, association, or organization whose net worth does not exceed $7.0 million and who employs no more than 500 workers.

The bill provides that the net worth limitations do not apply to tax-exempt organizations or agricultural cooperative associations.

Fee Awards

H.R. 2378 permits the agency rather than the adjudicative officer to make the final fee award decision at the agency level; fee claimants dissatisfied with the decision may appeal within 30 days. Fee awards must be paid out of funds made available to the agency from appropriations or otherwise.

The bill also broadens the standard for judicial review of administrative decisions on fees from "abuse of discretion" to "substantial evidence on the record," allows fees incurred in appealing such decisions to be recovered as part of the final fee award, postpones the fee determination until an appeal by the U.S. on the merits is decided, prohibits the U.S. from appealing fee award decisions of an adjudicative officer, and provides for payment of interest on an award that is appealed by the U.S.

The bill amends the Social Security Act to clarify that the existence of an attorney fee provision in that act does not prevent awards under EAJA. An attorney is precluded from receiving both Social Security Act and EAJA fees. In the case of dual entitlement, the attorney must refund the amount of the smaller award to the claimant.

Illustration 5.B. (continued)

Other Provisions

H.R. 2378 provides that proceedings before agency boards of contract appeals are covered by the act. The bill defines a final judgment as a judgment that is final and not appealable and includes an order of settlement (the meaning of final judgment is important because fee petitions must be filed within 30 days of such judgment), clarifies that condemnation cases are covered by the act, and provides a standard for determining who is the prevailing party in such a case.

The bill provides that cases pending on the date of its enactment, as well as cases filed on or after October 1, 1984, and disposed of before enactment, are covered by the act (in the latter case, the fee petitioner will have 30 days after enactment to apply for fees).

COSTS/COMMITTEE ACTION

CBO notes that costs under H.R. 2378 are dependent on the number of cases brought and awards made under the act. If current patterns continue, CBO estimates that the total cost of awards under the act would grow from $3.0 million in FY 1986 to $7.0 million in FY 1990, with the expansion authorized in the bill adding another $500,000 over the five-year period. If half of the winning parties were to apply, annual costs could reach $35.0 million or more.

The bill was ordered reported by voice vote on May 22, 1985.

ADMINISTRATIVE VIEW

The administration supports enactment of H.R. 2378.

RULE

H.R. 2378 will be considered under suspension of the rules. No amendments are in order, and a two-thirds vote is required for passage.

Staff Contact: David Mengebier, 226-7861

Illustration 5.B. (concluded)

Vol. XIV, #14
June 7, 1985

WEEK OF JUNE 10, 1985

TUESDAY AND WEDNESDAY

H.R. 2577--Supplemental Appropriations for FY 1985
FURTHER CONSIDERATION
UPDATE.. p. 1

THURSDAY AND BALANCE

H.R. 1555--Foreign Assistance Act Authorization for FY 1986
(see *Digest*, Vol. XIV, #11, May 10, 1985)
FURTHER CONSIDERATION

H.R. 1452--Refugee Assistance Authorization.............. p. 4

502 HOUSE OFFICE BUILDING ANNEX #1, WASHINGTON, D.C. 20515 (202) 226-2302

Illustration 5.C.
The House Democratic Steering and Policy Committee.

An important organ of the House Democratic machinery is the Steering and Policy Committee. The following excerpt from the *Preamble and Rules of the Democratic Caucus* gives an overview of this body.

PARTY COMMITTEES

Rule 41. Democratic Steering and Policy Committee

There shall be a House Democratic Steering and Policy Committee constituted as follows:

Membership

A. The Democratic Steering and Policy Committee shall consist of the Democratic Leadership (The Speaker, Majority Leader, Caucus Chairman, Caucus Secretary, Whip, and Chairman of the Democratic Congressional Campaign Committee), 12 Members who shall be elected from 12 equal regions as set forth below, not to exceed 8 Members who shall be appointed by the Speaker, the Chairman of the Committee on Appropriations, the Chairman of the Committee on the Budget, the Chairman of the Committee on Rules, and the Chairman of the Committee on Ways and Means.

Organization and Procedure

B. The Speaker shall serve as Chairman of the Committee, the Majority Leader as Vice Chairman, and the Caucus Chairman as Second Vice Chairman. The Committee shall adopt its own rules which shall be in writing; shall keep a journal of its proceedings; and shall meet at least once each month while the House is in session and upon the call of the Chairman or whenever requested in writing by four of its Members. In addition, the committee may authorize the Chairman to appoint ad hoc committees from among the entire membership of the Caucus to conduct special studies or investigations whenever necessary.

Functions

C. The Committee in the 98th Congress is vested with authority to report its nominations for committee memberships and chairmen and resolutions regarding party policy, legislative priorities, scheduling of matters for House or Caucus action, and other matters as appropriate to further Democratic programs and policies.

Regions

D. The 50 States (and other areas represented in the House) shall be divided into 12 compact and contiguous regions, each containing approximately one-twelfth of the Members of the Caucus. Following each election, the Chairman of the Steering and Policy Committee shall review the number of Members in each region, and if necessary, shall submit to the Caucus for its approval changes necessary to maintain, as near as practicable, an equal number of Members in each region. The proposed changes and a list of Members in each region indicating the total years of service for each as of the start of the new Congress shall be made available to Members of the Caucus at least 7 days before a Caucus which shall meet to approve or amend the regions.

Regional Elections

E. Each region shall meet to elect its representatives to the committee at a time determined by the Chairman of the Steering and Policy Committee and announced by written notice at least 7 days in advance. The Chairman shall also designate a Member from each region to call that region's election meeting to order and to preside until a permanent presiding officer is elected, which shall be the first order of business. If at such meeting, the election of a Member to the Steering and

Illustration 5.C. (concluded)

Policy Committee does not take place due to lack of a quorum, the Chairman shall reschedule the meeting as soon as practicable, provided Members are given at least 48 hours notice in writing of when and where the rescheduled meeting will be held. Nominations may be made from the floor or in advance of the election meeting by written notice signed by two Members from the region other than the nominee. Written nominations must be delivered to the Steering and Policy Committee office not later than 5 p.m. on the second day immediately preceding the day of the election meeting and mailed to all Members of the Caucus in the region not later than midnight of the second day immediately preceding the day of the election meeting. Following the close of advance nominations, a ballot shall be prepared for each region containing the names of candidates nominated in advance for election from the region. Candidates shall be listed in alphabetical order and all ballots shall contain space to write in the names of Members nominated from the floor. One-half of the Members of a region shall constitute a quorum for an election and a majority of those present and voting for a nominated candidate shall be required to elect. If more than one ballot be required, the candidate receiving the fewest votes on each ballot shall be eliminated from all succeeding votes until one candidate receives a majority of the votes cast.

Seniority Limitation

F. If a region's representative in the preceding Congress had completed 12 or more years service at the start of said Congress, he or she shall be succeeded by a Member who has less than 12 years service. This provision shall not apply to the reelection of an incumbent Member of the committee who is entitled to seek another term.

Terms of Service

G. Terms of service for Members of the Steering and Policy Committee shall expire when a successor is elected or appointed. In the event of a regional vacancy the region shall elect a successor to fill the unexpired term. No Member shall be elected to more than two consecutive full terms, and no regionally elected Member shall serve concurrently as a regional whip. Appointed Members shall not be eligible for reappointment in the next Congress. Provided, however, that this provision shall not preclude any appointed Member serving on the Committee in January 1983 from serving two consecutive full terms as previously permitted in this paragraph.

Source: "The House Democratic Steering and Policy Committee," *Preamble and Rules Adopted by the Democratic Caucus*, 1983. Reprinted from the public domain.

Illustration 5.D.
House Republican Policy Committee.

COMMITTEE ON POLICY

The Committee on Policy, an advisory body to the Republican members, discusses legislative proposals at the call of the chairman or Republican leader and presents plans for Republican action to the membership of the House Republican Conference. Republican members of appropriate standing and special committees, and other members the chairman may invite, meet with and participate in the committee's deliberations. In consultation with the Republican leader, the chairman of the committee may appoint subcommittees to focus on particular areas of interest. By conference resolution, traditions and privileges of seniority do not apply to members of the Committee on Policy.

The committee is composed of 31 members, derived from:

- Members of the House Republican Leadership;
- Representatives of eight regions;
- Seven members-at-large (appointed by the Republican leader to give balance to the Policy Committee);
- Representatives of the 99th and 98th Congressional Clubs

Source: Republican Conference Directory, U.S. House of Representatives, 99th Congress.

THE HOUSE REPUBLICAN POLICY COMMITTEE

DICK CHENEY, CHAIRMAN

TIM WYNGAARD, Executive Director
1620 Longworth House Office Building
Washington, D.C. 20515, (202) 225-6168

Statement No. 2
May 15, 1985

Continued strong economic growth must be a vital component of any realistic deficit reduction program. Lower interest rates are essential to achieve sustained high growth.

The House Republican Policy Committee notes that real interest rates in the United States remain at historically high levels, despite their recent decline. One cause has been the failure to apply a consistently sound monetary policy. Equally important is the failure of the Congress to enact an effective policy for controlling the federal deficit.

High real interest rates affect growth in a variety of ways, including the exchange rate of the dollar. The almost 15 per cent appreciation in the dollar last year was due, in part, to those abnormally high interest rates. In addition, the confidence of foreigners in the future of the U.S. economy, and the earnings opportunities President Reagan's economic policies offer, contributed to the rise of the dollar.

This rise in the dollar has made it increasingly difficult for American farmers and manufacturers to export their products. The price of agricultural exports alone fell by 6.9% last year. At the same time the rise in the dollar resulted in a flood of imports and a $123.3 billion merchandise trade deficit in 1984.

Continued growth is vital to America's economic health. Real economic growth will not only help us reduce the deficit, it will provide more jobs, more prosperity, more housing, and a better standard of living for Americans.

The House Republican Policy Committee supports President Reagan's call for a monetary policy which will promote price stability and the maximum amount of non-inflationary growth possible, and calls for a monetary policy that will not slow, but rather promote those policies for the good of all Americans. The House Republican Policy Committee reaffirms our belief that no policy-making body should place a ceiling on economic growth as a part of the nation's monetary policy. The Republican Policy Committee also supports President Reagan's program of deficit reduction through the containment of public expenditures. We see these as key elements of a strategy aimed at lowering interest rates, the creation of conditions conducive to more appropriate dollar exchange rates, and a much needed improvement in our foreign trade balance.

Illustration 5.E.
House policy committee endorsements.

The following illustrates endorsements sent to congressmen by their party's policy committee.

Thomas P. O'Neill, Jr., Mass.
Chairman

Jim Wright, Tex.
Vice Chairman

U.S. House of Representatives

Gillis W. Long, La.
2nd Vice Chairman

Democratic Steering and Policy Committee
114 House Office Building Annex 1
Washington, D.C. 20515

March 21, 1984

Dear Democratic Colleague:

This afternoon, the Democratic Steering and Policy Committee adopted the attached resolution calling upon all Democratic members to support the Democratic House Committee Budget Resolution and the Rule which will accompany the Resolution and to oppose any Republican substitutes or amendments.

The House Budget Committee proposal differs from the Republican plan in three important ways:

A lower deficit: It provides a three-year deficit reduction of $185 billion, compared to the President's $150 billion package. It achieves this lower deficit by limiting most federal spending to a rate of increase [3.5 percent] less than inflation [5 percent] and by putting all real spending growth on a pay-as-you-go basis, requiring that they be financed with additional revenues.

Tighter controls on military spending: It limits defense spending growth to 8.2 percent [inflation plus 3.5 percent]. Reagan supports a 13.2 percent increase [inflation plus 8.3 percent]. This reflects the priorities of the American people.

Less pain: Unlike the Reagan budget, we protect all "safety net" programs against the impact of inflation. We allow selected programs -- WIC, Headstart, child nutrition, compensatory education -- to grow on a pay-as-you-go basis.

The Democratic budget incorporates two important principles: fairness and pay-as-you-go.

As your Leadership in the House, we urge you to support our party on this critical matter.

Sincerely,

Jim Wright
Majority Leader

Thomas P. O'Neill, Jr.
Speaker

Gillis W. Long
Caucus Chairman

Thomas S. Foley
Majority Whip

Reading 5.3

The Senate Majority Leader/Senate Leadership

The following piece gives an overview of the major senate leaders, officials, and organizations.

THE MAJORITY LEADER

The Majority Leader of the Senate is the closest counterpart of the Speaker of the House, although the Framers of the Constitution apparently did not foresee such a development.

The Constitution's only references to leadership posts in the Senate are contained in two passages of Article I, Section 3. One passage provides that the Vice President "shall be President of the Senate, but shall have no vote, unless they be equally divided" (Clause 4). The other passage provides that the "Senate shall choose . . . a President pro tempore, in the absence of the Vice President, or when he shall exercise the office of the President of the United States" (Clause 5). With few exceptions, the Senate has been reluctant to place substantial political power in these offices. It has instead entrusted power to the Majority and Minority Leaders.

Historical studies attempting to explain the Senate's attitude toward these top offices have stressed the unwillingness of Senators to delegate power either to a nonmember (the Vice President), or to a member (the President pro tempore) who may preside only at times of the Vice President's absence. If the Vice President and President pro tempore are of different political parties, which has often been the case, the Vice President is able to neutralize the authority of the President pro tempore by merely assuming the chair. Consequently the Senate has vested the real leadership in its party floor leaders.

Source: From *The Capitol: A Pictorial History of The Capitol and of the Congress*, 8th ed., 1981, pp. 102–103, 108–109. Reprinted from the public domain.

Selection

Emergence of readily recognizable floor leaders in the Senate did not occur until 1911–1913. Designation of these positions was the culmination of an increasing party influence in the chamber which began around 1890. Before that time, leadership in the Senate was usually vested in powerful individuals or small factions of Senators.

In the early years of the 20th century each party elected its own chairman for the party caucus, but no Senator was elected to be the Majority or Minority Leader as we know these offices today. The "caucus" was in charge of putting through the legislative program.

The Majority and Minority Leaders today are elected by a majority vote of all the Senators in their respective parties. The practice has been to choose the leaders for a two-year term at the beginning of each Congress. After the parties have held their elections, the selection is made known through the press or by announcement to the Senate.

Powers and Duties

The Majority Leader is the elected spokesman on the Senate floor for the majority party. The office is a political one, and was not created by the rules of the Senate even though the rules do confer certain powers on the Majority Leader.

The Legislative Reorganization Acts of 1946 and 1970, and more recent amendments to the Senate rules, have given certain unique authorities to the Majority Leader.

The Majority Leader is responsible for the enactment of his party's legislative program. His role is an integral part of the effective functioning of the machinery of the Senate. The Majority Leader must keep himself informed on national and international problems in addition to pending legislative matters. On the floor of the Senate he is charged by his party members to deal with all procedural questions in consultation with them and his party's policymaking bodies. In turn, he must keep his party colleagues informed as to proposed action on pending measures. In more recent years, the Majority Leader also has been responsible for the scheduling of legislation.

The Majority Leader acts as a clearinghouse for his party as to the status of pending legislation. He works with party members to secure cooperation and unity in carrying out the party's program. The leader or his designee remains on the floor at all times while the Senate is in session to see that the program is carried out to the party's satisfaction.

When the Majority Leader is Democratic, he is also ex-officio chairman of all the party's policymaking and organizational bodies—that is, the Democratic Conference, the Democratic Policy Committee, and the Democratic Steering Committee.

The Majority Leader almost invariably: (*a*) offers motions to recess or adjourn from day to day; (*b*) calls up the *sine die* adjournment resolution and other resolutions relating to adjournment, including resolutions and motions to adjourn for periods of several days; (*c*) makes motions to proceed to the consideration of all proposed legislation (bills and resolutions); and (*d*) proffers routine requests to accommodate the Senate, including orders to permit standing committees to meet while the Senate is in session, notwithstanding the provisions of the rule. These are the parliamentary means which enable the Senate to conduct its day-to-day business.

Through the years, the Majority Leader has made the motions to recess or adjourn from day to day, until it is now assumed to be virtually his prerogative.

The Majority Leader keeps in close touch with the Minority Leader as to proposed legislation to be brought up, the procedure to be followed, and the legislative contests to be staged.

In earlier years, even in the 20th century, chairmen of committees usually submitted motions to proceed to the consideration of bills reported by their own committees. At the present time, however, nearly all such motions are made by the Majority Leader himself.

In summary, the Senate floor leader performs six basic functions of leadership. He is, or has the potential for being, the principal force in organizing the party, scheduling business for the Senate, promoting attendance on the floor, collecting and distributing information, persuading other Senators to unite on policy questions, and providing liaison with the White House.

SENATE LEADERSHIP

The Constitution requires that the Vice President is the President of the Senate. Since the Vice President is frequently not present in the Senate, except in the case of a close vote which may end in a tie, the Senate elects a President pro tempore, by custom, in recent decades, the most senior majority member of the Senate. The President pro tempore is a key member of his party's policymaking body. He usually designates a more junior Senator to preside over daily sessions in his place. The President pro tempore also has the responsibility for the

Legislative Counsel, a group of legal specialists who assist Senators in drafting bills.

Since the early days of the 20th century, the Senate has, by custom, developed the position of Majority Leader as a parallel in power to the Speaker of the House.

The real leader of the Senate is the Majority Leader. He is the legislative strategist and exercises considerable influence on committee assignments.

The Majority Leader is elected by the Senators who are members of the political party to which more than 50 percent of the Senators belong. The Senators of the party with the lesser number elect a Minority Leader.

In cooperation with their party organization, each Leader is responsible for the achievement of the legislative program. They manage the order in which legislation moves to passage and expedite noncontroversial legislation. They keep members of their party informed regarding pending business. Each Leader is an ex officio member of his party's policymaking and organizing body. Each is aided by an assistant leader, called the Whip, as in the House, and by the Majority or Minority Secretary, who are professional staff administrators, but not members of the Senate.

Each of the two major parties in the Senate is organized differently. The Democrats have a caucus which nominates the leaders, elects the Steering Committee, and approves Steering Committee nominations for committee chairmen. The Steering Committee nominates committee chairmen and assigns party members to committees. The Democratic Policy Committee develops legislative policy and positions.

The Republican Senators comprise the Republican Conference, which elects their leaders and deals with procedural matters. The Conference Committees assign party members to committees. They also elect the Republican Policy Committee, which handles the research and policy determination function of the party.

Reading 5.4

Leadership Roles in the Senate: Function and Change

Larry Burton

The floor leaders—especially the majority leader—are the main power brokers in the Senate. Although the majority leader lacks the presiding responsibilities of the speaker of the House, the Senate nonetheless gravitates around the majority leader much in the same way as the House does around the speaker. The following essay by a former assistant to Republican majority leadership in the Senate addresses both floor leader positions in the Senate: majority and minority leader, focusing on the 1984 race for majority leader to replace Howard Baker and contrasting the leadership style of winner Robert Dole with that of other recent majority leaders.

Source: Written for this volume.

INTRODUCTION

The majority and minority leaders of the United States Senate have profound influence in the formation of public policy. The roles performed are critical, yet not clearly defined. Majority and minority status is a function of relative numbers. The parties have experienced each status and have an historical sensitivity to the problems and responsibilities of these positions. Below is a description of the evolution of Senate leadership positions, the functions performed, obstacles to effective leadership, mechanics of elections, and the future of majority and minority leaders in the Senate.

HISTORY

Elected party leaders in the Senate are relatively new positions. Neither the U.S. Constitution nor the Standing Rules of the Senate officially prescribe the duties of majority or minority leaders. In fact, these positions are developments of the 20th century and are based principally upon practice and precedent.

Since 1893, both parties have had informal caucus conference chairmen. In 1903, the Democrats began electing a caucus chairman. The Republicans started this practice in 1911. The two caucus chairmen served as the party spokespersons. After a period during which the caucus chairmen clearly led the respective parties, in 1920 the Democrats formally elected a "leader." The Republicans followed suit in 1925.

Although today's two leaders occupy the front, center-aisle seats, this practice did not begin until the 1920s. The Democratic leader has continuously occupied that location since 1927. The Republican leader has maintained his position in the front, center aisle since 1937. This is symbolic of the party leadership position and the dialogue between the two leaders and the presiding officer regarding the operation of the Senate.

The Republicans have a more decentralized leadership, whereas the Democrats vest more power in their leader. The Democratic leader serves as the chairman of the Conference, Policy, and Steering Committees. The Senate Democratic leadership also includes a whip, conference secretary, and Democratic Senatorial Campaign Committee chairman.

The Republicans not only have different senators holding the Leader, Conference, and Policy Committee chairmanships, they have a conference secretary and a chairman of the Republican Senatorial Campaign Committee. In addition, the Republican Conference Rules preclude either the leader or assistant leader from concurrently holding a full committee chairmanship.

MAJORITY AND MINORITY LEADERSHIP ROLES

Historical momentum, the times, Senate rules, implicit versus explicit authority have influenced the roles of the two leaders. In addition, the personalities and temperaments of the two leaders affect these roles. What is clear is that, despite the institutional drive to create party leaders, there is a competing drive to maintain the power and prerogatives of senators as individuals.

A need has evolved in the Senate for creating party spokespersons. In 1789 there were only 26 senators. Each senator could be his own spokesperson due to the small numbers. Today, it would be unruly to have 100 senators trying to set the agenda. In spite of the development of leadership positions, nothing has eroded the individual rights of senators.

The times have enhanced the need for a focal point in the Senate. The issues debated, advancing technology, rapid information exchange, and constituent demand have created a need for a responsive Senate. The leaders provide a flow of information to individual senators so as to enable them to be responsive to their constituencies.

The Senate Rules do not specifically provide for the majority and minority leaders. Although some provisions of the Legislative Reorganization Acts of 1946 and 1970 were made part of the Senate Rules that conferred certain authority upon the two leaders, such authority relates more to procedure than to explicit grants of unusual power to the leaders.

The implicit authority conferred upon the leadership is founded upon practice and precedent. For example, the two leaders have the right to preferential recognition over other senators, although Rule XIX of the Standing Rules of the Senate directs the presiding officer to recognize the senator who shall first address him. The absence of explicit powers signals the reluctance of the Senate to create a "super" senator. There is an inherent institutional desire for the rights of all 100 senators to be equal.

The respective party leaders are the focal points of information. They serve as clearinghouses of information, and as spokespersons on national and international issues. The relationship between the two leaders can make this exchange of information helpful. Normally, they have a keen understanding of the Senate Rules and procedure and do not hesitate to exercise such knowledge, if it is required to protect the members of their party.

Both leaders are responsible for arranging votes, maximizing attendance of senators when necessary, and working out time agreements to consider bills, nominations, or treaties. Most legislation passed by the Senate is by unanimous consent. The two leaders strive to find legislative common denominators so that senators can act in a timely and responsible manner in formulating public policy.

The functions of the majority leader and the minority leader are different. The majority leader determines the legislative agenda. He has the votes on procedural matters and the responsibility to carry out the legislative program. In doing so, the majority leader coordinates the program with committee chairmen, since they determine committee priorities and because they are also members of the majority party. This coordination may be done in weekly scheduled meetings as former Senator Howard Baker did, or meetings may occur as needed, as practiced by Majority Leader Robert Dole. Efforts are made weekly, usually on Tuesdays, to inform the respective party caucuses about the legislative schedule and to provide a forum of exchange between members. In special circumstances, the party may hold a conference to discuss a critical issue. This is chaired by the party conference chairman. For example, in the spring of 1985, both parties caucused to resolve party positions with respect to the Budget Resolution.

The majority leader also has open communications with the White House to ascertain administration positions and priorities. This is helped in part by the fact that the current majority leader and the sitting President are of the same party. Past majority leaders of both parties have made efforts to communicate party and Senate concerns to the President. Institutionally, the majority leader confers frequently with his party counterpart in the House of Representatives.

The minority leader has a different function. While he cannot per se set the legislative agenda, he can use the rules of the Senate to prevent the majority from running roughshod over the minority. The concept of unlimited debate provides the minority with a significant check against the whim of the majority. The minority leader acts as the agent of the minority party in negotiating procedural as well as substantive agreements on legislation to be considered by the Senate. The major tool used is the so called time agreement, whereby the minority agrees to give up the right to unlimited debate in exchange for the right to offer alternatives to the legislation being debated. The minority leader has an important responsibility not only to protect the senators on his side of the aisle, but to protect against passage of unwise legislation.

OBSTACLES TO EFFECTIVE LEADERSHIP

The number in the majority sets the stage for effective leadership. By definition, if the majority has a one- or two-vote advantage, it is all the more difficult to win on every issue. Any defection from the majority on an issue could alter the outcome of the vote.

Social issues have been major obstacles to the leadership in recent years. Such issues as abortion, busing, and school prayer have often slowed the legislative flow because they have been offered as nongermane riders to various bills. Consideration of these issues delayed or prevented the leadership from accomplishing the goals on its legislative agenda.

Election-year politics also present problems for the majority leader. Presidential election years make a legislative agenda particularly difficult. The minority party can delay action, which may reflect poorly upon the majority. The majority party will press hard to accomplish as much as possible to demonstrate its ability to lead.

The administration can be a strong ally or a difficult foe in promoting an agenda. This depends upon the party in the majority, as well as in the White House. Partisan and/or bipartisan leadership meetings frequently occur at the White House—usually on Tuesday mornings—to discuss critical issues.

Interest groups play a major role in influencing the legislative program. If their agendas directly conflict with the Senate leadership or if an issue cuts across party lines in a timely way, well-organized advocacy or interest groups can force change. For example, passage of the Martin Luther King, Jr. Holiday legislation was a result of multifaceted, bipartisan pressure upon the leadership by outside interest groups to schedule this bill for floor action. These well-organized interest groups were responsible for breaking a filibuster and bringing this legislation to a final vote.

Finally, institutional memory affects the ability of the leadership to function. In 1983, 56 senators had served in the Senate less than one term. In 1968 however, 28 senators had served less than six years. This indicates that fewer members have the length of service and the sensitivity toward tradition in the Senate. Senators today are more likely to become active early in their first terms, unlike predecessors who waited for significant periods of time before even making their maiden speeches on the Senate floor.

WEAPONRY AVAILABLE TO THE MAJORITY AND MINORITY LEADERS

It is surprising how little power the leaders have. Their power is information; it is the ability to help and accommodate individual needs. The leaders must have the power of persuasion. Former Majority Leader Lyndon Johnson said:

> The only real power available to the leader is the power of persuasion. There is no patronage; no power to discipline; no authority to fire senators like a President can fire his members of cabinet . . . a good leader should not only know more about the workings of the committee and how the members arrived at the content of the bill as finally recommended, but he must also know the problems of each individual state and temperament of each individual senator.

Despite the lack of explicit authority, the majority leader influences the makeup of Senate offices and support staff. Although the majority leader does not directly appoint the secretary of the Senate, the secretary of the majority, the sergeant at arms, and the chaplain, he has significant influence over who fills these positions. In addition, the majority leader is consulted on the selection of the parliamentarian, postmaster, and pages as well as committee vacancies, special appointments, and appointments to commissions and special, joint, and select committees.

The two leaders have the weaponry of the Senate Rules, as do all senators, in addition to the right of preferential recognition, but they do not have "super" powers beyond tradition, practice, and precedent of the Senate. The leaders cannot hire and fire senators like a corporate CEO. The majority leader must carefully massage the party membership and persuade them to follow. Former Senate Majority Leader Howard Baker once referred to the "wet noodle" theory—unless the Senate were willing to act, nothing could force action.

CHARACTERISTICS OF PARTY LEADERS IN THE SENATE

No single answer describes the qualities needed in the Senate leadership. Former Senate Majority Leader Mike Mansfield was the longest serving majority leader in history (1961–1976). His mild manner sharply contrasted with that of his predecessor, Lyndon B. Johnson. Senator Howard Baker had a low-key managerial style, versus the strictly parliamentary style of Robert C. Byrd. Present Majority Leader Robert Dole has yet another style, forceful and partisan.

The basic characteristics of strong versus weak, team player versus independent, leader versus manager, fighter versus compromiser are factors in determining who is elected party leader. In addition, political philosophy, geographics, accessability, experience, communications skills, perceptions of fairness, presidential aspirations, and committee structure changes all have an influence upon leadership elections.

Democratic Leader Robert Byrd said that the greatest characteristic of a leader is "patience." But there is no doubt that the political climate emphasizes the necessary characteristics desired in a party leader.

MECHANICS OF LEADERSHIP ELECTIONS

Leadership elections are held every two years prior to the beginning of the new Congress. The chairman of the Republican Conference determines the date and time of the Republican leadership elections. The Conference Chairman presides unless he or she is a candidate for another office, in which case the secretary of the Conference presides.

Table 5.4.1.
Number of votes.

	Ballot			
	1	2	3	4
Dole	14	17	20	28
Stevens	12	14	20	25
Lugar	10	12	13	
Domenici	9	10		
McClure	8			

The Democratic Leader, who by tradition also serves as the Conference and Policy chairman, sets the date and presides over the Democratic leadership elections.

The way in which elections are conducted is realtively new. The Republicans use a precedent set in 1957 to elect their leaders in a multicandidate field. This precedent is known as the "low man out rule." The candidate with the fewest votes drops out until one candidate achieves a majority vote. In the event of a tie, the vote is taken again. The election of the majority leader for the 99th Congress clearly demonstrates that procedure. It took four ballots to elect a new Republican leader (see Table 5.4.1).

The Democratic leadership election for the 99th Congress saw Senator Robert Byrd defeat Chiles 36 to 11. It is not common for incumbent leaders to be challenged for the position they hold, although nothing prevents challenges.

The Republican leadership election for the 99th Congress epitomized the difference in characteristic qualities, expertise, strengths, weaknesses, and institutional perception of needs in the various candidates. The candidates included: Senators Jim McClure (Idaho), Pete Domenici (New Mexico), Richard Lugar (Indiana), Ted Stevens (Alaska), and Robert Dole (Kansas).

Election of any candidate other than Stevens would have resulted in a major reshuffle of committee chairmanships. His previous experience as the assistant leader, strong re-election in his home state, and moderate political philosophy made him an attractive candidate. His liabilities included a public perception of an inconsistent temper, as well as a need to service parochial concerns to the exclusion of more national issues.

McClure offered similar qualities to Stevens. More conservative than any other candidate, he had a core group of strong supporters, but had difficulty expanding beyond the core group. Many potential supporters preferred him in his position as the Energy Committee chairman, rather than as the party leader.

Domenici's candidacy invited a committee chairmanship change. In addition, his previous four years as Budget Committee chairman placed him in a position of being the "traffic cop" against higher spending. While he was in a position to prevent passage of legislation, he had the responsibility to insist on spending restraint. This did not allow him to perform political favors for his colleagues; therefore, they were not beholden to him.

Lugar offered the closest likeness to a Baker-style leadership. He had no enemies, yet no strong alliances because of his dearth of major legislative accomplishments. But he was in line to be the next chairman of the Foreign Relations Committee due to the re-election loss of Senator Percy. Insiders preferred Lugar to the next in line, Senator Helms. Therefore, in order to assure he would be chairman, Lugar lost votes for his bid to be majority leader.

Dole took the biggest gamble of all. Everyone knew he had presidential aspirations. He also faced his own re-election to the Senate in two years. His rival candidates used these as arguments against making Dole the new leader. But Senator Dole effectively turned that unspoken ambition into an asset, particularly with 22 Republicans slated to face re-election in 1986. These Republicans wanted a forceful, articulate advocate leading them into this important election. And, although many respected the leadership style of Senator Baker, many felt his successor should be more partisan.

Dole had proven his legislative acumen as Finance Committee Chairman. Many felt Senator Dole could use this experience to be a successful majority leader. The much-used argument that committee chairmanship changes would upset the Republican momentum of four years was in fact the major factor in Dole's election, since Dole was successful in making this a selling point in his favor rather than an argument against his candidacy. Senator Robert Packwood moved from being chairman of the Commerce Committee to chairman of the Finance Committee (Dole's position), and Senator John Danforth became chairman of the Commerce Committee.

Besides proving his legislative acumen as Finance Committee Chairman, Dole had also built up a substantial war chest in his political action committee, Campaign America, designed to help fund Republican campaigns. In the end, the Republican majority chose Senator Dole as their leader.

FUTURE

The positions of majority and minority leader continue to evolve, but are firmly entrenched as institutions within the U.S. Senate. The continued advancement of technology, the likelihood of televising Senate proceedings, constituent demands, and changes in Senate Rules will influence the roles of the party leaders. A former leader once said "the trouble with being a leader today is that you cannot be sure if senators are following you or chasing you." What is clear, however, is that Senate leaders play a critical role in the formation of public policy. They deal with inconsistencies, individual problems, and regional and parochial interests, yet try to maintain party cohesion, institutional foresight, and national leadership.

Reading 5.5

Duty of Senate Whips

Walter J. Oleszek

Here, Oleszek gives a summary of the functions of Senate party whips.

The duties of the Whip are formally spelled out only in the Republican Conference rules: "The assistant floor leader shall assist in securing the attendance of members at party conferences and upon the floor of the Senate when their presence is considered necessary by the chairman or the floor leader, and shall perform such other duties as the chairman or floor leaders may require."[1] This description, general as it is, underscores the chief duty of Whips—that of assisting the party's floor leaders.[2] In addition, the Republican Whip is given responsibility of conducting, either directly or with the help of the minority secretary, a whip check to determine how Republicans will vote on a particular issue.[3]

It was once the chief duty of a Whip to arrange pairs and know the whereabouts of Senate colleagues, but in recent years this task has been occasionally handled not by the Whip's office, but by the floor leader's staff, or more often, by the secretaries of the majority and minority parties. For example, in 1949 Senator Ralph E. Flanders (R–Vt.) delivered a note to his party's Whip, Kenneth S. Wherry, stating:

> Instead of arranging for a general pair as I told you on the floor, we have agreed to leave the pairing on specific questions up to Mark Trice (secretary to the minority) and his opposite number. I have left my instructions with him.[4]

Source: From Walter J. Oleszek, *Majority and Minority Whips of the Senate, The History and Development of the Party Whip System in the U. S. Senate* (Washington, D.C.: U.S. Government Printing Office, 1979, Senate Document No. 96–23), pp. 15–18. Reprinted from the public domain.

Because of the absence of any official formulation, the Whip's duties have been defined by precedent, with some variation developing from the different interpretations of the Whip's role by those who have held the position as well as from the feelings and attitudes toward the Whip's role held by whoever is Majority (Minority) Leader. For example, Republican Whip Thomas Kuchel stated that he learned the duties of his job from several sources: (1) the activities of previous party Whips; (2) the writings of former Senator Hiram Johnson (Calif.); (3) the advice given him by certain Senators; (4) suggestions offered by his party leader; and (5) his personal definition of what a Whip should do.[5] In the case of Senator Robert Griffin, his conception of a Whip's role developed from: (1) his previous service in the House, (2) his personal determination of what the Whip's duties should be, such as preparation of a whip notice, and (3) the need he felt as a junior senator to be more fully informed on what to expect in the way of Senate actions.[6]

Views concerning the work of a Whip by several Senators who have held this post help to illuminate the assistant floor leader's task. The first Democratic Whip, J. Hamilton Lewis (Ill.), wrote:

> The duties of the Senate whip demand his presence on the floor as constantly as possible. Sometimes the long hours test his

> physical capacity, but generally he is devoted to "watchful waiting." His is ex officio assistant floor leader, and in the absence of the floor leader, and other assistants, may be called upon to represent his party. At roll calls he reports absentees and pairs which have been brought to his attention. He is not supposed to introduce bills lest they may divert his attention from his floor duties. While the parliamentary whip is not supposed to engage in debate, there is no such restriction on the congressional whips. In fact, as assistant floor leader it often becomes necessary for them to do so.[7]

The biographer of the Republican party Whip from 1944 to 1949 wrote:

> Senator Kenneth S. Wherry saw himself as an official who was chosen by his party to assist in maintaining party discipline and united action in the day-to-day deliberations of the U.S. Senate. He viewed his position as being responsible for the attendance of party members and for the arranging and controlling of the "pairing" process. He reported the absentees, pairs, and voting attitudes of the members on roll calls. He consulted with and worked under the party floor leader in arranging the order of business of the Senate; and he handled the details of the weekly and day-to-day legislative programs, consulting with the floor secretary of his own party and with the whip of the Democratic party.[8]

Senator Leverett Saltonstall, Republican Whip from 1949 to 1957, stated that the Whip's chief responsibility was to do the "dirty work" as assistant floor leader—i.e., being on the Senate floor or ensuring that, in the Whip's absence, someone designated by him would be there to protect the party and national interest.[9]

In addition to his Senate leadership functions, a party Whip sometimes acts as Senate spokesman for major White House policies when his party controls the Presidency.[10] Senator J. Hamilton Lewis gave his view of the Whip's relationship to the White House:

> I particularly desire to stress that it is not sufficient as a justification for our opposition that we ourselves individually may feel that the President is wrong. The President of the United States, coming directly from the people has the right to be wrong. He may be wrong according to the estimate of some other man; he may be wrong according to the measure of some other community; but if he is fulfilling the directions of the people who placed him in office, at the same time giving him instructions as to the methods of relief they seek, however wrong it may appear to the individual here and there, that cannot be a justification for opposition to the measure.[11]

A Senate Whip may support a particular measure because his leadership position "requires" him to support his President, particularly on matters involving national security. On occasion, however, party Whips have taken positions opposed to those of their President, as witness the opposition of Minority Whip Robert Griffin (R–Mich.) to President Nixon's nomination of Clement F. Haynsworth to the Supreme Court. Former Minority Whip Griffin stated that, on those issues where the policy position of the White House differed from his own, a Republican leader who supported administration views defended them on the floor of the Senate.[12]

Finally, party Whips have underscored their responsibility to make the Senate work as efficiently and effectively as possible. "My most important responsibility," Majority Whip Alan Cranston said, "is to try to make the Senate work well, to make it strong and to preserve its independence."[13] In a similar vein, Minority Whip Ted Stevens stated his intention to seek improvements in the management of the Senate and to cooperate with the majority party in strengthening the Senate as an institution.[14]

The relation between the floor leader and his assistant parallels, in some ways, that between the President and Vice President of the United States. Both the Whip and Vice President depend to a great extent, though not completely, of course, upon the directions and duties given them by their party's leader; both have ill-defined responsibilities; and, at times, Whips and Vice Presidents have been selected more for political balance than for ideological compatibility.[15]

Just as a Vice President can be more effective in national affairs if he is close, personally and/or ideologically, to the President, the Whip can be more effective if he is close to the floor leader.

Illustration 5.F.
Senate Whip Notice and Policy Committee bulletin.

The following are examples of Senate party information publications: a Democratic Whip Notice and Policy Committee bulletin. They illustrate the kind of information disseminated by party organizations concerning floor voting in the U.S. Senate.

ALAN CRANSTON
CALIFORNIA

Whip Notice

United States Senate

OFFICE OF
THE DEMOCRATIC WHIP
WASHINGTON, DC 20510

Friday
December 13, 1985

Dear Colleague,

Monday, December 16

Senate convenes: 12 Noon

At 1 p.m. following the usual preliminary activities, the Senate will turn to items on the legislative and Executive Calendars which have been cleared for action. Conference reports will also be considered as they become available.

Roll calls: Are expected after 1:30-2 p.m.

The Week

Upon completion of work this week, the Senate will adjourn sine die until January. Measures which the Senate is expected to consider prior to adjournment include:

Conference report on the farm bill, H.R. 2100
Conference report on the Continuing Resolution, H.J.Res. 365
Conference report on the Budget Reconciliation Act, H.R. 3128

ALAN CRANSTON

Illustration 5.F (concluded)

DPC WEEKLY LEGISLATIVE UPDATE No. 33

DEMOCRATIC POLICY COMMITTEE
Robert C. Byrd, Chairman

T. Scott Bunton, Staff Director
(202) 224-5551

WEEK OF NOVEMBER 4, 1985

FLOOR SCHEDULE

Legislation in the following list is expected to be considered by the Senate this week. Times and details for floor action, if known, are listed. However, other legislation may be scheduled throughout the week. The Whip Notice and the Senate Calendar should be consulted for additional information on other measures which are eligible for action.

FARM BILL, S. 1714 (Cal. No. 328) The Senate will resume consideration of this bill on Monday morning at 11:45 a.m. Consideration of this bill is expected to continue throughout the week.

Other possible legislation includes but is not limited to:

COMMERCE, JUSTICE, STATE APPROPRIATIONS, H.R. 2965 (Cal. No. 338)

INTERIOR APPROPRIATIONS, H.R. 3011 (Cal. No. 318)

BUDGET RECONCILIATION, S. 1730 (Cal. No. 333)

COMPACT OF FREE ASSOCIATION, S. J. Res. 77 (Cal. No. 257)

COMMITTEE MARKUPS

APPROPRIATIONS COMMITTEE. To mark up proposed legislation appropriating funds for FY 1986 for the Department of Defense. November 5, 10 a.m., SD-192.

ENERGY COMMITTEE. To consider pending calendar business. November 6, 10 a.m., SD-366.

INDIAN AFFAIRS COMMITTEE. To mark up **S. 1684**, to declare that the U.S. holds certain Chilocco Indian School lands in trust for the Kaw, Otoe-Missouri, Ponca, and Tonkawa Indian Tribes of Oklahoma; **S. 1728**, to authorize the Cherokee Nation of Oklahoma to lease certain lands held in trust for up to ninety-nine years; **S. 1298**, to coordinate and expand services for the prevention, identification, and treatment of alcohol and drug abuse among Indian youth; **S. 1621**, to revise the Indian Education Act Amendments of 1978, by defining the eligibility of children who attend the Bureau of Indian Affairs funded schools; and **S. 1396**, to settle unresolved claims relating to certain alotted Indian lands on the White Earth Indian Reservation in Minnesota. November 7, 10 a.m., SR-385.

CONFERENCE COMMITTEE MEETINGS

INTELLIGENCE AUTHORIZATION, FY 1986, H.R. 2419. Conferees on H.R. 2419, authorizing funds for FY 1986 for the intelligence community. November 6, 10:30 a.m., SH-219.

COMMITTEE HEARINGS

AGRICULTURE COMMITTEE

ARMED SERVICES COMMITTEE

DEFENSE ACQUISITION PROCESS REFORM. Armed Services Subcommittee on Defense Acquisition Policy resumes oversight hearings to review the status and impact of certain legislative provisions to reform the defense acquisition process. Witnesses will be: Carl Harr, President, Aerospace Industries Association; Charles Steward, President, Machinery and Applied Products Institute; Vico Henrique, President, Computer and Business

Reading 5.6

The Context for a Leadership Role in Policy Analysis

Randall B. Ripley

Although congressional leadership is expected to perform important functions of policy coordination and congressional party integration, congressional party leaders possess little formal legislative authority and power. True, leaders have presiding, agenda-setting, and information-disseminating powers that place them in the center of the legislature's life and business. However, their limited patronage and perks leave congressional leaders with what David Truman calls "only the fragments of power" with which to work. In the following essay, Ripley addresses the many constraints that inhibit the influence of congressional party leaders.

THE NATURE OF CONGRESS AND ITS MEMBERS

Several facets of Congress as an institution are particularly relevant to the role of the party leaders in policy leadership.

First, Congress is, by design, pluralistic. In order to provide access for the many interests in a large and diverse society like ours and to cope with a mammoth agenda, responsibility for action (or inaction) and influence over outcomes is diffused throughout Congress to a variety of individuals and groups (especially the standing committees and subcommittees). But the exact form of the pluralism at any given time is not fixed. It can take, and has taken, many different shapes.

Source: From Randall B. Ripley, "Party Leaders Policy Committees, and Policy Analysis in the United States Senate," in *Policymaking Role of Leadership in the Senate: A Compilation of Papers Prepared from the Commission of the Operation of the Senate* (Washington, D.C.: U.S. Government Printing Office, 1976), pp. 18–27. Reprinted from the public domain.

Second, Congress is a partisan body. Despite blurring of party lines on most votes, despite the lack of party positions on many issues, and despite the functioning of many committees and subcommittees with a minimum of partisanship, there are still many times when the simple fact of formal party identification is critical in determining both a final legislative decision and its details. Partisanship is even more important on procedural matters.

Third, Congress is capable of conscious, self-directed change. Like any institution it changes in part in response to outside forces. But it also has a demonstrated capacity for considering internal institutional change in a rather orderly way and acting—sometimes effectively, sometimes not—to bring it about.

Fourth, Congress is powerful and important in terms of the substantive agenda it handles. It considers virtually everything in which the federal government is involved. More important, it need not be a rubber stamp on any issue for any other person or institution in the policymaking process if it does not want to be.

Several characteristics of the individual members of the Senate and House are also particularly relevant to the position of party leaders as potential policymaking leaders.

First, members are election-oriented. Most of them want to retain their seats, and a great deal of their activity is aimed at achieving that result. Most of the choices that confront members are looked at in part from the standpoint of their potential impact on the next election.

Second, members have created and sustained a set of norms for decision making founded on bargaining and compromise as the normal and preferred way of doing business. Bargaining and compromise takes place not only between members as individuals but also between members in special roles (committee chairmen, subcommittee chairmen, Whip, Majority Leader, delegation dean, and so on), and also between members and persons from outside Congress (bureaucrats, interest-group representatives, the President, a home-state newspaper editor, a home-state party leader or public official, and so on).

Third, members do care about policy. This concern may come from a variety of motivations. (Fenno, 1973, suggests, for example, that committee assignments may be sought to maximize re-election chances or to influence substantive policy, presumably because of personal interest in the subject matter.) But in some ways the motivations do not matter. What matters is that members care about substantive outcomes. These outcomes are far from being their exclusive concerns, but they are often important concerns and rarely totally absent.

Fourth, members care about their standing in their parties. This concern varies over time and is stronger among Representatives than among Senators, but it is rarely absent altogether for any member of either house.

Fifth, despite some grumbling and discontent, most members are or want to be proud of Congress as an institution. They develop a personal stake in having an institution to which they can be loyal.

Many observers of Congress look at the above factors (and others) and conclude that there are inevitable patterns of behavior in Congress that cannot be overcome. These patterns are often alleged to prevent party leadership from playing much of a substantive role. They are also alleged to lead virtually all members of the Senate and House to reject serious policy analysis as a meaningful input to their decision making. Oddly enough, what is proclaimed to be "inevitable" also turns out to be identical with whatever exists at any given time; earlier patterns of behavior and institutional arrangements are usually ignored.

To be sure, some of the above characteristics do limit policy analysis and substantive policy leadership by party leaders, but they do not absolutely prevent either from occurring. The characteristics produce tendencies and create a context. What is often forgotten is that tendencies are not inevitabilities and that any context offers opportunities as well as constraints.

THE NATURE OF PARTY LEADERSHIP

Throughout virtually all of the 20th century there has been a constant tension between those wanting a more important role for the party leadership and those wanting more autonomy for standing committees. On balance, more committee autonomy has been achieved, often at the expense of the influence of the leaders.

However, the situation is more complicated than a simple zero-sum balance between leaders and committees. There have also been demands for more influence for individual members of the Senate and the House and, at the same time, there have been demands for more aggressive and active leaders (often by members other than the leaders themselves). In some ways the demands for more autonomy for individual members and more influence for party leaders are not contradictory. Much as those thinkers attempting to weaken feudal controls in 17th- and 18th-century France linked the cause of individual freedom to a powerful monarchy acting against the nobility, so a number of persons in Congress have linked an increase in the importance of individual members to a simultaneous increase in the importance of the leadership. Those from whom power is to be taken are the committee chairmen, the counterparts of the nobles.

There are problems in maximizing the influence of individual members and party leaders at the same time, but there are also ways in which the two goals can be pursued simultaneously and serve to support each other. Strong leaders are needed if individual autonomy is to be aggregated into important impact on policy. If members are content with limited influence over relatively small aspects of policy, strong leaders may become irrelevant and perhaps threatening. What is critical is the degree to which large numbers of members seek to influence policy. Individuals by themselves cannot have much impact on policy. Those who want broader impact must find some method of aggregating their concern while not negating their individual importance. On balance, strong committee chairmen have not proved helpful to this goal.

The other option that some have taken is to look to aggregation through a strong caucus. But a caucus probably cannot operate with much impact without strong leadership of its own. In short, members of the House and Senate desiring enhanced individual influence on policy are likely to face the necessity of worrying about institutional influence over policy for the Senate or the House, or Congress as a whole. One major option for providing that institutionalized influence resides with the party leadership.

Many changes in recent years have created a situation in which individual members of the Senate and House can, in fact, pursue their own policy ends without being hostile to strong leaders. Indeed, in part they look to strong and active leaders for help (see Stewart, 1975, and Jones, 1976).

Strong leadership, however, has yet to emerge. Jones (1976:263) sums up the situation succinctly: "Whereas recent reforms have provided a greater potential for strong party leadership in Congress than at any time since 1910, seldom have leaders been as unassertive as Speaker Carl Albert and Senate Majority Leader Mike Mansfield." For those who think that party leaders have some potential role in policy leadership, Davidson (1976:305) puts the problem very well: "Party leaders, although stronger on paper than in the Rayburn-Johnson days, lack the political resources to induce coordination among the work groups, much less the analytical resources to foster coordination of policies." The question that remains is whether the political and analytical resources that are available can be used to their full potential to change this situation.

Reading 5.7

Majority Party Leadership in the Postreform House: Problems and Prospects

Barbara Sinclair

The postreform congressional environment of the 1980s poses many formidable challenges to congressional leadership. The following is the concluding chapter of an in-depth study of House majority party leadership. This excerpt focuses on the specific nature of these challenges and the coping strategies that have been employed by House Democrats. The final commentary on "the future of leadership" states well the primary fact of congressional leadership: that the ability of congressional leadership to influence legislative events is strongly conditioned by political forces and factors largely outside the Congress, within the context of the broader political environment.

LEADERSHIP PROBLEMS AND COPING STRATEGIES

Successful leadership always requires satisfying the expectations of followers. For leaders who do not control entry into the organization and who are directly dependent on their followers for their leadership positions, developing strategies consonant with member expectations is certainly a prerequisite to success.

Members of the postreform House expect to pursue their goals of reelection, influence, and policy with little restraint. They expect to participate broadly in the legislative process and to engage freely in other reelection-directed activities. Party maintenance requires that leaders facilitate rather than hinder members' high level of activity and broad participation; it dictates that they do so for all their members, not just for those whose participation is likely to be helpful to them. Yet extensive participation results in an unpredictable legislative process, which makes coalition building more difficult.

While members expect their leaders to pass legislation that satisfies members' reelection needs and policy goals, no member expects the leaders to tailor their legislative priority list to his or her individual preferences; members realize that the leadership must be responsive to the diversity of interests within the House Democratic membership and to significant actors outside the chamber. Yet the leadership is expected to be reasonably successful at coalition building on legislation of importance to its members.

When an intraparty policy consensus does not exist, building a winning coalition requires persuading some members to support a position other than their preferred position. The leadership cannot use direct rewards and punishments as a primary means of persuasion because its stock of them is limited and because party maintenance needs constrain the use of them. Highly desirable committee assignments and appointments to the Steering and Policy Committee, for example, cannot effectively be used as a quid pro quo simply because the number of such positions is too small. Furthermore, such use would contravene fairness norms and participation expectations and, consequently, would be costly in terms of

Source: From *Majority Leadership in the U.S. House* by Barbara Sinclair, pp. 237–55.

party maintenance. Similarly, the leadership cannot systematically use its control over legislative scheduling and floor procedure to reward or punish, because doing so would have a highly negative impact on party maintenance.

The leaders thus must balance the often conflicting dictates of party maintenance and coalition building. The current leaders lack both a strong intraparty policy consensus and resources sufficient to affect decisively members' goal attainment. They cannot count on members' goal-directed behavior being conducive to party maintenance or coalition-building success; nor can they assure desirable member behavior by the use of rewards and punishments.

In their attempts to cope with these problems, the current leaders have developed a three-pronged strategy; they are heavily engaged in the provision of services to members; they make use of their formal powers and influence to structure choice situations; and they attempt to involve as many Democrats as possible in the coalition-building process.

By providing services to members collectively and individually, the leaders help their members play the active role they desire in the chamber and facilitate their goal achievement. Leadership information dissemination helps members play an active role in the House. Legislative scheduling that is sensitive to members' needs conserves members' limited time and can contribute to the attainment of reelection, policy, and power goals. The many favors leaders do for individual members (such as making personal appearances in their districts) also further those members' goal attainment.

The leadership expects the collective services it provides to contribute to party maintenance and to produce a favorable climate for coalition building. Doing favors for individuals is expected to have the same effect; no direct quid pro quo is involved. Furthermore, the leadership will seldom withhold favors as a punishment. Members who have been helpful to the leadership will receive more and faster attention; the few members who almost never support the leadership do not ask for favors. The leaders will, however, do favors for members who frequently defect from the party position. Withholding favors from such members, the leaders believe, is likely to alienate them rather than produce leadership-desired behavior. Favors, then, are used to build up a psychological credit balance, a sense of obligation in the benefited members. So long as the resources the leadership commands are insufficient to affect decisively members' goal achievement, punishment, and even the withholding of rewards, is likely to be counterproductive. Party maintenance would be harmed without a commensurate gain in coalition-building success. Furthermore, coalition building is a continuing enterprise; to achieve success over the long run, the leadership needs to maintain ties to all sections of the party. In the process of doing favors, the leadership picks up information vital to effective coalition building. And even a frequent defector may occasionally provide an essential proleadership vote from a sense of obligation.

Most leadership favors—attending members' fund-raisers, helping a member obtain a district project—can be dispensed in a nondiscriminatory manner. Like representatives' casework, they may do some good and cannot do any harm. Some favors, however, have a direct effect upon coalition-building success; consequently, decisions about their distribution are considerably more complicated. In using its influence over committee assignments, especially assignments to the most important committees, the leadership must balance the need to accommodate all sections of the party against the need for a reliable committee majority. Sometimes by helping a frequent defector obtain such an assignment the leadership can co-opt him, thus contributing to coalition-building success. The Majority

Leader's support of Phil Gramm for a Budget Committee seat was in part thus motivated. As that case shows, attempted co-optation is a risky strategy but its occasional success complicates decision making on committee assignments. The current leadership has been reasonably successful in balancing the dictates of the two functions: even in the 97th Congress the key committees had reliable majorities.

In its relationships with the committees, the leadership is again faced with a delicate balancing act. Frequent or heavy-handed intervention into committee deliberations would violate old norms of committee autonomy and new participation norms; yet the form in which a bill emerges from committee strongly affects the probability of coalition-building success. The weakening of the committee autonomy norm allows the leadership to intervene, but it intervenes as discreetly as possible and on an ad hoc basis. When intervention fails, the leadership seldom opposes a Democratic committee majority on the floor. Using its resources against a committee would be too expensive in terms of party maintenance. Yet the leadership does exercise discretion over the amount of help it gives committees on the floor.

Because members and significant outside actors expect legislative results, party maintenance needs cannot be allowed to lead to immobility. Yet, lacking resources sufficient to affect decisively members' goal attainment, the leadership cannot base its coalition-building efforts on the employment of direct rewards and punishments. The reforms of the 1970s have augmented leadership resources for structuring members' choice situation. The Speaker's powers as presiding officer, leadership control over floor scheduling, and the leadership's decisive influence over the Rules Committee often make it possible for the leadership to advantage the party position.

Structuring the choice situation, through the use of a complex rule, for example, is a means of coercing members collectively. The strategy is limited by the requirement of overt or tacit member approval. When the strategy is skillfully used, members will acquiesce because what they gain is greater than what they lose by having their choices constrained. If, for example, members' policy goals dictate a proleadership vote but their reelection goal a contrary vote, leadership structuring of the choice situation so that the key roll call occurs on a procedural motion may allow members to vote their policy preferences.

From the leadership's point of view, the requirement of member acquiescence in the strategy of structuring the choice situation is both a disadvantage and an advantage. It limits the use of the strategy. Yet, coercion to which one has consented tends to be perceived as not unreasonably coercive. Because of the uncertain environment, leaders do not always know what their members will consider acceptable. Misjudgment may lead to a legislative defeat; members may, for example, vote down a rule. But, for the leadership, losing almost any particular legislative battle is preferable to creating serious dissatisfaction among the membership. Few legislative battles are worth winning if the price is a severe reduction in the probability of future coalition-building success.

The attempt to involve as many Democrats as possible in the coalition-building process is the third element of the current leadership's strategy. As rules and norms changes dispersed influence more widely in the chamber, more extensive vote mobilization efforts became necessary. The leadership could not rely on the traditional whip system for the help it needed because of the problematic loyalty of the elected zone whips. In response to these problems, Speaker Carl Albert began to enlist other members in specific coalition-building efforts. The current leadership's strategy of inclusion differs significantly from its predecessor's approach, though. It is a sustained, multifaceted strategy rather than an ad hoc response to a specific legislative battle, and its scale is much broader.

The current leaders' use of task forces, and of less formal ad hoc groups to work on specific legislation, and their use of the expanded whip system, the Steering and Policy Committee, and the Rules Committee are all elements of the strategy of inclusion. The leaders' regular interactions with members of the extended leadership circle provide them with information that is vital to successful coalition building in the unpredictable postreform House. By enlisting a large number and broad variety of Democrats in leadership efforts, the leaders acquire the help they so badly need. The large number involved makes one-on-one persuasion with a large proportion of the membership possible. The broad variety ensures that the group as a whole will have ties to all sections of the party. The strategy of inclusion, thus, contributes to coalition-building success.

The leaders believe that the strategy of inclusion also contributes to "keeping peace in the family." In the postreform House rules allow and norms dictate high rank-and-file participation. The leadership either channels such participation in directions that are helpful to the party effort or it will find itself by-passed and, consequently, will lose influence. Involvement in the extended leadership circle and in specific coalition-building efforts gives a large number of members the opportunity to participate actively, but in a way that helps rather than hurts the leadership.

The contrast between Speaker Rayburn's relationship to the Democratic Caucus and that of the current leadership illustrates how the transformation of the House has required changes in leadership strategies. Rayburn did not use the caucus because he believed that providing a forum in which the warring party factions could confront each other directly would only exacerbate intraparty conflicts. Instead, he acted as a negotiator among factional leaders. In contrast, the current leaders reacted to the intensified intraparty conflict in the 97th Congress by making much greater use of the caucus. All members now expect to be able to express their views to the leadership; all have considerable capacity to act upon their beliefs and, in so doing, can harm leadership efforts. Because leadership attempts to reduce the level of member participation would have severe negative consequences on party maintenance and would probably be unsuccessful, the leaders endeavor to satisfy members' desires for participation by providing forums in which members can attempt to influence leadership decisions and by including members directly in leadership coalition-building efforts. Doing so, the leaders believe, not only meets members' expectations about their roles in the chamber but also has a positive socializing effect, especially on junior members. The strategy of inclusion, the leadership believe, teaches junior members the value of joint action under the aegis of the party and may result in some identification with the leadership.

Although the strategy of inclusion contributes to both party maintenance and coalition-building success, it does not completely resolve the conflict between the dictates of the two functions. Party maintenance requires accommodating all sections of the party; it dictates drawing a broad cross-section of the Democratic membership into contact with the leadership and giving a diversity of members a voice in party decisions. The consequent heterogeneity of the group involved can hinder coalition-building efforts.

When constructing task forces and less formal vote mobilization groups, the leadership will attempt to enlist a diverse group of members, but support for the legislation at issue is a prerequisite to involvement. In its relationship with the structures of the extended leadership circle, the leadership must balance the need for loyalty and the need for diversity. The optimal balance is not obvious, and the leadership's solutions have been varied and ad hoc. In making appointments to the Rules Committee, O'Neill has emphasized the dictates of the coalition-building function. By refusing to appoint state delegation-endorsed members, the Speaker has sacrificed party maintenance objectives. He has been willing to do so because a loyal Rules Committee is essential to coalition building; the leadership's ability to structure the choice situation is dependent upon the Rules Committee being a true arm of the party leadership. Since O'Neill served on the committee during the period of conservative dominance, he is starkly aware of the dangers to the leadership of an unreliable Rules Committee.

The expansion of the whip system and the division of labor between elected and appointed whips were attempts to balance the dictates of the two functions. The leaders' interactions with the elected whips contribute to party maintenance. Because the zone whips are a diverse group, the whip meetings provide the leadership with information about the sentiments of most segments of its membership and provide a cross-section of the party with regular access to the leadership. The zone whips' heterogeneity precludes their effective use in coalition building, however; they take the initial count, but for persuasion, the leadership relies on the whips it appoints.

A comparison between the Steering and Policy Committee of the 95th (1977–1978) and the Steering and Policy Committee of the 97th Congress (1981–1982) shows that the broader political environment strongly affects the extent to which party maintenance and coalition building can be successfully reconciled. Because twelve members of the Steering and Policy Committee are elected by Democrats from twelve geographical zones, the committee's membership is diverse. In the 95th Congress the Speaker sought to balance party maintenance and coalition-building needs by appointing a relatively heterogeneous but nevertheless reliable group to fill the remaining slots. From the more conservative regions the Speaker chose members who had previous ties to the leadership. Partly as a result of his selections but even more because of a conducive political atmosphere, the committee was able to play an effective role in the coalition-building process. The Democrats had just won a presidential election and had maintained their large House majority. The Speaker received every legislative endorsement he requested; even such intensely controversial measures as Carter's energy program and common situs picketing legislation were endorsed without public dissent.

During the 97th Congress the changed political environment made balancing the functions more difficult. Not only had Democrats lost the presidency and thirty-three House seats, but many members read the election as a mandate for Reagan's program. Party maintenance needs required that the Speaker accede to conservatives' demands for greater representation on Steering and Policy. Although the three conservative members appointed by the Speaker were carefully chosen from among members the leadership considered responsible, the highly charged political climate prevented the more heterogeneous commitee from playing a meaningful role in coalition building. Neither the appointed nor the elected conservatives were willing to go along with leadership wishes as similar members had done in previous congresses. Doing so, such members believed, might be costly in terms of reelection. Aware that requesting endorsements on the key economic measures would only exacerbate intraparty conflicts, the Speaker did not bring such matters to Steering and Policy.

The extent to which the leadership's two primary functions can be successfully reconciled is highly dependent on the broader political environment, over which the leadership has little control. The size of the majority, which itself is determined by broader political forces, is one important factor. When the Democratic majority is large, accommodating all segments of the party without endangering coalition-building success is easier. In that case some unreliable members can be given desirable committee assignments; the size of the Democratic committee majority will assure that such members do not adversely affect outcomes. Floor success requires persuading fewer members to vote contrary to their preferences because, with a large majority, winning does not require high cohesion.

Successful reconciliation of the two functions depends even more on the extent of intraparty policy agreement. When a consensus exists, there is little conflict between the dictates of party maintenance and coalition-building success. In contrast, when the party is badly split, both functions are difficult to perform and reconciling the two is nearly impossible. Accommodating one section of the party is likely to embitter others, with a consequent negative impact on future coalition-building success. Floor success requires persuading a considerable number of members to vote contrary to strongly held preferences, which, if it can be accomplished at all, is costly in terms of party maintenance. Discussing leadership efforts in 1981, a perceptive junior member of the leadership explicated the costs involved in coalition building when the party is fragmented:

> There's a penalty for doing this, and the penalty is that the position taken is a very low common denominator that displeases everybody. You wind up with everybody feeling that he or she was overcompromised in order to come to that position, and if you continue to create that feeling, you're going to have people dissatisfied with themselves and ultimately with their party and their leadership. So there's a limit to the number of times you can take people through that. And the natural result of that is that people are going to feel badly not only that they lost, but that they wound up in a position they didn't really feel comfortable with, and that they gave up too much of their own true feeling to the group in order to conform to the group, and so leadership is going to get the bad rap. That's, I think, what's being expressed when people say the leadership stinks. Part of what they're saying is, "They made me adopt a position that is one-tenth of what I believe and nine-tenths things I don't believe in and what kind of leadership is that? If they were any good, they would have given me a position that's totally mine." And so that compromise process is a tough one, and the leadership loses a lot in terms of its own credibility driving people to those positions.

The current leaders' coalition-building strategies depend for success on some core intraparty policy consensus. Structuring the choice situation requires member acquiescence; the strategy of inclusion depends on members being willing to participate in leadership efforts. Because its resources are limited, the leadership's effect on coalition is always at the margins. When the party is badly fragmented, leadership resources, no matter how skillfully they are used, will be insufficient to produce success.

AN ASSESSMENT OF PARTY MAINTENANCE AND COALITION-BUILDING SUCCESS

Evaluating the leadership's coalition-building success would seem to be an easy task. The fate of bills in the House, after all, is a matter of the public record. Any assessment, however, must take into account the great variation in leadership interest and involvement. For the following analysis, two categories are used. The first includes the major bills that the president or a core party constituency declared top priority. The second category consists of measures that were less visible outside of Washington but that were important to the leadership's reputation within the Washington community and especially with the House membership. The choice of legislation is based primarily on interviews with House leaders and their staff, which skews the selection toward the tough issues. Some important measures that never became controversial, such as the multilateral trade agreements, are not included.

Table 5.7.1 is a list of the legislation included in the first category for the 95th Congress, the 96th Congress, and the first session of the 97th Congress. A rating of leadership success and an indication of the final disposition are included. In the 95th Congress the leadership scored nine successes and two defeats on top-priority legislation; results in three other cases were mixed. When the minimum wage bill was on the House floor the indexing of the minimum wage was deleted by amendment, but an amendment providing for a subminimum for youths, a provision strongly opposed by labor, was defeated. The Senate version was more generous than that passed by the House, and the conference agreement leaned toward the Senate provisions. To increase its chances on the House floor, the original concept of the Humphrey-Hawkins full employment bill was severely weakened by the committee. Although the bill sustained no further damage on the House floor, it was further weakened by the Senate. Neither the

Table 5.7.1.
House leadership record on top-priority legislation, 1977–1981.

Congress	Legislation	Result for House Leadership	Final Disposition
95th	Economic stimulus program	successful	enacted
	Hatch Act revision	successful	died in Senate
	Strip mining bill	successful	enacted
	Labor law reform	successful	died in Senate
	New York City aid	successful	enacted
	Social security bill	successful	enacted
	Lifting of Turkish arms embargo	successful	enacted
	Suspension of B-1 production	successful	enacted
	Energy program	successful	radically changed in Senate, then enacted
	Minimum wage bill	mixed	strengthened in Senate, then enacted
	Humphrey-Hawkins full employment bill	mixed	weakened in Senate, then enacted
	1978 tax bill	mixed	enacted
	Common situs picketing bill	unsuccessful	died
	Consumer protection agency	unsuccessful	died
96th	Chrysler loan guarantees	successful	enacted
	Synthetic fuels bill	successful	enacted
	Windfall profits tax	successful	enacted
	Busing constitutional amendment	successful	killed by House's action
	Taiwan Relations Act	successful	enacted
	Panama Canal implementation legislation	successful	enacted
	Fair housing bill	successful	died in Senate
	Welfare reform	successful	died in Senate
	Standby gas rationing bill	mixed	enacted
	Energy mobilization board	unsuccessful	died
	Hospital cost control	unsuccessful	died
	Oil import fee	unsuccessful	died
97th	First budget resolution	unsuccessful	enacted
	Reconciliation bill	unsuccessful	enacted
	Tax bill	unsuccessful	enacted

speaker nor President Carter liked the form in which the tax bill emerged from the Ways and Means Committee. The leadership's primary effort on the floor was to defeat an amendment embodying the Kemp-Roth 30 percent tax cut, and on this it was successful.

In the 96th Congress the leadership scored eight successes and three defeats; results in one case were mixed. Neither the Taiwan Relations Act nor the Panama Canal treaty implementation bill emerged from the House in a form totally satisfactory to the administration but they are counted as successes because the House leaders accomplished what they set out to do, which was prevent the adoption of "killer" amendments. The House vetoed Carter's standby gas rationing plan in the spring of 1979. A new bill providing for rationing authority and for a different congressional review process passed several months later. That bill, however, emerged from committee weaker than the president or the leadership wanted it to be, and it passed the House only after the leaders reversed the vote on what they believed to be a killer amendment.

In 1981 the new Reagan administration decided to use the congressional budget process to accomplish its priority objective of cutting spending. The three most critical measures that came to a House vote were the first budget resolution, the reconciliation bill, and the tax bill. In each case House Republicans offered administration substitutes for the committee versions that the leadership backed, and in each case the leadership was defeated.

On the big bills, then, the House majority party leadership was at least reasonably successful in the 95th and 96th congresses. The leadership won approximately 65 percent of its legislative battles in the two congresses and suffered defeats in 20 percent. In 1981, however, the decreased size of the Democratic House membership, a popular Republican president, and a change in the national political mood combined to hand the Democratic leadership three successive major defeats.

The second category of roll calls includes votes on budget resolutions (in the 95th and 96th congresses), debt limit increases, and measures of special personal interest to members of the House. Eighteen key budget resolution roll calls were identified in the 95th Congress. The leadership lost on four of the votes. During consideration of the first budget resolution in 1977, an amendment to increase defense spending—helped along by some covert lobbying from the administration—passed. Liberals retaliated by voting against passage of the resolution, which failed by a large margin. When a slightly revised resolution was brought to the floor, the defense spending amendment was defeated and the resolution passed. In 1978 a Republican amendment cutting HEW funds passed, but the vote was reversed before the first resolution was passed. During consideration of the second resolution in 1978 one amendment (which cut CETA and counter-cyclical aid) was adopted over the objections of the party leadership and the committee majority. Thus, only one of the eighteen roll calls resulted in a permanent defeat for the leadership. A loss that is later reversed is not, however, cost free. Resources must be expended to reverse the initial defeat, and every defeat tarnishes, at least temporarily, the leadership's reputation. For these reasons, debt limit votes have been a recurrent problem for the leadership. Every member knows the ceiling must be raised periodically, yet, especially in a time of high inflation, few like to vote for an increase. During the 95th Congress the need to increase the debt ceiling arose three times; in each case, the bill failed the first time it came to the floor and then, after heavy leadership lobbying, passed on the second attempt.

Four other measures in the 95th Congress fall into the second category. The Speaker staked his reputation on passage of a strong ethics code and of a substantial congressional pay increase; both were successfully enacted. The leadership also supported a bill providing for public financing of congressional elections and a measure recommended by the Obey Commission reforming the administration of the House. In both cases the rule for consideration of these measures was defeated. The leadership, then, won on only two of these four measures, though it was successful on the two most critical to the Speaker's reputation.

In the 96th Congress the leadership lost six of twenty-four key budget resolution roll calls, but all these defeats were reversed. During consideration of the first resolution in 1979, the Mattox amendment cutting counter-cyclical aid was adopted. Had that decision been allowed to stand, liberal Democrats would almost certainly have voted against the resolution, ensuring its defeat. The amendment was, however, largely nullified by the subsequent adoption of another amendment. Both the conference report on the first resolution and the second resolution were initially defeated but subsequently approved. In 1980 the conference report on the first resolution was again defeated, and in the aftermath the leadership lost two important procedural votes. These losses were particularly embarrassing, but a somewhat revised budget resolution was subsequently approved.

There were seven votes related to increasing the debt limit during the 96th Congress, of which the leadership lost two (both of the losses were, of course, reversed). Two of the wins were especially important. In early 1979 conservatives twice tried to defeat the previous question on the rule for consideration of the debt limit increases; their aim was to attach to the bill a provision requiring a balanced budget. The leadership's success on the previous question votes prevented the proposal (which, given the political climate, was almost irresistible) from coming to a vote.

Seven other roll calls in the 96th Congress fall into this category. The leadership twice successfully prevented the expulsion of Congressman Charles Diggs. Members of the Black Caucus were very much concerned that Diggs not be expelled before his appeals were exhausted; the leadership, by preventing such a move, built up credits with an important internal constituency. The leadership position also prevailed on the Obey-Railsback bill to limit political action committee (PAC) contributions in House races, but this measure died in the Senate. Of considerable importance to the leaders themselves was approval in 1979 of a change in the procedure for increasing the debt limit; under the new procedure, debt limit increases are included in the budget resolution, thus usually making a separate bill unnecessary and reducing the visibility of the decision. The leadership twice failed to win approval of a congressional pay increase but finally succeeded in late 1979.

From the leaders' point of view, winning is what is critical; the size of the margin and the sources of their support are of secondary importance. An analysis of such factors, however, contributes to our understanding of leadership coalition building. In the following analysis, voting patterns are examined within issue areas. The roll calls used are the key votes on the bills and other measures that were identified earlier. In the foreign and defense policy area, these have been supplemented by some additional votes that, although they were not taken on bills qualifying as top priority, were of unquestioned importance. Most of these additional roll calls represent attempts by congressional hard-liners to restrict President Carter's discretion in the foreign and defense policy area. During the 95th Congress, for example, an amendment expressing congressional opposition to Carter's plan to reduce ground troops in Korea came to a vote, a vote was taken on overriding the President's veto of a weapons procurement bill, and there were votes on two amendments restricting the nations to which foreign aid may go. During the 96th Congress there were a number of attempts to prohibit aid to Nicaragua and several to lift sanctions from Rhodesia. In all these cases the leadership took an active part in upholding President Carter's position.

Although the leadership won much more frequently than it lost in the 95th and 96th congresses, its winning margins tended to be slim (see Tables 5.7.2 and 5.7.3). On the sixty-nine key roll calls identified in the 95th Congress, the mean percentage of members supporting the leadership position was 53.2; in the 96th Congress on seventy-nine roll calls, the mean support percentage was 52.0. In the 95th Congress the leadership position was defeated on 21.7 percent of the roll calls; in the 96th, on 25.4 percent. Because many of the defeats were later reversed, these figures do not provide a true indication of leadership success, but they do indicate that coalition building in these congresses was no easy task. Of the roll calls won in the 95th Congress, 74 percent were won by less than 60 percent of the vote; in the 96th, 83 percent were won by less than 60 percent.

Examining support by issue area, one finds that only in the "other government management" area in the 95th Congress did mean leadership support reach a comfortable level. Included in this category are a number of roll calls on the 1977 economic stimulus program on which Democrats did agree. The other issue areas were much more difficult; a mean leadership support level of greater than 55 percent is unusual. In both congresses, mean support on budget resolution roll calls barely surpassed the 50 percent mark.

As can be seen in tables 5.7.2 and 5.7.3, southern Democrats are clearly the most troublesome segment of the party for the leadership. In three issue areas in each congress, the leadership received on the average less than one-half of southern Democratic votes. In the 95th Congress the mean leadership support percentage of southern Democrats on the total set of key roll calls was barely over 50; in the 96th, this increases to 59.2. Although northern Democrats as a group are much more supportive of leadership positions than their southern party colleagues, their support is far from unanimous. During the 95th Congress slightly less than 20 percent of northern Democrats defected on the average; during the 96th, slightly more than 20 percent defected. High cohesion among Republicans made the leadership's task even more difficult. During the the 95th Congress, the leadership received on the average only 13.7 percent of Republican votes, and during the 96th, only 16.6

Table 5.7.2.
Support for the leadership position in the 95th Congress (in percentages).

	Issue Area								
Group	Budget	Debt Limit	Energy	Other Government Management	Foreign and Defense	Labor	Social Security	Internal	All Issues
All	50.7	48.1	53.8	59.6	51.1	53.9	55.6	52.8	53.2
Democrats	72.8	67.6	74.8	81.2	64.1	74.1	77.4	74.5	73.6
Northern Democrats	79.7	74.3	82.3	89.1	71.6	87.3	86.3	80.1	80.6
Southern Democrats	53.1	48.3	53.4	57.9	42.8	36.5	52.9	58.7	50.6
Republicans	8.5	10.3	11.6	17.3	25.8	14.2	13.7	10.1	13.7
Number of roll calls	18	6	7	12	8	9	4	5	69

Table 5.7.3.
Support for the leadership position in the 96th Congress (in percentages).

	Issue Area								
Group	Budget	Debt Limit	Energy	Other Government Management	Foreign and Defense	Social Welfare	Civil Liberties	Internal	All Issues
All	51.8	50.6	46.5	54.0	54.0	52.6	50.5	56.0	52.0
Democrats	74.6	78.7	62.2	71.4	73.4	77.1	67.6	74.6	72.6
Northern Democrats	76.8	84.7	62.7	80.1	81.3	88.6	77.9	79.4	77.3
Southern Democrats	68.1	61.7	60.9	46.2	51.4	43.5	39.7	61.6	59.2
Republicans	13.0	1.5	19.6	23.5	20.7	9.9	21.2	23.7	16.6
Number of roll calls	24	7	12	2	22	2	2	8	79

percent. Only on foreign policy votes during the 95th did as many as 25 percent of Republicans typically support the Democratic position. However, given the narrow victory margins characteristic of these congresses, gaining even a small number of Republican votes was often essential to victory.

In the 95th and 96th congresses a highly but not totally cohesive Republican party faced a large but much less cohesive Democratic party. The leadership managed to corral enough votes from its members to win a substantial majority of the key votes, often with the help of a few Republican defectors. The victory margins, however, tended to be narrow. Given this situation, the losses in the 97th Congress are hardly surprising. The size of the Democratic party decreased and Republican cohesion increased. Democratic cohesion on the first of the key votes was about the same as the average for the 95th and 96th congresses; on the other two, Democratic cohesion was much higher than the average of the previous congresses (see Table 5.7.4). Thus in the 97th Congress the leadership was at least as successful in mobilizing Democratic votes as it had been in the two preceding congresses. However, winning would have required much higher Democratic cohesion than had prevailed in the previous congresses. Given the popularity of the president and the mandate interpretation of the 1980 election to which many Democrats subscribed, the leadership with its limited resources was incapable of engineering such extraordinary cohesion.

Assessing the leadership's success at party maintenance is considerably more

Table 5.7.4.
Support for the leadership position on key votes in the 97th Congress (in percentages).

Roll Call	All	Republicans	Democrats	Northern Democrats	Southern Democrats
First budget resolution—Gramm-Latta substitute	41.0	0	73.6	87.4	35.9
Reconciliation—previous question on rule	49.2	.5	87.8	97.1	62.5
Tax Bill—Republican substitute	45.0	.5	80.2	88.7	56.9

difficult than assessing coalition-building success, but members' evaluations of their leaders provide one basis for assessment. The Democrats interviewed do not constitute a random sample; as a group they are, however, representative of the Democratic House membership in terms of region, ideology, and seniority.

Asked what the membership wanted of its leadership, a top leader replied wryly, "A very strong leadership that pressures everyone else into doing what they want done." During interviews in 1979, 1980, and 1981, a number of Democrats expressed a desire for stronger leadership and complained that the current leaders were not tough enough. Asked if the leadership possessed sufficient resources to lead effectively, a senior member said, "The tools are there; I'm not sure the carpenter is. 'Tip' is such a nice man. I believe in using rewards and punishments. If you never help out, you shouldn't get the good committee assignments." But, while one group of members called for greater discipline, another complained that the leadership was insufficiently tolerant. These members believe the leaders discriminate against them in the awarding of committee assignments and other desirable positions. Ideology perfectly distinguishes the two groups. All the members who advocated more discipline are mainstream Democrats; all of those advocating greater tolerance are conservatives.

Clearly the leadership cannot fully satisfy both groups, and the smaller the size of their majority, the greater the problem the groups' conflicting expectations create for the leaders. When the majority is small, the minority conservatives have much greater bargaining power. Using negative sanctions against them is likely to be counterproductive; using inducements tends to breed resentment among the mainstream majority, especially if the inducements do not produce legislative victories. Peter Peyser's floor speech on the day after Democrats lost the key vote on the 1981 reconciliation bill provides some indication of mainstream Democrats' resentment toward the conservative defectors. "Rank and file Democrats in the House have had it," he said. "We have been abused and betrayed by those who have accepted and benefited by this party's support. We are really mad as hell, Mr. Speaker, and we are not going to roll over and play dead any more" (*Congressional Record*, 97th Cong., 1st sess., 26 June 1981, vol. 127, p. 3611).

Members' evaluations of their leadership are strongly related to whether the most recent major legislative battle was won or lost. This was evident throughout the interviews; sentiment sometimes altered massively almost overnight. The leaders are at least temporarily blamed for an important loss, regardless of whether their actions were a contributing factor. "They tend to fire the manager after the baseball team loses the pennant," a member said. "It's not unusual in America. Firing the manager doesn't make a 220-hitter hit 300, but there's always going to be dissatisfaction when you don't emerge successful." Legislative losses clearly have a negative impact on party maintenance.

Member dissatisfaction, if it is deep enough, can be politically fatal to the party leadership. A syndrome can develop in which intraparty splits lead to legislative defeats that in turn increase intraparty animosity that further decreases the probability of legislative victories. At some point the leaders' very positions as leaders become endangered. Yet even the mauling House Democrats took in 1981 did not lead to that syndrome. Certainly dissatisfaction was lessened by the improvement in Democratic political prospects by the fall of 1981. The leadership's strategy of inclusion also worked to keep dissatisfaction in check. The wide consultation and broad involvement that the strategy of inclusion entails results in a large proportion of Democrats being participants, rather than just followers, in leadership efforts. Because members of the postreform House want to participate actively and broadly in the legislative process, the opportunity to do so given them by the leadership mitigates dissatisfaction, even when the legislative battles in which they are involved do not end in success. Furthermore, although members blame the leadership when important legislative fights are lost, those members who have participated in the development and implementation of strategy tend to be somewhat more understanding after the initial disappointment has worn off. When the political environment imposes unusual stress on the House Democratic party, the strategy of inclusion cannot prevent, but does serve to mitigate, destructive intraparty dissatisfaction.

THE FUTURE OF LEADERSHIP

During the 95th and 96th Congresses the House majority party leadership was reasonably successful at building winning coalitions; but in 1981 it lost the major legislative battles. "Keeping peace in the family" was also much more difficult in the 97th Congress. A change in the broader political environment accounts for the leadership's decline in success. The 1980 election diminished the size of the Democratic majority, demoralized the membership, and further decreased the already shrinking intraparty policy consensus. The result was a series of legislative defeats which then further demoralized Democrats and exacerbated intraparty conflicts.

The political climate and, with it, the leadership's likelihood of success has since changed. The size of the majority tends to be cyclical; an increase makes the successful performance of leadership functions easier directly and, by alleviating members' reelection-related fears, indirectly. The reestablishment of a core intraparty policy consensus of some breadth would significantly increase leadership success; when such a consensus exists, members contribute to leadership success while pursuing their individual goals. Even the reestablishment of a narrower intraparty consensus when accompanied with the likely decline in Republican cohesiveness would increase leadership success. The cyclical character of national party politics assures cyclical variations in leadership success.

Leadership success and leadership influence are not, however, synonymous. A significant increase in leadership resources depends on members' perceiving such an increase to be conducive to their goal attainment. In the late 1970s and early 1980s a growing number of members were concluding that the reforms had gone too far. Many members believe that some subcommittees' lack of expertise, committee chairmen's inability to perform a quality control function, and the increased tendency to mark-up legislation on the floor have seriously impaired the House's capacity to legislate responsibly. Members for whom good public policy is an important goal seem increasingly willing to let the leadership assume a greater role in setting priorities and controlling quality.

Members are also beginning to believe that the attainment of their other goals is hampered by some of the effects of the reforms. The high rate of amending activity on the floor forces members repeatedly to go on the record on politically perilous issues. It also results in extremely lengthy floor sessions that impinge on the time members have for other tasks. In late 1979 a number of Democrats, including junior as well as senior members, sent the Speaker a letter requesting that he make more use of restrictive rules so as to decrease the length of floor sessions, and the Speaker has responded to this request by using restrictive rules more frequently.

To the extent that members become convinced that leadership-strengthening changes are necessary for the attainment of their individual goals, such changes will be made. However, given that impetus for change, it is extremely unlikely that members will alter fundamentally the participatory character of the postreform House. They may be willing to place some restraints on themselves and thereby give the leadership additional tools, but a return to anything approaching the Speakership of the 1890–1910 period is unimaginable.

As Cooper and Brady (1981) have pointed out, the powerful Speakership of the 1890–1910 period depended on the existence of a strong party system in the country and on the member norms attendant on such a system. Turn-of-the-century Speakers had powers that gave them significant influence over member goal attainment. Members supported the strong speakership because, within a strong party system, the attainment of individual goals is dependent on party success. As the strong party system and its attendant norms began to erode and the Republican party split, more and more members perceived the strong speakership as a barrier to their goal attainment. Speaker Cannon's spectacular failure to understand that the dictates of party maintenance had changed led to the revolt that stripped the speaker of much of his power. Barring the reestablishment of a strong party system, members will not again vest such extraordinary powers in their speaker.

Consequently, the majority party leadership in the foreseeable future will continue to be faced with the tasks of building winning coalitions and "keeping peace in the family" with limited resources and within an environment characterized by wide participation and thus high uncertainty. Leadership success will continue to require accommodating and making use of members' expectations of participation as well as employing limited resources as effectively as possible.

Yet the most important determinants of leadership's success will remain beyond the leaders' control. So long as the majority party leaders have little influence over members' individual goal achievement—and particularly over the reelection goal—their influence over members' behavior within the chamber will remain tenuous. On issues of some saliency, the perceived preferences of constituents and of other political actors who do affect the reelection goal will carry greater weight than the wishes of the leadership. The success of the majority party leadership, consequently, is highly dependent on the content of those perceived preferences. To large extent, the post-Cannon House receives its policy dynamics from the outside. When members perceive strong, clear signals favoring policy change from their constituencies, they respond with policy change. When signals are muted, confused, or contradictory, the House of Representative's capacity to make policy departures of any significance is extremely limited.

Illustration 5.G.
Informal congressional groups, 1984.

There is a multiplicity of formal and informal congressional leaders. In addition to the floor leaders and whips previously discussed, one must count committee leaders as formal party leaders. Committee chairmen and ranking minority members hold enormous sway over legislation emanating from their committees. The interaction between floor and committee leaders dramatizes the fragmentation of party authority, for these leaders are not always lined up in a monolithic way. Frequently, they are at loggerheads, providing members of their respective parties with contradictory cues.

The proliferation of leadership positions that has resulted from a deliberate strategy of inclusiveness by leadership in all four congressional parties has led, in many ways, to a kind of leadership vacuum. In this fragmented structure, each of the leaders develops his or her own following and does his or her own thing. In recent times, the void is being filled more and more by informal caucuses and groups. In both House and Senate, more than 100 such groups have developed by banding members together in bicameral and unicameral and partisan and bipartisan ways to pursue regional, ideological, issue, and ethnic causes. The attached illustration displays the major informal groups in Congress. A major question to be raised is the extent to which these groups aid or hinder the Congress in the performance of its lawmaking and representational functions.

Source: Samuel C. Paterson, Roger Davidson, and Randall Ripley, *A More Perfect Union*, 3d. ed. (Homewood, Ill.: Dorsey Press, 1985), p. 347.

Illustration 5.G. (concluded)

*Informal congressional groups, 1984.**

House

Democratic

Calif. Democratic Congressional Delegation (28)
Congressional Populist Caucus (15)
Conservative Democratic Forum ("Boll Weevils") (38)
Democratic Study Group (228)
House Democratic Research Organization (100)
Ninety-Fifth Democratic Caucus (35)
Ninety-Sixth Democratic Caucus (20)
Ninety-Seventh New Members Caucus (24)
Ninety-Eighth New Members Caucus (52)
United Democrats of Congress (125)

Republican

House Republican Study Committee (130)
House Wednesday Group (32)
Ninety-Fifth Republican Club (14)
Northeast-Midwest Republican Coalition ("Gypsy Moths")
Republican Freshman Class of the 96th Congress
Republican Freshman Class of the 97th Congress
Republican Freshman Class of the 98th Congress
Conservative Opportunity Society

Bipartisan

Ad Hoc Congressional Committee on Irish Affairs (110)
Budget Study Group (60)
Congressional Agricultural Forum
Congressional Automotive Caucus (53)
Congressional Border Caucus (12)
Congressional Coal Group (55)
Congressional Emergency Housing Caucus
Congressional Human Rights Caucus (150)
Congressional Mushroom Caucus (60)
Congressional Rural Caucus (100)
Congressional Steel Caucus (120)
Congressional Territorial Caucus (4)
Congressional Travel and Tourism Caucus (154)
Federal Government Service Task Force (38)
House Fair Employment Practices Committee
Local Government Caucus (22)
Northeast-Midwest Congressional Coalition (196)
Task Force on Devaluation of the Peso
Task Force on Industrial Innovation and Productivity
Conference of Great Lakes Congressmen (100)
Congressional Arts Caucus (186)
Congressional Black Caucus (21)
Congressional Caucus for Sciences and Technology (15)
Congressional Hispanic Caucus (11)
Congressional Metropolitan Area Caucus (8)
Congressional Port Caucus (150)
Congressional Space Caucus (161)
Congressional Sunbelt Council
Congressional Textile Caucus (42)
Export Task Force (102)
House Caucus on North American Trade
House Footwear Caucus
New England Congressional Caucus (24)
Pennsylvania Congressional Delegation Steering Committee (5)
Tennessee Valley Authority Caucus (23)

Senate

Democratic

Moderate/Conservative Senate Democrats (15)

Republican

Senate Steering Committee

Bipartisan

Border Caucus
Northeast-Midwest Senate Coalition (40)
Senate Caucus on the Family (31)
Senate Coal Caucus (39)
Senate Drug Enforcement Caucus (44)
Senate Footwear Caucus
Senate Steel Caucus (46)
Senate Wine Caucus
Concerned Senators for the Arts (35)
Senate Caucus on North American Trade
Senate Children's Caucus (18)
Senate Copper Caucus (18)
Senate Export Caucus
Senate Rail Caucus
Senate Tourism Caucus (60)
Western State Coalition (30)

Bicameral

Ad Hoc Congressional Committee on the Baltic States and the Ukraine (75)
Congressional Alcohol Fuels Caucus (90)
Congressional Clearinghouse on the Future (84)
Congressional Senior Citizens Caucus
Environmental and Energy Study Conference (37)
Long Island Congressional Caucus
New York State Congressional Delegation (36)
Pennsylvania Congressional Delegation (27)
Renewable Energy Congressional Staff Group (50)
Arms Control and Foreign Policy Caucus (129)
Coalition for Peace through Strength (232)
Congressional Caucus for Women's Issues (129)
Congressional Jewelry Manufacturing Coalition
Congressional Wood Energy Caucus
Friends of Ireland (80)
Military Reform Caucus
Pacific Northwest Trade Task Force
Pro-Life Caucus (60)
Senate/House Ad Hoc Monitoring Group on Southern Africa (53)
Vietnam Veterans in Congress (38)

*Numbers of members, where available, in parenthesis.
Source: Sula P. Richardson, Congressional Research Service.

Illustration 5.H.
The 1986 contest for elected house Democratic whip.

Leadership races and changes are important topics to consider when studying congressional political parties. In his many important works and statements concerning leadership succession and advancement, Robert Peabody emphasizes how both parties in both houses have very different structures and traditions of leadership changes. He also has revealed the high-theater politics of leadership races and contests. In 1986 the House Democrats will elect, for the first time, their third-ranking leader, the party whip. Previously an appointed position, the significance of the whip's job is that it puts the occupant within the inner circle of House leadership and in a succession line to the speakership. The following "news" article about the impending race reveals the nature of politics in leadership contests.

Another in the long line of Minnesota liberals has stepped forward to try to rally his party's diverse forces.

Rep. Martin Olav Sabo, who is seeking a House Democratic leadership position, displays a Norwegian reserve that makes Walter F. Mondale seem practically charismatic, by contrast. It is too early to say whether he will succeed, but he is an amiable and savvy legislator, with firm views on the steps Democrats should take to bolster their effectiveness.

"I believe in strong leadership, but not to give orders," said Sabo, who was Minnesota House Speaker for six years before winning his first congressional election in 1978. "For leadership to be strong, you have to maximize the avenues of communications, especially upward. . . . We get so preoccupied with running to meetings that we have little opportunity to talk to each other."

In particular, he called for more cooperation between committee chairmen and the party leadership. He cited the need for "an over-all strategy" for handling the 13 regular bills from the Appropriations Committee, on which he serves.

Sabo has been soliciting his colleagues' support for the Majority Whip post, which is scheduled to become vacant at the end of 1986 with the leadership changes following the retirement of Speaker Thomas P. O'Neill Jr., D-Mass. "It's amazing how many times I end up just listening" to their problems and suggestions during the meetings, he said.

Recent thinly veiled disagreements on how to handle budget and tax issues have offered renewed evidence of the difficulties in leading House Democrats. Since 1981, O'Neill's style has been marked by harsh criticisms of President Reagan coupled with his own policy alternatives that he occasionally promotes as widely held party positions. But he usually gives committee chairmen wide discretion to prepare legislation.

Working with former House Democratic Caucus chairman Gillis W. Long, D-La., who died in January, Sabo chaired its party effectiveness committee, which brought together Democrats of all ideological stripes for weekly lunches where they sought common ground on policy and tactics. Their efforts won attention with lengthy documents laying out a new agenda.

Because it is "very difficult for the majority party [in the House] to say that its program is different from what it already has passed," the more important result has been to allow Members to exchange ideas, Sabo said. Democrats must "build more responsibility" and "yield some individuality" to the House and their party, he added. "My sense is we don't have much of that now."

Although the idea sounds good in principle, many Members resist the broad consultation that he advocates. When Rep. Richard A. Gephardt of Missouri, the new Caucus chairman, early this year tried to win approval for regular Caucus discussions with committee chairmen of their forthcoming schedules, he encountered stiff resistance from several chairmen and eventually dropped the proposal.

Sabo's low-profile "insider" approach contrasts with that of Rep. Tony Coelho, D-Calif., whom many observers says is the front-runner of the six candidates competing to succeed Thomas S. Foley, D-Wash., as Democratic Whip. Foley is seeking to replace Jim Wright of Texas as Majority Leader, who in turn is bidding to replace O'Neill.

As chairman of the Democratic Congressional Campaign Committee, Coelho has often leveled vocal and highly partisan attacks against Reagan and the GOP. His critics contend that like O'Neill, he does not consult widely enough with his colleagues on political strategy or focus on legislative details. Coelho disputes those charges, and backers point to the wide support they say he has won in the early maneuvering for the Whip post and his support for Democrats calling for "new ideas."

Although such an assessment is highly speculative and subject to change, Sabo may be Coelho's principal opponent. In contrast to Coelho and Norman Y. Mineta of California, Bill Alexander of Arkansas and W.G. (Bill) Hefner of North Carolina, he offers regional balance and a distinctly liberal voice to a southern-western leadership team headed by Wright and Foley. He may have to battle on early ballots with Charles B. Rangel of New York, the sixth candidate, for regional and liberal support.

Another factor which makes these predictions tentative is the possibility that an active challenge to Wright or Foley, perhaps by Ways and Means Committee chairman Dan Rostenkowski of Illinois, could affect the Whip race because of deals or alliances that are struck. And some Whip candidates may bow out and other emerge before the selection; some House aides said, for example, that Mineta has not been campaigning actively, but Mineta contends that the contest has barely begun.

Sabo said that his prognosis of the race varies from one day to the next but cautions that it remains fluid. "On the whole, it's a very open race, and many Members won't come to a decision until a year from now or after the 1986 election," he said.

A postscript: A draft study of last year's race to replace Howard H. Baker Jr., R-Tenn., as Senate Majority Leader emphasizes the "blue smoke and mirrors" in congressional leadership contests, especially in the Senate.

"Most of the activity takes place behind the scenes," writes Robert L. Peabody, a political science professor at the Johns Hopkins University and noted author on the subject. "Commitments to one candidate or another remain essentially personal. . . . [Senators] have most trouble saying 'no' to a colleague, so they hedge. Almost inevitably, contenders are the last to find out that their counts are inflated and then only as revealed by the stark realities of a succession of secret ballots." In 1984, backers of Sen. James A. McClure, R-Idaho, contended he might lead the five candidates for Baker's post after the first ballot; instead, he finished last.

In an instructive note for next year's House contest, Peabody added that leadership races with more than three candidates are unusual because it is difficult for so many to engender "initial enthusiasm from a broad set of cohorts."

Source: Richard E. Cohen, "Congressional Focus," *National Journal*, May 25, 1985, p. 1,256.

Chapter Six

Structural Characteristics III: Legislative Procedures

The congressional decision process is labyrinthlike, involving multiple, successive decision stages and an abundance of decision points. For a bill to become a law, it must successfully circumnavigate numerous obstacles and hurdles. This affords opponents of legislation numerous opportunities for delay, deadlock, and defeat of a proposed bill. Once a proposed bill is introduced in both houses, it must be referred to committee, favorably reported by the relevant subcommittee and full committees in each house, scheduled on the floor, debated and voted on the floor, and, if necessary, sent to conference to iron out differences between the House and Senate before being forwarded for presidential approval. So complicated is the congressional process that Woodrow Wilson was moved to write, "Once begin the dance of legislation, and you must struggle through its mazes as best you can to the breathless end—if any there be."

Additionally, the legislative process is complicated by the requirement that Congress act twice if a government activity is to materialize; once in the form of an authorization, entitling the government to undertake certain actions; and second with an appropriation, allocating public money to fund such an action. Thus, this two-track requirement means that for almost every government purpose, Congress must complete two separate legislative processes in each house. Of course, all of this means that most legislation will be compromised and watered down as efforts are made by proponents to neutralize potential intensely opposed, strategically located opponents.

Selections in this chapter examine the functions and politics of rules and offer authoritative explications, with illustrations, of congressional procedures.

As one studies legislative procedures, it should be kept in mind that these rules are not neutral. Procedures significantly affect the group struggle by favoring one group rather than another, affecting who wins and thus affecting the distribution of policy benefits. Also, procedures frequently become the focus of the ploys and strategies of various interests as they aspire to increase their political advantage.

Reading 6.1

Functions of Rules and Procedures

Walter J. Oleszek

The rules and procedures of Congress satisfy important institutional requirements. Oleszek lists these and discusses how they facilitate the business of Congress and are augmented by the norms or informal rules of Congress.

FUNCTIONS OF RULES AND PROCEDURES

Any decision-making body, Congress included, needs a set of rules, procedures, and conventions, formal and informal, in order to function. In the case of Congress, the Constitution authorizes the House and Senate to formulate their own rules of procedure. Thomas Jefferson, who, as Vice President, compiled the first parliamentary manual for the U.S. Senate, emphasized the importance of rules to any legislative body.

> It is much more material that there should be a rule to go by, than what the rule is; that there may be uniformity of proceeding in business not subject to the caprice of the Speaker or captiousness of the members. It is very material that order, decency, and regularity be preserved in a dignified public body.[1]

Rules and procedures in an organization serve many functions. Among them are to provide stability, legitimize decisions, divide responsibilities, reduce conflict, and distribute power. Each of these functions will be illustrated both by examples drawn from a college or university setting and by parallel functions in Congress.

Stability

Rules provide stability and predictability in personal and organizational affairs. Individuals and institutions can conduct their day-to-day business without having to debate procedure. Universities, for example, have specific requirements for bachelor's, master's, and doctorate degrees. Students know that if they are to progress from one degree to the next they must comply with rules and requirements. Daily or weekly changes in those requirements would cause chaos on any campus. Similarly, legislators need not decide each day who can speak on the floor, offer amendments, or close debate. Such matters are governed by regularized procedures that continue from one Congress to the next and afford similar rights and privileges to every member.

Legitimacy

Students typically receive final course grades that are based on their classroom performance, examinations, and term papers. They accept the professors' evaluations if they believe in their fairness and legitimacy. If professors suddenly decided to use students' political opinions as the basis for final grades, there would be a storm of protest against such arbitrary procedures. In a similar fashion, members of Congress and citizens accept legislative decisions when they

Source: From Walter J. Oleszek, *Congressional Procedures and the Policy Process* (Washington, D.C.: Congressional Quarterly Press, 1978), pp. 5–12.

believe the decisions were approved according to orderly and fair procedure.

Division of Labor

Any university requires a division of labor if it is to carry out its tasks effectively and responsibly, and rules establish the various jurisdictions. Hence there are history, chemistry, and art departments; admissions officers and bursars; and food service and physical plant managers, all with specialized assignments. For Congress, committees are the heart of its legislative process. They provide the division of labor and specialization that Congress needs in order to handle the more than 20,000 measures introduced biennially, and to review the administration of scores of federal programs. Like specialized bodies in many organizations, committees do not make final policy decisions but propose recommendations to their respective chambers.

Conflict Resolution

Rules reduce conflicts among members and units of organizations by distinguishing appropriate actions and behavior from the inappropriate. For example, universities have procedures by which students may drop or add classes. There are discussions with faculty advisers, completion of appropriate paperwork, and the approval of a dean. Students who informally attempt to drop or add classes may encounter conflicts with their professors as well as sanctions from the dean's office. Most of the conflicts can be avoided by observance of established procedures. Similarly, congressional rules reduce conflict by, for example, establishing procedures to fill vacancies on committees when several members are competing for the same position.

Distribution of Power

A major consequence of rules is that they generally distribute power in any organization. As a result, rules are often a source of conflict themselves. During the 1960s, for example, many campuses witnessed struggles among students, faculty, and administrators involving the curriculum. The charge of irrelevance in course work was a frequent criticism of many students. As a result, the "rules of the game" for curriculum development were changed on many campuses. Students, junior faculty, and even community groups became involved in reshaping the structure and content of the educational program.

Like universities, Congress distributes power according to its rules and customs. Informal party rules, for example, establish a hierarchy of leadership positions in both chambers. And House and Senate rules accord prerogatives to congressional committee chairmen that are unavailable to noncommittee leaders. Rules are, therefore, not neutral devices. They help to shore up the more powerful members as well as protect the rights of the minority. Thus, efforts to change the rules are almost invariably efforts to redistribute power.

RULES AND POLICYMAKING IN THE CONGRESSIONAL CONTEXT

Rules play similar, but not identical, roles in most complex organizations. Congress has its own characteristics that affect the functions of the rules. First, members of Congress owe their positions to the electorate, not to their congressional peers or to influential congressional leaders. No one in Congress has authority over the other members comparable to that of university presidents and tenured faculty over junior faculty or to that of a corporation president over lower level executives. Members cannot be fired except by their constituency. And each member has equal voting power in committees and on the floor of the House or Senate.

Congress' rules, unlike those of many organizations, are especially sensitive to the rights of *minorities*, including the minority party, ideological minorities, and individual members. Skillful use of the rules enables the minority to check majority action by delaying, defeating, or reshaping legislation. Intensity often counts as much as numbers —an apathetic majority may find it difficult to prevail over a well-organized minority. Except in the few instances when extraordinary majorities are needed, such as overriding presidential vetoes (two thirds), Senate ratification of treaties (two thirds), and the decision to stop extended debate in the Senate (three fifths), the rules of the House and Senate require a simple majority to decide public policies.

Congress is also different from other organizations in its degree of responsiveness to external groups and pressures. The legislative branch is not as self-contained an institution as a university or a corporation. Congress is involved with every significant national and international issue. Its agenda compels members to respond to changing constituent interests and needs. Congress is also subject to numerous other influences, such as the President, pressure groups, political parties, and state and local officials.

Finally, Congress is a collegial and not a hierarchical body. Power does not flow from the top down, as in a corporation, but in practically every direction. There is only minimal centralized authority at the top; congressional policies are not "announced" but are "made" by shifting coalitions that vary from issue to issue. Congress' deliberations are also more accessible and public than those of perhaps any other kind of organization. These are some of the characteristics that set Congress apart from other organizations; inevitably these differences affect the decision-making process.

Procedure and Policy

Legislative procedures and policymaking are inextricably linked in at least four ways. First, procedures affect policy outcomes. Congress processes legislation by complex rules and procedures that permeate the institution and touch every public policy. Some matters are only gently brushed by the rules, while others become locked in their grip. Major civil rights legislation, for example, failed for decades to pass Congress because southern Senators used their chamber's rules and procedures to kill or modify such measures.

A second point is that very often policy decisions are expressed as procedural moves. Representatives and Senators, on various occasions, prefer not to make clear-cut decisions on certain complex and far-reaching public issues. Should a major weapons system be continued or curtailed? Should the nation's energy production needs take precedence over environmental concerns? Should financial assistance for the elderly be reduced and priority be given to aiding disadvantaged children? On questions like these, members may be "cross-pressured." (The President might be exerting influence one way while constituent interests dictate the opposite.) Legislators may lack adequate information to make informed judgments. They may be reluctant to oppose powerful pressure groups. Or the issue, they believe, does not lend itself to a simple yes or no vote.

As a result, legislators employ various procedural devices to handle knotty problems. A matter may be postponed on the ground of insufficient committee hearings. Congress may direct an agency to prepare a detailed report before an issue is considered. Or a measure may be "tabled" by the House or Senate, a procedural vote that effectively defeats a proposal without rendering a judgment on its substance. When the 95th Congress convened, for example, the Senate debated a proposal that would put it on record against blanket amnesty for Vietnam draft evaders. The controversial measure was tabled on a 48-to-46 vote, leaving the whole matter to the President.

Third, the nature of the policy can determine the use of certain procedures. The House and Senate generally consider noncontroversial measures under expeditious procedures, whereas controversial proposals normally involve lengthy deliberation. Extraordinary circumstances might prompt Congress to invoke rarely used practices to enact legislation with dispatch. For example, because of the severe winter of 1977, President Carter urged Congress to approve quickly a law granting him authority to order transfers of natural gas to states hard hit by gas shortages. On January 26, 1977, the measure was introduced in the Senate. To speed the bill's passage, the Senate employed a rarely used procedure that brought the measure immediately to the floor for debate, bypassing the usual committee stage entirely.[2] Moreover, under pressure from its leadership, the Senate rejected all substantive amendments and passed the measure 91 to 2 after two days of debate. As national issues change, moreover, some procedures become nearly extinct, while others are used more and more frequently to meet new needs.

Finally, policy outcomes are more likely to be influenced by members with procedural expertise. Members who are skilled parliamentarians are better prepared to gain approval of their proposals than those who are only vaguely familiar with the rules. Just as carpenters and lawyers must learn their trade, members of Congress need to understand the rules if they expect to perform effectively. And congressional procedures are confusing to newcomers. "To table, to refer to committee, to amend—so many things come up," declared freshman Senator S. I. Hayakawa (R–Calif.), "you don't know whether you are coming or going."[3] Former Speaker of the House John McCormack once advised freshmen House members:

> Learn the rules and understand the precedents and procedures of the House. The Congressman who knows how the House operates will soon be recognized for his parliamentary skills—and his prestige will rise among his colleagues, no matter what his party.[4]

Members who know the rules well always have the potential to shape legislation to their ends. Those who do not reduce their proficiency and influence as legislators.

Precedents and Folkways

Congress is regulated not only by formal rules, but by informal ones that influence legislative procedure and member behavior.[5] Two types of informal rules are precedents and "folkways." Precedents, the accumulated past decisions on matters of procedure, represent a blend of the formal and informal. They are the "common law" of Congress and govern many procedures not explicitly covered in the formal rules. For example, formal rules prescribe the order of business in the House and Senate, but precedents permit variations through the unanimous consent of the members. The rulings of the Speaker of the House and presiding officer of the Senate form a large body of precedents. They are given formal status by the parliamentarians in each chamber and distributed to Representatives and Senators.[6]

Folkways, on the other hand, are unwritten norms of behavior that members are expected to observe. "Without these folkways," concluded Donald Matthews, "the Senate could hardly operate with its present organization and rules."[7] Several of the more important are "legislative work" (members should concentrate on congressional duties and not be publicity seekers), "courtesy" (members should be solicitous toward their colleagues and avoid personal attacks on them), and "specialization" (members should master a few policy areas and not try to be a jack-of-all-trades). Those who abide by these and other norms are often rewarded with increased influence in the policy process, for example, by being appointed to prestigious committees. Conversely, legislators who persistently violate Congress' informal customs are apt to see legislation they support blocked in committee or on the floor. Congressional decision making, then, is shaped by each chamber's formal and informal structure of rules, precedents, and traditions.

Reading 6.2

Enactment of a Law: Procedural Steps in the Legislative Process

William F. Hildenbrand and
Robert B. Dove

The most authoritative treatment of legislative procedure is the following pamphlet, Enactment of a Law. *It is a publication of Congress, for the Congress, by people who do the business of Congress. In reading this, one should be aware that the Senate, which is more fully covered in this piece, differs markedly from the House. As noted in Reading 3.2, the House* does not *permit unlimited debate nor nongermane amendments; it* does *make more use of its committees and subcommittees,* does *have a Rules Committee that serves as a traffic cop,* does *have a more complex scheme of calendars for scheduling legislation for consideration on the floor, and* does *do most of its business in the committee of the whole.*

FOREWORD

Nothing can be of greater importance in a democracy than the dissemination of knowledge concerning the way that the government operates and how citizens can involve themselves in a meaningful fashion in that government. It is to that end that I am pleased that a new and expanded edition of this document, which has such a long and proud history, has been published. I can only hope that you the readers will find it helpful and enlightening as a primer on the legislative process and that your involvement in our American democratic process is aided as a result.

William F. Hildenbrand
Secretary, U. S. Senate

Source: William F. Hildenbrand and Robert B. Dove, *Enactment of a Law: Procedural Steps in the Legislative Process* Document No. 97–20. Washington, D.C.: U.S. Government Printing Office, 1982.

ENACTMENT OF A LAW, AND OTHER ASPECTS OF THE LEGISLATIVE BRANCH OF GOVERNMENT

The legislative branch of government has responsibilities which in many cases transcend the process of enactment of legislation. Among these are the Senate's power of advice and consent with regard to treaties and nominations and the power of either or both of the two Houses of Congress to veto various executive proposals through resolutions of disapproval, or the refusal to agree to resolutions of approval, for such activities as executive reorganization. The preeminent role of the legislative branch, however, is its concern with legislation.

"All legislative Powers" granted to the Federal Government by the Constitution, as stated in Article I, Section 1, are vested in a Congress of the United States, which shall consist of a Senate and House of Representatives. The Congress meets at least once a year, and has been doing so since 1789 in the following locations: from March 4, 1789 through August 12, 1790, in Federal Hall, New York City, New York; from December 6, 1790 through December 2, 1799, in Congress Hall, Philadelphia, Pennsylvania; from November 17, 1800 through the present, The Capitol, Washington, District of Columbia.

The Senate is composed of 100 Members. Each State, regardless of area or population, is entitled under the Constitution to two Senators. Constitutionally, the Senate's presiding officer is the Vice President of the United States, who is also the President of the Senate. Under prescribed circumstances, however, the Presiding Officer of the Senate can be any one of a number of officials of the Senate. The Senate chooses a President pro tempore who holds the office during the pleasure of the Senate and until another is elected or his term of office as a Senator expires. The very first act ever performed by the Senate (in 1789) was the election of a President pro tempore, who was elected "for the sole purpose" of opening the electoral vote in the absence of the Vice President-elect, who had not yet been installed. That appointment ceased 20 days later when John Adams appeared. From then through the 1860s vacancies occurred in the office of President pro tempore by reason of the return of the Vice President to the Chair.

The President pro tempore has the right to name a Senator as an Acting President pro tempore to perform the duties of the Chair. On January 10, 1977 the Senate adopted a resolution creating an Office of Deputy President pro tempore of the Senate. The resolution provided in part that: "any Member of the Senate who has held the Office of President or Vice President of the United States shall be a Deputy President pro tempore." Although the resolution did not specifically enumerate the duties and responsibilities of the office, the Deputy President pro tempore is authorized a legislative staff of three persons and an automobile with driver-messenger. Former Vice President Hubert H. Humphrey, then a Senator from Minnesota in 1977, received the special title, pay and allowances as a mark of respect for his former high office.

In the absence of the Vice President, and pending the election of a President pro tempore, the Secretary of the Senate, or in his absence the Assistant Secretary, shall perform the duties of the Chair.

The only exception to the constitutional right of the Vice President to preside occurs when the President of the United States, or the Vice President of the United States, upon whom the powers and duties of the Office of President shall have devolved, shall be impeached and the Chief Justice of the Supreme Court presides over the impeachment trial.

Senators are elected for terms of six years and are divided into three classes, so that the terms of one-third thereof expire every two years.

Membership of the House is apportioned on the basis of the population of the several States, the number now being fixed at 435, but each State shall have at least one Representative. The House is presided over by the Speaker, who is chosen by its Members at the beginning of a Congress or when a vacancy occurs in that office. Members of the House are elected for two-year terms, being the same as the duration of a Congress.

Vacancies in the representation of any State in the Senate may be filled at a special election called for such purpose or by a temporary appointment by the Governor. In the latter case the appointee serves until the vacancy is filled by election in the manner provided by law. Vacancies in the House of Representatives can only be filled by an election for that purpose.

In addition to the 435 Members of the House, there are in that body a Resident Commissioner from Puerto Rico, and one Delegate each from American Samoa, the District of Columbia, Guam, and the Virgin Islands. They have the same rights and privileges as a Representative with respect to attending sessions of the House, engaging in debate, and serving on committees, but they do not have the right to vote.

The life of a Congress is two years.

The Congress assembles at least once every year, as provided by the Constitution, beginning at noon on January 3rd, unless by law the two Houses shall otherwise provide.

The Senate's first day of the first session is largely ceremonial and organizational, including the administration of oaths of office; notification to the President and the House of the assembling of a quorum; adoption of resolutions electing Senate officials, fixing the Senate's hour of daily meeting, and providing for counting of the electoral vote for President and Vice President (occurring every other Congress); and getting unanimous consent agreements permitting the Senate to conduct routine housekeeping.

When the second session first meets, similar, though fewer, matters are provided for, since most requests for authority cover both sessions of a Congress, and officials are elected to serve at the pleasure of the Senate and until the election of a successor.

Upon reconvening after a sine die adjournment, the Chair lays before the Senate any letters of resignation of Senators and certificates of appointment of Senators to fill the vacancies caused by those resignations, together with the credentials of newly elected Senators.

The President, under the Constitution, may call a special session of Congress, or either body thereof, whenever in his judgment it is necessary. He may even adjourn them to such time as he shall think proper in case of "disagreement between them, with respect to the time of adjournment."

Both Houses ordinarily meet at noon each day, but either may change its hour of meeting. Each House terminates its daily session at its own pleasure, usually by 6:00 P.M.; however, evening sessions are held when necessary. Neither House can recess or adjourn for more than three days without the consent of the other.

Bills and resolutions started on their way to enactment but left unfinished at the end of any session of a Congress, except the last, are proceeded with at the next session as if no adjournment had taken place; however, at the end of a Congress all such measures die on which final action has not been taken. Treaties and protocols, which are considered by the Senate only, do not die, but remain from Congress to Congress until disposed of. Their consideration, however, must be resumed anew at the beginning of the next Congress. Nominations unacted upon in a session die and must be resubmitted to the Senate at the next session. A recess for more than 30 days also requires nominations to be returned to the President.

FORMS AND DESIGNATION OF LEGISLATIVE BUSINESS

All proposed legislation, and nearly all formal actions by either of the two Houses, take the form of a bill or resolution.

A bill is a legislative proposal of a general nature. A bill may propose either a public or private matter, but both are contained in the same numerical sequence. Public bills are the most numerous. They are designed to affect or benefit the general public. Private bills affect or benefit individuals or groups of individuals. Together, bills account for a large majority of the total of legislative proposals of each Congress. The Senate numbers bills in sequence starting with number 1, and each number is preceded by the designation "S." House bills are similarly numbered and prefaced by "H.R." Thus, bill number 100 in the Senate is written S. 100, and in the House, H.R. 100.

Joint Resolutions, which have the same effect as bills unless they are used to propose amendments to the Constitution, are designated "S.J. Res. ______." Concurrent Resolutions, which are designated "S. Con. Res. ______" for Senate concurrent resolutions, are chosen to express the sense of the Congress to the President or other parties; to attend to "housekeeping" matters affecting both Houses; or to carry proposals to correct the language of measures passed by one House (an engrossment), or both Houses (an enrollment). All concurrent resolutions, including corrective resolutions, must be agreed to in both the Senate and House. One House may seek to correct a measure it passed, or both Houses may wish to correct a measure awaiting the President's signature. The former may be accomplished merely by specifying what changes or additions are to be made and requesting the other House to make them, or requesting the return of the measure to the originating House for that purpose. Correction of measures already sent to the President, however, are made after agreement of both Houses to concurrent resolutions requesting their return from the White House. Such resolutions include a resolve that if and when a measure is returned, the action of the Presiding Officers of the two houses in signing the measure shall be deemed rescinded, and the Secretary of the Senate or the Clerk of the House is authorized and directed in the reenrollment of the measure to make the necessary corrections. The corrected measure (bill or joint resolution) is then again signed by the Secretary of the Senate or the Clerk of the House, the Speaker, and the Vice President and again delivered to the White House. Concurrent resolutions are not presented to the White House for the President's signature, because they do not become law.

Finally there is the designation of "S. Res. ______," for Senate resolutions. When the question of agreement to, or formal acceptance of, a resolution is raised, concurrent and simple resolutions are agreed to or adopted, whereas bills and joint resolutions are passed.

In the House of Representatives, they have the following designations: "H.R. ______," for House bills; "H.J. Res. ______," for House joint resolutions; "H. Con. Res. ______," for House concurrent resolutions., and "H. Res. ______," for House resolutions. The bills and resolutions are numbered ad seriatim, in the chronological order in which they are introduced.

Senate and House bills and Senate and House joint resolutions, when passed by both Houses in identical form and approved by the President, become public or private law—public laws affect the Nation as a whole; private laws benefit only an individual or a class thereof. The procedure on each is identical, with the exception of joint resolutions proposing amendments to the Constitution of the United States, which under the Constitution must be passed in each House by a two-thirds vote of the Members present and voting, a quorum being present. They are not sent to the President for his approval but to the Administrator of the General Services Administration, who transmits them to the various States for ratification by at least three-fourths thereof. When so ratified, such amendments are valid.

Concurrent resolutions by either House do not become law; they are not signed by the President, not by the Speaker and the Vice President. They are attested by the Secretary of the Senate and Clerk of the House and transmitted after approval to the Administrator of the General Services Administration for publication in the Statutes at Large. Concurrent resolutions have the force of both Houses and must be approved by them in identical form to be effective—they are used for joint housekeeping matters, such as the creation of a joint committee or to express the sense of Congress.

A House or Senate resolution (H. Res. ______ and S. Res. ______) only has the force of the House passing it, and the action by the one House is all that is necessary. Such resolutions are used for the housekeeping matters of the House passing it, such as creating an ad hoc investigating committee. They are also used to express the sense of the body passing them.

ORIGIN OF LEGISLATION

Legislation originates in several ways. The Constitution provides that the President "shall from time to time give to the Congress Information of the State of the Union, and recommend to their Consideration such Measures as he shall judge necessary and expedient; . . . ."

The President fulfills this duty either by personally addressing a joint session of the two Houses or by sending messages in writing to the Congress, or to either body thereof, which are received and referred to the appropriate committees. The President usually presents or submits his annual message on the state of the Union shortly after the beginning of a session.

In addition, there are many executive communications sent to the Congress. These are documents signed by the President, Agency, Department head or organization, and filed or submitted as a report to the Senate as directed by law or otherwise. These items are numbered sequentially for a Congress and assigned a prefix EC. They are described only by a brief statement of the contents in the *Congressional Record.*

The right of petition is guaranteed the citizens of the United States by the Constitution, and many individual petitions and memorials from State legislatures are sent to Congress. They are laid before the two Houses by their respective Presiding Officers or submitted by individual Members of the House and Senate in their respective bodies, and are usually referred to the appropriate committees of the House in which they were submitted.

Bills to carry out the recommendations of the President are usually introduced "by request" by the chairmen of the various committees or subcommittees thereof which have jurisdiction of the subject matter. Sometimes the committees themselves may submit and report to the Senate "original bills" to carry out such recommendations.

The ideas for legislative proposals may come from an individual Representative or Senator, from any of the executive departments of the Government, from private organized groups or associations, or from any individual citizen. However, they can be introduced in their respective Houses only by Senators and Representatives. When introduced, they are referred to the standing committees which have jurisdiction of the subject matter.

Members frequently introduce bills that are similar in purpose, in which case the committee considering them may take one of the bills and add the best features of the others for reporting to the parent body, or draft an entirely new bill and report it (known as an original bill) in lieu of the others.

A TYPICAL DAY AS IT ILLUSTRATES THE LEGISLATIVE PROCESS

Each day in the Senate begins as the Secretary of the Senate and the Presiding Officer for that day escort the Chaplain of the Senate or guest chaplain to the desk. The Chaplain is a clergyman chosen by the Senate, whose responsibility is to offer the prayer at the opening of each daily session, as well as to officiate at various ceremonies and respond to Senators' private needs. Various officials are present on the floor of the Senate when it convenes, including the Majority and Minority Leaders of the Senate, the Secretary and Assistant Secretary of the Senate, the Sergeant at Arms, the Legislative Clerk, the Journal Clerk, the Parliamentarian of the Senate, the Secretaries for the Majority and the Minority, the Official Reporters of Debate, and the Pages.

Secretary of the Senate

The Secretary of the Senate is the elected official of the Senate responsible for management of many legislative and administrative services. The Secretary is the disbursing officer for the Senate. The official seal of the Senate is in the custody of, and its use is prescribed by, the Secretary. In the absence of the Vice President, and pending the election of a President pro tempore, the Secretary performs the duties of the Chair.

Assistant Secretary of the Senate

The Assistant Secretary of the Senate is the chief assistant of the secretary of the Senate. The Assistant Secretary performs the functions of the Secretary in the latter's absence, and in the event of the death or resignation of the Secretary would act as Secretary in all matters except those duties as disbursing officer of the Senate.

Sergeant at Arms

On the day after the first organization of the Senate, a Doorkeeper was chosen whose title was eventually changed to Sergeant at Arms. His duties are to execute the Senate's orders as to decorum on the floor and in the galleries. He is responsible for the enforcement of all rules made for the regulation of the Senate wing of the Capitol. He is the custodian of all properties under the dominion of the Senate and supervises the messengers, pages, and other workers who labor for the Senate. If the Senate decides to issue warrants of arrest for its absent Members, it is the duty of the Sergeant at Arms to bring those Senators into custody.

Journal Clerk

Article 1, section 5, paragraph 3 of the Constitution provides that "Each House shall keep a Journal of its Proceedings, and from time to time publish the same, excepting such Parts as may in their Judgment require Secrecy; and the Yeas and Nays of the Members of either House on any question shall, at the Desire of one-fifth of those Present be entered on the Journal." The Journal Clerk is charged with maintaining the Senate Journal under the direction of the Secretary of the Senate.

Legislative Clerk

The Legislative Clerk has the responsibility of reporting all bills, messages from the House, conference reports, and amendments to the Senate. All record votes are taken by the Legislative Clerk and his assistants.

Parliamentarian

An appointed official of the Senate, the Parliamentarian functions under the direction of the Secretary of the Senate. The Parliamentarian's chief duty and responsibility is to advise the Presiding Officer on parliamentary aspects of Senate activity. The Parliamentarian advises Senators and senatorial committee staffs on matters, and is called upon by other branches of Government, the press, and the public for advice regarding procedural aspects of Senate activity.

Official Reporters of Debates

The Official Reporters prepare the material relative to the business of the Senate for inclusion in the *Congressional Record.* All proceedings in the Senate Chamber are reported verbatim by a staff of seven Official Reporters of Debates, who are under the supervision of the Editor in Chief. The Editor in Chief is the editor of all matter contained in the Senate proceedings. In addition to the verbatim proceedings in the Senate Chamber, the office of the Official Reporters processes for inclusion in the *Congressional Record* a description of the morning business conducted by the Senate (measures introduced, messages from the President and the House of Representatives, co-sponsors, communications received, and notices of hearings), and additional or unspoken statements of Senators. The Official Reporters of Debates are appointed by the Secretary of the Senate.

Secretary for the Majority

The Secretary for the Majority is an elected officer of the Senate who is responsible for providing many support services to the Majority Leadership and Members of the Senate. The floor-related duties of the Secretary include supervising the cloakroom, briefing Senators on votes and issues that are under consideration on the floor, obtaining pair votes for Senators, and polling Senators when the Leadership so desires. Additionally, the Secretary is responsible for assigning Senate Chamber seats to the majority party Members; maintaining a file of committee assignment requests; staffing the Steering Committee during arrangement of majority party committees; recommending to the Leadership majority party candidates for appointment to boards, commissions, and international conferences; maintaining records of such appointments; providing a repository for official minutes of majority conferences and meetings of the Policy Committee, Steering Committee, and committee chairmen; monitoring the nominations on the Executive Calendar; and other duties as directed by the Leadership.

Secretary for the Minority

The Secretary for the Minority is an elected officer of the Senate. His duties include supervising the cloakrooms, obtaining pair votes for Senators as requested, briefing Senators on issues under consideration and votes, polling Senators at the request of the Leadership, and assigning desk seats on the appropriate side of the aisle of the Senate Chamber. Additional responsibilities of the Secretary of the Minority include staffing of the Steering Committee during arrangement of minority party committees; maintenance of the request files for committee assignments; maintenance of Senate appointments to boards, commissions, and international conferences and recommendations of minority candidates to the Leadership; maintenance of repository for the official minutes of the Minority Conferences, Policy Committee, Steering Committee, and committee chairmen; monitoring of nominations on the Executive Calendar; and other duties as directed by the Leadership.

Republican Legislative Scheduling Office

The Republican Legislative Scheduling Office, under the direction of the Secretary for the Republicans, provides floor assistance to Republican Senators. The staff serves as a liaison between Republican Senators and the Republican leadership in dealing with Senators' legislative interests, unanimous consent requests, time agreements, and the scheduling of the Senate's proceedings. The staff also handles and schedules Republican Senators to preside over the Senate.

Democratic Policy Committee Floor Staff

Floor assistance for Democratic Senators is provided by the staff of the Democratic Policy Committee. This staff is available to provide information regarding the scheduling of legislation and to act as liaison between the legislative committees and the Democratic leadership. Assistance is given in the arrangement of unanimous consent requests on time agreements, amendments, and procedural issues on legislation being debated by the Senate. In addition, the staff provides advice on general parliamentary situations.

Policy Committees

The Policy Committees are party organizations within the framework of the Senate, functioning to provide services to their respective members in accordance with their needs as follows:

Democratic Policy Committee —detailed voting records available to each Democratic Senator; annual report on the major achievements of the session; extensive index of record votes on legislation both chronologically and by subject matter; and briefings on major bills and amendments.

Senate Republican Policy Committee —maintenance of research library; publication of legislative notices summarizing bills and resolutions on the Senate Calendar and proposed amendments thereto; publication of detailed analysis of all Senate record votes plus indexes, annual abstracts, and lists of voice votes; publication of the weekly Republican Counsel's Report; publication of policy papers on major issues; development ment of Republican legislative initiatives; research, legislative analysis, and speech writing for Republican senators upon request; personnel placement and counseling; briefing officials from State and local governments on national issues; assisting new Senators with staff orientation; and assistance to the party leader in preparation of the End-of-Year Report.

Pages

Senate pages, male and female, when appointed, must be at least 14 years of age and have completed the 8th grade of school. They may not be appointed or serve after attaining the age of 17, except when serving and enrolled in the Page School, they may continue their service through the session of the Senate in which the Page School terminates. Riding Page Service is provided by a separate service, through the Senate Post Office, several times a day for delivery of senators' letters to major Federal agencies in the District of Columbia only.

A NEW DAY

As the Senate begins its new day, it is important to note that the Senate recognizes two meanings for the word day, one known as "calendar" day, the other "legislative" day. A calendar day is recognized as each 24 hour period. Reference may be made to a day certain, as in a unanimous consent request to vote on passage of a measure on August 4, 1980 (a specific, determined, or fixed day), or a day not yet determined, as in a unanimous consent request or rule requiring action "on either of the next two days of actual session." Both, however, represent calendar days.

A legislative day is the period of time following an adjournment of the Senate until another adjournment. A recess (rather than an adjournment) in no way affects a legislative day; therefore, one legislative day may consume a considerable period of time—days, weeks, even months, but one or more adjournments from one day to the next would cause the calendar and legislative day to coincide. As used in the Rules of the Senate, unless specified as a calendar day, a day is recognized as a legislative day. There is, for example, the proviso that "no Senator shall speak more than twice upon any one question in debate on the same legislative day . . ." in Rule XIX, and yet Rule V, disallowing motions "to suspend, modify, or amend any rule . . . , except on one day's notice in writing . . . ," although not specifying the type of day, is interpreted as meaning one calendar day.

The Senate Majority Leader by unanimous consent customarily provides for a brief period of time (usually 10 minutes each) at the beginning of each daily session for himself and the Minority Leader to be used at their discretion for observations on current events, pending legislation, submission and agreement of various legislative matters, etc. They may yield all or part of their time to other Senators for sundry purposes.

It is with these orders that the day of the Senate begins.

During the morning hour of each legislative day, Rule VII of the Senate provides that, after the Journal is read, the Presiding Officer lay before the Senate messages, reports, and communications of various types.

Measures or matters are messaged between the two Houses, when transmitted in writing from one House to the other, on information pertaining to the passage of measures or other conduct of official business requiring concurrence or notification. The President of the United States transmits written messages to the Congress, which are brought to the Chamber and announced to the Senate by a messenger from the White House. Such messages are numbered sequentially for a Congress and assigned a prefix PM. They are printed in full in the *Congressional Record.* Messages from the President may be received at any stage of Senate proceedings, except during votes or quorums, while the Journal is being read, or while a question of order or a motion to adjourn is pending.

The Presiding Officer then calls for "The presentation of petitions and memorials."

These are documents memorializing the Government to do or not to do something. Memorials and petitions when laid before the Senate are numbered and assigned a prefix POM, and all memorials and petitions from State, Territory, and insular possession legislatures or conventions, lawfully called, are printed in full in the *Record* when presented. Those received from other memorialists or petitioners are described only by a brief statement of the contents.

The Presiding Officer then calls for "Reports of committees," "The introduction of bills and joint resolutions," and "The submission of other resolutions."

Under recent practices, however, nearly all of the bills and resolutions are presented by a Senator to the clerks at the Presiding Officer's desk for processing throughout the day, and without any comments from the floor.

The Majority Leader customarily secures unanimous consent at the beginning of each new Congress to allow receipt at the desk of all measures on days when morning business is conducted, at any time of the day. Such permission may be granted to allow Senators to bring measures to the desk, instead of following the procedure as set forth in Rule VII, requiring introduction of bills and joint resolutions only on a new legislative day during the transaction of morning business, followed by submission of other resolutions.

Bills and resolutions are still introduced from the floor, however, and any Senator, when making such introductions, usually discusses his proposal when he presents it. There can be only one prime sponsor of a bill or resolution, but commonly other Senators are included as co-sponsors.

The Senate Rules make no mention of multiple sponsorship, which has been a common practice for many years. Though custom permits unlimited numbers of senators to sponsor a wide assortment of measures, it prohibits more than one Member's name to appear on a reported bill or resolution and the printed report accompanying it. Co-sponsors are often shown on measures as introduced, but other names may be added, by unanimous consent, at their next printing. Since its inception, the practice of multiple sponsorship has been questioned by many Senators, and others have submitted resolutions to abolish its usage. The Committee on Rules and Administration has held hearings and favorably reported measures to amend the Rules to prohibit joint sponsorship, except under limited conditions, but to date, the full Senate has not voted its approval or disapproval. A former practice of holding measures at the desk for days, to permit the addition of names, has often met considerable opposition and was discontinued in the 1960s.

Measures can be submitted with the phrase "by request", a term found on bills and resolutions introduced or submitted at the request of the Administration or private organizations or individuals, following the name of its sponsor. Such proposals, though introduced as a courtesy, are not necessarily favored by the Senators sponsoring them. Drafts of proposed legislation from the President or an executive agency are usually introduced by the chairman of the committee of jurisdiction, who may on occasion be of the opposition party.

OVER, UNDER THE RULE

Newly offered resolutions or motions, when submitted, cannot be immediately considered when objection is heard. Rule XIV, paragraph 6, provides that they shall be placed on the Calendar under the heading "Resolutions and Motions Over, Under the Rule" and laid before the Senate on the next legislative day immediately before the close of morning business, unless by unanimous consent it is otherwise directed. Once laid before the Senate, if they are not disposed of before the close of the Morning Hour on the following legislative day, they are automatically placed on the Calendar for consideration at a later date in a similar fashion as other bills or resolutions thereon.

The rules require that every bill and joint resolution have three readings, each on a different legislative day, before passage—two of these to occur before reference to a committee. This is seldom done anymore, however, since all bills and resolutions are available in printed form. The reading requirement on different days is rarely invoked, usually only when there are procedural conflicts, but it can be forced on the Senate by a single Senator.

After the second reading of a bill, it is referred by the Presiding Officer to the standing committee of the Senate which, in his judgment, has jurisdiction of the subject matter, or a preponderance thereof. In the Senate, action by the joint leadership or unanimous consent is required to refer a bill jointly and/or sequentially to two or more committees having jurisdiction over the subject matter.

Some measures in the Senate are referred to as "companion measures." This term is used to describe a legislative document identical, or very similar, to another. Generally, companion bills or resolutions are introduced or submitted by design near or on a given day in both Houses. Similar or identical measures with the same intent, however, may be introduced in both the Senate and House at any time during a Congress as separate bills by one or more Members. Such measures, once having been reported from a Senate committee, are placed on the Calendar, and if their companion House measure is messaged to the Senate, it too is placed on the Calendar without being referred to committee.

The Senate committees deal with legislation in specific areas as set forth in Rule XXV, but sometimes the matter contained in certain measures significantly impinges on several areas, thereby necessitating consideration by more than one committee. When such need for joint jurisdiction occurs, a measure may be referred to two or more committees jointly or sequentially by motion of the majority and minority leaders or their designees, or by unanimous consent. When jointly referred, a measure must be jointly reported by the committees involved (except deferral resolutions and rescission bills), and a sequentially referred measure is reported in turn as specified in the motion or consent agreement by which it was so referred.

Endorsements showing the sponsor and reference are made at the Presiding Officer's desk on each bill. These various proceedings are shown in the *Congressional Record* of that day and are noted in the Minute Book kept by the Journal Clerk. After being referred, the bill is sent by a page to the Office of the Secretary of the Senate and numbered by the *Congressional Record* Clerk. He delivers it to the Bill Clerk, who makes entries in the Bill Book and the computer-controlled data storage and retrieval system, showing the number, sponsor, title, date, and reference. It is then turned over to the assistant Journal Clerk for proper notation in the Senate Journal of the proceedings of that day, and is subsequently sent to the Government Printing Office to be printed. Printed copies of the bill are delivered (usually the next morning) to the Secretary's Office, to the committee to which the bill was referred, and to the Senate and House document rooms, and are thus made available to the public. The original bill is then returned by the Printing Office to the Secretary of the Senate, who retains it in his files.

ANNUAL APPROPRIATIONS

After becoming law, legislative proposals are generally referred to as "legislative authority."

Funds for carrying on the work of the Government, which are generally in pursuance of this "legislative authority," are provided in general and special appropriation bills.

Although these appropriation bills usually originate in the House of Representatives, a report issued by the House Committee on the Judiciary in the 3d Session of the 46th Congress, entitled "Power of the Senate to Originate Appropriation Bills," said in part:

> The principal if not the only question submitted to your committee in this instance is, whether the Senate has the power to originate bills for the appropriation of money, and its correct solution depends solely upon the proper construction of the first clause of the seventh section of the first article of the Constitution, which contains the only restriction to be found anywhere upon the authority of that body to originate bills of any kind or description whatever. That clause provides that "all bills for raising revenue shall originate in the House of Representatives: but the Senate may propose or concur with amendments, as on other bills." And if the words in which it is expressed are to be taken in their ordinary acceptation, as required by the primary canon of legal interpretation, it is difficult to conceive how there could possibly be two opinions as to the idea they were intended to convey, for certainly the distinction between raising revenue and disposing of it after it has been raised is sufficiently obvious to be understood by even the commonest capacity.

The appropriations process has assumed a routine, however, which is briefly as follows: The heads of the various departments and agencies of the Government prepare estimates on the cost of doing their work for the year and submit these estimates to the Director of the Office of Management and Budget. He gives them careful consideration and then he prepares a budget for expenditures for each of the Government establishments based on their own official estimates. This budget is submitted to the President and, after his approval, is transmitted to the Congress.

The Committee on Appropriations of the House usually drafts the appropriation bills. After passage of these bills by that body, they are transmitted to the Senate where they are referred to its Committee on Appropriations. After due consideration by the latter committee, they are reported back to the Senate, usually with recommended amendments, for passage by the Senate.

The Government operates its business on a fiscal rather than a calendar year basis, beginning on October 1 of each year and ending on the following September 30.

When all appropriation bills have not been enacted by October 1, however, the Congress passes a continuing resolution or resolutions. These are a temporary expedient passed in the form of a joint resolution to cover expenditures for general support and administration of departments of the Government whose regular appropriation bills have not yet been enacted. Such resolutions provide "continuing appropriations" at rates generally based on the previous year's appropriations.

THE BUDGET ACT

The Congressional Budget and Impoundment Control Act was enacted in 1974 as a means for Congress to establish national budget priorities and the appropriate level of total revenues expenditures and debt for each year. Moreover, it provided for strict time limits in dealing with Presidential attempts to impound funds already appropriated either through deferrals or rescissions.

The Act established the Congressional Budget Office to provide the Congress with budget-related information. An agency of the Legislative branch, the Office does not make recommendations on matters of policy; its principal tasks are to present the Congress with options for consideration and to study the possible budgetary ramifications of those options.

Control of the budget is exercised through

the Senate and House of Representatives agreeing to a Concurrent Resolution on the Budget. In form this resolution can be:

A. A concurrent resolution setting forth the congressional budget for the United States Government for a fiscal year as provided in section 301 of the Congressional Budget and Impoundment Control Act of 1974;
B. A concurrent resolution reaffirming or revising the congressional budget for the United States Government for a fiscal year as provided in section 310 of the Congressional Budget and Impoundment Control Act of 1974; or
C. Any other concurrent resolution revising the congressional budget for the United States Government for a fiscal year as described in section 304 of the Congressional Budget and Impoundment Control Act of 1974.

The First Concurrent Resolution is adopted by May 15 preceding the fiscal year to which it applies, and it must be adopted before floor consideration of spending and revenue legislation for that fiscal year. The resolution sets levels of new budget authority, budget outlays, federal revenues, public debt, and any surplus or deficit. The joint explanatory statement of managers accompanying the conference report on the First Concurrent Resolution contains allocations of budget authority among major budget functions. These allocations of each of the amounts in the functional categories are then broken down by committee, or in the case of 'Appropriations, by subcommittee, and these breakdowns are referred to as "cross walks."

The Second Concurrent Resolution may retain or revise levels set out in the earlier resolution and is binding. It may also direct reconciliation, a process which mandates committees to locate savings within their areas of jurisdiction so that fiscal policies established by the resolution are reflected in congressional spending and revenue actions. In the case of reconciliation, if only one committee is required to reconcile, it reports a reconciliation bill directly to the floor. If multiple committees must reconcile, they report to the Budget Committee which aggregates such legislation, without making any substantive change, into an omnibus bill and reports such to the floor. The Senate may not adjourn sine die until the Second Concurrent Resolution and any reconciliation process it may direct have been completed.

Subsequent to the adoption of the Second Concurrent Resolution, Congress may pass further budget resolutions making necessary fiscal adjustments. This has happened on several occasions in which a First Concurrent Resolution for a forthcoming year revised figures in the previous concurrent resolution for the current year.

Section 311 provides for points of order against considering any bill, resolution, or amendment which would breach spending ceilings or revenue floors set forth in the Second Concurrent Resolution.

To retain flexibility, the Act contains general waiver authority against any provisions in Titles III or IV. This broad waiver is found in Section 904b.

Impoundment Control

A second principal purpose of the Act was to develop a mechanism to control Presidential impoundments. The Act recognizes two types of such impoundments: rescissions and deferrals.

In the case of a rescission, the President messages to Congress his determination that certain appropriated funds should not be spent. In a deferral, the President wishes simply to postpone the expenditure of funds.

The deferral of budget authority includes (A) withholding or delaying for a period not beyond the fiscal year the obligation or expenditure of budget authority (whether by establishing reserves or otherwise) provided for projects or activities; or (B) any other type of Executive action or inaction which effectively precludes the obligation or expenditure of budget authority, including authority to obligate by contract in advance of appropriations as specifically authorized by law.

A deferral resolution is a resolution of the House of Representatives or the Senate which only expresses its disapproval of a proposed deferral of budget authority set forth in a special message transmitted by the President under section 1013 of Public Law 93–344.

With regard to rescissions, the Act provides that funds proposed for rescission must be made available for expenditure if both Houses do not approve the rescission within 45 days after receipt of the President's message. The rescission bill is amendable, is subject to expedited procedures, and may approve a rescission in part as well as in whole.

EXECUTIVE BUSINESS AND EXECUTIVE SESSIONS

Nominations

A Presidential nomination requiring advice and consent must be approved by a majority vote of the Senate. After a nomination is received and referred to the appropriate committee, hearings may be held, and after the committee votes, it may be reported back to the Senate. If confirmed, a Resolution of Confirmation is transmitted to the White House and the appointment is then signed by the President.

In addition, Presidential nominations may be made during recesses of the Senate. The Constitution authorizes the President to "fill up" vacancies that may happen during such recesses "by granting Commissions which shall expire at the End of their next Session." Recess appointments to the Supreme Court, however, it was decided in a sense of the Senate resolution agreed to on August 29, 1960, "may not be wholly consistent with the best interests of the Supreme Court, the nominee who may be involved, the litigants before the Court, nor indeed the people of the United States." It further agreed "that such appointments, therefore, should not be made except under unusual circumstances and for the purpose of preventing or ending a demonstrable breakdown in the administration of the Court's business."

Executive Matters Generally

The executive business of the Senate includes both nominations and treaties submitted to the Senate by the President of the United States for its "Advice and Consent." This business of the Senate is handled separately from its legislative business.

Treaties are referred to the Committee on Foreign Relations and nominations are referred to one of the various committees of the Senate, basically determined on the grounds of which committee handled the legislation creating the position.

All confidential communications made by the President shall be kept secret, and all treaties which may be laid before the Senate, and all remarks, votes, and proceedings thereon, shall also be kept secret until the Senate shall, by their resolution, take off the injunction of secrecy. When the Senate is proceeding on treaty ratification, the treaty shall be read a first time. Only a motion to refer it to committee, to print it in confidence for the use of the Senate, or to remove the injunction of secrecy shall be in order.

When committees report treaties or nominations to the Senate, they are placed on the Executive Calendar, as distinct from the Calendar of Business, on which legislation is placed. These two calendars are printed separately.

When the Senate considers nominations and treaties, it goes into executive session, as distinct from legislative session, and a separate journal is kept of the proceedings thereon.

TREATIES

The rules for the consideration of executive business are different and distinct from the rules for the consideration and disposition of legislative business. For example, treaties are the only business considered by the Senate in the "Committee of the Whole."

Committee of the Whole

Rule XXX provides that the Senate, in executive session, when proceeding to consideration of treaties according to procedure included therein, shall consider them as in Committee of the Whole, and the question shall be put following any amendments therein proposed, "Will the Senate concur in the amendments made in Committee of the Whole?" after which new amendments may be proposed. At any stage of such proceedings the Senate may remove the injunction of secrecy from the treaty, and after passing through all other stages, finally consent to the ratification in the form agreed to, if an affirmative two-thirds vote of the Senators present shall so decide.

When there is no further debate or amendment to be proposed, the next step would be the proposal of the resolution of ratification.

Reservations are not in order while the treaty is being considered as in the Committee of the Whole or in the Senate. They should be offered to the resolution of ratification.

After the resolution of ratification has been proposed, no amendment to the treaty is in order except by unanimous consent. Reservations, etc., however, are in order at that stage, and not before.

The vote on the question of agreeing to the resolution of ratification or on a motion to postpone indefinitely requires a two-thirds vote of the senators present for adoption. All other motions and questions upon a treaty shall be decided by a majority vote.

Amendment to a Treaty

The Senate may stipulate conditions to a treaty in the form of amendments, reservations, understandings, declarations, statements, interpretations, and statements in committee reports.

Amendment An amendment makes actual changes in the language of the treaty.

Reservation The term "reservation" in treaty making, according to general international usage, means a formal declaration by a state, when signing, ratifying, or adhering to a treaty, which modifies or limits the substantive effect of one or more of the treaty provisions as between the reserving State and other States party to the treaty.

Understandings, Interpretations, Declarations, Statements, Etc. The term *understanding* is often used to designate a statement when it is not intended to modify or limit any of the provisions of the treaty in its international operation, but is intended merely to clarify or explain or to deal with some matter incidental to the operation of the treaty in a manner other than as a substantive reservation. They are part of the instrument of ratification no matter what they are called, even if their effect is solely of an internal domestic nature.

Ratification of Treaties

The word *ratification* when used in connection with treaties refers to the formal act by which a nation affirms its willingness to be bound by a specific international agreement. The basic purpose of ratification of a treaty is to confirm that an agreement which has been negotiated and signed is accepted and recognized as binding by those countries. Originally, when continuous and rapid communication between a government and its representatives abroad was not possible, ratification was the home government's endorsement of an agreement made by those representatives.

The procedure by which individual nations ratify treaties is a concern of domestic rather than international law. The Constitution does not use the word ratification in regard to treaties. It says only that the President shall have power, by and with the advice and consent of the Senate, to make treaties, and does not divide up the process into various component parts which can be identified today, such as initiation, negotiation, signing, Senatorial advice and consent, ratification, deposit or exchange of ratification and promulgation. From the beginning, however, the formal act of ratification has been performed by the President acting "by and with the advice and consent of the Senate." The President ratifies the treaty, but only upon the authorization of the Senate.

ADVICE AND CONSENT OF THE SENATE

This phrase refers to the Senate's approval of the resolution of ratification of treaties, or the approval of nominations. After a vote on a resolution of ratification, which must be by a two-thirds vote of the Senators present, the President, if he sees fit, may reject the treaty. With the President's approval, however, the ratification occurs with the exchange of the instruments of ratification between the parties to the treaty. Thus, the act of ratification for the United States is a Presidential act, but it may not be forthcoming unless the Senate has given its consent.

The scope of the Senate's approval of nominations sent to the Senate by the President is vast. It includes officers of the Government, specifically ambassadors, other public ministers and counsels, judges of the Supreme Court, all other officers of the United States as set forth in the Constitution, and such officers as Congress by law may designate. The President nominates individuals, and if the Senate by its advice and consent gives its approval by majority vote, they are then appointed by the President.

Treaties, unlike any other business considered by the Senate, stay before that body once they are submitted by the President until the Senate has acted thereon or unless the President requests, and/or the Senate adopts an order or resolution authorizing, their return to the President or the Secretary of State. In 1937, 1947, and 1952, numerous treaties were returned to the Secretary of State or the President of the United States pursuant to an order or resolution adopted by the Senate, including some dating back as early as 1910.

SENATE COMMITTEE CONSIDERATION

Senate committees are appointed by resolution at the beginning of each Congress, with power to continue and act until their successors are appointed. All Senate committees are created by the Senate. At present, Senate committees include 16 standing committees, 4 select committees, and 1 special committee. Standing committees are charged to report by bill or otherwise on matters within a defined jurisdiction and generally to study and review, on a comprehensive basis, certain matters relating thereto. Select and special committees have varying powers and obligations, and increasingly have been given legislative jurisdiction. Senate Members may also serve, along with House Members, on joint committees, whose duties and responsibilities are set forth in the respective resolutions creating them. There are currently four joint committees of the Congress. Conference committees, appointed when there is disagreement to a measure after passage by both Houses, like joint committees, are composed of Members of both the Senate and House, but votes in a conference committee are not as a body, but as two units. The committee chairman is normally a member of the majority party. He is chosen by order of the Senate, and is usually, but not always, the senior Member in point of service of the majority Members of the committee.

COMMITTEE RULES

Rule XXVI on committee procedure provides that each committee shall adopt rules (not inconsistent with the Rules of the Senate) governing the procedure of such committee. It provides also that the rules of each committee shall be published in the *Congressional Record* not later than March 1 of each year, except that if any such committee is established on or after February 1 of a year, the rules of that committee during the year of establishment shall be published in the *Congressional Record* not later than 60 days after such establishment. An amendment to the rules of any such committee shall be published in the *Record* not later than 30 days after the adoption of such amendment.

Once a bill has been introduced and has been referred by the Presiding officer with the advice of the Parliamentarian, the clerk of the committee enters it upon the committee's Calendar of Business.

Committees as a rule have regular meeting days, but they may meet at the call of their chairman or upon the request of a majority at other times. At these meetings matters on the committee calendar are usually the order of business, but any matter within the committee's jurisdiction may be considered—for example, an investigation of an agency of the Government over which it has jurisdiction, or to hear an official discuss policies and operations of his agency.

Any committee may refer its pending bills to its subcommittees for study and reports thereon. Most of the committees have standing subcommittees, and frequently ad hoc subcommittees are appointed to study and report on particular pieces of legislation or to make a study of a certain subject.

Committees or subcommittees generally hold hearings on all major or controversial legislation before drafting the proposal into a final form for reporting to the Senate. The length of hearings and the number of witnesses testifying vary, depending upon the time element, the number of witnesses wanting to be heard, the desires of the committee to hear witnesses, etc. Recommendations of the Administration, in conjunction with the Office of Management and Budget, are sought by the committees on nearly all major legislation, but they are in no way obligated to accept such recommendations.

For example, the Department of Agriculture, Office of Governmental and Public Affairs, providing liaison between the department and the Congress, would be addressed on a bill relating to inspection of livestock, meat, and agricultural products, and the Office of Congressional Affairs, General Services Administration, would be asked to comment on proposed legislation affecting small business, disadvantaged business, and related subcontracting programs. The responses are often used in support of or against matters pending before the Senate by being quoted on the floor or being inserted in the *Record* by Senators during debate.

A subcommittee makes reports to its full committee, and the latter may adopt such reports without change, amend them in any way it desires, reject them, or adopt an entirely different report.

After consideration of any bill, and the usual "markup" session, which is the committee session held just prior to reporting a bill or resolution back to the full Senate wherein final determination is made on the content and form of the measure, the full committee may report it to the Senate favorably with or without amendments, submit an adverse report thereon, or vote not to report anything.

The measure can be reported with committee amendments which may (*a*) insert, (*b*) strike, (*c*) strike part of the bill and insert other language, or (*d*) strike the entire text and insert a complete substitute, thereby rejecting in toto the language of a measure which was referred to, considered by, and reported by a Senate committee. The desired changes in the measure are indicated by use of italic type for additions and linetype for strike-outs, in contrast to the original introduced form of the measure which is printed as referred in Roman type.

Included may be additions, corrections, or modifications to the preamble of a resolution, the part(s) of a measure prefaced by the word "Whereas," which follow(s) the resolving clause. These are voted on after passage or adoption of the measure. Such clauses, which are introductory statements declaring the reasons for and the intent of the legislation, if amended, would reflect changes or modifications contained in the text of the measure. Also, the title may be amended.

Committees need not act on all bills referred to them. Under the rules, a Senator may enter a motion to discharge a committee from the further consideration of any bill, but this is rarely done. By unanimous consent, some bills are discharged from one committee and sent to another. If a motion to discharge is agreed to, the bill is thereby taken out of the jurisdiction of that committee and placed on the Senate Calendar of Business. It may subsequently be referred to another committee.

COMMITTEE REPORTS

The chairman, or some other Member of the committee designated for that purpose, reports bills to the Senate, and when reported they are placed on the Senate Calendar of Business, unless unanimous consent is given for immediate consideration.

The action taken by the committee appears on the copy of the bill reported, and a written report, which is numbered ad seriatim, nearly always accompanies the bill. The reports, like the bills, are printed by the Government Printing Office for distribution.

A reported bill passes through the same channels in the Secretary's Office as an introduced bill, for notation of the proper entries on the records. It is reprinted, showing the calendar and report numbers, the name of the Senator reporting it, the date, and whether with or without amendment. Matters proposed to be stricken out of a bill by the committee are shown in linetype, while matters proposed to be inserted are shown in italic. The committee report may include minority, supplemental, and/or additional views, and these are printed as a part of the committee report on the measure.

SENATE CONSIDERATION

The majority and minority leaders, as the spokesmen for their parties, and in consultation with their respective policy committees, implement and direct the legislative schedule and program.

Most measures are passed either on the call of the Calendar or by unanimous consent procedure. The more significant and controversial matters are considered under a unanimous consent agreement limiting debate and controlling time on the measure, amendments thereto, and debatable motions relating to it, when possible. This is done because otherwise debate is unlimited. Measures may be brought up on motion by a simple majority vote if they have been on the Calendar one legislative day. Such a motion is usually made by the majority leader or his designee and is usually debatable. The motion to proceed to the consideration of a measure on the Calendar is usually only made if unanimous consent to proceed to its consideration is objected to.

On highly controversial matters, the Senate frequently has to resort to "cloture" to work its will on the bill. Under Rule XXII, if three-fifths of the Senators duly chosen and sworn (sixty if the Senate is at full membership of one-hundred) vote in the affirmative, further debate on the question shall be limited to no more than one hour for each Senator, and the time for consideration of the matter shall be limited to 100 hours, unless increased by the same three-fifths vote indicated above. On a measure or motion to amend the Senate Rules, it takes two-thirds of the Senators present and voting, a quorum being present, to invoke cloture.

Although under Rule VIII, which governs the consideration of bills on the call of the Senate Calendar, there is supposed to be a Calendar call each day at the end of the morning business, under current practice this very rarely occurs—the Calendar is usually called pursuant to a unanimous consent order. Rule VII makes a call of the Calendar mandatory on Monday if the Senate had adjourned after its prior sitting. This requirement may only be waived by unanimous consent, and it has become the practice of the leadership to almost invariably request that the requirement be waived.

Once a bill or resolution is before the Senate, it is subject to the amendatory process, both by the committee reporting it and by individual Senators offering amendments from the floor. A committee amendment reported as a total substitute (strikes all after the enacting clause and inserts new language for the entire bill) for the pending measure is always voted on last, inasmuch as once a total substitute is agreed to, further amendments are precluded. With this exception, however, committee amendments take priority and are considered in order as they appear in the printed copy of the measure before the Senate. The only amendments from the floor in order during the consideration of these committee amendments are amendments offered to the committee amendments. Once the committee amendments have been disposed of, however, any Senator may propose amendments to any part of the bill not already amended, and while an amendment is pending, an amendment to the amendment is in order. By precedent, an amendment to an amendment to an amendment, being an amendment in the third degree, is not in order. However, the first amendment in the nature of a substitute for a bill, whether reported by a committee or offered by an individual Senator, does not kill a degree, being amendable in two more degrees.

There are certain special procedures in the Senate which limit the amendatory process. For example, during the consideration of general appropriation bills, amendments are subject to the strictures of Rule XVI under which amendments proposing new or general legislation, nongermane amendments, and amendments increasing the amount of an appropriation, which increase has not been previously authorized or estimated for in the President's Budget, are not in order. Likewise, when operating under a general unanimous consent agreement in the usual form on a bill or resolution, amendments must be germane. Germaneness of amendments is also required once the Senate has invoked cloture, and in addition, any amendments considered under cloture must have been submitted prior to the Senate's vote on cloture.

When all committee amendments and individual floor amendments offered by Senators have been disposed of, the bill is ordered engrossed and read a third time, which step ends the amendatory process.

The next step, after the amendment stage, is the engrossment and third reading of the bill. This reading is by title only. The question is then put upon its passage, which is carried by a majority vote. If a resolution has a preamble, sometimes referred to as "Whereas," it may be agreed to, amended, or stricken out, after the resolution has been adopted. The title to a bill is also acted upon after its passage, and if amendments are made that necessitate a change in the title, the bill is accordingly amended. At any time before its passage, a bill may be laid on the table or postponed indefinitely, either of which motions has the effect of killing the bill; made a special order for a day certain, which requires a two-thirds vote; laid aside temporarily; recommitted to the committee which reported the bill; referred to a different committee; or displaced by taking up another bill by a majority vote.

Most bills are passed by a voice vote only, but where a doubt is raised in such a case, the Presiding Officer, or any Senator, before the result is announced, may request a division of the Senate to determine the question. Before the result of a voice or division vote has been announced, a roll-call vote may be had upon the demand of one-fifth of the Senators present, but at least eleven—one-fifth of the presumptive quorum of fifty-one.

In the case of a yea-and-nay vote, any Senator who voted with the prevailing side or who did not vote may, on the same calendar day or on either of the next two days the Senate is actually in session, make a motion to reconsider a question. On a voice vote or division vote, however, any Senator may make the motion. If made before other business intervenes, it may be proceeded with and is debatable. It may be laid on the table without prejudice to the main question and is a final disposition of the motion. A majority vote determines questions of reconsideration. If the motion is agreed to, another vote may be taken on the question reconsidered; if disagreed to, the first decision of the Senate is affirmed. The making of such a motion is privileged and may be made while another matter is pending before the Senate, in which case its consideration cannot be proceeded with except by unanimous consent or on motion. In such latter case the pending business would be displaced by agreeing to the motion.

Only one motion to reconsider the same question is in order. Such a motion, under Rule XXI, may be withdrawn by the mover by leave of the Senate, which may be granted by a majority vote or by unanimous consent. A bill cannot be transmitted to the House of Representatives while a motion to reconsider remains unacted upon.

ENGROSSED BILLS

The printed bill used at the desk by the Senate during its consideration as the official desk copy, showing the amendments adopted, if any, and endorsed as having passed, is sent to the Secretary's Office and delivered to the Bill Clerk. Again the Bill Clerk makes the proper entries on his records and the data-retrieval system. He then turns it over to the Enrolling Clerk who makes an appropriate entry on his records and sends it to the Government Printing Office to be printed on special white paper in the form in which it passed the Senate. This printed Act is attested by the Secretary as having passed the Senate as of the proper date, and is termed the official engrossed bill.

After the passage of a bill by one body, it technically becomes an Act (not yet effective as a law), but it nevertheless continues to be generally referred to as a bill.

Bills Sent to House

Engrossed bills are messaged to the House of Representatives by one of the clerks in the Secretary's Office, who is announced by the doorkeeper of the House.[1] Upon being recognized by the Speaker, the clerk announces that the Senate has passed a bill (giving its number and title) in which the concurrence of the House is requested.

Upon receipt of the message from the Senate, the Speaker refers the measures contained therein to appropriate committees. If, however, a substantially similar House bill has been favorably reported by a committee, the Senate bill, unless it creates a charge upon the Treasury, may not be referred but remains on the Speaker's table. It may subsequently be taken up or substituted for such House bill when consideration of the latter occurs.

HOUSE COMMITTEE CONSIDERATION

Senate bills and resolutions when messaged to the House may be referred by the Speaker to the appropriate House committee, just as he refers all bills and resolutions introduced in the House. If referred, they are processed in much the same fashion as in the Senate

—that is, endorsed for reference, recorded in the Journal, listed in the *Congressional Record,* and printed by the Government Printing Office for distribution. The House committees, like the Senate committees, have committee calendars of business and usually have regular meeting days (but may also meet on the call of their chairman) for the consideration of business pending before them.

The procedure of House committees in considering and reporting bills is much the same as that of the Senate committees; they also have standing subcommittees and ad hoc subcommittees. Under new House rules (adopted in January 1975), a measure may be referred to a single committee, or jointly or sequentially to several committees, where more than one committee has jurisdiction over the subject matter.

After all House committees having jurisdiction have concluded consideration of a proposed bill, it may be reported to the House with or without amendments. A written report accompanies each reported measure. When reported it is placed on at least one of the four House calendars, namely: Union Calendar, House Calendar, Consent Calendar, and Private Calendar. If it is a noncontroversial public bill, it may at the same time be placed on either the Union or House and the Consent Calendars.

There is one other House calendar called the Discharge Calendar. Only bills discharged from committees are ever placed on this calendar.

HOUSE CONSIDERATION

The House calendars have little relationship to the order in which the House transacts its business.

In addition to the calendars, the House has special legislative days which have been established to expedite certain types of unprivileged business. The special legislative days are: Calendar Wednesday (every Wednesday), District of Columbia (considered on second and fourth Mondays), and Suspension of the Rules (considered first and third Mondays, and the Tuesdays following those days). The Consent Calendar business is transacted on the first and third Mondays, and Private Calendar business on the first and third Tuesdays. Discharge Calendar business, if any, comes up on the second and fourth Mondays.

The business privileged for consideration in the House on special legislative days is defined in each instance. Generally speaking, after the regular routine business each morning, including the reading of the Journal, the House proceeds to the consideration of bills or resolutions if any are to be acted on that day. The order varies somewhat, as follows: (1) On special calendar and special legislative days, bills and resolutions are called up in pursuance of the procedure defined by the rules in each instance as mentioned above; (2) under unanimous consent, bills are called up in pursuance of such requests made and granted by the House, regardless of the regular rules of procedure; (3) privileged matters, including general appropriation bills, conference reports, and the like, may be called up by the Members in charge of them at almost any time after they have been reported for three days, interrupting other less privileged business, providing the Representative in charge is recognized by the Speaker; and (4) the House can determine the order of its business and decide what bill to take up by adopting a special rule (simple House resolution) reported by the Rules Committee. The procedure for consideration of such measures is defined in each instance in the special rule. A special rule to call up a bill may be debated an hour before it is voted on.

Bills called up under the latter category are usually major or controversial pieces of legislation.

Bills which are first considered in the Committee of the Whole of the House are read for amendment under the 5-minute rule, after which the Committee of the

Whole reports them back to the House for action on any amendments that may have been adopted and for final passage.

In the House, as in the Senate, under the rules bills are read three times before they are passed. After a Senate bill is passed by the House, with or without amendment, it is returned to the Senate; if there are amendments, the amendments are engrossed before being messaged to the Senate. All House engrossments are printed on blue paper.

SENATE ACTION ON HOUSE AMENDMENTS

Senate bills returned with House amendments are held at the desk and almost always subsequently laid before the Senate by the Presiding Officer upon request or motion of a Senator (usually the manager of the bill). The Presiding Officer may also do this upon his own initiative, but this is rarely done. After the House message has been laid down, the amendments may be considered individually or en bloc by unanimous consent. Any one of the following motions relating to the amendment or amendments may then be offered, taking precedence in the order named: (1) A motion to refer the amendments to a standing committee of the Senate, (2) a motion to amend the amendments; (3) a motion to agree to the amendments; and (4) a motion to disagree to the amendments and ask a conference with the House. Usually number (4) includes authority for the Presiding Officer to appoint conferees on the part of the Senate, although the power to name conferees is in the Senate, not in the Chair. The number of conferees named varies widely. The usual range is seven to eleven, but occasionally a larger number is appointed, especially in the case of general appropriation bills.

In the case of motion number (2), the amendments made by the Senate to the House amendments are transmitted to the House, with a request for its concurrence therein. If the House concurs or agrees in all the amendments (the words being used synonymously), the legislative steps in the passage of the bill are completed. The House, however, may amend the Senate amendments to the House amendments, this being the second, and therefore the last, degree in which amendments may be made. The House amendments to the Senate amendments are transmitted to the Senate, usually with a request for concurrence therein. As in the case of the original amendments, the Senate may agree to some, disagree to others, or ask for a conference with the House thereon. A conference may be requested at any stage of the consideration of these amendments in disagreement. If the Senate agrees to all the House amendments to the Senate amendments, such action brings the two Houses into complete agreement, and likewise completes the legislative steps.

With respect to motion number (3), the concurrence of the Senate in the House amendments also completes the legislative steps.

With respect to motion number (1), the standing committee, after consideration, may recommend action indicated in motions (2), (3), or (4), and may make such motion accordingly.

BILLS ORIGINATING IN THE HOUSE

If a bill or resolution originates in the House, it follows the same steps as set forth above, except in reverse, i.e.: A House committee considers it first; it is passed by the House; it is messaged to the Senate and referred to a Senate committee; the committee reports it to the Senate and it is then acted on by the body. If amended, it is returned to the House for concurrence in the Senate amendments.

CONFERENCES

When the Senate requests a conference or agrees to a request for a conference and names its conferees, it informs the House of its action by message. After the second House agrees to the conference, appoints conferees, and apprises the first House of its action by message, all the papers relating to the measure sent to conference (referred to as the "official papers") are transmitted to the conference. This includes the original engrossed bill, engrossed amendments, and the various messages of transmittal between the Houses.

Since the conferees of each House vote as a unit, the House, like the Senate, may appoint as many conferees as it chooses to meet with the Senate conferees to reconcile the differences between the two Houses—the sole purpose of a conference. Thus, having a larger number of conferees than the other House does not provide an advantage.

After deliberation the conferees may make one or more recommendations: For example, (1) that the House recede from all or certain of its amendments; (2) that the Senate recede from its disagreement to all or certain of the House amendments and agree to the same; or (3) that they report an inability to agree in all or in part. Usually, however, there is compromise.

Conferees dealing with an amendment or a series of amendments are more limited in their options than conferees dealing with a bill passed by the second House with an amendment in the nature of a substitute. They can only deal with the matters in disagreement. They cannot insert new matter or leave out matter agreed to by both Houses, and if they exceed their authority, a point of order will lie against the conference report. Each House may instruct its conferees, but this is rarely done. Such instructions are not binding since conferences are presumed to be full and free—one House cannot restrict the other House's conferees.

Where one House passes a bill of the other House with an amendment in the nature of a substitute and the measure then goes to conference, the conferees have wider latitude since the entire matter is in conference. They may report a third version on the same subject matter; all of its provisions, however, must be a germane modification of either the House or Senate version, or it will be subject to a point of order.

Conference Reports

The recommendations of the conferees are incorporated in a written report and a joint statement of managers, made in duplicate, both of which must be signed by a majority of the conferees of each house. If there are amendments upon which they were unable to agree, a statement to this effect is included in the report. These are referred to as amendments in disagreement. The conferees cannot report amendments in disagreement where the bill had gone to conference after one House had amended it with a complete substitute for the other House's bill.

One report, together with the papers if the House is to act first, is taken by the House conferees, or managers, as they are termed in that body, and subsequently presented by them to the House, with an accompanying explanatory statement as to its effect upon the matters involved. The report must lie over three days in the House for printing, except during the last six days of a session. The Senate conferees take the other copy which is presented for printing under the requirements of the Legislative Reorganization Act as amended in 1970. To save time and expense, this requirement is frequently waived in the Senate by unanimous consent.

Normally, the House agreeing to a conference on a bill acts first on a conference report, but either House can act first if it has the official papers. Conference reports are privileged in both the Senate and the House. They cannot be amended, but must be voted upon as an entirety. If amendments in disagreement were reported by the conferees, they are acted on after the conference report is adopted and may be subject to amendment. After adoption by the first House, the conference report is transmitted with the official papers to the other House with a message announcing its action.

Assuming action by the House first, the Senate conferees could then present their report and ask for its immediate consideration. It does not have to lie over three days in the Senate, as it does in the House, and the motion to proceed to its consideration is not debatable; thus the Senate may act immediately. A motion to recommit a conference report may not be made in the second House acting on the report since the conferees of the first House were discharged when their body agreed to the report.

If conferees reach a complete agreement on all of the House amendments to a Senate bill, and the House adopts that report, the adoption of the report by the Senate completes the legislative action on the bill. If, however, there were amendments upon which an agreement had not been reached by the conferees, the adoption of the report by both Houses leaves the parliamentary status of these particular amendments in disagreement the same as if no conference had been held.

If the amendments on which an agreement could not be reached were House amendments, and the House acted on the report first, it could then recede from its amendments, eliminating the amendments in disagreement; then, if the Senate adopts the report, the bill would have been cleared for the President's signature. If they were Senate amendments and the House acted first, the House could concur in the Senate amendments or concur in them with amendments. If the Senate amendments were concurred in by the House, that would clear the amendments in disagreement, and when the Senate agreed to the conference report, the bill would be cleared for the President's signature. If the House should concur in the Senate amendments reported in disagreement with amendments, after the Senate agreed to the report, it could concur in the House amendments to the Senate amendments which would clear the bill for the President's signature. If the amendments reported in disagreement are not so disposed of, a further conference on these amendments could be requested by one House and agreed to by the other. When this happens, the two Houses usually appoint the same conferees. Until all the amendments in disagreement are reconciled by the two Houses, the bill cannot become a law.

If a conference report is rejected by one of the Houses, it so notifies the other body by message and usually requests another conference; however, it may merely notify the second body of its action without requesting a further conference, leaving further steps to be taken by the other House. Endorsements showing these various legislative steps, and when taken, are made on the engrossed bill.

When the two Houses reach a complete agreement on all the amendments, the papers are delivered to the Enrolling Clerk of the House where the bill originated. He prepares a copy of the bill in the form as finally agreed upon by the two Houses and sends it to the Government Printing Office for "enrollment," which means historically "written on parchment." The original papers on the bill are retained in the files of the originating House until the end of a Congress, when they are sent to the Archives.

SIGNATURES OF SPEAKER AND VICE PRESIDENT

Upon receipt of an enrolled bill from the Government Printing Office, either the Secretary of the Senate or the Clerk of the House endorses it, certifying where the bill originated. If, after examination by the Enrolling Clerk of that House, the bill is found to be in the form agreed upon by both Houses, a slip is attached thereto stating that the bill, identified by number and title, has been examined and found truly enrolled. It is then presented to the Speaker of the House for his signature, which is announced in open session. Usually, enrolled bills are signed first by the Speaker. The bill is then transmitted by messenger to the Senate, where it is signed by the Vice President.[2]

Under the rules of the House, the Committee on House Administration is charged, when an enrolled bill has been duly signed by the Speaker and the Vice President, to present the same, when the bill originates in the House, to the President of the United States for his signature "and report the fact and date of such presentation to the House." If it is a Senate bill, this responsibility of presenting the bill to the President falls on the Secretary of the Senate.

An error discovered in a bill after the legislative steps in its passage have been completed may be corrected by authority of a concurrent resolution, provided it has not been approved by the President. If the bill has not been enrolled, the error may be corrected in the enrollment; if it has been enrolled and signed by the Presiding Officers of the two Houses, or by the Speaker, such action may be rescinded by a concurrent resolution agreed to by the two Houses, and the bill correctly re-enrolled. If it has been presented to the President, but not acted upon by him, he may be requested by a concurrent resolution to return it to the Senate or the House for correction. If, however, the President has approved the bill, and it has thereby become a law, any amendment thereof can only be made by the passage of another bill, which must take the same course as the original.

PRESIDENTIAL ACTION—APPROVAL OR VETO

The President, under the Constitution, has ten days[3] (Sundays excepted)[4] after the bill has been presented to him in which to act upon it. If the subject matter of the bill is within the jurisdiction of a department of the Government, or affects its interests in any way, he may, in the meantime, at his discretion, refer the bill to the head of such department for investigation and a report thereon. The report of such official may serve as an aid to the President in reaching a decision on the question of approval. If the President approves the bill, he signs it, giving the date, and transmits this information by messenger to the Senate or the House, as the case might be. In the case of revenue and tariff bills, the hour of approval is usually indicated. The enrolled bill is delivered to the Administrator of the General Services Administration, who designates it as a public or private law, depending upon its purpose, and gives it a number. Public and private laws are numbered separately and serially. An official copy is sent to the Government Printing Office to be used in making the so-called slip law print. The enrolled bill itself is deposited in the files of the General Services Administration.

In the event the President does not desire to approve a bill, but is unwilling to veto it, he may, by not returning it within the ten-day period after it is presented to him, permit it to become a law without his approval. The Administrator of the General Services Administration makes an endorsement on the bill that, having been presented to the President of the United States for his approval and not having been returned to the House of Congress in which it originated within the time prescribed by the Constitution, it has become a law without his approval.

Where the ten-day period extends beyond the date of the final adjournment of the Congress, the President may, within such time, approve and sign the bill, which thereby becomes a law. If, however, in such a case, the President does not approve and sign the bill prior to the expiration of that period, it fails to become a law. This is what is known as a pocket veto. The United States Court of Appeals, in the case of *Kennedy* v. *Sampson,* 511 F.2d 430 (D.C. Cir., August 14, 1974), held that a Senate bill could not be pocket-vetoed by the President during an "intrasession" adjournment of

Congress to a day certain for more than three days, where the Secretary of the Senate had been authorized to receive Presidential messages during such adjournment.

If the President does not favor a bill and vetoes it, he returns it to the House of origin without his approval, together with his objections thereto (referred to as the "veto message"). It should be noted that after the final adjournment of the 94th Congress, first session, the President returned two bills, giving Congress the opportunity to reconsider and "override" the vetoes.

The constitutional provision for reconsideration by the Senate is met, under the precedents, by the reading of the veto message, spreading it on the Journal, and adopting a motion (1) to act on it immediately; (2) to refer it, with the accompanying papers, to a standing committee; (3) to order that it lie on the table, to be subsequently considered; or (4) to order its consideration postponed to a definite day. The House procedure is much the same.

If, upon reconsideration by either House, the House of origin acting first, it does not receive a two-thirds vote, the President's veto is sustained and the bill fails to become a law.

If a bill which has been vetoed is passed upon reconsideration by the first house by the required two-thirds vote, an endorsement to this effect is made on the back of the bill, and it is then transmitted, together with the accompanying message, to the second House for its action thereon. If likewise reconsidered and passed by that body, a similar endorsement is made thereon. The bill, which has thereby been enacted into law, is not again presented to the President of the United States, but is delivered to the Administrator of the General Services Administration for deposit in the Archives, and is printed, together with the attestations of the Secretary of the Senate and the Clerk of the House of its passage over the President's veto.

Illustration 6.A.
How a bill becomes a law.

This figure shows the long, complex, arduous, and multistaged process by which a bill becomes a law. It should be emphasized that each of these stages affords potential opponents of legislation opportunities to delay, defeat, or deadlock the legislative process. In order to cope, proponents of legislation must compromise, bargain, and accommodate with intensely opposed and strategically located would-be opponents.

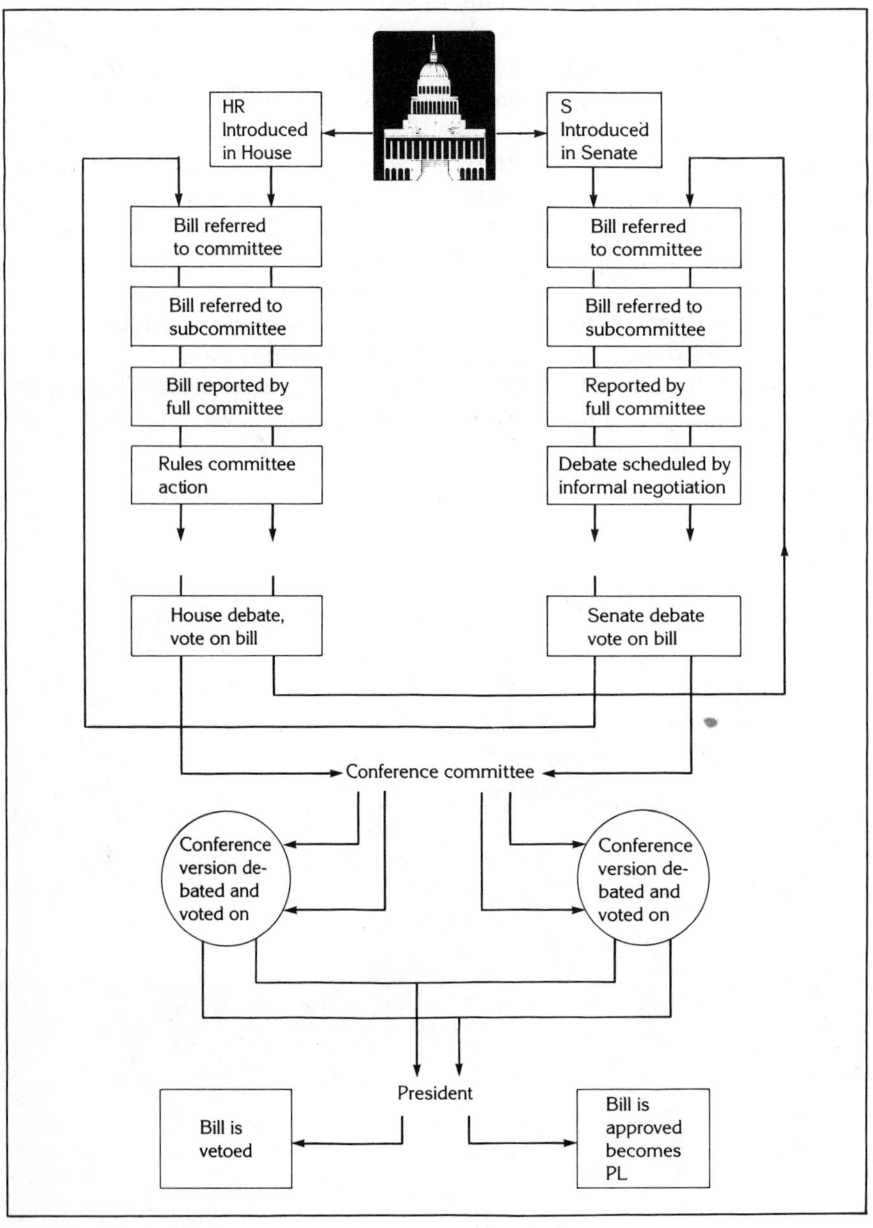

Illustration 6.B.
A House rule.

The House Rules committee functions as a traffic cop, governing the routing of bills to the floor and the general flow of traffic. Notice how the rule stipulates the time and means of debate and the way amendments can be offered.

House Calendar No. 127

96TH CONGRESS
1ST SESSION

H. RES. 368

[Report No. 96–347]

Providing for the consideration of the bill (H.R. 4040) to authorize appropriations for fiscal year 1980 for procurement of aircraft, missiles, naval vessels, tracked combat vehicles, torpedoes, and other weapons, and for research, development, test, and evaluation for the Armed Forces, to prescribe the authorized personnel strength for each active duty component and the Selected Reserve of each Reserve component of the Armed Forces and for civilian personnel of the Department of Defense, to authorize the military training student loads, to authorize appropriations for fiscal year 1980 for civil defense, and for other purposes.

IN THE HOUSE OF REPRESENTATIVES

JULY 17, 1979

Mr. FROST, from the Committee on Rules, reported the following resolution; which was referred to the House Calendar and order to be printed

---

RESOLUTION

Providing for the consideration of the bill (H.R. 4040) to authorize appropriations for fiscal year 1980 for procurement of aircraft, missiles, naval vessels, tracked combat vehicles, torpedoes, and other weapons, and for research, development, test, and evaluation for the Armed Forces, to prescribe the authorized personnel strength for each active duty component and the Selected Reserve of each Reserve component of the Armed Forces and for civilian personnel of the Department of Defense, to authorize the military training student loads, to authorize appropriations for fiscal year 1980 for civil defense, and for other purposes.

Resolved, That upon the adoption of this resolution it shall be in order to move that the House resolve itself into the Committee of the Whole House on the State of the Union for the consideration of the bill (H.R. 4040) to authorize appropriations for fiscal year 1980 for procurement of aircraft, missiles, naval vessels, tracked combat vehicles, torpedoes, and other weapons, and for research, development, test, and evaluation for the Armed Forces, to prescribe the authorized personnel strength for each active duty component and the Selected Reserve of each Reserve Component of the Armed Forces and for civilian personnel of the Department of Defense, to authorize the military training student loads, to authorize appropriations for fiscal year 1980 for civil defense, and for other purposes, and the first reading of the bill shall be dispensed with. After general debate, which shall be confined to the bill and shall continue not to exceed four hours, three hours to be equally divided and controlled by the chairman and ranking minority member of the Committee on Armed Services, and one hour to be equally divided and controlled by a Member opposed to, and a Member in favor of, the provisions of section 812 of the bill, the bill shall be read

Illustration 6.B. (concluded)

for amendment under the five-minute rule by titles instead of by sections. At the conclusion of the consideration of the bill for amendment, the Committee shall rise and report the bill to the House with such amendments as may have been adopted, and the previous question shall be considered as ordered on the bill and amendments thereto to final passage without intervening motion except one motion to recommit. After the passage of H.R. 4040, it shall be in order to move to take from the Speaker's table the bill S. 428 and it shall then be in order in the House to move to strike out all after the enacting clause of the said Senate bill and to insert in lieu thereof the provisions contained in H.R. 4040 as passed by the House.

Illustration 6.C.
Example of a Senate unanimous consent resolution.

The Senate, being less structured and more informal than the House, has no counterpart to the House Rules Committee which sets the terms of floor debate in the House. Although Senate rules permit unlimited debate (filibustering) and nongermane amendments, the time and terms of debate in the Senate are frequently agreed to informally through a unanimous consent rule of which the following is an example.

S. 1360 (ORDER NO. 310)

2.—*Ordered*, That when the Senate proceeds to the consideration of S. 1360 (Order No. 310), a bill to establish an Advisory Committee on Timber Sales Procedure appointed by the Secretary of Agriculture for the purposes of studying, and making recommendations with respect to, procedures by which timber is sold by the Forest Service, and to restore stability to the Forest Service timber sales program and provide an opportunity for congressional review, DEBATE on any amendment in the first degree shall be limited to 1 hour, to be equally divided and controlled by the mover of such and the manager of the bill, debate on any amendment in the second degree shall be limited to 30 minutes, to be equally divided and controlled by the mover of such and the manager of the bill, and debate on any debatable motion, appeal, or point of order which is submitted or on which the Chair entertains debate shall be limited to 20 minutes, to be equally divided and controlled by the mover of such and the manager of the bill: *Provided*, That in the event the manager of the bill is in favor of any such amendment or motion, the time in opposition thereto shall be controlled by the minority leader or his designee: *Provided further*, That no amendment that is not germane to the provisions of the said bill shall be received.

Ordered further, That on the question of FINAL PASSAGE of the said bill, debate shall be limited to 3 hours, to be equally divided and controlled, respectively, by the Senator from Idaho (Mr. Church) and the Senator from Oregon (Mr. Hatfield): *Provided*, That the said Senators, or any one of them, may, from the time under their control on the passage of the said bill, allot additional time to any Senator during the consideration of any amendment, debatable motion, appeal, or point of order. (July 28, 1977.)

Illustration 6.D.
A Senate bill.

The following is an example of an actual Senate bill. The lines on p. 262 indicate a modification of the original bill by the committee.

Calendar No. 240

96TH CONGRESS
1ST SESSION

S. 109

[Report No. 96–226]

To require the reinstitution of procedures for the registration of certain persons under the Military Selective Service Act, and for other purposes.

IN THE SENATE OF THE UNITED STATES

JANUARY 23 (legislative day, JANUARY 15), 1979

Mr. HARRY F. BYRD, Jr. (for himself, Mr. NUNN, Mr. CHILES, and Mr. CANNON) introduced the following bill; which was read twice and referred to the Committee on Armed Services

JUNE 19 (legislative day, MAY 21), 1979

Reported by Mr. NUNN, with an amendment to the text of the bill and an amendment to the title

[Strike out all after the enacting clause and insert the part printed in italic]

A BILL

To require the reinstitution of procedures for the registration of certain persons under the Military Selective Service Act, and for other purposes.

Be it enacted by the Senate and House of Representatives of the United States of America in Congress assembled,

Illustration 6.D. (continued)

~~That section 3 of the Military Selective Service Act (50 App. U.S.C. 453) is amended by inserting "(a)" before "Except at the beginning of such section and by adding at the end of such section a new subsection as follows:~~

~~"(b) The President, within one hundred and twenty days after the date of enactment of this subsection, shall institute procedures for the registration of citizens and other persons in accordance with the provisions of this title. After registration procedures have been instituted under this subsection, the President may thereafter suspend the registration of persons under this title only for the purpose of revising existing registration procedures or instituting new registration procedures, but in no event may the President suspend or otherwise discontinue the registration of persons required to be registered under this title for a period of more than ninety consecutive days, and in no event may the President suspend or otherwise discontinue registration under this title more than once in any one-year period.".~~

That section 3 of the Military Selective Service Act (50 App. U.S.C. 453) is amended by inserting "(a)" before "Except" at the beginning of such section and by adding at the end of such section the following new subsection:

"(b) The President shall commence registration of citizens and other persons in accordance with the provisions of this title by January 2, 1980. The President may suspend

the registration of persons under this title only for the purpose of revising existing registration procedures or instituting new registration procedures, but may not suspend or otherwise discontinue the registration of persons under this title for a period of more than ninety consecutive days. In no event may the President suspend or otherwise discontinue registration under this title more than once in any one-year period.".

SEC. 2. The President may not, after the date of enactment of this Act and before January 1, 1981, classify or examine any person registered under the provisions of the Military Selective Service Act (50 App. U.S.C. 451 et seq.) unless he determines that it is in the national interest to do so.

SEC. 3. The President shall submit a written report to the Congress not later than July 1, 1980, containing his recommendations (1) for revision of the categories and standards for deferment and exemption of persons under the Military Selective Service Act, (2) for the revision of the procedures to be followed for registration and classification under such Act, and (3) for other changes in such Act he determines necessary to improve the fairness and effectiveness of such Act. The President shall include in such report a certification to the effect that the Military Selective Service Act, including any changes recommended by him, is in his judgment, equi-

Illustration 6.D. (continued)

table and will provide the means necessary to meet effectively the military manpower needs of the United States.

SEC. 4. (a) The first sentence of subsection (b) of section 135 of title 10, United States Code, is amended to read as follows: "The Under Secretary of Defense for Policy shall supervise manpower mobilization planning in the Department of Defense and shall perform such other duties and exercise such other powers as the Secretary of Defense may prescribe.".

(b) Paragraph (3) of section 138(c) of such title is amended—

(1) by inserting "(A)" after "(3)" at the beginning of such paragraph;

(2) by redesignating clauses (A), (B), and (C) of the second sentence of such paragraph as clauses (i), (ii), and (iii), respectively;

(3) by striking out "It shall include" at the beginning of the third sentence of such paragraph and inserting in lieu thereof the following:

"(B) The Secretary of Defense shall also include in the report required under subparagraph (A) of this paragraph"; and

(4) by adding at the end of such paragraph the following new subparagraph:

Illustration 6.D. (concluded)

"(C) The Secretary of Defense shall also include in the report required under subparagraph (A) of this paragraph an assessment of the Nation's capability of mobilizing the military manpower that may be needed to meet national security requirements during periods of national emergency. In making such assessment, the Secretary of Defense shall determine the Nation's capability of mobilizing the active military forces, selected reserve forces, other reserve force personnel, retired military personnel, and persons not members of the armed forces and shall include in such assessment a statement and explanation regarding the Nation's capabilities for mobilizing each of the personnel categories named.".

Amend the title so as to read: "A bill to require the reinstitution of registration of certain persons under the Military Selective Service Act, and for other purposes.".

Calendar No. 240

96TH CONGRESS
1ST SESSION

S. 109

[Report No. 96–226]

A BILL

To require the reinstitution of procedures for the registration of certain persons under the Military Selective Service Act, and for other purposes.

JANUARY 23 (legislative day, JANUARY 15), 1979

Read twice and referred to the Committee on Armed Services

JUNE 19 (legislative day, MAY 21), 1979

Reported with an amendment to the text of the bill and an amendment to the title

Illustration 6.E.
House calendar.

The calendars of the two houses are a major information source concerning the flow of legislation. The following is an excerpted House calendar, revealing the major sources contained within it.

NINETY-NINTH CONGRESS

FIRST SESSION { CONVENED JANUARY 3, 1985
ADJOURNED DEC. 20 *(Legislative day of Dec. 19)*, 1985

SECOND SESSION { CONVENED JANUARY 21, 1986

CALENDARS
OF THE UNITED STATES
HOUSE OF REPRESENTATIVES
AND
HISTORY OF LEGISLATION

LEGISLATIVE DAY 150 CALENDAR DAY 152

Friday, December 20, 1985

INTERIM

This edition includes actions by both Houses as of their respective adjournments

Pursuant to S.J. Res. 255 the second session of the 99th Congress convenes at 12 o'clock meridian, Tuesday, January 21, 1986. *(Agreed to Dec. 20 (Legislative day of Dec. 19), 1985.)*

SPECIAL ORDERS

POSTPONE CONSIDERATION OF PRESIDENTIAL VETO OF H.R. 1562

On motion of Mr. Jenkins, by unanimous consent, *Ordered,* That consideration of the veto message received by the clerk on Tuesday, Dec. 17, 1985, on the bill H.R. 1562, Textile and Apparel Trade Enforcement Act of 1985, be postponed until Wednesday, Aug. 6, 1986. *(Agreed to Dec. 17, 1985.)*

(SEE NEXT PAGE)

PREPARED UNDER THE DIRECTION OF BENJAMIN J. GUTHRIE, CLERK OF THE HOUSE OF REPRESENTATIVES: BY THE OFFICE OF LEGISLATIVE OPERATIONS; THERON E. MORRIS, Tally Clerk; MAXINE W. SNOWDEN, THOMAS K. HANRAHAN, AND DOROTHY M. STUKES, Staff

Calendars shall be printed daily— Rule XIII: clause 6 } *Index to the Calendars will be printed on Monday of each week the House is in session: otherwise first day of session thereafter*

U.S. GOVERNMENT PRINTING OFFICE 1985 0—71-038

Illustration 6.E. (continued)

UNFINISHED BUSINESS

1985 H.J. Res. 192 Dec. 12	A joint resolution to designate Apr. 24, 1985, as "National Day of Remembrance of Man's Inhumanity to Man". *(Pending in the Committee of the Whole House on the State of the Union Dec. 12, 1985; Mr. Bonior of Michigan, Chairman.)*

SPECIAL LEGISLATIVE DAYS

Calendar Wednesday	Wednesday of each week, except during the last 2 weeks of a session (clause 7, rule XXIV).
Consent Calendar	First and third Mondays of each month (clause 4, rule XIII).
Discharge Calendar	Second and fourth Mondays of each month, except during the last 6 days of a session (clause 4, rule XXVII).
District of Columbia business	Second and fourth Mondays of each month (clause 8, rule XXIV).
Private Calendar	First and third Tuesdays of each month (clause 6, rule XXIV).
Suspension of rules	Mondays and Tuesdays and during the last 6 days of a session (clause 1, rule XXVII).

TABLE OF CONTENTS

Illustration 6.E. (continued)

BILLS IN CONFERENCE

Jefferson's Manual, sec. 555:
"And in all cases of conference asked after a vote of disagreement, etc., the conferees of the House asking it are to leave the papers with the conferees of the other * * *."
The House agreeing to the conference acts on the report before the House requesting a conference.

FIRST SESSION

S. 124—Safe Drinking Water Amendments of 1985.

Senate asked for a conference:
July 10 *(Legislative day of July 8)*, 1985.
Senate Conferees:
Messrs. Stafford, Durenberger, Simpson, Bentsen, and Baucus.

House agreed to a conference:
July 18, 1985.
House Conferees:
Messrs. Dingell, Waxman, Scheuer, Broyhill, and Madigan.

H.R. 1460—Anti-Apartheid Act of 1985.

House asked for a conference:
July 17, 1985.
House Conferees:
From the Foreign Affairs Committee on all provisions (Except Sec. 17 of the Senate amendment) and modifications committed to conference:
Messrs. Fascell, Solarz, Bonker, Wolpe, Crockett, Dymally, Berman, Weiss, Garcia, Broomfield, Siljander, Dornan, DeWine, and Burton of Indiana.
From the Banking, Finance and Urban Affairs Committee for Sec. 17 of the Senate amendment and modifications committed to conference as additional conferees for the following Sections: Sec. 3; Sec. 4, Sec. 5; Secs. 14(6) and 14(7) of the House bill; and Sec. 8; Sec. 15 of the Senate amendment:
Messrs. St Germain, Gonzalez, Annunzio, Mitchell, Neal, Barnard, Morrison of Connecticut, Wylie, McKinney, Leach of Iowa, and Hiler.

Senate agreed to a conference:
July 25 *(Legislative day of July 16)*, 1985.
Senate Conferees:
Messrs. Lugar, Helms, Mathias, Mrs. Kassebaum, Messrs. Garn, Heinz, Pell, Sarbanes, Cranston, and Proxmire.
For sec. 15 of the Senate amendment, Mr. Kennedy in lieu of Mr. Cranston.

House Report filed:
Aug. 1, 1985; Rept. 99-242.
Report agreed to in House:
Aug. 1, 1985.

S. 1128—Clean Water Act, amend.

Senate asked for a conference:
July 29 *(Legislative day of July 16)*, 1985.
Senate Conferees:
Messrs. Stafford, Chafee, Simpson, Durenberger, Bentsen, Mitchell, and Moynihan.

House agreed to a conference:
Sept. 4, 1985.
House Conferees:
Messrs. Roe, Anderson, Mineta, Oberstar, Edgar, Towns, Snyder, Hammerschmidt, Stangeland, and Clinger.
As additional conferees, Mr. Nowak solely for sections 59 and 73 of the House amendment and modifications committed to conference;
And Mr. Rowland of Georgia solely for sections 5, 16, 30(a), 34(b), and 45 of the House amendment and modifications committed to conference.

S. 1078—Trade Commission Act Amendments of 1985, Federal.

Senate asked for a conference:
Oct. 10 *(Legislative day of Sept. 30)*, 1985.
Senate Conferees:
Messrs. Danforth, Kasten, Gorton, Hollings, and Ford.

House agreed to a conference:
Oct. 31, 1985.
House Conferees:
Messrs. Dingell, Florio, Ms. Mikulski, Messrs. Broyhill, and Lent.
As additional conferees, solely for consideration of subsections 16(b), (c) and (d) and section 17 of the Senate bill and modifications committed to conference; Messrs. Waxman and Madigan.
As additional conferees, solely for consideration of sections 16 and 17 of the Senate bill and modifications committed to conference; Messrs. Moakley, Frost, and Lott.

H.R. 3037—Appropriations, Agriculture, Rural Development and Related Agencies, 1986.

Senate asked for a conference:
Oct. 16 *(Legislative day of Oct. 15)*, 1985.
Senate Conferees:
Messrs. Cochran, McClure, Andrews, Abdnor, Kasten, Mattingly, Specter, Hatfield, Burdick, Stennis, Chiles, Sasser, Bumpers, and Harkin.

House agreed to a conference:
Dec. 9, 1985.

(1-1)

Illustration 6.E. (continued)

1. UNION CALENDAR

Clause 1, rule XIII:
"First. A calendar of the Committee of the Whole House on the State of the Union, to which shall be referred bills raising revenue, general appropriations bills, and bills of a public character directly or indirectly appropriating money or property."

			No.
1985 Feb. 6	Referred to the Committee of the Whole House on the State of the Union.	Message of the President of the United States to the Congress on the subject of the State of the Union.	**1**
H. Rept. 99-4 Feb. 25	Mr. de la Garza *(Agriculture)*.	Report on allocation of budget totals for fiscal year 1985.	**5**
H. Rept. 99-5 Feb. 25	Mr. Whitten *(Appropriations)*.	Report on subdivision of budget totals for fiscal year 1985.	**6**
H. Rept. 99-25 Mar. 25	Mr. Brooks *(Government Operations)*.	Oversight plans of the committees of the U.S. House of Representatives.	**15**
H. Rept. 99-26 Mar. 25	Mr. Montgomery *(Veterans' Affairs)*.	Report pursuant to sec. 302(b) of the Congressional Budget Act of 1974.	**16**
H. Rept. 99-27 Mar. 26	Mr. Aspin *(Armed Services)*.	Allocation of budget authority and outlays by program.	**17**
H.R. 1532 Mar. 26	Mr. Swift *(House Administration)*. Rept. 99-28	To authorize appropriations for the Federal Election Commission for fiscal year 1986. *(Failed of passage under suspension of the rules June 26, 1985.)*	**18**
H. Rept. 99-45 Apr. 17	Mr. Brooks *(Government Operations)*.	Report on unnecessary firing of tactical missiles demands DOD's attention.	**28**
H. Rept. 99-46 Apr. 17	Mr. Brooks *(Government Operations)*.	Report on the impact of the budget process on Offices of Inspector General.	**29**
H. Rept. 99-47 Apr. 18	Mr. Brooks *(Government Operations)*.	The Federal response to the homeless crisis.	**30**

(3-1)

Illustration 6.E. (continued)

2. HOUSE CALENDAR

Clause 1, rule XIII:
"Second. A House Calendar, to which shall be referred all bills of a public character not raising revenue not directly or indirectly appropriating money or property."

1985			No.
H. Res. 72 Apr. 4	Mr. Hawkins *(Education and Labor).* Rept. 99-38	To reaffirm the House's commitment to the Job Corps Program.	**12**
H. Con. Res. 76 May 14	Mr. St Germain *(Banking, Finance and Urban Affairs).* Rept. 99-91	Expressing the sense of the Congress that the Export-Import Bank of the United States of America should continue to provide preliminary and advanced commitment for loans which may require approval on or after Oct. 1, 1985, in keeping with the Bank's mandate, unless and until the Congress of the United States changes that policy or directs the Bank to alter its programs.	**24**
H. Res. 171 June 12 *(Adverse).*	Mr. Hamilton *(Intelligence).* Rept. 99-171	Requesting the President to provide to the House of Representatives documents and factual information in his possession or under his control relating to certain counterterrorist units which received covert training or other support from the United States.	**34**
H. Res. 215 July 9	Mr. Wheat *(Rules).* Rept. 99-192	A resolution providing for the consideration of H.R. 2348, a bill to authorize appropriations to carry out the activities of the Department of Justice for fiscal year 1986, and for other purposes.	**40**
H.J. Res. 192 July 9	Mr. Ford of Michigan *(Post Office and Civil Service).* Rept. 99-193	To designate Apr. 24, 1985, as "National Day of Remembrance of Man's Inhumanity to Man".	**41**
H.J. Res. 3 July 24	Mr. Fascell *(Foreign Affairs).* Rept. 99-221	To prevent nuclear explosive testing.	**53**
H. Rept. 99-277 Sept. 19	Mr. Dixon *(Standards of Official Conduct).*	Investigation of alleged improper political solicitation.	**68**
H. Res. 281 Oct. 1	Mr. Pepper *(Rules).* Rept. 99-294	A resolution providing for the consideration of H.J. Res. 3, a joint resolution to prevent nuclear explosive testing.	**72**

(4-1)

Illustration 6.E. (continued)

3. PRIVATE CALENDAR

Clause 1, rule XIII:
"Third. A calendar of the Committee of the Whole House, to which shall be referred all bills of a private character."

Clause 6, rule XXIV:
"6. On the first Tuesday of each month after disposal of such business on the Speaker's table as requires reference only, the Speaker shall direct the Clerk to call the bills and resolutions on the Private Calendar. Should objection be made by two or more Members to the consideration of any bill or resolution so called, it shall be recommitted to the committee which reported the bill or resolution, and no reservation of objection shall be entertained by the Speaker. Such bills and resolutions, if considered, shall be considered in the House as in the Committee of the Whole No other business shall be in order on this day unless the House, by two-thirds vote on motion to dispense therewith, shall otherwise determine. On such motion debate shall be limited to 5 minutes for and 5 minutes against said motion.

"On the third Tuesday of each month after the disposal of such business on the Speaker's table as requires reference only, the Speaker may direct the Clerk to call the bills and resolutions on the Private Calendar, preference to be given to omnibus bills containing bills or resolutions which have previously been objected to on a call of the Private Calendar. All bills and resolutions on the Private Calendar so called, if considered, shall be considered in the House as in the Committee of the Whole. Should objection be made by two or more Members to the consideration of any bill or resolution other than an omnibus bill, it shall be recommitted to the committee which reported the bill or resolution and no reservation of objection shall be entertained by the Speaker.

"Omnibus bills shall be read for amendment by paragraph, and no amendment shall be in order except to strike out or to reduce amounts of money stated or to provide limitations. Any item or matter stricken from an omnibus bill shall not thereafter during the same session of Congress be included in any omnibus bill.

"Upon passage of any such omnibus bill, said bill shall be resolved into the several bills and resolutions of which it is composed, and such original bills and resolutions, with any amendments adopted by the House, shall be engrossed, where necessary, and proceedings thereon had as if said bills and resolutions had been passed in the House severally.

"In the consideration of any omnibus bill the proceedings as set forth above shall have the same force and effect as if each Senate and House bill or resolution therein contained or referred to were considered by the House as a separate and distinct bill or resolution."

1985			No.
H.R. 1598 Sept. 19	Mr. Glickman *(Judiciary).* Rept. 99-281	For the relief of Steven McKenna.	**5**

(5-1)

Illustration 6.E. (continued)

NUMERICAL ORDER OF BILLS AND RESOLUTIONS WHICH HAVE PASSED EITHER OR BOTH HOUSES, AND BILLS NOW PENDING ON THE CALENDARS

Complete history of all actions on each bill follows the number in chronological order. For subject of bill see index, using index key following bill number in this section.

NOTE. Similar or identical bills, and bills having reference to each other, are indicated by number in parentheses.
*Starred Bills are also located in section for Sequentially Referred Bills.

No. Index Key and History of Bill

HOUSE BILLS

H.R. 1.—Housing Act of 1985. Reported from Banking, Finance and Urban Affairs July 26, 1985; Rept. 99-230. Supplemental report filed Sept. 4, 1985; Pt. II.
Union Calendar.. Union 152

H.R. 6* (H. Res. 305) (H.R. 2494).—Water Resources Conservation, Development, and Infrastructure Improvement and Rehabilitation Act of 1985. Reported from Public Works and Transportation Aug. 1, 1985; Rept. 99-251, Pt. I. Bill referred to Interior and Insular Affairs Aug. 1, 1985 for period ending not later than Sept. 5, 1985; to Merchant Marine and Fisheries Aug. 1, 1985 for a period ending not later than Sept. 15, 1985; and to Ways and Means Aug. 1, 1985 for a period ending not later than Sept. 23, 1985. Referral to Interior and Insular Affairs and Merchant Marine and Fisheries extended Sept. 5, 1985 for a period ending not later than Sept. 16, 1985. Reported from Interior and Insular Affairs Sept. 16, 1985; Pt. II. Referral to Merchant Marine and Fisheries extended Sept. 16, 1985 for a period ending not later than Sept. 23, 1985. Reported from Ways and Means Sept. 23, 1985; Pt. III. Reported from Merchant Marine and Fisheries Sept. 23, 1985; Pt. IV. Union Calendar. Considered Nov. 5, 6, 1985. Passed House Nov. 13, 1985. In Senate, ordered placed on the calendar Nov. 21 *(Legislative day of Nov. 18)*, 1985.

H.R. 7 (H. Res. 262).—School Lunch and Child Nutrition Amendments of 1985. Reported from Education and Labor May 15, 1985; Rept. 99-96. Union Calendar. Considered Sept. 12, 1985. Passed House Sept. 18, 1985. In Senate, referred to Agriculture, Nutrition, and Forestry Sept. 19 *(Legislative day of Sept. 16)*, 1985. Committee discharged. Passed Senate amended Nov. 22 *(Legislative day of Nov. 18)*, 1985. Senate asked for a conference Nov. 22 *(Legislative day of Nov. 18)*, 1985. House agreed to a conference Dec. 3, 1985.

H.R. 8 (H. Res. 222) (H.R. 2493) (S. 1128).—Water Quality Renewal Act of 1985. Reported from Public Works and Transportation July 2, 1985; Rept. 99-189. Union Calendar. Considered July 22, 1985. Passed House July 23, 1985. Proceedings vacated. Laid on table July 23, 1985. S. 1128, as amended, passed in lieu July 23, 1985.

H.R. 10 (H. Res. 223).—Investment Act, National Development. (Referred jointly to Public Works and Transportation and Banking, Finance and Urban Affairs Jan. 3, 1985.) Reported from Public Works and Transportation May 15, 1985; Rept. 99-115, Pt. I. Passed House Sept. 4, 1985. In Senate, referred to Environment and Public Works Sept. 9, 1985.

No. Index Key and History of Bill

HOUSE BILLS—Continued

H.R. 14.—Commemorations and Memorials, "Perkins Federal Building and United States Courthouse, Carl D.", Federal building and United States Courthouse in Ashland, Kentucky as, designate. Reported from Public Works and Transportation Feb. 27, 1985; Rept. 99-10. House Calendar. Passed House Feb. 28, 1985. In Senate, referred to Environment and Public Works Mar. 5 *(Legislative day of Feb. 18)*, 1985. Reported May 7 *(Legislative day of Apr. 15)*, 1985; no written report. Passed Senate June 18 *(Legislative day of June 3)*, 1985. Approved June 26, 1986. Public Law 99-55.

H.R. 20.—Bank Definition Act of 1985. Reported from Banking, Finance and Urban Affairs June 18, 1985; Rept. 99-175.
Union Calendar.. Union 117

H.R. 37.—Commemorations and Memorials, Olmstead Heritage Landscapes Act of 1985. Reported from Interior and Insular Affairs May 24, 1985; Rept. 99-148. Union Calendar. Rules suspended. Passed House June 3, 1985. In Senate, referred to Energy and Natural Resources June 4 *(Legislative day of June 3)*, 1985.

H.R. 47.—Statue of Liberty-Ellis Island Commemorative Coin Act. Rules suspended. Passed House Mar. 5, 1985. In Senate, referred to Banking, Housing, and Urban Affairs Mar. 6 *(Legislative day of Feb. 18)*, 1985. Reported May 7 *(Legislative day of Apr. 15)*, 1985; no written report. Passed Senate amended June 21 *(Legislative day of June 3)*, 1985. House agreed to Senate amendments June 25, 1985. Approved July 9, 1985. Public Law 99-61.

H.R. 48.—Currency Design Act. Rules suspended. Passed House July 15, 1985. In Senate, referred to Banking, Housing, and Urban Affairs July 16, 1985.

H.R. 99 (H. Res. 195).—Conservation Corps Act of 1985, American. (Referred jointly to Education and Labor and Interior and Insular Affairs Jan. 3, 1985.) Reported from Interior and Insular Affairs Mar. 14, 1985; Rept. 99-18, Pt. I. Reported from Education and Labor May 2, 1985; Pt. II. Union Calendar. Passed House July 11, 1985. In Senate, referred to Energy and Natural Resources July 15, 1985.

Illustration 6.E. (concluded)

STATUS OF MAJOR BILLS—FIRST SESSION

Number of bill	Title	Reported	Passed House	Reported in Senate	Passed Senate	Sent to Conference	Conference report agreed to in—		Date approved	Law No.
							House	Senate		
	LEGISLATIVE BILLS	1985	1985	1985	1985	1985	1985	1985	1985	
H. Con. Res. 152	Budget, First, 1986 (Rept. 99-133)	May 20	May 23							
S. Con. Res. 32	Budget, First, 1986		May 23	Mar. 20	May 9	May 23 (1)	(2)	Aug. 1 (3)		
H.R. 2100	Food Security Act of 1985 (H. Rept. 99-271)	Sept. 18	Oct. 8		Nov. 23	Dec. 5	Dec. 18	Dec. 18		
H.J. Res. 372	Debt Ceiling Increase		Aug. 1	Sept. 26	Oct. 10	Oct. 15 Nov. 7	(4) (6) Dec. 11	Nov. 1 (5) Dec. 11	Dec. 12	99-177
H.R. 2817	Superfund Amendments of 1985 (H. Rept. 99-253)	Nov. 12	(8)							
H.R. 3500	Budget Reconciliation (H. Rept. 99-300)	Oct. 3	Oct. 24							
H.R. 3838	Tax Reform Act, 1985 (H. Rept. 99-426)	Dec. 7	Dec. 17							
	APPROPRIATION BILLS									
H.R. 1239	Supplemental Appropriations, African Relief (H. Rept. 99-2)	Feb. 21	Feb. 28	Mar. 5	Mar. 20	Mar. 27	Apr. 2	Apr. 2	Apr. 4	99-10
H.R. 2577	Supplemental Appropriations, 1985 (H. Rept. 99-142)	May 22	June 12	June 13	June 20	July 16	July 31	Aug. 1	Aug. 15	99-88
H.R. 2942	Legislative Branch, 1986 (H. Rept. 99-194)	July 10	July 18	July 25	July 31	Oct. 8	Oct. 29	Oct. 29	Nov. 13	99-151
H.R. 2959	Energy and Water, 1986 (H. Rept. 99-195)	July 10	July 16	July 25	Aug. 1	Oct. 1	Oct. 17	Oct. 17	Nov. 1	99-141
H.R. 2965	Commerce, Justice, State, Judiciary (H. Rept. 99-197)	July 11	July 17	Oct. 4	Nov. 1	Dec. 3	Dec. 5	Dec. 6	Dec. 13	99-180
H.R. 3011	Interior, 1986 (H. Rept. 99-205)	July 16	July 31	Sept. 24	(10)					
H.R. 3036	Treasury, Postal, 1986 (H. Rept. 99-210)	July 18	July 30	Sept. 9	Sept. 26	Oct. 8	Nov. 7	Nov. 7	(7)	
H.R. 3037	Agriculture, 1986 (H. Rept. 99-211)	July 18	July 24	Sept. 24	Oct. 16	Dec. 9				
H.R. 3038	HUD, 1986 (H. Rept. 99-212)	July 18	July 25	Aug. 28	Oct. 18	Nov. 6	Nov. 13	Nov. 13	Nov. 25	99-160
H.R. 3067	District of Columbia, 1986 (H. Rept. 99-223)	July 24	July 30	Sept. 9	Nov. 7	Dec. 4				
H.R. 3228	Foreign Assistance (H. Rept. 99-252)	Aug. 1								
H.R. 3244	Transportation, 1986 (H. Rept. 99-256)	Sept. 5	Sept. 12	Oct. 4	Oct. 23	Oct. 30				
H.J. Res. 388	Continuing, 1986 (H. Rept. 99-272)	Sept. 17	Sept. 18	Sept. 24	Sept. 25				Sept. 30	99-103
H.R. 3327	Military Construction, 1986 (H. Rept. 99-275)	Sept. 18	Oct. 17	Oct. 31	Nov. 7	Nov. 13	Nov. 20	Nov. 21	Dec. 10	99-173
H.R. 3424	Labor, Health, Human Services; 1986 (H. Rept. 99-289)	Sept. 26	Oct. 2	Oct. 4	Oct. 22	Nov. 5	Dec. 5	Dec. 6	Dec. 12	99-178
H.R. 3629	Defense, 1986 (H. Rept. 99-332)	Oct. 24	Oct. 30	Nov. 6						
H.J. Res. 441	Continuing, further, 1986		Nov. 12		Nov. 13				Nov. 14	99-154
H.J. Res. 465	Continuing, further, 1986 (H. Rept. 99-403)	Nov. 21	Dec. 4	Dec. 5	Dec. 10	Dec. 11 Dec. 17	(9) Dec. 19	Dec. 19		
H.J. Res. 476	Continuing, further, 1986		Dec. 12		Dec. 12				Dec. 13	99-179
H.J. Res. 491	Continuing, further, 1986		Dec. 17		Dec. 17					

[1] S. Con. Res. 32 became the budget vehicle subject to a House-Senate conference. [2] House receded from its amendment and concurred with a further amendment Aug. 1, 1985. [3] Senate concurred in further House amendment Aug. 1 *(Legislative day of July 16)*, 1985. [4] House receded and concurred with amendments in Senate amendments Nos. 1 and 2 Nov. 1, 1985. [5] Senate agreed to House amendments with amendments Nov. 2, 4, 6, 1985. [6] House disagreed to Senate amendments and asked for further conference Nov. 6, 1985. [7] Vetoed Nov. 15, 1985. *In House, referred to Appropriations Nov. 19, 1985.* [8] H.R. 2817 passed House Dec. 10, 1985. Pursuant to H. Res. 331, H.R. 2005 became the vehicle subject to a House-Senate conference. [9] House rejected conference report Dec. 16, 1985. [10] Laid on the table Dec. 4 *(Legislative day of Dec. 2)*, 1985.

Illustration 6.F.
Senate calendars.

The Senate has two calendars: General Business and Executive Business. The following are excerpts.

SENATE OF THE UNITED STATES

NINETY-EIGHTH CONGRESS

FIRST SESSION	CONVENED JANUARY 3, 1983 ADJOURNED NOVEMBER 18, 1983	DAYS IN SESSION 150
SECOND SESSION	CONVENED JANUARY 23, 1984	DAYS IN SESSION 88

CALENDAR OF BUSINESS

Thursday, June 28, 1984

(LEGISLATIVE DAY, JUNE 25, 1984)

SENATE CONVENES AT 10:00 A.M.

(IN RECESS)

PREPARED UNDER THE DIRECTION OF WILLIAM F. HILDENBRAND,
SECRETARY OF THE SENATE

By WILLIAM F. FARMER, JR., LEGISLATIVE CLERK

31-015 O

Illustration 6.F. (continued)

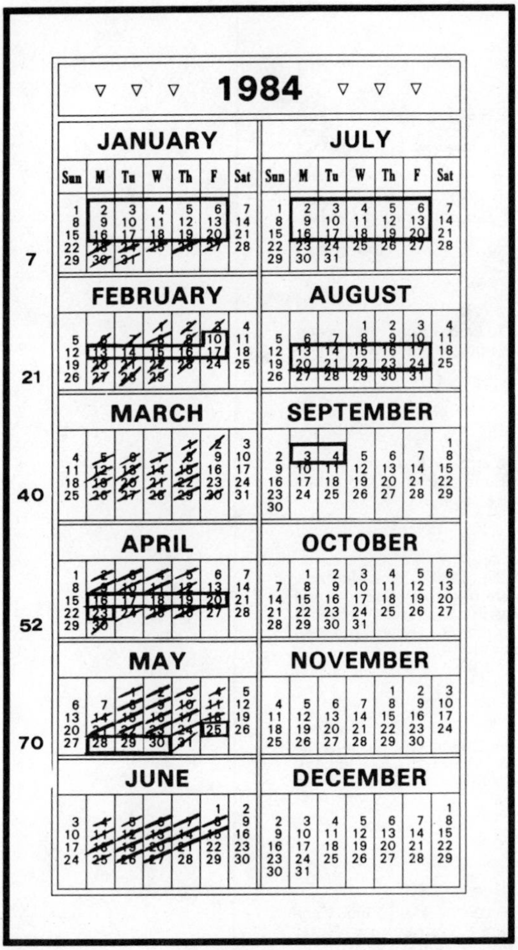

1984

JANUARY

	Sun	M	Tu	W	Th	F	Sat
	1	2	3	4	5	6	7
	8	9	10	11	12	13	14
	15	16	17	18	19	20	21
	22	23	24	25	26	27	28
7	29	30	31				

JULY

Sun	M	Tu	W	Th	F	Sat
1	2	3	4	5	6	7
8	9	10	11	12	13	14
15	16	17	18	19	20	21
22	23	24	25	26	27	28
29	30	31				

FEBRUARY

	Sun	M	Tu	W	Th	F	Sat
				1	2	3	4
	5	6	7	8	9	10	11
	12	13	14	15	16	17	18
	19	20	21	22	23	24	25
21	26	27	28	29			

AUGUST

Sun	M	Tu	W	Th	F	Sat
			1	2	3	4
5	6	7	8	9	10	11
12	13	14	15	16	17	18
19	20	21	22	23	24	25
26	27	28	29	30	31	

MARCH

	Sun	M	Tu	W	Th	F	Sat
					1	2	3
	4	5	6	7	8	9	10
	11	12	13	14	15	16	17
	18	19	20	21	22	23	24
40	25	26	27	28	29	30	31

SEPTEMBER

Sun	M	Tu	W	Th	F	Sat
						1
2	3	4	5	6	7	8
9	10	11	12	13	14	15
16	17	18	19	20	21	22
23	24	25	26	27	28	29
30						

APRIL

	Sun	M	Tu	W	Th	F	Sat
	1	2	3	4	5	6	7
	8	9	10	11	12	13	14
	15	16	17	18	19	20	21
	22	23	24	25	26	27	28
52	29	30					

OCTOBER

Sun	M	Tu	W	Th	F	Sat
	1	2	3	4	5	6
7	8	9	10	11	12	13
14	15	16	17	18	19	20
21	22	23	24	25	26	27
28	29	30	31			

MAY

	Sun	M	Tu	W	Th	F	Sat
			1	2	3	4	5
	6	7	8	9	10	11	12
	13	14	15	16	17	18	19
	20	21	22	23	24	25	26
70	27	28	29	30	31		

NOVEMBER

Sun	M	Tu	W	Th	F	Sat
				1	2	3
4	5	6	7	8	9	10
11	12	13	14	15	16	17
18	19	20	21	22	23	24
25	26	27	28	29	30	

JUNE

Sun	M	Tu	W	Th	F	Sat
					1	2
3	4	5	6	7	8	9
10	11	12	13	14	15	16
17	18	19	20	21	22	23
24	25	26	27	28	29	30

DECEMBER

Sun	M	Tu	W	Th	F	Sat
						1
2	3	4	5	6	7	8
9	10	11	12	13	14	15
16	17	18	19	20	21	22
23	24	25	26	27	28	29
30	31					

JUNE

Sun	Mon	Tue	Wed	Thu	Fri	Sat
					1	2
3	4	5	6	7	8	9
10	11	12	13	14	15	16
17	18	19	20	21	22	23
24	25	26	27	28	29	30

Days that Senate met in 1984 are marked (/).
Boxed areas indicate scheduled non-legislative period days.

Illustration 6.F. (continued)

GENERAL ORDERS

UNDER RULE VIII

Order No.	Number and Author of Bill	Title	Reported by
9	S.J. Res. 8 Messrs. Helms, East, and Denton	Joint resolution to amend the Constitution of the United States to guarantee the right to life.	Feb. 14, 1983.—Read the second time and placed on the calendar.
10	S.J. Res. 9 Mr. Helms and others	Joint resolution to amend the Constitution of the United States to protect the right to life.	Feb. 14, 1983.—Read the second time and placed on the calendar.
11	S. 26 Mr. Helms and others	A bill to provide legal protection for unborn human beings and for other purposes.	Feb. 14, 1983.—Read the second time and placed on the calendar.
30	S. 613 Mr. McClure	A bill to direct the Secretary of Agriculture to convey certain property to the city of Show Low, Arizona.	Feb. 28, 1983.—Mr. McClure, Committee on Energy and Natural Resources, without amendment. (Rept. 12.) (An original bill.)
36	S. Con. Res. 6 Mr. Boschwitz and others	Concurrent resolution expressing the sense of the Congress that the Federal Government should maintain current efforts in Federal nutrition programs to prevent increases in domestic hunger.	Mar. 8, 1983.—Mr. Hatfield, Committee on Appropriations, without amendment, and with a preamble. (Rept. 18.)
39	S. 17 Mr. Dole and others	A bill to expand and improve the domestic commodity distribution program.	Mar. 9, 1983.—Mr. Helms, Committee on Agriculture, Nutrition, and Forestry, with an amendment in the nature of a substitute. (Rept. 21.)
43	S. 784 Mr. Helms	A bill to restore the right of voluntary prayer in public schools and to promote the separation of powers.	Mar. 14, 1983.—Read the second time and placed on the calendar.

(12)

Illustration 6.F. (continued)

STATUS OF APPROPRIATION BILLS, SECOND SESSION, NINETY-EIGHTH CONGRESS

NUMBER OF BILL	SHORT TITLE	PASSED HOUSE	RECEIVED IN SENATE	REPORTED IN SENATE	PASSED SENATE	SENT TO CONFER-ENCE	CONFERENCE REPORT AGREED TO IN—		DATE APPROVED	NUMBER OF LAW
							SENATE	HOUSE	1984	
H.J. Res. 492	Urgent Supplemental, Agriculture, 1984	Mar. 6	Mar. 7	Mar. 14	Apr. 5	Apr. 11	June 25	May 24		
H.J. Res. 493	Urgent Supplemental, H.H.S., 1984	Mar. 6	Mar. 7	Mar. 8	Mar. 15	Mar. 21	Mar. 27	Mar. 27	Mar. 30	98–248
H.J. Res. 517	Urgent Supplemental, H.U.D., 1984	Mar. 29	Mar. 30	***						
H.R. 5653	Energy-Water, 1985	May 22	May 24	June 5	June 21	June 22	June 27	June 27		
H.R. 5713	H.U.D., 1985	May 30	June 5	June 7	June 21	June 22	June 27	June 27		
H.R. 5712	Commerce, Justice, State, Judiciary, 1985	May 31	June 5	June 13						
H.R. 5743	Agriculture, 1985	June 6	June 11							
H.R. 5753	Legislative, 1985	June 6	June 11	June 14	June 21	June 22				
S. 2793	Foreign Assistance, 1985	* * *	* * *	June 26						

Illustration 6.F. (concluded)

SENATE OF THE UNITED STATES

NINETY-EIGHTH CONGRESS

FIRST SESSION { *Convened January 3, 1983* *Adjourned November 18, 1983*

SECOND SESSION { *Convened January 23, 1984*

EXECUTIVE CALENDAR

Thursday, June 28, 1984

TREATIES

Calendar No.	Treaty Doc. No.	Subject	Reported By
1	EX. B, 95-1	Montreal Aviation Protocols Nos. 3 and 4	Feb 10 83 Reported favorably, by Mr. Percy, Committee on Foreign Relations, with a proposed resolution of advice and consent to ratification with conditions (Printed report--Ex. Rept. 98-1)

NOMINATIONS

Calendar No.	Message No.	Nominee, Office, And Predecessor	Reported By
		THE JUDICIARY	
514	664	James Harvie Wilkinson III, of Virginia, to be United States Circuit Judge for the Fourth Circuit, vice John D. Butzner, Jr., retired.	Mar 15, 84 Mr. Thurmond, Committee on the Judiciary, without printed report.

Illustration 6.G.
The Congressional Record.

An indispensable information source for the congressional researcher is the *Congressional Record.* It is a record of debate and floor action in both houses, as well as a calendar of events to come. The following excerpts show sections of the *Record.*

Congressional Record

PROCEEDINGS AND DEBATES OF THE 99th CONGRESS, FIRST SESSION

Vol. 131 WASHINGTON, WEDNESDAY, DECEMBER 11, 1985 *No. 171*

House of Representatives

A HARSH NEW YEAR'S GREETING FOR FARMERS

The SPEAKER pro tempore. Under a previous order of the House, the gentleman from Minnesota [Mr. OBERSTAR] is recognized for 30 minutes.

Mr. OBERSTAR. Mr. Speaker, shortly after January 1, 1986, farmers who have borrowed from the Agriculture Department and are $100 or more behind on loan payments will be receiving a letter from the Farmers Home Administration—and it won't be a New Year's greeting.

On the contrary, nearly 40 percent of FmHA borrowers in my State—those whose accounts are $100 or more delinquent—will be receiving FmHA form 1924-25, a copy of which I ask to include in the RECORD, "Notice of Intent To Take Adverse Action." In other words, Secretary Block is preparing to send a foreclosure notice to all farmers $100 behind on payments to the Federal Government. This callous action is the fruit of 5 years of this administration's stewardship of American agriculture, a process whose result is to dispossess the American farmer and to transfer his assets to investment trusts.

Upon receipt of form 1924-25, a farmer has 30 days to contact his county supervisor and request either a deferral of payments, and extension of the loan over a longer period of time, a debt restructuring, or a voluntary liquidation. Failure to contact FmHA within 30 days of receipt of the notice, will result in the adverse action threatened by form 1924-25—being taken.

Fifty percent of FmHA borrower's will be receiving these notices.

One FmHA official in my State referred to the upcoming letters as "merely an attention-getting device." The suspension of adverse actions pending resolution of the issues raised in Coleman versus Block may have required a revamping of loan servicing procedures, but to introduce those new procedures by threatening imminent foreclosure is cruel, callous, and without justification.

Throughout the course of my travels in northeastern Minnesota, I have met numerous officials of the FmHA, who on a daily basis personify the dilemma in agriculture today.

As agents of FmHA, these Federal employees must take adverse action against borrowers in their service areas who through no fault of their own cannot meet loan payment schedules. In carrying out these bleak duties, they earn the animosity of neighbors and community.

These officials are aware that most operators cannot compete at today's prices, and that liquidation of assets may be the best long-term strategy for the individuals they are forced to take action against. Yet they can offer no hope for employment, for retraining services, or for relocation assistance.

While agricultural economics—the fruit of the Reagan farm program—continue to force people off the land, no one—least of all the FmHA professionals—can answer the question, where do our farmers go from here? And to emphasize the depth of the problem, one county supervisor with whom I visited told me that he had only recently learned that his own father, an FmHA borrower in another Minnesota county, will soon be forced off the family's farmstead by adverse action.

I urge farmers in my district to respond promptly to FmHA's greeting card. Their future on the farm may depend on their ability to work out a refinancing plan with FmHA officials.

At the same time, I want my colleagues to be aware of Secretary Block's impending assault on those individuals who traditionally need the Federal Government—the small family farmer. And as we prepare to consider the conference report on the 1985 farm bill, we must realize that the plight of these individuals is in our hands. If we refuse to recognize and respond to the crisis in rural America our farm economy may well be triggered into a long, painful, downward spiral.

[U.S. Department of Agriculture, Farmers Home Administration]

(Date) ———

NOTICE OF INTENT TO TAKE ADVERSE ACTION

Dear:

We regret to inform you that a review of your Farmers Home Administration (FmHA) loan account indicates the need to take adverse action.

We have attempted to work out a satisfactory solution to your credit problems through the various servicing options available, but have not been able to do so. For your information and review, we have included with this material a copy of the FmHA notice entitled "Farmer Program Borrower Servicing Options Including Deferrals and Borrower Responsibilities" (Form FmHA 1924-14).

This "NOTICE OF INTENT TO TAKE ADVERSE ACTION" requires a response from you within 30 days, using the attached form entitled "Borrower Acknowledgement of Notice of Intent to Take Adverse Action" (Form FmHA 1924-26). That form offers you the opportunity to request for consideration a number of servicing options. Further details are provided below.

We have conducted a review of your Farmers Home Administration (FmHA) loan accounts and determined the following where checked:

☐ You are presently $——— behind schedule on your FmHA loan installments which is a violation of your note and mortgage and/or security agreement.

☐ You have made unapproved disposition(s) of property that is covered by security instruments which secure your FmHA indebtedness. The property in question is ———.

☐ You have stopped farming or ranching which is a violation of your loan agreements.

☐ You have ———.

If the above listed violation(s) is not corrected by one or more of the actions, described in the attached Form FmHA 1924-26, "Borrower's Acknowledgement of Intent to Take Adverse Action," FmHA intends to accelerate your FmHA debts and foreclose on your real estate and/or chattels. This

☐ This symbol represents the time of day during the House proceedings, e.g., ☐ 1407 is 2:07 p.m.

Boldface type indicates words inserted or appended, rather than spoken, by a Member of the House on the floor.

Illustration 6.G. (continued)

ing policies that meet the basic needs and priorities of the American people.

The SPEAKER pro tempore. The time of the gentleman from Wisconsin [Mr. OBEY] has expired.

The gentleman from Illinois [Mr. ROSTENKOWSKI] has 4 minutes remaining.

Mr. ROSTENKOWSKI. Mr. Speaker, I yield those 4 minutes to the gentleman from Texas [Mr. WRIGHT], the majority leader.

Mr. Speaker, I am asking the members of the Ways and Means Committee to please not leave the Chamber.

Mr. WRIGHT. Mr. Speaker, this bill is in a real sense an act of legislative desperation. The conferees on both sides who have struggled so valiantly deserve our commendation because they have done a very creditable job on an extremely difficult instrument.

This bill is drastic, it is painful. Let us know exactly what it does.

It seeks to place a political straitjacket on both the executive and the legislative branches of Government and force both branches to face unpleasant facts. To the degree that that may be necessary, it is the inevitable result of our fiscal excesses, particularly those of the last 5 years which have doubled the national debt.

In 1981, we deliberately chose to follow the siren call for tax cuts which reduced the Government's revenues by $135 billion a year.

No person, no family, no business, no country can indefinitely pursue a course of deliberately raising only $19 every time it spends $25, and yet that has been our course in the last 5 years. And it is not altogether the fault of an overspending Congress.

Yesterday at the White House, I heard the chairman of the Senate Appropriations Committee, Senator MARK HATFIELD, tell the President of the United States that every year for the last 5 years Congress has spent quite considerably less than the President himself has asked us to spend in aggregate. Senator HATFIELD explained that in those 5 years, we have cut discretionary domestic expenditures by 34 percent, and we have raised military spending by 89 percent.

Very soon we are going to have to renew the crumbling infrastructure of the country, roads and bridges, and water and sewer lines on which the Nation depends, and that will cost money. We face a real crisis in the rural economy of the United States. To correct that will cost money.

More Americans today live in poverty than did 5 years ago, and to attend to their needs will cost money. The average young American between the ages of 25 and 40 lives less well than his counterpart did 10 years ago.

What this says is that President Reagan is going to have to face one very hard fact, and face it clearly. If he insists on ever increasing levels of military expenditures to finance an escalating arms race, he is going to have to come forward with the sources of revenue to pay for them on a pay-as-we-go basis. It is just that simple. We are not going to put it on the cuff any longer, and that is what this amounts to.

Hard choices will have to be made. No longer can we place on our children and our grandchildren the responsibility to pay for things that we will have used up and worn out before they reach tax-paying age.

So that is the choice, what Harry Truman faced in the Korean war when he did not add to the national debt, what Lyndon Johnson faced during the years of Vietnam when he conducted that painful struggle and did not add appreciably to the national debt.

Here is what we say: To the extent that we need additional military spending, then it is going to have to be done on a pay-as-we-go basis. That is the choice, Mr. President, and that is the message of this vote tonight.

The SPEAKER pro tempore. All time has expired.

Mr. ROSTENKOWSKI. Mr. Speaker, I move the previous question on the conference report.

The previous question was ordered.

The SPEAKER pro tempore. The question is on the conference report.

The question was taken; and the Speaker pro tempore announced that the ayes appeared to have it.

Mr. OBEY. Mr. Speaker, on that I demand the yeas and nays.

The yeas and nays were ordered.

The vote was taken by electronic device and there were—yeas 271, nays 154, not voting 9, as follows:

[Roll No. 454]

YEAS—271

Akaka
Andrews
Anthony
Applegate
Archer
Armey
Atkins
AuCoin
Badham
Barnard
Bartlett
Barton
Bateman
Bates
Bedell
Bereuter
Bevill
Bliley
Boehlert
Boner (TN)
Bosco
Boucher
Boulter
Breaux
Broomfield
Brown (CO)
Broyhill
Bruce
Bryant
Burton (IN)
Byron
Callahan
Campbell
Carney
Carper
Chandler
Chapman
Cheney
Clinger
Coats
Cobey
Coble
Coleman (MO)
Coleman (TX)
Combest
Cooper
Coughlin
Courter
Craig
Daniel
Dannemeyer
Darden
Daschle
Daub
Davis
DeLay
DioGuardi
Dreier
Duncan
Durbin
Dyson
Eckart (OH)
Edwards (OK)
Emerson
English
Erdreich
Fascell
Fawell
Feighan
Fiedler
Fields
Fish
Flippo
Foley
Fowler
Franklin
Frenzel
Frost
Fuqua
Gallo
Gejdenson
Gekas
Gephardt
Gibbons
Gingrich
Glickman
Goodling
Gordon
Gradison
Gray (IL)
Green
Gregg
Grotberg
Gunderson
Hall (OH)
Hall, Ralph
Hamilton
Hammerschmidt
Hansen
Hatcher
Hefner
Heftel
Hendon
Henry
Hertel
Hiler
Hillis
Hopkins
Horton
Huckaby
Hutto
Ireland
Jacobs
Jeffords
Jenkins
Johnson
Jones (OK)
Jones (TN)
Kaptur
Kasich
Kindness
Kleczka
Kolbe
Kostmayer
Kramer
Lagomarsino
Lantos
Latta
Leach (IA)
Leath (TX)
Lent
Levin (MI)
Lewis (FL)
Lightfoot
Livingston
Lloyd
Loeffler
Lott
Lowery (CA)
Lujan
Luken
Lundine
Lungren
Mack
MacKay
Madigan
Manton
Martin (IL)
Mavroules
Mazzoli
McCain
McCandless
McCloskey
McCollum
McCurdy
McDade
McEwen
McGrath
McKernan
McMillan
Meyers
Mica
Michel
Miller (OH)
Miller (WA)
Molinari
Monson
Montgomery
Moore
Moorhead
Morrison (WA)
Mrazek
Murphy
Natcher
Neal
Nichols
Nielson
O'Brien
Olin
Oxley
Packard
Panetta
Pease
Penny
Petri
Pickle
Porter
Pursell
Quillen
Ray
Regula
Reid
Richardson
Ridge
Rinaldo
Ritter
Robinson
Roemer
Rogers
Rostenkowski
Roth
Roukema
Rowland (CT)
Rowland (GA)
Rudd
Russo
Saxton
Schaefer
Schuette
Schulze
Sensenbrenner
Sharp
Shaw
Shelby
Shuster
Sikorski
Siljander
Sisisky
Skeen
Skelton
Slattery
Slaughter
Smith (FL)
Smith (NE)
Smith (NJ)
Smith, Denny (OR)
Smith, Robert (NH)
Smith, Robert (OR)
Snowe
Snyder
Solomon
Spence
Spratt
Staggers
Stallings
Stangeland
Stenholm
Strang
Stump
Sundquist
Sweeney
Swift
Swindall
Tauke
Tauzin
Taylor
Thomas (CA)
Thomas (GA)
Torres
Valentine
Volkmer
Vucanovich
Walgren
Walker
Watkins
Weber
Whitehurst
Whitley
Whittaker
Wilson
Wirth
Wise
Wolpe
Wortley
Wright
Wyden
Wylie
Yatron
Young (AK)
Young (MO)
Zschau

NAYS—154

Ackerman
Addabbo
Alexander
Anderson
Annunzio
Aspin
Barnes
Beilenson
Bennett
Bentley
Berman
Biaggi
Bilirakis
Boggs
Boland
Bonior (MI)
Bonker
Borski
Boxer
Brown (CA)
Burton (CA)
Bustamante
Carr
Chappell
Clay
Coelho
Collins
Conte
Conyers
Coyne
Crane
de la Garza
Dellums
Derrick
DeWine
Dickinson
Dicks
Dingell
Dixon
Donnelly
Dorgan (ND)
Dornan (CA)
Dowdy
Downey
Dwyer
Dymally
Early
Eckert (NY)
Edgar
Edwards (CA)
Evans (IA)
Evans (IL)
Fazio
Florio
Foglietta
Ford (MI)
Ford (TN)
Frank
Garcia
Gaydos
Gilman
Gonzalez
Gray (PA)
Guarini
Hartnett
Hawkins
Hayes
Holt
Howard
Hoyer
Hubbard
Hughes
Hunter
Hyde
Jones (NC)
Kanjorski
Kastenmeier
Kemp
Kennelly
Kildee
Kolter
LaFalce
Lehman (CA)
Lehman (FL)
Leland
Levine (CA)
Lewis (CA)
Lipinski
Long
Lowry (WA)
Markey
Marlenee
Martin (NY)
Martinez
Matsui
McHugh
Mikulski
Miller (CA)
Mineta
Mitchell
Moakley
Mollohan
Moody
Morrison (CT)
Murtha
Myers
Nowak
Oakar
Oberstar
Obey
Ortiz
Owens
Parris
Pepper
Perkins
Rahall
Rangel
Roberts
Rodino
Roe
Rose
Roybal
Sabo
Savage
Scheuer
Schroeder
Schumer
Seiberling
Shumway
Smith (IA)
Solarz
St Germain
Stark
Stokes
Stratton
Studds
Synar
Tallon
Torricelli
Towns
Traficant
Traxler
Udall
Vento

Illustration 6.G. (continued)

United States of America

Congressional Record

PROCEEDINGS AND DEBATES OF THE 99th CONGRESS, FIRST SESSION

Vol. 131 WASHINGTON, THURSDAY, DECEMBER 12, 1985 *No. 172*

Senate

(Legislative day of Monday, December 9, 1985)

The Senate met at 9 a.m., on the expiration of the recess, and was called to order by the President pro tempore [Mr. THURMOND].

PRAYER

The Chaplain, the Reverend Richard C. Halverson, D.D., offered the following prayer:

Let us pray.

God of all comfort, be with Senator GOLDWATER, his two sons and two daughters, in the loss of his beloved wife Peggy.

This morning we feel the pain of the families of the 250 soldiers and the 8 crewmembers killed in the airplane crash at Gander Airport in Newfoundland, and we pray for them.

Father in Heaven, we beseech you for Your continued guidance—Your enablement—as the Senate works its way through controversial issues and clashing wills in a tough agenda. This room is occupied by 100 of the most powerful people in the Nation—for that matter, the world. Each is one, among many in his State, chosen and entrusted with the delicate, difficult stewardship of the democratic process. It is awesome to contemplate the immense potential when their power is united. It is tragic to observe the impotence when their powers collide and neutralize the power of each so that the whole is less than the sum of its parts.

You know the Senators, Lord, their motivation, purpose, sincerity, commitment. Protect them from the contradiction of national leaders victimized by their own power, position, prestige, and self-image. Protect their families from being victims. Renew the Senators in their dedication to the mandate which brought them to this Chamber and the will to be faithful to those who believed them and sent them here. Gracious God, transfigure these closing days of this session into a shining hour for the U.S. Senate. In His name Who was the Servant of all. Amen.

RECOGNITION OF THE MAJORITY LEADER

The PRESIDENT pro tempore. The distinguished majority leader is recognized.

SCHEDULE

Mr. DOLE. Mr. President, under the standing order, the leaders have 10 minutes each, and then routine morning business not to extend beyond the hour of 9:30, followed by, I guess, the OPIC conference report, S. 947, then the White Earth Indian Reservation bill under a 4-hour time agreement. Hopefully, today we can do the counterterrorism bill under a time agreement, possible trade legislation, if there can be a time agreement, and any conference reports that accompany the so-called must items. I think the only one that could possibly come before us today would be the continuing resolution.

We still, before we complete action this year, must come to grips with the farm bill. That means passing it. Hopefully, we could break the logjam on that in the conference this morning. Second, the farm credit legislation. There are a couple of ways we can approach that and dispose of that before we leave. And then reconciliation.

It would seem to me we would be walking away from all the work that many committees and many Members were engaged in throughout the year if we failed to pass a conference report on reconciliation. It involves a total of $35 billion in spending reductions over the next 3 years. I hope we will not say, "Well, that is something we can delay until next year."

There is little hope that we will adjourn this week. So it is now my hope that we may adjourn by midweek of next week. It seems to me that that would be the earliest time.

I will try to advise Members about this evening. I doubt that we will have a late evening, unless we are waiting on a conference report.

Also, because so many of our colleagues are involved in conferences, we would like to stack the votes, if there are any votes requested this morning, until about 1 o'clock and any other votes, maybe, until about 4 or 5 o'clock this afternoon to avoid Members' breaking up their conferences, coming back to the floor, and wasting a lot of their very valuable time in the last few days of the session.

Mr. President, I reserve the remainder of my time.

RECOGNITION OF THE ACTING MINORITY LEADER

The PRESIDING OFFICER (Mr. McCONNELL). The acting Democratic leader is recognized.

Mr. PROXMIRE. Mr. President, I ask unanimous consent that 2 minutes of the Democratic leader's time be reserved for his use at any time today.

The PRESIDING OFFICER. Without objection, it is so ordered.

THE NUCLEAR THREAT TO THE PACIFIC

Mr. PROXMIRE. Mr. President, the Prime Minister of New Zealand has said that he objects to the use of New Zealand ports by American ships carrying nuclear weapons. New Zealand may ban such American ships in the future. Our State Department has told New Zealand that if they prevent American ships from using New Zealand ports, we will regard this as a violation of our mutual defense agreements with New Zealand. The effect of that could exclude New Zealand from the protection of American naval and other military forces in the event of a Pacific war. Australia has announced

● This "bullet" symbol identifies statements or insertions which are not spoken by a Member of the Senate on the floor.

Illustration 6.G. (continued)

Thursday, December 12, 1985

Daily Digest

Senate

Chamber Action

Routine Proceedings, pages S17469–S17562

Measures Introduced: Eleven bills and eight resolutions were introduced, as follows: S. 1927–1937, S.J. Res. 245–248, S. Con. Res. 93, and S. Res. 271–273.

Page S17525

Measures Reported: Reports were made as follows:

H.J. Res. 450, to authorize and request the President to issue a proclamation designating April 20–26, 1986, as "National Organ and Tissue Donor Awareness Week."

S.J. Res. 235, to designate the week of January 26, 1986, to February 1, 1986, as "Truck and Bus Safety Week."

S. Res. 271, expressing the sense of the Senate regarding the furnishing of assistance for the Republic of Liberia, and for other purposes.

S. 1831, to amend the Arms Export Control Act to require that congressional vetoes of certain arms export proposals be enacted into law.

S. Con. Res. 93, commending the Government of Ireland and the Government of the United Kingdom for reaching agreement on measures which will lay the foundation for a just, durable, and peaceful solution to the problems of Northern Ireland.

S. 1912, to provide for a 6-month extension of certain temporary provisions relating to the Internal Revenue Code of 1954, with an amendment in the nature of a substitute and an amendment to the title. (S. Rept. No. 99–219)

H.R. 2694, designating the United States Post Office Building located at 300 Packerland Drive, Green Bay, Wisconsin, as the "John W. Byrnes Post Office and Federal Building."

Page S17524

Measures passed:

Further Continuing Appropriations, 1986: Senate passed H.J. Res. 476, making further continuing appropriations for fiscal year 1986.

Page S17515

Extension of Certain Tax Provisions: Senate passed H.R. 3918, to extend until December 18, 1985, the application of certain tobacco excise taxes, trade adjustment assistance, certain medicare reimbursement provisions, and borrowing authority under the railroad unemployment insurance program.

Page S17517

Panama Canal Authorizations, 1986: Senate passed H.R. 1784, to authorize funds for fiscal year 1986 for the operation and maintenance of the Panama Canal, after agreeing to a committee amendment thereto.

Page S17517

Reappointment of Carlisle H. Humelsine: Senate passed S.J. Res. 214, to provide for the reappointment of Carlisle H. Humelsine as a citizen regent of the Board of Regents of the Smithsonian Institution.

Page S17518

Reappointment of William G. Bowen: Senate passed S.J. Res. 215, to provide for the reappointment of William G. Bowen as a citizen regent of the Board of Regents of the Smithsonian Institution.

Page S17518

Kentucky Wilderness Lands: Senate passed H.R. 1627, to designate certain national forest system lands in the State of Kentucky for inclusion in the National Wilderness Preservation System, and to release other forest lands for multiple use management.

Page S17518

Protective Services for the Supreme Court: Senate passed H.R. 3914, to preserve the authority of the Supreme Court Police to provide protective services for Justices and Court personnel, after agreeing to Packwood (for Thurmond) Amendment No. 1417, in the nature of a substitute.

Page S17519

Request for Return of Enrolled Bill: Senate agreed to H. Con. Res. 247, requesting the President to return the enrolled bill (H.R. 3003), relating to the conveyance of certain land located in the State of Maryland to the Maryland National Capital Park and Planning Commission and providing for its reenrollment with technical corrections.

Page S17520

Condolences to the Goldwater Family: Senate agreed to S. Res. 273, expressing sincere condo-

D 1515

Illustration 6.G. (continued)

S. 1236, to make minor or technical amendments to provisions enacted by the Comprehensive Crime Control Act of 1984, with an amendment in the nature of a substitute;

H.R. 3511, to amend the Federal criminal code with respect to bribery involving financial institutions, with an amendment;

S. 1429, to authorize prosecution of terrorists who attack United States nationals in any foreign country, with an amendment in the nature of a substitute; and

S. 1562, to increase civil penalties for false claims and revise the procedure with regard to bringing suit under the False Claims Act, with an amendment in the nature of a substitute.

AUTHORIZATIONS—HIGHER EDUCATION

Committee on Labor and Human Resources: Subcommittee on Education, Arts, and Humanities approved for full committee consideration proposed legislation authorizing funds for fiscal years 1987 through 1991 for the Higher Education Act.

House of Representatives

Chamber Action

Bills Introduced: 21 public bills, H.R. 3917–3937; 1 private bill, H.R. 3938; and 11 resolutions, H.J. Res. 476–483, H. Con. Res. 259, and H. Res. 340–341 were introduced.

Page H11983

Bills Reported: Reports were filed as follows:

H.R. 2651, to amend section 504 of the Alaska National Interest Lands Conservation Act to promote the development of mineral wealth in Alaska, amended (H. Rept. 99–436);

H.R. 3851, to amend section 901 of the Alaska National Interest Lands Conservation Act (H. Rept. 99–437);

H.R. 2787, to extend through fiscal year 1988 SBA Pilot Programs under section 8 of the Small Business Act (H. Rept. 99–438); and

Conference report on H.R. 3037, making appropriations for Agriculture, Rural Development and Related Agencies programs for the fiscal year ending September 30, 1986.

Page H11983

Journal: By a yea-and-nay vote of 274 yeas to 111 nays with 3 voting "present," Roll No. 455, the House approved the Journal of Wednesday, December 12.

Page H11905

Supreme Court Police: House passed H.R. 3914, to preserve the authority of the Supreme Court Police to provide protective services for Justices and Court personnel.

Page H11905

Committee To Sit: Committee on Banking, Finance and Urban Affairs received permission to sit today during proceedings of the House under the 5-minute rule.

Page H11907

Lithuanian Independence Day: House passed H.J. Res. 409, to direct the President to issue a proclamation designating February 16, 1986, was "Lithuanian Independence Day."

Page H11916

Camp Fire Organization: House agreed to S. Con. 69, to recognize the National Camp Fire Organization for seventy-five years of service—clearing the measure.

Page H11917

Ethnic American Day: House passed and cleared for the President S.J. Res. 32, to authorize and request the President to designate September 21, 1986, as "Ethnic American Day."

Page H11918

Save for the U.S.A. Year: House passed H.J. Res. 436, to designate 1986 as "Save for the U.S.A. Year."

Page H11919

Agreed to the Garcia amendment that includes Congressional staff and constituents in the campaign to purchase United States savings bonds.

Page H11919

Jaycee Week: House passed and cleared for the President S.J. Res. 213, to designate January 19 through January 25, 1986, "National Jaycee Week."

Page H11920

Man's Inhumanity to Man: House completed all general debate and began consideration of amendments on H.J. Res. 192, to designate April 24, 1985, as "National Day of Remembrance of Man's Inhumanity to Man"; but came to no resolution thereon. Proceedings under the 5-minute rule are scheduled to continue at a later date.

Page H11931

Agreed to the committee amendments.

Page H11941

Rejected the Ford of Michigan amendment that sought to clarify the perpetrators of the Armenian genocide (rejected by a recorded vote of 206 ayes to 213 noes with 2 voting "present," Roll No. 459).

Page H11942

Illustration 6.G. (continued)

December 12, 1985 CONGRESSIONAL RECORD — DAILY DIGEST D 1521

as "Made in America Month." Signed December 11, 1985. (P.L. 99-175)

H.J. Res. 473, waiving the printing on parchment of the enrollment of H.J. Res. 372, increasing the statutory limit on the public debt. Signed December 11, 1985. (P.L. 99-176)

COMMITTEE MEETINGS FOR FRIDAY, DECEMBER 13, 1985

(Committee meetings are open unless otherwise indicated)

Senate

Committee on Armed Services, to hold hearings to review Navy promotion policies, 10 a.m., SR-222.

Committee on Governmental Affairs, to hold hearings on the nominations of J.H. Tyler McConnell, of Delaware, Barry D. Schreiber, of Florida, and Robert Setrakian, of California, each to be a Member of the Board of Governors of the United States Postal Service, 10 a.m., SD-342.

Committee on the Judiciary, Subcommittee on Immigration and Refugee Policy, business meeting, to consider pending private immigration relief bills, 11 a.m., SD-226.

House

Committee on Energy and Commerce, Subcommittee on Energy Conservation and Power, to mark up the following bills: H.R. 949, to amend the Energy Security Act and the National Energy Conservation Policy Act to repeal the statutory authorities administered by the Residential Energy Conservation Service and the Commercial and Apartment Conservation Service; and S. 410, Conservation Service Reform Act of 1985; and to continue markup of H.R. 44, Electric Consumers Protection Act of 1985, 10 a.m., 2123 Rayburn.

Committee on Foreign Affairs, to consider resolutions for Contempt of Congress for two recalcitrant witnesses, 1 p.m., 2172 Rayburn.

Subcommittee on Asian and Pacific Affairs, executive, to continue hearings regarding the investigation of Philippine investments in the United States, 9:30 a.m., 2172 Rayburn.

Committee on Government Operations, Subcommittee on Environment, Energy, and Natural Resources, hearing to examine the management of grazing on Federal Lands by the Bureau of Land Management and the Forest Service, 9:30 a.m., 2247 Rayburn.

Committee on Public Works and Transportation, to consider 2 11(B) Public Buildings and Grounds prospectuses, 9:30 a.m., 2167 Rayburn.

Illustration 6.G. (concluded)

D 1560 CONGRESSIONAL RECORD — DAILY DIGEST *December 19, 1985*

Next Meeting of the SENATE
11 a.m., Friday, December 20

Next Meeting of the HOUSE OF REPRESENTATIVES
12 noon, Friday, December 20

Senate Chamber

Program for Friday: Further consideration of H.R. 3128 and amendments thereto, Omnibus Budget Reconciliation Act of 1985.

House Chamber

Program for Friday: Legislative program is uncertain.

Extensions of Remarks, as inserted in this issue

HOUSE

Barnes, Michael D., Md., E5770, E5775, E5780
Biaggi, Mario, N.Y., E5761
Blaz, Ben Garrido, Guam, E5740
Bonker, Don, Wash., E5758
Broomfield, Wm. S., Mich., E5761
Chandler, Rod, Wash., E5735
Cheney, Dick, Wyo., E5764, E5769, E5775
Clay, William (Bill), Mo., E5736
Clinger, William F., Jr., Pa., E5799
Coats, Dan, Ind., E5795
Collins, Cardiss, Ill., E5749
Courter, Jim, N.J., E5762, E5793
Daschle, Thomas A., S. Dak., E5741
DioGuardi, Joseph J., N.Y., E5795
Dornan, Robert K., Calif., E5765
Downey, Thomas J., N.Y., E5797
Duncan, John J., Tenn., E5754
Dymally, Mervyn M., Calif., E5742
Dyson, Roy, Md., E5731, E5735, E5738
Edwards, Don, Calif., E5733, E5796
Fascell, Dante B., Fla., E5784
Fazio, Vic, Calif., E5796
Florio, James J., N.J., E5745, E5748, E5752, E5783, E5791
Ford, Harold E., Tenn., E5757
Fowler, Wyche, Jr., Ga., E5743
Frank, Barney, Mass., E5755
Frenzel, Bill, Minn., E5776
Gallo, Dean A., N.J., E5797
Garcia, Robert, N.Y., E5733, E5737, E5771
Gaydos, Joseph M., Pa., E5736, E5759
Gilman, Benjamin A., N.Y., E5734
Green, Bill, N.Y., E5744
Gunderson, Steve, Wis., E5797
Hamilton, Lee H., Ind., E5738, E5743, E5768
Hammerschmidt, John Paul, Ark., E5794
Hawkins, Augustus F., Calif., E5741, E5778
Howard, James J., N.J., E5779
Hoyer, Steny H., Md., E5749, E5753
Hyde, Henry J., Ill., E5766
Kasich, John R., Ohio, E5773
Kemp, Jack F., N.Y., E5763
Kennelly, Barbara B., Conn., E5740
Kindness, Thomas N., Ohio, E5737, E5789
Lagomarsino, Robert J., Calif., E5741
Levin, Sander M., Mich., E5745
Levine, Mel, Calif., E5739, E5756, E5757
Lewis, Jerry, Calif., E5799
Lloyd, Marilyn, Tenn., E5767, E5769, E5770
Lowry, Mike, Wash., E5745
McHugh, Matthew F., N.Y., E5734, E5781
McKernan, John R., Jr., Maine, E5751
Manton, Thomas J., N.Y., E5760
Moakley, Joe, Mass., E5742
Moody, Jim, Wis., E5756, E5792
Mrazek, Robert J., N.Y., E5786
Pickle, J.J., Tex., E5746
Porter, John Edward, Ill., E5732, E5749
Rodino, Peter W., Jr., N.J., E5798
Roe, Robert A., N.J., E5759
Rogers, Harold, Ky., E5751
Rowland, J. Roy, Ga., E5798
Russo, Marty, Ill., E5757
Shaw, E. Clay, Jr., Fla., E5791
Siljander, Mark D., Mich., E5793
Stokes, Louis, Ohio, E5746, E5752
Thomas, William M., Calif., E5744
Towns, Edolphus, N.Y., E5787, E5795
Whitehurst, G. William, Va., E5781
Williams, Pat, Mont., E5744
Wilson, Charles, Tex., E5747
Wirth, Timothy E., Colo., E5731, E5742
Wolf, Frank R., Va., E5745, E5794
Wolpe, Howard, Mich., E5798
Yatron, Gus, Pa., E5772

(House and Senate proceedings for today will be continued in the next issue of the Record.)

Congressional Record The public proceedings of each House of Congress, as reported by the Official Reporters thereof, are printed pursuant to directions of the Joint Committee on Printing as authorized by appropriate provisions of Title 44, United States Code, and published for each day that one or both Houses are in session, excepting very infrequent instances when two or more unusually small consecutive issues are printed at one time. ¶ The Congressional Record will be furnished by mail to subscribers, free of postage, for $109 for six months, $218 per year, or purchased for $1 per copy, payable in advance. The semimonthly Congressional Record Index may be purchased for $1 per copy, payable in advance. Remit check or money order, made payable to the Superintendent of Documents, directly to the Government Printing Office, Washington, D.C. 20402. ¶ Following each session of Congress, the daily Congressional Record is revised, printed, permanently bound and sold by the Superintendent of Documents in individual parts or by sets. ¶ With the exception of copyrighted articles, there are no restrictions on the republication of material from the Congressional Record.

Chapter Seven

Congressional Decision Making: The Micro Focus

In addition to studying congressional policymaking from the macro perspective of following how bills become law, congressional scholars also have employed a micro focus, studying how individual congressmen reach decisions.

Micro studies vary in terms of what they study and how they gather data. Four separate components of the member cognitive map—force field (communications), information sources, decision shortcuts and determinants, and role orientations—have been the object of study. Figure 7. 1 displays these different components and the facet of decision making on which they focus. Sources for micro studies have been content analysis, direct interviewing, and analyses of roll-call data. The selections that follow address these various components and give examples of studies based on these different sources.

Illustrations 7.A–7.F: Congressional Information Sources

The gathering and processing of information is an important facet of congressional decision making with regard to floor votes in the U.S. Congress. Numerous information sources are available to assist members. Some are valuable quite a while in advance of a vote while others avail themselves only right before the vote. Some involve personal contact with other actors and members while other information sources are in a less personal form. Some information is carried via in house congressional publications such as whip notices and advisories or the publications of the Democratic Study Group (DSG) and other informal caucuses. Personal staff provides, as well as processes, information. Of course, the personal reading and life's experiences of members also serve as information sources. Table 7.1 classifies major information sources by proximity to the vote and directness of approach.

Figure 7.1.
Four components of the member's cognitive map.

Component	Decision-Making Aspect	Component	Decision-Making Aspect
Fource field/policy arena	Communications input—attempts to influence to which members pays attention in making a decision.	Determinants	Actors/decision rules on which members rely when making a decision.
Information sources	Actors/sources from which member learns about the factual aspect of a bill.	Role orientations	Broad philosophical perspective with which members observe the representational aspects of a bill.

The following illustrations give examples of major congressional information sources on which members rely, in addition to previously displayed party publications such as whip notices and policy committee memos and legislative materials such as the bills themselves and committee reports. Illustration 7.A (p. 290) presents an example of a "Dear Colleague" letter of the type members send to other members in an effort to drum up support for particular bills and caucuses. These letters give a concise, albeit partisan, statement of the issue and the member's position on it.

The DSG, which originally was started by a group of liberal Democratic members of the House to counteract the "conservative coalition" of Republicans and southern Democrats, has evolved into perhaps the best information network on Capitol Hill. Now used by members across the spectrum and from both parties, the DSG distributes five different publications: Legislative Report, Daily Report, Special Reports, Facts Sheets, and Staff Bulletin.

Legislative Report is issued weekly. (See Illustration 7.B, p. 291) It gives a complete schedule of the upcoming week's activities together with a summary of all bills. The particular utility of the Legislative Report in comparison to party publications is that it anticipates the amendments that are expected to be offered. It also lists the arguments pro and con for each amendment. In a commentary section, the Legislative Report lists the support and opposition of the administration and major interest groups.

The Daily Report is issued each day and provides a detailed, updated schedule for the particular day plus a last-minute listing of possible amendments. The Special Reports (see Illustration 7.C, p. 295) are in-depth discussions of issues that, although not presently up for consideration, are imminent. They are compiled by the legislative staff of the DSG and are intended to provide background information on the major bills of the session. The Fact Sheets (see Illustration 7.D, p. 296) are detailed studies of major, controversial pieces of information that are coming up. Staff Bulletin (Illustration 7.E, p. 297) is a legislative newsletter designed especially for the staff community.

Illustration 7.F (p. 298) is an example of a staff-prepared legislative summary intended to brief members for floor voting. Through such information packages, staff filters and distills information received from DSG, committee, other members, interest groups, party organizations, the administration, and constituents.

Table 7.1.
Classification of major congressional information sources by proximateness and directness.

	Directness			Directness	
Proximity	Personal	Impersonal	Proximity	Personal	Impersonal
Proximate	Committee chairman Committee members Other members Party leaders State delegation Personal staff	Doormen Caucus recording Debate	Antecedent	Committee members Other members State delegation Personal staff Dear Colleague Interest groups Constituents	DSG publications Whip Notice Media/reading Committee report Policy committees

Illustration 7.A.
Dear Colleague letter.

CONGRESS
of the
United States of America

Andy Jacobs, Jr.

July 24, 1985

Dear Colleague:

For about six years I have been introducing annual amendments to do away with the slush funds for former Presidents.

This year will be no exception.

Former Presidents get pensions of $86,200. On top of that, each one has been getting about a third of a million dollars a year essentially to spend on secretaries and office rent to handle bookings for their $25,000 speech gold mines.

Why do they get $25,000 a speech? Because the American people have given them the privilege of having served as Presidents.

That strikes me as a little tacky for the fellow who is getting an $86,200 a year pension from the American public. But, at least the American taxpayers ought not be required to put up a third of a million dollars for each of these former Presidents to pay the overhead on the commercial aspects of the former Presidency.

Therefore, in accordance with professional polling indications that the overwhelming majority of the American public wants the slush funds cut out, I shall offer my amendment to the Treasury and Postal Service appropriation legislation, not to cut out some of the offending expenditure, but to cut out all of it.

The amendment I have proposed in the past has passed the House on one occasion. It should pass this year, if anybody really believes in cutting out wasteful government spending--especially for holy cows who have no official position with the government and no obligation to perform any duties.

Sincerely,

ANDY JACOBS, JR.

AJ/pc

THE ROAD TO PEACE IS PAVED WITH JUSTICE.

Illustration 7.B.
DSG Legislative Report.

DSG LEGISLATIVE REPORT

DEMOCRATIC STUDY GROUP - U.S. HOUSE OF REPRESENTATIVES - WASHINGTON, D.C. - Tel.: 225-5858
HON. JAMES L. OBERSTAR (Minn.) - Chairman RICHARD P. CONLON - Executive Director

SCHEDULE FOR THE WEEK OF DECEMBER 9, 1985

MONDAY, DECEMBER 9 (House meets at noon)

* Suspensions -- Eighteen bills are scheduled for consideration under suspension of the rules (page 1), including H.R. 3792, Farm Credit Act Amendments (page 4), and H.R. 1957, Ocean Dumping Amendments (page 9).

TUESDAY, DECEMBER 10 (House meets at noon)

* Superfund -- H.R. 2817, Superfund Amendments, complete consideration (page 29). See DSG Fact Sheet No. 99-16, December 3.

* U.S.-China Nuclear Pact -- S.J.Res. 238, Approval of U.S.-China Nuclear Cooperation Agreement (page 32).

* Uniform Poll Closing -- H.R. 3525, Uniform Poll Closing Time for Presidential Elections (page 35).

* Victims of Genocide -- H.J.Res. 192, Day of Remembrance of Man's Inhumanity to Man (page 39).

WEDNESDAY & BALANCE OF THE WEEK, DECEMBER 11, 12, & 13
(House meets at 10 a.m. each day)

* Debt Limit/Gramm-Rudman -- It is expected that conferees will reach agreement on H.J.Res. 372, Debt Limit Increase/Gramm-Rudman Balanced Budget Plan. DSG will issue a report on the agreement prior to Floor consideration.

* Tax Reform -- H.R. 3838, Tax Reform Act (page 41). See DSG Fact Sheet No. 99-17, December 5.

* Continuing Appropriations -- It is expected that conferees will also reach an agreement on H.J.Res. 465, Continuing Appropriations for FY 1986. DSG will report on the agreement prior to Floor consideration.

* Reconciliation -- Conferees hope to reach an agreement on H.R. 3128, Deficit Reduction Amendments, before the House adjourns this week. DSG will attempt to provide a report on a conference agreement before Floor consideration.

* Farm Bill -- It is possible that conferees may reach an agreement on H.R. 2100, Food Security Act, before adjournment for the Christmas District Work Period. DSG will attempt to report on any such agreement before Floor consideration.

Illustration 7.B. (continued)

DSG LEGISLATIVE REPORT

TUESDAY, DECEMBER 10, 1985

SUPERFUND AMENDMENTS (H.R. 2817; see DSG Fact Sheet No. 99-16, December 3)

FLOOR SITUATION: The bill is being considered for amendment. The two tax substitutes made in order by the rule and being offered by Reps. Downey and Duncan are pending. All other titles of the bill have been considered. An amendment to be offered by Rep. Frank to add a new Title 6 to the bill allowing persons to sue in federal court for injuries caused by toxic substances is also expected to be considered.

BACKGROUND: On December 5 and 6, the Committee of the Whole House considered the bill for amendment under the five-minute rule. Following is a summary of major amendments adopted:

* An amendment by Rep. Andrews that provides state employees who assist in cleanup actions the same exemption from liability that the bill grants to private contractors working on the cleanup action (agreed to by voice vote).

* An amendment by Rep. Wirth that requires on-site Superfund cleanup actions to conform to state laws governing the location of hazardous waste sites (agreed to by voice vote).

* An amendment by Rep. Edgar that requires companies to inventory and keep track of emissions of chemicals with chronic health effects, such as those that can cause cancer (agreed to by a vote of 183 to 166).

SUMMARY: Following is a brief summary of the bill's tax provisions, which are pending. For a complete summary of these and other provisions, see DSG Fact Sheet No. 99-16, December 3.

The bill establishes a new, broad-based manufacturers excise tax, called the Superfund excise tax (SET), that imposes an .08% tax on the sale of a product by a manufacturer. The tax, which is estimated to raise about $4.5 BILLION over five years, would be imposed on manufacturers with sales greater than $10 million.

Illustration 7.B. (continued)

TUESDAY

SUPERFUND AMENDMENTS (CONT'D)

Rep. Frank will offer an amendment to allow persons injured by the release of toxic substances to sue responsible parties in federal court. The amendment establishes uniform rules on liability, statutes of limitations, and the type of evidence that can be admitted. Under the amendment, victims would have to prove, by a preponderance of the evidence, that injury was caused by the toxic substance and that the person being sued placed that type of substance in the dump site. (Staff Contact: Bill Black, ext. 55931)

Rep. Glickman will offer an amendment to the Frank amendment to make the Frank amendment's provisions prospective only. The Frank amendment makes the right of persons to sue in federal court retroactive to 1975. (Staff Contact: Janet Potts, ext. 55741)

COMMENTARY: The Administration strongly opposes enactment of the bill unless it is amended to reduce the overall funding level from $10 BILLION to $5.3 BILLION, and provisions allowing citizens to sue and establish mandatory cleanup schedules are deleted. According to OMB, a veto will be recommended if the bill contains a broad-based tax (the bill as reported by the Ways and Means Committee contains such a tax), or if the bill contains "substantial increases in the existing feedstock and petroleum taxes" (the Downey amendment would increase such taxes).

DSG Contact: Michael Pryor

* * *

Illustration 7.B. (concluded)

DSG DAILY REPORT

DEMOCRATIC STUDY GROUP - U.S. HOUSE OF REPRESENTATIVES - WASHINGTON, D.C. - Tel.: 225-5858
HON. JAMES L. OBERSTAR (Minn.) - Chairman RICHARD P. CONLON - Executive Director

THURSDAY, DECEMBER 5, 1985

TODAY'S SCHEDULE

The House meets at 10:00 a.m. to consider the following:

* Conference Report on H.R. 3424, Labor-HHS-Education Appropriations for FY 1986

* H.R. 2817 Superfund Amendments (See DSG Fact Sheet No. 99-16, December 3)

ANTICIPATED AMENDMENTS

<u>Rep. Vento</u> will offer an amendment to authorize the use of money from the Superfund to reimburse municipalities that have incurred costs in developing alternative sources of water supplies because their existing groundwater drinking sources have been contaminated by hazardous substances traced to a federally owned site that has been placed on the National Priorities List. The EPA would be directed to recover Superfund expenditures from potentially responsible federal entities. (Staff Contact: Steve Francisco, ext. 56331)

<u>Rep. Markey</u> may offer an amendment to ensure that when private parties pay for the cleanup of Superfund sites, the cleanup will meet environment standards. The amendment also specifies that those standards cannot be waived on the basis on how much EPA would be willing or required to spend out of the Superfund to clean up the same site. (Staff Contact: Gerry Waldron, ext. 62424)

<u>Rep. Sikorski and Edgar</u> will offer an amendment to require companies to inventory and keep track of chemical emissions that have chronic as well as acute health effects. (The bill requires emission tracking only for those substances on a list of acutely toxic chemicals -- those capable of causing immediate injury or death. Chronic health effects take longer to become apparent, as in the case of cancer.) (Staff Contacts: Ron Apter, ext. 52271, or Dean Kaplan, ext. 52011)

<u>Rep. Carper</u> may offer an amendment to expand the potential list of acutely toxic chemicals whose emissions plants would be required by the bill to monitor. (Staff Contact: Christophe Tulou, ext. 54165)

Illustration 7.C.
DSG Special Reports.

DEMOCRATIC STUDY GROUP • U.S. HOUSE OF REPRESENTATIVES
225-5858 • 1422 HOUSE OFFICE BUILDING • WASHINGTON, D.C. 20515

HON. WILLIAM M. BRODHEAD (Michigan) – Chairman

RICHARD P. CONLON – Staff Director

SPECIAL REPORT

No. 97-23

June 17, 1981

THE CASE AGAINST BLOCK GRANTS

The Republican substitute to the reconciliation bill that may be offered on the House Floor next week is expected to contain President Reagan's block grant proposals.

The Administration's block grant proposals would consolidate nearly 100 categorical programs, slash funding levels, and repeal the authorizations for dozens of programs.

The Administration contends that its program would result in greater efficiency, responsiveness, and innovation. Critics contend that the net result would be the elimination of numerous federal health, education, social services, and community development programs, and the serious underfunding of many others.

This DSG Special Report contains the following sections:

<u>Note:</u> *See DSG evaluation form at end of report.*

December 12, 1985

THIRD SUPPLEMENT
TO THE DSG LEGISLATIVE REPORT
FOR THE WEEK OF DECEMBER 9, 1985

* *

<u>Waste Dump Insurance</u> -- H.R. ?, Hazardous Waste Facility Deadline Extension, is expected to be considered this week.

* *

Illustration 7.D.
DSG Fact Sheet.

DEMOCRATIC STUDY GROUP • U.S. HOUSE OF REPRESENTATIVES
225-5858 • 1422 HOUSE OFFICE BUILDING • WASHINGTON, D.C. 20515

HON. JAMES L. OBERSTAR (Minn.) Chairman   RICHARD P. CONLON Executive Director

FACT SHEET

No. 99-18   December 10, 1985

The Gramm-Rudman Compromise

THE DEFICIT CONTROL ACT

This DSG Fact Sheet deals with the conference agreement on the Balanced Budget and Emergency Deficit Control Act, which will be considered on Wednesday -- first by the Senate and then by the House. The measure has been incorporated into H.J.Res. 372, Debt Limit Increase, which must be enacted by Thursday.

The agreement, approved on Tuesday night, provides for a new process to lower the deficit to zero over the next five years. The compromise package establishes an automatic process to cut spending if the Congressional Budget Office, Office of Management and Budget, and General Accounting Office project that the deficit limits will not be met without further action.

The agreement, while retaining the basic features of the original Gramm-Rudman proposal, includes House provisions to protect certain low-income programs from further cuts, limits automatic cuts in Medicare, and requires the Pentagon to absorb 50% of the cuts.

This report contains the following sections:

Illustration 7.E.
DSG Staff Bulletin.

DEMOCRATIC STUDY GROUP - U.S. HOUSE OF REPRESENTATIVES - WASHINGTON, D.C. - Tel.: 225-5858
HON. JAMES L. OBERSTAR (Minn.) - Chairman   RICHARD P. CONLON - Executive Director

NOVEMBER 19, 1985

The DSG Staff Bulletin is published weekly while Congress is in session as a service to DSG members and staff. The Bulletin contains the following eight sections:

I. COMMITTEE AND SUBCOMMITTEE ACTION — Summaries of important bills reported by committees and subcommittees during the previous week.

II. LEGISLATION REPORTED — Major legislation which has been reported by committees and is available for Floor scheduling.

III. HEARINGS AND MARKUPS — Selected hearings and markup sessions scheduled for the current week.

IV. MEMBERS' PROJECTS — Legislative proposals being circulated for cosponsorship and other activities initiated by individual Members.

V. RESEARCH MATERIALS — References to useful insertions and articles that appear in the *Congressional Record* and elsewhere.

VI. RULINGS AND REGULATIONS — References to key rulings and regulations that appear in the *Federal Register*.

VII. CONSTITUENT MAIL RESPONSE — Examples of Members' responses to constituent and pressure-group mail on controversial issues.

VIII. JOB OPENINGS — Announcements of job openings in congressional and related offices.

Illustration 7.F.
Staff-prepared legislative summary for Representative Jim Santini (D–Nev.).

COMPLETE LEGISLATIVE SUMMARY

Number: H.R. 3965

Title: Federal Aviation Administration Authorization Act: FY 78

Date: March 24, 1977

Cost: $85 M in authorization for FY 78
Plus pay raise & benefits costs for FY 78

Floor situation: Open rule: 1-hour debate

Summary: Authorizes $85 M in FY 78 appropriations from Airport & Airway Trust Fund for research, development, & demonstration projects. Restricts funding for Aerosat program to $1.5M for feasibility study, although FAA requested $14.7M in its FY 78 budget. Terminates $50M annual FAA R&D authorization for RY 78-80 by amending Airport & Airway Development Act and initiates a requirement for annual authorization for FAA R&D commencing with this bill for FY 78. Reduce FY 76 authorization by $0.4M & FY 77 by $0.4M.

Amendments: 1. to raise funding level for Aerosat to FAA's original request of $14.7M (Rationale for program was based on increases in trans-Atlantic air routes & limitations of existing communications systems, but now travel levels have been reduced. Committee has reservations about high cost of total program & its effect on other expenditures)

Support Opposition: FAA supports the bill. State Department supports continuation of Aerosat program. Air Transport Association & International Air Transport Association oppose continuation of Aerosat.

Prior votes:

Nevada concern: None noted

Recommendation comment:

Reading 7.1

Congress and Computers

Steve Blakely

As is the case with all major endeavors and enterprises, the U. S. Congress has been swept by the data processing revolution. The following article illustrates the uses of computers in Congress.

Barely a decade ago, a tourist visiting Congress would have been hard pressed to find a single computer terminal sitting on any desk.

Today, an estimated 7,500 units have been plugged into House and Senate offices, at a cost to taxpayers of some $30 million a year—a testament to the technological revolution that has swept the legislative branch of government into the computer age.

While computers may never alter the basic political nature of Congress, they have made some fundamental changes in how the institution does its work: writing the federal budget, watching over executive agencies, dealing with special-interest groups and constituents back home.

The technology's greatest impact has been in the way Congress handles the budget and its mail. Many members credit computers with breaking the White House monopoly on budget information that existed during the 1970s, and helping Congress reassert its powers over the federal purse.

"We're all equal now," said Sen. Ted Stevens, R-Alaska, chairman of the Senate Appropriations Defense Subcommittee. "Before, we were at the mercy of OMB [the Office of Management and Budget] because they had the computers long before we did."

Source: Steve Blakely, "Congress and Computers," *Congressional Quarterly*, July 13, 1985, pp. 1379–82.

Even OMB Director David A. Stockman acknowledges that computers have helped the legislative branch catch up.

"I don't think it [computer technology] has made much difference in Congress in a political sense. But it has made them more competent adversaries," said Stockman, a Republican representative from Michigan between 1977 and 1981.

Technology has touched almost every other aspect of Congress. Consider that:

- Computers have fundamentally changed the way lawmakers deal with constituent mail. The machines maintain sophisticated mailing lists organized by constituents' particular interests. Using those lists and very specific computer-generated messages, lawmakers can target letters to constituents for maximum political impact. In the Senate, contractors help maintain mailing lists, freeing staff from part of the burdensome chore of answering mass-mail lobby campaigns.
- Virtually every administrative function in Congress is computerized: voting in the House, printing the *Congressional Record*, tracking federal programs, communicating with district offices, even reserving a parking space in the Senate. Congressional experts report a move toward shifting some constituent services—such as answering letters and prodding the bureaucracy—away from Washington and back to lawmakers' state offices, because so much can now be done electronically.
- Computers are being used in political campaigns to help challengers blunt some of the powers of incumbency. For instance, almost every GOP House challenger in 1984 was hooked into a national Republican computer network that dispensed quotes by Democratic incumbents, information on their controversial votes, political strategy and

campaign advice. Republicans plan to make extensive use of computerized demographic data and mailing lists in 1986 to help defeat incumbent House Democrats.

- Private industry is turning to computers to monitor Congress. At least three firms currently offer computer data bases that allow users to produce selective ratings of lawmakers, based on their recorded votes: Legi-Slate, owned by *The Washington Post*; Lobbyist Systems Corp., owned by a small group of investors; and Washington Alert Service, owned by Congressional Quarterly Inc.

COMPUTERS ARE EXPENSIVE

No revolution is without its costs, and the computer revolution in Congress has not been cheap.

According to the Congressional Research Service, the House and Senate spent a mere $732,000 on computers in 1970, mostly for clerical tasks such as payroll and bookkeeping. By 1984, reflecting the technology's growing use, the annual cost had jumped to $29.5 million.

Much of the demand for sophisticated computer services can be attributed to the Congressional Budget Office (CBO)—Capitol Hill's professional economic adviser, which was created by the Congressional Budget and Impoundment Control Act of 1974 (PL 93-344). CBO's computer costs alone currently run just under $5 million a year.

On a wider scale, Congressional Research Service figures show that in fiscal 1970, $4.9 million was spent on computers in all corners of the legislative bureaucracy, which includes the House and Senate, the Library of Congress, the General Accounting Office, and parts of the Government Printing Office.

In fiscal 1985, total legislative branch spending on computers will hit $75 million —a growth rate of 1,500 percent over 15 years.

That money has put computers in the hands of virtually every committee and subcommittee in Congress, as well as the overwhelming majority of members' offices.

All but 20 or so of the 435 House members have computerized offices. Only half a dozen of the 100 senators do not, and those holdouts will not last long. Just this year, the Senate launched a three-year, $30 million office automation project to install the latest computer equipment in each senator's office.

A major reason why the Senate decided to computerize all its personal offices at once was a strong desire to catch up with the House.

"The House is quantum leaps ahead of us in the Senate in computerizing individual offices," said Stevens, a self-described computer buff.

"Our budget staff and some individual committees may be better . . . but the House has been ahead of the Senate for a long time," Stevens said.

The House has been far more generous in allowing members to lease or purchase equipment for their offices. Representatives can choose from an "approved vendors list"—a 28-page smorgasbord of office goodies; fully 21 pages of it are devoted to computers and related gear.

Observers say that House policies have led to a complex, expensive, and occasionally wasteful procurement system that has left the House with some poor equipment and bad service, but it has also allowed the House to keep up with rapidly changing computer technology. In 1983, in response to severe problems with several computer vendors, the House Administration Committee tightened its approval standards.

COMPUTERS AND THE BUDGET

For both the House and the Senate, one major event sparked the drive to computerize: the 1974 Budget Act. Besides creating a new procedure for handling the budget, the law pushed Congress to acquire the same kinds of computer skills that OMB had been perfecting since 1969. To obtain and use those skills, the law created the Congressional Budget Office.

"By 1975, it wasn't a question of whether to use computers. It was a question of how," said former CBO Director Alice M. Rivlin. "The budget is a very complicated thing. . . . You could not do what CBO does without computers."

Her successor, Rudolph G. Penner, continues to expand CBO computer capability. He is said by staff to be more comfortable with the technology than Rivlin, and regularly uses the terminal on his desk.

Perhaps the major function computers play is helping to translate the different budgetary languages used by the White House and Congress. The president's budget, a single product that is prepared just once a year, focuses on appropriatons—money actually approved and spent.

But Congress must analyze budget data for two appropriations panels, and rearrange it for the authorizing committees, which share jurisdiction over thousands of programs.

The OMB Computer Tape

One of the most important tools CBO uses to deal with the complexity is a copy of the master computer tape of the president's budget, prepared every year by OMB.

The tape contains far more detail than the printed budget released to the public. CBO computers use it to quickly break out every federal program by committee jurisdiction.

This is significant in three ways:

First, the six major budget and tax-writing committees in Congress now have their pieces of the federal pie carved out and waiting almost as soon as the president delivers it.

Second, it allows for extremely fast comparison to past and alternative spending plans.

And third, it gives authorizing committees a complete report on every federal account in their bailiwicks—something many panels never had, until computers made it possible.

"The authorizing committees, nine times out of 10, didn't know which accounts were within their jurisdiction," said Robert D. Harris, CBO deputy assistant director.

LEGISLATIVE OVERSIGHT

Because the 1974 Budget Act gave authorizing committees low priority for CBO help, they turned to the House and Senate computer centers to design new ways of monitoring federal programs. The result was a number of highly specialized computer programs that help Congress perform its legislative oversight functions.

The Geographic Reporting System is used in the House to track how much federal aid goes to each state, county or congressional district. The Program Review System, developed by the Senate Labor and Human Resources Committee and used by several other panels, tracks the cost and performance of federal programs within each panel's jurisdiction.

Computers are especially effective at projecting the effect of changes in federal aid formulas, such as price supports for farmers, Social Security for retirees, or Medicaid for the poor. The Joint Committee on Taxation uses a program, created by the Treasury Department, to project the consequences for taxpayers of proposed changes in tax rates.

One current trend in Congress is the growing use of small but powerful minicomputers by individual committees to produce extremely sophisticated (and sometimes partisan) reports on how their particular programs would be affected by different budget plans.

Some of the most controversial products of Capitol Hill computers are CBO's economic projections of the federal budget and national economy.

CBO bases those reports on its own

experience tracking the budget, and on a consensus of four major econometric computer models. Because CBO uses different economic assumptions from OMB, its reports often contradict White House estimates.

The most bitter dispute over computer projections came in 1981, when CBO accurately predicted far higher deficits from the Reagan administration's spending and tax cut package than what the White House was suggesting. And last month, a CBO report disputed White House claims that President Reagan's tax simplification plan would not add to the deficit.

COMPUTERS AND MAIL

Just as House and Senate committees gradually became more computerized during the last decade, so did individual member offices. They had to, because of the phenomenal growth during the last decade in the amount of congressional mail.

"When I first came to Congress [in 1972] we used to get between 6,000 and 8,000 a year," said Rep. James R. Jones, D-Okla., who was House Budget Committee chairman from 1981 through 1984.

"Just in 1981, we got 400,000 letters. Without computers, we couldn't have kept up with the mail."

It is no accident that the rapid growth of computers in Congress over the last decade has been accompanied by an explosive increase in the amount of mail leaving Capitol Hill.

According to the House Appropriations Committee, about 30 million letters were mailed from Congress in 1977. That more than tripled by 1985, to more than one billion letters a year.

In the past, lobby-by-mail campaigns have brought congressional offices to a virtual standstill, as staff worked overtime to answer all the letters. Lawmakers remember with some bitterness the crushing load of mail in 1983 generated by banks against withholding taxes on dividend and interest income. The campaign worked, and the provision was repealed.

In response to that incident, the Senate Rules Committee decided in 1984 to let an outside contractor handle the job of computerizing names and addresses from direct-mail campaigns. This new service is in use continually, and has proven to be "a great release valve for senators," according to John K. Swearingen, director of technical services for Senate Rules.

Members of the House have a similar arrangement, which allows them to lease computer services to update and print their mailing lists.

"Direct mail used to paralyze members' offices, but [it doesn't] anymore," said Rep. Charlie Rose, D-N.C. "Now, it's looked upon as an opportunity to improve your mailing list."

Political Mail

Coupled with the free mailing privilege that members of Congress enjoy, computerized letters can be a powerful political weapon. So powerful, in fact, that in 1973 Common Cause sued the federal government, claiming that free postage gave incumbents an unfair and illegal advantage over challengers.

One of the alleged abuses Common Cause cited was "self-generated" mail—computerized letters sent by lawmakers to constituents who had not written in the first place. The suit noted that in 1972 Sen. Robert P. Griffin, R-Mich., used a list of owners of high-priced cars to direct a letter opposing school busing to upper-income, and presumably white, households.

Common Cause ultimately lost in the courts. But the lawsuit prompted Congress to restrict the kinds of mail that can be sent out free, and prohibit mass mailings 60 days before elections.

Still, there are few strict limitations, and some critics say the new computer system now being installed in Senate offices will provide new opportunities for political abuse. That is because senators will have total control over their mailing lists—something they do not have now, since the current centralized mailing system limits their access.

With the new computers, staff experts say, the major restrictions on imaginative use of mailing lists will be the fear of getting caught.

"Remember, these letters go through the mail to a lot of people," said Swearingen. "Sooner or later they're going to fall into unfriendly hands."

Reading 7.2

Decision Settings in Congress

David C. Kozak

This piece emphasizes variations in congressional decision making at the micro level. It contends that different patterns of congressional decision making correspond to different kinds of issues. An epilogue, written upon the completion of the author's service as a Congressional Fellow, discusses the initial findings in light of a year's experience as a House and Senate staffer.

ABSTRACT

This paper attempts to document contextual decision behavior in House floor voting and to foster an approach to congressional decision making that emphasizes decision settings. After presenting a synopsis of recent interview research among House members that reveals variable decision behavior, this paper argues that congressmen encounter at least five different decision settings during the act of floor voting: hot votes, nonvisible votes, complicated bills, grant aid votes, and routine votes. Each setting is associated with distinctive decision behavior and decision rules. Therefore, universal or general models of legislative behavior that attempt to describe typical, normal, or modal behavior, although providing a significant glimpse of legislative life, necessarily oversimplify what is a highly complex and contextual process. A sophisticated approach to congressional decision making requires a multiple model approach and an appreciation for the decision setting within which each model is likely to apply. The paper concludes with an optimistic assessment of the potential for constituency-representative linkages in House voting, and an epilogue based on actual staff work experience.

Source: Published here for the first time, this paper is an edited and revised version of one prepared for delivery at the 1980 annual meeting of the Legislative Studies Group, held in conjunction with the 1980 annual meeting of the American Political Science Association, Washington, D.C., August 28–31, 1980.

INTRODUCTION

Congressmen make up their minds in different ways on different kinds of issues. Although this is a rather obvious conclusion, it has not been emphasized or researched in the scholarly literature of congressional voting behavior.

Previously, various authors have focused

on what they conclude is the dominant behavioral pattern or decision determinant affecting congressional decision making. For example, Julius Turner, in his roll-call study, *Party and Constituency: Pressures on Congress*, argues that "party continues to be more closely associated with congressional voting behavior than any other discernible factor."[1] For Donald Matthews and James A. Stimson in *Yeas and Nays*, as the subtitle of their work states, cue-taking (i.e., following the position of another actor presumed to be an expert) is the "normal" decision-making procedure in the House.[2] For Aage Clausen in *How Congressmen Decide*, most decisions are made on the basis of policy dimensions. In his words,

> Legislators reduce the time and energy requirements of policy decision making by (1) . . . sorting specific policy proposals into a limited number of general policy content categories and by (2) establishing a policy position for each general category of policy content, one that can be used to make decisions on each of the specific proposals assigned to that category.[3]

John Kingdon, in *Congressmen's Voting Decisions*, develops a consensus model of decision making. To him,

> Congressmen begin their consideration of a given bill or amendment with one overriding question: Is it controversial? . . . When there is no controversy in the Congressman's environment at all, his decision rule is simple: vote with the herd. . . . If the Congressman does see some conflict in total environment . . . he proceeds . . . to the next step in the decisional flow chart.[4]

Usually, findings have been presented in terms of general propositions that attempt to describe typical or normal behavior, such as:

- A congressman hears from few actors when making a decision, "most often from those who agree with him."[5]
- "Fellow congressmen appear to be the most important influence on voting decisions, followed by constituency."[6]
- "Other members are the major source of a congressman's information."[7]
- "Congressmen confine their searches for information only to the most routine and easily available sources."[8]
- Congressmen generally are not well informed when making a decision.[9]
- Party affiliation is the factor most strongly related to congressional voting.[10]
- Members base most votes on ideology.[11]
- Most members have a "politico" style of representation and a district focus.[12]

The result of these research efforts has been both informative and frustrating—informative because each author gives us a glimpse of the forces and decision rules that affect congressional voting, but frustrating because we are presented with a series of conflicting, single-factor theories and single-eye interpretations with little attempt to integrate them. For example, four different single-eye interpretations have evolved as alternative explanations for congressional decision making. They are the organizational explanation (cue-taking), the representational (instructed delegate) explanation, the trustee (public-interest statesman) model, and the ideologist model. With few exceptions, there have been no concentrated efforts to reconcile these disparate perspectives. This lack of integration frequently has been lamented by those who have made epistemological inventories of the legislative process field.[13] For example, Robert Peobody has emphasized that "the critical need is for theory at several levels for, quite clearly, in congressional research the generation of data has proceeded much more rapidly than the accumulation of theory."[14] Norman Meller has written that:

> Like raindrops on a dirty windowpane, legislative-behavior studies afford brief glimpses at a broader vision of the legislative process, but have failed to furnish a framework enabling its full comprehension. Studies are yet too disperse and lack replication; conflicting findings have not always served as stimuli for subsequent clarificatory research. Also, there has been

> too ready a subsuming of the basic unity of the legislative process and too little attention given to the generation of an inclusive theory.[15]

Recently, students of the policy process have taken to formulating a contextual approach to congressional decision making that offers the opportunity for overcoming the static quality of previous research. Examples are works by Theodore Lowi,[16] Randall Ripley and Grace Franklin,[17] John Bacheller,[18] Michael Hayes,[19] Charles O. Jones,[20] David Price,[21] and James Q. Wilson.[22] These works emphasize that there are different decision tracks or arenas in Congress, each associated with distinctive decision behavior. Through the construction of typologies—such as Lowi, and Ripley and Franklin's distinction between distributive, regulatory, and redistributive policy processes—they implicitly argue that no one model of legislative behavior is best. To them, congressional scholars are best served by multiple models and interpretations, each of which best explains congressional decision making in a specific issue context.

Although the contextual approach has the potential for synthesizing divergent perspectives on decision making, it has been neither adequately conceptualized nor thoroughly researched. The most detracting limitation has been the failure to translate the typologies to the micro level of member decision making. For example, what is different about the decision environment of (again, to use Lowi's typology) distributive, regulatory, and redistributive issues that leads legislators to behave differently? What are the differences in the cognitive map of members when they decide on different kinds of issues? These concerns simply are not addressed in the aforementioned works that employ a contextual approach.

This paper will report some major findings of a research project that attempted to both explicate and test, at the micro level, propositions inherent in the contextual approach. It will be divided into two parts. The first part will give an overview of the project and its findings.[23] The second part will present some suppositions, drawn from the research, concerning decision settings in Congress.

RESEARCH SYNOPSIS

The micro-level theory deduced from work utilizing a contextual approach is that congressmen utilize different decision rules, depending on the incentives for involvement present in different decision settings. On low-grade issues where few actors are involved or heard from, the member will make a decision by deferring to someone he perceives to be an expert in the field. Thus, the decision will reflect a narrow "subgovernment" phenomenon. Conversely, on hot, emotional, visible, controversial votes, where many are involved, members will feel sufficiently motivated to develop issue positions with which to cast, explain, and justify the vote. In David Price's words:

> The degree of conflict an issue is thought to entail and its perceived salience to the electorate . . . influence both the distribution of legislators' policy-making "investments" and the extent to which they take their bearings from broader interests.[24]

To test the theory, John Kingdon's method of direct interviewing of members was employed with three modifications. First, Kingdon asked questions about communications and then drew conclusions about decision determinants. In contrast, this research design asked questions about four separate components of the cognitive map: communications, information, decision rules, and role orientations. Second, this research design asked questions about issue characteristics (i.e., how the member perceived and defined the vote at hand). Third, Kingdon studied only, in his words, "big votes"[25]—those that were politically interesting and important. This research attempts to select a mixture of votes. Noncontroversial and routine votes, as well as

Table 7.2.1.
Questionnaire.

1. Re the __________ vote, who did you hear from or talk to concerning how to vote?
2. Was there anyone else to whom you paid attention?
3. I imagine that these kinds of communications and information sources are helpful to you in different ways.
   a. Who was helpful in informing you about the facts of the bill?
   b. In your estimation, who/what was most decisive in helping you make up your mind?
4. What kind of issue do you feel this is?
   a. Do you feel it is complex? yes no
   b. Do you feel it is technical? yes no
   c. Is there a lot of conflict and disagreement on this bill? yes no
   d. Is it major legislation? yes no
   e. (1) Is this legislation important to the people of your district? yes no
   (2) Are they aware of it? yes no
   f. Did you receive a lot of mail on it? yes no
   g. Do you feel that your vote on this could affect:
   (1) Your renomination? yes no
   (2) Your re-election? yes no
   h. Do you feel that this is a routine matter? yes no
   i. How strongly do you personally feel on this issue? 1 2 3
   j. When did you make up your mind on this issue?
   k. Is it a tough decision? yes no
5. When making up your mind on this piece of legislation, on what did you rely?
   a. Constituency wishes.
   b. Your own opinion.
   c. Something else.
6. Was your focus the national interest, local interest, or both?
7. How informed do you feel about the issues raised in this legislation?
   a. Not at all.
   b. Somewhat.
   c. Very well.
8. Did you put much thought into it? yes no

high-profile votes, were studied. Table 7.2.1 displays the questionnaire used in this study. The appendix at the conclusion of this article provides a synopsis of each of the votes.

Interviewing was undertaken in the first session of the 95th Congress (March-July 1977) under the sponsorship of Rep. Jim Lloyd (D-Calif.). Research efforts yielded 361 interview protocols from 80 sampled members concerning 31 separate House votes. Tables 7.2.2a and 7.2.2b display both the stratification of U.S. House at the time of interviewing and the distribution of interviewees per the different strata. As can be seen, there was considerable overrepresentation of northern Democrats with short service and underepresentation of northern Democrats with long tenure. Other strata were fairly representative.

The results document contextual decision behavior in Congress, but in ways *more complicated* than the hot/low-profile distinction implied by contemporary contextual approaches.

With regard to communications, members heard from an average of three sources per vote. The actors most frequently mentioned as making input to congressional decision making were personal staff, constituency, committee members, and other members not on the committee. Table 7.2.3

Table 7.2.2a.
Stratification of U.S. House of Representatives, 95th Congress, per two variables.

Length of Service	Northern Democrat	Southern Democrat	Republican	Total
Short (0–5 years)	111 (27%)	38 (9%)	71 (17%)	220 (53%)
Medium (6–11 years)	30 (7%)	17 (9%)	38 (9%)	88 (21%)
Long (12+ years)	57 (14%)	22 (5%)	26 (6%)	105 (25%)
	198 (48%)	77 (19%)	135 (33%)	410 (100%)

Table 7.2.2b.
Stratified Distribution of Interviews.

Length of Service	Northern Democrat	Southern Democrat	Republican
Short (0–5 years)	135 (38%)	22 (6%)	63 (18%)
Medium (6–11 years)	23 (6%)	31 (9%)	35 (10%)
Long (12*a* years)	23 (6%)	16 (4%)	11 (3%)

Note: Both tables based on 359 questionnaires. Due to an oversight, two questionnaires were not collated with the number with whom the interview was obtained.

displays the frequency with which various actors were mentioned. Interviews revealed that there were different kinds of communications to members. First, a distinction can be made on the basis of when the input was received. There are inputs proximate to the time of the vote, such as the partisan members who man the doorways, and inputs more antecedent to the decision, such as constituency mail, staff briefing, and correspondence from interest groups. Second, communications vary according to whether or not there is an attempt to exert pressure. Some inputs involve active attempts to sway and influence. Examples are lobbying activities by those competing for a member's attention, such as other members, the President, constituents, and interest groups. Other inputs do not involve intense pressure. Rather, they are best thought of as latent factors and a member's self-referents for decision making. Examples are perceptions of constituency interests, opinions obtained through member-sponsored polls, inquiries a member makes to a trusted colleague, staff work on an issue, and communications received from congressional agencies such as the Library of Congress, Congressional Budget Office, and General Accounting Office.

Table 7.2.3.
Percentage of the interviews in which each actor was mentioned by members in response to the question "Who did you hear from, pay attention to, consider concerning this decision?"

Actor	Responses (Percent)
Committee chairman	20
Ranking minority	3
Committee members	36
State delegation	31
Party leader	13
Other congressmen	36
Committee staff	5
Personal staff	42
Individual constituents	37
Inspired mail	8
Group constituents	26
Private groups	22
Public-interest groups	5
Public groups	3
Bureaucrats	3
White House	14
Media	14

Note: Based on 361 interviews. Multiple responses permitted.

The volume of communications a member receives and the sources he hears from vary by the kind of vote at hand. On hot votes, members received input from many sources; on low-grade issues, members heard from only a few sources. Variations in the mention of various sources are captured by the distinction between routine, grants to localities, hot, and specialized hot votes. On routine votes, members hear from staff and committee sources. On grant votes, members pay attention to staff, state delegation members, and the affected clientele in the district. On hot votes, members hear from major political actors: interest groups, congressional leaders, constituents, and the White House. Specialized hot issues involve imput from segmental constituencies.

Three aspects of the congressional information process were studied: volume, sources, and level. With regard to volume, members acknowledged the use of an average of two sources for each vote. With regard to sources, information was received from direct contact with members, impersonal contact with members, in-house publications, staff, outside sources, and the general experience and reading of members. As noted in Illustrations 7.A–7.E, information sources can be classified as being personal or impersonal and proximate to or distant from the vote. The most frequently utilized references were personal staff, Democratic Study Group (DSG) publications, party Whip Notices, and floor debate. Table 7.2.4 exhibits the frequency with which various information sources were mentioned. Concerning level or adequacy of information, on most votes members feel generally well-informed.

Variations in volume occur according to complexity, technicality, and parliamentary scheduling, as well as the low-profile/hot distinction. Members searched for more information when the vote was low-grade but hard to understand, hot, or did not come up at the last minute. Variations in the use of sources occurred according to a member's knowledge and need. If a member was unfamiliar with an issue but it was politically important to him, he would consult normal sources (*i.e.*, staff and in-house publications). If a member was unfamiliar with a bill and it was not important to him, he would consult no source, save for members on the floor. Finally, if a member was unfamiliar with a bill but he perceived his vote to be very important, he would consult special, supplemental sources (*i.e.*, members on the committee). Variations in the level of information occur according to the hot/low-profile distinction. On hot issues members feel better informed. On low-profile votes they feel less informed.

The decision rule (or decision "determinant" or "referent," as it is sometimes called) most frequently cited was, confirming Aage Clausen, ideology, or what might be called policy predisposition (i.e., standing committments to support or oppose certain programs, policies, or agencies). In 65 percent of the decisions studied, members mentioned ideology as a decision referent. The next most frequently mentioned

Table 7.2.4.
Aggregate frequency distribution of information sources: The percentage of interviews in which members mentioned various information sources.

Source	%
Committee chairman	5%
Committee members	13
State delegation	4
Party leader	4
Party Whip Notice	22
Floor debate	18
Committee report	14
Other members	9
Committee staff	3
Personal staff	33
Constituents	5
Interest groups	5
White House	3
Media/reading	18
Democratic Study Group (DSG)	30
Republican ad hoc group	1
Steering/Policy Committee membership	1
Person experience/learning	5
Membership on other committee	2
Committee membership	6
Dear Colleague letter	5
Environmental study group (ESG)	2
Last time through	8

Note: 361 interviews were conducted.

referents were constituency (13 percent), philosophy—support or opposition on moral grounds—(11 percent), and committee members (10 percent). The frequency with which various determinants were mentioned is displayed in Table 7.2.5. Determinants cited can be classified as proximate to or distant from the vote and internal or external to the legislator and legislature. Actors internal to or within the legislature and proximate to the vote that were identified as influential in congressional voting were the committee system, fellow members, party leaders, and a member's personal staff. Internal forces somewhat remote from the vote were party, ideology, legislator's demography, legislative procedures, and norms/folkways. External actors proximate to the vote were constituents, the President, bureaucrats, and lobbyists. Factors external to the legislature and antecedent to the vote were constituency characteristics, media, electoral outcomes, and public opinion. Table 7.2.6 classifies the major, identified causes according to the four possible categories.

Some variation in the mention of decision rules does occur according to a hot/low-profile distinction, although ideology is used as a decision rule in both issue contexts. For

Table 7.2.5.
Frequency distribution of determinants: The percentage of interviews in which various decision determinants were mentioned.

Actor	Responses (Percent)
Committee chairman	6%
Committee members	10
State delegation	3
Party leader	2
Other congressmen	4
Personal staff	4
White House	6
Constituency	13
Compromise	7
Consistency	7
Consensus	7
Philosophical convictions	11
Policy assessments (ideology)	65
Campaign promises	3
Miscellaneous:	
Testimony before committee	1
Bureaucrats	2
Media/reading	1
Rule	1
No choice	2
Family/friends	1
Personal experience	2
On committee	7
Other items	1
Protect the process	2
Prioritization	2

Note: Based on 361 interviews. Multiple responses permitted.

Table 7.2.6.
Forces, factors, and actors identified as determinants of legislative voting.

	External to the Legislature or Legislator	Internal to the Legislature or Legislator	
Proximate to the vote	Constituents President Bureaucrats Lobbyists	Committee system Fellow members Party leaders Personal Staff	{ Election classes Friends Ideological groups State delegations
Distant from the vote	Constituency characteristics Media Electoral outcomes Public opinion	Party Ideology Legislator's demography Legislative procedures Norms/folkways	

hot votes, decisions were likely to be based on ideology, philosophy, constituency interests, or constituent demands, and the member's assessment of the adequacy of the compromise. Low-profile votes were based on cue-taking and perception of consensus, as well as ideology.

Although ideology was overwhelmingly the most cited determinant, it was most frequently used in conjunction with other determinants. Thus, it seems that there are perhaps eight different, identifiable ways or modes of congressional decision making: philosophy, ideology, consensus, campaign promise, assessment of compromise, constituency representation, cue-taking from personal staff, and cue-taking from members. Each tended to be more frequently mentioned on certain kinds of issues.

With regard to role orientations, members mentioned a trustee (self-referent) style much more frequently than a delegate (constituency referent) or broker (combination of self and constituency) style. Table 7.2.7 displays the frequency of role orientation responses. Variations in role orientations occur according to hot votes with and without constituency relevance, grants to localities, and low-profile votes. On hot votes that are perceived by the member to be important to his constituency, a broker role is more prevalent. On hot votes without constituency relevance, members utilize a trustee role. On grant votes, members employ the broker role, while on low-profile votes a trustee style prevails.

An additional aspect of congressional decision making—time of decision—was researched starting midway through the study at the urging of several members. The most frequently cited times of decision were "on the floor" and "the last time the bill was up." Table 7.2.8 exhibits the frequency distribution of various temporal responses. Variations in time of decision occur according to the hot/low-profile distinction, member's information, parliamentary scheduling, and floor maneuvering. Early decisions are made when the vote is hot, has been scheduled well in advance, has been seen before, and does not involve last-minute floor wrangling. Late decisions are made on low-profile votes, new issues, votes that are brought up quickly, and votes on which there is some doubt concerning the final outcome due to the amendment process. It should be emphasized that the precise time at which a member makes up his mind is also a function of his own idiosyncratic information process. If a member is briefed early in the week on that week's legislative activity, he will make up his mind early. If

Table 7.2.7.
Frequency distribution of role conceptions in response to the question, "On what did you base your decision: constituency, self, a combination of both?"

Actor	Responses (Percent)
Constituency (delegate)	2%
Self (trustee)	74
Both self and constituents (politico)	19
President	2
Staff	1

Note: Based on 352 interviews.

Table 7.2.8.
Frequency distribution of responses to the question: "When did you reach a decision of this vote?"

When Decided	Percent
When member first entered politics	7%
Last time vote was up	18
During campaign	9
Automatic (when heard it was up)	6
On committee	5
Week before	3
Day before	3
When read about it	6
When heard from constituents	4
On the floor	25
When change was made	5
Late	9

Note: Based on 141 interviews.

he is briefed day to day, he will make up his mind late.

Four major conclusions are supported by the research. First, there is contextual decision making in Congress. Neither the mode nor the mean yields a sophisticated view of congressional voting. The voting behavior of congressmen is best understood in terms of decision contexts. Second, many of our major generalizations concerning congressional decision behavior—such as cue-taking is the normal mode of congressional decision making, congressmen hear from only a few when making a decision, congressmen engage in only a perfunctory search when making a decision, congressmen do not feel informed when making a decision, members base voting on ideology, members have a broker role orientation, and other members are a major source of information—are highly contextual. These propositions are valid under certain conditions but invalid under others. Third, the hot/low-profile distinction implied by Lowi and by Ripley and Franklin is not the only difference that drives variations in legislative behavior. Variations occur according to a variety of factors, depending on the component of the cognitive map in question. Fourth, the involvement, contribution, and influence of various actors in congressional decision making varies by issue contexts and components of the cognitive map. For example, personal staff, which is mentioned in 33 percent of the decisions as an information source, is mentioned in only 4 percent of the decisions as a decision determinant. An emphasis on general patterns of influence fails to pick up these nuances.

SUPPOSITIONS CONCERNING ISSUE SETTINGS

There are two major limitations to the research design and the way data were analyzed. One is that there was no opportunity to interrelate the different components of the cognitive map. Another is that, in analyzing the results, the congressman is portrayed as a passive actor when an emphasis on the congressman as an "active" contextual decision maker is perhaps more illuminating.

Moving away from the data arrays, it seems that—on the basis of this author's extensive interviewing among members concerning congressional decision making—there are at least five different settings that members encounter when voting on the floor. They are hot votes, nonvisible votes, complicated bills, votes on grant aids to localities, and routine votes. Although these settings may not be completely mutually exclusive (for example, a grant vote may also be routine or complicated), they seem to capture the major variations in decision making relayed by members during the interview sessions. For each setting there is a unique demand pattern that leads members to devise distinctive behavioral routines and shortcuts. Therefore, each decision setting is associated with a different combination of demand patterns, information search, level of information, decision rule, time of decision, and role orientation. Moreover, interview sessions indicate that members perceive and define the various settings with a degree of unanimity. For example, most will agree that a certain vote is hot and another is nonvisible.

Hot Votes

A hot, or high-profile, vote is one that members feel is "controversial," "emotional," "salient," "major," and "visible." This kind of vote involves a lot of mail from the district, general constituency awareness, and a close, hard-fought battle based on strongly held positions. Examples of "hot" legislation in this study were votes on ethics, tax reform, the Hatch Act revisions, clean air (Dingell Amendment), abortion (Hyde Amendment), congressional pay raise, the saccharin ban, Rhodesian chrome, and common situs picketing. Several members also emphasized that other frequently seen hot votes involve minority and women's rights, military conscription, and gun control. Several members and staffers indicated that there are usually 10 or so extremely hot issues each session of Congress.

The input to members on hot legislation is extremely broad and voluminous, for it is these kinds of issues that attract heavy mail, press coverage, and party and presidential involvement. Most members recalled receiving a broad spectrum of input from a wide variety of interests. As one member stated:

> If there is an existence of contrary approaches on a bill, you do talk to a lot of people on it. When a lot of people are interested, when the range of opinion is wide, many attempt to talk to you and you have no alternative but to talk to them. On big, important bills, you will always hear from people.

For most members, the information search on hot issues is lower than normal, because most members are very familiar with the issues due to experience with the bill either in previous sessions of Congress or on the campaign trail. As one member stated, "On this kind of thing you don't need an extensive search for information. We know it already. Usually you've seen all the big ones before." If members utilize any information source on these votes it is usually a scan of normal materials (briefing by personal staff, DSG publications, Whip Notices, or committee reports) to learn the facts of a specific bill and possible amendments.

The level of a member's information on a hot vote is quite high. Several members addressed the reasons for this. One member noted,

> We are usually prepared on major bills and significant amendments to them. Divisions in committee which occur on important votes provide safeguards by communicating to the member that there will be a fight, and he better inform himself.

Another argued,

> The more controversy, the more you'll know about it. If you are to be respected by your colleagues, you should be able to talk the pros and cons on an issue.

Another noted,

> On major bills you get stuff from the Library of Congress, Congressional Research Organization, and party and factional groups. There is usually an abundance of information that allows you to get familiar with basic issues.

On hot votes, members will cast a vote on the basis of one of five decision rules: personal philosophy, ideology, campaign promise, constituency representation, or assessment of the adequacy of compromise. Many members state that on hot votes they rely on their own personal values or philosophy (e.g., "I believe it is morally wrong to have the government finance abortion"). If the member's personal values are not relevant, then he will cast the vote on the basis of ideology/policy predisposition (support for or opposition to certain programs and policies), a campaign pledge or commitment, and/or constituency representation (responding to citizen mail or voting what one perceives to be the interests or preferences of constituents). On a few hot issues, some members will employ the decision rule of voting their assessment of the adequacy of compromise. The statement, "I think it is a good compromise—all parties were able to deal" is given as the determinant of the vote. It should be emphasized that on hot votes members make no mention of cue-taking or following a consensus.

The time of decision on hot votes is usually very early, often stemming back to when one first got involved in politics. As one member elucidated,

> On these kinds of decisions you constantly are pressed for your opinion during primary and election campaigns and speaking engagements. Hell, I've been asked my

> opinion on ERA as much as I've been asked my name. By the time it comes up, I don't have to agonize. I know my position.

Several members emphasized that on hot votes they would reserve judgment only if major changes in the basic bill seemed a possibility.

Most members contend that on hot votes they employ a broker role that incorporates their own and their constituents' preferences. As a member stated, "On hot issues, you better be in accord with your constituents or you may find yourself in trouble. But, you usually get to Congress because you are in agreement already."

Nonvisible Votes

Most of the votes congressmen face are not hot issues. They are not publicized and there is not much interest in them. Those kinds of votes are frequently referred to by members as "low-grade," "inside," or "nonvisible" votes.

Examples of nonvisible votes covered by this study were House Assassination Committee extension, regulation of the Arab boycott, the Debt Collection Practices Act, the Goldwater Amendment to a housing bill, and Rumanian earthquake relief.

On nonvisible bills, the input to members is low—almost nonexistent—and narrow, usually from only those interested or affected.

The search for information is confined primarily to normal, in-house sources or the usual pattern. The level of information is atypically low. Given the low political stakes involved, the floor voting member rarely will engage in an extensive search on this type of legislation.

The distinctive decision rule frequently employed in this setting, especially when the vote lacks controversy, is consensus —"following the herd," "moving with your crowd," or "flowing with the trend." For many members, this means watching the House voting board and paying attention to who is for or against and moving with the group with whom one identifies. Several members emphasized that consensus voting is an outshoot of the way Private, Consent, and Suspension Calendar items are handled. As one member stated, "On those, I just float with the tide, figuring that if there are problems they would have come out in the committee report." Since many nonvisible votes pass by wide margins, many members acknowledge that consensus voting often involves "voting yes unless you have a reason to vote no" and "staying out of a minority of 30 to avoid being targeted by the benefiting group." Members also stress that given their heavy load with committee work and case work, consensus voting is both an expeditious and rational way to decide.

The time at which members make up their minds on nonvisible votes depends on when they first learn or read about it. This, in turn, depends on the member's idiosyncratic staff system. However, many report on-the-floor decisions.

On nonvisible votes, members most frequently cite a trustee role orientation, arguing that they rarely get input from constituents. A few, with a basic delegate orientation, argue that they cast the vote on the basis of their perception of constituents' preferences. This, however, seems to be a rare practice in floor voting on these kinds of issues.

Complicated Votes

Frequently, members must vote on bills that are "difficult," "confusing," "complex," "hard to handle," and "hard to zero in on." These usually are multifaceted votes that "require a lot of thought" on the member's part. Examples of complicated votes uncovered in this study were both the FAA and EPA reauthorization, strip mining regulations, the creation of the new Energy

Department, and votes on budget targets. Either a hot or low-profile vote can be complicated.

The input pattern is moderate to high. Usually only those immediately affected communicate with floor voting members.

Because this type of vote is "hard to understand," members engage in an extended search. They turn not only to normal sources of information, but frequently approach committee sources, either going directly to members or committee staff or relying on personal staff to check for detail and clarification. The level of information is best characterized as "medium." After the extended search, members feel fairly comfortable with the vote.

The decision rule most utilized is cue-taking from members on the committee, who are also frequently in the cue-taker's state delegation and/or election class and have a similar ideological bent and a like constituency. "I voted that way because Congressman X on the committee assured me the bill was OK and recommended that I vote for it" is a frequently heard justification of the vote on complicated bills.

The time of decision for complicated votes occurs "late," after the extended search. The role orientation is almost always a trustee one. Given the technical nature of many complicated votes, members usually base the decision on their interpretation of the issue simply because constituency input is lacking.

Routine Votes

Many of the bills that members vote on can be classified as routine. They are less controversial but more salient than nonvisible votes. Routine votes are ones that "have been seen before" and therefore might be considered "normal" or "the usual." Examples from this study were votes on school lunch, a nuclear navy, snow removal, marine mammals, and the Miller Amendment of foreign aid reductions. The numerous uncontroversial, recurring authorization and appropriation measures that members see each year also serve as examples of routine votes.

The input pattern is low and narrow on routine votes. Only those affected are heard from. However, the lobbying activities of affected publics are usually very selective, zeroing in on those members who are bloc leaders, uncommitted, or wavering. Therefore, the force fields of average floor voting members are empty.

The information search process is a very normal one. Only normal sources are referenced. The level of information is very low due to a general lack of concern, interest, and relevance.

The decision is almost always based on ideology—standing policy positions to vote for or against certain programs. As one member noted,

> On recurring matters you simplify by attempting to achieve a consistent record pro or con certain programs. This allows you to develop little categories with which to classify and then act on relatively minor legislation that a member not on the committee can't affect anyway.

The time of decision on routine votes is either the time of the staff briefing that alerts members to a vote coming up or, for more experienced members, the last time the issue was before the Congress.

Like the nonvisible setting, the role orientation used on routine votes is a function of a member's basic orientation. Most use a trustee orientation, given the lack of communications from constituents, but a small minority of members attempt to represent their perceptions of constituency sentiment.

Grant Votes

Votes most relevant to members are those pertaining to federal grants to localities. These are high in political salience for the member and involve constituency awareness of the member's activities. The community development bloc grants, countercyclical aid, and public works are examples of grant votes studied during this research. Although grant votes may be routine, hot, complicated, or nonvisible, it is felt that members' behavior is so distinctive as to warrant classifying grants as a separate setting.

The communications members receive on grant votes come primarily from segmental constituencies—i.e., organized beneficiaries, including local public officials, in the district.

Members engage in an extended and intense information search on grant votes. Normal sources of information are supplemented by an exchange of information within the state delegation that involves interaction, both direct and through staff, with committee and agency sources.

On grant votes, members have a medium level of information. They do not know all facets, but the extended search yields more than average information—especially in terms of how the bill will affect the district.

Members follow two decision rules when making a decision on grant votes: cue-taking from staff and/or constituency representation. Usually members will assign personal staff to work on proposed grant formulas to ascertain how it affects their district. The vote is then made with deference to staff recommendations and with an effort to further constituency interests.

The time of decision for grant votes is typically the day before, once the mist has cleared on the likely impact of alternative schemes. Sometimes members suspend judgment, waiting to see the outcome of last-minute maneuvering and compromising on the allocation sections of a bill.

For almost all members, the role orientation used on grant votes is the delegate style. Members attempt to serve and further their perception of constituency interest.

SUMMARY, CONCLUSIONS, AND INTERPRETATIONS

The major conclusion to be drawn from this research is that congressional decision behavior varies according to different decision contexts. No single force drives decision making. No single model has a monopoly on truth. Congressmen do not all make up their minds in the same way or in a set fashion on each and every vote. This research provides the first empirical verification (based on systematic interviewing) for the proposition that different decision settings are associated with different behavior patterns and decision rules.

Members cast more than 1,500 votes on a wide variety of topics in the span of a single Congress. This research has detected five different decision settings that members confront when making these votes. It is felt that each is associated with rather distinguishable forms and styles of decision behavior. To cope with the high volume of decisions they are asked to make, members develop different programmed courses of behavior for each of the settings. On hot votes, members usually base the decision on their own personal values. If the member does not have strong feelings on a bill or if the bill is one on the vast majority that is not major, the vote will be cast on the basis of one of several decision shortcuts (constituency representation, cue-taking, consensus, or ideology) depending on (*a*) the member's familiarity with a bill, and (*b*) the bill's complexity, controversiality, and relevance to constituency.

Table 7.2.9 summarizes the suppositions concerning variations in members' cognitive maps associated with the five different decision settings. It should be emphasized that both the complicated and nonvisible settings approximate the subgovernment model (ratification of committee decisions), but the others do not. Only one setting (complicated) conforms to classic notions of cue-taking. Only two (hot and

Table 7.2.9.
Variations in the configuration of legislators' cognitive map associated with different decision settings.

Decision Setting	Input Pattern	Information Search	Level of Information	Decision Rule	Role Orientation	Time Decision
Nonvisible	None	Atypically low due to lack of concern	Low	Consensus	Trustee or delegate (depending on basic inclination)	Floor
Complicated	Moderate to high	Extended	Medium	Cue-taking: members	Trustee	Late
Grant Aid	Low	Extended	Medium	Cue-taking: staff or constituency representation	Delegate	Day before
Routine	Low	Normal	Low	Ideology	Trustee (depending on basic inclination)	When briefed/ last time up
Hot	High	Atypically low due to familiarity	High	Assessment of compromise, campaign promise, philosophy, ideology, and/or constituency representation	Broker	Early (except when crucial amendments are pending)/ last time up

Note: This table summarizes suppositions, based on the research, concerning how each decision setting is associated with a distinctive input pattern, time of decision, information search procedure, level of information, decision rule, and role orientation.

routine) approximate the model of ideological voting. All of this is to argue that a multiple model approach must be utilized if students of the legislative process are to have a complete understanding of congressional decision making, for each setting constitutes a very different kind of congressional decision-making process.

This documentation of contextual decision making in Congress confirms the speculation of several organization theorists that decision makers in large, complex organizations employ variable decision rules. For example, James D. Thompson emphasizes that there are different "types of decision issues" and "it seems clear that each type of decision issue calls for a different strategy."[26] Fredrick Cleaveland speculated in 1969 about "issue contexts" in Congress. For him, "issue contexts" are

> . . . the way members of Congress perceive a policy proposal that comes before them, how they consciously or unconsciously classify it for study, and what group of policies they believe it related to.[27]

To Cleaveland, "Such issue contexts strongly influence legislative outcomes because their structure helps determine the aproach for analysis . . . as well as the advice and expertise that enjoys privileged access."[28] Surprisingly, until now there has not been much research on variable decision making in Congress.

The implications of a major finding presented here—that most floor decisions are based on ideology or extensions of it, such as cue-taking[29]—necessarily lead to a rather optimistic assessment of the potential for democratic linkage between representative and represented. A member's ideology, or policy predispositions as referred to here, better than any other factor predicts (*a*) the voting behavior of a member and (*b*) the sources of input and information on which he will rely. Although there are numerous ways representatives can evade public accountability, the opportunity for mass control of congressional elites is afforded by the ability of the masses to choose among competing policy approaches as presented in the debate of campaign issues, published voting records, and the ideological differences between political parties.

Finally, the five decision settings

identified here may not be the only ones with which members must come to grips. Subsequent research may uncover additional settings—especially in the realm of foreign or defense policies, areas not covered by this study—or patterns of variation more refined than those offered here. One can only hope that others will contribute to a more sophisticated study of congressional behavior by attempting to identify decision contexts. As Roland Young sagaciously wrote more than two decades ago:

> Legislative theories do not develop by themselves, as if wishing would make them so. . . . Unfortunalety for those who want a general or easy answer, the dynamics of the legislative process do not relinquish their secrets readily.[30]

POSTSCRIPT: CONGRESSIONAL DECISION BEHAVIOR IN THE 1980s (WITH SOME SENATE COMPARISONS)

In 1981–1982 I had the privilege of serving as an American Political Science Association Congressional Fellow on the staffs of Congressman Andy Jacobs (D-Ind.) and Senator James Exon (D-Neb.). This experience gave me the unique inside opportunity to test the conclusions of the 1977 research and to re-examine them in light of the many changes that had occurred in Congress in the interim. These changes included the beginning and fall of the Carter administration, the large turnover of members, and the emergence of new issues. The fellowship also afforded a glimpse of decision behavior in the U.S. Senate.

My service in both offices, conversations with other fellows, and meetings with members from the 1977 sample who are still in office confirmed contextual decision behavior. Members and staffers constantly distinguished between what *they* refer to as "hot" and "low-profile" votes. A vote is considered hot if it is, for the member, politically important and controversial. Hot and low-profile votes are handled quite differently. One congressman from the original sample, when given an overview of the study's results, commented: "You've got it right. That's how it's done. There are hot votes which we decide on the basis of philosophy, ideology, and high-level politicking and there are votes not so hot that we handle with all kinds of simplifying aids." My service as a legislative assistant (LA) in the House also confirmed other major findings: that few actors are heard from on most votes, that the DSG is the pre-eminent information source, and that ideological voting often involves the member's attempt to be consistent with what he or she did the last time the bill was up.

A new insight provided during this stay on the Hill was the relative unimportance of floor voting. Congressional offices are preoccupied with five major activities: (1) servicing and working the district, (2) answering the mail, (3) attending to committee work, (4) interfacing with other members, groups, and other external players, and (5) handling and voting on floor legislation. The attention each is given appears roughly in that order. Everyone in Congress seems to understand that only a handful of votes are decided on the floor. For most votes, the fight is over in committee and the margin of passage on the floor is high.

A major refinement in the original findings brought to light was the different uses of ideology or policy voting on hot versus low-profile votes. On hot issues, a policy vote is made with regard to the members' rather strongly held views. Policy votes on low-profile issues seem to be based more on either a desire to be consistent or on some instrumental values that are only tangentially related to ideology.

Another qualification that emerged was the use of party quotas for passing necessary but unpopular legislation. Evidently, on votes such as those funding the Occupational Safety and Health Administration (OSHA) or foreign aid reauthorization, the leadership of the two parties decide how many votes each party must provide to secure passage. Leaders then get enough votes lined up, first from among supporters already favorably inclined and next among party loyalists, leaving the remainder of the party members to make political hay with a nay vote. Such quota voting, the calling in of IOUs, and other efforts to get people to go along do not show up in interviews with individual members.

This service in Congress gave me the impression that there have been three related developments in Congressional decision behavior since 1977. One is the decline of cue-taking from other members. Several members mentioned that the classic cue-taking practice of asking other members "what's my vote" is not as prevalent as it once was. One said, "It just isn't done anymore. It jeopardizes your credibility." A second development is the increased use by the member of personal staff for assistance in reaching decisions on floor votes. More and more, members cast floor votes through in-office procedures.

Finally, personal staff have increased their utilization of internal sources of information when providing assistance for floor votings. Televised floor proceedings are an indispensable source for following debate and amendments. CRS studies are widely circulated and seem to provide a more basic grounding on issues than was detected in 1977. The best source for all LAs, however, is the staff of the committee (subcommittee) of origin. These staffers have become the best bet and the most-often consulted source.

The original project by-passed the Senate for the reasons listed earlier. However, some superficial comparisons with the Senate are useful because of (1) the importance of the Senate in the legislative process and (2) the desire to develop and test a legislative theory that transcends the House.

The differences between the House and Senate in terms of structure, organization and procedure[31] and policy role[32] have been well-documented. Although Ornstein has convincingly argued that each is tending to behave like the other in the last few sessions,[33] there is an essential character unique to each house—especially with regard to floor voting. The most meaningful difference in micro decision making on the Senate side is greater uncertainty and unpredictability in parliamentary process due to the informality of the smaller body, the lack of a "traffic cop" Rules Committee, the possibility of nongermane amendments, and the practice of passing House-passed bills without extensive committee deliberations. With this as a backdrop, major differences in the two houses were observed in communications flow, information search, decision modes, and role orientations.

With regard to communications, the major difference between House and Senate pertains to staff networks. Senators have much larger staffs than House members. Staffs of senators tend to be bureaucratized and functionally oriented. As a result, communications tend to be more filtered by staff in the Senate.

There are three major differences with regard to information flow. First, the comprehensive coverage afforded floor voting in the House by DSG publications is not provided by any source on the Senate side. Bills and votes pop up so quickly that it is impossible to anticipate all legislation and the many germane and nongermane amendments. Second, most information for floor voting on the Senate side comes from floor debate monitored through closed circuit radio to Senate offices (squawk boxes), party policy committee publications, inquiries to staffers of the parent committees, and meetings of party caucuses and conferences. Third, the realm of the member is much more remote from the realm of staff in the Senate. Frequently, senators get and exchange important information from other senators that leads them to vote for reasons not clearly evident to staff.

Like the House, many modes of decision

making are used in the Senate and the major determinant of floor voting seems to be ideology or policy predispositions. But the shortcut procedures of cue-taking and ratification of compromise seem to be more prevalent in the Senate. Perhaps, due to the uncertainty with which votes come up in the Senate, policy voting is not as feasible because of the lack of time for study and codification. Hence, there is more cue-taking on bills that come up quickly. Ratification of compromise is prevalent on bills of major national significance. Senators want to know, "How have the major players—the White House, party leadership, committee leaders—lined up on this? Has a deal been struck?"

The role orientations found in the House also appear in the Senate, but in the Senate, state orientation seems more pronounced. Senators seem more energized by parochial concerns for state interests and boodle and local protectionism than House members.

A final thought afforded by the fellowship opportunity is that congressional decision making in the 1980s will be challenged by the fluidity of political ideology in America. Thus far, the major issues of the 1980s that the Congress faces are those of macro budgeting and finance. Major issues concerning the extent of government programs in various sectors (energy, environment, urban) and national strategy (places and extent of commitment abroad) have been displaced by debates concerning deficits, revenues, defense versus domestic spending, and entitlements versus discretionary spending. Traditional policy positions do not seem to apply. It is difficult for members to know what is and is not a Democratic or liberal policy position, especially amidst attempts by "neo-liberals" and "neo-Republicans" to redefine their parties' ideologies. As a result, for many members, policy voting seems to have been supplanted by a ratification of compromise that involves cue-taking from party and committee leaders and leaders of factions. More and more, on hot votes Democrats in Congress look to Speaker O'Neill or Congressmen Claude Pepper, Jim Jones, or Gillis Long, while Republicans look to Congressmen Barber Conable, Robert Michel, or Senators Robert Dole and Peter Domenici to see if the right deal has been worked out.

On low-profile votes, members don't have as easy a time as they used to in applying policy positions, for it is tougher to know what a middle-of-the-road Republican or a populist Democrat should be for or against. For members, short-term solutions for the problems posed by floor voting seem to lie in cue-taking and the ratification of compromise. Long-term relief will come only from the development and clarification of party positions and the stabilization of currently shifting party conditions.

APPENDIX: SYNOPSIS OF SAMPLED VOTES

1. H Res 287. House Ethics Code (14 interviews). Adoption of the resolution to require comprehensive financial disclosure by House members, ban private office accounts, increase office allowance, ban gifts from lobbyists, limit outside earned income and impose other financial restrictions on members. Accepted, 402–22. March 2, 1977.
2. HR 3839. Second Budget Rescission, fiscal 1977 (10 interviews). Chappell (D-Fla.) amendment to the committee amendment to restore $81.6 million in the previously appropriated long-lead-time funds for a Nimitz-class nuclear aircraft carrier. Rejected, 161–252. March 3, 1977.
3. HR 3477. Stimulus Tax Cuts (10 interviews). Passage of the bill to provide for a refund of 1976 individual income taxes and other payments, to reduce individual and business income taxes, to increase the individual standard deduction, and to simplify tax preparation. Passed, 282–137. March 8, 1977.
4. HR 3843. Supplemental Housing Authorization (10 interviews). Goldwater Amendment to delete Title II of the bill establishing a National

Commission on Neighborhoods. Adopted, 243–166. March 10, 1977.

5. HR 1746. Rhodesian Chrome Imports (11 interviews). Passage of the bill to halt the importation of Rhodesian chrome in order to bring the United States into compliance with U. N. economic sanctions imposed on Rhodesia in 1966 (repeals Byrd Amendment). Adopted, 250–146. March 14, 1977.
6. HR 4088. NASA Authorization (10 interviews). Passage of the bill to authorize $4.05 billion for NASA for fiscal 1978. Accepted, 338–44. March 17, 1977.
7. HR 4250. Common-Site Picketing (11 interviews). Passage of the bill to permit a labor union with a grievance with one contractor to picket all contractors on the same construction site and to establish a construction industry collective bargaining committee. Rejected, 205–217. March 23, 1977.
8. HR 3965. FAA Authorization (10 interviews). Passage of the bill to authorize $85 million for research and development programs for fiscal 1978. Accepted, 402–6. March 24, 1977.
9. HR 5045. Executive Branch Reorganization Authority (13 interviews). Passage of the bill to extend for three years presidential authority, which expired in 1973, to transmit to Congress plans for reorganization of agencies in the executive branch. Accepted, 395–22. March 29, 1977.
10. H Res 433. House Assassination Committee (13 interviews). Adoption of the resolution to continue the Select Committee on Assassinations. Adopted, 230–181. March 30, 1977.
11. HR 5294. Consumer Credit Protection (11 interviews). Pasage of the bill to prohibit debt collection agencies from engaging in certain practices alleged to be unfair to consumers. Passed, 199–198. April 4, 1977.
12. HR 5717. Rumanian Earthquake Relief (9 interviews). Motion to suspend the rules and pass the bill to authorize $120 million for the relief and rehabilitation of refugees and other victims of the March 4, 1977, earthquake in Rumania. Passed, 322–90. April 18, 1977.
13. HR 5101. Environmental Protection Agency Research and Development (6 interviews). Passage of the bill to authorize $313 million for fiscal 1978 research and development activities of the EPA and to promote coordination of environmental research and development. Accepted, 358–31. April 19, 1977.
14. HR 5840. Export Administration Act (10 interviews). Passage of the bill to revise U.S. export controls on sensitive materials and to prohibit U.S. firms from complying with certain aspects of the Arab boycott against Israel. Passed, 364–43. April 20, 1977.
15. HR 4877. First Regular Supplemental Appropriation, fiscal 1977 (11 interviews). Brademas (D-Ind.) motion that the House recede and concur with a Senate amendment to provide an additional $20 million to reimburse state and local governments for the costs of snow removal incurred during the 1976–77 winter emergency. Defeated, 124–279. April 21, 1977.
16. H Con Res 195. Fiscal 1978 Budget Targets (12 interviews). Passage of the resolution, as amended, providing for fiscal 1978 budget targets of revenues of $398.1 billion, budget authority of $505.7 billion, outlays of $466.7 billion and a deficit of $68.6 billion. Rejected, 84–320. April 27, 1977.
17. HR 2. Strip Mining Regulation (13 interviews). Passage of the bill to regulate surface coal mining operators and to acquire and reclaim abandoned mines. Passed, 241–64. April 29, 1977.
18. HR 11. Public Works Jobs Programs (9 interviews). Adoption of the conference report for the bill to authorize an additional $4 billion for the emergency public works employment program as requested in President Carter's economic stimulus package. Accepted, 335–77. May 3, 1977.
19. H Con Res 214. Fiscal 1978 Budget Targets (7 interviews). Adoption of the budget resolution setting fiscal 1978 targets of revenues of $398.1 billion, budget authority of $502.3 billion, outlays of $464.5 billion, a deficit of $66.4 billion, and binding limits for fiscal 1977. Adopted, 213–179. May 5, 1977.
20. HR 6655. Housing and Community Development Programs (12 interviews). Passage of the bill to authorize $12.45 billion for the Community Development

Block Grant Program for fiscal 1978-1980 and to authorize more than $2 billion for federally assisted, public and rural housing and to contiue FHA mortgage and flood insurance programs. Passed, 369–20. May 11, 177.

21. HR 6810. Countercyclical Assistance Authorization (13 interviews). Passage of the bill to extend for an additional year, through fiscal 1978, a program of countercyclical grants to help state and local governments avoid cutbacks in employment and public services and to authorize a maximum of $2.25 billion for the five quarters, beginning July 1, 1977. Passed, 243–94. May 13, 1977.
22. HR 1139. Child Nutrition Programs (9 interviews). Passage of the bill to extend through fiscal 1979 the summer food program and to make other changes in the school lunch and child nutrition programs. Passed, 393–19. May 18, 1977.
23. HR 6161. Clean Air Act Amendments (15 interviews). Dingell (D-Mich.) substitute for Title II to delay and relax automobile emissions standards, to reduce the warranties for emissions control devices, and to make other changes in existing law regarding mobile sources of air pollution. Adopted, 255–139. May 26, 1977.
24. HR 6970. Tuna-Dolphin Protection (12 interviews). Passage of the bill to limit the total number of dolphins that could be accidentally taken during the 1977 commercial tuna fishing operations, to authorize significant further reductions after 1977, to establish a 100 percent federal observer program on tuna boats, and to establish certain incentives and penalties to encourage conservation of dolphins. Adopted, 334–20. June 1, 1977.
25. HR 6804. Federal Energy Department (16 interviews). Passage of the bill creating a Cabinet-level Department of Energy by combining all powers currently held by the FPC, FEA, ERDA, and various other energy authorities and programs currently scattered throughout the federal bureaucracy. Passed, 310–20. June 3, 1977.
26. HR 10. Hatch Act Amendments (12 interviews). Passage of the bill to revise the Hatch Act to allow federal civilian and postal employees to participate in political activities and to protect such employees from improper solicitations. Approved, 244–164. June 7, 1977.
27. HR 7553. Public Works—ERDA Appropriations, Fiscal 1978 (16 interviews). Conte (R–Mass.)–Derrick (D–S.C.) Amendment to delete funding for 16 water projects and reduce funding for one more project, but to retain the total appropriations amount in the bill. Rejected, 194–218. June 14, 1977.
28. HR 7555. Labor-HEW Appropriation, fiscal 1978 (14 interviews). Hyde (R-Ill.) Amendment to prohibit the use of federal funds to finance or encourage abortions. Adopted, 201–155. June 17, 1977.
29. HR 7558. Agriculture Appropriations, fiscal 1978 (12 interviews). Voice vote to delay for one year the HEW-proposed saccharin ban. June 21, 1977.
30. HR 7797. Foreign Aid Appropriations, fiscal 1978 (11 interviews). Miller (R–Ohio) Amendment to cut 5 percent from the $7,046,454,000 recommended by the Appropriations Committee for foreign aid programs. Adopted, 214–168. June 23, 1977.
31. HR 7932. Legislative Branch Appropriations, fiscal 1978 (198 interviews) Grassley (R–Iowa) Amendment to prohibit use of funds appropriated in the bill for the 29 percent pay increase for high-level federal officials that took effect March 1, 1977. Rejected, 181–241. June 29, 1977.

Reading 7.3

The U.S. Senate and Federalism Policy: An Examination of Selected Roll Call Votes in the 96th and 97th Congress

Rodney Hero

An enormous amount of scholarly effort has been expended studying recorded congressional roll call votes. A dozen or so major studies have called attention to the correlation of party and constituency variables with congressional voting. In this essay, specifically written for this volume, Hero employs roll call analysis to explore the correlates of U.S. Senate votes on selected issues involving federalism policy. This piece usefully illustrates how this type of analysis is done.

Federalism has long been recognized as a central characteristic of the American political system. At the same time, Congress has been identified as probably the major institutional influence on federalism (Walker, 1981:107–13; Wright, 1982:161). It is, therefore, surprising how little systematic attention has been given to what factors influence the formulation of and voting on federalism issues in Congress (Caraley, 1976, 1978; Cleaveland, 1969; Nathan et al., 1977: Ch. 1; Dommel, 1974:23–27). This research is an initial effort to address the question of what variables explain congressional voting on federalism issues. More specifically, it examines Senate roll call votes on federalism issues in the 96th and 97th Congresses. Before turning to that major question, however, why federalism has not been examined as a policy issue warrants attention.

Source: This article was specifically written for this edition of this volume.

FEDERALISM AS A POLICY ISSUE

Part of the reason that federalism has seldom been examined as a policy issue may be that it is often not perceived as such. Wright (1982:6), for example, suggests that intergovernmental relations, while a pervasive and constant influence, are a "hidden dimension" of government policy. Writing about related issues, Cleaveland (1969:3–5, 357–59, 363–65) contends that federalism concerns are "easily sidetracked or subsumed under more salient political issues" and that federalism issues are "often a byproduct" of other substantive policy issues. Nonetheless, Cleaveland concludes that policies related to intergovernmental issues are "a distinct—though not isolated—field of public policy" (Elazar, 1984:4, 9–10; Edner, 1976; Weidner, 1967).

A related question concerns federalism as a policy type. Federalism issues do not fit neatly into Lowi's (1964) typology of distributive, redistributive, and regulatory policy (Kettl, 1983; Hale and Palley, 1981), nor do federalism issues appear to coincide well with the policy dimensions of congressional voting identified by Clausen (1973; Clausen and Cheney, 1970)—government management, civil rights, social welfare, and agriculture. Federalism policy would appear to be relevant for virtually all of these policy types and dimensions. For example, intergovernmental grants-in-aid are often evaluated as to how widely or narrowly they distribute, or redistribute, money (e.g., Stein, 1981; Dye and Hurley, 1978). At the same time, however, scholars have increasingly characterized intergovernmental relationships concerning grants-in-aid as regulatory in nature (Kettl, 1983; Hale and Palley, 1981; Wirt, 1980). Similarly, the civil rights issue has historically generated much national-state conflict. Yet Clausen and Cheney (1970:141–42) found that several "federalism" issues, such as tidelands oil rights and pre-emption of state legislative powers, were relevant to a different policy dimension, social welfare policy (Clausen, 1973:40–41, 46–48; see also Collie, 1984:15; Kozak, 1984: Ch. 1).

Whatever policy type or dimension federalism issues represent, several major American political thinkers have stressed that the scope of political competition/conflict and *where* decisions are made significantly influence substantive policy outcomes (Madison, 1961; Schattschneider, 1975:3–10; Lowi, 1984:35–36). This alone is sufficient grounds to examine the variables that influence how senators vote on federalism issues. The Senate is especially interesting to examine because it is very much a federal institution: members are elected from states to serve in a major institution of the national government (Riker, 1955).

CONGRESS AND VOTING DECISIONS

A voluminous body of research has attempted to explain congressmen's voting decisions (e.g., Kingdon, 1973; Clausen, 1973; Kozak, 1984). Among the major explanatory factors that have been identified are party, region, constituency, ideology, and issue visibility. Policy domain or type is another variable that has been examined, but because this analysis focuses solely on the domain of federalism policy, that variable is controlled for.

The few analyses that have focused on the domain of urban aid and/or policy (e.g., Caraley, 1976, 1978; Cleaveland, 1969) or other federalism-related issues (Dommel, 1974; Nathan, et al., 1977) have stressed the significance of party, constituency, ideology, and region. These variables need to be considered in the present research, although, as is developed and emphasized below, this research examines the broader issue of federalism policy. Other variables that seem especially appropriate to consider, given the particular focus of this research, will also be included.

DATA AND HYPOTHESES

The dependent variable to be examined is the senators' federalism scores. The federalism scores were constructed by several congressional staff persons for the scholarly journal that deals most extensively and carefully with issues of federalism and intergovernmental relations, *Publius: The Journal of Federalism*. (For further information as to how the scores were constructed, see Schechter, 1983:97–128; 1981:155–92.)

The score is based on whether a senator's roll call votes evince a federalist stance. A federalist stance means (*a*) a "yes" vote on a measure enabling states and localities to exercise their political authority flexibly in ways that do not jeopardize the legitimate ends of the measure, or (*b*) a "no" vote on a measure enabling an unwarranted federal intrusion into or collision with legitimate state and local authority.

It is very important to note that the roll call votes analyzed by those who constructed the federalism scores were chosen because the overriding issue raised in these votes is the division or sharing of responsibility between the national and state/local governments, not simply the distribution of financial resources (Caraley, 1976, 1978; Wirt, 1980). For example, a "no" vote on an amendment to retain provisions in the existing Community Development legislation requiring communities to file a detailed application for community development block grant funds was considered a vote to uphold federalist policy (Schechter, 1983: 127). Questions might be raised about this particular definition of federalist stance, given the considerable practitioner and scholarly uncertainty as to the meaning of federalism (Elazar, 1981; Rothman, 1978; Stewart, 1982; Walker, 1981). So long as that definition is applied consistently, however, it seems a useful tool with which to consider initially the important questions of interest here.

Twelve Senate roll call votes were examined to construct the federalism score for the 96th Congress, and 10 for the 97th Congress (see Appendix).

The independent variables measure party, ideology, constituency demographic characteristics, and the state's political culture. Two additional variables focus most directly on intergovernmental influences. Party is simply the senator's party affiliation. In light of the actions of past Democratic presidential administrations, particularly the Roosevelt (New Deal) and Johnson (Great Society) initiatives, Democratic senators would be expected to have lower federalism scores. Previous research would suggest this, as well (Caraley; Nathan, et al., 1977; Dommel, 1974).

Ideology is measured by the senator's score on the Americans for Democratic Action rating and the Conservative Coalition score for 1980 (for the 96th Congress) and 1981 (for the 97th Congress) (Ornstein et al., 1982:226–41). Previous research would lead one to expect a positive relationship between conservatism and federalism voting and, conversely, a negative relationship between liberalism and federalism voting (Caraley; Nathan, et al., 1977; Dommel, 1974). Several measures of constituency characteristics were collected: state's percent urban, percent black, median family income, and education levels (percent with 12+ years of education).

Elazar (1984: Ch. 5) has argued that a state's "political culture" influences attitudes toward national government policies, particularly when those policies may impinge on state-local authority. Elazar suggests that "traditionalistic" states are the most averse to national government "intrusion." To examine this assertion, the 50 states were divided into two categories based on their predominant political culture, "traditionalistic" and "nontraditionalistic" (Elazar, 1984:135–36). This is also, essentially, a measure of region because all but one of the traditionalistic states are in the South.

Because the interest here is on intergovernmental and federalism policy, two other variables were included: (1) a measure of state-local centralization within the states (Stephens, 1974) and (2) the total number of local governments within a state (Nathan and Nathan, 1979). The former variable is included on the presumption that senators are products of particular political environments, including particular state-local traditions within states, that might predispose them in certain directions when considering national action affecting state and local governments. (It is recognized, of course, that national/state-local and state/local relations are legally different relationships.) The number of governments within a state is included on the assumption that more governments implies more government officials who might pressure senators to enact legislation that permits those local officials the greatest authority and discretion. The actual number of governments, rather than the number of governments per capita, was used because, from a theoretical standpoint, this measure seems more appropriate given the present concern with inter*governmental* policy.

Finally, several other variables were included to test for the marginality hypothesis—the hypothesis that how electorally safe a senator is might influence voting behavior. The primary measure for this is the senator's margin of victory in the most recent election; two related variables are the number of years since the senator last faced election and the level of interparty competition within the state (Patterson and Caldeira, 1984).

The federalism votes analyzed were for the 96th (1979–1980) and the 97th (1981–1982) Congresses. These two Congresses seem especially interesting to compare. The 96th included the last two years of the Carter administration, the 97th the first two years of the Reagan administration. The years 1981–1982 were notable for the considerable attention to, and certain legislative achievements of, Reagan's "New Federalism." Ideally, longer-term analysis would be undertaken, but federalism scores and the like are not readily available for past Congresses. The author hopes, however, to analyze similar issues in future Congresses to help ascertain the stability of parameters over a period of time. The data are analyzed through simple correlation and regression analysis.

FINDINGS

The simple relationships between independent variables and federalism score are shown in Table 7.3.1 on p. 326). The data suggest that party and ideology are strongly related to federalism voting. Democrats and those with liberal voting records tend to have lower federalism scores, and Republicans and those with conservative voting records tend to have higher federalism scores. The only other variables that show even a moderate relationship to the federalism score are political culture and the number-of-governments measure for the 97th Congress.

To control for the impact of the several independent variables, the relationships were further analyzed through regression analysis. However, because a number of the independent variables were themselves interrelated, factor analysis was used to create several scales. These scales are called ideology/party, constituency, and urbanization/state centralization. (Information, such as factor loadings, is not included to conserve space. This information is available upon request from the author.)

The results of the regression analysis for the 96th and 97th Congresses are shown in Tables 7.3.2 and 7.3.3 on (p. 326), respectively. For both Congresses, it is clear that the ideology/ party scale is strongly related to a senator's roll call votes on federalism policy. Only one other variable, the number of governments in a state, seems to have much explanatory power, but its explanatory power is evident only in the 97th Congress, and, contrary to expectations, it is inversely related to senators' federalism scores. Despite the fact that only the ideology/party variable emerges as a major explanatory variable, the total explained variance for the two Congresses, particularly the 96th (with an R^2 = .655), is impressive. (Other variables noted in Table 7.3.1, but not cited in Tables 7.3.2 and 7.3.3, were dropped because they did not contribute to any of the scales and were, alone, only very weakly related to the dependent variable.)

To further clarify the relationships, partial correlation analyses of federalism scores with party and ideology were undertaken. As seen in Table 7.3.4 (on p. 327), ideology is clearly more strongly related to federalism voting than is party affiliation. When ideology is statistically controlled, the impact of party decreases considerably. On the other hand, the impact of ideology remains rather strong when party is controlled.

The inability of the other independent variables to account for any major part of the variation also is important to consider. First, Riker (1955) argued that at least since the 17th amendment, which provided for the direct election of senators, the Senate has largely been divorced from state government. This may explain the weak relationship of the federalism score with the number-of-governments measure. Similarly, Clausen and Cheney (1970:150) argued that because senators have heterogeneous and ambiguous constituencies, constituency may not be a major factor in many voting

Table 7.3.1.
Simple correlation results: Senators' federalism score with the independent variables.

	96th Congress (1979–1980)	97th Congress (1981–1982)
Party (0 = Rep.; 1 = Dem.)	–.502	–.522
ADA (liberalism) score	–.707	–.644
Conservative Coalition score	.808	.615
State's percent urban (1980)	–.117	–.133
State's percent black (1980)	.148	.070
State's education levels (1980)	–.071	.047
State's median family income (1980)	–.150	–.160
State's political culture (1982) (0 = traditionalistic; 1 = nontraditionalistic)	–.294	–.214
State's centralization score (1974)	–.007	.037
Number of local governments (within the state)	–.028	–.214
Senator's percent of total vote in most recent election	.084	–.121
Years since election	–.188	–.108
Party competiton (within state)	–.047	–.083

Table 7.3.2.
Regression analysis results: Senators' federalism score for 96th Congress with the independent variables.

Independent Variables*	B	Beta
Party/ideology scale	–16.4800	–.818†
Constituency scale	.7760	.032
Number of governments	.0003	.019
Urbanization/state centralization scale	–.5870	–.009
R^2	.655	

*Variables loading on the several scales were: Party/Ideology—party affiliation and the ideology (ADA and Conservative Coalition) measures; constituency—party competition, percent black, education levels, political culture, and median family income; urbanization/state centralization—percent urban and state centralization score. The number-of-governments measure is included because it appeared to be somewhat important in the simple case, but did not load on the scales.
†p = .001

Table 7.3.3.
Regression analysis results: Senators' federalism score for 97th Congress with the independent variables.

Independent Variables*	B	Beta
Party/ideology scale	–11.8130	–.629†
Number of governments	–.0019	–.160‡
Urbanization/state centralization scale	–.6050	–.038
Constituency scale	.6030	.031
R^2	.446	

*Variables loading on the several scales were: Party/Ideology—party affiliation and the ideology (ADA and Conservative Coalition) scores; urbanization/state centralization scale—percent urban and state centralization score; constituency scale—party competition, percent black, education levels, political culture, and median family income. Regarding the number-of-governments measure, see the footnote to Table 7.3.2.
†p = .001
‡p = .01

decisions. That seems to be the case concerning federalism policy. Finally, Kozak (1984) has suggested that intergovernmental issues are only moderately visible votes and, therefore, provide congressmen considerable discretion in their voting decisions.

It can also be noted that votes on federalism issues appear to be primarily related to variables other than those that influence voting on the several domestic policy dimensions (social welfare, government management, etc.) identified by Clausen. Thus,

Table 7.3.4.
Partial correlation results: Senators' federalism scores with party and ideology.

Federalism score	Ideology (ADA)*	Ideology Controlling for Party	Party†	Party Controlling for Ideology (ADA)
96th Congress	−.707	−.604	−.502	−.225
97th Congress	−.645	−.455	−.522	−.116‡

*Because the ADA scores and Conservative Coalition scores were so strongly correlated ($r = -.87$ and $r = -.94$ for the 96th and 97th Congresses, respectively), the partial correlation analysis was performed with only the ADA scores.
†Party is coded Republican = 0; Democrat = 1.
‡This relationship is not significant at .10. All the other relationships in the table are significant at .01 or better.

federalism appears to be a unique domestic policy area. Clausen and others have found that foreign policy, like federalism policy, is most affected by ideology. This is particularly interesting because several scholars have likened federal relations in the United States to the foreign aid-giving process between donor and recipient nations (e.g., Pressman, 1975: Ch. 5).

SUMMARY AND CONCLUSION

There is frequently a link between the policy process (and where decisions are made) and policy outcomes (what decisions are finally implemented). The variables that affect legislative voting concerning how authority and responsibility are shared within the federal system are thus important to understand. Therefore, the factors that influence congressional voting on federalism matters deserve systematic attention. This analysis, one of the first to focus explicitly on federalism issues, indicates that ideology and party, especially the former, are the major influences on senators' voting.

The relationship between ideology and federalism voting supports some previous perceptions (Nathan, et al., 1977). However, there is a need to ascertain more precisely how government practitioners, including congressmen, understand federalism. It may be that what practitioners perceive as a federalist stance is only administrative decentralization (Elazar, 1981:17–18; Walker, 1981; Hero, 1986). In this regard, it is notable that the highly conservative Reagan administration, which has often proclaimed a deep concern for federalism, has deviated from a federalist stance in several significant instances. This suggests either a poor understanding of federalism, that federalism is secondary to other value and substantive policy concerns, or both (Lowi, 1984).

Other variables, including several that attempt to focus directly on intergovernmental factors, do not appear to influence senators' federalism votes. Possible reasons for this were cited. Moreover, the influences on senators' federalism votes appear somewhat distinct from those that influence other domestic policies.

Future research needs to consider the question of Congress and federalism further. Beyond examining the understanding that policymakers have of the concept, efforts should be undertaken to examine the relative saliency of federalism to other substantive policy concerns. An examination of the House of Representatives, as well as state legislatures, similar to that undertaken here for the Senate might also be useful. Only then will scholars begin to fully understand how major political institutions perceive and create, or recreate, federalism's contemporary meaning.

APPENDIX: VOTES USED TO CONSTRUCT FEDERALISM SCORES

96th Congress

1. S. 210 Department of Education Organization Act of 1979
2. S. 210 Amendment No. 139 to the Department of Education Organization Act of 1979
3. S. 1030 Emergency Energy Conservation Act of 1979
4. S. J. Res. 28 Direct Popular Election of the President
5. S. 1149 Amendment No. UP 348 to the Housing and Community Development Amendments of 1979
6. S. 1308 Priority Energy Project Act of 1979
7. H.R. 4986 Amendment No. 543 to the Depository Institutions Deregulation Act of 1979
8. S. 1648 Amendment No. 730 to the Airport and Airway System Development Act of 1979
9. H.R. 10 (S. 10) Civil Rights of Institutionalized Persons
10. S. 2882 Amendment No. UP 1371 to the Budget Reconciliation of Congressional Budgets for the Federal Government for Fiscal Years 1980–1983
11. S. 1177 Amendment No. UP 1416 to the Mental Health Systems Act
12. S. 1280 Amendment No. UP 1448 to the Energy Management Partnership Act

97th Congress

1. S. 197 Housing and Community Development Act amendments

2, 3. S. 1377 Budget Reconciliation (two votes)

4. S. 1204 Noise Control Authorization
5. S. 1503 Standby Petroleum Allocation Act
6. S. 1086 Older Americans Act
7. H. J. Res. 357 Continuing Appropriations, Fiscal 1982
8. S. Con. Res. 60 Disapproval of Federal Trade Commission Used-Car Rule
9. H.R. 4961 Budget Reconciliation Tax Increases/Spending Cuts
10. H.R. 7019 Transportation Appropriations, Fiscal 1983

Chapter Eight

Policy Relationships in Congress: Constituents, Interest Groups, and the Executive Branch

Policy making in Congress does not occur in a vacuum. Congress is the focus of lobbying efforts by individual constituents, organized interests, executive branch personnel, and the President. Thus, to understand the congressional policy process, one must have an appreciation for the policy relationships that exist between Congress and other actors and institutions seeking to influence congressional outcomes. Articles offered in this chapter examine policy relationships with constituents, groups, and the President.

A major point to be emphasized in studying policy relationships is that the activity, involvement, and influence of different actors is highly variable, depending on situational factors. Groups are most apt to be influential on highly particularized and nonvisible legislation. The President is likely to influence legislative affairs when his popularity is high, he has strong support in Congress, and a featured plank in his program is at stake. Congressional party leaders usually are most successful on procedural and low-profile votes not involving ideological, state, or constituency concerns.

Another point is that executive branch lobbying is not monolithic. Not all executive branch lobbyists are pursuing the administration's package. Frequently, agencies pursue their own narrow self-interests in the congressional process, even if at odds with or out of step with the President's program.

Reading 8.1

U.S. House Members in Their Constituencies

Richard Fenno, Jr.

Interaction between members of Congress and their constituents back home has been a much neglected topic in the study of Congress. In this article, Fenno is the first really to systematically study the "home style" of members of Congress.

ABSTRACT

The paper addresses itself to two questions left underdeveloped in the literature on representative-constituent relations. First, what does the representative see when he or she sees a constituency? Second, what consequences do these perceptions have for his or her behavior? The paper reverses the normal Washington-oriented view of representative-constituent relations and approaches both questions by examining the representative in his or her constituency. The paper's observations are drawn from the author's travels with seventeen U.S. House members while they were working in their districts. Member perceptions of their constituency are divided into the geographical, the reelection, the primary and the personal constituencies. Attention is then given to the home style of House members. Home style is treated as an amalgam of three elements—allocation of resources, presentation of self, explanation of Washington activity. An effort is made to relate home style to the various perceived constituencies. Some observations are made relating constituency-oriented research to the existing literature on representation.

Source: From "U.S. House Members in Their Constituencies: An Exploration," by Richard F. Fenno, Jr., *American Political Science Review* 71 (September 1977), pp. 883–917. Reprinted with permission of the American Political Science Association.

Despite a voluminous literature on the subject of representative-constituency relationships, one question central to that relationship remains underdeveloped. It is: what does an elected representative see when he or she sees a constituency? And, as a natural follow-up, what consequences do these perceptions have for his or her behavior? The key problem is that of perception. And the key assumption is that the constituency a representative reacts to is the constituency he or she sees. The corollary assumption is that the rest of us cannot understand the representative-constituency relationship until we can see the constituency through the eyes of the representative. These ideas are not new. They were first articulated for students of the United States Congress by Lewis Dexter.[1] Their importance has been widely acknowledged and frequently repeated ever since. But despite the acceptance and reiteration of Dexter's insights, we still have not developed much coherent knowledge about the perceptions members of Congress have of their constituencies.

A major reason for this neglect is that most of our research on the representative-constituency linkage gets conducted at the wrong end of that linkage. Our interest in the constituency relations of U.S. senators and representatives has typically been a derivative interest, pursued for the light it sheds on some behavior—like roll call voting—in Washington. When we talk with our national legislators about their constituencies, we typically talk to them *in Washington* and, perforce, in the Washington context. But that is a context far removed from the one in which their constituency relationships are created, nurtured, and changed. And it is a context equally far removed from the one in which we might expect their perceptions of their constituencies to be shaped, sharpened or altered. Asking constituency-related questions on Capitol Hill, when the House member is far from the constituency itself, could well produce a distortion of perspective. Researchers might tend to conceive of a separation between the representative "here in Washington" and his or her constituency "back home," whereas the representative may picture himself or herself as a part of the constituency—me *in* the constituency, rather than me *and* the constituency. As a research strategy, therefore, it makes some sense to study our representatives' perceptions of their constituencies while they are actually in their constituencies—at the constituency end of the linkage.[2]

Since the fall of 1970, I have been traveling with some members of the House of Representatives while they were in their districts, to see if I could figure out by looking over their shoulders what it is they see there. These expeditions, designed to continue through the 1976 elections, have been totally open-ended and exploratory. I have tried to observe and inquire into anything and everything the members do. Rather than assume that I already know what is interesting or what questions to ask, I have been prepared to find interesting questions emerging in the course of the experience. The same with data. The research method has been largely one of soaking and poking or just hanging around. This paper, therefore, conveys mostly an impressionistic feel for the subject as befits the earliest stages of exploration and mapping.

As of June 1976, I had accompanied fourteen sitting House members, two House members-to-be and one House member-elect in their districts for a minimum of two, a maximum of ten, and an average of five days each—sometimes at election time, sometimes not. In eleven cases I have accompanied the member on more than one trip; in six cases I have made only one trip. Since I am a stranger to each local context and to the constellation of people surrounding each member, my confidence in what I see and hear increases markedly when I can make similar observations at more than one point in time. In ten cases I have supplemented my trips to the district with a lengthy interview in Washington. In the district, I reconstruct my record from memory and from brief jottings, as soon after the event as is feasible. In Washington, I take mostly verbatim notes during the interview and commit them to tape immediately thereafter.

I have tried to find a variety of types of members and districts, but I make no pretense at having a group that can be called representative, much less a sample. The seventeen include nine Democrats and eight Republicans. Geographically, three come from two eastern states; six come from five midwestern states; three come from three southern states; five come from three far western states. Since I began, one has retired, one has been defeated and one has run for the Senate. There is some variation among them in terms of ideology, seniority, ethnicity, race, sex,[3] and in terms of safeness and diversity of district. But no claim is made that the group is ideally balanced in any of these respects.

PERCEPTIONS OF THE CONSTITUENCY

The District: The Geographical Constituency

What then do House members see when they see a constituency? One way they perceive it—the way most helpful to me so far—is as a nest of concentric circles. The largest of these circles represents the congressman's broadest view of his constituency. This is "the district" or "my district." It is the entity to which, from which, and in which he travels. It is the entity whose boundaries have been fixed by state legislative enactment or by court decision. It includes the entire population within those boundaries. Because it is a legal entity, we could refer to it as the legal constituency. It captures more of what the congressman has in mind when he conjures up "my district," however, if we label it the *geographical constituency.* We retain the idea that the district is a legally bounded space and emphasize that it is located in a particular place.

The Washington community is often described as a group of people all of whom come from somewhere else. The House of Representatives, by design, epitomizes this characteristic; and its members function with a heightened sense of their ties to place. There are, of course, constant reminders. The member's district is, after all, "the Tenth District of *California.*" Inside the chamber, he is "the gentleman from *California*"; outside the chamber he is Representative X (D–*California*). So, it is not surprising that when you ask a congressman, "What kind of district do you have?", the answer often begins with, and always includes, a geographical, space-and-place perception. Thus, the district is seen as "the largest in the state, twenty-eight counties in the southeastern corner" or "three layers of suburbs to the west of the city, a square with the northwest corner cut out." If the boundaries have been changed by a recent redistricting, the geography of "the new district" will be compared to that of "the old district."

If one essential aspect of "the geographical constituency" is seen as its location and boundaries, another is its particular internal make-up. And House members describe their districts' internal makeup using political science's most familiar demographic and political variables—socioeconomic structure, ideology, ethnicity, residential patterns, religion, partisanship, stability, diversity, etc. Every congressman, in his mind's eye, sees his geographical constituency in terms of some special configuration of such variables. For example,

> Geographically, it covers the northern one-third of the state, from the border of (state X) to the border of (state Y), along the Z river—twenty-two counties. The basic industry is agriculture—but it's a diverse district. The city makes up one-third of the population. It is dominated by the state government and education. It's an independent minded constituency, with a strong attachment to the work ethic. A good percentage is composed of people whose families emigrated from Germany, Scandinavia and Czechoslovakia. I don't exactly know the figures, but over one-half the district is German. And this goes back to the work ethic. They are a hardworking, independent people. They have a strong thought of "keeping the government off my back, we'll do all right here." That's especially true of my out-counties.

Some internal configurations are more complex than others. But, even at the broadest level, no congressman sees, within his district's boundaries, an undifferentiated glob.[4] And we cannot talk about his relations with his "constituency" as if he did.

All of the demographic characteristics of the geographical constituency carry political implications. But as most Representatives make their first perceptual cut into "the district," political matters are usually left implicit. Sometimes, the question "what kind of district do you have?" turns up the answer "it's a Democratic district." But much more often, that comes later. It is as if they first want to sketch a prepolitical background against which they can later paint in the political refinements. We, of course, know for many of the variables just what those political refinements are likely to be. (Most political scientists would guess that the district just described is probably more Republican than Democratic, which it is.) There is no point to dwelling on the general political relevance of each variable. But one summary characterization does seem to have special usefulness as a background against which to understand political perceptions and their consequences. And that characteristic is the relative homogeneity or heterogeneity of the district.

As the following examples suggest, members of Congress do think in terms of the homogeneity or heterogeneity of their districts though they may not always use the words.

> It's geographically compact. It's all suburban—no big city in the accepted sense of the word and no rural area. It's all white. There are very few blacks, maybe 2 per cent. Spanish surnamed make up about 10 per cent. Traditionally, it's been a district with a high percentage of home ownership. . . . Economically, it's above the national average in employment . . . the people of the district are employed. It's not that it's very high income. Oh, I suppose there are a few places of some wealth, but nothing very wealthy. And no great pockets of poverty either. And it's not dominated by any one industry. The X County segment has a lot of small, clean, technical industries. I consider it very homogeneous. By almost any standard, it's homogeneous.

> This district is a microcosm of the nation. We are geographically southern and politically northern. We have agriculture—mostly soy beans and corn. We have big business—like Union Carbide and General Electric. And we have unions. We have a city and we have small towns. We have some of the worst poverty in the country in A County. And we have some very wealthy sections, though not large. We have wealth in the city and some wealthy towns. We have urban poverty and rural poverty. Just about the only thing we don't have is a good sized ghetto. Otherwise, everything you can have, we've got it right here.

Because it is a summary variable, the perceived homogeneity-heterogeneity characteristic is particularly hard to measure; and no metric is proposed here. Intuitively, both the number and the compatibility of significant interests within the district would seem to be involved. The greater the number of significant interests—as opposed to one dominant interest—the more likely it is that the district will be seen as heterogeneous. But if the several significant interests were viewed as having a single lowest common denominator and, therefore, quite compatible, the district might still be viewed as homogeneous. One indicator, therefore, might be the ease with which the congressman finds a lowest common denominator of interests for some large proportion of his geographical constituency. The basis for the denominator could be any of the prepolitical variables. We do not think of it, however, as a political characteristic—as the equivalent, for instance, of party registration or political safeness.[5] The proportion of people in the district who have to be included would be a subjective judgment—"enough" so that the congressman saw his geographical constituency as more homogeneous than heterogeneous, or vice versa. All we can say is that the less actual or potential conflict he sees among district interests, the more likely he is to see his district as homogeneous. Another indicator might be the extent to which the geographical constituency is congruent with a natural community. Districts that are purely artificial (sometimes purely political) creations of districting practices, and which pay no attention to pre-existing communities of interest are more likely to be heterogeneous.[6] Pre-existing communities or natural communities are more likely to have such homogenizing ties as common sources of communication, common organizations, and common traditions.

The Supporters: The Re-election Constituency

Within his geographical constituency, each congressman perceives a smaller, explicitly political constituency. It is composed of the people he thinks vote for him. And we shall refer to it as his *re-election constituency.* As he moves about the district, a House member continually draws the distinction between those who vote for him and those who do not. "I do well here"; "I run poorly here." "This group supports me"; "this group does not." By distinguishing supporters from nonsupporters, he articulates his baseline political perception.

House members seem to use two starting points—one cross-sectional and the other longitudinal—in shaping this perception. First by a process of inclusion and exclusion, they come to a rough approximation of the upper and lower ranges of the re-election constituency. That is to say, there are some votes a member believes he almost always gets; there are other votes he believes he almost never gets. One of the core elements of any such distinction is the perceived partisan component of the vote—party identification as revealed in registration or poll figures and party voting. "My district registers only 37 per cent Republican. They have no place else to go. My problem is, how can I get enough Democratic votes to win the general election." Another element is the political tendencies of various demographic groupings.

> My supporters are Democrats, farmers, labor—a DFL operation—with some academic types. . . . My opposition tends to be the main street hardware dealer. I look at that kind of guy in a stable town, where the newspaper runs the community—the typical school board member in the rural part of the district—that's the kind of guy I'll never get. At the opposite end of the scale is the country club set. I'll sure as hell never get them, either.

Starting with people he sees, very generally, as his supporters, and leaving aside people he sees, equally generally, as his nonsupporters, each congressman fashions a view of the people who give him his victories at the polls.

The second starting point for thinking about the re-election constituency is the congressman's idea of who voted for him "last time." Starting with that perception, he adds or subtracts incrementally on the basis of changes that will have taken place (or could be made by him to take place) between "last time" and "next time." It helps him to think about his re-election constituency this way because that is about the only certainty he operates with—he won last time. And the process by which his desire for re-election gets translated into his perception of a re-election constituency is filled with uncertainty. At least that is my strong impression. House members see re-election uncertainty where political scientists would fail to unearth a single objective indicator of it. For one thing, their perceptions of their supporters and nonsupporters are quite diffuse. They rarely feel certain just who did vote for them last time. And even if they do feel fairly sure about that, they may perceive population shifts that threaten established calculations. In the years of my travels, moreover, the threat of redistricting has added enormous uncertainty to the make-up of some re-election constituencies. In every district, too, there is the uncertainty which follows an unforeseen external event—recession, inflation, Watergate.

Of all the many sources of uncertainty, the most constant—and usually the greatest—involves the electoral challenger. For it is the challenger who holds the most potential for altering any calculation involving those who voted for the congressman "last time." "This time's" challenger may have very different sources of political strength from "last time's" challenger. Often, one of the major off-year uncertainties is whether or not the last challenger will try again. While it is true that House members campaign all the time, "the campaign" can be said to start only when the challenger is known. At that point, a redefinition of the re-election constituency may have to take place. If the challenger is chosen by primary, for example, the congressman may inherit support from the loser.[7] A conservative southern Republican, waiting for the Democratic primary to determine whether his challenger would be a black or a white (both liberal), wondered about the shape of his re-election constituency.

> It depends on my opponent. Last time, my opponent (a white moderate) and I split many groups. Many business people who might have supported me, split up. If I have a liberal opponent, all the business community will support me. . . . If the black man is my opponent, I should get more Democratic votes than I got before. He can't do any better there than the man I beat before. Except for a smattering of liberals and radicals around the colleges, I will do better than last time with the whites. . . . The black vote is 20 per cent and they vote right down the line Democratic. I have to concede the black vote. There's nothing I can do about it. . . . [But] against a white liberal, I would get some of the black vote.

The shaping of perceptions proceeds under conditions of considerable uncertainty.

The Strongest Supporters: The Primary Constituency

In thinking about their political condition, House members make distinctions within their re-election constituency—thus giving us a third, still smaller concentric circle. Having distinguished between their nonsupporters and their supporters, they further distinguish between their routine or temporary supporters and their very strongest supporters. Routine supporters only vote for them, often merely following party identification; but others will support them with a special degree of intensity. Temporary supporters back them as the best available alternative; but others will support them regardless of who the challenger may be. Within each re-election constituency are nested these "others"—a constituency perceived as "my strongest supporters," "my hard core support," "my loyalists," "my true believers," "my political base." We shall think of these people as the ones each congressman believes would provide his best line of electoral defense in a primary contest, and label them *the primary constituency.*[8] It will probably include the earliest of his supporters—those who recruited him and those who tendered identifiably strong support in his first campaign—thus, providing another reason for calculating on the basis of "last time." From its ranks will most likely come the bulk of his financial help and his volunteer workers. From its ranks will least likely come an electoral challenger.

A protected congressional seat is as much one protected from primary defeat as from general election defeat. And a primary constituency is something every congressman must have.

> Everybody needs some group which is strongly for him—especially in a primary. You can win a primary with 25,000 zealots. . . . The most exquisite case I can give you was in the very early war years. I had very strong support from the anti-war people. They were my strongest supporters and they made up about 5 per cent of the district.

The primary constituency, I would guess, draws a special measure of a congressman's interest; and it should, therefore, draw a special measure of ours. But it is not easy to delineate—for us or for them. Asked to describe his "very strongest supporters," one member replied, "That's the hardest question anyone has to answer." The primary constituency is more subtly shaded than the re-election constituency, where voting provides an objective membership test. Loyalty is not the most predictable of political qualities. And all politicians resist drawing invidious distinctions among their various supporters, as if it were borrowing trouble to begin classifying people according to fidelity. House members who have worried about or fought a primary recently may find it somewhat easier. So, too may those with heterogeneous districts whose diverse elements invite differentiation. Despite some difficulty, most members—because it is politically prudent to do so—make some such distinction, in speech or in action or both. By talking to them and watching them, we can begin to understand what those distinctions are.

Here are two answers to the question, "who are your very strongest supporters?"

> My strongest supporters are the working class—the blacks and labor, organized labor. And the people who were in my state legislative district, of course. The fifth ward is low-income, working class and is my base of support. I grew up there; I have my law office there; and I still live there. The white businessmen who are supporting me now are late converts—very late. They support me as the least of two evils. They are not a strong base of support. They know it and I know it.

> I have a circle of strong labor supporters and another circle of strong business supporters. . . . They will "fight, bleed and die" for me, but in different ways. Labor gives you the manpower and the workers up front. You need them just as much as you need the guy with the two-acre yard to hold a lawn party to raise money. The labor guy loses a day's pay on election day. The business guy gets his nice lawn tramped over and chewed up. Each makes a commitment to you in his own way. You need them both.

Each description reveals the working politician's penchant for inclusive thinking. Each tells us something about a primary constituency, but each leaves plenty of room for added refinements.

The best way to make such refinements is to observe the congressman as he comes in contact with the various elements of his re-election constituency. Both he and they act in ways that help delineate the "very strongest supporters." For example, the author of the second comment above drew a standing ovation when he was introduced at the Labor Temple. During his speech, he spoke directly to individuals in the audience. "Kenny, it's good to see you here. Ben, you be sure and keep in touch." Afterward, he lingered for an hour drinking beer and eating salami. At a businessman's annual Christmas luncheon the next day, he received neither an introduction nor applause when the main speaker acknowledged his presence, saying, "I see our congressman is here; and I use the term 'our' loosely." This congressman's "circle of strong labor supporters" appears to be larger than his "circle of strong business supporters." And the congressman, for his part, seemed much more at home with the first group than he did with the second.

Like other observers of American politics, I have found this idea of "at homeness" a useful one in helping me to map the relationship between politicians and constituents[9]—in this case the perception of a primary constituency. House members sometimes talk in this language about the groups they encounter.

> I was born on the flat plains, and I feel a lot better in the plains area than in the mountain country. I don't know why it is. As much as I like Al [whom we had just lunched with in a mountain town], I'm still not comfortable with him. I'm no cowboy. But when I'm out there on that flat land with those ranchers and wheat farmers, standing around trading insults and jibes and telling stories, I feel better. That's the place where I click.

It is also the place where he wins elections, his primary constituency. "That's my strong area. I won by a big margin and offset my losses. If I win next time, that's where I'll win it—on the plains." Obviously, there is no one-to-one relationship between the groups with whom a congressman acts and feels most at home and his primary constituency. But it does provide a pretty good unobtrusive clue.[10] So I found myself fashioning a highly subjective "at homeness index" to rank the degree to which each congressman seems to have support from and rapport with each group.

I recall, for example, watching a man whose constituency is dominantly Jewish participating in an afternoon installation-of-officers ceremony at a Young Men's Hebrew Association attended by about forty civic leaders of the local community. He drank some spiked punch, began the festivities by saying, "I'm probably the first tipsy installation officer you ever had," told an emotional story about his own dependence on the Jewish "Y," and traded banter with his friends in the audience throughout the proceedings. That evening as we prepared to meet with yet another and much larger (Democratic party) group, I asked where we were going. He said, "We're going to a shitty restaurant to have a shitty meal with a shitty organization and have a shitty time." And he did—from high to low on the "at homeness index." On the way home, after the meal, he talked about the group.

> Ethnically, most of them are with me. But I don't always support the party candidate, and they can't stand that. . . . This group and half the other party groups in the district are against me. But they don't want to be against me too strongly for fear I might go into a primary and beat them. So self-preservation wins out. . . . They know they can't beat me.

Both groups are Jewish. The evening group was a part of his re-election constituency, but not his primary constituency. The afternoon group was a part of both.

The Intimates: The Personal Constituency

Within the primary constituency, each member perceives still a fourth, and final, concentric circle. These are the few individuals whose relationship with him is so personal and so intimate that their relevance to him cannot be captured by their inclusion in any description of "very strongest supporters." In some cases they are his closest political advisers and confidants. In other cases, they are people from whom he draws emotional sustenance for his political work. We shall think of these people as his *personal constituency*.

One Sunday afternoon, I sat in the living room of a congressman's chief district staff assistant watching an NFL football game—with the congressman, the district aide, the state assemblyman from the congressman's home county, and the district attorney of the same county. Between plays, at halftime, and over beer and cheese, the four friends discussed every aspect of the congressman's campaign, listened to and commented on his taped radio spots, analyzed several newspaper reports, discussed local and national personalities, relived old political campaigns and hijinks, and discussed their respective political ambitions. Ostensibly they were watching the football game; actually the congressman was exchanging political advice, information, and perspectives with three of his six or seven oldest and closest political associates.

Another congressman begins his weekends at home by having a Saturday morning 7:30 coffee and doughnut breakfast in a cafe on the main street of his home town with a small group of old friends from the Rotary Club. The morning I was there, the congressman, a retired bank manager, a hardware store owner, a high school science teacher, a retired judge, and a past president of the city council gossiped and joked about local matters—the county historian, the library, the board of education, the churches and their lawns—for an hour. "I guess you can see what an institution this is," he said as we left. "You have no idea how invaluable these meetings are for me. They keep me in touch with my home base. If you don't keep your home base, you don't have anything."

The personal constituency is, doubtless, the most idiosyncratic of the several constituencies. Not all members will open it up to the outside observer. Nine of the seventeen did, however; and in doing so, he usually revealed a side of his personality not seen by the rest of his constituencies. "I'm really very reserved, and I don't feel at home with most groups—only with five or six friends," said the congressman after the football game. The relationship probably has both political and emotional dimensions. But beyond that, it is hard to generalize, except to say that the personal constituency needs to be identified if our understanding of the congressman's view of his constituency is to be complete.

In sum, my impression is that House members perceive four constituencies, geographical, re-election, primary, and personal—each one nesting within the previous one.

POLITICAL SUPPORT AND HOME STYLE

What, then, do these perceptions have to do with a House member's behavior? Our conventional paraphrase of this question would read: what do these perceptions have to do with behavior at the other end of the line—in Washington? But the concern that disciplines the perceptions we have been talking about is neither first nor foremost a Washington-oriented concern. It is a concern for political support at home. It is a concern for the scope of that support—which decreases as one moves from the geographical to the personal constituency. It is a concern for the stability of that support—which increases as one moves from the geographical to the personal constituency. And it ultimately issues in a concern for manipulating scopes and intensities in order to win and hold a sufficient amount of support to win elections. Representatives, and prospective representatives, think about their constituencies because they seek support there. They want to get nominated and elected, then renominated and re-elected. For most members of Congress most of the time, this electoral goal is primary. It is the prerequisite for a congressional career and, hence, for the pursuit of other goals. And the electoral goal is achieved—first and last—not in Washington but at home.

Of course, House members do many things in Washington that affect their electoral support at home.[11] Political scientists interpret a great deal of their behavior in Washington in exactly that way—particularly their roll-call votes. Obviously, a congressman's perception of his several constituencies will affect such things as his roll-call voting, and we could, if we wished, study the effect. Indeed, that is the very direction in which our conditioned research reflexes would normally carry this investigation. But my experience has turned me in another—though not, as we shall see an unrelated—direction. I have been watching House members work to maintain or enlarge their political support at home, by going to the district and doing things there.

Our Washington-centered research has caused us systematically to underestimate the proportion of their working time House members spend in their districts. As a result, we have also underestimated its perceived importance to them. In all our studies of congressional time allocation, time spent outside of Washington is left out of the analysis. So, we end up analyzing "the average work week of a congressman" by comparing the amounts of time he spends in committee work, on the floor, doing research, handling constituent problems—but all of it in Washington.[12] Nine of my members whose appointment and travel records I have checked carefully for the year 1973—a nonelection year—averaged 28 trips to the district and spent an average of 101 working (not traveling) days in their districts that year. A survey conducted in 419 House offices covering 1973, indicates that the average number of trips home (not counting recesses) was 35 and the number of days spent in the district during 1973 (counting recesses) was 138.[13] No fewer than 131, nearly one-third, of the 419 members went home to their districts *every single weekend.* Obviously, the direct personal cultivation of their various constituencies takes a great deal of their time; and they must think it is worth it in terms of winning and holding political support. If it is worth *their* time to go home so much, it is worth *our* time to take a commensurate degree of interest in what they do there and why.

As they cultivate their constituencies, House members display what I shall call their *home style.* When they discuss the importance of what they are doing, they are discussing the importance of *home style* to the achievement of their electoral goal. At this stage of the research, the surest generalization one can make about home style is that there are as many varieties as there are members of Congress. "Each of us has his own formula—a truth that is true for him," said one. It will take a good deal more immersion and cogitation before I can improve upon that summary comment. At this point, however, three ingredients of home style appear to be worth looking at. They are: first, the congressman's allocation of his personal resources and those of his office; second, the congressman's presentation of self; and third, the congressman's explanation of his Washington activity. Every congressman allocates, presents, and explains. The amalgam of these three activities for any given representative constitutes (for now, at least) his home style. His home style, we expect, will be affected by his perception of his four constituencies.

HOME STYLE: ALLOCATION OF RESOURCES

Every representative must make a basic decision with regard to his home style: "How much and what kinds of attention shall I pay to home?" Or to put it another way: "Of all the resources available with which to help me do my job, which kinds and how much of each do I want to allocate directly to activity in the district?" There are, of course, many ways to allocate one's resources so that they affect the district. Our concern is with *resources allocated directly to the district.* Of these, we propose to look first, at the congressman's *time* and second, at the congressman's *staff.* The congressman's decision about how much time he should spend physically at home and his decision about how much of his staff he should place physically in the district are decisions which give shape to his home style.

Of all the resources available to the House member, the scarcest and most precious one, which dwarfs all others in posing critical allocative dilemmas, is his time. Time is at once what the member has least of and what he has the most control over. When a congressman divides up his time, he decides by that act what kind of congressman he wants to be. He must divide his time in Washington. He must divide his time at home. The decision we are concerned with here is the division of his time between Washington and home. When he is doing something at home, he must give up doing some things in Washington, and vice versa. So he chooses and he trades off; and congressmen make different allocative choices and different allocative trades. In this section, we shall focus on the frequency with which various congressmen returned to their districts in 1973.

"This is a business, and like any business you have to make time and motion studies," said one member. "All we have is time and ourselves, so we have to calculate carefully to use our time productively." It is not true, of course, that "all" the congressman has is time and himself. The office carries with it a large number of ancillary resources—a staff, office space, office expense allowances, free mailing privileges, personal expense allowances, etc.—all of which draw attention when the advantages of incumbency are detailed. Each congressman chooses how he will utilize these resources. The most important of these choices are choices about how to use his staff. And among the key choices about staff is how to allocate them between Washington and the district. In this section we shall focus particularly on one indicator of that decision—the percentage of his total expenditures on staff salaries allocated by him to the salaries of his district staff.[14]

The information on trips home and staff allocation was collected on Capitol Hill in June 1974. Six students, each of whom had just finished working for four months, full-time in a congressman's office, conducted a survey by visiting each member's office and talking to his or her administrative assistant or personal secretary. The question about trips home usually produced an educated estimate.[15] The questions about staff yielded more precise answers. Each student presented the Clerk of the House's *Report* for 1973, with its list of each representative's

Table 8.1.1.
Trips home and electoral margin.

	Frequency of Trips Home (1973)			
Election Margin (1972)	Low (0–23)	Medium (24–42)	High (43+)	Total
Less than 55%	21 (29%)	28 (38%)	24 (33%)	73 (100%)
55–60%	18 (32%)	18 (32%)	20 (36%)	56 (100%)
61–65%	22 (27%)	17 (20%)	44 (53%)	83 (100%)
More than 65%	68 (33%)	66 (32%)	73 (35%)	207 (100%)
	129	129	161	419

Note: Gamma = −.03

staff members and their salaries; and the respondents simply designated which staff members were located in the district. A briefer, follow-up survey was conducted by four students with similar "Hill experience" in May 1975. This survey added to the store of information on those 1973 members who were still in Congress.[16] For 1973, it should be noted, each member was allowed a maximum of sixteen staff members and a maximum payroll of $203,000. And for the two-year period 1973–1974 (the 93d Congress) each member was reimbursed for thirty-six round trips to his district. Members were not, of course, required to use any of these allowances to the maximum.

On the matter of trips home, there is evidence of personal attentiveness to the district and of variation in that attentiveness. The average number of 1973 trips per member was thirty-five, and the median was thirty. The range went from a low of four trips to a high of three hundred and sixty-five.[17] One can ask: "for which kinds of House members is their frequent physical presence in the district an important part of their home style and for which kinds is it less so?" At this early stage, we can present only a few suggestive relationships. In order to do so, we have categorized the frequency of trips home into *low* (less than 24), medium (24–42), and high (more than 42). The categories are based on the responses to the question and to the appearance of reasonable cutting points in the data.[18] These categories have been cross-tabulated with a number of variables that should be expected to correlate with the frequency of home visits.

One standard supposition would be that representatives in electoral jeopardy will decide to spend more of their time at home than will representatives whose seats are well-protected. As a generalization, however, this supposition receives no confirmation when our conventional measures of electoral safeness are used. As Table 8.1.1 shows, the frequency of trips home does not increase as electoral margins decrease. Indeed, there is just not much of a relationship at all.[19] It might be noted, in this connection, that objective measures of marginality have not fared particularly well in producing consistent findings whenever they have been used.[20] My own experience leads me to believe that only *subjective* measures of electoral safety are valid. House members feel more uncertainty about re-election than is captured by any arbitrary electoral margin figures. Furthermore, uncertainty about their primary election situation is totally untouched by such figures. The point is that subjective assessments of electoral safeness might be more strongly correlated with trips home.

Table 8.1.2.
Trips home and seniority.

Seniority	Frequency of Trips Home Low (0–23)	 Medium (24–42)	 High (43+)	Total
Low (1–3 terms)	34 (22%)	44 (28%)	78 (50%)	156 (100%)
Medium (4–7 terms)	43 (28%)	59 (38%)	52 (34%)	154 (100%)
High (8+ terms)	52 (48%)	26 (24%)	31 (28%)	189 (100%)
	—	—	—	—
	129	129	161	419
Mean seniority	7.0 terms	5.0 terms	4.7 terms	

Note: Gamma = −.30

A related hunch would be that the longer a congressman is in office, the less time he will spend at home. Part of the argument here overlaps with the previous one —the longer in office, the more secure the seat. But the more important part of the reasoning would be that with seniority comes increased influence and responsibility in the House and, hence, the need to spend more time in Washington. These suppositions are supported by our data—but not as strongly and as consistently as we had imagined would be the case. A simple correlation between terms of service and number of trips home shows that as seniority increases, home visits decrease—as we would expect. But the correlation coefficient (Pearson's r) is an exceedingly weak—.235. When the data are grouped, however, the nature and strength of the relationship becomes clearer.

Table 8.1.2 pictures the relationship between the three categories of personal attentiveness and three levels of seniority. The summary statistics continue to be unimpressive, because for the middle levels of seniority no allocative pattern is evident. But looking at the lowest and highest levels of seniority, it is clear that the frequency of home visits is much greater for the low seniority group than it is for the high seniority group. The relationship between length of service and trips home, we conclude, is not a consistent, linear relationship. But for those at the beginning of their House careers and those farthest along in their House careers, their longevity is likely to be one determinant of their decisions on time allocation. Congressional newcomers appear to be more single-minded in pursuing of the electoral goal than are the veterans of the institution.

A third reasonable guess would be that the more time-consuming and expensive it is to get to his district, the less frequently a congressman will make the trip. Leaving money aside (but recalling that for 1973–1974, each member was provided with a "floor" of thirty-six trips), we would expect to find that as distance from Washington increases, the number of trips home decreases. It is not easy to get a measure of distance that captures each member's travelling time. For now, we shall use region as a surrogate for distance, on the theory that if any relationship is present, it will show up in a regional breakdown. And it does. Table 8.1.3 indicates that the members nearest Washington, D. C. (East) spend a good deal more time at home than do the members who live farthest away from the Capitol (Far West). The less of his Washington time a member has to give up in order to get home, the more likely he is to go home—at least at the extremes of distance. If distance is a factor for the other three regional groups, it does not

Table 8.1.3.
Trips home and region.

Region	Frequency of Trips Home Low (0–23)	 Medium (24–42)	 High (43 +)	Total
East	5 (5%)	20 (20%)	76 (75%)	101 (100%)
South	36 (35%)	32 (30%)	36 (35%)	104 (100%)
Border	9 (26%)	10 (29%)	16 (45%)	35 (100%)
Midwest	29 (28%)	47 (44%)	30 (28%)	106 (100%)
Far West	50 (69%)	20 (27%)	3 (4%)	73 (100%)
	—	—	—	—
	129	129	161	419

Regions:
East: Conn., Me., Mass., N.H., N.J., N.Y., Pa., R.I., Vt.
South: Ala., Ark., Fla., Ga., La., Miss., N.C., S.C., Tenn., Texas, Va.
Border: Del., Ky., Md., Mo., Okla., W.Va.
Midwest: Ill., Ind., Iowa, Kans., Mich., Minn., Neb., N.D., Ohio, S.D., Wisc.
Far West: Alaska, Ariz., Calif., Colo., Hawaii, Idaho, Mont., Nev., N.M., Oregon, Utah, Wash., Wyo.

Table 8.1.4.
Trips home and family residence.

Family Residence	Frequency of Trips Home Low (0–23)	 Medium (24–42)	 High (43 +)	Total
Wasinghton area	87 (41%)	89 (42%)	37 (17%)	213 (100%)
District	3 (4%)	6 (8%)	69 (88%)	78 (100%)
Unmarried	5 (14%)	12 (32%)	20 (54%)	37 (100%)
	—	—	—	—
	95	107	126	328

show up here. Our guess is that the distance is a far more problematical factor in those cases. We shall, however, return to the regional variable shortly.

A persistent dilemma facing every member of Congress involves the division of time between work and family. And one of its earliest manifestations comes with the family decision whether to remain at home or move to Washington. If (for whatever reason) the family decides to remain in the district, we would expect the House member to go home more often than if the family moves to Washington. Table 8.1.4 shows that this is very much the case.[21] Five times the percentage of representatives whose families remain at home fall into the high category of trips home as do representatives whose families are in Washington—88 per cent to 17 per cent. To put the finding somewhat differently, the average number of 1973 trips for members with families in Washington was twenty-seven, for members with families in the district it was fifty-two, and for unmarried members it was forty-four trips. Whether family decisions produce the home style or whether a home style decision produces the family decision remains an unanswered question. Either process seems perfectly plausible. It is clear, however, that

Table 8.1.5.
Trips home and district staff expenditures.

	Frequency of Trips Home			
District Staff Expenditures	Low (0–23)	Medium (24–42)	High (43 +)	Total
Lowest 1/3	53 (39%)	42 (31%)	40 (30%)	135 (100%)
Middle 1/3	42 (30%)	55 (40%)	41 (30%)	138 (100%)
Highest 1/3	31 (23%)	32 (23%)	75 (54%)	138 (100%)
	126	129	156	411

Note: Gamma = .28

some decisions about home style are family-related decisions.

To sum up, a House member's decision on how to allocate his time between home and Washington is affected: (1) by his seniority, if it is very low or very high; (2) by the distance from Washington to home, if that distance is very long or very short; and (3) by the place where his family is located, whether his family moves to Washington or remains in the district. A congressman's electoral margin, objectively measured, has little effect on his time allocations. How, if at all, these factors are interrelated, and how strongly each factor contributes to the allocative pattern are matters for later analysis.

Members of Congress also decide what kind of staff presence they wish to establish in the district. Here, too, we find great variation. On the percentage of total staff expenditure allocated to district staff, the range, in 1973, went from 0 to 81 per cent. We might think that a member who decides to give a special degree of personal attention to "home" would also decide to give a special degree of staff attentiveness to "home." But the relationship between the two allocative decisions does not appear to be strong. Using percentage of total staff expenditure on district staff (as we shall throughout this section) as the measure of district staff strength, we find a very weak correlation (Pearson's r = .20) between a congressman's decision on that matter and the number of trips he takes home. Table 8.1.5 clusters and cross-tabulates the two allocative decisions. For our measure of district staff strength we have divided the percentage of expenditures on district staff into thirds. The lowest third ranges from 0 to 22.7 per cent; the middle third ranges from 22.8 to 33.5 per cent; the highest third ranges from 33.6 to 81 per cent. The cross-tabulation also shows a pretty weak overall relationship. For now, therefore, we shall treat the two decisions as if they were made independently of one another and, hence, are deserving of separate examination.

What kinds of members, then, emphasize the value of a large district staff operation? Once again, it turns out, they are not members in special electoral trouble. Table 8.1.6 displays the total lack of any discernible impact of electoral situation (objectively measured) on district staff strength. Nor, as indicated in Table 8.1.7, does seniority make any difference in staff allocative decisions. That it does not adds strength to the idea that the relationship between seniority and home visits discovered earlier is accounted for—as we have suggested—by career-and-goal factors rather than by electoral factors.

The other variables discussed earlier —family residence and distance—do not have the obvious implications for staff allocation that they have for the member's

Table 8.1.6.
District staff expenditures and electoral margin.

Electoral Margin 1972	District Staff Expenditures (1973)			
	Lowest 1/3	Middle 1/3	Highest 1/3	Total
Less than 55%	20 (27%)	28 (38%)	26 (35%)	74 (100%)
55–60%	20 (36%)	20 (36%)	16 (28%)	56 (100%)
61–65%	24 (29%)	29 (35%)	29 (35%)	82 (100%)
More than 65%	72 (36%)	61 (30%)	68 (34%)	201 (100%)
	—	—	—	—
	136	138	139	413

Note: Gamma = −.04

Table 8.1.7.
District staff expenditures and seniority.

Seniority	District Staff Expenditures			
	Lowest 1/3	Middle 1/3	Highest 1/3	Total
Low (1–3 terms)	44 (29%)	54 (35%)	56 (36%)	155 (100%)
Medium (4–7 terms)	44 (29%)	56 (37%)	51 (34%)	151 (100%)
High (8+ terms)	47 (44%)	28 (26%)	32 (30%)	107 (100%)
	—	—	—	—
	136	138	139	413

Note: Gamma = −.13

own time dilemmas. It might be that if his family is in the district, and if he plans to be home a lot, a congressman might decide to have a big district staff operation to work with him there. That supposition receives some support in Table 8.1.8. Another possibility is that members might decide to use a strong district staff to compensate for their lack of personal attention via trips home. However, this idea is not supported in Table 8.1.8, nor in Table 8.1.9, which seeks to uncover regional and distance patternings of district staffs. Representatives who live nearest to Washington (East) and who tend to go home the most do tend to have large district staffs. But representatives who live farthest away and tend to go home the least show only a slight tendency to compensate by allocating heavy expenditures to their district staffs.

Table 8.1.9, however, does reveal some regional allocation patterns that did not appear when we looked for regional patterns in home visits. Region, it appears, captures a good deal more than distance, particularly in relation to staff allocations. The southern and border regions emerge with distinctive patternings here. To a marked degree, House members from these two areas eschew large staff operations in their districts. Scanning our two regional tabulations (Tables 8.1.3 and 8.1.9), we note that every region save the Midwest reveals a noteworthy pattern of resource allocation. In the East we find high frequency of home visits and large district staffs; in the Far West, we find a low frequency of home visits; in the southern and border regions, we find small district staffs. Again, the two types of allocative decisions appear to be quite distinct and independent.

Table 8.1.8.
District staff expenditures and family residence.

Family Residence	District Staff Expenditures			
	Lowest 1/3	Middle 1/3	Highest 1/3	Total
Washington area	85 (40%)	77 (37%)	48 (23%)	210 (100%)
District	21 (28%)	17 (23%)	37 (49%)	75 (100%)
Unmarried	8 (22%)	10 (28%)	18 (50%)	36 (100%)
	—	—	—	—
	114	104	103	321

Table 8.1.9.
District staff expenditures and region.

Region	District Staff Expenditures			
	Lowest 1/3	Middle 1/3	Highest 1/3	Total
East	16 (16%)	31 (31%)	52 (53%)	99 (100%)
South	47 (46%)	36 (35%)	19 (19%)	102 (100%)
Border	18 (55%)	8(24%)	7 (21%)	33 (100%)
Midwest	39 (37%)	34 (32%)	33 (31%)	106 (100%)
Far West	16 (22%)	29 (40%)	28 (38%)	73 (100%)
	—	—	—	—
	136	138	139	413

Regions:
East: Conn., Maine, Mass., N.H., N.J., N.Y., Pa., R.I., Vt.
South: Ala., Ark., Fla., Ga., La., Miss., N.C., S.C., Tenn., Texas, Va.
Border: Del., Ky., Md., Mo., Okla., W.Va.
Midwest: Ill., Ind., Iowa, Kans., Mich., Minn., Neb., N.D., Ohio, S.D., Wisc.
Far West: Alaska, Ariz., Calif., Colo., Hawaii, Idaho, Mont., Nev., N.M., Oregon, Utah, Wash., Wyo.

Region, we tentatively conclude, has a substantial effect on home style.

But regions are composites of several states; and while regional regularities often reflect state regularities, they can also hide them. Both situations have occurred in this instance. Figure 8.1.1 displays state-by-state allocation patterns of personal and district staff attentiveness. For each state delegation, we have computed the mean number of trips home made by its members in 1973; and we have divided the state delegations into those whose averages fell above and below the median number of trips for all House members, i.e., 30 trips. Also, for each state delegation, we computed an average of the percentage of staff expenditures allocated to the district staff by its members, and we have divided the state delegations into those whose averages fell above and below the median percentage for all House members, i.e., 29 per cent. The result is a crude fourfold classification of states according to their combined personal and staff resource allocations to "home." The underlined states fall strongly into their particular patterns; the others display weaker tendencies. Each state is identified, also, by its regional classification.

There are, as Figure 8.1.1 shows, distinctive state allocative patterns. Some were foreshadowed in the regional patterns discussed earlier. For example, the eastern states cluster in the high-trips home

Figure 8.1.1.
Allocation patterns: By state.

District Staff Attentiveness	Personal Attentiveness: Above the median in trips home	Personal Attentiveness: Below the median in trips home
Above the median in district staff expenditures	*Connecticut (E)* *Massachusetts (E)* *New York (E)* *Tennessee (S)* Illinois (MW) Maine (E) New Hampshire (E) Pennsylvania (E) Rhode Island (E) South Carolina (S) Vermont (E)	*California (FW)* Colorado (FW) Hawaii (FW) Idaho (FW) Iowa (MW) Kansas (MW) New Mexico (FW) Wyoming (FW)
Below the median in district staff expenditures	*Kentucky (B)* *Maryland (B)* *North Carolina (S)* *Virginia (S)* *West Virginia (B)* Delaware (B) Indiana (MW) Montana (FW) Ohio (MW)	*Alabama (S)* *Arizona (FW)* *Florida (S)* *Louisiana (S)* *Minnesota (MW)* *Oklahoma (B)* *Oregon (FW)* *Washington (FW)* *Wisconsin (MW)* Arkansas (S) Michigan (MW) Nebraska (MW) South Dakota (MW) Texas (S) Utah (FW)

N.B. States which fall five trips or more above or below the median *and* whose district staff expenditures fall 5 percent or more above or below the median are *italicized.* States not listed fall on the median in one or both instances. Regional classifications are in parentheses.

category; and the far western states cluster in the low-trips home category. Southern and border states cluster in the weak-district staff category. Other state patterns, however, appear here for the first time. The large number of states clustering in the low-trips-home/small-district-staff category, for example were totally obscured in our regional data.

Explanations for these various state clusters are more difficult; and only a few guesses can be made here. The sharp separation between eastern and far western states in trips home is doubtless a function of distance. And—it now appears more strongly—some far western state representatives do compensate for the infrequency of their home visits by maintaining a relatively large staff presence in the district. Yet if California members invest heavily in this compensatory allocative strategy,[22] why don't the members from Washington and Oregon do likewise?

The decision of most southern and border state representatives to spend relatively little on their district staff operations may be explainable by a tradition of nonbureaucratized, highly personalized politics in those areas. Northeasterners may be accustomed to coping with bureaucrats—legislative or otherwise—whereas southern and border state residents would expect to deal directly with the elective officeholder. Yet, in terms of the amount of personal attentiveness to their districts, southern delegations vary widely. At first glance, that variation seems to be related to distance—with states in the near South receiving more attention than states in the far South. But the marked difference among, say, Kentucky,

Tennessee, and Alabama would seem to require a more complex explanation. And, speaking of complexity, the similar disposition of resources by the unexpected mix of delegations in the low-trips-home/small-district-staff category (in the lower right hand corner of Figure 8.1.1) defies even an explanatory guess at this stage of our study.

The allocative elements of home style vary across regions and among states within regions. The relevance of state delegations to patterns of resource allocation at home will come as no surprise to students of Congress. For there is virtually no aspect, formal or informal, of the legislative process on Capitol Hill that has not already revealed the importance of the state delegation.[23] How much that importance is the product of extensive communication among delegation members and how much the product of similar expectations emanating from similar districts, has not been definitively answered. Nor can it be here. All we can say is that both are probably involved. State delegation members probably talk to one another about their allocative practices and follow one another's example and advice. Also, certain expectations and traditions probably develop within states, or sections of states, so that members feel constrained to make resource allocations that are not too far out of line with those expectations.

The ambiguity of this discussion raises one of the broadest questions concerning home style. Is a congressman's home style something he chooses and then imposes upon his district or is it something that is imposed upon him by the kind of district he represents? We shall worry that question and work our way toward an answer as we proceed. At this point it appears that either or both patterns can hold: for, while state regularities testify to district influences on home style, some states display no regularities; and all states display enough idiosyncratic behavior to testify to the presence of individual choice.

Home style is, then, partly a matter of place—i.e., it is affected by the nature of the congressman's geographical constituency. That constituency is, after all, the closest thing to a "given" in his nest of perceptions. But home style is also partly a matter of individual choice. And in this respect, it can be affected by his perception of his other three constituencies. That, indeed, is what we expect to find as we move to discuss the other elements of home style.

HOME STYLE: PRESENTATION OF SELF

Most House members spend a substantial proportion of their working time "at home." Even those we placed in the "low frequency" category return to their districts more often than we would have guessed—over half of them go home more than once (but less than twice) a month.[24] What, then, do they do there? Much of what they do is captured by Erving Goffman's idea of *the presentation of self.*[25] That is, they place themselves in "the immediate physical presence" of others and then "make a presentation of themselves to others." A description of all the settings in which I have watched members of Congress making such presentations or "performances" as Goffman calls them, would triple the size of this article. But, surely, I have logged—during my thirty visits and ninety-three days in seventeen districts—nearly every circumstance concocted by the mind of man for bringing one person into the "immediate physical presence" of another.

In all such encounters, says Goffman, the performer will seek to control the response of others to him by expressing himself in ways that leave the correct impressions of himself with others. His expressions will be of two sorts, "the expression that he gives and the expression that he gives off." The first is mostly verbal; the second is mostly nonverbal. Goffman is particularly interested in the second kind of expression—"the more theatrical and contextual kind"—because he believes that the performer is more likely to be judged by others according to the nonverbal than the verbal elements of his presentation of self. Those who must do the judging, Goffman says, will think that the verbal expressions are more controllable and manipulable by the performer; and they will, therefore, read his nonverbal "signs" as a check, on the reliability of his verbal "signs." Basic to this reasoning is the idea that, of necessity, every presentation has a largely "promissory character" to it. Those who listen to and watch the presentation cannot be sure what the relationship between them and the performer really is. So the relationship must be sustained, on the part of those watching, by inference. They "must accept the individual on faith." In this process of acceptance, they will rely heavily on the inferences they draw from his nonverbal expressions—the expressions "given off."

Goffman does not talk about politicians; but politicians know what Goffman is talking about. Goffman's dramaturgical analogues are appropriate to politics because politicians, like actors, perform before audiences and are legitimized by their audiences. The response politicians seek from others is *political support.* And the impressions they try to foster are those that will engender political support. House member politicians believe that a great deal of their support is won by the kind of individual self they present to others, i.e., to their constituents. More than most people, they believe that they can manipulate their "presentation of self." And more than most other people, they consciously try to manipulate it. Certainly, they believe that what they say, their verbal expression, is an integral part of their "self." But, like Goffman, they place special emphasis on the nonverbal, "contextual" aspects of their presentation. At least, the nonverbal elements must be consistent with the verbal ones. At most, the expressions "given off" will become the basis on which they are judged. Like Goffman, members of Congress are willing to emphasize the latter because, with him, they believe that their constituents will more readily discount what they say than how they say it or how they act in the context in which they say it. In the member's own language, constituents want to judge you "as a person." The comment I have heard most often from the constituents of my representatives is: "He's a good man," or "She's a good woman," unembossed by qualifiers of any sort. Constituents, say House members, want to "size you up" or "get the feel of you" "as a person," or "as a human being." And the largest part of what members mean when they say "as a person" is what Goffman means by "expressions given off."

So members of Congress go home to present themselves "as a person"—and to win the accolade, "He's a good man," "She's a good woman." With Goffman, they know there is a "promissory character" to the presentation. And their object is to present themselves "as a person" in such a way that the inferences drawn by those watching will be supportive ones. The representative's word for these supportive inferences is *trust.* It is a word they use a great deal. If a constituent trusts a House member, the constituent says something like: "I am willing to put myself in your hands temporarily; I know you will have opportunities to hurt me—though I may not know when those opportunities occur; I assume that you will not hurt me and I'm not going to worry about your doing so until it is proven beyond any doubt that you have betrayed that trust." The ultimate response members of Congress seek is political support; but the instrumental response they seek is trust. The presentation of self—what is "given" in words and "given off" as a person—will be calculated to win trust. "If people like you and trust you as an individual," members often say, "they will vote for you." So trust becomes central to the congressman-constituent relationship. Constituents, for their part—as Goffman would emphasize—must rely on trust. They must "accept on faith" that the congressman is what he says he is and will do what he says he will do. House members, for their part, are quite happy to emphasize trust. It helps to allay the uncertainties they feel about their support relationship with their various constituencies. If they are uncertain about how to work for support directly, they can always work indirectly to win a degree of personal trust that will increase the likelihood of support, or decrease the likelihood of opposition.

Trust is, however, a fragile relationship. It is not an overnight or a one-time thing. It is hard to win; and it must be constantly renewed and rewon. So it takes an enormous amount of time to build and maintain constituent trust. That is what House members believe. That is why they spend so much of their working time at home. Much of what I have observed in my travels can be explained as a continuous and continuing effort to win (for new members) and to maintain (for old members) the trust of their various constituencies. Most of the communication I have heard and seen is not overtly political at all. It is, rather, part of a ceaseless effort to reinforce the underpinnings of trust in the congressman or congresswoman "as a person." Viewed from this perspective, the archetypical constituent question is not "what have you done for me lately" but "how have you looked to me lately." House members, then, make a strategic calculation that helps us understand why they go home so much. Presentation of self enhances trust; enhancing trust takes time; therefore, presentation of self takes time.

Of the "contextual," "expressions given off" in the effort to win and hold constituent trust, three seem particularly ubiquitous. First, the congressman conveys to his constituents a sense of his *qualification*. Contextually and verbally, he gives them the impression that "I am qualified to hold the office of United States representative." "I understand the job and I have the experience necessary to do a good job." "I can hold my own—or better—in any competition inside the House." All members try to convey their qualifications. But it is particularly crucial that any nonincumbent convey this sense of being "qualified." For him, it is the threshold impression—without which he will not be taken seriously as a candidate for Congress. Qualification will not ensure trust, but it is at least a precondition.

Second, the congressman conveys a sense of *identification* with his constituents. Contextually and verbally he gives them the impression that "I am one of you." "I think the way you do and I care about the same things you do." "You can trust me because we are like one another." The third is a sense of *empathy* conveyed by the congressman to his constituents. Contextually and verbally, he gives them the impression that "I understand your situation and I care about it." "I can put myself in your shoes." "You can trust me because—although I am not one of you—I understand you." Qualification, identification, and empathy are all helpful in the building of constituent trust. To a large degree, these three impressions are conveyed by the very fact of regular personal contact at home. That is, "I prove to you that I am qualified," or "I prove to you that I am one of you," or "I prove to you that I understand you" by coming around frequently "to let you see me, to see you, and to meet with you." Contrariwise, "if I failed to come home to see and be seen, to talk and be talked to, then you would have some reason to worry about trusting me." Thus do decisions about the allocation of resources affect the frequency of and opportunity for the presentation of self.

Once he is home, what kind of a presentation does he make there? How does he decide what presentation to make? How does he allocate his time among his perceived constituencies? How does he present himself to these various constituencies? What proportion of competence, identification, or empathy (or other expressions) does he "give off"? In short, what kinds of home styles are presented; and how do they differ among

House members? I shall work toward an answer to these questions by discussing the styles of two representatives.

Presentation of Self: A Person-to-Person Style

While it is probably true that the range of appropriate home styles in any given district is large, it is also probably true that in many geographical constituencies there are distinct limits to that range. Congressman A believes there is a good "fit" between his kind of district and his kind of home style. He thinks of his geographical constituency as a collection of counties in a particular section of his state—as southern, rural, and conservative. And he believes that certain presentations of self would not be acceptable there. "I remember once," he told a small group at dinner before a college lecture,

> when I was sitting in the House gallery with a constituent listening to Congressman Dan Flood speak on the floor. Dan is a liberal from Wilkes Barre, Pennsylvania. He is a former Shakespearian actor and his wife is a former opera singer. Dan was wearing a purple shirt and a white suit; and he was sporting his little waxed moustache. My constituent turned to me and asked 'what chance do you think a man like that would have of getting elected in our district?' And I said, 'exactly the same chance as I would have of getting elected in Wilkes Barre, Pennsylvania.'

The expressions "given off" by a former actor with a purple shirt, a white suit, and a waxed moustache would be suicidal in Congressman A's district. Indeed, two days earlier as we got out of the car in one of his county seats, Congressman A said apprehensively, "see my brown shirt? This will be the first time that these people have ever seen me in anything but a white shirt." Brown—possibly; purple—never.

Congressman A sees his geographical constituency as a homogeneous, natural community. And he thinks of himself as totally at one with that community, a microcosm of it. Three generations of his family have lived there and served as its leaders and officeholders. He himself held two elective offices within the district before running for Congress. He has been steeped in the area he represents.

> I should write a book about this district—starting with the Indians. It's a very historic district and a very cohesive district—except for Omega County. Nobody knows it like I do.
>
> One thing that ties the district together is the dominance of the textile industry and the dependence of the people of the district—employer and employee—on the textile industry. . . . If I were hostile to the textile industry, it would be fatal. But that could never happen because I feel so close to the textile industry.
>
> I represent a district in which my constituents and I have total mutual confidence, respect and trust—95 per cent, nearly 100 per cent.

Congressman A feels a deep sense of identification with his constituents. It is this sense of identification that he conveys—verbally and nonverbally—when he presents himself to them.

"In my state," he says, "only a person-to-person campaign will work." So, when he goes home, he "beats the bushes," and "ploughs the ground," in search of face-to-face contact with the people of his district. From county to county, town to town, up and down main street, in and out of county courthouses, through places of business, into homes and back yards, over country roads and into country stores, from early morning till late at night: ("Anyone who hears a knock on the door after 11:00 p.m. knows it's me") he "mixes and mingles" conveying the impression that he is one of them. In each encounter, he reaches (if the other person does not provide it) for some link between himself and the person he is talking with—and between that person and some other person. There is no conversation that does not involve an elaboration of an interpersonal web and of the ties that bind its members one to the other. In the forefront, always, are ties of family: Congressman A possesses an encyclopedic memory for the names and faces, dates and places of family relations, and for the life-cycle events of family—birth, marriage, moving, sickness, and death. His memory and his interest serve him equally well in finding other common ground—be it rivers, plants and trees, farms, crops and businesses, hunting, fishing and football, land, buildings and automobiles, home, church, and country. He devours the district's history; on one trip he was absorbed in a county history and genealogy, on another the memoirs of U.S. Grant. He continually files, sorts, arranges and rearranges his catalogues of linkages—person-to-person, place to place, event to event, time to time.

The Congressman muses a lot about the keys to success in person to person relationships.

> Do you remember Miss Sharp back in the post office? She had never met me before, but she called me Sam. That's the way people think of me. No person will ever vote against you if he's on a first name basis with you. Did you know that?
>
> When I'm campaigning I sometimes stop in a country store and buy some salmon and crackers and share them with everyone there—and buy more if need be. Do you know that a man who eats salmon and crackers with you will vote for you? And if a man takes a bite of your chewing tobacco—or better still if he gives you a bite of his chewing tobacco—he'll not only vote for you, he'll fight for you.
>
> People feel they can talk to me. When they are talking, they feel that I'm listening to what they have to say. Some people have the ability to make others feel that way and some don't. They feel that if they come to me with a problem, I'll do everything I can to help them.

The expression he tries to give off in all his person to person dealings is that he knows them, that they know him "as a person," that they are all part of the same community, and that his constituents, therefore, have every reason to make favorable inferences about him. "They know me," he says, "and they trust me."

Since he perceives his geographical constituency as a group of counties, it is natural to find him conveying this sense of identification in terms of counties. In three different counties—none of them his place of residence—he verbalized his relationship with the people who lived there as follows: Chatting with a group of businessmen riding to lunch after a meeting with the officials of Alpha County on water and sewer problems, he said,

> Did you know that an Alpha County man saved my grandfather's life in the Civil War? In the battle of Williamsville, my grandfather was badly wounded and Lieutenant Henry from Henryville picked him up and carried him off the field—just a bloody uniform with pieces of bone sticking out. An orderly stopped him and said, 'What are you doing carrying that corpse?' Lieutenant Henry said, 'That's no corpse; that's Captain McDonough; and so long as there's a spark of life in him, I'm going to try to save him.' He did and my grandfather lived. My roots go deep in Alpha County.

Giving an after dinner speech to the Women's Business and Professional Club of Beta County, he said,

> I feel as much at home in Beta County as I do any place on earth. I can't begin to describe to you the frustrations I feel when I see these crazy social experiments (in Washington).... These frustrations would make me a nervous wreck or worse if I could not come back home to be with you, my friends and neighbors, my supporters and my constituents. I come home to refresh my spirit and renew my strength, here in the heart of our district, where my family's roots go deep. To me, this truly is 'holy ground.'

Speaking to a sesquicentennial celebration in adjacent Gamma County, he began,

> I have never recognized the artificial boundaries that separate our two counties. I have felt as much at home in Gamma County—our county—among my friends and neighbors as if I had been born here, raised here, and lived here every day of my life.

Later that evening, he reflected on his appearance at the sesquicentennial, which he ranked as the most important event of my four-day visit. "When Marvin introduced me today and said that there weren't five people out there, out of 4000, who didn't know me, he was probably right. And those who don't know me think they do."

His repeated use of the term "at home" suggests that Congressman A perceives the people whom he meets as his primary constituency. When asked to describe "his very strongest supporters," he explained: "My strongest supporters are the people who know me and whom I have known and with whom I have communicated over the years . . . in my oldest counties, that means 30–40 years." He does not perceive his primary constituency in demographic terms but in terms of personal contacts. In a district seen as homogeneous there are few benchmarks for differentiation. And the one clear benchmark—race—is one he never mentions in public and only rarely in private. His primary constituents are the rural and small town whites who know him (or feel that they know him) personally. He seems to be, as he was once introduced, "equally at home with blue denim and blue serge, with rich folks and po' folks"—so long as the blue denim is nonunion. Standing around in a dusty, brown field swapping hunting jokes with a group of blue-collar friends and sitting in an antique-filled living room talking business with the president of a textile company rank equally high on his "at homeness" index. His primary constituency, as may be the case in homogeneous districts, is quite amorphous—as demographically amorphous as V. O. Key's classic "friends and neighbors" victory pattern. But it is sizeable enough and intense enough to have protected Congressman A, for a considerable number of terms, from any serious primary challenge.

Congressman A does not come home a lot, falling into our low-frequency category (0–23) of trips home. He spent eighty working days there in 1973. When he does, he spends most of his time where it is strategically profitable (and personally comfortable)—with his primary constituency. There, he reinforces his ties to the group of greatest importance to him in his traditionally one-party district. He explained, for example, why he took time out of a crowded Washington work week to fly home to the installation of officers of a Boy Scout Council.

> I wanted to make it because of who they were. They were Boy Scout leaders from six of my counties—the men who make scouting here a viable movement. They have given me some of my strongest support since I have been in politics. And they have never asked anything of me but to give them good government. So when they ask, I sure don't want to pass up the opportunity to meet with 90–100 of them. I knew about 90 percent of them. And the other 10 per cent I know now. Some of those I hadn't met were sons of men I had known.

The scout leaders, of course, want more from him than "good government." They want his time and his personal attention. And he, believing these to be the essence of his home style, happily obliges.

When he mentioned that he had also left Washington once to speak at a high school graduation, I asked whether a high-paid staff assistant in the district might relieve him of some of these obligations. (Some members in my group have just such an assistant who attends meetings "in the name of the congressman" when he cannot come.) Congressman A answered,

> It wouldn't work. People want to see the congressman—me. At the high school commencement exercises, I could have sent the most scholarly person I could find, to make a more erudite, comprehensive and scholarly exposition than I made. If I had done so, the people there wouldn't have enjoyed one bit of anything he said. And they would never have forgiven me for not being there.

He has a small district staff—three people, one full-time office. and one-half time office—and when he is home, he is as apt to pick up someone's personal problems and jot them down on the back of an envelope as he tours around as he is to find out about these problems from his district aides. Congressman A, at home, is a virtual one-man band. His home style is one of the hardest to delegate to others, and he has no inclination to do so.

He allocates relatively little of his time to his larger-re-election constituency. Omega County, singled out earlier as out of the district's mold, is not rural, is populated heavily by out-of-staters, and has experienced rapid population growth. Congressman A admits he does not feel "at home" there. Yet he still gets a sizeable percentage of Omega County's votes on grounds of party identification. He explained why he didn't spend time among these re-election constituents.

> It is so heterogeneous, disorganized, and full of factions. . . . I don't spend very much time there. Some of my good friends criticize me and say I neglect it unduly. And they have a point. But I can get 50 per cent of the vote without campaigning there at all; and I couldn't get more than 75 percent if I campaigned there all the time. If I did that, I would probably lose more votes than I gained, because I would become identified with one of the factions, and half the people would hate me. On top of that, I would lose a lot of my support elsewhere in the district by neglecting it. It's just not worth it.

There is another reason besides time costs and political benefits. It is that Congressman A's home style is totally inappropriate for Omega County, and he avoids the personal unpleasantness that would be involved in trying to campaign there. Strategically, Congressman A will accept any increment of support he can get beyond his primary constituency. ("The black people who know me know that I will help them with their problems.") But he allocates very little of his time to the effort.

Congressman A's presentation of self places very little emphasis on articulating issues. The congressman's own abilities and inclinations run to cultivating personal, face-to-face relationships with individuals. The greater the social, psychological, and physical distance between himself and others, the less he is at home, regardless of the situation. And he was clearly least "at home" at a college, in a lecture-plus-question-and-answer format. He accepts invitations of this sort to discuss issues. But he does nothing to generate such engagements; nor does he go out of his way to raise issues in his dealings with others at home. On the single occasion when he broke this pattern, he tested out his potentially controversial position with his primary constituents (i.e., the American Legion post in his home town), found it to be acceptable, and articulated it often thereafter. Congressman A's home style does, however, take place *within an issue context*. There is widespread agreement in the district, and very strong agreement within his primary constituency, on the major issues of race, foreign aid, government spending, and social conservatism. The district voted for George Wallace in 1968. Thus while Congressman A's home style is apparently issueless, it may depend for its very success on an underlying issue consensus.

There are, therefore, strategic reasons as well as personal reasons for Congressman A not to focus heavily on specific issues. To do so would be unnecessary and potentially divisive. Congressman A is protective of his existing constituency relations and will not want to risk alienating any of his support by introducing or escalating controversy of any kind. He is a stabilizer, a maintainer. And so, when asked to speak formally, he often responds with communitarian homilies. "I believe if ever there was a promised land, that land is America; and if ever there was a chosen people, those people are Americans." "If a man isn't proud of his heritage, he won't leave a heritage to be proud of. And that goes for his family, his community and his country." These utterances are not the secret of his success. But they do testify, again, to his continuing efforts to articulate a sense of community, to construct and reconstruct a web of enduring personal relationships and to present himself as totally a part of that web. If he gets into electoral difficulty, Congressman A will resort not to a discussion of "the issues," but to an increased reliance on his person-to-person home style. And, so long as his strategic perceptions are accurate, he will remain a congressman.

Presentation of Self: An Issue-Oriented Style

If Congressman B's geographical constituency places any constraints on an appropriate home style, he is not very aware of them. He sees his district as heterogeneous.

> It is three worlds; three very different worlds. . . . It has a city—which is an urban disaster. It has suburbs—the fastest growing part of the district. . . . It has a rural area which is a place unto itself.
>
> We spent all afternoon talking to the Teamsters in the city; and then we went to a cocktail party in a wealthy suburb. That's the kind of culture shock I get all the time in this district—bam! bam! bam!

The "three worlds" are not just different. They are also socially and psychologically separated from one another.

> Actually the people in the three worlds don't know the others are even in the district. They are three separate worlds. In the city, they call it the city district; in the rural area, they call it their district. And both of them are shocked when they are told that they each make up only one-quarter of the district.

The other half are the suburbs which are themselves very disparate. A few suburbs are linked to the city, most are not. Some are blue collar; others are affluent. Some are WASP; others are ethnic. The district is, then, perceived not only as diverse and artificial, but as segmented as well. The possibilities for an acceptable presentation of self would seem to be limitless.

Congressman B's past associations in the district do not incline him toward a style peculiar to any one of "the three worlds." His district ties are not deep; he is a young man who went to college, worked and got his political feet wet outside his district and his state. Nor are the ties strong; he grew up in a suburb in which he probably feels less "at home" ("We lost that stupid, friggin' town by 1000 votes last time.") than anywhere in the district. When he first thought about running, he knew nothing about the district. "I can remember sitting in the living room here, in 1963, looking at the map of the district, and saying to myself, 'X? Y? I didn't know there was a town called X in this district. Is there a town called Y?' I didn't know anything about the district." Furthermore, he didn't know any people there. "We started completely from scratch. I was about as little known in the district as anyone could be. In the city, I knew exactly two people. In the largest suburb, I didn't know a single person." He has (unlike Congressman A) absolutely no sense that "only a person like myself" can win in his district. Indeed, he thinks the opponent he first defeated was better suited to the district and should have won the election. "If I were he, I'd have beaten me." In terms of a geographical constituency and an individual's immersion in it, it is hard to imagine two more different perceptions of me-in-the-constituency than those of Congressman A and Congressman B.

Congressman B has not been in office very long. Not only did he begin from scratch, but he has been scratching ever since. He lost his first race for Congress; he succeeded in his second; and he now represents an objectively (and subjectively) marginal district. His entire career has been spent reaching out for political support. As he has gone about identifying and building first a primary and then a re-election constituency, he has simultaneously been evolving a political "self" and methods of presenting that "self" to them.

His earliest campaign promises were promises about the allocation of resources. He pledged to return to the district every week and to open three district offices, one in each of the "three worlds." These commitments about home style were contextually appropriate, if not contextually determined. For a candidate who neither knew nor was known in the district, pledges of attentiveness would seem almost mandatory. Furthermore, they allowed him to differentiate his proposed style from that of the incumbent—who was not very visible in the district and who operated one office there staffed by two people. Also, these pledges allowed him to embroider his belief that "a sense of distance has developed between the people and the government," necessitating efforts to "humanize" the relationship. And finally, his pledges gave him a lowest common denominator appeal based on style to a district with palpably diverse substantive interests. In 1973, Congressman B made thirty trips home, spent 109 working days there, operated three district offices and assigned one-half of his total staff of fourteen to the district. Promises have turned into style. "We have given the impression of being hardworking—of having a magic carpet, of being all over the place. It's been backbreaking, but it's the impression of being accessible."

Congressman B's actual presentation of self, i.e., what he does when he goes home, has evolved out of his personal interests and talents. He was propelled into active politics by his opposition to the Vietnam War. And his political impulses have been strongly issue-based ever since. He is severely critical of most of what has gone on in American public life for the last ten years. And he espouses a series of programmatic remedies—mostly governmental—for our social ills. He is contemptuous of "old line" politicians who are uninterested in issues and who campaign "by putting on their straw hats and going to barbeques." Riding to a meeting at which he was to address one of his aging town committees, he shouted, "We don't want any old pols or town committees. Give me housewives who have never been in politics before." Whereupon, he rehearsed the opening lines of "the speech I'd like to give" to the town committee. "It will be a stirring speech. 'My fellow political hacks. We are gathered together to find every possible way to avoid talking about the issues.'" This comment, together with his running mimicry of the "old pols," exemplifies what Goffman calls a performance in the "back region," i.e., behind the scenes where the individual's behavior is sharply differentiated from, and serves to accent, his presentation of self to the audience in the "front region."[26]

Congressman B presents himself in the "front region," i.e., in public, as a practitioner of an open, issue-based, and participatory politics. It was his antiwar stand particularly, and his issue-orientation generally that attracted the largest element of his primary constituency. These were the antiwar activists—young housewives, graduate students, and professionals—who created, staffed, and manned the large volunteer organization that became his political backbone. In the end, his volunteers became skilled in the campaign arts—organizing, coordinating, polling, canvassing, targeting, mailing, fund raising, scheduling, advancing, leafleting—even "bumper-stickering." "We organized and ran a campaign the likes of which people in this district had never seen. Neither party had done anything like it." Lacking a natural community to tie into and lacking any widespread personal appeal (or basis for such), Congressman B turned to the only alternative basis for building support—an organization. The "strongest supporters" in his organization did not support him because they knew him or had had any previous connection with him. The bond was agreement on the central issues and on the importance of emphasizing the issues. That agreement was the only "qualification" for the office that mattered to them.

Within this group, the sense of identification between candidate and supporters was nearly total. He was "one of them." They trusted him. And they, with some trade union help (especially financial), gave him a victory in his initial primary.

In reaching for broader electoral support, Congressman B has been guided, in addition to his commitment to "the issues," by a personal penchant for talking about them. That is, he is an exceptionally verbal person and he has evolved a suitably verbal home style. He places special emphasis on articulating, explaining, discussing, and debating issues. In each campaign (whether he be challenger or incumbent) he has pressed for debates with his opponent; and his assessment of his opponents focuses on their issue positions and their verbal facility. ("He's very conservative and, I understand, more articulate than the last guy. I felt sorry for him; he was so slow.")

In his first two campaigns the main vehicle for presenting himself to his prospective election-re-election constituency was "the coffee." He would sit in a living room or a yard, morning, afternoon, and evening (sometimes as often as eight or ten times each day) with one or two dozen people, stating his issue positions, answering their questions, and engaging in give and take. At the verbal level, the subject was substantive problems. But Congressman B knew that expressions "given off" were equally important.

> People don't make up their minds on the basis of reading all our position papers. We have twenty-six of them, because some people are interested. But most people get a gut feeling about the kind of human being they want to represent them.

Thus, his display of substantive knowledge and his mental agility at "the coffees" would help convey the impression that "as a human being" he was qualified for the office. And, not relying wholly on these expressions given off, he would remind his listeners, "No congressman can represent his people unless he's quick on his feet, because you have to deal with 434 other people—each of whom got there by being quick on his feet." Coffees were by no means the only way Congressman B presented himself. But it was his preferred method. "The coffees are a spectacular success. They are at the heart of the campaign." Strategically, they were particularly successful in the suburban swing areas of the district. But he tried them everywhere—even in the city, where they were probably least appropriate.

Once in office, he evolved a natural extension of the campaign coffee—a new vehicle which allowed him to emphasize, still, his accessibility, his openness and his commitment to rational dialogue. It is "the open meeting," held twice a year, in every city and town in the district—nearly 200 in each session of Congress. Each postal patron gets an invitation to "come and 'have at' your congressman." And, before groups of 4 to 300, in town halls, schools, and community centers, he articulates the issues in a question and answer format. The exchanges are informative and wide-ranging; they are punctuated with enthusiasm and wit. The open meetings, like the coffees, allow Congressman B to play to his personal strengths—his issue interests and his verbal agility. In the coffees, he was concerned with conveying threshold impressions of qualification, and his knowledge and status reinforce that impression in the open meetings. But in the open meetings, he is reaching for some deeper underpinnings of constituent trust. He does this with a presentation of self that combines identification and empathy. "I am not exactly one of you," he seems to tell them, "but we have a lot in common, and I feel a lot like you do." He expresses this feeling in two ways.

One expression "given" and "given off" in the open meetings is the sense that the give-and-take format requires a special kind of congressman and a special kind of constituency and involves them, therefore, in a special kind of relationship. In each meeting I attended, his opening remarks included two such expressions.

> One of the first pieces of advice I got from a senior member of my party was: "Send out lots of newsletters, but don't mention any issues. The next thing you know, they'll want to know how you vote." Well, I don't believe that.
>
> My colleagues in Congress told me that the questionnaires I sent you were too long and too complicated and that you would never answer it. Well, 5,000 have been filled out and returned already—before we've even sent them all out.

At the same time that he exhibits his own ability to tackle any question, explain any vote, and debate any difference of opinion, he massages the egos of his constitutents by indicating how intelligent, aware, and concerned they are to engage with him in this new, open, rational style of politics. At the conclusion of an emotional debate with a group of right-to-lifers, whose views he steadfastly opposed, he summed up: "I don't want to pat myself on the back, but there aren't too many congressmen who would do what I am doing here today. Most of them dig a hole and crawl in. I respect your opinions and I hope you will respect mine." The "pat on the back" is for *them* as well as him. And the expression "given off" is that of a special stylistic relationship. From that relationship, he hopes, will flow an increasing measure of constituent trust.

A second, related, expression "given off" is the sense that Congressman B, though he is a politician, is more like his constituents than he is like other politicians. It is not easy for him to convey such an impression, because the only thing his potential reelection constituents know about him is that he is a politician. They do not know him from any prior involvement in a community life. So he works very hard to bind himself to his constituents by disassociating himself from "the government" and disavowing his politician's status. He presents himself as an antipolitician, giving off the feeling that, "I'm just as fed up with government and the people who run it as you are." Since he is a congressman-politican, he is unrelentingly harsh in his criticism of Congress and his fellow legislators.

> As you know, I'm one of the greatest critics of Congress. It's an outrageous and outmoded institution.
>
> All Congress has ever done since I've been in Congress is pass the buck to the president and then blame him for what goes wrong. . . . Congress is gutless beyond my power to describe to you.
>
> Most members of Congress think that most people are clods. . . . Most of the guys down there are out of touch with their districts. . . . We aren't living in the 1930's anymore. Of course some members of Congress are. . . . I could never understand the lack of congressional sensitivity to the problems of the elderly. There are so many of them there.

A politician seeking to convey the impression that he is not a politician, Congressman B hopes to build constituent trust by inviting them to blend their cynicism with his.

The presentation of self—an accessible, issue-oriented, communicative antipolitician—at the open meetings is a lowest common denominator presentation. It can win support in each of "the three worlds" without losing support in any. For it is the style, not the issue content that counts most in the re-election constituency. Congressman B is completely comfortable in the setting. "That was fun," he says after each open meeting. And, occasionally, "it's more fun when there's some hostility." But it is the format more than the audience that makes him feel really "at home." He is not a person-to-person campaigner. "Two of my friends in Congress hold office hours and see people one at a time. That would be a horribly inefficient use of my time. I can see fifty at once. Besides, they don't want to get involved in a give and take." He, on the other hand, keeps his distance from the personal problems of his constituents, inviting them to talk with the staff members who accompany him to the open meetings. Of course, he meets people face-to-face—all the time.

But he does not know or seek out much about them as individuals, not much that would build anything more than a strictly political connection. An aptitude for names and faces, a facility with tidbits of personal information and small talk, an easy informality in face-to-face relations—these are not his natural personal strengths. But they are not the keys to his success with his re-election constituency. He has evolved a home style that does not call for person-to-person abilities in large supply.

The open meetings remain the centerpiece of his home style. "They are the most extraordinary thing we've ever done, and the most important." He sees them as vehicles which help him reach out to and expand his re-election constituency. For he remains a builder instead of a stabilizer in his constituency relations.

> Politically, these open meetings are pure gold. Fifty may come, but everybody in town gets an invitation. . . . I do know that none of our loyalists come to the meetings. They know the meetings are nonpartisan. Maybe one or two of them will show up, but mostly they are new faces.

They have given him entree into the least supportive, rural areas of his district, where he recruits support and neutralizes the more intense opposition. At first, he says, "in some of these towns they didn't know what to say to a Democrat. They probably hadn't met one except for people who fixed their toilets." Yet at the open meetings, "we've had better turnouts, proportionately, in the rural area." "And we get a lot of letters from people there who say they disagree with us but respect our honesty and independence." In time—but only in time—interest and respect may turn into the supportive inferences that connote trust.

But as Congressman B spends more and more of his time at home cultivating an expanding re-election constituency, his oldest and strongest supporters have felt neglected. So Congressman B has a more complex strategic problem, in terms of allocating his time, than Congressman A.

> When we began, we had the true believers working their hearts out. It was just like a family. But the more you gain in voters, and the more you broaden your constituency, the more the family feels hurt. Our true believers keep asking me. 'Why don't you drink with us?' 'Why don't you talk to me personally anymore?' I have to keep talking to them about the need to build a larger majority. I have to keep telling them that politics is not exclusive; it is inclusive. It is not something that can be done in the living room.

The true believers are not threatening a total loss of support; but declining enthusiasm would present a serious support problem. One way Congressman B may deal with the problem is to come home more, so that he can give the necessary time to the true believers. He does come home more than Congressman A, perhaps partly because his strategic problems at home require it. Still, Congressman B emphasizes identifying and building support beyond the primary constituency in the "the three worlds." And he finds the open meetings the most effective (and most comfortable) vehicle for him. "What more could anyone ask," he says, "than to have the congressman come to their town personally?" His primary constituents do ask something more. And, so long as he gives it to them, he will remain a congressman.

Presentation of Self: Constituency Constraints and Constituency Careers

Our description of the person-to-person and the issue-oriented styles is exemplary, not exhaustive.[27] Speculatively, however, presentation of self would seem to be explainable by three kinds of factors—*contextual, personal, and strategic.*

Contextually, a representative thinks about his constituency relations in terms of me-in-the-constituency. That perception predates his service in Washington and cannot be understood by drawing inferences from his Washington behavior. Part of the content of that perception involves a sense of fit—a good fit as in the case of Congressman A, a nonfit as in the case of Congressman B, and a bad fit as in the case of one congressman (not in my group) who refers to his district as "outer Mongolia." A congressman's sense of fit will, in turn, be affected by whether he sees the district as homogeneous or heterogeneous. Good fits are more likely in homogeneous districts. But the reverse side of the coin is that home styles are more likely to be imposed upon the congressman in homogeneous districts. If Congressman A did not represent his district, someone who performed similarly at home probably would. In a heterogeneous district—Congressman B's case—home style is much more a matter of individual choice, and is more likely to be imposed by the congressman on his district. Thus, upon further analysis of the state-by-state resource allocation data, we would expect to find the most idiosyncratic patterns appearing in the most heterogeneous districts. Homogeneous districts, in sum, impose more stylistic constraints on a congressman than do heterogeneous districts.

A second contextual impact on the presentation of self, however, may produce contrary tendencies. Once a congressman has imposed a particular presentational style upon his district, his successors may feel constrained to continue that style. That is, a congressman's home style may be influenced by the previous congressman's home style. Congressman B deliberately chose a style that contrasted with his predecessor's in order to help develop an identifiable political self. It is equally plausible (and it happened in my group) that expectations about style could be so strongly implanted in the district by a predecessor that the new congressman dare not change. Similarly, a choice of home style by imitation or by contrast can occur with reference to a neighboring congressman—if the congressman choosing a style has reason to believe that some of his constituents are likely to compare him to that neighbor. Regardless of district make-up, then, under certain conditions one congressman's style may be shaped by the style of another congressman, past or present.

From the cases of Representatives A and B, it seems clear that the presentation of self is also shaped by each individual's inclinations and talents. Every congressman has some latitude in deciding how to present himself "as a person." That is not to say that House members *like* to do all the things they do at home. More members than I would have expected described themselves as "shy," "reserved," or "not an extrovert." But they go home and present themselves anyway. And they try to do what they are most comfortable doing and try not to do that which they are most uncomfortable doing. Congressman A seeks out person-to-person relationships, but does not encourage issue-oriented meetings. Congressman B seeks out issue-oriented meetings, but does not encourage person-to-person relationships. Experience, interest, abilities—all the personal attributes of a congressman's self—help shape his presentation of that self to others.

Strategically, each congressman must decide how he will allocate his time when he is at home. And it is of some help to think of this strategic problem in terms of his perceived constituencies. From our two cases, we might generalize that a man in a homogeneous district will spend most of his time with his primary constituency. Homogeneous districts are most likely to be perceived as protected in the general election, so that the strategic problem is to hold sufficient primary constituency support to ward off a primary challenger. By the same token, the primary constituency in a homogeneous district is probably more amorphous and less easily defined than it is in a heterogeneous district. Thus a concentration of effort in the primary constituency does not mean that any less time will be required to cultivate it.

By contrast, in a district perceived to be both heterogeneous and electorally unprotected, the congressman will spend relatively more time in his re-election constituency. But he faces a problem of balance. He will play "the politics of inclusion" by spending time expanding his re-election constituency, partly on the assumption that his strongest supporters have no inclination to go elsewhere. Yet he cannot neglect the primary constituency unduly, since their loyalty and intensity of commitment are necessary to sustain a predictably difficult election campaign. He may, of course, be able to allocate resources other than his time, i.e., votes, to keep his primary constituency content.[28] But there is every evidence from my experience that the congressman's strongest supporters are more—not less—demanding of the congressman's time than his other constituencies.

A strategic problem in allocating time, alluded to briefly in discussing Congressman B, involves the presentation of self to one's strongest opponents—to the people each congressman believes he "will never get." House members handle the problem differently. But most of them will accept (and some will solicit) opportunities to present themselves before unfriendly constituents. The strategic hope is that displaying themselves "as a person" may reduce the intensity of the opposition, thus neutralizing their effect with the district. Intense opposition is what every congressman wants least of. Any time spent cooling the ardor of the opposition is time usefully spent, for it may mean less intense support for the challenger. Functionally, the same accents used in presenting one's self to supporters apply to a presentation to opponents—the emphasis on qualification, the effort at identification, the projection of empathy. In other words, the process of allaying hostility differs little from the process of building trust. That makes it easier for House members to allocate some time—probably minor—to a strategy of neutralization.

Students of Congress are accustomed to thinking about a congressman's *career in the House*—his early adjustments, his rise in seniority, his placement on the ladders of committee and party, the accumulation of his responsibilities, the fluctuations of his personal "Dow Jones Average." But House members also pursue a *career in the constituency.* Congressman B's evolution from "scratch" to a concern with his primary constituency to a concern with his re-election constituency gives evidence of such a constituency career. He was as much a newcomer in the district as newcomers are (or were) purported to be in the House. He had to work out an appropriate home style there just the way each new House member adapts to the House as an institution. Congressman B has been, and is, in the expansionist phase of his career, continually reaching out for increments of support. Congressman A, by comparison, is in a more protectionist phase of his constituency career. He believes that he has, over a considerable period of time, won the trust of his constituents (i.e., his primary constituents). He is working mainly to reinforce that trust, to protect the support he already has. Congressman B does not talk about constituent trust; he never says, "my constituents trust me." His presentation of self is designed to build trust, but, as we have said, it takes time.

The idea of a career in the constituency helps to highlight an important fact about the congressman as an elective politician. As any textbook treatment of incumbency tells us, the congressman is a particularly long-lived political species. He has been making or will make presentations of self to his constituents *for a long time.* And they have been looking at or will look at him "as a person" for a long time. Relative to politicians with briefer constituency careers

—like Presidents—a congressman's political support will depend especially heavily upon his presentation of self. That, of course, is precisely what House members themselves tell us whenever we have asked. They tell us that their "personal record and standing" or their "personalities" are more important in explaining their election than "issues" or "party identification."[29] They tell us, in other words, that their home style—especially their presentation of self—is the most important determinant of their political support. The idea of a lengthy constituency career helps us understand why this might be true. For it makes home style into a durable, consistent long term factor in congressional electoral politics. In any congressional electoral analyses patterned after our presidential electoral analyses, home style may have to be elevated to a scholarly status heretofore reserved only for party identification and issue voting.[30]

HOME STYLE: EXPLANATION OF WASHINGTON ACTIVITY

When members of Congress are at home, they do something that is closely allied with, yet separable from, the presentation of self to their constituencies. They explain what they have done in Washington. For some House members, their Washington activities are central to their presentation of self. One congressman, for example, routinely began every speech before every district group as follows:

> I have represented this district for the last twenty years. And I come to you to ask for a two-year renewal of my contract. I'm running because I have a twenty-year investment in my job and because I think you, as my constituents, have an investment in my seniority. In a body as large as the House of Representatives with 435 elected, coequal members, there has to be a structure if we're ever going to get anything done. And it takes a long time to learn that structure, to learn who has the power and to learn where to grease the skids to get something done. I think I know the structure and the people in the House better than any newcomer could. And I believe I can accomplish things for you that no newcomer could.

He wants his constituents to see him "as a person" in terms of his importance in Washington. By contrast, neither Congressman A nor Congressman B makes his Washington activity central to his presentation of self. But whether or not his behavior in Washington is central to his presentation of self, every House member spends some time at home explaining and justifying his Washington behavior to his various constituencies. He tells them what he has done and why. What he says, how he says it, and to whom can be viewed as a distinctive aspect of his home style.

The objective of every congressman's explanations—our usage of *explanation* incorporates the idea of *justification* as well—is political support. And just as a congressman chooses, subject to constraints, a presentational style, so too does he choose, subject to constraints, an explanatory style. When most people think of explaining what goes on in Washington to constituents, they think of explaining votes. But we should conceptualize the activities subject to explanation more broadly than that. A House member will explain any part of his activity in Washington if he thinks that part of his activity is relevant to the winning and holding of support at home. Just what kinds of behavior he thinks his various constituencies want or need to have explained to them is an empirical matter; but one which bulks especially large among my representatives is their effectiveness (or lack of it) inside the House on behalf of their constituencies. Often this explanation of one's internal influence also entails a more general explanation of the workings of Congress.

In the case of our Congressman A, for example, press reports that he had lost a committee assignment of importance to the district because of his lack of power within the House, posed a major explanatory problem.

> Nothing is more damaging to a congressman in his district than to have his constituents believe that he doesn't have the power to get something he wants of that nature. . . . It might have been the only issue in the next campaign. . . . That would have been all that was needed—and only that—to defeat me. . . . No one in the world would believe my explanation, so I had to try for the next vacancy on the committee and I had to win. [Which he did, before the next election.]

For Congressman A, that is, explaining his internal House influence (or lack of it) might be more crucial to protecting his home support than explaining his votes. "I worked my head off to get that building," he said, as we drove by a new federal building in one of his county seats. "The people here were fixing to run someone against me if I hadn't produced it. People think you just have to wave a magic wand to get an appropriation, when most of it is just standing in line waiting your turn." Obviously, such an explanation of "how Congress really works" would not have satisfied his constituents in that county. So he had to produce.

The range of possible activities requiring a home explanation extends well beyond voting. Still, voting is the Washington activity we most easily recognize; and we can make most of our comments in that context. From John Kingdon's splendid discussion of "explaining,"[31] we know that, at the time they decide to vote, House members are very aware that they may be called upon to explain their vote to some of their constituents. Moreover, says Kingdon, the anticipated need to explain influences their decision on how to vote. They may cast a certain vote only if and when they are convinced that they have a satisfactory explanation in hand. Or they may cast a certain vote because it is the vote least likely to require an explanation. Kingdon is interested in finding out why members of Congress vote the way they do. But along the way, he helps make the case for finding out why members of Congress explain the way they do. For, if the anticipated need to explain has the effect on voting that Kingdon suggests—i.e., if it makes voting more complicated and more difficult that it otherwise would be—then the act of explaining must be as problematical for House members as the act of voting. House members believe that they can win and lose constituent support through their explanations as well as through their votes. To them, therefore, voting and explaining are interrelated aspects of a single strategic problem. If that is the way House members see it, then it might be useful for political scientists to look at it that way, too—and to spend a little less of our time explaining votes and a little more of our time explaining *explanations.*

Members are, of course, called upon to vote much more often than they are called upon to explain. That is, they are never called upon to explain all their votes. Their uncertainty about which votes they will have to explain, however, leads them to prepare explanations for more votes than they need to, the need being enforced on them by dissatisfied constituents and, primarily, by the electoral challenger. The challenger, particularly, controls the explanatory agenda —or, better, tries to do so. All the uncertainty that the challenger produces for the perception of constituency, the challenger also brings to the problem of explanation.

Representatives will strike different postures regarding the need to explain. Some will explain their votes only when they feel hard pressed by constituents and/or challenger to do so. They will follow the congressional adage that "if you have to explain, you're in trouble." And their explanatory practices, if not their voting practices, will be calculated to keep them out of trouble. Other members bend over backward to explain every vote that any constituent might construe as controversial—sometimes well in advance of the vote. It is our hunch that the more issue-oriented a congressman's presentation of self, the more voluminous will be his explanations. Our Congressman B, for example, produces a heavy volume of explanation. "We have explained every difficult vote. Anyone who gives a twit about how I vote has the opportunity to know it. We have explained our votes on all the toughies." Given his presentational style, it is hard to see him adopting any other explanatory style. In both cases, the content of what he says is less important than the fact that he says it—i.e., than his style.

I shall resist the temptation to spell out all the possible relationships between the presentational and explanatory aspects of home style. But it seems obvious that they exist. We would, at the least, expect to find a "strain toward compatibility" operating between the two. And we would expect to find the presentation of self—as the centerpiece of home style—to be the more controlling aspect in the relationship. We would further expect both aspects of home style to be influenced by the same constituency constraints. For example, we would expect the broadest perception of me-in-the-constituency—the sense of fit the congressman has with his various constituencies, to underlie the choice of explanatory styles, just as it underlies the choice of presentational styles. A good illustration of this latter point lies outside my particular group of House members. It lies, instead, in the explanation of their historic impeachment vote by two members of the House Judiciary Committee.

In the face of extraordinary constituency interest, two Judiciary Committee Republicans took to statewide television and radio to explain their upcoming vote in favor of impeaching their own party's president. Representative Lawrence Hogan of Maryland cast his explanation heavily in terms of voting his individual conscience against the acknowledged wishes of many prospective constituencies—primary and re-election—in his announced try for the Maryland governorship. To accent his act of conscience, he acknowledged the grave risks to his career.

> I know that many of my friends, in and out of Congress, will be very displeased with me. I know that some of my financial contributors (who have staunchly supported Richard Nixon and me) will no longer support me. I know that some of my long-time campaign workers will no longer campaign for me. But to those who were my campaign workers back in my first campaign, I want to remind you of something. Remember, I was running for Congress as a Republican in an area that was registered 3–1 Democratic, and in an effort to convince Democrats that they should vote for me, a Republican, I quoted John F. Kennedy who said: 'Sometimes party loyalty demands too much.' Remember that? Well, those words have been coming back to haunt me in recent weeks. Clearly, this is an occasion when "party loyalty demands too much." To base this decision on politics would not only violate my own conscience, but would also be a breach of my own oath of office to uphold the Constitution of the United States. This vote may result not only in defeat in my campaign for governor of Maryland, but may end my future political career. But that pales into insignificance when weighted against my historic duty to vote as my conscience dictates.[32]

Representative William Cohen cast his explanation in terms of voting as the people of his state of Maine would vote if they were in his shoes. He did not say they were pressuring him to vote, but that he and they, as members of the same community, thought alike on fundamental matters.

> I have tried to put all of these events into the context of a political system that I know well, that of the State of Maine. I have asked myself some questions.
> What if the governor of Maine ordered his aides to keep a list of those people who supported his opponents? What if he tried to have the state treasurer's department conduct audits of those who voiced dissent? What if he ordered that state police to investigate those who were critical of his policies or speeches? What if he asked aides to lie before legislative committees and judicial bodies? What if he approved of burglaries in order to smear and destroy a man's credibility? What if he obtained information that was to be presented to a grand jury for the purpose of helping his advisors design a strategy for defense?
>
> What would the people of Maine say? You and I both know that the people of Maine

> would not stand for such a situation, for it is inconsistent with our principles and our constitutional system of government.[33]

Hogan and Cohen offered their listeners very different kinds of explanations for the same vote. It is our hunch that underlying the difference in their explanatory styles are different perceptions of me-in-the-constituency. Cohen sees himself, we would guess, as part of a fairly homogeneous re-election-plus primary constituency. He identifies strongly with it and he has a comfortable sense of fit with this broad constituency. That being so, he would neither perceive nor explain his vote in terms that set his conscience against theirs. His explanation was, therefore, communitarian. "I am one of you, and the issue is our conscience as a community." Hogan, we would guess, perceives his geographical constituency to be heterogeneous, and has no strong sense of fit with any large or differentiable element of it. Almost surely he feels uncertainty about his prospective statewide constituency; but it seems that he feels uncertainty, even, about his relationships with the primary constituency in his district. It is hard, therefore, for him to find any communitarian bases for explanation. His explanation was individualistic. "I am following my conscience and disregarding the opinions of my constituents."

Neither explanation is inherently "better" than the other. Each had an element of strategic calculation to it. That is, each man chose his words deliberately, and, presumably, neither wanted to lose the next election by virture of his explanation. That being the case, the acceptability of the two explanations by the Maryland and Maine constituencies becomes a question of some moment. We lack sufficient information to assess the actual impact of the two explanations on each man's political support. But we can try a more general answer. To the degree that Maryland voters already perceived Hogan to be "a man of conscience," and to the degree that Maine voters already perceived Cohen to be "one of us," their explanations probably would have been accepted. On the other hand, to the degree that Maryland voters had already come to view Hogan as a self-serving opportunist, and to the degree that Maine voters had already come to view Cohen as a spineless follower of the herd, their explanations probably would not have been accepted. That is, the credibility of any given explanation probably depends less on the content of the explanation itself than on its compatibility with some previously established perception of the explainer "as a person." "Issues" said one member, "are not as important as the treatment of issues."

Their reasoning goes something like this: There probably are, in every district, one or two issues on which the congressman is constrained in his voting by the views of his re-election constituency. (Whether he *feels* constrained—which depends on whether or not he agrees with those constituent views—is beside the point.) But on the vast majority of votes, a congressman can do as he wishes—provided only that he can, if and when he needs to, explain his vote to the satisfaction of interested constituents. The ability to get his explanations accepted at home, is then, the essential underpinning of his voting leeway in Washington. Thus the question arises, how can the congressman act so as to increase the likelihood that his explanations will be accepted at home. And the answer the House members give is: he can win and hold constituent trust. The more your various constituencies trust you, House members reason, the less likely they are to require an explanation of your votes and the more likely they are to accept your explanation when they do require it. The winning of trust, we have said earlier, depends largely on the presentation of self. Presentation of self, then, not only helps win votes at election time; it also makes voting in Washington easier. So Congressmen make a strategic calculation. Presentation of self enhances trust; trust enhances the acceptability of explanations; the acceptability of explanations enhances voting leeway; therefore, presentation of self enhances voting leeway.

When I asked Congressman C if he wasn't more liberal than his district, he said:

> Hell, yes, but don't quote me on that. It's the biggest part of my problem— to keep people from thinking I'm a radical liberal. How do you explain to a group of Polish Catholics why you voted to abolish the House Internal Security Committee or why you voted against a bill to keep Jane Fonda from going to North Vietnam? How do you explain that? You can't.

When queried, later, on a TV interview to comment on his opponent's charge that he was "ten times more radical than George McGovern," Congressman C answered in terms of identification and trust. He said simply, "if he means by that that I'm some kind of wild-eyed radical, people around here know me better than that." Later still, he mused out loud about how he managed this problem.

> It's a weird thing how you get a district to the point where you can vote the way you want to without getting scalped for doing it. I guess you do it in two ways. You come back here a lot and let people see you, so they get a feel for you. And, secondly, I go out of my way to disagree with people on specific issues. That way, they know you aren't trying to snow them. And when you vote against their views, they'll say, "Well, he's got his reasons." They'll trust you. I think that's it. If they trust you, you can vote the way you want to and it won't hurt.

A pair of examples from two different types of districts will illustrate variations on this theme.

Congressman D perceives his urban, predominantly black district to be homogeneous. His re-election constituency is "the whole black community"; and his primary constituency consists of the civic-minded, middle-class activists who have organized black politics in his city. As tends to be the case in homogeneous districts, the line between his re-election and his primary constituencies is not sharp. Congressman D, who was born, raised, and employed in his district, sees himself as a microcosm of both groups. Voting in Congress, therefore, is rarely problematical for him. "I don't have any trouble knowing what the black community thinks or wants. . . . I don't have any trouble voting. When I vote my conscience as a black man, I vote right for the district." Though he does not feel constrained, he, of course, is. "If I voted against civil rights legislation, my people would probably ask me why I did that. But I never would do it." On one occasion when it might have looked to them as though he had, he explained and they were satisfied.

> When I come home, I go to the church groups and tell them what's been going on in Washington and explain to them why I voted as I did. For instance, I explained to them that I voted against the Voting Rights Bill (1970) because it was a fraud. Nixon wanted to get the fifty-seven Registrars working in the South out of there. After they heard me on the Voting Rights Bill, they went home mad. I know my people will agree with me.

Congressman D falls in the "medium frequency" category in trips home, having made thirty such trips in 1973. "I meet with church groups and other groups; and I let people see me just to let them know I haven't lost touch with them." The "other group" with which he meets most frequently (once a month formally and more often informally) is his district's political organization—"my political lifeline." "The more people see me working for them in our organization, the more popular I become, the more they trust me and are proud of me." From this presentation of self comes, then, the essential condition for his voting leeway in Washington.

> The fact is that I have the freedom to do almost anything I want to do in Congress and it won't affect me a bit back home. My constituents don't know how I vote, but they know me and they trust me. . . .They say to themselves, "Everything we know about him

tells us he's up there doing a good job for us." It's a blind faith type of thing.

Congressman E describes his district as "heterogeneous—one-third urban, one-third suburban, one-third rural." His primary constituency is the rural area, where three generations of his family have lived. At the very moment we turned off a four-lane highway onto a back road on our way to a small town fair, he said,

> It must be terrible to be without roots, without a place to call home. I have a profound sense of identification with these rural people. My wife still worries about me a little bit in this respect—that I'm too much of a country boy. But life's too short to play a role or strike a pose. This will be fun. I'm really going to enjoy myself.

Not only is he clearly most "at home" in the rural part of the district, but it casts a strategically disproportionate 40 percent of his party's primary vote. "If these city people (in my party) with their slick city ways think they could go out to Mrs. O'Leary's cow pasture and get the farmers to throw out the local boy, they're crazy." His presentation of self is skewed toward his primary constituency. During his 35 trips and 100 working days at home in 1973, his scheduled appearances were allocated as follows: 41 in the urban area, 38 in the suburban area and 70 (or about 50 per cent) in the rural one-third of the district. His accessibility—especially to his primary constituency—is the essence of his presentational style and, hence, he believes, the basis for constituent trust.

> Sometimes I do my talking to the same people over and over again. But they talk to others and they speak favorably about me. They tell others that 'old George' is always available and accessible. And I get a reputation in that way. That's how I succeed in this kind of district. People think of me as a nice guy, one of the boys, and they make presumptions in my favor because I'm a nice guy.

It is sometimes argued that representatives from heterogeneous districts enjoy a special degree of voting leeway because no single constituency interest controls their electoral future. Congressman E makes this argument. When asked if any single vote could defeat him in his district, he replied, "No, not in my district. It's too diverse, not all urban ghetto or Idaho potato farmers. That gives me a chance to balance interests in my votes. There really aren't any dominant interests." The crucial extra ingredient in the argument—one usually left out—is this: The congressman must be able to explain his voting pattern to his constituencies and have that explanation accepted. And this is especially true as regards his primary constituency. Congressman E commented,

> If I want to vote for an urban program, I can do it, and the people in the rural area will say, "He does have an urban constituency and he has to help them, too." And they will still vote for me so long as they think I'm a nice fella. But if I had no urban constituents—if I had all countryside—and I voted for an urban program, people in the rural areas would say, "He's running for governor, he's forgotten who his friends are." The same is true in the urban area. They know I'm a country boy and that I have a lot of rural area. So they say, "He gives us a vote once in a while; he's probably all right."

Congressman E is not unconstrained. He would, he admits, lose his primary constituency if he voted consistently for urban programs.[34] He will also lose his primary constituency if they stop trusting him as "a nice fella" and no longer make "presumptions in my favor" when he explains his few urban votes. If we are to understand a congressman's voting patterns in Washington, it seems that we must also understand his presentational and explanatory patterns at home.

As a final note, two general patterns of explanation deserve mention. One I had expected to find but have not, and one I had not expected to find but have. Both invite further research. In view of the commonly held notion that elective politicians "talk out of both sides of their mouths" (which Goffman discusses in terms of performances before "segregated audiences"),[35] I had expected to find members of Congress explaining their activity somewhat differently to their various constituencies. The likelihood seemed especially strong in heterogeneous districts, where the opportunity and temptation would be greatest. But I have found little trace of such explanatory chameleons in my travels. The House members I observed give the same explanations for their Washington activity before people who disagree with them as before people who agree with them—before nonsupporters as well as supporters, from one end to the other in the most segmented of districts. The lack of this kind of demagoguery, and the patient doggedness with which members explained their activities to unsympathetic audiences surprised me. I do not mean they went out of their way to find disagreement (though such a practice is of central importance to the presentation of self in some cases—such as Congressman C). I only mean that when disagreement was present, members offered the same explanation for their vote that they offered under all other conditions. Their presentation of self may vary from group to group in the sense that the basis for demonstrating identification or empathy will have to differ from group to group. As they reach out to each group in a manner appropriate to that group, they may take on some local coloration; and they may tailor their subject matter to fit the interests of their audience. However, they rarely alter their explanations of their Washington activity in the process.

An explanatory pattern I had not expected to find was the degree to which the congressman at home explains his Washington activity by disassociating it from the activity of his colleagues and of Congress as a whole. I had assumed that home styles would be highly individualized. And I should not have been surprised, therefore, when I heard every one of my seventeen members introduced at home as "the best congressman in the United States." But I was not prepared to find each of them polishing this individual reputation at the expense of the institutional reputation of the Congress.[36] In explaining what he was doing in Washington, every one of my House members took the opportunity to portray himself as "different from the others"—the others being "the old chairmen," "the inexperienced newcomers," "the tools of organized labor," "the tools of big business," "the fiscally irresponsible liberals," "the short-sighted conservatives," "the ineffective leadership," "the obstructionist minority," "those who put selfish concerns before country," and so on. The diversity of the House provides every member with plenty of collegial villains to flay before supportive constituents at home. Individual members do not take responsibility for the performance of Congress; rather each portrays himself as a fighter against its manifest shortcomings. Their willingness, at some point, to stand and defend their votes contrasts sharply with their disposition to run and hide when a defense of Congress is called for. Congress is not "we"; it is "they." And members of Congress run *for* Congress by running *against* Congress. Thus, individual explanations carry with them a heavy dosage of critical commentary on Congress.

Conclusion: Political Support, Home Style, and Representation

"A congressman has two constituencies," Speaker Sam Rayburn once said. "He has his constituents at home and he has his colleagues here in the House. To serve his constituents at home, he must serve his colleagues here in the House." For over twenty years, political scientists have been researching the "two constituencies." Following the thrust of Rayburn's comment, we have given lopsided attention to the collegial constituency on Capitol Hill. And we have neglected the constituency at home. Knowing less than we might about one of the two constituencies, we cannot know all that we should about the linkage between them. This paper argues for opening up the home constituency to more political science investigation than it has received. It suggests that students of Congress pay more attention to "home" as a research focus and research site. No one can say what we might learn if the suggestion were heeded. But a few speculations will serve as a conclusion to this exploratory effort.

For one thing, it appears that a congressman's constituency is more complicated than our normal treatment of it in our literature suggests. We have not, of course, obtained a constituent's-eye view of the constituency, having tried to keep the congressman's perceptions as our sole vantage point. But from that vantage point alone, it seems that we must be more precise about what we mean by "his (or her) constituents." If we are going to continue to talk in the language of role orientations—in which the "trustee's" votes are not determined by his constituents, and in which the "delegate" does follow the wishes of his constituents—we shall have to know just which "constituents" we (and he) are talking about. If we are going to continue to do survey research—in which we match the attitudes of the congressman with the attitudes of his constituents, or with his perceptions of the attitudes of his constituents—we shall, again, have to know just what "constituents" we (and he) are talking about. The abstraction "his (or her) constituents" is only slightly more useful as an analytical variable than the abstraction "the people." It may be that the distinctions attempted here are not the most useful ways of dividing up the home constituency for analytical purposes. But the days when our literature acknowledges the complexities of politics on Capitol Hill while accepting the most simplistic surrogates for political reality at home—those days ought to be numbered.

While this article has not dwelled directly on the topic of representation, our exploration has implications for the family of questions, both descriptive and normative, raised by studies of representation. For people studying the conditions of electoral accountability, this study has something to say about the electoral accountability of members of Congress. They are not among Kenneth Prewitt's "volunteerists."[37] House members work hard to get the job and work hard to keep it. In the course of that effort, they expend a great deal of time and effort keeping in touch with their various constituencies at home. Furthermore, they feel much more uncertain, insecure, and vulnerable electorally than our objective measures reveal. When a congressman describes his seat as "safe," he implicitly adds: "because, and so long as, I work actively to keep it so." And many a House retirement decision is made in anticipation of electoral difficulty. Surely, then, some of the necessary conditions for electoral accountability are present in Congress as they are not in certain other representative bodies in this country. But the existence of such conditions does not, by itself, tell us whether House members are as responsive to constituent desires as democratic theory may require. Our study can provide, however, some perspectives with which to pursue this normative inquiry.

For example, it appears that members of Congress feel a good bit more accountable—and, hence, I would guess, are more responsible—to some constituents than to others. House members feel more accountable to some constituents than to others because the support of some constituents is more important to them than the support of others. Thus, the process by which people become and remain representatives is closely related to their activity while they are representatives. In a representative democracy, the process is electoral; and the central problem for the representative is that of winning and holding voter support. From the viewpoint of this paper, problems of representation and problems of support are inseparable. It is precisely because a congressman's right to represent depends on his cultivation of electoral support that he develops such a complex and discriminating set of perceptions about his constituents. In a representative democracy, the representative learns who his, or her, various constituencies are by campaigning for support among them. The one deficiency in Hanna Pitkin's splendid book is the undifferentiated, uncomplicated idea of the constituency which she employs in her study of representation.[38] And her monolithic view of "the constituency" remains viable only because she separates the process of running for office from the problems of representation. The traditional view of representation is somewhat more static and structural than the process-oriented view one gets by focusing on the cultivation of constituent support. To the congressman, the very word "political" connotes the ongoing problem of support. A "political vote" is one calculated to win (or to avoid losing) support. A "politically unwise move" is one that will lose support, etc. Focusing on the problem of support keeps the dynamism and the politics in the subject of representation. If politics is about "who gets what, when, and how," then the politics of representative democracy is about "who supports whom, when, and how—and how much." And, "what do various constituencies get in return for their support?"

A more inclusive, process-oriented view of representation has the effect of making it less exclusively a policy-centered subject. Traditionally, representation has been treated mostly as a structural relationship in which the congruence between the policy preferences of the represented and the policy decisions of the representative is the measure of good representation. The question we normally ask is: "How well does Representative X represent his or her district?" And we answer the question by matching and calibrating substantive policy agreement. But our view here is that there is an intertwining question: "How does Representative X carry his or her district?" To answer that question, we shall need to consider more than policy preferences and policy agreements. We shall need to consider the more encompassing subject of home style and constituent trust generated by home style. We shall need to entertain the possibility that constituents may want good access as much as good policy from their representative. They may want "a good man" or "a good woman" whom they judge on the basis of home style and whom they trust to be a good representative in terms of policy. Indeed, the growing political science literature on voter behavior in congressional elections contains both evidence and speculation—usually under the rubric of the rising pro-incumbent vote—that voters are looking increasingly to just such candidate-centered bases for tendering electoral support.[39] The point is not that policy preferences are not a crucial basis for the representational relationship. They are. The point is that we should not start our studies of representation by assuming they are the *only* basis for a representational relationship. They are not.

This last comment may be as valid normatively as it is empirically. What reason is there to believe that a relationship based on policy is superior to one based on home style—of which policy is, at most, only a part—as a normative standard for representative democracy? It may be objected that a search for support that stresses stylistic compatibilities between the representative and the represented easily degenerates into pure image-selling. And, of course, it may. But the search for support that emphasizes policy compatibilities between the representative and the represented easily degenerates into pure position-taking. It is, perhaps, the signal contribution of David Mayhew's elegant essay to make exactly this point.[40] Position taking is just as misleading to constituents and as manipulative of their desires as image selling. Both representational bases, we conclude, may take a corrupt form. Appearing to do something about policy without a serious intention of, or demonstrable capacity for, doing so is no less a corruption of the representative relationship, no less an impediment to accountability and responsiveness than is the feigning of a personal relationship without a serious intention of establishing one. They are equally corrupt, equally demagogic. They are substitutes for any real effort to help make a viable public policy or to establish genuine two-way communication and trust. At the least, normative theory ought to take account of both policy and extra-policy standards of good representation, and acknowledge their respective corruptions.

Our concentration on and our preference for the policy aspects of representation carries a related implication. For a people who profess an attachment to representative democracy, we have always seemed curiously uncomfortable when our representatives devote themselves to contact with their constituents. We tend to denigrate the home part of the representational process as mere "errand-running" or "fence-mending" and to assume that it takes the representative away from that which he, or she, really should be doing, i.e., making public policy in Washington. As one small example, we have always criticized, out of hand, the "Tuesday to Thursday Club" of House members who go home for long weekends—on the assumption, presumably, that going home was *ipso facto* bad. But we never inquired into what they did at home or what the consequences (other than their obvious dereliction of duty) of their home activity might have been. Predictably, the home activities described in this paper will be regarded, by some, as further evidence that members of Congress spend too little of their time "on the job." But this paper asks that we entertain the alternate view that the Washington and the home activities can be mutually supportive. Time spent at home can be time spent developing leeway for activity undertaken in Washington. And it may be that leeway in Washington should be more valued than the sheer number of contact hours spent there. It may be, then, that the congressman's effectiveness in Washington is vitally influenced by the pattern of support he has developed at home and by the allocational, presentational, and explanatory styles he displays there. To put the point most strongly, perhaps we cannot understand his Washington activity without first understanding his perception of his constituencies and the home style he uses to cultivate their support.

No matter how supportive of one another their Washington and home activities may be, House members still face constant tension between them. Members cannot be in two places at once. They cannot achieve legislative competence and maintain constituency contact, both to an optimal degree. The tension is not likely to abate. The legislative workload and the demand for legislative expertise are growing. And the problems of maintaining meaningful contact with their several constituencies—which may make different demands upon them—are also growing. Years ago, House members returned home for months at a time to live with their supportive constituencies, soak up the home atmosphere, absorb local problems at first hand. Today, they race home for a day, a weekend, a week at a time. The citizen demand for access, for communication, for the establishment of trust is as great as ever. The political necessity and the representational desirability of going home is as great as ever. So members of Congress go home. But the quality of their contact has deteriorated. It is harder to sustain a genuine two-way relationship—of a policy or an extra-policy sort—than it once was. They worry about it and as they do, the strain and frustration of the job increases. Many cope; others retire. Indeed, retirements from the House appear to be increasing. Political scientists do not know exactly why.[41] But the research reported in this article points to the possibility that an inability or an unwillingness to improve the quality of the home relationship may be a contributing factor. Those who cannot stand the heat of the home relationship may be getting out of the House kitchen. If so, people prepared to be more attentive to home are likely to replace them. Thus, our focus on home activity may help us understand some changing characteristics of House members.

Our professional neglect of the home relationship has probably contributed to a more general neglect of the representational side of Congress's institutional capabilities. At least it does seem to be the case that the more one focuses on the home activities of its members, the more one comes to appreciate the representative strengths and possibilities of Congress. Congress *is* the most representative of our national political institutions.[42] It mirrors much of our national diversity, and its members maintain contact with a variety of constituencies at home. While its representative strengths surely contribute to its deserved reputation as our slow institution, the same representative strengths give it the potential for acquiring a reputation as our fair institution. In a period of our national life when citizen sacrifice will be called for, what we shall be needing from our political institutions are not quick decisions, but fair decisions. Some of the recent internal congressional reforms have increased the potential for both representativeness and fairness. They have increased the equality of representation by distributing influence more broadly inside Congress. They have increased the visibility of representation by opening up congressional proceedings to public view. This is by no means all that is needed. But it is enough to place an added obligation on the members of Congress to educate their constituencies in the strengths as well as the weaknesses of the institution. Members should participate in consensus building in Washington; they should accept some responsibility for the collective performance of Congress; and they should explain to their constituents what an institution that is both collective and fair requires of its individual members.

The evidence of this study indicates that members have the leeway to educate their constituents if they have the will to do so. The evidence of this study also shows that they may not have that will. Instead, they often seek support and trust for themselves by encouraging a lack of support and trust in the Congress. By refusing to accept responsibility for an institutional performance, they simultaneously abdicate their responsibility to educate their constituents in the work of the institution. Instead of criticizing House members for going home so much, we should criticize them for any failure to put their leeway to a constructive purpose —during the legislative process in Washington and during the explanatory process at home. The trust of his, or her, supportive constituents should be viewed by a House member as his, or her, working capital—not just to be hoarded for individual benefit but to be drawn on, occasionally, for the benefit of the institution. So long as House members explain themselves but not the institution, they help sustain (wittingly or unwittingly) the gap between a 10 percent approval level for Congress and a 90 percent re-election record for themselves. If this imbalance seems unhealthy for both Congress and the Republic, we have yet another justification for an increased scholarly attentiveness to our House members at home.

Reading 8.2

Introduction to Interest Groups

Bundett A. Loomis
and Allan J. Cigler

The American political system is best thought of as a "pluralistic" or "interest-group" democracy. With a comparatively weak political party system, interest groups have emerged in modern times as major intermediaries between the governed and government. Interest-group politics carry both strengths and weaknesses into the U.S. policy process. The good is that such groups and their lobbyists provide a major source of communication and input to representatives from the represented, affording a sense of participatory democracy. The bad is that they frequently convey highly distorted and particularistic demands. The interest-group environment has drastically changed over the past two decades, with major implications for the U.S. Congress. The following introduction to a major study of U.S. interest groups focuses on this changing interest-group environment.

From James Madison to Madison Avenue, political interests have played a central role in American politics. That is a great continuity in our political experience, as is the ambivalence with which citizens, politicians, and scholars have approached interest groups. James Madison's warnings on the dangers of faction echo in the rhetoric of reformers ranging from Populists and Progressives near the turn of the century to contemporary "public interest" advocates.

If organized special interests are nothing new in American politics, can today's group politics be seen as changing in fundamental ways from the past? Acknowledging that many important, continuing trends do exist, we seek to place in perspective a broad series of changes in the modern nature of interest group politics.

Among the most substantial of these changes are:

1. A great proliferation of interest groups since the early 1960s,
2. A centralization of group headquarters in Washington, D.C., rather than New York City or elsewhere,
3. Major technological developments in information processing that promote more sophisticated, timely, and specialized grassroots lobbying,
4. The rise of single-issue groups,
5. Changes in campaign finance laws (1971; 1974) and the ensuing growth of political action committees (PACs),
6. The increased formal penetration of political and economic interests into the bureaucracy (advisory committees), the Presidency (White House group representatives), and the Congress (caucuses of members),
7. The continuing decline of political parties' abilities to perform key electoral and policy-related activities,
8. The increased number, activity, and visibility of so-called "public interest" groups, such as Common Cause, and the Ralph Nader-inspired public interest research organizations.

All these developments have their antecedents in previous eras of American political life; there is little genuinely new under the interest group sun. Political action committees replace (or complement) other

Source: From Bundett A. Loomis and Allen J. Cigler, *Interest Group Politics*, pp. 1–7.

forms of special-interest campaign financing. Group-generated mail directed at Congress has existed as a tactic since at least the early 1900s.[1] Many organizations have long been centered in Washington, D.C., members of Congress have traditionally represented local interests, and so on.

At the same time, the level of group activity, coupled with growing numbers of organized interests, leads us to see contemporary group politics as distinct from the politics of earlier eras. Current trends of group involvement lend credence to the fears of scholars such as political scientist Theodore Lowi and economist Mancur Olson, who view interest-based politics as contributing to governmental immobilism and reduced accountability.[2] If accurate, these analyses point to a fundamentally different role for interest groups than those suggested by Madison and later group theorists.

In addition, several contemporary studies, such as those by Olson and political scientists Robert Salisbury and Terry Moe, illustrate the weakness of much interest group analysis that does not adequately account for the reasons groups form and persist.[3] Only during the last 20 years, in the wake of Olson's path-breaking research, have scholars begun to examine realistically why people join and become active in groups. It is by no means self-evident that citizens should naturally become group members—quite the contrary, in most instances. We are faced, then, with the paradoxical and complex question of why groups have proliferated, as they certainly have, when it is economically unwise, ordinarily, for individuals to join them.

The agenda for students of interest groups is full. New groups, ranging from computer software associations to Moral Majority, have formed while existing groups, such as the Chamber of Commerce, the Sierra Club, and the National Rifle Association, have become increasingly sophisticated and aggressive.

INTEREST GROUPS IN AMERICAN POLITICS

Practical politicians and scholars alike generally have concurred that interest groups (also known as factions, pressure groups, and special interests) are natural phenomena in a democratic regime. That is, individuals will band together to protect their interests.[4] If it is thus agreed that, in Madison's words, "the causes of faction . . . are sown in the nature of man," controversy continues as to whether groups and group politics are benign or malignant forces in American politics. "By a faction," Madison wrote,

> I understand a number of citizens, whether amounting to a majority or minority of the whole, who are united and actuated by some common impulse of passion, or of interest, adverse to the rights of other citizens, or to the permanent and aggregate interests of the community.[5]

Although Madison rejected the remedy of direct controls over factions as "worse than the disease," he saw the need to limit their negative effects by promoting competition among them and by devising an elaborate system of procedural "checks and balances" to reduce the potential power of any single, strong group, whether representing a majority or minority position.

Hostility toward interest groups became more virulent in an industrialized America, where the great concentrations of power that developed far outstripped anything Madison might have imagined. After the turn of the century, many progressives railed at various monopolistic "trusts" and intimate connections between interests and corrupt politicians. Later, in 1935, Hugo L. Black, then a senator (and later a Supreme Court justice), painted a grim picture of group malevolence:

> Contrary to tradition, against the public morals, and hostile to good government, the lobby has reached such a position of power that it threatens government itself. Its size, its power, its capacity for evil, its greed,

> trickery, deception and fraud condemn it to the death it deserves.[6]

Similar sentiments remain intact today. Many citizens, journalists, and reformers continue to view interest groups with great suspicion, especially in light of PAC contributions to escalating campaign expenditures. By October 1982, for example, PAC spending in the 1982 elections had already surpassed by 60 percent the total PAC contributions to 1980 campaigns. One typical expression of dismay comes from Common Cause, the self-styled public interest lobby:

> The special Interest State is a system in which interest groups dominate the making of government policy. These interests legitimately concentrate on pursuing their own immediate—usually economic—agendas, but in so doing they pay little attention to the impact of their agendas on the nation as a whole.[7]

Despite the considerable popular distrust of interest group politics, political scientists and other observers have often viewed groups in a much more positive light. This perspective also draws upon Madison's *Federalist* writings, but it is more tied to the growth of the modern state. Political science scholars, such as Arthur Bentley, circa 1910, and David Truman, 40 years later, place groups at the heart of politics and policy making in a complex, large, and increasingly specialized governmental system. The interest group becomes an element of continuity in a changing political world. Truman notes the "multiplicity of co-ordinate or nearly co-ordinate points of access to governmental decisions," and concludes that

> The significance of these many points of access and of the complicated texture of relationships among them is great. This diversity assures various ways for interest groups to participate in the formation of policy, and this variety is a flexible, stabilizing element.[8]

Derived from Truman's work, and that of other group-oriented scholars, is the notion of the pluralist state in which competition among interests, in and out of government, will produce policies roughly responsive to public desires, and no single set of interests will dominate. As one student of group politics summarizes,

> Pluralist theory assumes that within the public arena there will be countervailing centers of power within governmental institutions and among outsiders. Competition is implicit in the notion that groups, as surrogates for individuals, will produce products representing the diversity of opinions that might have been possible in the individual decision days of democratic Athens.[9]

In many ways the pluralist vision of American politics corresponds to the basic realities of policy making and the distribution of policy outcomes, but a host of scholars, politicians, and other observers have roundly criticized this perspective. Two broad (although sometimes contradictory) critiques have special merit.

In the first place, some interests systematically lose in the policy process, while others habitually win. Without making any elite-theory contentions that a small number of interests and individuals conspire together to dominate societal policies, one can make a strong case that those interests with more resources (money, access, information, etc.) usually will obtain better results than those who possess fewer assets and employ them less effectively. The numerically small, cohesive, well-heeled tobacco industry does well, year in, year out, in the policy-making process; marginal farmers and the urban poor produce a much less successful track record. Based on the continuing inequalities of results, critics of the pluralist model argue that interests are still represented unevenly and unfairly.

A second important line of criticism generally agrees that inequality of results remains an important aspect of group politics. But this perspective, most forcefully set out by Theodore Lowi, sees interests as generally succeeding in their goals of influencing government—to the point that the government itself, in one form or another, provides a measure of protection to almost all societal interests. Everyone thus retains some vested interest in the ongoing structure of government and array of public policies. This does not mean that all interests obtain just what they desire from governmental policies; rather, all interests get at least some rewards. From this point of view, the tobacco industry surely wishes to see its crop subsidies maintained, but the small farmer and the urban poor also have pet programs, such as guaranteed loans and food stamps, which they seek to protect.

Lowi labels the proliferation of groups and their growing access to government "interest-group liberalism," and he sees this phenomenon as pathological for a democratic government:

> Interest-group liberal solutions to the problem of power [who will exercise it] provide the system with stability by spreading a *sense* of representation at the expense of genuine flexibility, at the expense of democratic forms, and ultimately at the expense of legitimacy.[10]

Interest-group liberalism is pluralism, but it is *sponsored* pluralism, and the government is the chief sponsor.

On the surface, it appears that the "unequal results" and "interest-group liberalism" critiques of pluralism are at odds. But reconciliation is relatively straightforward. Lowi does not suggest that all interests are effectively represented. Rather, there exists, in many instances, only the appearance of representation. As political scientist Murray Edelman points out, a single set of policies can provide two related types of rewards—tangible benefits for the few and symbolic reassurances for the many.[11] Such a combination encourages groups to form, become active, and claim success.

A CLIMATE FOR GROUP PROLIFERATION

Substantial cleavages among a society's citizens are essential for interest group development. American culture and the constitutional arrangements of the U.S. government actively encourage the emergence of multiple political interests. In the pre-Revolutionary period, sharp conflicts existed between commercial and landed interests, debtor and creditor classes, coastal residents and those in the hinterlands, and citizens with either Tory or Whig political preferences. As the new nation developed, its vastness, characterized by geographical regions varying in climate, economic potential, culture, and tradition, contributed to a great heterogeneity. Open immigration policies further led to a diverse cultural mix with a wide variety of racial, ethnic, and religious backgrounds represented among the populace. Symbolically, the notion of the United States as a "melting pot," emphasizing group assimilation, has received much attention, but a more appropriate image may be the "tossed salad."[12]

The Constitution also contributes to a favorable environment for group development. Guarantees of free speech, association, and the right to petition the government for redress of grievances are basic to group formation. Because political organization often parallels government structure, federalism and the separation of powers principles embodied in the Constitution greatly influence the existence of large numbers of interest groups in the United States.

The decentralized political power structure in the United States allows important decisions to be made at the national, state, or local levels. Even within governmental levels, there are various points of access. For example, business-related policies such as taxes are acted upon at each level, and interest groups may affect these policies in the legislative, executive, or judicial arenas. Because several organizations, like the U.S. Chamber of Commerce, are federations, their state and local affiliates often act independently of the national organization. Numerous business organizations thus focus upon the multiple channels for access.

The American governmental structure also indirectly encourages the proliferation of interest groups. Political parties in the United States, organized along the lines of a decentralized framework, are less unified and disciplined than parties found in many other nations. The resulting power vacuum in the decision-making process offers great potential for alternative political organizations such as interest groups to influence policy.

Finally, American cultural values may well encourage group development. As Alexis de Tocqueville observed 150 years ago, values such as individuality and need for personal achievement underlie the propensity of citizens to join groups. And the number of access points, especially local ones, probably contributes to Americans' strong sense of political efficacy when compared with that expressed by citizens of other nations.[13] Not only are Americans joiners, but they tend to belong to more political groups than do people of other countries.[14]

Reading 8.3

Politicians, Hired Guns, and the Public Interest

Rich Roberts

Lobbying is a very important activity in Congress. The following original essay, written by a professional lobbyist, gives an overview of the nature and tools of the lobbying business.

I–495, the Washington beltway, is an asphalt moat that separates Washington from the country it governs. Inside that circle are political operatives known as "hired guns." They are the lobbyists who are hired to represent the points of view of their clients and who use their experience, resources, and contacts to shape both legislation and public policy. Their organizations may be called trade associations, councils, think tanks, public interest groups, and a host of other names. Their purpose is to protect the client's turf, whether that means saving whales, creating park lands, dredging harbors, or protecting tax benefits.

They orchestrate an intricate mix of strategies, personalities, tactics, and resources in order to serve their clients. The term "special-interest group," most often used in describing many of them, is very misleading. Every individual citizen who joins any organization, which in turn contacts a congressman, constitutes a special interest, and virtually every political opinion expressed by any citizen has some group to forward it to in Washington. As a result, there are over 5,000 registered lobbyists and organizations in the city, as well as a host of others in state capitals and major cities, seeking to influence legislation.

For all the complaints of the press and the self-appointed "public-interest" groups (who in their own right influence legislation)

Source: Specifically written for this collection.

the system works and the public is ultimately served. The first amendment to the Constitution justifies the lobbyists' existence through the proviso that all citizens are guaranteed the right to petition the Congress for redress of grievances. Lobby organizations simply provide a focus and clarity to the petitioning process. The petitioning can range from a massive mail campaign organized by a trade association and generated from a grass-roots membership, to a single lobbyist speaking to a city councilman in a quiet corridor on behalf of a specific client.

An elderly woman in a small town in middle America may write her congressman complaining about a proposed change in social security policy at the same time that her neighbor may be writing protesting a cutback in defense spending. Both are "special interests." She is not concerned with broad national policy so much as she is with her ability to pay her rent. Her neighbor is really concerned with his own safety more than the strength of the nation. She can turn to the American Association of Retired Persons and multiply her voice a thousandfold, just as he can send a copy of his letter to the National Commander of the American Legion whose membership in turn supports his position with thousands of voices. In the same way, labor, business, environmentalists, and a host of other American citizens have joined associations or hired lobbyists to make certain that they are heard, and, they hope that they will be protected from the vagaries of government.

There is a practical value in a politician's having access to these groups. Every year, thousands of individual bills are introduced in both houses in Congress. Congressional staffs are limited in number, constantly overworked, and cannot possibly analyze every bill that crosses their boss's desk. Smart staffers learn to select those bills that affect their state or district and seek out the lobbyists with an interest in the bills. Professional lobbyists have the luxury of concentrating on limited subject areas and can provide detailed analyses and briefings unavailable to the congressman and his staff. By obtaining briefings from lobbyists from several sides of an issue, the smart staffer can balance the inherent biases against the constituencies' needs and provide a cogent, and usually accurate, briefing for his or her boss. It is the congressman's job to sort out the merits of the positions and vote according to the best interest of the broad constituency that elected him. That is what we vote for and what we pay him to do.

A long-held myth outside of Washington is that money buys votes. Even inside Washington some of the fading dinosaurs of the pre-Watergate era still believe it. Money is one of three key elements of any campaign that must be balanced against the merits of the arguments, and the wishes and attitudes of the voters. The triangle of money, arguments, and votes is never equilateral or even isosceles, but however unequal any given leg may be, all three must be present. One lobbyist may be able to deliver substantial campaign contributions and even meritorious arguments but be unable to deliver a single block of constituents. An opposing lobbyist may be short on contributions, have equal merit to his arguments, and, because he has a large grass-roots following of registered voters, he may offset the other's monetary strength. As a general rule, business comes up stronger on the money and arguments side and weak on the constituent side, while public-interest groups appear to be strongest on arguments and grass-roots support. In the past, organized labor appeared to be strong on all three counts, although recently there has been some erosion of money and a lack of cohesiveness in grass-roots political organization.

Of the three elements of successful lobbying, meritorious arguments are consistently important and too often overlooked. The right facts to support a lobbyist's case can offset limited money by bolstering the politician's ability to answer both supporters and critics in justifying his vote. In those cases where the lobbyist has solid financial backing and a weak voter base, the proper arguments justifying the legislation can effectively dilute the accusation that the money was the decisive factor.

In fairness, the old cliché that "money is the mother's milk of politics" still holds true. However, between the Federal Election Commission's stringent reporting requirements and the clerk of the House and the secretary of the Senate's own reporting requirements, demanded of both lobbyists and congressmen alike, any exchange of political money is subject to public scrutiny. The best way to determine if Congress is in recess or having a slow news day is to count the number of reporters getting eye strain reading microfilm reports in the public rooms of those offices.

All of this information is a matter of public record and available to private citizens, reporters, or opposition candidates on demand. Slush funds and payoffs effectively died with the reform of Watergate, and the coup de grace was delivered with Abscam. If there is an occasional backslider in the political congregation, those lessons will be hammered home from the American pulpit as strongly as any pentecostal message is roared under canvas on the sawdust trail.

With the advent of pollsters, campaign consultants, media advisors, and the high cost of media time and space, there is no such thing as a cheap campaign. (Cost of any hotly contested House race will run to six figures, and a Senate race may run well into millions. To impose limits on campaign contributions instead of spending is like packing a feverish victim in ice. It makes them somewhat comfortable and reduces the physical damage by reducing the severity of the symptoms, but does nothing to address the disease itself.) No candidates will ever be such media darlings that they can capture enough regular news coverage (read "free") to offset an effective advertising campaign by his opponent. The absolute political fact of life is that if candidates are serious about winning, they had better be serious about raising the money with which to do it. In order for a man or woman of less than millionaire status to hope to achieve high office, outside contributions are a necessity. Even wealthy candidates seldom spend their own money. There are only two legal sources for those funds—personal contributions by individual citizens or PAC contributions. In all cases, the law specifically prohibits using corporate money in federal campaigns.

In addition, the FEC has imposed strict contribution limits on both personal and PAC contributions. No individual can give more than $1,000 to any candidate for any single election or spend more than $25,000 in any two-year political cycle. Even a wealthy individual contributing $1,000 in a primary and $1,000 in a general election per candidate can only spread $25,000 among a federal field of 535 incumbents and an undetermined number of challengers. In a minimal race costing over half a million dollars, even a wealthy contributor's influence is significantly diluted. By spending the maximum, one individual can only contribute to 12 candidates out of 1,000 or more. That exerts influence over less than 2 percent of the total field.

In order to focus their influence, individuals must amplify their financial clout through an organization's registered political action committee (PAC). Those like-minded individuals can pool their financial resources to contribute as much as $5,000 per candidate per election, or a total of $10,000 per two-year cycle.

Even with this amplification of resources, controls are still in place. No corporate money is allowed; all contributions must be reported semi-annually in off years and as many as nine times in election years, and details as to the names, addresses, and occupations of contributors and the size of each contribution must be reported—all within the $1,000 limitation.

While large blocks of money can be raised through events ranging from $250-per-person cocktail parties and $1,000-a-plate dinners, a major portion still comes from coffee klatches and other events at $25 to $50 per contributor, usually at the local level. Another method that raises a large volume of campaign money is direct mail. However, between administrative, creative, and production costs, direct mail is more likely to be an advertising campaign that pays for itself, than a major fundraising technique. With the exception of the major national mail houses espousing senior Senators or presidential candidates, the contributions still fall well under $100 per contributor.

The only other legal source of political money is honoraria. Corporate funds can be used as an honorarium, but still must meet several reporting requirements. Honoraria are treated as part of a candidate's personal earned income by the IRS and must be reported by the company in the same manner as any payment to an outside consultant or subcontractor. The recipient must declare this as taxable income to the IRS and simultaneously report it to the clerk of the House or the secretary of the Senate.

In addition, the Congress has imposed a $25,000 annual limit on total honoraria, with no more than $2,000 coming from a single occasion. The actual dollar limit is in fact a percentage of the total congressional salary and will change proportionately with the annual salaries of the members of Congress. In all cases, honoraria figures are recorded in the public domain and subject to public scrutiny by citizens, reporters, or opponents, just as campaign contributions are of public record.

In order to raise campaign money, a candidate relies on supporters among both lobbyist and constituents to plan and conduct events and beat the bushes. Many members of Congress loathe this unavoidable aspect of campaigns and reluctantly approach people for money. Fortunately for them, key campaign staff and strong supporters do not show that reluctance.

The prudent lobbyist joins steering committees, often formed by campaign staffs, to use his or her contacts among like-minded individuals or groups to sponsor breakfasts, lunches, cocktails, and dinners where supporters can gather and contribute to candidates who agree with their position. There is rarely any altruism involved, regardless of the supposed purity of the issue. Environmentalists and industrialists alike analyze the voting records of members, consider their personal knowledge, speculate on the candidate's chances, and look at the candidate's jurisdiction before committing time, effort, and money to a campaign.

At this point, it is a cold-eyed business that is only occasionally tempered by personal loyalty. On rare occasions, a lobbyist will support a candidate facing almost certain defeat out of old, established loyalties. Still, campaign support is a high-stakes game and, with only a very few exceptions, it is a calculated decision, made under cool analysis.

Grass-roots contributions are usually made with more emotion, but with no more altruism. Local contributions are stimulated by personal contact with the candidate, by his reputation as perceived from press coverage and word-of-mouth, or by well-designed solicitations.

In any case, the motives for contributing come less from concern for great international issues of world peace, military strength, and the common good as they do from the need for lower taxes, better highways in a given town, or the protection of a local stream. A nation of close to a quarter of a billion people is, in fact, an amalgam of special-interest groups. The saving grace of the system is that the varied voices provide a counterpoint that prevents any single voice from holding sway long enough to cause irreparable damage.

A mitigating factor that prevents money from being the sole source of political influence is still the voter. If lobbyists are able to raise substantial money for campaign contributions, their opponents with limited resources can counter them by marshalling grass-roots voters in numbers sufficient to sway an election. The one thing a politician needs more than money is a majority at the polls. Swaying public opinion doesn't come cheaply, but if an organization can capture the sympathetic attention of the press, it can effectively offset paid political announcements.

This has given rise to the most pernicious loophole in campaign finance law. The FEC permits "independent expenditures," that is, any expenditures used to support a candidate or attack his opponent, so long as they are made without the permission of, or consultation with, the candidate or his staff. This technique has been most successfully adopted by the far right and their bedfellows among the fundamentalist electronic ministers.

In a kind of guerrilla politics, they produce commercials and mailings attacking the character and policies of a candidate without advocating his opponent. Too often, these campaigns have escalated hostilities between two bona fide candidates to the point of 19th century, bare-knuckle mudslinging, to the disservice of the public because the real issues are obscured. As a rule, the intended victims of these attacks best survive with controlled humor that mocks the attacks.

A classic case in the 1982 campaign between Senator Melcher of Montana and his Republican challenger. Without the foreknowledge or permission of Melcher's opponent, an arch-conservative group launched a television campaign based on false information and emotion. The scene opened with a "hippie" couple using food stamps to buy a packed basket of groceries, followed by a clean cut "logger/rancher" couple and appealing child with a skimpy basket carefully doling out cash. The voice-over claimed that Melcher had aided and abetted profligate spending and was "too liberal" for Montana.

Rather than fall prey to an almost certainly fatal response of denials and cries of foul play, Melcher's campaign countered with a classic in its own right. The opening scene of the response showed suited figures with briefcases leaving an airplane. As the voice-over let you know that "outsiders" were trying to influence Montanans, their briefcases broke open and cash fluttered across the runway. The scene immediately cut to a corral where two cows and a calf were talking. Playing on Melcher's popular down-home style and his profession as a veterinarian, one cow concluded that the outsiders were "steppin' in what they'd been throwing at Doc." The final cut clinched the Montana image with Melcher walking tieless, silhouetted against a broad evening Montana sky.

While this single commerical may not have been the sole difference between winning and losing a hotly contested race, it effectively turned a liability into an asset. It does point out two key aspects of the race. It is a case of Melcher's having to spend more money than anticipated to counter an outside attack and of a successful attempt of pitting legitimate dollars effectively against questionable dollars.

Unfortunately, independent expenditures enjoy the existing loopholes in campaign law and have successfully resisted change by hiding behind the first amendment. In any case, they cause more money to be spent than should be necessary and the public is not served.

Those cases aside, the majority of the effort to sway and hold voters' loyalties are a part of the legitimate political process. In order for a lobbyist to capture a block of votes and bring it to the attention of the candidate, he must organize any grass-roots support his client has available on behalf of the candidate.

Hosting events where the candidate can press the flesh is a time-honored technique. Personally escorting a candidate on a tour of a client's facility, factory, office, or institution and introducing him to workers and staff who are potential voters provides two benefits. First, the candidate has received free exposure to a block of voters identified with the lobbyist's interest and secondly, the lobbyist has demonstrated his client's personal stake in the candidate's district.

Public endorsement of a candidate can be helpful, but must be treated as a two-edged sword. Either through press announcements or an organization's in-house organs, endorsements are another method of giving the candidate free assistance. However, a lobbyist must be absolutely certain that the general public is at least neutral toward the client's interests. Any organization engaged in a cause or business that is controversial among the electorate can cause a candidate as much harm as good with a public endorsement. A good lobbyist must make certain that his client knows his standing in the community and does not embarrass the candidate. An anti-gun group in an Alaska campaign could do as much damage by supporting a candidate there as a chemical company might in a district populated predominately by environmentalists.

The third leg of the lobbyist's triangle is often the most overlooked, and yet is the pivot point that determines the effectiveness of the other two. Regardless of the ability of any interest group to raise money or generate campaign support, a sound and credible argument is critical to the reception a lobbyist will get.

With the exception of joint resolutions lauding motherhood and apple pie, or castigating known enemies of the Republic, all other votes cast by elected officials lay them open to criticism from one quarter or another. Any successful politician knows that the best defense against critics is carefully crafted and believable reasons for a specific vote. Those reasons must demonstrate that the approval or defeat of a bill would save the public money; protect their health, welfare, or safety; or adhere to a basic constitutional principle. Especially in cases where a specific interest seeks special treatment—a tax break, loan guarantee, or regulatory relief—the public may resent that special treatment. A good lobbyist will anticipate that attitude and provide the congressmen who might support him with arguments that they can use to respond to press or constituent inquiries. A tax break can be justified on the grounds that it will protect a vital industry and therefore workers' jobs; a loan guarantee could encourage the economic development of a depressed area and create jobs; regulatory relief could prevent an industry from closing its doors and throwing large numbers of people out of work and onto the welfare rolls.

In formulating these arguments, a lobbyist may find that his client's position doesn't perfectly fit a public justification without some alteration of the legislative language. Compromise is often inevitable, if not desirable. All initial legislation should have a "gimme" factor tucked away, some part of it that the proponents can give up without sustaining damage or drastically altering the final effect. The "gimme" point may be given up grudgingly, but any purely hard-line position of no compromise by both parties is doomed to failure. Whenever possible, a lobbyist should avoid getting caught in a stalemate with each party pointing a pistol at the other's head, waiting for the first guy to blink.

Once an issue reaches a stalemate position, many congressional supporters will lose heart and turn in frustration to other matters on their extremely full agendas. The issue will either waste away out of apathy or be killed by a frustrated committee chairman who wishes to be rid of it. In the worst cases, a potential ally will be angered by the intransigence of the lobbyists and arbitrarily swing to the other side merely to dispense with the issue.

There is a big difference between trying to pass legislation and trying to defeat it. It takes a clear majority of votes to pass legislation and often requires a coalition of diverse interests. It takes only a strong and committed minority to kill a bill. To succeed at either one requires the ability to carefully count heads well in advance of an anticipated vote. Knowing how each member is going to vote on an issue is an unquantifiable combination of art and science.

First, a lobbyist has to build a network of staff contacts that will call him, or on whom he calls, at a moment's notice. They have to trust the lobbyist enough to speak with candor and in confidence. Senior staff contribute to their bosses' decisions and are the best bellwether as to their directions. A sudden coolness or lack of availability on the part of a staffer can signal a shift in position by his or her boss. Other lobbyists who may not work the same issues, but deal with the same players, are also a valuable source of information, and can provide valuable introductions to both members and staff. However, there is no free lunch in Washington. Every favor done is a chit to be called in at a later date. Good lobbyists never seek favors unless they are prepared to pay back on demand.

If the network is working right and the lobbyist accurately reads the head count, a good appraisal of the position can be made. If the head count shows strong opposition and the vote is obviously going wrong, there are several fallback positions. If there is a large number of undecided or publicly uncommitted congressmen, the lobbyist may get a solid supporter to seek a procedural delay. During that time, arguments can be adjusted and the neutral members can be courted.

If the count runs clearly against a lobbyist's position and the vote is in subcommittee, supporters can be released from any commitment. This enables the lobbyist to save those crucial chits for a later battle while re-forming strategies. By releasing supporters, especially shaky ones, from a public commitment, it is possible to seek support further along the legislative process in committee or on the floor. A lobbyist may find limited support among the 15 members of a subcommittee, but have depth among the remaining members on the larger full committee who have a later crack at the issue. Relinquishing supporters at the early stages of the process puts opponents offguard as to the real strength that may lie ahead.

In opposing legislation, a walk can be as good as a vote. In a closely contested vote with only one or two members in a position to swing the results either way, the failure to show up and vote could well deny the advocates a clear majority. This is where an accurate head count is of paramount importance. Given the right arguments, a member who personally sympathizes with a lobbyist's position but does not want to be on record as publicly supporting it may be persuaded to attend some other meeting or attend to "more pressing matters."

In order to strengthen a position with a member, constituent contact is extremely valuable. Most members maintain a mail count of constituent letters on any subject and use the pro and con count to help decide which side of an issue to support. The key factors are to keep the letter short and to a single issue, the sender must be a registered voter in the member's district, and the points should appear original. That, coupled with clips from the media—articles or editorials—that present the position in a favorable light, can also be a part of the arsenal. These are especially effective if they were published in the member's district.

Key players in the political arena cover a broad variety of congressional staff positions and too many lobbyists underestimate staff influence. Whether dealing with the office manager, legislative director, administrative assistant, or scheduling secretary, every office has its own dynamics. Scheduling secretaries are crucial because they are often the only ones who know how to reach members on a moment's notice. Sometimes the office manager or press secretary has a closer relationship to the member and, therefore, better access to the member's ear than the administrative assistant or legislative director. Short visits of a social nature, including brief lunches with a variety of staff, usually let a lobbyist know the dynamics of an office quickly.

It is equally important to determine

which committee and subcommittee have jurisdiction over a client's issue. Subcommittee generally has first crack at legislation and the chief of staff or chief counsel will be attuned to the nuances long before anyone else. However, with the massive work load they face and the volume of legislation, regular contact is necessary to make sure a client's concerns don't slip through the cracks because staff was distracted by any of a number of other issues. Given the limited time available during the working day, cultivating staff is done best during recess, slack time, or after hours. Lobbyists should never interfere with the flow of staff work, unless immediate attention is critical to impending action.

Most social events are good settings for cultivating staff and members alike. However, members are more likely to respond to invitations to fundraisers, honoraria situations, or events held in close proximity to their offices on Capitol Hill. Conventions and meetings with a group of clients or other lobbyists are good forums, especially if an honorarium speech is involved. There are no purely social situations in Washington, but detailed business discussions should be avoided during those events that appear to be social in nature. Their purpose is to allow staff and members to relax in friendly surroundings, leaving a favorable impression of the lobbyist and the client. When serious discussions become necessary, members and staff will be more comfortable in listening to the specific points a lobbyist is making if they feel they are dealing with someone who understands their own situations at a personal level.

Lobbying is a people-oriented service business that requires a sensitivity to the feelings and personal traits of the people involved. A lobbyist must be professionally comfortable with a client's position and the practicality of the requests. A good lobbyist has to be prepared to fine-tune those requests if they are unrealistic or unreasonable and to convince the client of the realities of the arena. Any lobbyist who is uncomfortable with the client's position or who feels that he cannot reach a reasonable accomodation with a sufficient number of members should resign the account or face certain failure and possible damage to his reputation among the congressional community.

While government agencies are expressly forbidden to engage in direct political advocacy, governmental bodies can adapt the same techniques in their need to influence legislation. If a particular agency is concerned about upcoming appropriations, it should have already laid the groundwork by having quickly, carefully, and politely responded to prior congressional requests. Every member of Congress gets a high volume of mail asking him or her to act as an intermediary or ombudsman between a constituent and a government agency. Even if the agency legitimately has to deny a request, by doing so promptly and with precise reasons it is letting the congressman off the hook. As far as the constituent is concerned, the agency said no, not the congressman.

Field hearings, well-handled, are the government's equivalent of the factory gate or coffee klatch. Visits to field facilities with photo-opportunities and good briefings are usually appreciated for their political value. From the White House on down, government agencies maintain congressional liaison officers who are in fact government lobbyists. With some fine-tuning, basic lobbying techniques are as applicable to a congressional liaison officer as they are to a private-sector lobbyist.

In lieu of prohibited campaign contributions, money can legally be spent providing members with travel and access to government facilities and personnel so that their constituents are aware that their congressman is working in their behalf. If the agency provides the access, the congressman's staff will make certain that the public is aware of his or her activities.

Liaison officers and their staffs, like lobbyists, are responsible for marshalling effective arguments in support of an agency's position, though they are usually restricted to presenting arguments at a congressman's request. However, if a liaison officer is prepared in advance and has done his or her homework on the Hill, those arguments will bear weight.

So long as there is representative government and so long as like-minded members of the public body seek to address that government, lobbyists will fill a legitimate role by representing the individual wishes of a variety of interest groups. Whether it is a business, labor union, public-interest group, or government agency, the size and complexity of government requires that they have effective professional representation. No matter what euphemism is used, be it federal relations representative, public affairs specialist, or government liaison officer, the "hired gun" is here to stay.

Reading 8.4

The Open Congress Meets the President

Norman J. Ornstein

The late, pre-eminent constitutional historian Edwin Corwin aptly characterized the Constitution as "an invitation to struggle" for the President and Congress. The founding framers, through the separation of powers doctrine and the system of checks and balances, intentionally created an adversarial relationship between the legislature and the executive branch in order to minimize tyrannical and capricious authority in government. This tension between the President and Congress is exacerbated by the differences in the constituencies, time frames, and policy roles of the two branches.

Over history, the rivalry between the President and Congress has demonstrated a cyclical nature. Sometimes conflict is most intense, as in periods of divided government when the two branches are controlled by different parties. At other times, conflict is attenuated, such as under conditions of crisis and emergency, during the "honeymoon period" immediately following presidential elections, or when both branches are controlled by the same political party in a majoritarian alignment of power.

The reforms of the 1970s pose exceptional challenges in presidential-congressional relationships for both branches. The following essay by a renowned authority on the Congress pinpoints the new wrinkles in this enduring struggle.

Source: Norman J. Ornstein in *Both Ends of the Avenue: The Presidency and the Executive Branch, and Congress in the 1980's*, pp. 185–211, ed. by Anthony King.

It is January 1980. Imagine Sam Rayburn materializing suddenly on Capitol Hill, nineteen years after he last set foot on it. He first has considerable trouble getting his bearings. There is the familiar old Capitol, and the Cannon and Longworth Buildings. But what are all these other new buildings and parking lots, not to mention once-familiar hotels and apartments that seem to be office buildings now? And look at the bottom of the hill at that monstrosity that bears his name! He enters his Capitol and feels a little better, although it is awfully crowded; the mere handful of members, staff, and lobbyists that he remembers are surrounded by hundreds of unknown people milling around, dashing down the corridors and in and out of the chamber. Entering the chamber, he feels still more comfortable—it looks pretty much the same as it did when he last saw it, and with Tip O'Neill in the speaker's chair the Democrats are obviously still in control. Rayburn smiles contentedly. "Tip's a good man," he says to himself. "He learned a lot from me." He positively grins when he sees that good ol' Jim Wright of Fort Worth is the majority leader. So the venerable Boston-Austin connection in the leadership is still there.

A young, unfamiliar member is managing a bill; Rayburn sidles up to an old colleague and learns to his shock that the bill manager is in his second term in the House. Not only that, the bill and the manager are from the Ways and Means Committee! Rayburn feels a bit better when he sees Tip O'Neill get up on the floor and warmly endorse the bill. But he is horrified again as he witnesses a succession of young Democrats get up and denounce, in blunt language, O'Neill, the Ways and Means chairman, and the Democratic president. He watches, stunned, as the bill goes down in flames, largely on the votes of Democrats. A second-termer managing a bill? From Ways and Means? Supported by the Speaker, the committee, and the President? And it gets rolled on the floor? What's going on here, anyhow? But then again, Rayburn can remember times when he and a young Democratic president had been humiliated, too—also with the help of Democrats. But it usually did not happen so openly, so publicly on the floor!

Rayburn's mortification is compounded by his confusion at the vote. Not only does no clerk call out the roll, but members are not calling out aye or nay. They seem instead to be sticking pieces of plastic in fancy machines, and, suddenly, the familiar House chamber is surrounded by unfamiliar lights and signs. The tapestry on an entire vast wall is covered with names, with red or green lights beside them. Large electronic scoreboards at each side of the chamber tick off fifteen minutes and indicate vote tallies, overall and by party. And up in the corners —can it really be?—television cameras. When it is all over, Rayburn is dumbstruck. What hath Congress wrought?

On a walk through the Capitol corridors and over to the Cannon Building, Rayburn is somewhat assuaged. Party offices—Speaker, majority leader, whip, and so forth—seem to be unchanged, and the names of the committees on the doors, from Appropriations to Veterans Affairs, are all familiar. But he keeps getting jostled by a series of mostly unfamiliar people (who seem to be members) running out of one subcommittee room and into another, or running to the floor when the bells ring, and they are ringing all the time. All this frenetic activity—and it is not even the end of a session. Not only that, but his newspaper tells him that today is *Friday*! Why, even the people from New York and Pennsylvania are here! He passes an open committee room door, stops, looks in, and sees a markup session in progress on an energy bill. "They must have forgotten to lock the door," he thinks, but then sees that the room is filled with staff, reporters, and spectators. "An open markup on a major bill. I can't believe it," he mutters to himself.

Rayburn walks into an office. Seeing three connecting rooms filled with desks, files, electronic equipment, and staff people, he assumes it must be the main quarters of the Appropriations Committee. He reels back in astonishment when a receptionist tells him that, no, this is the office of a freshman congressman from Texas. On his way out, Rayburn counts staff people and notices a computer terminal and a television set playing the floor proceedings. Out in the hall, a set of blinding klieg lights ring several television cameras and reporters. "Oh," Rayburn thinks, "It must be the Speaker, or the Ways and Means chairman." The interviewee turns out to be a freshman Democrat, criticizing the windfall profits tax proposed by President Jimmy Carter and endorsed by O'Neill. Rayburn goes outside, sits on a park bench, slowly shakes his head, and drifts off into a troubled sleep.

He wakes up with a start. This was a comparative catnap; now it is April 1981. Rayburn is afraid to go into the House again. There may be even more frightening changes in store. So he strolls to the Senate side of the Capitol, picking up a newspaper on the way. He discovers, that while he slept, a Republican president has been elected—unfortunate, though nothing terribly unusual there—and along with him, a Republican Senate. Now that *is* unusual; Rayburn had seen only two others, for two years each, in his twenty-one years as House Democratic leader. To his relief, he reads that his beloved House of Representatives, at least, remains in the hands of the Democrats.

As Rayburn reaches the Senate side, he notices a door labeled "Budget Committee." "So they went back to the idea of separate budget panels," he muses. He walks inside to find Republicans voting in a solid bloc to support their president's budget package and thinks to himself that this new president is having an easier time with his own party in the Senate than Eisenhower did. When he discovers that the budget package calls for nearly $40 billion in budget cuts, he is doubly impressed. Why, these cuts total nearly half the entire budget when he left Congress! He notes that Democrats are deeply and bitterly divided on the budget question. "It's a good thing Lyndon isn't around to see this," he mutters.

Rayburn heads to the Foreign Relations Committee, where a confirmation hearing is going on. He is startled to see a Republican senator from North Carolina—politics have certainly changed in the South! But he is even more startled when the senator (Jesse Helms, a conservative like the president, he is told by a reporter) lambastes the nominee for assistant secretary of state for his leftist views and warns him—and the administration—that Senator Helms is not happy with the administration's nominees and will hold a large number of them in limbo indefinitely in protest. He thinks to himself that maybe this president is not in such great shape with his own Republicans, especially the conservatives.

A trip to the Senate floor presents a similar picture. A parade of self-identified conservative Republican senators criticize the president and his priorities, as well as their own Senate majority leader, arguing passionately that social issues cannot be delayed and that they will not sit idly by. "Ah," says Rayburn, "looks like we still have civil rights filibusters." No, he is told, the senators refer to such things as abortion, family planning, and prayer in the schools. But there is a marathon filibuster planned in the Senate over civil rights—conducted by liberals to prevent a rollback of major civil rights laws.

Continuing his stroll around the Senate, Rayburn is struck by the large number of people scurrying around the corridors of the numerous office buildings (including such converted landmarks as the Carroll Arms Hotel and the Senate Courts Apartment Building). These are not tourists, he realizes; they are staff. A tour of a typical senator's office shows five large rooms filled with staff, computer terminals, and equipment, along with three additional rooms in an annex. Rayburn is also struck by his realization that neither party nor ideology affect the sizes or apparent activities of the staffs—conservative Republican offices are as bureaucratic, overcrowded, and busy as those of liberal Democrats. Moreover, Southern senators do not seem to differ from Northerners in their use of staff. In a committee hearing, Rayburn sees senators constantly in whispered conferences with staff; staff feeding their bosses questions for witnesses; staff preparing speeches and amendments for their senators. "I saw *some* of this in the 1950s," he muses, "but not nearly so much, nor so universal!"

Rayburn walks outside again and finds another park bench. He prepares to drift off to sleep again, but this time he takes a sleeping pill first. After what he has seen, he does not want to wake up again for a very long time.

Our brief Rip van Rayburn fable, not the first spun by a scholar to highlight change in Congress, is designed to introduce a key question for this book—What has changed inside Congress that affects presidential leadership? We can first address this question by asking, Why was Rayburn so surprised, even stunned, by what he saw in 1980 and 1981? Obviously because much that characterized Congress in his heyday had changed. What changed—and what did not—can help us sort out the problems and potentialities that contemporary presidents face in dealing with Congress. Rayburn was a strong leader who worked closely with presidents from Franklin D. Roosevelt to John F. Kennedy. Our best place to start is with the core Rayburn era—the Congress of the 1950s.

INSIDE CONGRESS IN THE 1950s

In the 1950s, as in the decade before and some years afterward, Congress was a closed system. Incentives, rewards, and sanctions all were internal to the congressional process. First, the absence of an outside focus of attention forced legislators to look inside their own system. Without an intense national media presence—especially a television presence—in Washington, relatively little public attention was paid to congressional proceedings or congressional members. A battle over policy between a committee baron and a maverick junior legislator, say, or a scandal involving one or more congressmen was paid little heed outside the confines of the Capitol. William Proxmire gained notoriety among political scientists as the quintessential "outsider" in the Senate after Ralph K. Huitt's seminal article in 1961,[1] but he was not a well-known figure outside Wisconsin or the political science fraternity.

As Michael Robinson has noted, a bribery scandal involving a prominent senator, Daniel Brewster of Maryland, was given virtually no coverage in the national media, even when Brewster was convicted and sent to prison (leaving Brewster both broken personally and obscure nationally).[2] Such goings-on—on the Hill, at least—were of only passing interest to a Washington press corps more involved with the behavior of the president and his coterie, and of even less interest to television networks centered in New York and attempting to establish a credible presence as sources of national nightly news.

This relative congressional obscurity was underscored in the social arena. Inside the Washington community at this time, social circles were more concentric than overlapping. While the style section of the *Washington Post* would report on fancy soirees attended by legislators, this was news of significance only to a handful of D.C. cognoscenti. The *Post* in the 1950s was not a national newspaper, with its stories syndicated nationally. Its focus on Washington social lions and lionesses would capture attention outside the capital only when the socializing involved the presidential circle (hence, Perle Mesta's notoriety). Only the handful of senators who sought presidential nominations were able to move into a more public spotlight—and even this was much less likely before 1960.

All of this meant that legislators could not easily find power, attention, publicity, or celebrity status away from the confines of the Capitol. To a member of Congress, virtually the only way to get ahead was to ride up the power structure inside the House or Senate. But the elevators were not self-run; rather, the operators were the senior party leaders and committee chairmen. These people pushed the internal button for numerous internal reasons. The formal rules of the House and Senate enhanced their power and influence in a variety of ways.

First, they protected committee chairmen

from sanction or removal by their colleagues. Chairmen were basically selected at the beginning of each new Congress by a secret ballot vote in the majority party caucus, based on recommendations made to the caucus by a party committee. For House Democrats, in the majority for nearly the entire 1950s and 1960s, the group was called the Committee on Committees and consisted of the Democratic members of the Ways and Means Committee; the counterpart Senate group was the Democratic Steering Committee, chaired by the majority leader, who appointed the other members. In each chamber, the caucus was presented with a single slate of nominees for chairmanships, all routinely chosen on the seniority principle—that is, the Democrat with greatest continuous service on the committee—and arranged to provide for a single in toto vote. No procedure existed for a separate vote on any individual choice for a chairmanship. Though no rules mandated it, the party selection panels implicitly were governed by the seniority criterion. The same patterns prevailed for Republicans in the minority and on the rare occasions (1947–1948 and 1953–1954) when they were in the majority.

Second, formal rules gave the chairmen a near-monopoly over committee resources, especially committee staff. Chairmen could use the rules to control their committee agendas and to shape policy emphases and outcomes through their dominance over subcommittees (they could name the panels, choose the majority members, and select the chairmen) and through their ability to control when and if their committee would meet. Chairmen also controlled what other perquisites existed inside Congress for committee members: appointment to a conference committee, the ability to travel or "junket" on committee business at committee expense, and the giving of permission to hold a hearing in a member's home state or district.

Rules that kept most congressional negotiations closed to all except members and privileged staff multiplied the "inside" influence of chairmen. Chairmen were there overseeing their colleagues, making deals, and compromising or refusing to bend, while outside forces, such as the media and lobbying groups, were not present. True, lobbyists could still apply pressure and could always find out what went on in the closed rooms. But they could not supply their expertise or relevant data to members during the process of decision making, while chairmen had their expert staffs immediately at hand. Furthermore, with closed sessions, the members could put the best face on their actions or inactions when recounting them to groups or constituents.

Formal rules, especially in the House, also extended the control that chairmen had in their committees to actions on the floor. Chairmen controlled the time of debate for a bill, allocating the limited minutes to their designated spokesmen. Most important, House rules made amendments to bills difficult to attach and rarely subject to outside, or extra-congressional, influences. Chairmen, who tended to shape the bills in committee to their liking, did not want amendments added to their bills. The rules, which forced most amendments to be unrecorded, made it difficult for interest groups and the public to track the votes for or against their interests (while chairmen, who were there on the floor, could watch the voting more closely). The rules also placed a burden on anticommittee forces to get their allies to the floor to vote when amendments came up. Chairmen, however, merely had to convince potential opponents not to vote at all, an easy task since no records of attendance were kept.

Formal rules were supplemented by informal norms. Junior members were to be seen and not heard, to serve an apprenticeship until they were well-steeped in the system. Violators of this norm received no great benefits in terms of public attention, but were quite likely to feel the sting of internal disapproval, with the amount of pain inflicted varying according to the gravity of the offense. The continuum of possible sanctions was large: no access to committee staff, no opportunity to ask questions of witnesses in a hearing, no room at the witness table for an important constituent who wanted to testify, no invitation to an interparliamentary exchange in Madrid, and no action on a coveted piece of legislation or amendment. With very limited resources available to the rank-and-file legislators, each of these perquisites was important. Sam Rayburn's most famous phrase was his admonition to junior colleagues: "to get along, go along." In this closed congressional system, few doubted the truth of his adage.

It is not surprising, then, that the House and Senate our fantasy Sam Rayburn saw in 1980 and 1981 came as a jolt. The latter-day Congress was oriented toward and dominated by junior members; open, to an incredible degree, to press, lobbies, and public; replete with overt challenges to the authority of party leaders, committees, chairmen, and the president; and filled with a seemingly endless army of staff and technical resources for everybody.

To a leader like Rayburn (or to a president for that matter), the most important contrast with the old was the fluidity of the new Congress. One key consequence of the old, closed system was that Congress had been quite predictable, at least to the relative handful of close and seasoned observers (including the speaker, the Senate majority leader, and usually the President's key staff aides). Bills from one set of committees were certain to pass easily and intact *if* they were reported out at all; bills from other committees were sure to elicit conflict, controversy, and amendment in committee and on the floor. How most members would vote or react was predictable long before the actual votes were cast. What amendments would be offered (and by whom) and which would be successful could usually be forecast. Of course, no one could determine the precise outcome of every piece of legislation or policy initiative. But one knew which votes would be close and which bills had no chance—and, on the close calls, which twenty or thirty members of the House or which five or six members of the Senate were the crucial swing votes.

The decisions governing these final outcomes were usually made at earlier stages of the process, shaped behind closed doors in committees, in conditions forged by committee chairmen, often negotiated with party leaders and presidential representatives. If and when agreements were worked out, the chairmen used their formidable resources within their committees, either to report a bill out with a united front or to quash a bill outright.

If the predictability of the system failed —if a bill that seemed certain to pass intact foundered on the floor—party leaders could swiftly withdraw the offending article from consideration and return to the proverbial drawing board, with few tremors that the embarrassment would make the front pages or the nightly television news. Indeed, it might not even make the wire services, given the small number of journalists closely following Congress and the general propensity of news editors to regard such stories as petty and boring internal congressional warfare.

This did not mean—as Rayburn himself would have readily admitted—that leaders like the Speaker ran Congress or that, as conventional wisdom would have it, the president could sit down with Sam Rayburn and Lyndon Johnson, work out an agreement, and that would be that. Rayburn's influence, and Johnson's, stemmed first from their relationship with committee chairmen and other senior powers—their ability to negotiate, to logroll, and to compromise with the oligarchs, to know when to back off and when to push.

Second, their influence was greater because they knew every member's political environment, strengths, weaknesses, and predilections. Thus they knew what could pass when. Lyndon Johnson was not powerful enough to push through the 1965 Voting Rights Act in 1957 or the 1957 Civil Rights Act in 1955. But he and Rayburn knew when *a* civil rights bill—any civil rights bill—could get through Congress, what it could contain, and what it would take to get the bill past a filibuster and the other major hurdles.

Third, the power of the leaders was enhanced by the closed nature of the congressional system. The Speaker and Senate leader could minimize overt defeats by their ability to control access of bills to the floor, and they could know with some reasonable certainty when they would win or lose. In the absence of substantial public or group attention to voting patterns, there was usually enough flexibility in the votes of their colleagues for the leaders to have a "reserve" in case things were going unexpectedly badly. The reserve of support included members who owed the leaders favors or who were afraid of sanctions or who were simply predisposed to help if needed. Moreover, the more often it appeared the leaders won and the less the attention paid when they lost, the more Rayburn and Johnson enhanced their reputations as powerful leaders. Thus they were all the more able to parlay those reputations into even more concrete successes, as rank-and-file legislators acted without prodding in anticipation of what the leader might want.

The formula for presidential success was not much different. The successful president, to begin, worked closely with congressional leaders, using their strength to expand his own. He accepted their judgments about what would pass and what to push, and he compromised with them, as they in turn compromised with committee barons. He provided his resources to them when necessary. As Senate Secretary Bobby Baker put it about the LBJ style of leadership:

> Much of the work of putting together a simple majority consisted of logistics. A senator who's for your cause down to his toenails is of no help if you can't produce him when the vote is taken. My first goal always was to produce one hundred percent of those senators who'd promised to help us; if I did that, no way in hell we'd lose—because LBJ was not one to call for a vote until he knew he had the horses. . . . When we had a Democratic President in the White House, I had Air Force One available to fetch them on short notice. Even when Republicans ruled the White House, we could command police cars and wailing sirens to round up the strays.[3]

Most important, the successful president emulated the successful congressional leader. He buried his failures in committee or in a conference in the Oval Office, before they escalated into embarrassing reversals in public forums. He only proposed initiatives he thought he could win (or, at least, he understood and publicized only the likely successes). He built his reputation as a winner with Congress and used it to achieve more success, often with legislators acting on their own in anticipation of presidential action or approval.

Still the basic fact confronting presidents and congressional party leaders alike was that the constraints on them far outweighed their freedom to do what they wanted in the policy arena. When Rayburn and Johnson met with Eisenhower, it was most often to tell him what could *not* be accomplished—what was out of the question in Ways and Means; sure to be killed in Rules; absolutely unacceptable to Senator Richard Russell or Senator Robert Kerr. When Rayburn met with his own committee chairmen, it was not to tell them what the Speaker demanded or what the president insisted upon; it was to negotiate. Rayburn recognized full well the strong cards the chairmen held in their hands. Rarely would he take on a powerful chairman in a public setting. When he did, as with the challenge to Rules Chairman Howard "Judge" Smith in the attempt in 1961 to enlarge the Rules Committee, undertaken with the full backing of the popular new president, the outcome was very much in doubt until the actual vote (taken after a long postponement to enable Rayburn to scratch for more votes to provide a slender majority).

Johnson and Rayburn knew their systems well and could operate as masters within them. But even before both left Congress—LBJ to move to the vice-presidency in 1961, Rayburn upon his death later that year—they saw the beginnings of change. Both saw it coming with the 1958 election, a "critical" election for Congress. While the 1958 elections ostensibly helped both party leaders, giving each of them many more members to fatten their majorities, they presaged greater problems for them and their successors. The Democrats gained forty-nine House seats and fifteen senators, most of the newcomers being liberals from the Northeast, the Midwest, and the West.

In the House, the freshman bloc, led by representatives like James G. O'Hara, helped form a new, structured liberal caucus, the Democratic Study Group (DSG). DSG became an ally of Rayburn's after liberal Democrat John F. Kennedy moved into the White House in 1961, but more important it became the moving force behind internal reforms implemented in the 1970s. These measures, which transformed the House, eliminated one by one the formal rules and informal norms that had created and nurtured the closed congressional system. In the Senate, the famous "class of '58" endured for nearly two decades, spurring the Senate toward the decentralized, democratized, junior-oriented institution that still prevails in 1982.[4]

CHANGES INSIDE CONGRESS IN THE 1960s AND 1970s

Changes in the internal rules, power, and customs of Congress began in the 1960s and culminated in the 1970s. The House of Representatives generally led the day in formal rules changes, the Senate lagging a bit behind.[5] The thrust of change, however, was the same in both houses.

First, power was decentralized. The insulation from removal of full committee chairmen provided by the rigid custom of seniority and by the omnibus-vote system of selection in the Democratic caucus was taken away by caucus reforms in 1971 and 1973. At the same time, the ability of chairmen to control their committees through subcommittees was hamstrung by reforms that took away the chairman's power to structure the subcommittees, to pick the subcommittee chairmen and members, and to control their jurisdictions and staffs. Subcommittees were given independent status and authority; their members were selected automatically according to set criteria; and their chairmen were elected individually by the committees' Democratic caucuses. Rules limiting legislators to one subcommittee chairmanship apiece gave an unprecedented number of gavels to rank-and-file members.

Second, resources available to subcommittees, to their chairmen and ranking members, and to all legislators were expanded. Chairmen in the past had been able basically to hire and fire all the committees' staffs—and the staffs had been small. In 1965, standing committees employed 571 people in the House and 509 in the Senate, an average per committee of 28 and 32, respectively. Reforms in the early 1970s allowed subcommittees and their leaders to hire their own personnel. Staffs then expanded rapidly; by 1979, the standing committees employed 1,959 in the House and 1,098 in the Senate, or an average per committee of 89 and 73, respectively.[6]

Personal staffs expanded rapidly as well. In the late 1960s, each House member could hire up to nine or ten employees, with a staff budget of about $150,000. By the end of the 1970s, House members were each entitled to hire eighteen employees, with a budget of nearly one-third of a million dollars. Adjunct research staffs—the Library of

Congress's Congressional Research Service, the Office of Technology Assessment, the Congressional Budget Office—also mushroomed. So, too, did other resources available to members, such as computers, fancy telephone systems, data-processing equipment, and so forth. The net result was that each member of Congress, down to the lowliest minority freshman, became resource-rich, the possessor of enough staff and equipment to "stroke" all constituents, to monitor the legislative activities in all committees and other forums, to maintain a steady stream of press releases and media contacts, and to get involved, through speeches, bills, hearings, and amendments, in the full range of policy areas.

A third important change in the 1970s was that internal congressional deliberations were opened to public scrutiny. In both houses, reforms dramatically changed the nature of committee business. Before 1973, an open committee markup session, when a bill was actually put together, line by line, was as rare as a whooping crane. They were closed to all but committee members and a handful of staff (all beholden to the chairman). After 1973, nearly all the markups in the House and Senate were open to outside observers, whether press, lobbyists, or tourists wandering by.

This change further chipped away at the power of chairmen. They lost their near-monopoly of expertise; all the other committee members now had their own staff or even lobbyists whispering advice and amendments in their ears during the markups. Also, the chairmen's inside persuasion was less effective on members who faced conflicting outside pressures as well, because the members' actions were now directly viewed by the outsiders. Legislators could no longer put the best face on their votes or their rhetoric, as they had been able to do when the action took place behind closed doors.

It was not only meetings that were opened: in the House, votes, too, were opened. Before the 1970s, virtually all votes on amendments to bills were handled in a nonrecorded fashion, using a parliamentary procedure known as teller voting. To expedite business, members would walk down separate aisles, for ayes and nays, counted by colleagues as they passed. This took six minutes as opposed to the thirty or forty minutes for a roll call. Only the total number of votes was tallied, not who voted or how. With no records kept, attendance was low—less than half, on average, than for roll-call votes.

In the Legislative Reorganization Act of 1970, these votes were changed to recorded teller votes. Members signed cards—green for aye, red for nay—and dropped them in boxes, saving time while allowing votes and attendance to be published. This change doubled voting attendance at teller votes. More important, it reduced again the power of committees and their chairmen, this time to wheel and deal on the floor. A chairman in the past had been able generally to structure bills in his committee to his liking. Thus, amendments on the floor were discouraged, and nonrecorded votes helped in this regard. The burden was on the proponents of the amendment to get their supporters on the floor and voting. Chairmen could merely say to wavering members, "Don't cross me and don't violate your principles or constituents: don't vote at all. Without records, no one will know if you voted or how you voted—except me." With recorded, open votes, everybody knew who voted and how. Outside influences thus had more leverage, and many more amendments were offered and passed.

Fourth, in combination with these formal changes, informal norms and ways of behavior changed, too. The first to disappear was apprenticeship, the admonition long given to junior legislators to be seen and not heard. Tom Foley, initially elected to the House in 1964, described well his own experience at a time when apprenticeship was still strong:

> My first day on the Agriculture Committee . . .was spent listening to the strictures of the chairman, Harold Cooley of North Carolina. In the public arena of the committee room with the press present, he told us that he hated to hear new members interrupt senior members when they were asking questions. He went on to say that we would find, if we would only remain silent, that the senior members of the committee would ask all the important questions, discuss all the relevant issues, and decide them without our interference. He added that, unfortunately, for some it would take years; other, more clever individuals might learn in months, some of the basic information of the committee necessary for constructive participation. But, in the meantime, they could all help us—that is, the senior bench—by being quiet and attentive.[7]

In the years after Foley's initiation, committee chairmen lost their power to enforce such admonitions. Junior legislators expanded in number, and their resources expanded even faster. Party leaders became—out of both conviction and necessity—more indulgent in their attitudes toward the juniors. By the late 1960s, few sanctions existed to chastise the overzealous freshman. By the early 1970s, the norm of apprenticeship itself had disappeared: Junior members were encouraged to speak out and play an active role. Starting with 1974, freshman classes in the House organized, elected chairmen, took on staff, and aggressively acted to promote their interests, which included top committee assignments for class members and some substantive policy goals.

Through the 1970s and into the 1980s, freshmen offered amendments on the floor without ostracism and with legislative success. Some, like the Harkin Amendment specifying conditions for U.S. foreign aid, had important policy consequences. Likewise, freshmen pushed their own bills and sometimes chaired their own panels. Nothing happened to reverse this pattern when the conservative Republicans captured the Senate in 1980.

As a norm of behavior, apprenticeship wholly disappeared. Other norms continued to exist as ideals, but faded in their expression and lost any power of sanction for violation. One such was reciprocity: the notion that a member should and would defer to the expertise and desires of committees and their leaders, and that the member in turn would be deferred to for his own committee recommendations.[8] Reciprocity had at times in the past been honored only in the breach, breaking down mainly for committees that were internally divided, like House Education and Labor. More often than not, it worked well, bolstering such panels as Ways and Means, Appropriations, Commerce, and Foreign Affairs on the floor. But by the late 1970s, the most prestigious panels, including Ways and Means and Appropriations, were suffering on the floor.

"Closed" rules, which bolstered the results of reciprocity by curtailing amendments to key bills, were virtually eliminated, and important committees were increasingly unable to keep their handiwork from being changed drastically on the floor by nonmembers of the committee, or rejected altogether. Ways and Means in the Carter years saw its proposal for a five-cents-a-gallon gasoline tax rudely rejected by the House; Foreign Affairs had its human-rights policy rewritten on the floor by nonmember Tom Harkin of Iowa; Commerce saw its version of the Clean Air Act redrawn on the House floor; Appropriations' proposals to cut back on impact aid for education were rebuffed by a broad bipartisan cross section of legislators. Some bills still emerged unscathed, of course, but the path of any given piece of legislation became more unpredictable, and the prospect diminished that a coalition built in a committee would hold together on the floor.

Reciprocity as an institutional norm had in the past gone hand in hand with specialization as an individual norm. Legislators were expected to dig into their committee work, learn it well, and devote their time and legislative activity to the relative handful of areas within their panel assignments. Dilettantes—those who were active in other areas and offered bills or, worse, floor amendments outside their specialties—were frowned upon, chastised, or ostracized. Their efforts were rarely successful.

Specialization, like reciprocity, worked in a system in which senior members (especially committee chairmen) dominated, in which staff resources were scarce and the substantive experts were monopolized by the committee seniors, and in which rules discouraged outsiders' efforts. Rank-and-file legislators would suffer if they challenged the committees; in any event, few had the time or staff to follow in sufficient detail the activities or issue areas of other panels, much less to draft the appropriate amendments or bills.

In the 1970s, of course, conditions changed. Senior authority waned, staff resources multiplied, rules opened things up. Every legislator had the opportunity and the ability to track every issue area and to introduce timely amendments to all bills as they hit the floor. Over time, the sanctions against such behavior declined. The norm remains in the legislature in the 1980s; specialization is still considered theoretically desirable and still has some meaning to many members. But its reach is far less than it was in the 1950s and 1960s, and, more important, it has little effect on actual congressional behavior.

One other norm that has recently been honored mainly in the breach is courtesy. Members of Congress used to go to very great lengths to praise their colleagues, even in disagreement. Former Speaker of the House John McCormack used to note proudly that he always referred to a fellow legislator as "the most distinguished member from . . ." or "the truly honorable gentleman." Once, in the heat of anger, he ignored his own advice and went so far as to disparage a colleague by saying, "I hold the gentleman in minimum high regard."

This restraint has changed. In the past decade, there have been many more incidents of personal animosity reflected in heated comments on the floor or in committee. Epithets like "liar" are used; personal motives or abilities are questioned. Shouting matches, if not commonplace, are no longer remarkable or notable. We have by no means returned to the physical violence of the nineteenth century Congress, nor are such incidents of public acrimony applauded in the cloakrooms or accepted by members as necessary or inevitable. But clearly the norm of courtesy means less and is ignored more than it was in the 1950s. More open conflict means less ability for the legislature to compromise or even to act.

Along with changes in rules, resources, and norms, there have been significant changes in attitudes. The closed system of the 1950s had as an essential element a universally accepted sense of respect by rank-and-file members for their seniors. Party leaders and committee chairmen were revered, venerated, feared. So, too, were presidents and other such authority figures.

With the 1970s—and with Vietnam and Watergate—respect was replaced by distrust. Those with formal titles of authority or with age, status, or expertise were not to be given an additional measure of consideration by members of Congress, or the benefit of the doubt. To the contrary, they were to be discounted and downplayed. Party leaders, from the Speaker of the House on down, suffered from this change in attitude toward authority and leadership. So did the president and by extension the entire executive branch.

OUTSIDE CHANGES AFFECTING CONGRESS IN THE 1960s AND 1970s

Formal and informal changes inside Congress were accompanied by related and reinforcing changes beyond its confines. First, there were changes in the party system and thus the recruitment patterns for congressional candidates, resulting in different kinds of people getting nominated and elected. The political shakeups of the late 1960s (including disagreements over Vietnam and the riotous 1968 Democratic convention in Chicago) resulted in broad party reforms that diluted the roles of public officials in the parties and strengthened the hands of grass-roots activists. Many of these same activists used their political organizing experiences, the assistance of their fellow activists, and their new clout to run in congressional primaries. Many won. By 1974, the mix of new members of Congress included a large number with no prior elective experience, little or no background in party affairs, and a deeper commitment to issue positions than to party or legislative organization. By the late 1970s, antiwar activists were drying up as a pool for new Democratic members—only to be replaced on the Republican side by anti-gun-control, anti-abortion, and pro-morality activists.

To many observers, the arrival of this new breed of legislator brought a decline in interest in compromise in Congress, a growing sense of personal acrimony, an enhanced distrust of leadership, and a growing pressure for more decentralization and democratization. Complained one veteran Democratic House member in 1975: "These new guys don't appreciate the value of compromise, don't believe there's a history of actions around here to learn from, don't trust anybody who's a chairman, and don't give a damn about the party." Virtually the identical words were uttered by a senior Republican congressman about his colleagues in 1980! The new legislators tended to be less predictable in their voting patterns, too—less likely, in other words, to be easily added to the columns of consistently liberal or conservative. This added to the unpredictability of action in the new Congress.

A second major outside change occurred in the mass media. Coverage of Congress, Washington, and government increased in importance and public visibility when the network news shows moved from fifteen minutes to a half-hour in 1963. But a more profound change occurred in the 1970s, as tension between citizens and government over the Vietnam War grew, tension between president and Congress mounted, and Watergate exploded. The press "discovered" Washington.

In 1957, there were 876 journalists accredited by the general Congressional Press Gallery, and 261 accredited by the Radio and TV Press Gallery, and 306 by the Periodical Press Gallery. By 1967, the comparable numbers were 986, 512, and 591. In 1981, they were 1,331, 1,028, and 1,004. The radio, television, and periodical press corps almost quadrupled in twenty-four years.[9]

Washington coverage was increasing rapidly before Watergate, but public interest in the nationally televised hearings by the Ervin Committee in the Senate and the Rodino Committee in the House, and in the investigative reporting of Bob Woodward and Carl Bernstein, added a new dimension to media attention. Coverage of Washington and of Congress moved beyond the front pages and the nightly news shows to the personality columns and prime time. The fact that Watergate was followed closely by congressional scandal—notably Wilbur Mills and the famed Tidal Basin incident, and Tongsun Park and "Koreagate"—accentuated and refocused the media coverage of Congress. A new generation of "Woodsteins"—investigative reporters inspired by the Watergate duo—began to zero in on scandal and sloth as well as policy on Capitol Hill.

This new media interest in Washington had several effects on Congress. Most important, it opened up Congress more than ever before to public attention and thereby created more opportunities than ever before for individual members to receive national publicity. In the 1970s, the high-circulation personality journal, *People* magazine, opened a Washington bureau and began to feature regular pictorials on congressmen in the news. The "Today" show, "Good

Morning America," and "Nightline" expanded their coverage of Washington personalities. It became possible for any member of Congress to get national coverage and become a nationally recognized figure. Unshackled by norms or rules, aided by staff resources and new procedures, every member down to the most junior had the opportunity to seize attention.

Essentially, there were three ways to do this: become a victim of scandal, defy conventional wisdom and conduct, or publicize an issue. In the first category, we could put in recent years Wilbur Mills, Bob Bauman, Michael Myers, Charles Diggs, and many others. In the second category, there were members who denounced party leaders (Lowell Weicker and John LeBoutillier), denounced their institutions and colleagues (Bruce Caputo and Shirley Chisholm), denounced Washington (Ed Zorinsky and Paula Hawkins), defied Presidents (Dennis DeConcini), used profanity (Bella Abzug), moved into their offices (Jim Jeffords), and tried singlehandedly to free U.S. hostages in Iran (George Hansen). The third group includes among others Jack Kemp (tax cuts), Les Aspin (Pentagon cost overruns), William Proxmire (government waste, a.k.a. the "fleece of the month"), Tom Harkin (human rights), Henry Hyde (abortion), and Jeremiah Denton (teenage sex).

Television and the mass media were not, of course, new phenomena on the Capitol scene. Such luminaries as Joe McCarthy, Estes Kefauver, and John McClellan had gained national attention through televised investigations in the 1950s. But the 1970s were different. As media coverage expanded, the number of members of Congress who were brought to public attention mushroomed, and more and more of the publicized members came from the rank and file. For Caputo, Hyde, Zorinsky, DeConcini, Denton, and LeBoutillier, fame of sorts came in their freshman terms. It came in every instance because of maverick behavior that in the old Congress would have resulted in ridicule and ostracism.

This trend toward personal publicity provided, in contrast to the Rayburn era, a range of tangible and possible outside incentives. No longer did a member have to play by inside rules to receive inside rewards or avoid inside setbacks. One could "go public" and be rewarded by national attention; national attention in turn could provide ego gratification, social success in Washington, the opportunity to run for higher political office, or, by highlighting an issue, policy success.

A third major change in the 1970s outside Congress was a striking expansion in the number, range, and activity of interest groups. The anti-Vietnam War movement fostered the growth in the 1970s of a number of groups claiming to represent the public interest in areas like consumer protection, environmental and defense policy, and general government reform.[10] The decentralization, democratization, and staff growth in Congress encouraged the creation and perpetuation of these and other groups, since more members of Congress, along with their staff, could provide access and assistance to groups. As the access points expanded, the access process opened up, aided by recorded teller voting, open meetings, and open hearings.

It was not just (or mainly) public interest groups that grew in number and presence in and around Congress. Every type of group expanded. From 1970 to 1980, over 800 national trade associations moved to Washington, while the number of cities and towns directly represented tripled, to over 100. Another indication of the growth of groups during this period is the expansion of nongovernmental office space in Washington; this mushroomed from 39 million square feet in 1970 to 70 million square feet in 1980. The growth was not in commercial enterprises. By 1980, fully 40 percent of that office space was occupied by lawyers, accountants, and associations—compared with 19 percent in Chicago and 20 percent in Los Angeles.[11]

The growth in groups, combined with the "sunshine" reforms in Congress, contributed to the pressure for decentralization, strengthened the hand of junior members by giving them access to group information and resources, and added additional, outside pressures on members' voting decisions. Groups began to suggest or draft amendments to committee bills, to see that their friends introduced them, then to watch carefully when the votes—recorded votes—occurred in committee and on the floor. Groups began to pressure members of Congress on particular issues, using such weapons as targeted grass-roots support from constituents, issue-based "hit lists" of members on the wrong side, and contributions from political action committees (PACs) created after the passage of campaign finance reform laws.

In sum, as the result of a series of interrelated changes in internal operations and outside forces, Congress has become an *open system*. External incentives and rewards now compete with internal ones for members' time, attention, and behavior. The internal rewards, such as staff, trips, or chairmanships, have been democratized—they come automatically to legislators, without long waiting or testing. They cannot be withheld or removed for errant behavior. Moreover, what would have been defined as errant or maverick behavior in the past—challenging a committee's recommendations or expertise with amendments on the floor, criticizing the leadership or Congress itself, challenging the motives of other legislators—is no longer grounds for chastisement or even murmurs of disapproval. It may even bring two minutes of television exposure on the evening news, which would elicit widespread envy among colleagues.

In the open system, a high proportion of members (a majority of the Senate and 40 percent or so of the House) have chairmanships of one sort or another, usually with freedom to range widely in the scope of their hearings or investigations and with ample staff resources to assist. All 535 members have ample personal staff resources, which afford them the freedom to be active in all legislative issues and still attend to the more mundane constituency servicing. Inside committees, the open system spreads power and initiatives from the once-autocratic chairmen out to subcommittee leaders and rank-and-file members. Internal dissension in committees is not discouraged or quashed. Open meetings and hearings provide new opportunities for a variety of groups to observe members talk, deal, and vote and to influence members' actions as bills are marked up.

No longer internally cohesive or disciplined, committees are also unprotected on the floor. Major amendments to a bill might come from any direction, ranging from a dissident committee member challenging his own panel's product to an unknown freshman, whose foray into this policy area comes as a surprise to everyone. In an open system, unpredictability is the norm.

THE OPEN SYSTEM AND THE PRESIDENT

Rayburn, in our fable, was dazzled by these changes—accustomed, as he was, to operating within a closed system. But we can be confident that, in spite of his initial shock, he would quickly have adapted. Rayburn was a leader who worked in whatever system he was presented with, adapting himself and his resources to the available opportunities and constraints. And he would have realized that the open system of Congress, while unpredictable, erratic, diffused, and decentralized, also offered new openings for leadership and policy success that had been unavailable in the old era.

It is not much different for presidents. When Congress was characterized by a closed system, presidents had to work out deals and coalitions with the committee barons, or on occasion, find a broader group to persuade. The style that successful past presidents used was identical to that of the congressional leaders like Rayburn; indeed, the presidents would often rely on the leaders as brokers.

The challenge for a president in an open congressional system is, likewise, the same as the challenge to the contemporary party leaders. It requires a combination of new sensitivities and traditional skills. To prevail these days, a president first must accept a cardinal premise: he will be required to know and to deal regularly with a much wider array of players in the process, members *and* staff. Such dealings require a congressional liaison staff that works to know not just who the members are, but what they like and dislike, who needs to be sweet-talked and who can be bullied, who will be satisfied with a special White House tour for constituents or an invitation to a state dinner and who will insist on a substantive concession. Knowing the members also means maintaining an active, ongoing intelligence operation to achieve early warning of who might introduce a surprise amendment or oppose a presidential initiative or be vulnerable at a given future moment to a particular presidential plea.

Second, the open system requires much more frequent use of the most precious presidential resource—the president himself. Telephone calls to wavering members, meetings with important congressional groups, intimate give-and-take sessions with important legislators, and close working arrangements with congressional leaders are all necessary to maintain the broad net of relationships a president needs in Congress to get things done. A president who wishes to be successful with Congress will be willing to commit precious personal time to persuading members and will carry out the task of persuasion eagerly and cheerfully. While members of Congress have changed, and their institutions and incentives have changed, they are still human beings who respond to attention and favors, who understand political give and take, and who remain respectful and a bit awed by the presidency.

In knowing the members of Congress and in working closely with them, Jimmy Carter was deficient, while Ronald Reagan (at least at the beginning) was superb. Carter, selected and retained a congressional liaison staff chief who was organizationally inept and ignorant of Congress. Frank Moore stories are legion—the unreturned phone calls, the gaffes—but the problem went far beyond Moore. One story epitomizes the Carter White House relationship with Congress: Congressman Norman Mineta, a Japanese-American Democrat from San Jose and a bright young Carter loyalist, was inadvertently and embarrassingly left off the guest list for the White House state dinner for the Japanese prime minister—because the White House thought Mineta was Italian! And this from a White House that included a key congressional liaison staff member who had once been Mineta's administrative assistant.[12]

In spite of the presence of at least a few savvy lobbyists, the Carter liaison team had a difficult time assessing the members of Congress and keeping track of each one's needs and preferences. They were not helped by Carter's well-known distaste for personal politicking and friendly regular chats with legislators. They were hampered as well by Carter's lack of close friends on or from Capitol Hill.

Ronald Reagan, in part responding to the Carter experience, quickly established a strong and knowledgeable congressional liaison team, headed by Hill veteran Max Friedersdorf. Early in the administration, Friedersdorf and his colleagues made direct contact with all the members of Congress (sixteen months into the Carter term, one key Republican House member complained to me that he still had not been called by anyone from the Carter congressional liaison operation). The Friedersdorf team also began to size up the 535 members of Congress in the ways we have discussed above. They recognized early that long-term success is dependent on the accumulation of little things, such as returning calls and doing small favors for members.

They have been aided enormously by their president. Ronald Reagan likes to visit with congressmen and enjoys bargaining and bantering. He is charming and persuasive. Some of his best friends serve in Congress. He willingly devotes long hours to calling legislators and relying on personal persuasion. By all accounts, Reagan's personal efforts added at least a dozen Democrats to his side in the key vote on the budget reconciliation rule on June 25, 1981. As a *Congressional Quarterly* newsletter noted, "Reagan's prowess in the rule fight was undeniable. Vote counts by the GOP and Democrats the day before the House rules showdown . . . showed that the GOP had no more than 15 of 26 Democrats needed for their victory. That was before Reagan spent hours phoning undecided conservatives."[13] Similar comments were made after Reagan's stunning tax cut victory on July 29, 1981.[14]

Good political intelligence, political favors, and personal "stroking" of legislators are not always sufficient. There are too many members, too few inducements, and too many other persuasive elements out there. So a good president will also know to limit his priorities and to order them carefully. The new Congress is an anthill of activity, but that means much motion, and little movement. A president can use his resources, prestige, and power to focus congressional (and public) attention and to put a handful of his items at the top of the congressional agenda for action. Then, if he is lucky and skillful, he can use his abilities to succeed in these key areas. This has always been so, but Congress today is much more active and much less ordered—and everything is open and public. If a president asks for too many things and fails to put them in any strong order of preference, Congress will become overloaded, and much of his program will founder. Worse, it will look, under the glare of intense media coverage, as if the president said, "Do this," and Congress responded, "No." This is precisely what happened to Jimmy Carter, who early in his term proposed, among other things, a total overhaul of the tax system, a plan to contain health care costs, a major change in the welfare system, a new trade bill, a gasoline tax, and a fifty-dollar tax rebate. All of these proposals—some vague pronouncements, other specific bills—were referred en masse to the House Ways and Means Committee. Most stayed there, the victims of committee gridlock. There were no specific instructions from the president on the order of consideration. Ironically, Carter's major early success—House passage of his comprehensive energy bill—was diluted because other, equal priorities of the president's simultaneously went nowhere. Carter looked like a weak leader as a result.

Reagan, on the other hand, started his presidency with one overriding issue to press: the economy. This focus translated into two initiatives, a budget proposal and a tax cut proposal. Reagan as President gave a nationally televised speech in February 1981, addressed Congress (also on television) in February, addressed Congress again (once more on prime-time television) in April, and spoke to the public via national television in late July—all on the subject of his economic recovery program and his two specific proposals. He set up timetables for action, devoted the full scope of his own and his administration's resources to get these two proposals ready for Congress and to persuade Congress to meet his deadlines and vote his way. The issues were magnified as a result of the Reagan emphasis, and his successes thus underscored and celebrated by press and public alike.

Just as important, the focus on the economic issue meant that simultaneous

Reagan failures in other areas—the rejection of State Department nominee Ernest Lefever by the Senate Foreign Relations Committee; the postponement of advanced weapons sales to Saudi Arabia after overwhelming congressional protest; the passage of near-unanimous House and Senate resolutions condemning the adminstration's vote in an international organization on infant formula regulation; the rejection by House committees of administration proposals on surface mining, park land acquisition, and mineral leasing; the rebuff of the White House's proposals for funding cuts for public broadcasting; the rejection of the Reagan proposal to repeal the Clark Amendment banning American involvement in Angola—were downplayed in the press and ignored by the public, and thus had little negative effect on Reagan's overall image in Congress.

Reagan's early handling of the economic issue underscores another, traditional skill of presidential leadership, the ability to capitalize on political timing. A seasoned, savvy leader knows that momentum is a real force in politics and that reputation is more important than reality in the leadership game. It is as true today as it was in the 1950s that a president who can exaggerate his victories and mimimize his losses is considered a leader, while a president who gets more blame and less credit than he deserves is dismissed as inept or is vilified.

Congressional cloakrooms still exist, and cloakroom banter about a president has a very real influence on how fearful legislators feel when they cast votes with or against the White House. The fear may be less than it was a few decades ago, given the reality that a president has fewer sanctions to apply to the recalcitrant. But it still exists.

Moreover, the president's reputation is not built entirely on the personal experiences of the legislators. Like the rest of us, they get most of their news and impressions of people and politics from the mass media: the *New York Times, Washington Post, The Wall Street Journal,* and the networks. Thus, it is most important for a president to have a strong reputation with the media as a leader. It helps him not only with the public at large, but also with the Washington community. In the contemporary era, the access a president has to the enormous television audience multiplies the potential advantages he has in raising and fulfilling expectations, thus enhancing his reputation for further political leverage.

So, the sophisticated president knows how to maximize his public or political attention when success or drama are at hand. In Congress, Lyndon Johnson and Sam Rayburn were masters at delaying votes until just the right psychological and political moment. In the White House in 1964 and 1965, Johnson knew enough to take advantage of the momentum given him by the Kennedy assassination and his landslide election to steamroll legislation through and to look like a master doing it. Nixon timed his China trip and recognition announcement superbly, to disarm his foes and capture full world attention.

Jimmy Carter, in contrast, showed a consistent ability to deflate his opportunities—to bring public attention, interest, and expectation to a peak, only to follow with inaction. Energy policy is the best example. Michael J. Malbin elaborates on Carter's handling of energy policy elsewhere, but it is useful here to recount a little of one episode to show the importance of timing. After a few weeks of Senate and conference committee deadlock over his first comprehensive energy plan in 1977, Carter announced dramatically on national television on November 8 of that year that he was canceling his four-continent tour to stay in Washington to get the plan passed. At the time, the stalemate was with the Senate, where conferees were deadlocked 9–9 on natural gas pricing. They stayed that way for six and a half months, when the conferees finally voted 10–7 for a compromise. Much evidence suggests that during November 1977

—incredibly—Carter did not apply face-to-face pressure to any of the nine opposing senators. Whether or not this is true, no savvy leader would dramatically cancel a trip, causing the public, Congress, and press to take notice, before first arranging for a breakthrough to be imminent. Instead, as a result of Carter's inattention to political timing, he not only was unable to take credit for his plan and his persuasion, but his dramatic move served rather to highlight his ineptitude!

Note that we are not talking about charisma here. *Any* president has the ability to suddenly capture public and media attention, as Carter did. Note also that the energy plan ultimately passed; it does go down as a Carter accomplishment. But he received little or no credit for it, and his reputation in fact declined.

Carter repeated this pattern in July 1979, when he abruptly canceled a planned energy speech and retreated to Camp David, emerging days later to address the nation. The drama was palpable. Interest in this prime-time Sunday presidential address was as high as for any recent times. The result was not wild enthusiasm, but still, mild approval. While well-delivered, the Carter speech gave few specifics and made no striking proposals or calls for sacrifice. But even worse, the president tripped over his own momentum a couple of days later by abruptly firing several members of his cabinet. The rather favorable response to his speech was forgotten, and once again the Carter reputation suffered.

In the "new" Congress, stage-managing is far more difficult than in the old, and far more risky. Reagan came within four votes of losing on his 1981 budget reconciliation vote; many things beyond his control could have occurred to turn a dramatic presidential victory into an equally important presidential defeat. The same is true of the vote in August 1982 on the Reagan tax increase bill. The point is, however, that a president must be sensitive to the importance of timing and must devote his resources to using it to his advantage. No matter how skillful a president is as a communicator, there are only a limited number of times that he can wholly capture public, press, and congressional attention, and heighten everybody's expectations. The successful president will hoard these opportunities judiciously, use them only when he can gain from them, and tie them directly to his expenditure of resources to persuade congressmen.

Finally, the savvy president will look at the new, open Congress and will devise ways of taking advantage of the permeability in the system. If Congress is more diffuse, no committee or "little group of willful men" can any longer bottle up completely and without recourse a pet presidential proposal, the way that chairmen like Wilbur Mills on Ways and Means, "Judge" Smith on Rules, and others did to pet initiatives of Truman, Eisenhower, Kennedy, and Johnson. In the old closed system, Jimmy Carter would never have gotten a vote in the House on his hospital cost containment plan; it would have died a definitive death in committee. In the new open system, he found ways to get the bill to the floor (even if he did end up losing on the vote there). Reagan's dramatic budget plan required bypassing many committees, overruling others, and turning the usual congressional decision-making process upside down. The new reformed budget process made his bold plan feasible technically; the fluid, unfocused atmosphere of the open congressional system allowed it to work politically.

The new Congress poses both new problems and new opportunities for a president. New sensitivities, creative leadership, and traditional political skills can overcome the problems and result in success. It will not be total success: no president in modern history has won all or even most of his legislative battles. But a skillful president today can do as well as his successful predecessors from the good old days. Even Sam Rayburn would acknowledge that.

Reading 8.5

The President as Coalition Builder: Reagan's First Year

Hedrick Smith

In the 1970s, the Presidency encountered a most assertive Congress. In response to excesses of executive authority during both the Vietnam War and Watergate crisis, Congress reared up on its hind legs. Restraints were imposed on the President by the Congress in the form of a War Powers Act, National Commitments Resolution, denial of funds for continued involvement in Southeast Asia and Angola, a new budget process with restrictions on presidential spending authority, and increased, aggressive general congressional oversight and micromanagement of executive authority.

The intensity of this bold, balky, and independent Congress led many to conclude that the United States had entered an era of an "imperiled" or "no-win" Presidency, so constraining were the shackles placed on executive power by the Congress. Many wrote of the Presidency as "an illusory, impossible job," an institution that was no match for the fragmented yet assertive Congress. The Reagan administration, especially during its first two years with a series of impressive legislative victories, at least temporarily put an end to notions that modern Presidents were hopeless matches for Congress.

The following insightful case study by a well-known journalist gives an in-depth view into the Reagan successes. In reading this, it should be kept in mind that some see in the Reagan administration a return to a more conventional mode of presidential-congressional relations, quite different from the Johnson-Nixon-Ford-Carter Presidencies, during which, respectively, Presidents conducted business in roles as majority leader, foreign minister, minority leader, and layman outsider. The current question to ask is: Does the Reagan administration represent a new era in presidential-congressional relations or only a brief respite from the agonizing frustrations of congressional assertiveness and stalemated legislative-executive relations?

Source: *The New York Times Magazine,* August 9, 1981.

In his stunning first-year drive to push through Congress a radical program of budget and tax cuts, President Ronald Reagan faced a pivotal and revealing moment of decision on the warm, humid morning of June 18, 1981. Meeting with a handful of aides in the Oval Office, the President was under pressure from David Stockman, his tireless and combative budget director, to throw down the gauntlet once more to the Democratic leadership of the House of Representatives—to reject the budget cuts developed by the Democratic-dominated committees of the House and send up a second package of his own to make the House toe the line of the original budget resolution passed in early May.

"The committees have broken faith with the first budget resolution," Stockman argued. "What they have done is sadly deficient. It could jeopardize your entire economic program. We have to make a major fight to restore the provisions in your first budget."

Others cautioned the President about the perils of treading on congressional prerogatives and of kindling institutional animosities. "We just have to understand we're running a very great risk here," warned James A. Baker III, the White House Chief of Staff. "If we throw down the challenge and lose, it will sap our momentum. It will have very damaging effects on the tax program." David Gergen, the tall, lanky communications director, pointed out that this time, unlike in the first budget fight, the White House would have "precious little time" to generate broad public support.

But Stockman was insistent. He sensed that the President felt sandbagged by the Democratic leaders' pretended support of his earlier budget victory, and he played to Mr. Reagan's instinct to show them now that they could not get away with partial measures. Some of the Democratic cuts, Stockman asserted, were "phony" because they left the eligibility and entitlement rules of many big federal programs largely unchanged, which meant that these programs would grow automatically in future years.

"If you can't get those entitlement cuts," Stockman declared, "it will add to the deficits in 1983 and 1984. If you want to balance the budget in '84, you can't live with the cuts they've made."

That hooked the President, who asked to look at Stockman's figures. "Well, if that's the case," he declared with irritation, "we can't accept it."

That was the call to battle. The White House swung into action. By noon, the President was going over his options at a hastily assembled luncheon of his staff, House Republican leaders, and four of the dissident conservative Southern Democrats who had broken party ranks and given him vital support for his first budget victory. These "boll weevil" Democrats now formed a crucial component of his working coalition though some of them were "a little goosey" about a new budget fight, as one White House official later recalled. But the President's legislative advisers were telling him that while Stockman's complete budget substitute would not make it, a more modest partial package could pass the House.

To prepare the way, the President put in a call the next morning to Speaker O'Neill, the shaggy Irish politician and New-Deal Democrat with whom Mr. Reagan has both kidded and clashed. Most recently they had had a public spat over Mr. O'Neill's implication that the President was insensitive to the poor. Since then the air had cleared, but, as it now turned out, their morning telephone talk again fired the President's mood for combat.

"I want a chance to send some substitute language up there on the budget and have it voted on," the President told the Speaker. "The House has worked hard and done a good job, but it hasn't gone far enough, and I. . . ."

Aides saw irritation and frustration flash across the President's face as the Speaker interrupted to remind the President that the Congressional committees had completed their work.

"Did you ever hear of the separation of powers?" Mr. O'Neill asked. "The Congress of the United States will be responsible for spending. You're not supposed to be writing legislation."

"I know the Constitution," Mr. Reagan broke in.

"Can you be specific about what you're going to send up?" The Speaker pressed on. "You always talk to me in vague generalities. I don't want to see the Republicans trying to shove something through without full consideration."

"Oh, come on, you mean the Democrats," tweaked the President. "I was a Democrat myself, longer than I've been a Republican, and the Democrats have been known to make a few power plays."

The Speaker backed off. "O.K., we'll have a look," acceded Mr. O'Neill. "I'll get back to you." The President inserted a belated anniversary congratulations, and the Speaker closed by advising him, "Have your people talk to Jones and Bolling" (the Democratic chairmen of the Budget and Rules Committees).

Despite the genial sign-off, the President's dander was up. He became further irritated, aides said later, when O'Neill did not get back to him, though that may have been the result of a misunderstanding. (O'Neill may have thought his comment about Jones and Bolling would take care of that.) But now the die was cast, and any thought of compromise, on either budget or tax cuts, was dashed. Eager for confrontation, Mr. Reagan was ready to concentrate on his battle to beat the Democrats.

Six days later, on the eve of the crucial budget vote, the President arrived in his penthouse suite at the Century Plaza Hotel in Los Angeles after an all-day cross-country trip that had him stumping for his budget and tax proposals at the National Jaycee Convention in San Antonio. Jim Baker and others had ruled out a national television address on the second budget package because they did not want the President's prestige so totally on the line in this nip-and-tuck battle.

But the Jaycees provided a good forum. They had whooped and cheered like a political pep rally at Mr. Reagan's sallies against big spenders in "these puzzle palaces on the Potomac." It was time, the President had insisted, to "restore economic sanity" and to send a message to Congress to "finish the job."

By now, the budget battle turned on an intricate parliamentary fight over the rules, and Speaker O'Neill, sensing favorable terrain, was telling reporters he expected a Democratic victory the next day.

At his hotel suite, the President was relaxing over vodka and orange juice with his chief personal aide, Michael K. Deaver, when a call came from the White House reporting a new burst of insurrection among conservative Democrats. They were angered over the way the leadership was chopping up the Reagan package, thus reviving the President's prospects for victory. Stockman and Max Friedersdorf, the smoothly efficient chief of congressional liaison at the White House, were urging the President to telephone some of the undecided Congressmen. But after the long trip from Washington, Mr. Reagan's voice was hoarse, and Deaver was unsure how he would take to more politicking that night.

"It's pretty close back there," Deaver reported, "and if you made a few calls, that could swing it."

"Get them on the phone," the President offered quickly.

"It may be as many as 20 calls," Deaver said, testing him.

"What time is it back there?"

"About 9 o'clock back East," Deaver said.

"Well, we'd better get going."

The President sat down in slacks and an open-necked shirt at a little desk with a lamp and note pad while the White House switchboard tracked down 16 members of the House at dinner parties, in restaurants, or at home. For two and a half hours he stalked votes.

"Gee, I know it's late back there and I'm sorry to bother you," Mr. Reagan would begin. "I hear you're still on the fence. If I could answer any questions, I'd be happy to. I know you've been under a lot of pressure. But I hope you can find your way clear to supporting us tomorrow." If someone had a specific problem, he'd make a note and say, "I'll get the fellows back to you on that one."

He caught John Breaux, an influential sixth-term Louisiana Democrat, at a downtown dinner party. "The President comes across on the phone as smooth as he does on TV," Breaux would recall later. "He's a generalist, doesn't talk details. But he knows enough of the big picture. He's easygoing, not strong-arm like Lyndon Johnson. It's a soft sell and it's very effective."

The next day, the President sweated out each vote, pestering Deaver for results or asking why there were so many procedural ballots before the House actually got to his budget package. But he won what turned out to be his toughest fight in the long economic offensive, telling reporters: "I've never felt better in these last five months than I feel in this particular moment."

Reagan the convinced conservative crusader, Reagan the strategist, Reagan the battler, Reagan the cheerleader, Reagan the political charmer, has staked the fate of his presidency on his single-minded campaign to enact a radical turn in the nation's economic policy. Using his capacity to persuade Congress to enact the largest budget and tax cuts in American history, he was able to move Congress on this one central issue, and establish his national leadership. In slightly more than six months, he achieved far more than political Washington had dreamed possible on the day of his Inauguration.

His accomplishment was striking not only because it came in spite of a Democratic majority in the House, but also because such political mastery of the legislative branch eluded the last three occupants of the White House—Carter, Ford, and Nixon. For not since Lyndon B. Johnson's Great Society surge in the mid-sixties had Washington seen a president perform so persuasively with the legislature, devising a working political coalition of Republicans and conservative southern Democrats for a program that has put the country on a new political course.

In his first six months as chief executive, Mr. Reagan had been bold and purposeful, firm about his major objectives but flexible at the margins. As a public figure, he had enjoyed an extended honeymoon and warm popularity. Sheer luck had also helped. His presidency was born in the special upsurge of national emotion that greeted the release of the American hostages from Iran. It got another boost from the successful Columbia space shuttle. Public sympathy and support rose further in response to his gallant geniality after the attempt on his life, an event that he turned to political advantage with a dramatic appearance before Congress. Fate also spared Mr. Reagan any major foreign crisis up to that point and had given him a global oversupply of oil that helped ease the fires of inflation.

To the electorate, he had come across as Mr. Nice Guy with the Eisenhower grin and the infectious optimism of the boy next door. But on Capitol Hill, legislators had discovered his political grit and competitive streak. He may have had a reputation for 8:30 to 5:30 office hours, but when the chips were down, he was willing to roll up his sleeves. As political chairman of the board, he delegated wide latitude to his lieutenants and left the details to others, but the administration's programs indisputably bore his philosophical hallmarks. Comments in Washington about his age quickly evaporated. Nor did other politicians disparage him as a former actor. Many expressed amazed respect for his deft salesmanship and his taste for political combat, both vital ingredients to his success.

"In dealing with Congress, he's closer to Lyndon Johnson than anyone else," observed Senate Majority Leader Howard H. Baker, Jr. "Johnson had a feel for the way the legislature works. He was a product of the legislature. Reagan understands it instinctively. He understands legislative politics, but he doesn't try to bull his way through the way Johnson did. Carter never understood the legislative process. Ford understood but he couldn't do anything about it. Nixon never paid enough attention to it to be successful. For give-and-take with Congress, Reagan is the best I've ever served with."

Grudgingly, experienced Democrats also tipped their hats; though they contended Mr. Reagan's success was temporary. "Reagan's six months is comparable with Johnson's first six months on the Great Society," conceded Representative Morris K. Udall, the liberal Arizona Democrat, in August 1981. "On the budget, it was a brilliant one-shot marriage. Overall, on his dealing with Congress, I'd give him a B-plus. He's been good. He still doesn't know Congress all that well. He's got some good people who do. But I don't see this as a permanent coalition for Reagan. I don't think that because he got through a budget that he can count on a new political alignment in October on some other issue. I think the disillusionment is going to set in this fall."

Whether Reagan's economic policy will eventually cure the nation's ills or will ultimately backfire economically and polarize Americans politically is a critical question for his presidency and the Republican party. But, initially, he not only prevailed politically and pulled the entire public debate in his direction, but he also altered the political chemistry in Washington. He projected genial optimism to the public and injected a sense of motion in government.

Only four times this century has a president had such effective sway with Congress, according to James Sundquist, a presidential scholar at the Brookings Institution. He cites Woodrow Wilson after his first election, Franklin D. Roosevelt at the start of the New Deal period, President Johnson in his Great Society heyday, and now Mr. Reagan.

"The system works well at only one time—right after a landslide election," Mr. Sundquist observed. "This is one of those brief periods in our history when a president comes riding a great tide of personal popularity. I think this will change when the president's popularity begins to go down. But he has it now."

From the perspective of late 1981, it is hard to step back into the dark mood of pessimism in 1980 and to recall the flow of worried essays about the breakdown of government and the weakness of the American presidency as an institution. Just after the November election, former President Gerald Ford epitomized the concern in an essay for *Time* magazine in which he wrote: "We have not an imperial Presidency but an imperiled Presidency."

Many shared his mood, Republicans and Democrats alike. Lloyd Cutler, former President Carter's White House counsel, found there was a "structural inability" to govern under the American system of separated powers. He longingly eyed the European parliamentary model and proposed several electoral remedies to the Congress closer to the Chief Executive. Former Treasury Secretary John B. Connally, Jr., prescribed a single, six-year term for the president. Former Vice-President Walter Mondale, lamenting that the presidency had become the focus of popular discontent, called it "the fire hydrant of the nation."

The common diagnosis was that any president was institutionally crippled not only because of the impossibility of managing the sprawling federal establishment, but more importantly because of the unwieldy inertia of Congress. Presidential programs got lost, defeated, or simply mired down, it was said, because Congressional leaders had lost their former clout, power had become dispersed and disorganized among a labyrinth of committees, party discipline had broken down, and the main business of the legislature was snarled in the incessant crossfire of special-interest lobbying and single-issue politics. All these prevented the formation of an effective governing coalition between the White House and Capitol Hill.

How, then, does one explain the dramatic turnaround that President Reagan achieved?

National Consensus In the amalgam of causes, the most fundamental is that President Reagan picked as his first priority the issue on which he found a strong consensus and a palpable conservative trend—the urge to cut back government and the sense of a pocketbook squeeze at all levels of society. He profited greatly from a pent-up sense of frustration at the Carter government, perhaps because the Vietnam War, Watergate, and Nixon's resignation had deferred the normal rhythmic swing toward conservatism and consolidation in American politics.

The November 1980 election represented a frustrated rejection of the "ins" and their old economic policies and a demand for something new. The Reaganites have contended that their man won a clear mandate for his package of budget and tax cuts. In fact, from the opinion polls on election day, it seems that the message was less precise than that—less a mandate for a specific economic blueprint than an urge for change and a willingness to grant a new President greater-than-usual tolerance to experiment. And shrewdly, President Reagan and his lieutenants fed that sentiment and built their own mandate with their constant preachments against "politics as usual" to nourish public support for Mr. Reagan's radical shift in policy.

Clear Presidential Objectives With an economic program fashioned during the campaign, President Reagan immediately conveyed a sense of self-confidence and direction. He not only had exploited vacillation and zig-zag policies under Mr. Carter as a campaign issue, but he also had profited from the contrast with his predecessor once he moved into the White House.

Mr. Reagan's own clarity of purpose gave unity and thrust to his administration from the outset. It also simplified his legislative agenda. For the Reagan team deliberately avoided Jimmy Carter's early mistake of inundating Congress and confusing the public with a profusion of proposals. The priority was clear. The message was simple. Mr. Reagan concentrated his early fire on the economic package and pushed foreign policy and controversial social issues into the background. Later, in the fall, he was unable to keep the legislative agenda as sharply focused, for the battle over arms sales to Saudi Arabia helped disrupt congressional momentum on his economic program.

A Fast Opening The President's political braintrust—Counselor Ed Meese, III, Baker, Deaver, Stockman, Gergen, and Richard Wirthlin, the pollster, understood that Mr. Reagan's opportunity to achieve radical change was perilously short. "Normally," said Gergen, "a new president has an open window for just so long and it shuts very quickly in terms of public interest and support." To capitalize on the traditional honeymoon with the Congress, the press and the public, they felt compelled to move fast with major proposals, seize the initiative, and keep momentum rolling.

With the Administration's first $50 billion budget-cut package, the Reagan team stunned the opposition and captured political momentum before congressional Democrats fully appreciated what was happening. Soon the Democratic leaders, belatedly responding to the public's conservative fiscal mood, scrambled in disarray to play catch-up, me-too politics with the President. By then, Mr. Reagan got a second lease from the public with his graceful handling of the attempt on his life. Rather than daring to oppose him outright, the Democrats resisted him at the margins. Their budget and tax proposals ultimately became variations on basic Reagan themes, an indication of how thoroughly he had dominated the political arena. For even if he lost, the President stood to get most of what he wanted.

Assiduous Courting of Congress Knowing that success depended on congressional support, the President and his entourage began courting goodwill on Capitol Hill and among the Washington establishment well before taking office. On Inauguration Day, it was not lost on Capitol Hill, where courtesies and symbolic gestures are warmly appreciated, that the President's first official acts were to sign a hiring freeze and the certificates for his cabinet officers in the President's room of the Capitol, where he stayed to have his inaugural lunch.

In the early weeks, senior House Democrats were invited to the Oval office for a presidential chat and came away murmuring that Democratic presidents had never treated them so well. In his effort to strike up acquaintances with adversaries as well as with allies, Mr. Reagan spent roughly 20 percent of his time on congressional relations.

In the week before his first House vote on the budget, he sat down personally with 60 Democrats and 12 Republicans, either in head-to-head sessions or in such small groups that each felt the flattery of his attention, and many left with a gift of presidential cuff links or seats in the presidential box at the Kennedy Center. When the going got tougher in the second budget fight, the fence-sitters got juicier sweeteners—White House backing for a sugar price support, more funds for Medicaid, Conrail, energy subsidies for the poor, or a slowdown on mandatory conversion to coal for industrial boilers in oil-producing states. The President and his lieutenants were not skittish about the kind of horse-trading that Jimmy Carter had found so distasteful and that Lyndon Johnson had so expertly exploited.

Louisiana's John Breaux, who zig-zagged in his support of the Reagan program, was lured into the President's camp on the crucial second budget vote with a promise of higher sugar support prices, an issue of great importance to his home state. And others went along with Breaux. "I went for the best deal," Breaux admitted candidly after the vote. But he denied that his vote had been bought. "I can be rented," he quipped puckishly, and then later proved it by voting against the President in the tax-cut fight.

The Legislative Vehicle At the suggestion of Senator Pete Domenici, the New Mexico Republican who heads the Senate Budget Committee, the Reagan strategists fastened on the unique vehicle of budget reconciliation to force the legislature to dance to a disciplined drum beat. The process was set up in 1974 to provide a central mechanism to force congressional committees to abide by some overall spending ceilings and central guidance. It had been used only once before, modestly in 1980, but Domenici and Stockman saw it as a vital lever for the Reagan program.

"The driving force has been the national consensus for a program that became a magnet for support in Congress," Stockman commented afterward. "Reconciliation was the action-firing mechanism that overcame the natural inertia of Congress." Some people question whether it can be used so extensively in years to come, and it works only with the budget process—not on other legislation.

Using Presidential Popularity from the Bully Pulpit At the time of his success on his economic package, Reagan was winning about a 65 percent approval rating from the American people—slightly higher than Nixon and Carter, but lower than Kennedy and Eisenhower in their early months. He used the leverage of his early popularity to go over the heads of Congress to sell his program with simple, evocative language. The acme was his dramatic televised reappearance before Congress on April 28 after the shooting incident. That produced what House Republican leader Robert Michel called "the kind of reception that makes a few of the waverers feel, 'Gosh, how can I buck that?'"

Dan Rostenkowski, the veteran Democratic leader in the tax battle, conceded the point. "My problem is that the President can gear up his army with just one television appearance," Rostenkowski moaned before the final showdown. "That's fighting the Army, Navy, Marines and Air Force." Among southern Democrats, the President's public following had a noticeable effect. "Reagan won 72 percent of the vote in my district and he's a lot more popular there now than he was on Election Day," remarked Kent Hance, a West Texas Democrat who cosponsored the Reagan tax program. "It's mighty tough to go against a popular president in a district like mine, especially when he's pushing the same kind of economic policies I've been talking about all along."

A First-Rate Political Team Once again, President Reagan has profited by contrast with former President Carter. His legislative operation was widely regarded as well-organized, purposeful, attentive, and usually ahead of the Democrats on tactics. As a former Congressman, Dave Stockman brought to the budget maneuvering an intimate understanding of both the budget and the congressional process. As point man on the budget, he not only overwhelmed opponents with expertise but absorbed criticism, sparing the President.

Friedersdorf, who previously served as President Ford's congressional liaison, is known as one of Washington's most experienced, best-organized and quietly effective experts on Congress. Jim Baker, another experienced political strategist, has shepherded the whole operation and teamed up well with Treasury Secretary Donald T. Regan on tax legislation. On the Hill, Senator Howard Baker and Representative Michel are given high marks for keeping Republicans in line and stepping in with advice to save the Administration from legislative pitfalls. When the fall round of budget cutting began, however, Reagan's inner circle did not work so closely with the congressional leaders, and this cost the White House setbacks on intended budget-cutting plans. But, overall, the Reagan team was strong.

Hardball Politics in the Home Districts One of the least visible weapons in the Reagan arsenal is the political operation masterminded by Lyn Nofziger, the puckish, rumpled California conservative. As White House political director, he carried the budget and tax battles into the home districts of wavering members of Congress, softening them up for presidential persuasion.

The theory was that pressure from home, especially from local officials or big campaign contributors has more impact on a member of Congress than any other political force.

From 15 years of criss-crossing America in the cause of conservatism, Ronald Reagan has developed the most potent network of political activists in the nation. "That's why Reagan is not a man to trifle with," asserts Lee Atwater, the South Carolina political organizer who is Nofziger's deputy. "He's got more people committed to him than anyone else. They're ready, able and willing to go into action on a moment's notice, and technically they're well organized."

Drawing on this network during the first budget fight of last April 1981, Nofziger ran a political blitz in 54 swing congressional districts, 45 of them in the South. His operation tapped wealthy, organized groups like the Republican National Committee, the Republican Congressional Campaign Committee, the National Conservative Political Action Committee, the Moral Majority, the Fund for a Conservative Majority, business political action committees linked with the national Chamber of Commerce, National Association of Manufacturers, Business Roundtable, National Federation of Small Businessmen, National Jaycees, American Medical Association, local civic clubs, and scores of other groups interested in cutting federal spending and taxes. They were spearheaded by a team of high-level administration and congressional speakers, direct mail, and phone banks generating grass-roots support.

"The premise of the whole operation is that political reforms and the impact of media have made it so that a congressman's behavior on legislation can be affected more by pressure from within his own district than by lobbying here in Washington," explains Atwater. "The way we operate, within forty-eight hours any Congressman will know he has had a major strike in his district. All of a sudden, Vice-President Bush is in your district, Congressman Jack Kemp is in your district. Ten of your top contributors are calling you, the head of the local AMA, the head of the local realtors' group, local officials. Twenty letters come in. Within forty-eight hours, you're hit by paid media, free media, mail, phone calls, all asking you to support the President."

More potent, perhaps, is the implication

that the big political action money will oppose incumbents who line up against the Reagan program. A House Republican task force under Representative Stan Parris of Virginia cross-checked people who had contributed more than $100 both to the Reagan Presidential campaign and to the local Democratic Congressman's campaign. Computerized letters went out to get these pro-Reagan contributors to pressure their Representative to go along with the President.

"The key to these Congressional victories, of course, is muscle," says Senator Paul Laxalt of Nevada, a close friend of the President. "People here feel that most of the public is with the President. One of the greatest things that was done was to go through the lists of big contributors and get them to lean on swing people. If a key contributor calls and says, go along with this, it has an effect."

The reach of the White House political operation has astonished some fence-sitters. Representative Ronnie Flippo of Alabama was reportedly turned around by a call from Governor Fob James, a pro-Reagan Democrat. Representative Dan Mica, a Democrat representing the Palm Beach area, was leaned on by his former campaign manager. "I had a call, too, from a local mayor, a Democrat very active in the party and associated with liberal causes, and he asked me to vote with the President," Mica said. "That surprised me that they would get to him."

Sometimes ardent Reaganites have been overly zealous. Mica and Bill Nelson, another swing Florida Democrat, squawked after William Wirthlin, a lobbyist for the National Taxpayers Union, told them that unless they committed themselves to the second Reagan budget package, even before it had been publicly surfaced, his group would run radio ads in their home districts. Mica was infuriated after Worthlin played for him a tape asserting that Speaker O'Neill was enlisting him to "destroy" the President's program. When Nelson protested directly to the President at a White House meeting, Mr. Reagan shook his head in disbelief. "That's about the lousiest tactic I ever heard of," he said. "We don't condone it. We don't have anything to do with it." White House aides advised the National Taxpayers Union the maneuver was backfiring and it was dropped.

Reagan aides believe that one reason the President has fared so well in his first long legislative drive was his effort to understand the predicament of the "boll weevil" Democrats. At a breakfast on June 4, John Breaux of Louisiana voiced a common fear that the "boll weevils" were getting cut off from their own party and might have to face President Reagan campaigning against them in 1982. "I don't want to end up like a turkey with an eagle (the nickname of big Republican contributors) chasing me," Breaux said.

Instantly, the President gave a widely quoted response. "I could not oppose someone who supported my principles," he said. "I could not look myself in the mirror if I campaigned against you." Even though the President left himself the loophole of fund raising in their states and stopped short of offering them immunity from Republican opposition, one aide said, "You could sense a real sigh of relief around that table."

The Reagan camp does keep score among friends and foes, meting out rewards and punishment. Because of a campaign pledge and good Republican backing in Michigan last November, Mr. Reagan went along with import relief for the automobile industry and United Auto Workers Union through seeking reduction of Japanese exports. But in June he lifted import quotas on shoes from Taiwan and Korea, a move that hit the American shoe industry in Massachusetts, home territory of Speaker O'Neill and Senator Edward M. Kennedy.

Party-Line Support So much attention has focused on Reagan recruitment of Democratic dissidents that an even more impressive feat has been largely overlooked—*the* *near perfect party-line support among 53 Republican Senators and 191 House members.* (The Democrats have 243 in the House, 46 in the Senate, and there is one Senate independent.) Neither Eisenhower, Nixon, nor Ford achieved close to that kind of party loyalty and discipline. Indeed, some scholars say that the Republican party-line votes this spring have not been equaled since the hard-headed rule of "Czar" Joseph G. Cannon, the Republican speaker, back in 1910.

The congressional leaders, Howard Baker in the Senate and Bob Michel in the House, were extremely effective in persuading Republicans that political success is affected by President Reagan's success when it comes time for reelection. One impetus is that many newly elected Republican conservatives in Congress feel special allegiance to Mr. Reagan because they rode his coattails into office in 1980. Occasionally, Michel went to House Republicans to call for a party-line vote with the admonition that there would be "retribution" against dissidents. None was meted out in the budget and tax battles because the economic issues were the best for unifying Republicans; they split more naturally over social and foreign policy questions. Beyond that, the new experience of partisan victory fostered loyalty.

Among the first- and second-term House Republicans, partisan spirit was especially strong. "The freshman and sophomore classes make up almost half of our 191 members," observes Max Friedersdorf. "They are extremely aggressive to make their mark. They want to win and they are fully aware that they have power in unity. They have an influence on the more senior Republicans who have developed a 'minority complex' over the years and have been inclined to go off on their own. They sense that they're getting close to having a majority in the House. This makes for an esprit that I've never seen before."

On the budget votes, holding two dozen northeastern and midwestern moderate and liberal Republicans led by Carl Purcell of Michigan and William Green of New York was a delicate task. Like other Republicans they chafed over the attention the White House lavished on renegade southern Democrats.

Nofziger's office tried to meet their desires for political appointments. Stockman and Michel met repeatedly with their group to adjust the budget cuts to appease them. Ultimately the frost-belt Republicans won increases in funds for Amtrak, Conrail, energy subsidies to the poor, the National Endowment for Arts and the Humanities, nurses' training, and a less stringent cap on the growth of Medicaid spending. "When you're dealing with the entire budget, there are things along the margin that give way to making the overall goal," Stockman later explained. "We were willing to make adjustments at the margin."

That approach worked well through the summer, but when the White House and Stockman came back with a new round of proposed cuts in domestic social programs and the idea of deferring the annual cost-of-living increase in Social Security benefits, they touched a raw nerve. These moderate Republicans, who called themselves the "gypsy moths," rebelled. Bill Green talked of a "double-cross" by the administration. With Purcell and others, he called for $9 billion in defense cuts as a protest against the President's choice of priorities. With close to two dozen Republicans in rebellion, Michel could no longer hold the House coalition together and pressed the White House to backtrack. The constant risk for Reagan was that as he kept pressing further on his budget-cutting, he was losing his Congressional consensus. The Gypsy Moths, facing the 1982 elections in many pro-Democratic districts, had gone about as far as they could go with Reagan fiscal conservatism.

In all the maneuvering, President Reagan has left the horse-trading to others and stayed out of the details of legislative maneuvering. His generalized approach caused

Speaker O'Neill to quip that Mr. Reagan does not know very much about the specifics of his own legislation. Emerging from one meeting with the President in early June, O'Neill told reporters that when the Democratic leadership would try out variations on the President's tax program, Mr. Reagan would look at Ed Meese, his counselor, for a lead on how to reply, a charge denied at the White House.

"The President's really not as well posted on the specifics and on the machinery as Johnson, Nixon, or Ford, who used to be more intimately involved in how it all worked," observed Michel, the House Republican leader. "Sometimes I'm a little apprehensive. I think, 'My Gosh, he ought to be better posted. Where are his briefing papers?' But he's chairman of board. He's not going to be hassled over details, and anyway you get the feeling that he's just so intent that he's going to get along with Congress and get as much out of Congress as he can."

Friedersdorf credited the President's early successes to his amiable manner, his willingness to listen, and his investment of time. "Congressional relations is not just a haphazard, occasional thing with the President," he said. "It's constant. He's very willing to take advice not only from the White House staff but the Congressional leaders. Plus, he's sold on his program and he transmits that enthusiasm in his contacts."

Both cohorts and competitors have discovered, too, that Mr. Reagan's amiability is disarming; it masks a certain toughness. Governor Hugh Carey ran into the hard side of President Reagan during one session that the President held with state governors back on February 23. Carey criticized the Reagan tax plan of ten percent personal tax rate reductions for each of the next three years, on grounds that it would fuel inflation. He urged Mr. Reagan to reconsider the plan.

"You could hear a pin drop in that room," said Rich Williamson, the White House aide for intergovernmental relations. "It was a very forceful challenge. They all wanted to see if Reagan was for real. While Carey was talking, Reagan got red in the face. He glared at Carey, and then he burst out: 'What you've been talking about, business as usual, has given us an economic mess. Double-digit inflation. Double-digit interest rates. High unemployment. Let's try something new.' Then he cited past examples of regenerative tax cuts, and ended: 'I'd say with vehemence that I support 10–10–10.'"

Over the next four months, the President was persuaded to drop that 30 percent tax cut to 25 percent and to delay the first effective date from January 1 to October 1 to gain support from the "boll weevil" Democrats. But that was not enough; he was still under pressure from other Democrats to go lighter and later with his tax cut.

At one session with Democrats on the Senate Finance Committee Senator Fritz Hollings of South Carolina voiced renewed concern that the Reagan tax cut would add to federal deficits. Moreover, he said, public opinion polls showed that a tax cut ranked behind inflation, a balanced budget, unemployment, and American prestige abroad in the public's view. He urged the tax cut be put off until January 1, 1982.

"We've already split the difference by moving it to October," the President demurred. "I believe very strongly that all of the things they've listed will be helped by the tax cut." He then recalled that tax cuts under President Kennedy had not only stimulated the economy but generated more tax revenues. He wanted to follow the Kennedy model.

"But Jack Kennedy did it in steps," Hollings objected. "He lowered the capital gains tax first and then moved on to personal tax cuts."

"I've come to learn over the years that government doesn't get the money it needs," the President countered. "Government spends all the taxes it gets. So if we reduce the amount of taxes, we will reduce spending."

Senator Bennett Johnston, the Louisiana Democrat, suggested having the third year of the tax cut conditional—triggered only by the success of the first two years. But Mr. Reagan rejected that tactic. "We will have difficulty convincing people that it [the third year] will really happen," he said. "If you have any loophole, we will have trouble."

Charming as he can be in private sessions, the President becomes more combative in public. He enjoys the cut-and-thrust of debate. He seems to relish political hyperbole. Visiting Capitol Hill in mid-July, he taunted the Democrats, who had been accusing him of offering a "rich man's tax bill," with the charge that they were providing a more generous tax shelter than he for the intricate tax dodges of the wealthy known as commodity straddles. Their tax bill, he mocked, was "a make-believe tax cut . . . a wolf in sheep's clothing" because it was not as big as his.

Jousting with Speaker O'Neill has occasionally gotten under the President's skin, but he is quick to patch things up. As O'Neill has said, they put aside their disagreements at 6 P.M. and mix cordially. "They can disagree and still be friends," said one White House official. "I think that sets an atmosphere for cooperation and communication. It shows junior members of Congress that some of this is political posturing and there's no real animosity."

Two terms as Governor of California gave Mr. Reagan solid awareness of the need for legislative compromise, for during most of his tenure in Sacramento, Democrats controlled both houses of the state legislature. He emerged with a more moderate record than his campaign rhetoric had foreshadowed. His method, Ed Meese said, was "to stand firm on principle but be flexible enough to negotiate within the framework of principle."

As President, Mr. Reagan has left it to others to do most of the active negotiating for him. "Ronald Reagan gives more latitude to subordinates than any president I ever saw but when it comes time to make a decision, he makes it," commented Senator Howard Baker. Dave Stockman improvised many of the particulars of his budget cut package, especially after the first program was put together. Jim Baker, the White House staff chief, and Treasury Secretary Regan worked out the tax compromise. They came to him with an expanded package, adopting several items worked up by the mainstream and boll weevil Democrats, as well as a proposal to cut in half the first of his own three years of 10 percent individual tax cuts.

As a decision-maker, the President had preferred to have his inner circle thrash out the alternatives and come to him with a consensus recommendation, if possible. Usually he has ratified their proposal but if they could not agree, he has prodded them to argue their cases in front of him. "I've seen members of Congress and his staff go at it hard with the President there," Senator Baker reported. "He listens. There's almost a sense of pleasure and amusement as he watches different people argue the point. He lets it go on to a certain point and he makes a decision. The implication I draw is that this man is not afraid of controversy. He doesn't feel the need to placate anybody."

Occasionally, President Reagan has been ill-served by merely ratifying the consensus brought to him by advisers and hurt by his own lack of independent Washington experience. Thus, Stockman and Friedersdorf wanted to rush through the final stage of the budget process by having the Senate merely pass the House version and bypassing the usual House-Senate conference. At their suggestion, President Reagan called Senator Baker, who disagreed and got the support of 19 Senate Republican committee chairmen. The White House had to back down.

Far more costly was the failure of the White House to anticipate the aroused Senate reaction to the administration's proposed cuts in the Social Security program. Stockman and Richard S. Schweiker,

Secretary of Health and Human Services, were anxious to send a proposal to Congress on this issue before a House subcommittee began hearings. The President's political aides were not paying close attention to the controversial dynamite in this package. They acquiesced and the President gave the go-ahead. Immediately, the Senate voted down the idea 96–0. Senate Republicans were outraged at not having been consulted in advance, and the administration had to retreat and revise its plan. Again, in the fall, Stockman and the White House team were prepared to tinker with Social Security and the revenue-sharing program, and Reagan went along (only to have to back down when the Republican leaders in Congress balked).

Those episodes illustrate that in spite of the Reagan victories and in spite of the President's solicitude toward Congress, institutional differences remain strong and plenty of problems confront the White House, despite early success. Budget and tax-cutting have been the most favorable issues for the President. Once the first stages of the economic battle had been fought, the legislative agenda could never again be so tidy, so focused, or so favorable. The single-mindedness of the administration and Congress was bound to dissipate. Legislative momentum was inevitably much harder to maintain.

It is only natural that on other issues, centrifugal political forces began to wear away at the winning coalition the Reagan forces constructed on the economic issues. Liberal and conservative Republicans had already split on such emotional and controversial issues as busing and were increasingly unhappy over further efforts to cut social programs. Similar rifts arose over abortion, school prayer, voting rights, and other social issues. Out in the country, the supporting political network also faced strains. Many business conservatives were likely to part company with the Moral Majority on social issues. Boll weevil Democrats who sided with Mr. Reagan on economics, quickly acknowledged that they differed with him on social issues. Representative G.V. "Sonny" Montgomery of Mississippi, a leader of the Conservative Democratic Forum, predicted that the group's support for the President—only partial on economic issues—would not extend to social issues.

Other divisions arose on foreign policy. One harbinger of trouble, not sufficiently heeded by the White House came when majorities in both Houses signed a letter opposing the administration's planned sale of advanced electronic reconnaissance planes [AWACS] to Saudi Arabia. Much of the President's time and energy and the legislative muscle of the White House was sapped fighting a rearguard effort to save that deal. To almost everyone's surprise, President Reagan won the AWACS fight narrowly, and spared himself a costly setback. Once again he proved his pervasive power with Congress, but the price may have been lost momentum and even some lost support on subsequent economic votes. On other issues, foreign relations committees in both Houses had made further aid to El Salvador conditional on "significant progress" on human rights in that country. They resisted the President's appeal for a $350 million "contingency" fund for responding to foreign crises. These were all warning signals to the White House.

In short, the President's success in Congress on 1981 budget and tax cuts struck many observers as a one-year phenomenon, hard to transfer into other areas. If the economy performs badly in 1982 and 1983, Mr. Reagan's first-year victories on economic issues would become difficult to repeat.

"If there was any mandate, it was pretty well confined to economics," commented Thomas E. Cronin, a presidential scholar at Colorado College. "And it is on the economic issues that Reagan has swung from the heels. But once they get into the social issues like abortion, or even policy issues like the MX missile, he's going to have trouble keeping his own party together. This is the only period, this six months, that he's going to be able to have his own way. The Reagan team has kept the other issues off the agenda and that's how they've been so impressive."

The top White House expert on Congress, Max Friedersdorf, essentially agreed, even while he was reaping the harvest of support on the economy. "I think it's too early to say we have a working coalition for the President," he said. "It's potentially there. But we've only dealt with two issues —the budget and tax cuts. On dozens of other issues—foreign policy, the environment, social issues, we haven't tested the water yet."

That assessment, made at the higher-water mark of Reagan's success in early August 1981, could hardly have been more prophetic. The pressure of persistent high interest rates, the pessimism of investors of Wall Street, talk of a recession instead of a spurt of economic growth, and the wary vulnerability of northern congressional Republicans raised obstacles that forced the Reagan White House to slow its legislative pace and curb its ambitions by mid-October. The stunning confessions of doubt about the effectiveness of the Reagan program and the admission of sometimes dubious political tactics by Budget Director David Stockman in November were another jolt to the Reagan cause.

Although the President did make some headway on further budget trims, the coalition that Reagan's team had so carefully stitched together in spring and summer began to unravel. Only by being willing to backtrack and compromise as well as talk the tough tactics of presidential vetoes could the President make even modest progress with his economic program. He had to settle in the fall session in Congress for considerably less action than he proposed in his nationally televised address on September 24. His growing difficulties seemed to confirm Lyndon Johnson's judgment that if a new president wants to achieve significant results, he must accomplish them in his first year—because after that the opportunity vanishes.

Chapter Nine

Congress and Public Policy: Contributions, Processes, and Impacts

Congress's contribution to public policy cannot be overemphasized. Almost all that the government does can be traced to some congressional action. Congress serves as policy incubator and initiator, formulator and legitimator. As a grand forum for debate and deliberation, Congress is the great coalition builder for the American polity.

The policy tools of Congress include much more than passing legislation. Among the extra legislative tools are oversight responsibilities, the variations of congressional veto, the power of the purse, advise-and-consent authority, and the "new" congressional budget process.

Selections in this chapter address these various formidable policy tools. Also examined are analytical perspectives on Congress's contributions to the broader political system and the total policy process.

The subject of congressional policymaking can be examined as both an independent and a dependent variable. As dependent variable, congressional policymaking can be viewed as the result of a combination of congressional organizational qualities and the re-election imperative. In other words, much of what Congress does in a policy sense can be explained by referencing the organization and underlying incentive system of Congress. As an independent variable, congressional policymaking can be studied with an eye toward detecting bias in policy outcomes, impacts, and consequences. From this vantage point, an effort is made to ascertain who wins and who loses from the configuration of power in Congress.

Illustration 9.A.
Powers of Congress.

POWERS OF CONGRESS

Article I, Section 8 of the Constitution defines the powers of Congress. Included are the powers to assess and collect taxes—called the chief power; to regulate commerce, both interstate and foreign; to coin money; to establish post offices and post roads; to establish courts inferior to the Supreme Court; to declare war; to raise and maintain an army and navy. Congress is further empowered "to provide for calling forth the Militia to execute the laws of the Union, suppress insurrections and repel invasions;" and "to make all laws which shall be necessary and proper for carrying into execution the foregoing powers, and

Illustration 9.A (continued)

all other powers vested by this Constitution in the government of the United States, or in any department or officer thereof."

AMENDMENTS TO THE CONSTITUTION

Another power vested in the Congress is the right to propose amendments to the Constitution, whenever two-thirds of both houses shall deem it necessary. Should two-thirds of the state legislatures demand changes in the Constitution, it is the duty of Congress to call a constitutional convention. Proposed amendments shall be valid as part of the Constitution when ratified by the legislatures or by conventions of three-fourths of the states, as one or the other mode of ratification may be proposed by Congress.

SPECIAL POWERS OF THE SENATE

Under the Constitution, the Senate is granted certain powers not accorded to the House of Representatives. The Senate approves or disapproves certain presidential appointments by majority vote, and treaties must be concurred in by a two-thirds vote.

SPECIAL POWERS OF THE HOUSE OF REPRESENTATIVES

The House of Representatives is granted the power of originating all bills for the raising of revenue.

Both houses of Congress act in impeachment proceedings, which according to the Constitution, may be instituted against the President, Vice President, and all civil officers of the United States. The House of Representatives has the sole power of impeachment, and the Senate has the sole power to try impeachments.

PROHIBITIONS UPON CONGRESS

Section 9 of Article I of the Constitution also imposes prohibitions upon Congress: "The privilege of the writ of habeas corpus shall not be suspended, unless when in cases of rebellion or invasion the public safety may require it." A bill of attainder or an ex post facto law cannot be passed. No export duty can be imposed. Ports of one state cannot be given preference over those of another state. "No money shall be drawn from the Treasury, but in consequence of appropriations made by law. . . ." No title of nobility may be granted.

Source: From "Powers of Congress," *United States Government Manual*, 1985–1986, pp. 40–41. Reprinted from the public domain.

Reading 9.1

Legislative Oversight of Bureaucracy

Morris S. Ogul

Congress possesses a very awesome array of powers and policy tools with which to exercise its constitutional roles and responsibilities and make its imprint on public policy. Among the most impressive are authority for lawmaking, control of the government's purse-strings, and countervailing of the executive branch, or what is commonly called "congressional oversight." The following article gives an overview of congressional

Source: From Morris S. Ogul, "Legislative Oversight of Bureaucracy." Working papers on House Committee Organization and Operation, Select Committee on Committees, 1973. Reprinted from the public domain.

oversight of the executive. Here, Ogul offers several important conclusions concerning oversight activities: (1) that oversight is a rather desultory activity in Congress, (2) that much oversight is latent as well as manifest, ie., it occurs often as a by-product of other activities, and (3) that the conduct of oversight is affected by the political and structural circumstances of various congressional committees and subcommittees.

Legislative oversight of bureaucracy involves some of the most complex forms of behavior that the Congress undertakes. Not surprisingly then, legislative oversight is less understood than almost any other aspect of congressional behavior. Both Congressmen in interviews and scholars in their writings concede this lack of sustained insight. In this vortex of incomplete knowledge (recognizing that the best experts on congressional behavior are often Congressmen) an outsider may make a contribution by looking at familiar questions from a more detached viewpoint than that of the immersed participant.

What follows is based on perspectives derived from a variety of sources, from general reading and observation of the Congress and especially from intensive research in 1965 and in 1966 into the behavior of several committees and subcommittees. Then, and since, the writer has interviewed in depth some 40 House members, an equal number of staff persons, and more than a score of lobbyists and officials in the Executive Branch concerned with oversight.

Statements embodying general laws about oversight are scarce. It is possible, however, to provide some useful insights into the conduct of oversight. The materials that follow may qualify under this latter heading. Oversight is defined as the behavior of legislators, individually or collectively, formally or informally, which results in an impact on bureaucratic behavior in relation to the structure and process of policy implementation.

LEGAL EXPECTATIONS AND ACTUAL BEHAVIOR

There is a large gap between the oversight the law calls for and the oversight actually performed. The clearest single statement about the oversight that the law requires the Congress to perform comes from that often quoted and seldom heeded statement in the Legislative Reorganization Act of 1946 assigning each standing committee the responsibility to "exercise continuous watchfulness of the execution by the administrative agencies concerned of any laws, the subject matter of which is within the jurisdiction of such committee."

Members of the Congress agree that this provision provides a full and direct legal obligation to act. In addition, all those interviewed saw that obligation as an appropriate one for the Congress. In brief, there is consensus in the Congress that extensive and systematic oversight *ought* to be conducted.

One reason for the gap between expectations and behavior lies in the nature of the expectation. The plain but seldom acknowledged fact is that this task, as least as defined above, is simply impossible to perform. No amount of congressional dedication and energy, no conceivable increase in the size of committee staffs, and even no extraordinary boost in committee budgets will enable the Congress to carry out its oversight obligations in a comprehensive and systematic manner. The job is too large for any combination of members and staff to completely master. Congressmen who feel obligated to obey the letter of the law are doomed to feelings of inadequacy and frustration and are laid open to charges of neglect. Fortunately, at least for their own morale, the members of the Congress tend to focus on the immediate more than on the impossible.

The statements above are not intended to suggest that the Congress ignores the oversight function but rather that it performs it selectively. In fact, the Congress oversees formally and informally in many ways on a daily basis. The most visible and perhaps the most effective way is through the appropriations process; the most unnoticed is latently as it considers authorizations, performs casework, and goes about business not directly labeled as oversight.

The remaining part of the gap between expectations and behavior narrows as one considers why Congressmen act as they do. Two topics will be given central attention: the multiple priorities of the members of the Congress, and the impact of their policy preferences on their behavior. A discussion of these topics will reveal that there are sound reasons for this gap to exist and that most members do not really mind too much that the gap is as large as it is. Hence, their lack of willingness to do much about it.

MULTIPLE PRIORITIES

Although they seldom seem to articulate it, most members do seem to realize that the performance of oversight is best discussed not in the vacuum of legal expectations but in the more proximate context of multiple priorities and policy preferences. Each member is faced with a variety of obligations that are generally agreed to be legitimate, important, and demanding in time and energy. In principle, he should be working hard at all of them. In fact, since he does not weigh them equally, he is unlikely to give them equal attention.

When any action is perceived to contribute directly and substantially to political survival as well as to other legitimate functions, it is likely to move toward the top of any member's priority list. Extra incentives to oversee come from problems of direct concern to one's constituents or from issues that promise political visibility or organizational support. Conversely, problems not seen as closely related to political survival are more difficult to crowd onto the member's schedule. In the choice phrase of one member: "Our schedules are full, but flexible."

Not all congressional activity is linked directly to political survival. A Congressman seems to gain interest in pushing oversight efforts onto his active calendar under the following conditions: New executive requests are forthcoming calling for massive new expenditures or substantial new authorizations in controversial policy areas; a crisis has occurred that has not been met effectively by executive branch departments; the opposition political party is in control of the executive branch; he has not been treated well either in the realm of personal attention or in the servicing of his requests; he has modest confidence in the administrative capacity of Department or agency leaders. If key members have confidence in the way that executive branch department leaders are running their programs, pressure for oversight eases. Comparing the experience of two former heads of the now defunct Post Office Department is instructive. Because most members of the House Post Office and Civil Service Committee had great respect for Postmaster General Lawrence O'Brien, their willingness to give him wide latitude to run his department was immense. Because these same members lacked such confidence in John Gronouski, they probed somewhat more carefully into the affairs of the Post Office Department when he ran it. At issue was not comparative executive competence, but congressional perceptions about that competence.

In making his choices about what to do, each Congressman applies his own standards of relevance; all will be doing those things that they consider most important to them at that time. Problems seen as less pressing may be recognized but may remain untouched. In these calculations, oversight frequently falls into the semineglected category. Choice, not accident, governs this decision.

If one judges from the behavior of Congressmen rather than from their words alone, the conclusion seems clear that in oversight as in other congressional activities, selection and choice among worthy tasks is always necessary. Absolute mandates, even if accepted as desirable, will be obeyed only in relative terms. The price of effective action in one area may be the neglect of another.

Members of the Congress, like most other people, manage to compartmentalize their various beliefs and behaviors. Even in the face of continuing imperfect performance, Congressmen retain their belief in the desirability of doing a good job at oversight. Yet, concurrently, many members seem comfortable while not doing much to narrow the gap between expectations about oversight and the actual performance of it. One might reasonably conclude then that the main spurs to the conduct of oversight do not come from any abstract belief about its necessity or desirability, but from other sources.

Congressmen through their actions implicitly rank their priorities. A glance at the rules that many seem to use provides some help in trying to understand oversight.

All members have many tasks that they feel should be pursued. The finite limits set by time and energy require that some of these expectations will be met more fully than others. If there is widespread agreement about the contents of a list of high-priority tasks, there is less consensus on the relative ranking of them. Only a few things are known about why members choose to give primary attention to some activities and less to others. Even if we can presume that the omnipresent desire to survive politically serves as a major inspiration, still, member selection of other priorities remains a murky area of political analysis.

Because these factors change, the interests of each Congressman in oversight will wax and wane despite his continuing adherence to the notion that oversight is an important function for the Congress to be performing.

POLICY PREFERENCES

Examining the policy preferences of members of the Congress moves us toward a more adequate explanation of the gap between expectations and behavior. From interviews and observation, I conclude that Congressmen are seldom anxious to monitor those executive activities of which they approve. Oversight efforts to support administrative programs are the exception. A member essentially indifferent to a program is not likely to press for oversight efforts. One of the most important pressures to oversee flows from disagreements on policies, especially those that are of intense concern to the member. The words of members express the abstract desire to oversee; it is when that desire combines with policy disagreement that oversight is more likely to ensue.

A classic example is the experience of the House Judiciary Committee in 1965 and 1966 with civil rights issues relating to race relations. This committee was an able group vitally interested in civil rights policymaking and administration. Emanuel Celler ran the committee as a strong chairman. Superficially, the Committee was conducting almost no oversight activity on questions of civil rights. What was strange was that the civil rights concerns of the Committee were known to be strong and deep. Several not so obvious factors helped to explain the situation. First, the Committee chairman felt that he was having an impact on the activities of the Justice Department through informal consultation. Second, the chairman agreed in essence with what the Justice Department was doing and thus had no desire to interfere. Third, in the judgment of Chairman Celler, the net effect of any formal investigations would be harmful to the cause of civil rights since anti-rights forces might find the forum useful to articulate and publicize their views. In this case, the absence of formal oversight could be explained by a simple formula: When policy interests and the obligation to oversee clash, policy preferences will normally prevail as a guide to conduct.

The discussion thus far of member priorities, choices, and policy preferences concerns each member. The fact is that in oversight efforts, as in other activities, all Congressmen are not equal. So even an intense desire to oversee, clearly a rarity in the Congress, depends for its fruition on factors other than the individual member's wants. The ability to oversee depends on where one is situated in the legislative process. Individual members, on their own, conduct very little oversight. For reasons of authority, money, and staff, oversight efforts are centered in the standing committees and subcommittees. Where one is placed in the committee system becomes a vital element in translating desires into effective action. A brief look at committees and their oversight activity is thus warranted.

COMMITTEES AND OVERSIGHT

One key to understanding oversight can be discovered by examining those places in the Congress where the division of labor and specialization can most easily be found, the committees and subcommittees. Members individually rarely can expect to conduct much legislative oversight. A comment later in the paper will indicate how even individual members can partially overcome this limitation. The heart of legislative oversight lies in the committees and subcommittees. How and why these units function as they do will tell us a great deal about how legislative oversight is performed. How the committees function is related to their structures for decision making.

Perhaps the most effective means to enhance a committee's oversight performance is through the presence of an alert, shrewd, active chairman who wants to conduct oversight broad in scope and profound in depth. Most reforms pale in significance before this seemingly simple solution. No one, of course, really knows how to pretest prospective chairmen for these talents and interests. Nor is it clear that the members would want to pick their chairman on the basis of these criteria even if they could. The best practical bet seems to be to assume that a list of committee chairmen and subcommittee chairmen will include a few who are intensely interested in oversight and highly talented in pursuing it and a large number who are less keen and less talented.

Assuming some such mix of committee chairmen, is there any way to enhance the oversight efforts of those committees headed by chairmen whose appetites and talents for oversight are unimpressive? At least one suggestion merits discussion. The odds for active oversight are better, in the absence of an eager chairman, if there are some semiautonomous subcommittees with established jurisdictions, budgets, and staffs. The objective is to create additional fields in which ambition may flower. Visibility and ambition are as effective stimulants for subcommittee chairmen as for any other members. An active subcommittee within a quiescent full committee is not an unknown phenomenon in the Congress.

Innovation always has its price. The flexibility of the full committee chairman, his personal power, and perhaps even committee efficiency could possibly suffer. Whether enhancing the prospects for oversight may be worth these costs has to be decided by the Congressmen themselves.

What promotes the personal power of the chairman is not necessarily good for committee oversight efforts. Fixed subcommittee jurisdiction may indeed remove some flexibility from the full committee chairman, but the price may be right: promoting the competence prerequisite to oversight activity. Numbered subcommittees without fixed jurisdictions may impede the development of expertise. Besides, from an oddsmaker's perspective, the presence of several subcommittee chairmen with defined jurisdictions, separate staffs, and separate budgets, increases the field from which an interest in oversight may emerge. This analysis does not ignore the problems that may arise in some decentralized communities, but merely adds another weight to the scales.

Committee leaders may not dominate all committee behavior, but they do control much of it. What they are willing to do is central. Of course, committee members may press committee leaders to act. One type of situation minimizes the likelihood of member pressure for leadership action: where the members of a committee are there involuntarily. Members view some committee assignments as highly desirable; other assignments are viewed as burdens to be endured. Members appointed to unsought committees frequently transfer to more satisfactory assignments as soon as they can muster sufficient seniority. Given the normal problems in allotting their time and energy, we can expect that few members who see their assignments as undesirable are likely to exert maximum effort on such committees. Some oversight behavior, or the lack of it, is explainable in part by the priority that members assign to their work on a particular committee. In low-status committees, those few members who choose to remain probably do so for reasons unrelated to any desire to actively pursue oversight.

SOME GRIST FOR CONTEMPLATION AND DISCUSSION

Four Myths about Oversight

Perhaps the first necessity in thinking more generally about oversight is to suggest that some widely held and deeply cherished ideas are myths. The first of these is that the Congress lacks sufficient authority to oversee properly. In fact, one can argue that the Congress has all of the authority that it needs to oversee much more extensively and effectively.

A second myth holds that the Congress lacks the budget to oversee effectively. With few exceptions, committees have the money that they need even if they wish to sharply augment their oversight efforts. One can uncover, of course, some relatively deprived committees or subcommittees, but these are the exceptions.

A third cherished belief states that the answer to how to improve oversight efforts is more staff. This answer might hold in a few cases, but not generally. Committee staff persons are hired to satisfy a variety of needs. If committee chairmen choose to take on staff exclusively for subject-matter competence, research skills, and investigative talents, they can quickly improve the prospects for oversight. But even then, staff behavior is largely a function of member preferences. A chairman passive about oversight is unlikely to have staff persons, however talented, who view oversight as a high priority. With a few conspicuous exceptions, staff behavior is more a function of member preferences than a determinant of them.

The Legislative Reorganization Act of 1970 spelled out some relationships between the Congress, its committees, and the GAO. The actual impact of the GAO on legislative oversight would be an intriguing study in itself. Such an analysis might well suggest useful paths in a rethinking of how the oversight function is performed.

Legal authority, staff, and money are all important prerequisites to congressional action, but none of these are grossly lacking now. Genuflections before the trilogy of authority, money, and staff do not reach the basic problems.

In my judgment, a fourth myth about oversight is that members of the Congress and their staffs lack the experience, training, intelligence, or creativity to conduct more and better oversight. To put it more bluntly, some critics charge that the members and their staff simply lack the competence, defined broadly in the terms just mentioned, to do the necessary work. One can unearth situtations where members lack the competence needed for specific tasks, but one finds little evidence to support the proposition that these deficiences are universal or, when found, that normally they are beyond remedy. As has been demonstrated in actual performance, useful oversight is practicable in the Congress. Deficiences in competence in specific circumstances can frequently be remedied if the committees or subcommittees desire to do so.

It is true that even talented generalists (viz., the members of the Congress) can be intimidated by mountains of data, by exotic or technical vocabularies, or by arcane analyses. It is also true that some technical experts at times seem to relish prolix analyses presented in nearly incomprehensive language. The expert may indeed understand that obfuscation is his first line of defense. But legislators and their staff are predestined neither to succumb nor to be deceived. Effective legislative oversight does not require that all members and all staff persons be competent in all aspects of public policy. If that were necessary, the task indeed would be hopeless. The dual practices of division of labor and specialization provide the classical solution to this problem.

SOME SUMMARY PROPOSITIONS

1. Oversight is neither comprehensive nor systematic because that goal is beyond achievement.

2. Oversight is performed intermittently because the factors most relevant to stimulating it are not constantly present. Thus the quality and quantity of oversight varies between the two branches of the Congress, among the committees and subcommittees within each house, and in the same committees and subcommittees from session to session and from issue to issue.

3. It is not too difficult to produce a syndrome of factors which tend to maximize the possibilities for effective oversight. The elements might be: there is a legal basis for committee activity and there is an adequate budget for it; adequate staff resources, defined in terms of numbers, skills, and attitudes are present; the subject matter is not unusually complex or technical; the issue involved has high political visibility; the committee with relevant jurisdiction is decentralized in structure unless the chairman is a strong advocate of oversight in the given area; key committee members are unhappy with their treatment by executive branch personnel; key committee members lack confidence in top executive branch personnel; committee senior members harbor personal antipathy toward executive officials; the executive branch proposes vast changes in existing programs; committee control rests in the political party opposite to that of the President.

The ease of creating such a list obscures the more difficult problem of assigning weights to each element and to predicting the possible consequences of its presence or absence. Perhaps that is because the primary elements of explanation may well vary from case to case. There seems to be no single pattern which explains legislative oversight in all circumstances. There are only common factors which combine in different ways under specified sets of circumstances. Moreover, even casual inspection of congressional behavior suggests that all the conditions which are part of this syndrome are rarely present simultaneously.

4. Oversight is not a high priority much of the time for most members.

5. Congressional staff behavior is primarily determined by member priorities and policy preferences. The best way to alter staff behavior is to focus on its major determinant.

6. A sense of realism demands recognition of the fact that most members are relatively satisfied with the conduct of legislator oversight of the bureaucracy. They feel little stimulus to alter existing patterns.

SOME PROPOSALS PERHAPS WORTHY OF DISCUSSION

Casework and Oversight

For very fundamental reasons, most oversight activity will come from congressmen acting not as individuals, but as members of committees and subcommittees. But congressmen acting as individuals in their own offices can do something that most do not do now. Priorities are basic. Most members now view the mountains of casework processed in their offices simply as service for constituents. Members could instruct their caseworkers to be more alert to the patterns of problems revealed in cases so that this information could be passed on to the appropriate committees and subcommittees. Congressmen collect routinely a mother lode of information potentially useful for oversight. Members either have not understood the value of what they have or have not cared enough to order the modest effort that would make this information more useful.

Committee Structure and Oversight

Committees that are serious about improving their potential for oversight should carefully examine their subcommittee structure to see if more autonomy might be provided.

Recognition of the Full Dimensions of Oversight

Much oversight that now occurs in the Congress is not recognized. Because a session is called a legislative hearing, or because processing of constituent complaints is called casework does not mean that these activities are unrelated to oversight. Oversight should be viewed from a broader perspective than that of formal investigations.

Are Oversight Subcommittees Worthwhile?

Perhaps the most obvious step taken by a few standing committees to enhance their oversight efforts has been to create specific oversight subcommittees. To my knowledge, no one has systematically or intensively looked at whether having such subcommittees makes any appreciable difference in the conduct of oversight. Here is a structural solution which one could suspect has not had any great impact. But nobody knows for sure. The topic does deserve attention.

A FINAL NOTE

The standard answer to improving the conduct of the congressional oversight function usually seems to be: Elect smarter people to the Congress, make them work harder, and give them bigger staffs. After extensive observation of the Congress at work, it seems to me that most members have the talent necessary to perform their jobs well; many Congressmen probably cannot work much harder than they do now, although they can change what they do if they want to; few Congressmen argue that increasing staff size would have any significant impact on the conduct of oversight. Apparently, those members who publicly proclaim the general virtue of having more staff seemingly do not have the improvement of oversight specifically in mind.

Surely a more accurate answer than the standard one (although still not a fully satisfactory one) might be: If more and better oversight is to be achieved, members need to alter their priorities for allocation of their time and they need to insist on *better* staffs. In practice, how to achieve either of these objectives is far from obvious.

The idea that no problem, given human effort and enough money, is beyond solution stands at the center of the American ethos. As a goad to improve things, this view may have great utility; as an observation about reality, it may be sadly defective. If the goal is to increase the quantity of oversight and to improve its quality, one needs to look at underlying causes. From this perspective, structural changes in the Congress, by themselves, are unlikely to do the job. The basic limits to more adequate oversight seem to me to lie not in defective structures but peripherally in excessive expectations and centrally in an imperfect will to act. The latter comment necessarily implies neither a general criticism nor a weakness. Congressmen do what they do and slight what they slight for reasons that seem persuasive to them. In the words of an astute Senate staff member discussing staff behavior on oversight matters:

> Specialists in departmental interference must judge both the merits of the case and the costs in time, effort, and their own or the Congressman's "credit" with the agency, of attempting to achieve a given solution.

In other words, reality is complex. The bases for choice are many. Balancing reasonable requests for time and action is central. Most Congressmen feel that they can justify much of what they do in terms that their constituents would find quite acceptable. Most staff members feel that what they are doing is what their employers, the members of Congress, want them to do. Merely telling members or staff persons to do something else is just not much help. The incentives for conducting more intensive and extensive oversight are great in the abstract and yet are modest in most concrete situations. Any analysis of legislative oversight has to be grounded in these stern facts.

Reading 9.2

Judicial Misjudgments about the Lawmaking Process: The Legislative Veto Case

Louis Fisher

Refereeing disputes between the President and Congress is a major function assigned federal courts by the Constitution. In 1983 in the Chadha case, the U.S. Supreme Court invalidated Congress' exercise of the so-called legislative veto in the area of naturalization policy. The legislative veto is a policy tool Congress has used since the 1930s. Proliferating greatly in the 1960s and 1970s, legislative vetoes are an attempt by Congress to retain control of policy beyond the passage of a bill. Basically, they involve a broad statutory delegation of power to the executive branch in various functional areas. In exercising its discretion under the legislation, the executive branch must report its decisions to the Congress, which stand unless Congress "vetoes" them. The veto is accomplished through a two-house, one-house, or even committee vote, depending upon the provisions of the enabling legislation. The Chadha case is sure to be a landmark, for it cast doubt on the constitutionality of all such vetoes as violations

Source: From "Judicial Misjudgments About the Lawmaking Process: The Legislative Case" by Louis Fisher in Special Issue on "Law and Public Affairs," *Public Administation Review* (1985). Reprinted by permission of the American Society for Public Administration.

of the separation of powers doctrine. The following article by a leading student of the U.S. Constitution discusses the aftermath of the Chadha case, how Congress is coping, and castigates the courts for denying Congress an important policy tool.

The Supreme Court's decision in *INS* v. *Chadha* (1983) set up unrealistic expectations about the disappearance of the legislative veto. Instead of sounding its death knell, the legislative veto is alive and well. The decision stimulated the executive and legislative branches to find ingenious and novel methods of achieving basically the same results: broad delegations of legislative power by Congress to the agencies, checked by congressional controls that do not need enactment of another law. Some of the new legislative vetoes are informal and nonstatutory. A few rely on convoluted uses of the rulemaking powers available to the House and Senate. Others are indistinguishable from the legislative veto supposedly struck down by the court. The adoption of joint resolutions as a substitute for one-House and two-House vetoes has introduced complex strategies between the branches, often putting the president in a weaker position than before. These consequences, sometimes of a surprising and bizarre nature, flow from a court decision that was broader than necessary.

In past years the Supreme Court has damaged its reputation by issuing decisions based on misconceptions about the political and economic system. After trying to impose archaic and mechanical concepts about federalism, the taxing power, the commerce power, and other clauses of the Constitution, the court was forced to retreat from pronouncements that were simply unacceptable for a developing nation. To minimize what Charles Evans Hughes once called the court's penchant for "self-inflicted wounds," justices evolved a number of rules to limit their exercise of judicial review. One mainstay is the principle that the court will not "formulate a rule of constitutional law broader than is required by the precise facts to which it is to be applied."[1]

That guideline was not followed in 1983 when the Supreme Court issued *INS* v. *Chadha*, which declared the legislative veto unconstitutional in all its forms. The court announced that future congressional efforts to alter "the legal rights, duties and relations of persons" outside the legislative branch must follow the full lawmaking process: passage of a bill or joint resolution by both Houses and presentment of that measure to the president for his signature or veto.[2] The court lectured Congress that it could no longer rely on the legislative veto as "a convenient shortcut" to control executive agencies.[3] Instead, "legislation by the national Congress [must] be a step-by-step, deliberate and deliberative process."[4] According to the court, the framers insisted that "the legislative power of the Federal Government be exercised in accord with a single, finely wrought and exhaustively considered, procedure."[5]

A HISTORY OF ACCOMMODATIONS

All three branches reached agreement long ago that the step-by-step, deliberate and deliberative process is not appropriate for each and every exercise of the legislative power. Despite occasional invocations of the nondelegation doctrine, the court itself has accepted the inevitable delegation of legislative power to executive agencies and independent commissions. Administrative bodies routinely "make law" through the rulemaking process. Efforts are made to subject this lawmaking activity to procedural safeguards, but the persistence of the Administrative State is ample proof that the theoretical model of legislative action envisioned by the framers applies only in the most general sense to the 20th century.

Notwithstanding 50 years of delicate accommodations between the executive and legislative branches regarding the legislative veto, the Supreme Court decided to strike it down in one fell swoop. In his dissent, Justice White claimed that the court "sounds the death knell for nearly 200 other statutory provisions in which Congress has reserved a 'legislative veto.'"[6] Although White demonstrated better than his colleagues an appreciation of the realities and subtleties of lawmaking in contemporary times, he too framed the issue too starkly. He argued that without the legislative veto, Congress "is faced with a Hobson's choice: either to refrain from delegating the necessary authority, leaving itself with a hopeless task of writing laws with the requisite specificity to cover endless special circumstances across the entire policy landscape, or in the alternative, to abdicate its lawmaking function to the Executive Branch and independent agencies."[7] In fact, Congress and the agencies have access to a number of middle-range options that serve much the same purpose as the legislative veto. In some cases, current practices are difficult to distinguish from what supposedly vanished with the death knell.

Lower courts were more alert than the Supreme Court to the complexities of the lawmaking process. Many of the courts handled the legislative veto issue in gingerly fashion, preferring to decide only the particular statutory provision before them. They deliberately refused to consider the legislative veto as an abstract proposition, susceptible to an across-the-board answer.[8] In 1982, however, the D.C. Circuit issued three broadsides against the legislative veto.[9] In one of the cases, two judges with prior experience in the legislative and executive branches warned their brethren about the dangers of overbroad decisions. Patricia Wald, who served in the Justice Department during the Carter years, and Abner Mikva, former member of Congress from Illinois, asked that an earlier case decided by a three-judge panel be reheard *en banc* "because vitally important issues of executive-legislative relations are articulated too broadly and explored inadequately in the panel opinion."[10] They urged the court to avoid a black-and-white treatment of unique accommodations that had proven useful for both the executive and legislative branches, such as the Reorganization Act, the Impoundment Control Act, and the Federal Salary Act.[11]

Opponents of the legislative veto viewed it as a blatant attempt by Congress to intrude upon executive prerogatives. This critique overlooked the fact that the legislative-veto procedure was an effort to balance the interests of both branches: the desire of administrators for greater discretionary authority and the need of Congress to maintain control short of passing another public law. Those interests persist after *Chadha*.

Under the legislative-veto accommodation, Congress delegated authority on the condition that certain adminstrative actions be delayed for a specified number of days. During that period Congress had an opportunity to approve or disapprove without further presidential involvement. Congress acted by a one-House veto (by a simple resolution of either House), a two-House veto (by concurrent resolution of both Houses), and committee veto. The very essence of the legislative veto is that it could be invoked without risk of a presidential veto. Congressional approvals and disapprovals were not submitted to the president.

This procedure obviously benefited Congress, but it was part of an accommodation with distinct advantages also to the executive branch. Executive officials accepted the legislative veto because they received discretionary authority that might otherwise have been withheld by Congress. While it is true that Congress gained a "shortcut" because its approval or disapproval was not sent to the president, the executive branch also enjoyed shortcuts. At the close of the legislative review period, administration proposals automatically became law as if they had been enacted by Congress.

It is often forgotten that the legislative

veto was used initially to advance the interests of the president. President Hoover wanted to reorganize the executive branch without having to go to Congress for a public law. He proposed that his reorganization proposals become the law of the land unless one House disapproved within a fixed period of time. The lawmaking procedure was thus expedited to favor the president.[12] The procedure did not threaten vital principles of constitutional government. If one House disapproved, the structure of the executive branch remained as before. Exercise of the one-House veto merely preserved the *status quo*.

This type of legislative shortcut contained benefits for both branches. Even with *Chadha*, the need for a *quid pro quo* continues. Some of the new accommodations are statutory; others are non-statutory. The persistence of these executive-legislative compacts demonstrates the distance between the court's decision and the operational realities of government. Both executive officials and legislators are finding ways to avoid the theory of lawmaking espoused by *Chadha*.

THE PERSISTENCE OF LEGISLATIVE VETOES

It came as a surprise to some observers that Congress continued to place legislative vetoes in bills after the court's decision and President Reagan continued to sign the bills into law. In the 16 months between *Chadha* and the adjournment of the 98th Congress, an additional 53 legislative vetoes were added to the books.

A flagrant case of non-compliance? A sign of disrespect for the courts? An alarming challenge to the time-honored belief that the Supreme Court has the last word on constitutional questions? Perhaps, but the court painted with too broad a brush and offered a simplistic solution that is unacceptable to the political branches. Its decision will be eroded by open defiance and subtle evasion. Neither consequence is attractive, but much of the responsibility for this condition belongs on the doorstep of the court.

Some of the legislative vetoes enacted since *Chadha* are easy to spot. Most of them vest control in the appropriations committees. For example, construction grants by the Environmental Protection Agency are subject to the approval of the appropriations committees (97 Stat. 226). The approval of the appropriations committees is required before exceeding certain dollar amounts in the National Flood Insurance Fund (97 Stat. 227). With the approval of the appropriations committees, up to 5 percent may be transferred between specified accounts of the National Aeronautics and Space Administration (NASA) (97 Stat. 229). Reimbursement of certain funds for the Ventura Marina project, administered by the Corps of Engineers, requires the prior approval of the appropriations committees (97 Stat. 312). Appropriations may not be available for the acquisition, sale, or transference of Washington's Union Station without the prior approval of the appropriations committees (97 Stat. 462).

Other legislative vetoes are more subtle. A continuing resolution provided that foreign assistance funds allocated to each country "shall not exceed those provided in fiscal year 1983 or those provided in the budget estimates for each country, whichever are lower, unless submitted through the regular reprogramming procedures of the Committees on Appropriations" (97 Stat. 736). Those procedures provide for committee prior-approval. The District of Columbia Appropriations Act for fiscal 1984 prohibited funds from being obligated or spent by reprogramming "except pursuant to advance approval of the reprogramming granted according to the procedure set forth" in two House reports, both of which require prior approval by the appropriations committees (97 Stat. 827).

One year after *Chadha*, President Reagan received the HUD-Independent Agencies Appropriations bill which contained a number of committee vetoes. In his signing statement, he took note of those vetoes and asked Congress to stop adding provisions that the Supreme Court had held to be unconstitutional. He said that "the time has come, with more than a year having passed since the Supreme Court's decision in *Chadha*, to make clear that legislation containing legislative veto devices that comes to me for my approval or disapproval will be implemented in a manner consistent with the *Chadha* decision."[13] The clear import was that the administration did not feel bound by the statutory requirements to seek the approval of congressional committees before implementing certain actions.

The House Appropriations Committee responded to the president's statement by reviewing an agreement it had entered into with NASA four years previously. Caps were set on various NASA programs, usually at the level requested in the president's budget. The agreement allowed NASA to exceed the caps with the approval of the appropriations committees. The House Appropriations Committee thought that the procedure had "worked well during the past four years, and has provided a mechanism by which the Congress and the Committee can be assured that funds are used solely for the purpose for which they were appropriated." Because of Reagan's statement and the threat to ignore committee controls, the committee said it was necessary to repeal the accommodation that had lasted for four years. Repeal language was inserted in the second supplemental bill for fiscal 1984. Both sides stood to lose. The appropriations committees would not be able to veto NASA proposals; NASA would not be able to exceed ceilings without enacting new language in a separate appropriation bill.[14]

Neither NASA nor the appropriations committees wanted to enact a separate public law just to exceed a cap. To avoid this kind of administrative rigidity, NASA Administrator James M. Beggs wrote to both committees on August 9, 1984. His letter reveals the pragmatic sense of give-and-take that is customary between executive agencies and congressional committees. His letter also underscores the impracticality and unreality of the doctrines enunciated by the Supreme Court in *Chadha*:

> We have now operated under the present operating plan and reprogramming procedures for several years and have found them to be workable. In light of the constitutional questions raised concerning the legislative veto provisions included in P.L. 98-371 [the HUD-Independent Agencies Appropriations Act], however, the House Committee on Appropriations has proposed in H.R. 6040, the FY 1984 general supplemental, deletion of all Committee approval provisions, leaving inflexible, binding funding limitations on several programs. Without some procedure for adjustment, other than a subsequent separate legislative enactment, these ceilings could seriously impact the ability of NASA to meet unforeseen technical changes or problems that are inherent in challenging R&D programs. We believe that the present legislative procedure could be converted by this letter into an informal agreement by NASA not to exceed amounts for Committee designated programs without the approval of the Committees on Appropriations. This agreement would assume that both the statutory funding ceilings and the Committee approval mechanisms would be deleted from the FY 1985 legislation, and that it would not be the normal practice to include either mechanism in future appropriations bills. Further, the agreement would assume that future program ceiling amounts would be identified by the Committees in the Conference Report accompanying NASA's annual appropriations act and confirmed by NASA in its submission of the annual operating plan. NASA would not expend any funds over the ceilings identified in the Conference Report for these programs without the prior approval of the Committees.

In short, the agency would continue to honor legislative vetoes. But they would be informal rather than statutory. Beggs ended his letter by assuring the appropriations committees that NASA "will comply with any ceilings imposed by the Committees without the need for legislative ceilings which could cause serious damage to NASA's ongoing programs." By converting the legislative veto to an informal and nonstatutory status, NASA is not legally bound by the agreement. Violation of the agreement, however, could provoke the appropriations committees to place caps in the appropriation bill and force the agency to lift them only through the enactment of another public law.

INFORMAL LEGISLATIVE VETOES

The NASA agreement describes a world of informal agency-committee accommodations that were solidly in place before *Chadha*. No doubt these agreements will continue (and probably increase), notwithstanding the court's strictures on the proper steps for lawmaking. The reprogramming procedure has been followed for at least three to four decades. As an informal accommodation between the branches, it allows agencies to shift funds within an appropriation account provided they obtain committee approval for major changes.

The arrangement is mutually beneficial to Congress and the agencies. Without such an understanding, Congress would have to appropriate with far greater itemization. With it, Congress can appropriate in lump sums and monitor major deviations through the reprogramming procedure. Line itemization is an unattractive solution because neither branch can forecast with adequate precision the financial needs of government agencies. There is a need for flexibility as the fiscal year unfolds and new requirements emerge.

Reprogramming is called informal in the sense that the procedures are not included in public laws. And yet the procedures are highly formalized, spelled out in great detail in committee reports, committee hearings, and correspondence between the committees and the agencies. Agencies place these understandings in their instructions, directives, and financial management manuals, alerting agency personnel to the types of reprogrammings that may be done internally with only periodic reports to Congress and the reprogrammings that require prior approval. Dollar thresholds are used at times to identify the latter. Certain matters of special interest are singled out for prior approval. With the growth of annual authorizations after World War II, the reprogramming process has come to require the prior approval not merely of the appropriations subcommittees but of the authorizing committees as well.[15]

Statutes after *Chadha* may rely more heavily on notification to designated committees before an agency acts. Notification does not raise a constitutional issue, since it falls within the report-and-wait category already sanctioned by prior court rulings.[16] In an informal sense, however, notification in a statute can become a code word to indicate the need for committee prior approval. For example, the Military Construction Appropriation Act for fiscal 1985 prohibits the use of funds to transfer or relocate any activity from one base or installation to another, or to initiate a new installation overseas, without prior notification to the appropriations committees.[17] For these kinds of matters, it is difficult to conceive of a situation in which the Pentagon would proceed against the opposition of its appropriations subcommittees.

The lower courts have recognized the need for informal clearance procedures between agencies and congressional committees. The General Services Administration (GSA) is required by statute to notify appropriate committees of the Congress in advance of a negotiated sale of surplus government property in excess of $10,000. The review panels are the House Government Operations and Senate Governmental Affairs committees. Agency regulations further provide that in the "absence of adverse comment" by a committee or subcommittee, the disposal agency may sell the property on or after 35 days.[18] The U.S. Claims Court found "compelling similarities" between the GSA procedure and the practices prohibited by *Chadha*. It regarded the combination of congressional statute, agency regulation, and agency deference to committee objections as tantamount to committee disapproval and therefore an unconstitutional violation of the doctrine of separated powers.[19]

Congressmen Jack Brooks and Frank Horton, the chairman and ranking minority member of the House Committee on Government Operations, respectively, filed an *amicus curiae* brief which argued that it was improper to characterize as a legislative veto the self-imposed agency deference to congressional sentiment. Such reasoning, they said, would render virtually every statute requiring notification an unconstitutional interference with agency decisions. Their brief also cited instances in which GSA had proceeded despite committee opposition to proposed sales.

The Claims Court was reversed on appeal. The U. S. Court of Appeals for the Federal Circuit found nothing unconstitutional about the decision of agencies to defer to committee objections:

> Committee chairmen and members naturally develop interest and expertise in the subjects entrusted to their continuing surveillance. Officials in the executive branch have to take these committees into account and keep them informed, respond to their inquiries, and it may be, flatter and please them when necessary. Committees do not need even the type of "report and wait" provision we have here to develop enormous influence over executive branch doings. There is nothing unconstitutional about this: indeed, our separation of powers makes such informal cooperation much more necessary than it would be in a pure system of parliamentary government.[20]

Chadha does not affect these non-statutory legislative vetoes. They are not legal in effect. They are, however, in effect legal. Agencies are aware of the penalties that can be invoked by Congress if they decide to violate understandings and working relationships with their review committees.

INTERNAL CONGRESSIONAL RULES

What is now prohibited directly by *Chadha* can be accomplished indirectly through House and Senate rules. As highlighted by a dispute in the 1950s, rules governing authorizations and appropriations can serve as the functional equivalent of the legislative veto. President Eisenhower had objected to statutory provisions that required agencies to come into agreement with committees before implementing an administrative action. Such provisions, claimed the Justice Department, violated the constitutional principle of separated powers.[21] Congress retaliated by changing its internal procedures so that funds could be appropriated for a project only after the authorizing committees had passed a resolution of approval. The form had changed; the substance of committee veto remained unscathed. Nevertheless, the Justice Department accepted the committee resolution as a valid form of action because it was directed at the internal workings of Congress (the appropriations committees) rather than at the executive branch. By relying on the authorization-appropriation distinction, Congress retained its committee veto.

At the start of the 99th Congress, Congressman Joe Moakley introduced a House concurrent resolution to strengthen legislative oversight over agency rulemaking. He explained that the resolution "seeks to respond to constitutional issues raised in connection with recent Court decisions relating to traditional legislative vetoes."[22] The resolution invokes two constitutional powers: the power of each House to determine the rules of its proceedings, and the requirement that no money be drawn from the Treasury but in consequence of appropriations made by law. The resolution would create a Joint Committee on Regulatory Affairs with authority to review all federal agency rules. If Congress adopted a concurrent resolution objecting to a regulation, it would be a rule in each House that the appropriations committees could not report new appropriations to carry out the regulation. The appropriations committees would be acting as agents for their respective Houses. The procedure contemplates a two-House veto directed at the internal workings of each House rather than at the executive branch.

Congress retains the right to place language in an appropriations bill to deny funds for agency activities. Although House and Senate rules generally prohibit the insertion of substantive language in appropriations bills, these rules are not self-enforcing. Members of both Houses find it convenient at times to attach legislation and limitations to the most available appropriations bill. Since a president is unlikely to veto an appropriations bill simply because it contains an offensive rider, the practical effect is at least a two-House veto. Because of accommodations and comity between the House and the Senate, the reality in many cases is a one-House veto.

The Trade and Tariff Act of 1984 includes an intriguing use of congressional rules to control the executive branch. The statute authorizes either tax committee —Senate Finance or House Ways and Means —to disapprove the negotiation of certain trade agreements.[23] The actual effect is not to prevent negotiation but to withdraw the president's authority to submit trade agreements for expedited consideration by Congress.[24] These expedited procedures offer major conveniences for the president. His bill implementing a trade agreement is assured automatic introduction in both Houses; neither House may amend the president's bill; the bill will be discharged from the tax committees if they fail to act within a specified number of days; motions to consider the implementing bill are privileged and not debatable; and debate in either House is limited to not more than 20 hours. These procedures represent an exercise of the rulemaking power of each House "and as such they are deemed a part of the rules of each House." The two Houses retain the right to change the rules "at any time, in the same manner and to the same extent as in the case of any other rule of that House."[25]

If one of the tax committees objected to the negotiation of a trade agreement, would the Justice Department and the president complain about congressional interference with executive duties or challenge the committee action as an invalid legislative shortcut incompatible with *Chadha*? Probably not. Unless the executive branch is willing to swallow this arrangement, Congress can repeal the fast-track procedure and force the president to submit an implementing bill subject to all the uncertainties and "indignities" of the regular legislative process: having a bill buried in committee, or amended until the executive branch cannot recognize its own creature, or filibustered to death on the floor.

JOINT RESOLUTIONS: SHIFTING THE BURDEN

After *Chadha*'s invalidation of the legislative veto, members of Congress and the agencies searched for statutory alternatives that would satisfy their institutional needs. The joint resolution is a tempting substitute, since it meets *Chadha*'s requirement of bicameralism and presentment. Like an ordinary bill, joint resolutions must pass both Houses of Congress and must be presented to the president for his signature or veto.

Depending on the type of joint resolution, the burden shifts to Congress or the president. A joint resolution of disapproval usually weakens legislative control because it requires Congress to act and the resolution is vulnerable to the president's veto. Congress cannot be expected to pass joint resolutions to stop every agency action it opposes. The workload is too heavy and veto overrides too difficult.

On the other hand, a joint resolution of approval shifts the burden to the president, who would have to obtain the approval of both Houses within a set number of days. The results could be ironic. For example, reorganization plans submitted to Congress by the president since 1949 were subject to a one-House veto. If one House failed to disapprove within a specified number of days, a reorganization plan became law. The Reorganization Act Amendments of 1984 reverses the burden. A reorganization plan could not take effect unless Congress passed a joint resolution of approval within 90 days. As the statute notes: "Failure of either House to act upon such resolution by the end of such period shall be the same as disapproval of the resolution."[26] The practical effect is that Congress still has a one-house veto, but it can be invoked by inaction rather than action. The new procedure puts the president at a definite disadvantage. He must secure the support of both Houses within a limited number of days.

Joint resolutions of approval are also being used for such controversial issues as the MX missile. Before *Chadha,* Congress made use of legislative vetoes to control the timetable for the MX program. Legislation in 1981 prohibited the obligation or expenditure of funds to develop the basing mode after November 18, 1981, if before that date the two Houses agreed to resolutions expressing disapproval of the president's plan.[27] Congress strengthened its hand the following year by prohibiting the obligation or expenditure of funds to initiate full-scale engineering development of a basic mode until *approved* by both houses in a concurrent resolution.[28] This change required the president to lobby both houses for support.

After *Chadha,* Congress turned to the joint resolution of approval to protect its institutional interests. At the end of 1984, Congress authorized the use of $1.5 billion in prior-year, unobligated funds for the MX missile. However, the funds could not be obligated unless Congress passed two joint resolutions of approval after March 1, 1985. The first resolution would be handled by the armed services committees, and the second by the appropriations committees. Action on the joint resolution was subject to certain fast-track procedures spelled out in the statute: procedures to discharge committees, time limits on floor debate, and prohibitions on amendments.

A similar approach was used for Nicaragua. A proscription on the use of intelligence-agency funds would cease after February 28, 1985, if Congress passed a joint resolution of approval, again subject to expedited procedures.[29] A joint resolution of approval, although it conforms to the court's decision, offers not the slightest benefit to the president. It is functionally identical to a concurrent resolution of approval. In either case the president must obtain the support of both houses; doubtless the president would sign a joint resolution giving him the authority he sought.

Congress must be selective in its use of the joint resolution of approval. It cannot serve as an all-purpose substitute for the legislative veto. On November 3, 1983, the House of Representatives voted down the use of a joint resolution to approve certain rules promulgated by the Environmental Protection Agency. During hearings the following year, Congressman John Dingell expressed his satisfaction with the House action and warned against overuse of joint resolutions of approval: "if you want to see the Congress clogged, overloaded, incapable of action, because of a new effort to review a prodigious number of actions by the Executive and regulatory structure, that is a fine way to do it."[30]

To protect Congress from being overloaded, combinations of joint resolutions of approval and disapproval are possible. A few months after *Chadha,* Congressman Trent Lott introduced legislation to require a joint resolution of approval for major rules and a joint resolution of disapproval for minor rules.[31] This hybrid approach subjects major rules to a heavy burden, but allows minor rules to take effect unless disapproved by Congress. Senator Charles E. Grassley has also recommended this approach for agency rules.[32]

Prior to *Chadha,* major arms sales were subject to a joint resolution of disapproval. Both houses had to disapprove within a limited number of days. In response to the court's decision, Congressman Stephen Solarz introduced legislation to divide arms sales into two categories. The president would be prohibited from selling arms to certain countries and international organizations unless Congress enacted a joint resolution authorizing the sale. This procedure would force the White House to enlist the support of both houses. Whereas both houses had to disapprove under the previous system, the Solarz bill would allow one House to stop an arms sale simply by refusing to support a joint resolution of approval. The administration would face not a two-House but a one-House veto. As for the second category in the Solarz bill, arms sales for NATO, Japan, New Zealand, Australia, and Israel would be allowed to go forward unless Congress disapproved by joint resolution within 15 days.[33]

Congress and the executive branch reached an interesting compromise on the D.C. Home Rule Act. The Reagan administration usually preferred that Congress use joint resolutions of disapproval as a substitute for the legislative veto. If Congress failed to act, administration proposals would automatically take effect. If Congress managed to pass a joint resolution of disapproval, the president could veto it. In the case of the District of Columbia, however, the strategy was reversed. The use of a joint resolution by Congress to disapprove certain laws passed by the D.C. Council effectively eliminated presidential participation. If Congress disapproved and the president vetoed the joint resolution, his action would merely reinstate the D.C. law. The president would have little leverage through his veto to influence D.C. legislation.

The Justice Department pressed for a joint resolution of approval to allow the president to veto changes in the D.C. criminal code. However, the D.C. government and members of Congress opposed this procedure as a step backward from home rule. The administration eventually acquiesced and accepted the use of joint resolutions of disapproval as substitutes for the one-House and two-House vetoes in the D.C. Home Rule Act.[34]

CONCLUSIONS

Through its misreading of history, congressional procedures, and executive-legislative relations, the Supreme Court has commanded the political branches to follow a lawmaking process that is impracticable and unworkable. Neither agencies nor committees want the static model of government offered by the court. The inevitable result is a record of noncompliance, subtle evasion, and a system of lawmaking that is now more convoluted, cumbersome, and covert than before. In many cases the court's decision simply drives underground a set of legislative and committee vetoes that had previously operated in plain sight. No one should be misled if the number of legislative vetoes placed in statutes gradually declines over the years. Fading from view will not mean disappearance. In one form or another, legislative vetoes will remain an important method for reconciling legislative and executive interests.

Reading 9.3

Explaining Congressional Casework Styles

John R. Johannes

Members of Congress expend an enormous amount of time and effort doing what people in Congress call casework—i.e., responding to complaints about government or requests for services from individual constituents. Casework or what some call errand-boy functions is also a major institutional activity. In performing these functions, members in effect become ombudsmen, attempting to get relief or redress from government on behalf of citizens and constituents.

There is a good deal of variation in how various members engage in casework. The following article identifies different patterns of casework styles and attempts to account for them. This article is a good introduction to this important congressional function. It is also an excellent example of an empirical-quantifying study of the Congress.

ABSTRACT

Using questionnaire and interview data from 1977 to 1978 on 146 House and 72 Senate offices, this study examines five aspects of congressional casework activity: the amount of time members personally devote to casework, the size of their casework staffs, the percentage of casework done in home offices, the degree to which congressmen attempt to solicit cases, and their propensity to use casework for electoral or public relations purposes. Multiple regression analysis shows significant but substantively minor effects on casework decisions for a number of member-related and constituency-related independent variables. The most important findings are that (1) only a small proportion of the variance in casework activities can be explained by the variables used here, (2) member seniority proves to be the most consistent factor in explaining such activities, and (3) "demand-side" factors (constituency demands, traditions, expectations) are more important than previous research indicated.

Source: From *American Journal of Political Science* 27 (1983), pp. 530–47.

Casework and other forms of constituency service and attentiveness have been recognized as vital elements of legislative life in parliaments around the world, the U.S. Congress, and state legislatures. Constituency service is a major form of responsiveness and representation (Eulau and Karps, 1977). It raises questions concerning legislative organization, member and staff behavior, and legislative-executive relationships. And it is a distinct type of output, potentially relevant to both electoral and policy purposes.

The most recent studies of constituency service have focused on two sets of questions. The first concerns the *purposes* that lay behind, and the factors that distinguish among, differing levels of constituency service. Thus are raised questions relevant to member-constituent relationships, constituency needs and demands (that is, the representational process), role theory, and rational choice theory. The dominant view among scholars is that constituency service activities are purposeful, and that members of Congress engage in them primarily as a means to secure reelection (or widen election vote margins). The second set of questions deals with the electoral, institutional, and policy *effects* of efforts to serve constituents (Mayhew, 1974; Fiorina, 1977; Johannes and McAdams, 1981; Yiannakis, 1981; Jacobson, 1981; Parker, 1981; Powell, 1982; Parker and Parker, 1982). With several exceptions (Elling, 1979, 1980; Jewell, 1982; Macartney, 1975; Peterson and Dutton, 1981), the focus of scholarly investigations of constituency service in the United States has been the House of Representatives. This article departs slightly from that practice, examining both the House and Senate to test two general theories that purport to explain why certain congressmen devote greater effort and resources to constituency service than others. The form of constituency service studied is congressional casework.

DATA

For the purposes of this paper, "casework" includes (1) individual and group casework and (2) federal projects or grants assistance. The first category encompasses most of what one normally associates with the European ombudsman: specific intervention with agency bureaucracies by congressmen and their staffs on behalf of constituents who seek benefits, ask for preferments, or register complaints. The second category refers to helping state and local governments obtain discretionary grants from executive agencies. The essence of the definition employed here is the role of a congressional office as an intermediary between the needy or aggrieved constituent and the government's executive bureaucracy, programs, and operations. Such activities as making appointments to military academies, mailing out pamphlets on child care, flooding constituents with newsletters, obtaining special White House tour tickets, sending congratulatory messages, and answering routine inquiries for information are not included.

Data for this study come from mail questionnaires and interviews (both personal and telephone) in 1977–78, as described elsewhere (Johannes, 1979; Johannes and McAdams, 1981). Responses sufficiently complete for coding on at least some of the variables were received from or interviews were conducted with 11 senators and representatives, 106 Senate staff members (32 in Washington and 74 in home offices), and 248 House aides (87 in Washington and 161 in district offices). Of these, there were 108 face-to-face interviews and 38 telephone interviews (including 4 with members themselves). At least partial data were obtained for the casework operations in 75 Senate and 178 House offices, although for the analyses below the figures are lower owing to missing data. The overall sample is not random, but it is very representative on all important dimensions in the 95th Congress (party, region, seniority, ideology, electoral marginality, and constituency demographic traits).[1]

MEASURES OF CASEWORK ACTIVITY

Scholars studying constituency service and incumbents' electoral advantages in the U.S. House have focused on a variety of variables: trips home and time spent in the district (Fenno, 1978; Parker, 1980; Powell, 1982; Parker and Parker, 1982; O'Donnell, 1982); mailing of newsletters and press releases (Cover, 1980; Yiannakis, 1979); communication patterns (Rundquist and Kellstadt, 1982); size of constituency service staffs (Cavanagh, 1979); staff salaries (Powell, 1982); allocation of such staffs to district offices (Cavanagh, 1979; Fiorina, 1981; Cain, Ferejohn, and Fiorina, 1981; Born, 1982); staff activities (Cranor and Westphal, 1978; Brown, Fuchs, and Hoadley, 1979; Macartney, 1975); efforts to solicit cases from constituents (Cain, Ferejohn and Fiorina, 1981); "advertising" of casework successes (Cain, Ferejohn and Fiorina, 1981); and members' personal involvement in handling cases (Cavanagh, 1979; Cain, Ferejohn, and Fiorina, 1981). This study followed these lines of research, employing five different indicators of casework orientation, effort, and activity as dependent variables. These five indicators are outlined in the next five paragraphs.

1. *The amount of time senators and representatives personally spend on case and project work when in Washington* measures members' own commitments to constituency service and, perhaps, personal role orientations. Focusing on this variable runs the risk of overlooking what might be a good deal of activity by senators and representatives when they are back home with their constituents, but both practical and theoretical reasons lead to using the variable as measured here. On the one hand, obtaining reasonable estimates of time spent on casework when members are back home is much more difficult than getting estimates from their Washington staffs (unless one merely assumes that all time in the constituency is dedicated to casework—an extremely risky assumption). On the other hand, (1) if members refuse to handle cases when in Washington, it is doubtful that they spend large amounts of time on them when back home, and (2) to the extent that one may be concerned with the forced trade-off between efforts devoted to constituent problems and efforts devoted to legislation and oversight duties, examining time in Washington seems appropriate. The measure of time is the estimated number of hours per week senators and representatives spent on casework.[2]

2. *The number of devices (newsletters, WATS lines, mobile offices, and so on) used to stimulate casework requests from constituents* indicates the amount of effort congressmen put into "hustling" cases—for whatever reason they do so.[3] Perhaps members believe that casework pays off in reelection; perhaps traditions of diligent service have been built up by their predecessors or by their own previous efforts; perhaps they seek to contrast their records with those of neighboring senators and representatives; or perhaps, as one staffer said of his boss, the typical congressman "has a soft heart for the poor schmuck getting screwed by the bureaucrats," and realizes that too many citizens are afraid to complain directly.

3. *The number of staff members assigned to cases and projects* (not merely the number of "caseworkers," but all staffers in Washington and the field who "regularly" engage in case and project work) measures the importance members attach to the diligent handling of cases and projects. A decision by a senator to move one or two more aides into the casework business is, generally, not earthshaking. But in the House, where a limit of eighteen exists for staffs, allocating resources to casework represents resources lost to other functions (Cavanagh, 1979); thus, it is a consequential indicator.

4. *The percentage of casework handled in state or district offices,* as opposed to Washington, represents an effort to move casework operations closer to constituents. Most scholars studying congressional resource allocation have assumed that congressmen place staffs in home offices and do casework there in order to ingratiate themselves with constituents. It may be equally plausible to suggest that congressmen do so to accommodate their casework efforts to the decentralized structure of executive agencies, to get casework "out of their hair" (or that of their legislative assistants), or simply to relieve the congestion in Capitol Hill offices while taking advantage of lower salaries and other reduced costs back home. Although other studies have used the number of staffers assigned to district offices as a measure, this analysis uses the percentage of casework handled there, on the grounds that staffers in field offices do have other duties.[4]

5. *Whether or not members use the results of successful casework for politically beneficial purposes* (i.e., whether or not they mention successes in newsletters, various media advertisements, or campaign literature and speeches; whether or not they add

casework recipients' names to various mailing lists; or whether or not they call upon casework recipients for help at election time) indicates an appreciation for the educational and electoral benefits of casework, and it may be a dead giveaway of a congressman's motives. Ninety-two percent of House offices and 77 percent of Senate offices reported making at least some use of casework for electoral or publicity purposes.

These five measures are related to each other, but hardly as much as one might expect. The zero-order correlations among the five variables range from .01 to .40 in the House and from −.10 to .43 in the Senate. Of 20 possible correlations, only six exceeded .20. Clearly, members can rank high on some dimensions of casework activity while placing near the bottom on others. Each is a distinct activity.

INDEPENDENT VARIABLES AND HYPOTHESES

Explanations of casework and other constituency service activities in the United States and elsewhere have focused almost exclusively on member-related ("supply side") factors. Thus any model seeking to explain casework activism must include appropriate member-related variables. What has been largely ignored are the "demand side" or constituency characteristics, except when scholars have sought to explain casework loads. The argument here is that *both* sets of factors need to be included in any satisfactory explanation.

Member-Related Explanations for Casework Activism

Electoral and Seniority Factors Virtually all studies of constituency service and perquisite use begin with the assumption that electorally marginal and junior members would be most likely to court their constituents assiduously; and some, indeed, have found these expected relationships—much more commonly for seniority than for electoral marginality (Mayhew, 1974; Fiorina, 1977; Mohapatra, 1976; Kumbhat and Marican, 1976; Fenno, 1978; Cranor and Westphal, 1978; Cover, 1980; Parker, 1980; Cain, Ferejohn, and Fiorina, 1981; Cavanagh, 1979; McAdams, 1981; Powell, 1982; Parker and Parker, 1982; Born, 1982). Specific hypotheses are that the safer and the more senior the members, the less likely they are to spend their own time on casework, to solicit cases, to devote large staffs to casework and decentralize them, and overtly to seek political benefits from cases and projects. The difficulty in applying the electoral criterion is the problem of reciprocal causality. On the one hand, electorally insecure members may hustle cases, build larger staffs, decentralize casework operations, use casework for electoral purposes, and devote more of their own time to casework, but electorally secure members would not. On the other hand, it may be that safe members are safe *because* they have been attentive to constituents, although that prospect has been questioned recently (Johannes and McAdams, 1981). In the absence of any easy way out of this dilemma (Fiorina, 1981), the analyses below have been undertaken with and without the electoral factor. The electoral margin (safety) variable for the House is the average percentage of the vote received by the 1977–1978 incumbent or the candidate of the member's party in the four elections, 1970–1976. For the Senate, the results of the immediately preceding election for incumbents have been used.

Partisanship and Ideology Several studies have used ideology and partisanship to explain constituency service, but with mixed results (Clark, Price, and Krause, 1975; Clark, 1978; Dowse, 1972; Yiannakis, 1979; LeDuc and White, 1974; Cain, Ferejohn, and Fiorina, 1981; Powell, 1982; Parker and Parker, 1982). Hypotheses are difficult to formulate. Conservatives presumably oppose big government and would be active in trying to help constituents against the bureaucracy; therefore, conservatives should be active in soliciting cases and spending their own time on casework. But their aversion to "big government" might translate into having smaller casework staffs as a matter of principle and into holding back from trying to generate more cases. Similarly, one would not expect them to have numerous home offices or to move casework operations to them. Liberals, perhaps being more policy oriented, might move casework away from Washington to free up their staffs for legislative work. No hypothesis exists to link ideology to the use of casework for political purposes. Even greater problems exist in developing hypotheses for the partisan dimension. (For that reason, as well as the high correlation between party and ideology, the party variable is not included in the analysis below.) The measure for ideology is *Congressional Quarterly's* conservative coalition support score.

Power, Career Trends, and Institutional Responsibilities A narrow focus on the electoral incentive may ignore member orientations toward policy or internal congressional power and may overlook the common House career progression from worry about reelection (and thus a constituency focus), to concern about public policy, to a desire to wield influence over other congressmen (Dodd, 1977; Fenno, 1973, Ch. 1). Two variables—leadership and policy activism—can be isolated for analysis.

A dummy variable for leadership position was created by lumping together all members in the sample who held official party leadership positions, chaired committees or subcommittees, or served as ranking minority members on such panels. The expectation is that leaders would be unlikely to spend their own time on casework, to hustle cases, or to use cases overtly for political purposes. However, they would be able to devote larger personal staff resources to casework, since they have access to extra legislative staff members by virtue of their leadership positions. Since they have additional office space in Washington, one does not expect them to have to put casework operations in district offices. Two problems here are that practically all senators hold leadership positions and, in the House, leadership and seniority correlate highly. Therefore, equations have been run with both variables, and separately, with each.

Congressmen and senators differ, somewhat systematically, in their levels of policy activism (Walker, 1977; Frantzich, 1979). Policy activism might affect casework operations and attitudes, but the direction of the effect is not so clear. Policy activists might be just that—policy entrepreneurs and negotiators who care little for constituency service. At the same time, perhaps the price one must pay to be an activist is assiduous attention to one's constituency. If that is true, strong positive relationships would be expected between activism and all measures of casework except the time variable. Similar positive relationships would be expected if the measure of activism used here (introduction and cosponsorship of bills in 1977) was merely a ploy to attract attention from the media and key interest groups back home. Given this ambiguity, a two-tailed test of significance was appropriate for the analyses below.

Electoral margin, seniority, ideology, leadership, and policy activism represent the major member-related characteristics available for use in this analysis. Certainly others might be used, such as roles (Davidson, 1969; Clark, Price, and Krause, 1975; Kumbhat and Marican, 1976) or political ambition (Clark, 1978; Parker and Parker, 1982). Such concepts, however, have not proved terribly useful in dealing with constituency service; and at any rate, adequate measures are not available for role orientations. An analysis was done with respect to ambition: members leaving the House to run for higher office in 1978 were compared with those seeking reelection, but no differences emerged with respect to any of the dependent variables.

Constituency Characteristics

The only theory to rival a member-based explanation for constituency service activity evolves from the assumption that congressmen must, or do, *react*: constituency characteristics, expectations, demands, and traditions may also affect casework activism.

Socioeconomic Conditions One might suppose that states and districts with generally low average income and low education (as indicated by 1970 census data) have a greater objective need for casework but are populated by constituents less inclined, or able, to make demands. Whereas letter writing and opinion expressing are positively correlated with socioeconomic status, an investigation of the Obey Commission's 1977 national opinion survey and of the 1978 and 1980 Center for Political Studies (CPS) National Election Studies found the reverse to be true for requesting help on personal problems. Districts having constituencies with less education generate more cases (Johannes, 1980), and voters of lower socioeconomic status have slightly higher expectations of casework service. Thus one would hypothesize that districts and states with constituencies of low income and low education would be "hustled" more for cases, that they would have casework operations located in them, and that their congressmen might believe that such constituents could be influenced by successful casework (better educated districts might care more about policy) and that congressmen would attempt to use casework results politically. One expects, then, that either because districts with constituents having less education produce more cases (a simple stimulus-response model) or because their representatives are more committed to helping them, their congressmen would spend more personal time on and devote greater staff to casework. Since the correlation between income and education is high (.61 in the Senate and .68 in the House), only education will be used here.

Population Density Rational senators and congressmen would be less likely to locate casework operations in states and districts that are sparsely populated and widely spread out, since the impact of having staffers back home and of doing casework in district offices is maximized in compact, urban areas where personal visits and phone calls by constituents are facilitated. One thus expects to find a positive relationship between the degree to which a district is "urban" (measured as the percentage of the population living in Standard Metropolitan Statistical Areas) and the location of casework operations in field offices.

Demand Presumably, the greater the demand for casework services (measured by staff estimates of the average weekly case and project loads), the more time the member will spend on casework, the larger the case and project staff, and the more likely the member is to decentralize casework operations.

Regional and Cultural Traditions The East and the upper Midwest have experienced relatively hard economic times of late, while the Sunbelt has been booming. These conditions might translate into more or less attentiveness, respectively, by their congressmen to casework and projects. Moreover, each region tends to be characterized by one more or less dominant political culture (Elazar, 1972). The eastern culture tends to be individualistic, implying that congressmen from that region would be more opportunistic and more aggressive concerning casework. One also expects that the East's history of urban political machines would leave a strong commitment to casework. Many areas of the Midwest have moralistic cultures, in which policymaking

Table 9.3.1.
House members' casework activities.

Independent Variables	Members' Time	Number of Devices to Solicit Cases	Total Casework Staff	Percentage of Casework Done in Home Offices	Use of Casework for Political Purposes
Seniority	−.197* (−.199)	−.038* (−.234)	−.073* (−.159)	−1.234† (−.258)	−.014* (−.226)
Conservatism	.015 (.072)	−.002 (−.004)	.014 (.129)	−.229† (−.210)	−.001 (−.052)
Legislative activism	−.002 (−.004)	−.002‡,§ (−.178)	−.001 (−.035)	.030 (.088)	−.001‡,§ (−.215)
Constituent education	−1.552§ (−.201)	−.015 (−.011)	−.495 (−.121)	3.225 (.074)	−.170* (−.282)
Case load	−.000 (−.006)	—	.008* (.197)	−.034 (−.081)	—
Percentage urban	—	—	—	.281† (.275)	—
East	3.544§ (.245)	.485§ (.199)	.939 (.130)	15.935* (.209)	.243 (.246)
South	.493 (.032)	−.001 (−.000)	−.675 (−.081)	15.016* (.178)	−.097 (−.087)
Midwest	−1.516 (−.108)	.143 (.059)	−1.350§ (−.188)	4.602 (.060)	−.028 (−.028)
West	−.276 (−.017)	−.171 (−.064)	.049 (.006)	8.998 (.102)	6.638 (.058)
Constant	24.883	2.431	12.211	12.670	3.009
N	82	133	117	137	79
R^2	.16	.10	.18	.35	.16
Adjusted R^2	.06	.04	.09	.30	.06

Note: Standardized regression coefficients appear in parentheses below ordinary least squares coefficients.
*$p < .05$.
†$p < .01$.
‡Two-tailed test of significance.
§$p < .10$.

would take precedence over service and in which using casework for political purposes would be frowned upon. In short, one anticipates distinct regional effects upon casework operations. For this analysis, the country was divided into five regions: East, South, Border, West, and Midwest.[5]

ANALYSIS

The analysis is straightforward. Tables 9.3.1 and 9.3.2 present coefficients from ordinary least squares (OLS) regression equations. For the analysis of whether or not congressmen employ casework results to gain publicity or for other electoral purposes, a more appropriate statistical procedure would be dichotomous PROBIT. Since the regression analysis in this case yields the same results as PROBIT, the OLS coefficients are presented for ease of comparison with the other measures.

First, the most striking finding of the analysis is the overall weakness of these

Table 9.3.2.
Senator's casework activities.

Independent Variables	Senators' Time	Number of Devices to Solicit Cases	Total Casework Staff	Percentage of Casework Done in Home Offices	Use of Casework for Political Purposes
Seniority	.048 (.118)	−.068* (−.389)	−.168 (−.143)	−2.890† (−.533)	−.014 (−.249)
Conservatism	−.003 (−.027)	−.004 (−.125)	−.065‡ (−.317)	−.216 (−.170)	−.002 (−.128)
Legislative activism	−.005 (−.068)	.002 (.060)	.047§ (.290)	.167 (.182)	.001 (.089)
Case load	.005* (.539)	—	.007* (.359)	.018 (.152)	—
Constituent education	−1.361 (−.296)	−.301 (−.156)	.195 (.016)	−5.588 (−.097)	.341 (.424)
Percentage urban	—	—	—	.338‡ (.215)	—
East	−1.100 (−.087)	1.090 (.294)	−6.849‡ (−.271)	−18.190 (−.149)	.011 (.010)
South	.096 (.013)	.758 (.226)	−.794 (−.045)	−2.293 (−.023)	−.125 (−.097)
Midwest	.331 (.045)	.570 (.237)	−4.318‡ (−.312)	−7.274 (−.082)	−.231 (−.222)
West	3.270‡ (.494)	1.159* (.483)	1.053 (.066)	2.847 (.031)	−.181 (−.187)
Constant	17.676	4.856	7.107	128.196	−3.000
N	28	41	38	52	28
R^2	.39	.24	.38	.39	.35
Adjusted R^2	.09	.05	.18	.24	.08

Note: Standardized regression coefficients appear in parentheses below ordinary least squares coefficients.
*$p < .05$.
†$p < .01$.
‡$p < .10$.
§Two-tailed test of significance.

models—and those used by other scholars—in explaining casework activity. Either key variables are left out, the measures used are inadequate, or many of the decisions concerning constituency service are idiosyncratic. Addition of other variables (party, constituency income, and the percentage of constituents employed by government) does increase the proportion of variance explained in several equations, but only slightly (the largest adjusted R^2 was .30) and inconsistently. One is sorely tempted to agree with Fenno (1978, p. 48), Breslin (1977, p. 24), and Hammond (1977, p. 5) that constituency service decisions and resource allocations are highly individualized. Perhaps some of these decisions are controlled not by members but by staffers who are influenced by considerations other than those represented in the models.

Second, the measures of casework activity seem to be affected by different independent variables. Given the weak correlations among them, this is not surprising. Apparently, casework decisions are differentially motivated and are not the effects of coherent strategies adopted by most members. Certainly, scholars investigating constituency service activities must be sensitive to the different influences at work.

Third, to the extent that the models have at least some explanatory power, member-related *and* constituency-related factors help to account for casework behavior. Of member-related factors, seniority stands out as the only consistently important independent predictor of casework activity, juniors being more active than seniors. House juniors, and especially freshmen, spend more time on casework than senior members. There is a bigger difference in time spent on cases and projects between first and second termers, on the one hand, and middle-seniority members, on the other, than between middle and high seniority congressmen.

Seniority also is inversely related to casework solicitation, use of casework for political purposes, size of staff, and decentralization. The same is true for the Senate, although the coefficients are not always significant. The pattern is clear: juniors do more. Analysis of data on time spent on casework and on numbers and location of caseworkers reported in the House Commission on Administrative Review's 1977 survey of over 140 offices (excluding, unfortunately, party leaders and committee chairmen) confirms these findings, except for time spent on casework. If other scholars are correct (Parker, 1980; Parker and Parker, 1982; Born, 1982), these results may represent cohort or generational replacement effects more than life-cycle or aging effects, since it is improbable that seniors, having once had large casework staffs, would reduce them. Rather, newcomers, especially those elected in the last decade, seem to begin legislative life with a more aggressive stance toward casework, spending more time and staff (in their districts) on serving constituents. This contrasts with seniors, who began their careers in an age when staffs were smaller and tied to Washington offices and who have not adapted as thoroughly or quickly to the newer styles.[6]

What of electoral safety or marginality? Although bivariate correlations between electoral margin and casework solicitation and staff decentralization are negative, they are modest ($r = -.21, -.24$) and disappear when controls are imposed in regression equations (not shown). The lack of significant effects may be due to the simultaneity or multicollinearity factors explained above. Or it could simply mean that electoral insecurity, as measured here, does not itself affect casework activities. Perhaps *perceptions* of insecurity are more important; perhaps the measure used here (a four-election average) is a poor indicator;[7] or perhaps—incredible as it seems—members do not systematically let electoral margins dictate casework behavior.

Ideology helps to explain several casework activities. Its coefficient carries a negative sign in eight of ten equations, suggesting a rather consistent, but weak, effect. Conservatism clearly is negatively related to casework decentralization in the House, and the same may hold true for the Senate (the coefficient is not significant). In the upper chamber, conservatism led to smaller casework staffs in 1977 and 1978.

Since House leadership is so intertwined with seniority, it is impossible to get a clear reading of leadership's effects on casework. Substituting leadership for seniority in the equations, one observes that leaders, as expected, spend less time on cases, hustle cases less aggressively, and tend to keep casework operations and staffs on Capitol Hill. When both leadership and seniority are included—a genuine test of leadership's effects despite the risk of multicollinearity—it becomes clear that leaders still spend less of their own time on constituent problems and go to fewer lengths to solicit cases. As hypothesized, leaders average about one more casework-related staff member than back-benchers.

Legislative activism is associated with several casework activities. In the House, activists tend to do less to stimulate new case requests and are less inclined to try to milk political advantage from serving constituents. Perhaps they believe, correctly, that legislative activism itself will garner attention and credit (Johannes and McAdams, 1981). Conversely, were the introduction of many bills and resolutions merely part of an overall strategy to seek visibility and political credit, one would expect positive coefficients. The negative signs may suggest that, even given this scenario, the two sorts of reelection-oriented activities (introduction of legislation and casework) are independent. And that might mean that casework is valued as something other than merely a means of ingratiating oneself with voters.

Although the coefficients are not statistically different from zero, the signs hint that activists decentralize casework activities, suggesting perhaps a desire to remove the "distraction" from their Washington offices. The virtual lack of any relationship between activism and either time spent on casework or the size of casework-related staffs may indicate that legislative activity and casework are not inevitably at odds. Were there a forced trade-off, one would expect to see some stronger negative correlations.

Turning to constituency characteristics, we see a bit more light shed on the problem. Regional considerations, at least in the House, seem important. Representatives from the East spend more time, do more to stimulate cases, more consistently locate casework operations in district offices, and (the coefficients are less clear) seem to have larger staffs and to use cases for political gain. The coefficients for the Senate are inconclusive. Interestingly, being from the Midwest—perhaps influenced by its moralistic culture—seems to discourage allocating large staffs to the casework enterprise in both chambers.

Casework loads, as expected, are useful predictors of the size of staffs working on cases and projects; and in the Senate, they also seem to be linked to the time senators spend dealing with cases. The implication is that congressmen respond to constituent demands by increasing the number of staffers who regularly handle constituent problems.[8]

Congressmen and senators from urban areas in 1977 and 1978 were unusually likely to decentralize casework operations to home offices. There are economies of scale and other conveniences in working out of district offices that are easily accessible to constituents, as is the case in densely populated areas. Moreover, many department and agency offices are found in large cities; the staffs of congressmen and senators from such constituencies can deal directly with executive officials who may be located just across the street or even in the same federal building.

House constituency education levels, as predicted, are inversely related to the amount of time representatives spend on casework and to their use of casework for political purposes. The signs for the education coefficients in the equations modeling casework solicitation and size of casework-related staffs also are in the predicted directions. Congressmen at once are responsive to and solicitous of constituencies with less education, but apparently they also believe that such districts can be influenced by careful service and attention.

CONCLUSION

Rational choice theorists have sought to explain constituency service in terms of electoral threats and seniority. This study, too, finds the expected effect for seniority, but it finds little support for the electoral connection hypothesis. Members demonstrably are rational and responsive when it comes to allocating larger staffs to deal with heavy casework demands, to meeting constituency expectations and traditions, to doing casework in those districts and states (urban) where doing so is efficient, and to adjusting their political use of casework to the educational levels of their constituents. Leaders in the House are able to allocate greater personal staff resources to dealing with constituents and rationally do so.

If the analysis here is accepted, it means that future efforts to explain constituency service behavior will have to pay greater attention to demand-side (constituency) factors. Even then, however, it is unlikely that a clear and consistent picture will emerge. Much—perhaps most—of casework activity seems to be idiosyncratic, with the various components largely unrelated to each other. Some political phenomena, it seems, defy systematic explanation.

Reading 9.4

Congress and Budgeting

Howard Shuman

Preoccupation with fiscal, tax, budgetary, and deficit issues is another important characteristic of the contemporary Congress. Congress handles money matters through a framework established by the 1974 Congressional Budget and Impoundment Control Act. The following original essay by a noted expert on congressional budgeting examines the modern history of budgeting and the budget process, the major provisions of the 1974 act, and the origins and features of the most significant Gramm-Rudman deficit reduction package.

More than a decade after the landmark Budget and Impoundment Control Act of 1974 became law, the budget, the budget process, and the Budget Act were in a mess.

Since 1946 the budget had been balanced only eight times—four times under Truman, three times under Eisenhower, once in the transition year (FY 1969) between Johnson and Nixon, and never since then.

Source: This article, original to this collection, is based in part on Howard E. Shuman, *Politics and the Budget: The Struggle Between the President and the Congress* (Englewood Cliffs, N.J.: Prentice-Hall, 1984).

In fiscal years 1985 and 1986, not one of the regular 13 major appropriations bills had been signed by the President when the new fiscal year began on October 1. Worse, Congress had great trouble passing the continuing resolution, the catch-all temporary appropriations bill designed to keep the government going when Congress fails to pass the regular money bills.

There was a deficit of more than $200 billion and there was no chance the budget could be balanced during the decade of the 1980s. The national debt had risen to more than $2 trillion, double the amount of only five years before.

Finally, out of sheer frustration, the Congress proposed and the President signed a Draconian measure called the Gramm-Rudman-Hollings Act, which instructed the President and future Congresses to do in a mechanical way what the President and the sitting Congress refused to do in an intelligent way, namely to come to grips with the

Table 9.4.1.
Total number and percentage of the 13 regular appropriations bills passed by the House and by the Senate and/or signed by the President in the first 11 years of the 1974 Budget Act (fiscal years 1976–1986).

Fiscal Years 1976–1986 (Ford, Carter, Reagan)	House	Senate	President
Total number of regular appropriations bills introduced in the House or Senate or proposed by the President	143	143	143
Total number passed or signed into law by October 1	119	79	45
Percentage passed or signed into law by October 1	83%	55%	31%
Fiscal Years 1976–1981 (Ford, Carter)			
Total number of regular appropriations bills introduced in the House or Senate or proposed by the President	78	78	78
Total number passed or signed into law by October 1	74	56	37
Percentage passed or signed into law by October 1	95%	72%	41%
Fiscal Years 1982–1986 (Reagan)			
Total number of regular appropriations bills introduced in the House or Senate or proposed by the President	65	65	65
Total number passed or signed into law by October 1	45	23	8
Percentage passed or signed into law by October 1	70%	35%	12%

budget crisis. Ironically, the act provides an unprecedented shift of power over budget matters from Congress to the President, only a decade after Congress passed the 1974 act in order to regain congressional budget power lost to the President. Under Gramm-Rudman-Hollings, Congress provides the President with the power to impound or "sequester" funds. When President Nixon exercised such power, Congress proposed Articles of Impeachment.

Not all these problems were caused by Congress alone. President Reagan's 1981 tax bill, supported by both political parties in the Congress, gave away $150 billion a year in government revenues, enough even with the military build-up to have provided an overall balance in the budget during President Reagan's first five years. In addition, delays in passing money bills were caused by at least three other procedural factors. First, President Reagan proposed more controversial budget issues to the Congress than it was conceivable for Congress to deal with in any fiscal year. Second, controversial social issues (abortion, prayer in the schools, busing) were proposed to money bills in the form of "riders," which brought filibusters and threats of filibusters. Finally, as table 9.4.1 shows, the President and his Senate Republican supporters deliberately delayed passing money bills on the political grounds that the President would have more leverage over specific budget matters during arguments over the continuing resolution when he could threaten the veto than during the regular procedures. (For FY 1986, for example, the House passed 8 of the 13 major money bills by July 30 and a 9th on September 12, but the Senate had acted on only 3 by October 1.)

Table 9.4.1, compiled from the Status of Appropriation Bills, Calendar of Business, Senate of the United States for the appropriate fiscal years, indicates the declining number of appropriation bills reaching the President's desk by the beginning of the fiscal year 1976–1986.

But there is a more important, fundamental reason for the impasse. It's called Madisonian democracy. The government of the United States with its division of powers, two-house legislature, and federal-state system, is designed to prevent action until political consensus is reached. In the case of the budget, there is a consensus about the problem, but not about the answer. In the first session of the 99th Congress, a Republican Senate was prepared to attack the problem courageously by proposing a cut in the rate of military spending, a freeze on entitlements including social security, and a modest tax increase to reduce the deficit. Neither a Republican President, however, nor the Democratic and Republican members of a Democrat-controlled House, were willing to go along.

The President opposed any tax increase and a freeze on social security. The House Democrats were unwilling to vote for tax increases not proposed by the President, and both Deomocrats and Republicans in the House were unwilling to touch the sacred social security cost of living allowance for the ever-increasing aging population.

Confronted with obstruction, deadlock, and delay, Congress and the President abandoned their individual responsibilities and passed Gramm-Rudman. Some of its supporters voted for it in the desperate hope that it would force the consensus that regular procedures had failed to bring about.

THE PRESIDENT'S BUDGET

The Budget of the United States Government, traditionally released in January or early February, is the President's, not the government's budget. Provided for under the Budget and Accounting Act of 1921, which many scholars believe was the beginning of the modern Presidency, each year it gets more sustained attention from the press and media than the Super Bowl, the World Series, the U.S. Tennis Open, and the Master's Golf Tournament combined.

It consists not of a single small document, but of at least five principal documents of more than 3,000 pages. The day they are released to the press is called "shopping bag day" in Washington because a shopping bag is required to carry them away.

On the day of release, at least one-third of the evening network news programs are devoted to the budget. The next morning the major national newspapers devote as much as four front-page stories and five full inside pages to the substance and politics of the budget. Why is there so much interest in these turgid documents, the details but not the thrust of which are often added to the list of great unread literature of the world?

The first reason is that the budget is now the country's number one political document. Certainly since 1980, the budget has been the major domestic political issue. Presidential elections are fought over the issues of taxes, spending, debt, and deficit. Entire congressional sessions are devoted to it.

Second, the budget is the nation's chief priority-setting document. Economic and political benefits are received by every person and institution in the country from the Fortune 500 to the lowliest citizen. Here are found the funds for the water projects, weapons systems, farm price supports, highways, food stamps, export subsidies, credit programs, housing grants, social security and Medicare payments, education loans, and energy grants. The budget determines who gets the gravy. It is the bread and butter and the mother's milk of politics. Some of the benefits go to the weak and the poor, but most go to those who are powerful enough to get them and to keep them.

Third, the budget is the country's chief economic instrument. It affects both domestic and foreign economic policies and relations with the rest of the world. It influences, although it does not always control, counter-cyclical fiscal policy, inflation or deflation, economic growth at home, the balance of payments, the balance of trade, and the price of the dollar of the world currency exchanges.

A SHORT BUDGET HISTORY

Historically, the budget was neither dominated by the President nor the major influence in domestic economic policy.

The founding fathers gave virtually every power over the budget to the Congress. Article I, Section 8 of the Constitution states that "Congress," not the President, "shall have power to:

- Lay and collect taxes.
- Pay the debts, provide for the common defense and general welfare.
- Borrow money on the credit of the United States.
- Coin money and regulate the value thereof.
- Raise and support armies.
- Provide and maintain a Navy."

Article I, Section 9, which delineates the "prohibitory powers," says that "No money shall be drawn from the Treasury except in consequence of an Appropriation made by law."

From 1789 until the beginning of the 20th century, Congress dominated budget procedures and exercised the powers of the purse strings, except for short periods of wars or panics, without let or hindrance. From 1789 until 1921, there was no presidential budget, except for one President Taft sent to Congress in 1912, which was dutifully ignored. Instead, officials in each agency or department compiled something called the "Book of Estimates," which they then marched up to Capitol Hill where it was presented to key congressional committee leaders, usually without benefit of review by either the President or the Treasury. The results were interesting.

From 1789 until 1893, the budget was in surplus every year except for years of wars and panics, that is for 77 of the 104 years.

By the end of 1836, the U. S. government was free of all debts, principally those it had accumulated when it assumed the debts of the original 13 states and those brought about by the War of 1812.

From 1867 to 1893, or for 27 years, the budget was balanced every year. Total spending was routinely below $400 million a year.

Virtually all the revenues of the government were provided by customs and tariffs on the one hand, or excise taxes on the other. An income tax helped for a short period during the Civil War, but basically customs and excises provided all the revenues.

After 1893 things began to change. From 1894 to the end of the 19th century, there was a deficit every year. From 1900 until World War I, there was a deficit almost every other year. In these periods expenditures doubled to slightly less than $800 million a year.

These conditions were brought about by the panic of 1893–1894, the increase in government because of the second wave of immigrants, the flowering of the industrial revolution and the growth of such businesses as steel and railroads, the cost of the Spanish American War, and the increase in funds for Civil War veterans and their families. The world was more complex and Congress found difficulty in dealing with the new issues that arose.

As a result, Congress began to delegate its powers. In 1913 it delegated its power to coin money and regulate the value thereof, the monetary power, to the Federal Reserve System. In 1917 Congress delegated to the Treasury vast powers over funding the debt and deficit under the First and Second Liberty Bond Acts of that year, which established the debt ceiling. This became necessary as spending increased because of World War I from the $700 to $800-million-a-year level in 1913 to $18.5 billion by 1919, and the budget deficit grew to $13.4 billion in the latter year.

Finally, after a series of study commissions and pressures from both the business community and progressive reformers, the Congress passed the Budget and Accounting Act of 1921. "The modern Presidency," wrote James L. Sundquist, "judged in terms of institutional responsibilities, began on June 19, 1921, the day that President Harding signed the Budget and Accounting Act."[1] It provided for the presidential budget and the Bureau of the Budget (now the Office of Management and Budget) and its Director.

Congress also established under the 1921 act both the General Accounting Office (GAO) and the Comptroller General of the United States as its head, to act as the congressional watchdogs over the massive power Congress had delegated to the President.

During the 1930s, Congress delegated much of its power over the right "to borrow money on the credit of the United States" to a variety of established and new executive agencies such as the Farmer's Home Administration, the Federal Housing Administration, the Rural Electrification Administration, and dozens of others. By the 1980s, funds provided through direct loans, guaranteed loans, and loans by government-sponsored enterprises equalled the total amount of spending in the annual budget.

Finally, in the Employment Act of 1946 Congress called on the President to exercise responsibility over the economy by proposing each year "all practicable means to promote maximum employment, production, and purchasing power."

These actions by Congress over a third of a century gave the President vast initiative over public policy. It concentrated power and the initiative over the budget and economic policy in the hands of the President in lieu of the diffusion of power and the cacaphonous pronouncements of 535 individual members of Congress.

The President's command of the initiative, or what Theodore Roosevelt called "the bully pulpit," were further institutionalized through four events that occur at the beginning of the year. Every fourth year in the inaugural address and every year in the State of the Union message, the President proclaims his policies from the steps of Capitol Hill or from the dais in the chamber of the House of Representatives. The President's budget is released shortly thereafter. Within a few more days the President's Economic Report is sent to Congress. These events allow the President to dominate and monopolize public, fiscal, and economic policies in a way the founding fathers never contemplated.

THE BUDGET AND IMPOUNDMENT CONTROL ACT OF 1974

The 1974 Budget Act was not only the result of a budget war between President Nixon and a Democratic Congress; it was also a child of the constitutional crisis called Watergate. It encompassed greater issues than those that drove previous budget crises. President Nixon, in a series of actions produced the crisis that infuriated the Congress and threatened the Constitution.

First, the President authorized the secret bombing of Cambodia in March 1969. The money came not from funds provided for this purpose, but from those Congress authorized for Air Force operations in Vietnam. Funds authorized under foreign aid for Taiwan, Turkey, the Philippines, and Greece were used to invade Cambodia in April 1970. Money to continue the war in Cambodia in 1972 and 1973 came through transfer authority over $750 million of appropriated funds, which was contingent on the House and Senate Appropriations Committees being both notified and giving approval. By the time Congress found out about the "transfer," all the funds had been spent.

Second, on the domestic side, President Nixon declared a moratorium on spending funds Congress had appropriated for housing and the cities. Then he refused to allocate $9 billion of the $18 billion Congress had provided for clean water projects. He then refused to spend money for a series of farm programs to which he objected, but which Congress had both authorized and funded.

Congress was furious. Through his actions, President Nixon alienated Republicans and Democrats, liberals and conservatives, and members from both the North and South, urban and rural constituencies.

Congress was equally unhappy with its own and the President's inability to deal with the budget. Congress was concerned with the 34 deficits in the previous 40 years. Congress was unhappy at its inability to examine the budget on an overall basis. It had to look at it piecemeal and with little opportunity to decide between and among competing priorities. Congress was frustrated that authority was splintered between spending and revenues. It was even more unhappy that two-thirds or more of the budget was outside its jurisdiction or "relatively uncontrollable" in the absence of a change in a specific law. Congress also agonized over the backlog of unspent budget authority, which essentially equalled the amounts requested in each new budget.

As a result, Congress passed the Budget and Impoundment Control Act of 1974. The final version passed the House by 401 to 6 and the Senate by a vote of 75 to 0. Its purpose was both to set its own house in order and to retrive power from the President that, since 1913, it had so easily delegated away.

The act is really two acts. Titles I through IX are cited as "The Congressional Budget Act of 1974." Title X is called "The Impoundment Control Act of 1974." The purpose of the first was for Congress to discipline itself. The purpose of the second was for Congress to discipline the President.

Provisions of the 1974 Act

Essentially the act did four things. First, through a concurrent resolution on the budget, required to be passed by May 15, Congress set overall budget goals or limits for itself. The concurrent resolution is not a law, but a set of instructions by the House and Senate to their committees and members. The act does not call for a balanced budget or even for cuts in spending. Instead it provides that Congress set the "appropriate levels" of budget authority, outlays, surplus or deficit, and public debt, and the "recommended level" of federal revenues. In addition, it calls for Congress to set forth the amount, if any, "of the surplus or deficit in the budget *which is appropriate in light of economic conditions and all other relevant factors.*" It canonized counter-cyclical fiscal policy. *The first concurrent resolution on the budget is the cornerstone of the act.*

Second, the act provided for a new congressional superstructure. It did not do away with any existing institutions. It provided for two new budget committees, one in each house. It established the Congressional Budget Office (CBO) as its own source for facts and information to offset those provided by the President. It also changed the fiscal year by moving its starting date from July 1 to October 1 to give Congress three more months from the time the President released his budget to work its will.

Third, the act provided a new budget timetable. There were five key dates in the timetable as originally passed. They were:

1. The release of the President's budget 15 days after Congress convenes in January (usually the first Monday in February).
2. Passage of the nonbinding First Concurrent Resolution on the Budget by May 15.
3. Passage of the binding Second Concurrent Resolution on the Budget by September 15.
4. Completion of action on a reconciliation bill or resolution to implement the Second Budget Resolution by September 25. Its purpose was to make certain that the budget actions of Congress were in harmony with its professed goals.
5. The beginning of the new fiscal year on October 1.

By the early 1980s, Congress had in practice done away with the Second Budget Resolution, made the First Budget Resolution binding, and provided for reconciliation as a part of the First Resolution.

Fourth, the act provided two methods to deal with presidential impoundments. They were called deferral and rescission. Deferral refers to the slowing down or temporary delay in the spending of funds. A rescission occurs with a proposal that money appropriated by Congress not be spent either in whole or in part, such as when a program, project, or weapons system is cancelled.

Under the act, the President must inform the Congress in writing of his intention either to defer or rescind money. If the President fails to report, the Comptroller General is required to do so instead. In the case of deferral, the President's action is approved unless either house passes an "impoundment resolution" disapproving the deferral. In short, funds are deferred unless one house of Congress objects.

With respect to a rescission, both houses of Congress must give their approval within 45 days or the funds must be spent. Thus, affirmative action of both houses is necessary to rescind. These provisions have worked very well indeed, but are now threatened by the recent Supreme Court decision in *Chada* v. *Immigration and Naturalization Service (INS)* calling the legislative veto into question.

THE REAGAN BUDGET REVOLUTION

President Reagan, in his first year in office, instituted a budget revolution. He had a purpose, a program, and a method to achieve his goals.

His *purpose* was to shift budget resources from civilian to military programs, to shift financial burdens from the federal to the state and local governments, to shift some programs from the government entirely to the private sector, and to shift the tax burden from the wealthy and relatively well-to-do to middle and lower income citizens. The latter was justified on the grounds that tax cuts for upper-income classes would result in greater incentives to save, and hence to invest in new machinery and equipment, which would stimulate the economy and produce new jobs.

The *program* had three prongs. Domestic programs were to be cut by $40 billion in the first year. This would produce additional billions of domestic savings in future years. The military budget was to be increased to provide outlays of $1.5 trillion over five years or at an average level of $300 billion a year. Finally, a tax cut of $750 billion over five years, or an average of $150 billion a year, was proposed.

Finally, the President devised a *method* or a set of *tactics* to achieve his purpose and his program. These consisted of three elements. The program was started in the Senate where the gain of 12 seats in the 1980 election gave the Republicans control. In addition, the new Budget Act provision for "reconciliation" was used in a new and radical way at the beginning of the year to push through the President's program. Further, the provisions for majority rule and limited debate on budget matters provided for under the 1974 act were invoked in both houses to prevent filibuster and delay. As a result, the President was highly successful.

What President Nixon attempted to do illegally and unconstitutionally, President Reagan did legally and constitutionally with majorities behind him at every step. In doing so, the President turned the 1974 Budget Act on its head. The act, designed by Congress to discipline itself and to regain power from the President, ironically enlarged the power of the President and allowed him to discipline Congress.

But the President's successes were also his failures. The successful domestic spending cuts were more than offset by the increases in the military budget so that there was no overall decrease in the level of federal spending. In the meantime, the $750-billion five-year tax cut, combined with fluctuating economic conditions, provided an annual deficit that exceeded $200 billion a year by FY 1986.

THE GRAMM-RUDMAN-HOLLINGS ACT OF 1985

The Gramm-Rudman-Hollings Act had its origins in two major events. The first was the aborted effort by Senate Republicans to confront the deficit issue in 1985 by freezing domestic programs, limiting military spending to the previous year's level plus a 3 percent inflation adjustment, and a small tax increase. Having confronted and voted on the toughest domestic political issues, the Senate Republicans sought protective covering after the Republican President and the combined House Democrats and Republicans pulled the rug out from under them and refused to go along.

The second was the proposed increase in the federal debt limit to over $2 trillion dollars presented to the Republican Senate by the Democratic House in the last weeks of the 1985 fiscal year. Members of Congress returned to Washington after Labor Day convinced that their constituents were far more concerned with the ultimate effects of the debt and deficit than the President's initiative for tax reform.

When the bill increasing the debt ceiling to $2,088 billion came to the Senate, the 22 Republicans up for re-election in 1986 were seeking a political device to save face when, to keep the government going, they were required to vote to increase the debt ceiling. The solution was the Gramm-Rudman-Hollings amendment, which provides a balanced budget by 1991. Some called it the Republican Incumbent Protection Act of 1985.

While it wound its way through the Senate, the House, and the Conference Committee it provided a moving target, but as finally passed and signed into law by the President it set a number of budget requirements.

1. It mandates a specific budget deficit for six fiscal years beginning October 1, 1985. Except for the first year, the President must propose and Congress must approve a budget whose maximum deficit is reduced by $36 billion a year until the budget is balanced in fiscal year 1991. The following table lists the maximum deficit allowed for the critical years.

Fiscal Year	Maximum Deficit ($ Billions)
1986	$171.9
1987	144
1988	108
1989	72
1990	36
1991	0

2. If Congress fails to approve a budget that meets the annual deficit, an emergency deficit-cutting procedure is triggered by the combined action of the Office of Management and Budget, the Congressional Budget Office, and the Comptroller General of the General Accounting Office. The OMB and the CBO estimate the amount by which the deficit exceeds legal limits. The Comptroller General of the GAO then issues a report to the President setting forth the areas in which the act requires specific reductions in budget programs, projects, and activities (PPAs).

3. Based on these findings, the President is required to issue an order—called a "sequestering order"—largely ministerial in nature, that must "strictly adhere to the determinations set forth in the GAO report" as to where cuts must take place in budget accounts. The timetable for the "sequestering" provisions for FY 1987[2] and beyond is as follows.

- August 15—The "snapshot" of the deficit by the OMB and the CBO is taken.
- August 20—OMB and CBO Report to GAO.
- August 25—GAO issues the report to the President, based on the findings of OMB and CBO.
- September 1—The Presidential Order is issued based on the GAO report.
- October 1—The order takes effect.
- October 5—OMB and CBO issue a revised report to reflect final congressional action.
- October 10—GAO issues a revised report to the President.
- October 15—The final order, based on the revised report, is effective.
- November 15—GAO issues a compliance report.

Under this timetable, the month of September would be set aside for a congressional response to the sequestration order. The conferees expect the CBO and OMB will take the final snapshot as close to October 5th as possible.

4. While the law provides exemptions for some programs (social securty, low-income programs, veterans and health benefits, etc.) and limited cuts for others, it effectively provides that the cuts called for in the President's order will be equally divided between civilian and defense programs.

A recession would postpone the six-year schedule. A war would negate it.

The mechanism appears to be both automatic and Draconian. Tightly drawn, there appears little leeway for maneuvering. It is a procedure designed to force action.

While most critics see it as an unprecedented shift of power from Congress to the President, its supporters deny this by pointing to its largely ministerial aspects. In any case, it is a clear abandonment of power by Congress either to the President or to a faceless and mindless mechanistic procedure. What Congress sought to impeach President Nixon for doing, it now requires President Reagan and his successor to carry out.

5. Gramm-Rudman sets a new budget timetable. Its effect is to require both the President's budget and the First Concurrent Resolution to be submitted and passed a month earlier than under the 1974 act.

Starting in January 1987, the new timetable is as follows.

- First Monday after January 3—President submits his budget.
- February 15—Congressional Budget Office submits its report to Budget Committees.
- February 25—Committees submit their views and estimates to Budget Committees.
- April 1—Senate Budget Committee reports concurrent resolution on the budget.
- April 15—Congress completes action on the concurrent resolution on the budget.
- May 15—Annual appropriation bills may be considered in the House.
- June 10—House Appropriations Committee reports the last annual appropriation bill.
- June 15—Congress completes action on reconciliation legislation.
- June 30—House completes action on annual appropriation bills.
- October 1—Fiscal year begins.

During the debate over its passage, the amendment's sponsor, Senator Warren B. Rudman (R—N.H.) said it was "a bad idea whose time had come." Majority Leader Robert Dole (R—Kan.) reportedly told a colleague (said to be Senator Rudman) during a Republican caucus, "Don't get up and explain it again. Some of us are for it."

Mainstream economists fear sequestration would trigger a recession or depression if exercised during a period of economic slowdown short of a recession. Proponents of a military build-up, including the Secretary of Defense, have referred to its effects as "devastating." Virtually no one has a good word for it.

Some of its active proponents believe the consequences will force President Reagan to come to terms with the budget problem and advocate a more balanced program of domestic freezes, a more modest Pentagon budget, a tax increase, and a more modest goal of cutting the deficit in half by 1991, rather than an impossible attempt to eliminate it.

CONCLUSIONS

If there are any lessons to be drawn from the 1974 Budget and Impoundment Control Act and the Gramm-Rudman-Hollings Act of 1985, they would seem to be these.

In the American political system based on Madisonian democracy, no tinkering with "process" can substitute for a general political consensus on substantive matters. Neither in domestic nor budget policies, on the one hand, nor foreign policy, on the other, can process be substituted for general agreement on policy. This may explain why the results of the 1974 Budget Act are so disappointing and the prospects for Gramm-Rudman-Hollings appear so dismal.

For a quarter of a century from 1941 to 1965, there was general consensus on American foreign policy and debate and disagreement did "stop at the water's edge." But for at least the next 15 years, and with respect to Central America for the following two decades, there was no consensus.

When the Gramm-Rudman Act was passed, there was no consensus on budget policy. There was a general consensus in Congress that the solution required a freeze on most domestic programs, a major reduction in the rate of the military build-up, and a necessity for more revenues, but few congressional politicians were willing to risk their political lives to advocate a tax increase or a social security freeze while the President, wielding his veto pen, remained obdurate against both. To vote for either, only to see the result defeated by presidential veto, was to risk the worst of all worlds.

It is fair comment to predict that, until the budget deadlock between the President and Congress is resolved and budget consensus is reached, no process provided by either the 1974 Budget Act or the 1985 Gramm-Rudman-Hollings provisions can be substituted for a substantial agreement on public policy by the American people and their political representatives. This is especially true now that the automatic enforcement provisions of the Gramm-Rudman-Hollings Act were declared unconstitutional by the U.S. Supreme Court in the summer of 1986. The opinion stated that the act, in giving power to the Comptroller General to tell the President what specific cuts to make under the "sequestration order," was a violation of the Constitution's separation of powers requirements.

The back-up provisions of the act would apply. The Comptroller General's "sequestration order" would go to Congress instead of the President on September l. Under the act's provisions, the House and Senate are required to vote up or down on the "sequestration order." To vote to cut tens of billions of dollars from specific military and civilian programs within a few weeks of a congressional election might require unrealistically heroic acts by members of Congress. Further, even if Congress were to pass a joint resolution containing the order, especially if the cuts were deep, the President might veto the resolution on grounds that the cuts threatened military security.

Without the automatic nature of the original "sequestration order," a consensus among Republicans and Democrats, and the House, the Senate, and the President will be more difficult to fashion and the enforcement of the act may become a more formidable task.

Reading 9.5

Policy Contributions of Congress

Charles O. Jones

The major policy activities of the Congress—lawmaking, representation, and oversight—are perhaps conceived of best in terms of the broader policy process. Here, utilizing policy concepts and employing a policy-process framework, Jones identifies the major functional activities through which Congress is involved in the making of public policy.

CONGRESS AND PROGRAM DEVELOPMENT ACTIVITIES

We turn now to consider congressional involvement in program development activities—those associated with getting problems to government (perception, definition, aggregation, representation, and agenda setting) and with acting on them once there (formulation, legitimation, and appropriation)—see Table 9.5.1. Bear in mind that the focus in this section is on the *activities*, not on the *institution*. That is, we are not solely trying to explain how, for example, Congress establishes means for defining problems or setting an agenda, but rather how the actions of members and staff contribute to achieving these functions for a particular issue. It may well be, of course, that Congress will be the center of such activity for certain issues (see below), but we may not discover that fact unless attention is directed more broadly to the activity rather than to the institution.

Source: From Charles O. Jones, *The United States Congress: People, Places, and Policy* (Homewood, Ill.: Dorsey Press, 1981), Chapter 13, pp. 365–78.

PROBLEM TO GOVERNMENT

Perception/Definition of Problem

Members of Congress are highly sensitive to public problems. The demands of the office itself insure that the successful Representative and Senator will organize his or her political life to search for and receive public problems (principally those in the state or district). Most notable in this regard is the campaign. For Representatives these events come so frequently that they are in a virtually perpetual search for district problems. The campaign experience is instructive but so are the frequent visits to the district, the mail, phone calls, and the work of the district office.

Table 9.5.1.
The policy process.

Phase		Activities	Initial Product
Program development activities	Problem to government	Perception	Problem
		Definition	
		Aggregation/ organization	Demand
		Representation	
		Agenda setting	Priorities
	Action in government	Formulation	
		Research	
		Analysis	Proposal
		Selection	
		Legitimation	
		Identification of interests	
		Communication	Program
		Bargaining	
		Compromise	
		Appropriation	
		Formulation	Budget
		Legitimation	
Program execution activities	Government to program	Implementation	Structure
		Organization	Rules
		Interpretation	Service, payment, controls, etc.
		Application	
	Program to government	Evaluation	Support, adjustment, cancellation, etc.
		Specification	
		Measurement	
		Analysis	
		Recommendation	
	Problem resolution or change	Resolution	Relative solution, social change
		Termination	

Source: Adapted from similar table in Jones (1981: 335).

Much of this intelligence about state or district problems is gained by the members through an unsystematic but normally reliable process of personal absorption. Representatives in particular often know more about the geographical area that constitutes their district than anyone else. This knowledge is typically honed by the threat posed by a primary or general-election opponent. An exception to the more personally developed information is that gained by polls, a device increasingly used by members of both houses.

Members also can claim expertise in problem definition by virtue of their work in Washington. Personal staffs may be directed to study particular problems—often those affecting the state or district. And, of course, the committees and subcommittees are constantly engaged in problem identifying and defining activities in the hearings and staff reports. Similarly, the various congressional research agencies may also be requested to prepare analyses of the causes and effects of public problems.

These Washington-based definitional activities tend to be more systematic than those associated with the state- or district-based activities mentioned above, but less systematic than those of the bureaucracy. It is also the case that, whereas Representatives typically have an advantage over Senators in knowing their constituency, Senators have a staff advantage over Representatives that sometimes prepares them to comprehend better the relationships among various problems.

Aggregation and Representation

Senators and Representatives are likewise very active and experienced in facilitating the aggregation of those whom they perceive to be affected by a problem. This talent follows from their need for electoral support at home and their experience in enacting legislation in Washington. In some cases, members insist that those affected get together so as to present a stronger, more united front in Washington. And, conversely, they may discourage presentation of demands if groups are divided and in conflict. Again I must stress that we are merely noting how and why *members of Congress* get involved in other than the familiar policy approval activities. Policy actors from elsewhere in the government and from the private sphere are also involved in these early-stage activities of definition and aggregation.

It should also require no more than a brief mention that the members of Congress and their staffs are experts in representing. Just as they are well trained and organized to campaign and get reelected, so too are they well-prepared to represent. In fact, the one activity follows from the other. This is not to say that they are always good at representing, or that others are not also involved in that activity, but only to stress that the members are predictably and legitimately active here.

Agenda Setting

Members of Congress, in particular the party and committee leaders, are often actively involved in the process of setting priorities among public problems to be treated. The leaders can provide important information about the mood and interests of the membership. They can supply predictions about how members will react to certain priorities. But not even party leaders are normally in a position to establish priorities on their own. As Richard E. Neustadt observes: "Congressmen need an agenda from outside, something with high status to respond to or react against. What provides it better than the program of the President?" (1960: 6–7).* The President and his aides often consult with members of Congress and their staff, but priority setting has typically been an executive-centered activity.

What about those instances when the President is of a different party from that of the majority in Congress? As Neustadt mentions, the presidential program may also be something for Congress to react to. But what if the President doesn't want much of anything from Congress—or intends to let present programs expire, programs that a majority in Congress support? In such cases, members of Congress have been much more active in establishing priorities. For example, in his study of the Eisenhower Administration, James L. Sundquist concludes that congressional Democrats definitely established priorities to counter those of the Republican President, and in spite of a lack of cooperation by their own party leadership. Speaker Sam Rayburn and Senate Majority Leader Lyndon B. Johnson worked rather closely with the popular President.

> The [Democratic] activists were constrained to proceed independently to organize their own bloc in each house of the Congress, rally support for specific measures inside and outside the legislature, and press for action on them. They could also work with the Democratic National Committee . . . and particularly with the Democratic Advisory Council established by [Paul] Butler late in 1956.

*Reference list in Endnotes.

> The Senate activist bloc, the corresponding House bloc (organized as the Democratic Study Group), and the national committee and advisory council came to comprise a triangle of communication and mutual reinforcement that bypassed the party's leadership in Congress. By 1960 it had come close to isolating the leadership. (Sundquist, 1968:395–96.)

The Nixon Administration also encouraged congressional Democrats to be more active in setting priorities. Ralph K. Huitt describes the situation as follows (in Mansfield, ed., 1975:76).

> Nixon did not seem to want anything from Congress. To be sure, he initiated domestic programs and proclaimed priorities, but he seemed to lose interest in them quickly. In fact, Congress found itself upbraiding him for not really trying to get what he said he wanted, which many members wanted more than he did.

Nixon's style and lack of programmatic drive may have encouraged many congressional Democrats to establish their own priorities but they were not successful in creating a process for doing so. Weak party leadership and rather continuous reform were but two many factors preventing the development of a coherent counterprogram.

In summary, neither house of Congress is well-structured to set priorities. Bicameralism, the decentralized committee system, and a highly dependent party leadership are obstacles to this end. At the same time, members can provide information about what their constituents think is important. They can provide equally useful information on the many special interests likely to be touched by government programs. It is for these reasons, as well as the realization that Congress must approve government programs, that the members are drawn into agenda-setting activities.[1]

ACTION IN GOVERNMENT

Formulation

As indicated in Table 9.5.1, program formulation may involve doing research on the various options for treating a problem, analyzing the advantages and disadvantages of these options (to include review of the effects from each), and eventual selection of one option or a combination of options. Members of Congress can bring a great deal of wisdom to these activities, again working in concert with others. Congressional hearings are often designed to explore policy options—typically including that of continuing an existing program. Committees and subcommittees are structured by membership and staff operations to provide political analysis of political options. Over time these units become impressive banks of information on the feasibility of proposals.

Political feasibility is a crucial consideration for program formulation. But Ralph K. Huitt questions whether it makes sense to speak of a total "legislative system" to include Congress, the interest groups, executive agencies, and the press, in making strategic choices on what is feasible (in Ranney, 1968:272)

> It is more accurate, I think, to begin with the committees and speak of the *policy system*, which is focused about each pair of committees House and Senate that shares similar, if not identical jurisdiction.

Huitt observes that there are large national interest groups and high-level executive departments "ranging across a broad sweep of the legislative spectrum."

> More common than the giants by far are the groups with a single interest (albeit a broad one, like higher education), and the executive agency with one or a handful of bills, all of whose business is done with a single committee in each house. (in Ranney, 1968:272.)

According to Huitt, "this organization . . . around specialized concerns shapes the entire system that makes legislation" (in Ranney, 1968: 274). For present purposes we can interpret these comments as reinforcing the view that it is the member's knowledge of specialized interests that contributes to program formulation—from the research into options to the selection of one proposal over another.

It should be pointed out that the participation of members of Congress in formulation activities is often highly subjective. The evidence they offer is biased in favor of the interests they represent. One is expected to have preferences on Capitol Hill. Selective presentation of data is a common and accepted practice. Staff reports are typically prepared for some one or some group and for a clearly specified purpose. The objectivity or fairness is presumed to be a result over time of subjective arguments forcefully presented.

The reforms during the 1970s increased Congress' capacity to formulate programs independent of the executive. The creation of the Congressional Budget Office and the Office of Technology Assessment, the provision for a stronger research agency in the Library of Congress (the Congressional Research Service), and the large increases in personal and committee staff contributed to greater research and analytical skills on Capitol Hill. Program formulation has been centered in Congress for certain issues in the past. We may expect it to occur there in the future, both as a consequence of inaction elsewhere and in response to, or as a counterforce to, proposals developed elsewhere. A further result of this increased analytical capacity may well be more active participation by members in executive-centered program formulation—partly due to demands by the members themselves, perhaps due as well to a recognition of their growing competence.

Legitimation

It is within this set of legitimation activities that legislators typically excel. Given the nature of our constitutional system, most national government programs must be traceable to majority support in Congress. Others besides legislators participate in building legislative majorities however, and there are all kinds of approval processes which take place outside Congress—in letting contracts, setting standards, issuing licenses, etc. (Jones and Matthes, 1982).

The activities associated with majority building in a legislature include the identification of the principal interests to be satisfied, communication among those interests, bargaining, and determination of a compromise. Virtually the entire legislative process as described in the previous chapters is designed to accomplish these goals—the organization and appointment of committees and subcommittees, assigning bills, the hearings and markup sessions, the scheduling of bills for floor debate, the amending process, and voting. The Congress is composed of two majority-building machines, which then must meld their products before legitimation is complete.

One must not be misled, of course, into believing that each proposal for government action on a public problem represents a significant challenge to the majority building talents of legislators. There are such cases, to be sure. It took several decades before majorities were fashioned for federal aid to education, medical care for the aged, federal civil and voting rights laws. If all legislative proposals were so conflictual, congressional turnover would no doubt be high—the result of fatigue. As it is, however, most proposals are to do a bit more of what is already being done, extend what is being done for some to others, or do something like that being in another area. As Huitt notes (in Ranney, 1968:274):

> What is most feasible is what is purely incremental, or can be made to appear so. Paradoxically, it is politically attractive to tout a proposal as "new" so long as it is generally recognized that it is not new at all, but a variation on a familiar theme.

The advice contained in this wisdom is: Try to go where the majority already is. Even if you want to do something truly new, you are advised to begin with what is feasible. Huitt speaks of "finding halfway houses . . . which supply at least part of what is needed under the guise of doing something else" (in Ranney, 1968:274). A classic case is the means by which we finally got a federal aid to education program. Having just enacted a popular "War on Poverty" program, the education aid proposal was based on the number of persons in a school district below the poverty line rather than the number of students, the economic base, the condition of the schools, etc.

R. Douglas Arnold notes a distinction between "separate coalitions for each new expenditure program" and "a single umbrella coalition for a whole collection of diverse programs" (1979:210). In the first the necessary support is garnered by extending the program to each state and congressional district, regardless of need. The second "umbrella" type coalition relies on what Arnold calls "multiple-program logrolls." The exchange of support between urban and rural Democrats for programs affecting each is an example of the umbrella coalition. Of course, building and maintaining such a group typically depends on strong party leadership and structure. As Arnold notes, however (1979:212):

> The days of Lyndon Johnson and Sam Rayburn passed, and their successors, Mike Mansfield and Carl Albert, were much less inclined to function as coalition leaders. Yet party leaders are the only ones who *could* arrange and enforce the complex series of trades necessary to assemble an umbrella coalition for diverse programs.

We may also expect to find members of Congress getting involved in other legitimation processes. Certainly they will be attentive to federal contracts to be awarded in their states and districts. They may show up at public hearings for setting pollution standards or licensing a nuclear power plant (or be instrumental in organizing others to testify). And they may challenge the expertise of a government technician who has been given the authority to develop a procedure, build a dam, set a standard, design a weapon. The rationale for involvement by a member may again be constituency interest but it may also be the result of the member's understanding of the law which provides for the bureaucratic approval process.

Appropriation

The budgetary process runs parallel to the substantive lawmaking process. Few laws can be enforced, few program goals can be realized without money. Until the passage of the Budget and Impoundment Control Act of 1974, the formulation of a budget was centered primarily in the executive. Though sensitive to the views of members, the Office of Management and Budget (and its predecessor, the Bureau of the Budget) had the responsibility of preparing the document for submission to Congress.

In essence, the 1974 act created a budgetary formulation process in Congress. Budget Committees were established in each house, a Congressional Budget Office with a professional staff was authorized, and a procedure was developed for setting money limits for the authorizing and appropriations committees. Congress now takes a comprehensive view of taxing and spending and seeks to control both. As Dennis S. Ippolito sees it, the new congressional participation in budget formulation offers several advantages (1978:119):

> First, the new budget process provides Congress with the mechanism to act on fiscal policy and to challenge executive dominance in economic management. Second, Congress can use the budgetary process to make priority choices by considering spending decisions in relation to each other. The budget resolutions therefore also make it possible for Congress to specify how its priorities differ from those of the President. Third, Congress has developed budgetary staff and information resources that reduce considerably its reliance on the executive for budget data and analysis.

Approval of the taxing proposals is centered in the House Committee on Ways and Means and the Senate Committee on

Finance. Authorization of expenditures must precede appropriations and this action is taken in the several authorizing committees. And appropriations are handled in the two Appropriations Committees. All of these actions are legitimation processes like those described above—i.e., actions requiring majority support in both houses. We needn't repeat the earlier discussion. But two points are worth mentioning.

First, approval of appropriations is a separate action from approval of a program. Therefore they may not come out the same. That is, the money appropriated for a program may be less (it can't be more) than the amount authorized. Thus different forces may be at work in the two legitimation processes.

Second, the new budget system has affected the approval processes for taxation, program authorization, and appropriation. When Congress approves budget resolutions, it is, in essence, establishing limits for the standing committees—limits which did not exist in the past. The potential for conflict is considerable (LeLoup, 1980; Schick, 1980). Thus, for example, in 1980 the House passed a budget resolution directing its committees to reduce spending by $6.4 billion. Appropriations Committee Chairman Jamie L. Whitten (D–Miss.) defied the resolution in regard to appropriations for Saturday mail delivery. Much to the chagrin of Budget Committee Chairman Robert N. Giaimo (D–Conn.), Speaker O'Neill appeared to support Chairman Whitten: "If the Budget Committee was to say to the Appropriations Committee, 'You can't do this,' they would be transgressing on the rights of the Appropriations Committee." Chairman Giaimo responded by charging that the Speaker was undermining the budget process. "It undermines what the leadership told us to do. The Budget Committee didn't dream this up by itself."[2]

To summarize, one may expect to find members of Congress and their staff actively involved in all functional activities associated with program development. They can justify involvement because of their knowledge and understanding of constituencies, and the many private and public interests affected by government programs, as well as expertise on the special topics of their committees and subcommittees, and, ultimately, their authority to approve laws. This general survey of activities suggests quite varied participation. We may expect:

1. Active participation by many members and staff in legitimation activities (including appropriations).
2. Variable participation by members and staff in problem definition, interest aggregation, program formulation, and formulation of the congressional budget.
3. Limited participation by members and staff in agenda setting.

COMPARING ACTION ON SPECIFIC BILLS

The tremendous variation in legislator involvement in program development is illustrated by comparing what happens on specific bills at any one time or what happens over time in regard to a particular program. Consider a few of the many available studies of a bill becoming a law—campaign finance reform by Robert L. Peabody and colleagues (1972), the federal aid to education program by Eugene Eidenberg and Roy Morey (1969), civil rights legislation by Daniel M. Berman (1966), a national health service corps by Eric Redman (1973), and the classic study of the Employment Act of 1946 by Stephen K. Bailey (1950). Each of these studies provides quite different answers to the following questions.

1. Who participated in what program development activities?
2. Did this participation vary between the House and Senate? If so, how did it vary?
3. Which activities were centered in Congress? Which in the executive branch?
4. How and when did legislators and staff communicate with each other? With other participants?
5. How aware of program development were the less active legislators and staff?

These are but a few of the more obvious questions one might ask, with quite variable results.

David E. Price has conducted one of the few systematic analyses of legislators' participation in program development activities. Based on a study of 14 major bills, Price, like Huitt, first warns against generalizing about participation in policy activities, "particularly if the unit of analysis remains the entire executive or legislative establishment."

> Legislative initiatives are diverse and scattered phenomena, while various policymakers hardly find themselves possessed of equal incentives and resources, the system does display considerable "slack." Differences between individuals, committees, and agencies sometimes display fixed patterns attributable to "external" determinants. But the freedom of individuals and decision-making units to determine their own legislative roles is often considerable. (Price, 1972:292.)

In what was a most useful exercise for our purposes, Price identified who was involved in six program development activities for fourteen bills. The activities closely parallel those relied on in Table 9.5.1

Those listed in Table 9.5.1	Price's Counterparts
Perception/definition	Information gathering
Aggregation/organization	Interest aggregation
Representation/agenda-setting	Instigation/publicizing
Formulation	Formulation
Legitimation	Mobilization Modification

Table 9.5.2 summarizes Price's observations about the relative involvement of executive, legislative, and interest-group participants—whether actors from these sources were primarily involved or whether they worked together with others, hence the several "mixed" categories. Several conclusions emerge from this table.

1. Information gathering tended to be centered more in the Executive Branch—six bills where executive actors were primarily involved, six others where they worked with others (a,b and a,c)
2. Interest aggregation and modification tended to be centered more in the legislature—the latter heavily so.
3. Instigation/publicizing, formulation, and mobilization were characterized by considerable mixing of participants.
4. Lesiglators were primarily involved in more activities than either executive or interest-group actors—information gathering being the only activity in which they were not the principal actors for at least one bill.

The three groups of participants also varied in their involvement across policy activities for the different bills studied by Price. I assigned scores to each group depending on whether they were primarily involved in an activity (3 points), shared involvement with another group (1½ points each), or shared with the other two groups (1 point each). By this simple scoring system the following variations were identified:

1. Congressional dominance (members of Congress active in all activities, little sharing with others):
   Fair packaging
   Campaign finance
   Cold War GI benefits
2. Congressional sharing with interest groups (members of Congress active in most activities, some sharing with lobbyists):
   Traffic safety
3. Congressional sharing with executive (members of Congress active in most activities, some sharing with members of Executive Branch)
   Cigarette labeling
   Oceanography
   Poverty amendments
4. Executive sharing with Congress (members of Executive Branch active in most activities, some sharing with members of Congress):
   Foreign investors' tax
   Medical complexes (heart disease, cancer, and stroke research)
5. Sharing among all groups (significant involvement of groups in several activities):
   Medicare

Table 9.5.2.
Variation in participation in program development activities (14 bills, 89th Congress).

	Source of Participants (Number of Bills)						
	(A)	(B)	(C)	Mixed			
Program Development Activity	Primarily Executive	Primarily Legislative	Primarily Interest Groups	A, B	B, C	A, C	A, B, C
Information gathering* (perception/definition)	6†	—	1	4	1	2	—
Interest aggregation (aggregation/organization)	—	7	—	7	—	—	—
Instigation/publicizing (representation/agenda-setting)	1	2	—	3	2	5	1
Formulation (same)	2	3	—	2	—	—	7
Mobilization (legitimation)	—	2	—	8	1	—	3
Modification (legitimation)		13	—	1	—	—	—

*The labels in parenthesis represent the policy activities used here—see Table 9.5.1.
†Figure represents the number of bills on which participants drawn from the executive were primarily involved (N = 14).
Source: From David Price, *Who Makes the Laws?* (Cambridge, Mass.: Schenkman, 1972), Table 7, pp. 290–91.

Sugar Act amendments
Unemployment insurance
Elementary and secondary education
Fair labor standards

James L. Sundquist also found important differences in policy responsibility and participation among several major bills during the Eisenhower, Kennedy, and Johnson administrations. Though Sundquist's analysis of program development activities is less systematic than Price's, his rich descriptive material provides further support for the impressive variation in congressional policy participation (Sundquist, 1968:390–91 and *passim*). Ripley and Franklin likewise identify variations among important bills—Executive Branch dominance, joint program development, congressional dominance, and stalemate—but as noted earlier they do not discriminate among the several program development activities (1980:219).

The point to be emphasized from these variations is that they reinforce the utility of viewing Congress as a population variably drawn into the policy process as associated with different issues. It is clear that the members and their staffs participate broadly in policy activities and this participation varies greatly among various types of issues. Price contributes even more evidence to support this conclusion when he examines differences among congressional committees. As with individual members, he found that certain committees and subcommittees were active in different types of activities. He cautiously concluded that some committees specialize in "the formulation and publicizing of legislation," and others specialize in "the 'maturing' and compromising of proposals with an eye to eventual mobilization (Price, 1972:311–12).

CONCLUSION

The Congress is the most critical government institution for maintaining a constitutional democracy. Its legitimacy as the lawmaker stems from the electoral connections with the people. This authority to pass on all government programs justifies congressional involvement in other program development activities (problem definition, aggregation, agenda-setting, formulation) and guarantees that those responsible for and benefitting from these programs (political executives and bureaucrats at all levels of government, as well as public and private interest groups) will often draw members and their staffs into fuller participation in the early stages of program development. For the student of legislatures the policy process perspective offers a different view of the role those institutions play in the political system. The formal structure and procedures of the lawmaking process are undeniably important for maintaining the legitimacy of government programs, thus justifying the scholar's attention. But focusing on issues, how they get to government and who acts on them there, provides quite a different window for studying legislative behavior. We have done no more in this chapter than provide clues as to where to look and what to look for. In summary, these clues are:

1. Look for congressional involvement (members and staff) in all activities logically associated with developing a government program.
2. Look for congressional participation in policy-associated networks (cozy little connections, cozy little triangles, sloppy large hexagons).
3. Above all, look for variation—in who participates in what, in how this participation changes over time, in how the participation differs between issues, bills, committees, the two chambers, the political parties.

Reading 9.6

Different Kinds of Policies Get Handled Differently: Policy Process Differences

Randall B. Ripley
and Grace A. Franklin

Ripley and Franklin promote a sophisticated interpretation of congressional policymaking by arguing that different kinds of policy gets handled in different ways. They contend that policy relationships in a given area vary by type of issue. The significance of this is to place in perspective certain models of policymaking. For example, the subgovernment model (that policy is thrashed out in a tripartite subsystem comprised of congressional subcommittees, relevant bureaus, and affected publics) is applicable only for distributive and structural policies. Other kinds of policies are made in different ways.

Source: From Randall B. Ripley and Grace A. Franklin, *Congress, the Bureaucracy, and Public Policy*, 3d ed. (Homewood, Ill.: Dorsey Press, 1984), pp. 22–30.

The basic notion behind our categorizations is that each type of policy generates and is therefore surrounded by its own distinctive set of political relationships. These relationships in turn help to determine substantive, concrete outcomes when policy decisions emerge. Table 9.6.1 summarizes the characteristics of the political relationships surrounding policymaking for each type of policy. The main features of the political relationships that we are concerned with in Table 9.6.1 are the identity of the primary actors, the basic nature of the interaction among those actors, the stability of their interaction, the visibility of the policy decisions to individuals not immediately involved or concerned, and the relative influence of different actors.

We have excluded competitive regulatory policy from Table 9.6.1 because it is a type of policy that is rarely formulated and legitimated; rather, competitive regulatory policy is concerned primarily with issues of implementation. Responsibility for competitive regulatory policy is almost totally delegated to bureaucratic agencies, regulatory commissions, or courts for implementation. It focuses on decisions about individual cases, and the actors involved are limited to relevant bureaucratic, judicial, or quasi-judicial agencies, the individuals competing for benefits being awarded, and occasional members of Congress who have a specific interest in the outcome. We have included a discussion of competitive regulatory policy in the sections immediately following to contrast it with the other types of policy, but because this book focuses on the formulation and legitimation of policymaking, we have not included competitive regulatory policy in the analysis.

DOMESTIC POLICY

Distributive Policy

Distributive policies and programs are aimed at promoting private activities that are said to be desirable to society as a whole and, at least in theory, would not or could not be undertaken otherwise. Such policies and programs provide subsidies for those private activities and thus convey tangible government benefits to the individuals, groups, and corporations subsidized. (A subsidy is a payment designed to induce desired behavior.) Many government policies turn out to be subsidies, even if they do not seem to be subsidies at first glance. Decisions about subsidies are typically made with only short-run consequences considered. The decisions are not considered in light of each other; rather they are disaggregated. Thus there appear to be only winners and no losers.

The case of characters (usually individuals or groups that comprise a subgovernment) involved in distributive decisions in a particular field (such as agricultural price supports, water resources, or subsidies for health research) is fairly stable over time, and their interactions are marked by low visibility and a high degree of cooperation and mutually rewarding logrolling. The congressional subcommittee generally makes the final decisions after receiving input from the other actors. The recipients of distributive subsidies are not aware of each other, and there is no sense of competing for limited resources—anyone can potentially be a recipient, and resources are treated as unlimited. Distributive decisions embody the federal pork barrel in its fullest sense, giving many people a bite of the federal pie. Distributive decisions, both within a field and between different substantive fields, are made individually, without consideration for their interrelation or overall impact—they are decentralized and uncoordinated.

Examples of distributive policies include direct cash payments for purchase of agricultural commodities; grants for scientific research in universities and private laboratories; grants to localities for airport construction, hospital construction, sewage facilities, and mass transit facilities; promoting home ownership through tax provisions allowing deductions for interest on home mortgages and local property taxes; and issuing low-cost permits for grazing on public lands.

Competitive Regulatory Policy

Competitive regulatory policies and programs are aimed at limiting the provision of

Table 9.6.1.
Political relationships for policymaking.

Policy Type	Primary Actors	Relationship among Actors	Stability of Relationship	Visibility of Decision
Distributive	Congressional subcommittees and committees; executive bureaus; small interest groups	Logrolling (everyone gains)	Stable	Low
Protective regulatory	Congressional subcommittees and committees; full House and Senate; executive agencies; trade associations	Bargaining; compromise	Unstable	Moderate
Redistributive	President and his appointees; committees and/or Congress; largest interest groups (peak associations); "liberals, conservatives"	Ideological and class conflict	Stable	High
Structural	Congressional subcommittees and committees; executive bureaus; small interest groups	Logrolling (everyone gains)	Stable	Low
Strategic	Executive agencies; President	Bargaining; compromise	Unstable	Low until publicized; then low to high
Crisis	President and advisers	Cooperation	Unstable	Low until publicized; then generally high

specific goods and services to only one or a few designated deliverers who are chosen from a larger number of competing potential deliverers. Some of the potential deliverers who want the business win, some lose. Some decisions allocate scarce resources that simply cannot be divided, such as television channels or radio frequencies. Some decisions maintain limited rather than unlimited competition in the provision of

Table 9.6.1. (concluded)

Influence of				
President, Presidency, and Centralized Bureaucracy	Bureaus	Congress as a Whole	Congressional Subcommittees	Private Sector
Low	High	Low (supports subcommittees)	High	High (subsidized groups)
Moderately high	Moderate	Moderately high	Moderate	Moderately high (regulated interests)
High	Moderately low	High	Moderately low	High ("peak associations" representing clusters of interest groups)
Low	High	Low (supports subcommittees)	High	High (subsidized groups and corporations)
High	Low	High (often responsive to executive)	Low	Moderate (interest groups, corporations)
High	Low	Low	Low	Low

goods and services by allowing only certain potential deliverers to provide them and excluding other potential deliverers. Some decisions are aimed at regulating the quality of services delivered through choosing the deliverer periodically and imposing standards of performance. If those standards are not met, a new deliverer can be chosen. This type of policy is a hybrid, which subsidizes the winning competitors and also tries to regulate some aspects of service delivery in the public interest. Examples of competitive regulatory policies include the granting and review of licenses to operate television and radio stations; authorizing specific airlines to operate specified routes; and authorizing specific trucking companies to haul specified commodities over specified routes.

Decisions on basic overall policy in this area are rare. Most decisions are delegated to bureaus, regulatory commissions, and courts. The influence of the competitors is high and over time most of them can be expected to get some benefits. Thus in application at the general level the policy resembles one of subsidy, especially for the largest competitors that can enter many specific competitions. For example, a major airline will not win every route from the Civil Aeronautics Board for which it competes but it will win enough routes over time to enhance its profitability. Congressional influence on individual decisions is present but usually in the form of intervention from specific Senators and Representatives.

Protective Regulatory Policy

Protective regulatory policies and programs are designed to protect the public by setting the conditions under which various private activities can be undertaken. Conditions that are thought to be harmful (air pollution, false advertising) are prohibited; conditions that are thought to be helpful (the publication of interest rates on loans) are required.

Protective regulatory policies are not as disaggregatable as distributive decisions because they establish a general rule of law and require that behavior among a certain segment of the population conform to the law. The actors (coalitions of members of the full House and Senate, executive branch agencies, and representatives of trade associations) involved in protective regulatory decisions are much less stable than in the distributive arena, partially because of constantly shifting substantive issues. The ultimate decisions get made on the floor of the House and Senate.

Examples of federal protective regulatory policies include the requirement that banks, stores, and other grantors of credit disclose true interest rates; prohibitions of unfair business practices, unfair labor practices, and business combinations that lessen competition; limits on the conditions under which strip mining can be undertaken and requirements for the postmining restoration of land; the prohibition of harmful food additives; and high taxation to reduce the consumption of scarce commodities such as gasoline.

Redistributive Policy

Redistributive policies and programs are intended to manipulate the allocation of wealth, property rights, or some other value among social classes or racial groups in society. The redistributive feature enters because a number of actors perceive there are "winners" and "losers" in policies and that policies transfer some value to one group *at the expense* of another group. Thus the more well-off sometimes perceive themselves to be losers in relation to a program that seeks to confer some benefits on the less well-off. Whites sometimes perceive themselves to be losers in relation to a policy or a program that confers special benefits on minority groups.

Redistribution runs in several directions. Some programs redistribute items of value from the less well off to the more well off or from minorities to whites, but usually such programs are not perceived as redistributive. They do not generate the hot political controversy that is associated with redistributive attempts in the other direction. Thus the politics of redistribution almost always involves situations in which the intended beneficiaries are the relatively disadvantaged in society.

Since redistributive policy involves a conscious attempt to manipulate the allocation of wealth, property, rights, or some other value among broad classes or groups in society, the actors perceive that there will be distinct winners and losers. The stakes are thought to be high and this fact means that the policymaking process will be marked by a high degree of visibility and conflict. The coalitions that form over any redistributive issue may change in composition depending on the issue (integrated schools, open housing, public welfare programs) but they can generally be identified as a proponent ("liberal") group and an opponent ("conservative") group. Their debate on the issue at hand is cast in ideological terms. Whether redistributive policy will emerge from the coalitions' conflicting viewpoints depends on the presence of strong presidential leadership and the willingness of participants to retreat from ideological stances and adopt compromises. The principal political consideration among the participants during the process is who gets what at the expense of whom.

Examples of redistributive policy include setting progressive personal income tax rates so that more affluent people pay a higher percentage of their incomes in taxes than do less affluent people; requirements that housing, public accommodations and facilities, and public education be available to all, without racial discrimination; requirements of affirmative action in hiring by federal contractors to increase the employment of women and minorities; the provision of employment and training programs, food stamps, or special legal services for the disadvantaged; and government-sponsored health insurance to help the elderly meet the costs of medical care.

FOREIGN AND DEFENSE POLICY

Policy typologies in nondomestic issue areas are less clear-cut than in domestic areas. Lowi (1967: 324–25)* suggests that there are three distinctive patterns of politics in foreign policy. The first is crisis foreign policy. In this situation the perception of a threat to the national security cuts across normal channels of decisions, and an elite of formal officeholders within the executive branch makes the decisions with a minimum of conflict. In the absence of a crisis, there is time for "normal" patterns and concerns to emerge. Institutions become involved and interactions occur over a number of questions. Foreign policy then is basically either distributive or regulatory, with much the same sets of characteristics as domestic distributive or regulatory policy types.

In the area of defense policy, which has both domestic and foreign policy aspects, Huntington (1961) has identified two types —strategic and structural defense policy. Strategic defense policy is oriented toward foreign policy and international politics, and it involves the units and use of military force, their strength, and their deployment. Structural defense policy focuses on domestic politics and involves decisions about the procurement, allocation, and organization of personnel, money, and materiel that constitute the military forces. Structural decisions are made primarily within the context of strategic decisions and are made to implement those decisions.

We have drawn on both Lowi and Huntington in developing our ideas about the three categories of foreign and defense policy: structural, strategic, and crisis.

Structural Policy

Structural policies and programs aim primarily at procuring, deploying, and organizing military personnel and materiel, presumably within the confines and guidelines of previously determined strategic decisions. Since the federal government has no competitors in providing defense, the element of total subsidy for the enterprise is a given. But the details of that subsidy can vary greatly. Thus, as indicated in Table 9.6.1,

*Reference list in Endnotes.

structural policies are closely related to distributive policies. The process is characterized by the presence of subgovernments, by decentralized decision making, by nonconflictual relationships among the actors, and by decisions that treat internal resources as unlimited and separable. Policy decisions emerge from the formal legislative process (bill introduction, committee hearings, passage by the House and Senate). Although Congress is generally responding to executive branch requests rather than initiating policy in this area, it nonetheless has final decision power.

Examples of structural policies include specific defense procurement decisions for individual weapons systems: the placement, expansion, contraction, and closing of military bases and other facilities in the United States; the retention, expansion, or contraction of reserve military forces; and the creation and retention of programs that send surplus farm commodities overseas.

Strategic Policy

Strategic policies and programs are designed to assert and implement the basic military and foreign policy stance of the United States toward other nations. Policy planning and proposals resulting from that planning stem primarily from Executive Branch activities. A number of Executive Branch agencies compete, bargain, and sometimes engage in conflict during policy development. Decisions are made by these agencies, with the final approval of the President. Public debate and congressional involvement usually occur after the formal decisions are announced. Congress may get involved in several ways—committees or individuals may lobby executive branch agencies for particular decisions, Congress may respond to an executive branch request for legislation to implement a decision already made, or Congress may protest and alter an action already completed. Congress does not make strategic decisions by itself; thus the influence of Congress as a whole can be high, but that potential influence is often used to respond supportively to Executive Branch initiatives.

Examples of strategic policies include decisions about the basic mix of military forces (for example, the ratio of ground-based missiles to submarine-based missiles to manned bombers); foreign trade (tariffs and quotas for specific goods and nations); sales of U.S. arms to foreign nations; foreign aid; immigration; and the level and location of U.S. troops overseas (both in general and in relation to specific "trouble spots").

Crisis Policy

Crisis policies are short-run responses to immediate problems that are perceived to be serious, that have burst on the policymakers with little or no warning, and that demand immediate action. The occurrence of crisis situations is unpredictable and tied to external (nondomestic) events. The principal actors are elite officeholders who work cooperatively together with a minimum of publicized conflict. Visibility of the decision-making process is also low, except to the extent that press releases and press conferences inform the public. The involvement of Congress is informal and limited and is usually made in the mode of consultation with key individuals. The full body may get involved formally, usually after the crisis, to make the action legitimate or to forbid similar exercises of executive power in the future.

Examples of crisis policies include decisions about the U.S. response to the Japanese attack on Pearl Harbor in 1941, the impending French collapse in Indochina in 1954, the Soviet Union's placement of missiles in Cuba in 1962, the North Korean seizure of a U.S. Navy ship in 1968, the Cambodian seizure of a U.S. merchant ship in 1975, and the Iranian seizure of U.S. hostages in late 1979.

Reading 9.7

Policy Consequences

David R. Mayhew

In this second selection from Mayhew's important book, congressional policymaking is treated as a dependent variable. According to Mayhew, "assembly coherence" (certain characteristics of policymaking) is necessitated by the organizational features of Congress and by the electoral connection.

Now, if these are the impulsions behind legislating and overseeing, what are the effects? What seems to happen is that congressional policymaking activities produce a number of specifiable and predictable policy effects. Taken together these effects display what might be called an "assembly coherence"—an overall policy pattern that one might expect any set of assemblies constructed like the U.S. Congress to generate.[1]

One effect is *delay*—or, more properly, since the eye of the beholder creates it, a widespread perception of delay. Not too much should be made of this, but it is fair to say that over the years Congress has often lagged behind public opinion in enacting major legislation.[2] Thus a perceived "inaction" was the major source of dissatisfaction with Congress in a survey of a generally dissatisfied public in 1963.[3] Or the delay may exist in the eyes of elites; President Kennedy's tax cut proposal of 1963 and President Johnson's tax increase proposal of 1967, both set forth for the purpose of fiscal management, each took a year to wend its way through a Democratic Congress.[4] Recurrent perceptions of congressional delay on nonparticularized matters should cause little surprise. Mobilization may be halfhearted; there are so many other things to do; some issues may be uncomfortable to vote on at all; a live issue may be better than a live program; the effects are not important anyway.

A second effect is *particularism*—that is, a strong tendency to wrap policies in packages that are salable as particularized benefits. Not only do Congressmen aggressively seek out opportunities to supply such benefits (little or no "pressure" is needed), they tend in framing laws to give a particularistic cast to matters that do not obviously require it. The only benefits intrinsically worth anything, after all, are ones that can be packaged.[5] Thus in time of recession Congressmen reach for "accelerated public works" bills listing projects in the various districts; Presidents prefer more general fiscal effects. In the education field a Congressional favorite is the "impacted areas" program with its ostentatious grants to targeted school districts; again, Presidents prefer ventures of more diffuse impact. Presidents are capable of closing a hundred veterans' hospitals like a shot in the interest of "efficiency"; Congressmen combine to keep them open. The handling of revenue policy is particularistic; in Manley's exhaustive treatment of congressional tax processes there is hardly any mention of an interest in fiscal effects (though of course the members must worry about how it *looks* to vote for a tax cut or tax increase). Rather the concern is with distributive effects. The highly

Source: From David R. Mayhew, *Congress: The Electoral Connection* (New Haven, Conn.: Yale University Press, 1974), pp. 125–32.

talented staff of the Joint Committee on Internal Revenue Taxation, serving both Senate Finance and House Ways and Means, is in the business of "explicating . . . how individuals and groups will be affected by changes in the Internal Revenue code."[6] Across policy areas generally the programmatic mainstay of Congressmen is the categorical grant. In fact the categorical grant is for modern Democratic Congresses what rivers and harbors and the tariff were for pre-New Deal Republican Congresses. It supplies goods in small manipulable packets. "Congressmen . . . like categorical programs because of the opportunities they afford to interfere in administration and thus to secure special treatment, or at least the appearance of it, for constituents among whom . . . state and local as well as federal agencies sometimes figure prominently."[7] The quest for the particular impels Congressmen to take a vigorous interest in the organization of the federal bureaucracy. Thus, for example, the Corps of Army Engineers, structured to undertake discrete district projects, must be guarded from Presidents who would submerge it in a quest for "planning."[8]

A third effect is the *servicing of the organized*.[9] This takes two familiar forms. First there is a deference toward nationally organized groups with enough widespread local clout to inspire favorable roll-call positions on selected issues among a majority of members. Thus, under four Presidents in a row—Harding through Roosevelt—Congress passed veterans' bonus bills, the Presidents vetoed them, and the House voted decisively to override the vetoes.[10] In recent years the National Rifle Association has weighed in against gun control legislation.[11] Second, there is deference toward groups with disposable electoral resources whose representatives keep a close watch on congressional maneuvers. Clientelism at the committee level is the result, with its manifestations across a wide range of policy areas. Agriculture is an obvious example.[12] Clientelism, like particularism, gives form to the federal bureaucracy. Congressmen protect clientele systems—alliances of agencies, Hill committees, and clienteles —against the incursions of Presidents and Cabinet Secretaries.[13]

A fourth effect is *symbolism*. The term needs explication. It is probably best to say that a purely symbolic congressional act is one expressing an attitude but prescribing no policy effects. An example would be a resolution deploring communism or poverty. But the term *symbolic* can also usefully be applied where Congress prescribes policy effects but does not act (in legislating or overseeing or both) so as to achieve them. No doubt the main cause of prescription-achievement gaps is the intractability of human affairs. But there is a special reason why a legislative body arranged like the U.S. Congress can be expected to engage in symbolic action by this second, impure construction of the term. The reason, of course, is that in a large class of legislative undertakings the electoral payment is for positions rather than for effects.

Chapter Ten

Congress: Change, Issues, and the Future

A concluding discussion of Congress inevitably raises a number of important and interesting polemics: What have been the consequences of recent reforms and changes? Are they desirable? What are the major ethical problems Congress now faces and what might be done about them? What does the future portend for the Congress? What might be the nature of future Congresses? Will they be materially different? Readings in this last section present essays by prominent congressional scholars and in-house congressional self-studies that address these major questions.

Reading 10.1

Congress the Peculiar Institution

Samuel C. Patterson

Despite the recent decade of change and transformation, there is an essential congressional character that, because of its uniqueness, seems to pass the test of time. The following brief excerpt from a major essay by Samuel C. Patterson speculates about Henry Clay's recognition of this essential character in a Congress much changed from the one within which he served.

THE REINCARNATION OF HENRY CLAY

Henry Clay was America's most remarkable congressional politician. Just after the turn of the 19th century he served in the Kentucky legislature, which twice sent him to the U.S. Senate. Then he was elected to the 12th Congress as a member of the House of Representatives. As a freshman Congressman, he was elected Speaker, and he served as Speaker off and on between 1811 and 1825. His leadership contributed importantly to the development of the House as an autonomous and politically unified policymaking body. After his House service, he was a presidential candidate in 1824, 1832, and 1844, and a U.S. Senator from Kentucky from 1831 to 1842 and from 1849 to 1852.

Clay was a Congressman and Senator during the years when Congress was becoming an imposing and powerful national legislative body. Although what we might call the "modern" Congress was not fully developed until after the 1880s, the institution came to be, in many fundamental ways, much as it is today during the period of Clay's service.[1]

If Henry Clay were alive today, and he were to serve again in the House and Senate to which he was chosen so many times in the 19th century, he would find much that was very familiar. He would certainly recognize where he was, and perhaps after some initial shock he surely would be reasonably comfortable in the modern congressional envelope. Of course, things have changed. Congress has a much larger membership. There were only 186 members of the House that Clay first entered as member and Speaker; there were only 52 Senators in the 1830s. Members and committees have vastly more staff help. A far greater array of policy decisions is required of Congress nowadays than before the Civil War. There is a fancy electronic gadget for voting in the House. The party memberships are less coherent, and the committee system is much more complex. Many more Congressmen are professionals now, in contrast to the relative amateurism of the pre-Civil War Congresses. The scale of things has grown; but the fundamental character of the institution has not changed so very much.

Congress is an extraordinarily stable institution. Many changes have occurred in the party leaderships, the committee systems, and the norms of the Congress, but the intrinsic internal order of the institution

Source: From Samuel C. Patterson, "The Semi-Sovereign Congress," in *The New American Political Systems*, ed. by Anthony King (Washington, D.C.: American Enterprise Institute, 1977), pp. 131–33, 176–77.

has shown enormous continuity. Although relationships between Congress and the executive branch were altered as the country came to be an urban, industrial society with a pivotal role in international affairs, Congress, unlike the legislative bodies of many other industrial nations, continues to be a highly autonomous institution. Certainly since the mid-19th century Congress has been embedded in its environment; this feature and its responsiveness as it performs its constituent function have become profoundly institutionalized. It has been said that the United States is a modern country with an antique political system, and in a sense that is true.[2] American governing institutions emerged in a particular way in the 19th century, and many of their present-day core features are readily traceable to earlier times. That is why Henry Clay, if he were a Congressman today, would surely find that Congress had not become unrecognizable. Institutions simply do not change very much, which is why they are called institutions.

Keeping that in mind is helpful to understanding the Congress of the 1970s. Congress has never experienced a "revolutionary" change. Congress is very stable. Stable institutions change as they adapt themselves to changes in the world around them. Thus, congressional changes are most appropriately viewed as the adaptations through which a very stable system maintains itself. Accordingly, reforms of Congress, relatively small in magnitude, are consequential largely in the ways in which they maintain the existing congressional structure. A marked transformation of a political institution like the Congress is not impossible, but it simply has not occurred in the whiggish context of American political history. As a result, it is the stability of Congress, and not changes in it, that is the most remarkable in the long term. Perhaps, therefore, we should distinguish between adaptive and transformative institutional change; changes in Congress are all adaptive.

CONCLUSION

It is an open question whether Henry Clay would find the Congress of the 1970s an improvement over the Congress in which he served. But there is reason to believe that he would be impressed. While retaining its basic shape and form, Congress has adapted itself in many important ways to the demands of a changing society. Thirty years ago, the architect of the Legislative Reorganization Act of 1946 wrote:

> Congress lacks adequate information and inspection facilities. Its internal structure is dispersive and duplicating. It is a body without a head. Leadership is scattered among the chairmen of 81 little legislatures who compete with each other for jurisdiction and power. Its supervision of executive performance is superficial. Much of its time is consumed by petty local and private matters which divert its attention from national policy-making. Elected by the people to protect the public interest, it yields too often to the importunities of lobbyists for special-interest groups. It lacks machinery for developing coherent legislative programs and for promoting party responsibility and accountability. Its posts of power are held on the basis of political age, regardless of ability or agreement with party policies. And its members are overworked and underpaid—the forgotten men of social security.[3]

Congress has acquired impressive staffs and information processing facilities; improvements have been made in its system of committees; oversight of the executive branch has expanded measurably; because of the growth in the scope and immediacy of national policy issues and the professionalization of its membership, far less of its time is spent on merely parochial issues; mainly on account of its extensive and expert staffs, it is substantially more impervious to special-interest pressure; seniority is no longer an automatic guarantee of committee power; and certainly its members are not underpaid (a 1977 increase raised members' pay to $57,500 a year).

Congress has great political power and

an enormous capacity to frustrate the legislative ambitions of the President, as President Jimmy Carter discovered in the course of his first year in the White House. It tasted sovereignty during the exhilarating days of 1973 when it nearly removed a President, Richard Nixon, from office, and surely would have had he not resigned. We do not have congressional government in the United States in the sense that an omnipotent Congress makes all the laws, which the President and the executive branch merely enforce. Such a simplistic system never existed. But Congress is far more formidable as a political body today than it was in the more quiescent days of the 1950s and early 1960s. Congress is semisovereign.

It remains, nevertheless, a peculiar institution. The electoral connections of its members are highly individual and localized. Although its membership has become more ideologically homogeneous, and accordingly somewhat more partisan, its party leadership remains relatively weak. Its internal power structure continues to be highly dispersed, with legislative influence over policy decisions scattered over a large number of members manning its many subcommittees and conducting business in a remarkably open and public manner. It jealously guards its independence, enlarges the scope of its legislative activities, strengthens its capacity to scrutinize the executive, and demands a greater role in realms of policy previously left largely to the President. Its aggregate decision making is "individualistic" in the sense that party or committee influence on members' voting is not compelling. In short, Congress is an unusually democratic legislative institution. This makes it a very frustrating policymaking body for those politicians and intellectuals who have the "received truth." And its democratic character makes it often seem painfully slow and incompetent to its attentive constituents. Its own internal dynamic, along with these external frustrations and annoyances, brings about cyclical pressures for reform. So it surely will be true that the Congress of the 1980s will not be very different from the Congress of the 1970s—but, equally, it will not be the same.

Reading 10.2

The Impact of Recent Reforms

William J. Keefe

In this brief excerpt from a major text on Congress, a leading student of legislative life speculates about the impact of recent reforms and encourages more study of the policy consequences of institutional change.

Change in political institutions always leaves tracks. The problem for the analyst is that years may be required to distinguish which way they are headed, and sometimes the direction never becomes clear. The rash of changes in Congress is a case in point. We are still a long way from knowing exactly what kind of Congress these changes, taken together, have produced. Their lasting power, moreover, remains to be seen. But if allowance is made for generality, certain broad observations about the thrust of these reforms can be made.

The upheavals involving the seniority system, coupled with the revival of the caucus, have brought an end to government by standing committee chairmen—the dominant pattern from the Presidency of Roosevelt to that of Johnson. A chairman who leans noticeably toward autocracy will encounter difficulty surviving in the new Congress. In essence, the committee chairmanship is a new office, sharply reduced in independent authority, and reduced as well in its attractiveness for the occupant.

The decline in the authority of committee chairmen has been accompanied by a diffusion of power among numerous members, improving their opportunities for influencing legislative decisions. The increase in the number, independence, and importance of subcommittees has been spectacular. Concretely, these changes have pushed up the value of subcommittee chairmanships. At the same time, the proliferation of leadership positions and the antimonopoly stipulations concerning their distribution have produced a dramatic change in the opportunity structure of Congress. It now takes new members less time to gather power in their own right; for those in the majority party, a subcommittee chairmanship (in many committees) is not much farther than around the corner. Overall, the fragmentation of power has contributed to a condition under which individual members have greater opportunities to do what they want to do, free to ride all manner of hobbyhorses, relatively insulated from leadership controls. Perhaps at no time in the history of Congress have the individual preferences of members counted for as much as they do now.

In spite of the rediscovery of the caucus as an instrument of party, party management has become much more difficult in both houses. The eclipse of party machines, the decline of party loyalty in the electorate, the fierce independence and antiparty posturings of many candidates—all converge to drain vitality from the congressional parties. For most members, the element of party has rusted out in their electoral connection. Their incumbent status (with its awesome advantages) is likely to prove much more important to their reelection than their party affiliation or their record of support for party leaders, including the President. What counts, members know, is pleasing the voter by developing an "appropriate" image, addressing matters of high moment to them, responding to the claims of key interest groups, concentrating on local and state matters, and taking care of constituent problems with government.

Organizational change in Congress has also weakened the parties. The emergence of subcommittee government means that leaders have more bases to touch, more independent power centers with which to reckon, more interests to be accommodated, more "one-on-one" games to play. Finally, the pervasive openness of Congress undoubtedly diminishes the opportunities for party leaders to press hard on members, hoping to bring them into line. When exposed to too much light, party controls wither.

In certain respects, Congress has become a more independent institution, better able to fend for itself, better able to resist the pressures and blandishments of the President and the bureaucracy. Its growing independence results in part from the sharp growth in professional staff and from the creation of two new research arms, the Office of Technology Assessment and the Congressional Budget Office. In addition, it can call on the experts of the Congressional Research Service of the Library of Congress and on those of the General Accounting Office. Congress now has more experts responsible to it and to its members than could have been imagined just a few years ago, a resource that lessens its reliance on the experts of the executive branch.

But probably of greater significance is simply the spirit of independence within Congress. Most members manage to get elected on their own, forming their own electoral organizations, raising their own campaign money, and creating their own personal followings. Their success as solitary political entrepreneurs has habituated them to the need to guard their own careers. To enhance their independence, they have shaped a Congress in which old hands count for less and in which even the newest members must be taken seriously. For members who are more concerned with their reelection than with majority-building, this is the best of all worlds.

Their freedom, of course, creates problems in the system. The independence of Congress has added to the tensions between the branches. Congressional responses to presidential initiatives have become more unpredictable. There are fewer incentives for members to go along with the leadership, and party has become a less reliable link for bridging the separation of powers. The result is that it has become measurably more difficult to put together the firm majorities necessary to make decisions and to adopt new policies. Immobilization occurs all too commonly.

Of related interest is the question of whether the independence that Congress has achieved from the chief executive has been matched by a comparable distancing between Congress and interest groups. The overwhelming impression among observers is that it has not. Probably at no time has Congress been whipsawed so frequently by single-interest, nonclass, high-intensity groups, arrayed on such passionate issues as gun control, abortion, conservation, nuclear power, equality, school prayer, and a thin slice of domestically volatile foreign policy questions. Emerging in one context after another, these issues crowd the congressional agenda and inflame the debate. The independence that Congress and its members have won from the chief executive and from the parties has been diminished by a new vulnerability to narrow pressure groups that regard anything less than complete accord with their positions as betrayal, or worse yet, as reason to carry on the fight where it hurts, among the voters in the next campaign. Weary of the "rectitude" issues and the "new politics" encirclement, it is no wonder that some members, not only elderly ones, slip out between the wagons, headed back home to stay.

Democratization of the congressional system was a major objective of the reform movement. Proceeding along two dimensions, it led to opening up congressional workings to public view and to a redistribution of power among members and units. As a result of various "sunshine" provisions adopted in the 1970s, secrecy has been virtually eliminated—in committees and caucuses and in voting. The broad consequence of openness has been to change the way members do business, putting them "on the record" much more often than in the past and presumably increasing their responsiveness and accountability to the public. At the same time, openness has increased the risks for members, at least as many perceive it, and added to the explanations (concerning positions, votes, and even personal finances) which they must make to those who pay attention and ask questions. It appears probable that the new openness has made members more likely to succumb to conspicuous displays of public pressure. Similarly, it may contribute to the success of interest groups in wringing larger accommodations out of Congress.

The redistribution of power brought about by alterations in the position of committee chairmen and in committee-subcommittee relations has pushed Congress toward extreme decentralization, offset only to the extent that party leaders, skillfully drawing on limited resources, can convince members to fall into line. The changes made in the name of democratization have contributed significantly to the further devolution of power in Congress.

The lasting importance of the changes made in Congress over the last decade remains to be seen. The immediate consequences, however, stand out, and are familiar by now. What is not clear is whether these changes have led to significantly different policy outcomes. That is the main question, and it is also the one on which there is the least systematic evidence. Investigation of the consequences of congressional reform for the political system, particularly in terms of public policy, ought to carry high priority for students of politics.

Reading 10.3

The Two Congresses in an Age of Limits

Roger H. Davidson

In this essay, Davidson lists major sources of congressional change and presents several conclusions concerning their consequences. He distinguishes between two Congresses—(1) the institution, with its focus on legislation, and (2) the individuals, driven by a desire to represent constituents and gain reelection.

The U.S. Congress has a persistent image problem. The other branches of government have nothing quite comparable to the comic-strip figure of Senator Snort, the overblown and incompetent windbag. Pundits and humorists find Congress an inexhaustible source of new material. Seemingly, the public shares this disdain toward the institution.

The view of Congress held by serious commentators—seasoned journalists, scholars, and other commentators—is often scarcely more flattering than the public image. The currently fashionable textbook portrait of Congress, for example, depicts a collection of politicians obsessed by re-election fears and surrounding themselves with staff and facilities for constituency errand-running—not a wholly erroneous picture, to be sure, but a caricature nonetheless. Legislators themselves contribute to this shabby image by often portraying themselves to their constituents as gallant warriors against the dragons back on Capitol Hill; as political scientist Richard F. Fenno, Jr., notes, they "run *for* Congress by running *against* Congress."

Fenno's observation is a reminder that the U.S. Congress has a dual character: It is both a "deliberative assembly of one nation" and a "congress of ambassadors," using Edmund Burke's words to describe what is a most un-Burkean institution. It is not extravagant to observe that there are two Congresses, not just one. They are analytically and even physically distinct, yet they are inextricably bound together. What affects one

Source: Appearing as an original essay in the first edition, this paper was updated by the author in December 1985. The views expressed are his own and do not necessarily represent those of the Congressional Research Service.

sooner or later affects the working of the other.

One of these two entities is Congress as an institution. It is Congress the lawmaking and policy-determining body. It is Congress acting as a collegial body, performing its constitutional duties and debating legislative issues. Of course, as a large institution with a demanding work load, Congress functions more often in subgroups than as a single body. Yet its many work groups (there are now hundreds of them) are attending to public business, and the outcomes, whatever form they take, affect the citizenry at large.

Yet there is a second Congress, every bit as important as the Congress of the textbooks. This is the Congress of 535 (actually 540) individual senators and representatives. They possess diverse backgrounds and follow varied paths to win office. Their electoral fortunes depend not upon what Congress produces as an institution, but upon the support and goodwill of voters hundreds or thousands of miles away—voters whom they share with almost none of their Capitol Hill colleagues. Journalist Richard Rovere once described members of Congress as tribesmen in an extraterritorial jungle whose chief concern while in Washington was what was going on around the council fires back home.

The dual character of Congress, though underscored by recent trends, is in fact dictated by the Constitution. Congress was intended as a lawmaking body, and it is no accident that the writers of the Constitution enumerated the powers of government, as understood in the 18th century, in that portion (Article I) devoted to the legislative branch. Yet frequent elections tightly bind the House of Representatives to popular needs and opinions. The Senate, although not originally conceived as a popularly representative body, has become so in the 20th century.

The dichotomy between institutional and individual activities surfaces in legislators' role orientations and daily schedules. Like most of us, senators and representatives suffer from a scarcity of time in which to accomplish what is expected of them. No problem plagues the two houses more than balancing constituency work with legislative work (that is, committee and floor deliberations). Despite scheduling innovations for partitioning Washington and constituency work, Tuesday–Thursday Capitol Hill schedules persist. Legislators themselves acknowledge the primacy of the twin roles of legislator and constituency servant, though assigning different weights to these roles and budgeting their time differently to cope with them.

Citizens, for their part, view the Congress in Washington through different lenses than they do their own senators and representatives. Congress as an institution is perceived mainly as a legislative body. It is evaluated largely on the basis of citizens' generalized attitudes about policies and the state of the union: Do people like the way things are going, or do they not? By contrast, citizens see their own representatives as agents of local interests, evaluating them on the basis of such factors as their ability to serve the district materially, their communication with constituents, and their "home style."

Significantly, citizens profess to be far happier with the performance of their individual legislators than with the performance of Congress as a whole. This is the source of the observation that Americans love their congressmen, but denigrate their Congress, and it explains why incumbents can be overwhelmingly returned to office while Congress itself falls behind in public esteem.

Notwithstanding its reputation for inertia, Congress, in both its manifestations, was dramatically transformed in a reformist era that lasted roughly from the mid-1960s through the mid-1970s. The changes touched virtually every nook and cranny on Capitol Hill—membership, structures, procedures, folkways, and staffs. Some changes resulted from pressures built up over many years; others occurred suddenly and almost casually. Some have been well-chronicled by journalists and scholars; others are still little known or understood.

In cataloging the major forces for change and analyzing their consequences, it is useful to continue the metaphor of the two Congresses. What forces have impacted upon the Congress-as-institution? What forces have affected Congress-as-political-careerists? What innovations have these forces produced, and what new generation of problems have these innovations created?

CONGRESS AS INSTITUTION

If ours is an antiparliamentary age, it is surely because of profound and ever-shifting challenges emanating from the larger economic, social, and political environment. These take the form of pressing national problems, rising public expectations, fast-moving events, competing institutions, or simply a burgeoning agenda. Like most of the world's legislative bodies, the U.S. Congress faces a prolonged crisis of adaptation to this larger environment. On this point most analysts are agreed, although they differ over the exact causes and outlines of the crisis. Whatever its origins, the crisis is acutely felt on Capitol Hill and stretches legislative structures and procedures to their limits, and sometimes beyond. Contributing to this state of affairs are several salient features in Congress's external environment.

Forces for Change

First, the government and Congress in turn continue to be asked to resolve all manner of problems. House and Senate work loads, in absolute terms, are impressive. In the 98th Congress (1983–1984), for instance, more than 10,000 bills and resolutions were introduced in the two chambers and more than 8,000 committee hearings were held. Even in an era when scarcely any programs are authorized, review of ongoing programs and their budgets is a persistent, time-consuming challenge.

Second, relative to these policy demands, resources for resolving them in politically attractive ways have contracted. In the 1970s the United States faced a painful transition from a growth-oriented society with cheap resources to a steady-state society of costly resources. Rather than distributing benefits, politicians found themselves having to assign costs. This involved, in political scientists' terminology, a shift from distributive to redistributive politics—an uncomfortable predicament for politicians, and comparatively novel for those in America.

Third, contemporary problems do not come in familiar packages or admit of traditional solutions. Many of them transcend traditional categories and jurisdictions, not to mention the two-year legislative timetable. For example, about 17 percent of all bills and resolutions reported by House committees in the 98th Congress (1983–1984) were handled by more than one committee. Multiply referred measures are a growing portion of the legislative work load, and are more apt to become law than in the past.

Fourth, challenges from the executive establishment cause acute stresses on Capitol Hill. On the one hand, legislators have grown accustomed to White House leadership and grumble when it is not forthcoming; on the other hand, they chafe under vigorous leadership, sensing a threat to legislative prerogatives. The Nixon period represented a high-water mark in the constitutional struggle between White House and Capitol Hill, with presidential incursions in impoundment, executive privilege, the war powers, dismantling of federal programs, and even abuse of the pocket veto.

Although in the post-Watergate year the pendulum swung toward Capitol Hill, the Reagan era saw the return of aggressive presidential leadership. Reagan's ability to steer his 1981 economic package onto a fast legislative track showed how presidential leadership, backed by skill and grass-roots support, could turn Congress around. Reagan's later legislative record was mixed, but he challenged Congress at every turn over war powers, taxing and spending, executive rulemaking, and executive and judicial appointments. Moreover, the mix of economic policies adopted in 1981 and thereafter, including new defense commitments, continued entitlement programs, and broad tax reductions, squeezed federal spending and further frustrated the distributive instincts of the elected politicians on Capitol Hill. Whether or not this was a deliberate stratagem of the Reagan administration (as some critics charged), the effect was to place further strains on congressional work groups and procedures.

A final impetus for change, external in the sense that it emanates from electoral decisions, is the nation's shifting partisan and factional structure. Within both parties, regional variations have become muted while other groups have fought to be heard. Partisan and ideological ties, never overwhelming in the American system, have been gradually diluted. Interest groups are flooding into the vacuum left by the political parties' decline—not just the few traditionally powerful lobbies, but a bewildering and shifting profusion of groups organized around all manner of issues and programs.

Institutional Innovations

In the wake of these shifts in its external environment, Congress has adopted a variety of innovations. Several of these are noteworthy: work load adjustments, committee and subcommittee proliferation, a framework for budgetary discipline, "democratization" of the two houses in reaction to the seniority system, and the growth of staff bureaucracies.

Work Load Adjustments From all accounts, the House and Senate are working as diligently as ever. By the 1970s Congress was locked into a virtually year-long schedule. While somewhat fewer measures are now being introduced and processed, they are longer and more complex than ever before. Most other workload indicators, moreover, including length of floor sessions and number of hearings, show little sign of slacking off.

Congress has adapted to its burgeoning work load by manipulating its structure: concentrating on fewer but more complex issues, delegating many decisions to executive-branch agents, and shifting its own role to one of monitor, vetoer, and overseer. Typically, legislation delegates vast powers, but directs executives to report and recommend, oftentimes subjecting their actions to formal legislative review by one or both chambers or even a committee. (The so-called "legislative veto" was invalidated by the Supreme Court in the 1983 case of *INS* v. *Chadha,* but that decision has not halted formal or informal procedures having the same effect. Indeed, some legislative veto mechanisms are still enacted into law despite their tenuous constitutional position.)

Relying upon executive agents carries its own costs. To recover power they sense is slipping away, legislators grasp for new instruments of control. In the wake of the Watergate and Vietnam crises, and propelled by an anti-government mood, legislators of all persuasions proclaim their fealty to the concept of oversight. Predictably, cries of congressional "meddling" are heard from the White House, and some of the more ambitious oversight techniques have proven to be cumbersome and time-consuming.

Sometimes, as in the 1973 War Powers Resolution or the Budget and Impoundment Control Act of 1974, Congress seeks to recapture power, but ends up giving formal recognition to de facto shifts toward the executive. The budget process, though designed in part to curb executive impoundments of funds, actually legitimized them in certain forms (called rescissions and deferrals) and provided a new lever (reconciliation) for presidential influence. By the mid-1980s, long-term despair at budgetmaking in an environment of scarcity pushed Congress to the point of ceding new budget authorities to the executive branch.

Work Group Proliferation Perhaps the most significant organizational phenomenon on Capitol Hill has been decentralization among its numerous work groups. The 99th Congress was divided into 178 committees and subcommittees in the House (actually, the number constantly changes) with the average member serving on seven of them. Since 1977, the Senate has succeeded in paring its 175 subcommittees to 92. This has been achieved by coupling consolidation with limits on the number of subcommittee assignments and chairmanships each senator can hold, thus assuring a more equitable distribution of committee posts. The average number of assignments per senator was cut from approximately 18 (4 committees and 14 subcommittees) to approximately 10 (3 committees and 7 subcommittees).

Still, Congress boasts an impressive number of work groups, and no one familiar with the ways of the Hill expects the number to decline drastically. Senators and representatives are spread very thinly. Virtually any day the houses are in session, a large majority of legislators face schedule conflicts. Members are tempted to committee-hop, quorums are hard to maintain, and deliberation suffers. Committee specialization and apprenticeship norms have been diluted, casting doubt on the committees' continued ability to give in-depth consideration to detailed measures that come before them.

Jurisdictional competition among committees is the order of the day, resulting in member complaints about the need for tighter scheduling and coordination. Attractive issues often cause an unseemly scramble for advantage, sometimes breaking into open conflict, more frequently simply escalating decision-making costs by necessitating complicated informal agreements or formal referrals involving two, three, or more committees.

The "Democratization" of Congress Democracy is in full flower in the House and Senate. Formal positions of power still remain, as do inequalities of influence, but the Senate boasts nothing to match its bipartisan conservative "inner club" of the 1950s, which so vexed the tiny band of liberal Democrats. Over on the House side, the old committee barons have been replaced by a horde of committee and subcommittee baronets. Decision-making processes have been opened up and are no longer monopolized by the committees having jurisdiction on a given subject.

The war over the "seniority system" was fully recounted both in academic studies and in the mass media. Seniority recorded past electoral triumphs, rewarding a party's centers of strength as they existed in an earlier generation. When a party's factional balance shifted, the seniority system distorted its leadership ranks, causing a generation gap between leaders and backbenchers. Such a gap—in region, district type, ideology, and even age—lay at the heart of the Democrats' seniority struggles. By the late 1960s, internal contradictions within the congressional party became untenable and were resolved, inevitably, in favor of youth and liberalism. In the House, the revolts were spasmodic and occasionally bloody, punctuated by a series of intracommittee revolts against recalcitrant chairmen, dispersion of power into the subcommittees (1971 and 1973), and, finally, overthrow of several unpopular committee chairmen (1975). Since then only one committee chairman has been removed by the caucus, although several subcommittee chairmanships have been contested in committee caucuses.

In the Senate the transformation was more peaceful, hastened by caucus and chamber rules that dispersed desirable committee assignments, not to mention permissive leadership styles that have prevailed since Lyndon Johnson left the Senate in 1961.

Republicans experienced similar tensions, although they were more generational than ideological. For the GOP, however, seniority was never the burning issue it was among Democrats. Because of the GOP's prolonged minority status (which ended in the Senate in 1981), its seniority posts were simply less valuable than those of the Democrats. As long as senior GOP members had no hope of changing committees, they were more apt to retire, yielding more rapid generational turnover.

Reforms have not really eliminated seniority. As H. Douglas Price has remarked, "seniority, like monarchy, may be preserved by being deprived of most of its power." The benefits of seniority have simply been extended to far more members. At the latest count, all Republican senators and a majority of Democratic representatives were committee or subcommittee chairmen. Thus, there are more seniority leaders in the House and Senate than ever. If Woodrow Wilson were around to revise his classic book, *Congressional Government*, he would no doubt be led to observe that "Congressional government is subcommittee government."

The Growth of Staff Bureaucracies To help cope with escalating work loads, proliferating work groups, and executive-branch challenges, Congress has created an extensive staff apparatus. No visitor to the Hill these days can fail to be impressed by the hoardes of people who work there. More than 13,000 staff aides now work for members and committees, and some 25,000 more in congressional support agencies like the Congressional Research Service, the General Accounting Office, the Office of Technology Assessment, and the Congressional Budget Office. Simply housing them is a major logistical problem.

The Capitol Hill bureaucracy has grown in ways betraying the character of Congress as a decentralized, nonhierarchical institution. Congress has begotten not one bureaucracy, but many clustered about centers of power, in one sense defining those centers. Efforts to impose a common framework upon the staff apparatus have thus far been stoutly resisted.

The Future Agenda

The shifts in congressional organization and procedures that came to a head in the early 1970s reinforced the historic decentralization in the House and Senate. Congressional history is a struggle of the general versus the particular, in which the particular seems the most powerful force. This particularism, so characteristic of Congress from its beginnings, and with rare exceptions ever since, has been further formalized and institutionalized.

These changes have made the House and Senate more democratic bodies, and they have given members more channels for participating. What this recent generation of reform did not solve, however, was how to orchestrate the work of separate, semi-autonomous work groups into something resembling a coherent whole. Indeed, the advent of subcommittee government compounds the dilemmas of congressional leadership. The next generation of reform politics will have to direct its energies to unifying what the last generation of reforms has dispersed.

Two related problems of coordination will form the pivots for tomorrow's innovative efforts. These are strengthening the central leadership and structuring the committee system.

The Leadership Gap Congressional leadership embodies a paradox, for on paper today's leaders are actually stronger than any of their recent predecessors. The Speaker of the House, if a Democrat, has significant powers conferred by the Democratic Caucus. He chairs the Democratic Steering and Policy Committee and appoints nearly half of its members. He nominates all Democratic members of the Committee on Rules, subject to ratification by the caucus. For the first time since the days of Speaker Cannon, the Rules Committee serves as a leadership arm in regulating access to the House floor.

The speaker also exercises crucial new powers under the House rules. He may now make joint, split, or sequential referrals of bills to two or more committees with jurisdictional claims, options that are invoked hundreds of times each session. In sequential referrals, he may also lay down time limits upon the committees' deliberations. He is also empowered to create *ad hoc* legislative committees to handle bills claimed by two or more committees.

Over in the Senate, however, leadership is more fragile. That chamber's rules and traditions accord great latitude to individuals or small groups of senators in scheduling business, delaying legislation or nominations, offering floor amendments, and closing debate. Floor leaders are expected to protect the interests of colleagues from their side of the aisle, and to be honest brokers in efforts to expedite business. It is little wonder that Senator Howard H. Baker, Jr. (R—Tenn.), majority leader from 1981 to 1985, compared his job to that of a janitor: the first to arrive in the morning, the last to leave at night, and in between busy cleaning up other people's messes.

Central leadership remains suspect on Capitol Hill, and in today's political atmosphere, decentralizing and fragmenting forces are ascendant. The next few years will no doubt see reform battle lines drawn around the question of leadership prerogatives.

Because a majority of members in both houses now have immediate stakes in preserving the present decentralized structure, efforts to centralize leadership will be hazardous. Moreover, party discipline is tenuous. Every legislator, it seems, is intent upon forging a unique voting record; blocs of members cluster less around the parties than around special-purpose caucuses to exchange information, develop legislative stands, and even operate whip systems. According to a recent estimate, about 100 of these groups are in operation.

Leaders, for their part, seem not to know which way to turn. Oftentimes they seem reluctant to accept new prerogatives, preferring to rely on informal powers. Yet they sense that, although publicly held responsible for congressional performance, they lack the power to coordinate or schedule the legislative program. That is why virtually every House and Senate leader of recent vintage has favored reforms aimed at increasing their leverage on the legislative process.

Committee Revitalization Reorganization efforts have thus far failed to recast House or Senate committees to dovetail with contemporary categories of public problems. A wide-ranging House committee realignment proposed by a House select committee in 1974 fell victim to intense lobbying by committee leaders who opposed curbs on their jurisdictions and by allied lobbyists who feared that structural shifts would unwire their mutually beneficial alliances. The reorganization plan was defeated by a reverse-lobbying process, in which committee members and staffs, seeking to preserve their positions, mobilized support from groups that had previously benefited from committee decisions. An effort to revive committee organization three years later was struck down summarily, partly because of the same forces. Another reorganization effort, launched in 1979, proposed one structural change—an energy committee—that was defeated by a coalition of committee leaders bent on protecting their turf.

The Senate was somewhat more successful when it adopted a 1977 realignment package. This realignment left jurisdictional lines pretty much untouched, concentrating instead on consolidating several obsolete committees. The scheme was accepted because, by limiting assignments and leadership posts, it succeeded in spreading the work load more equitably among the Senate's more junior members.

Senators and representatives have expressed profound dissatisfaction with the committee system. In a survey of 101 House and Senate members conducted during the 93d Congress, a foreign-policy commission discovered that 81 percent of the legislators were dissatisfied with "committee jurisdictions and the way they are defined in Congress." Only 1 percent of the legislators were "very satisfied" with the jurisdictional situation, while 13 percent were "very dissatisfied." In a House study conducted in 1977, committee structure was the most frequently mentioned "obstacle" preventing the House from doing its job. "Scheduling" and "institutional inertia" were next in line. In short, although aware of the committee system's disarray, legislators have not as yet brought themselves to pay the price for remedying the problem. Meanwhile, costs of operating under the present structure are escalating.

Dramatic evidence of the committee system's vulnerability occurred during President Reagan's first months in office. Rather than choosing the lengthy, laborious path of pushing proposals through the authorizing committees, Reagan and his advisers cleverly focused on the budget process as a short-cut way of shifting spending priorities. Time was short, they reasoned, and committees would be unwilling to curtail programs they had developed and nurtured. Committees were thus given spending ceilings and told to conform. When the painful process yielded results somewhat short of the administration's goals, a new budget resolution was prepared and pushed through. Both the process and the product unsettled many lawmakers on both sides of the aisle, especially more senior members who had invested heavily in committee specialization.

Fiscal frustration persisted in the 1980s, although the exact pattern of the 1981 reconciliation was not repeated. Stalemate among the multitude of budget claimants, all backed by committee allies on Capitol Hill, continued until the mounting deficit crisis produced in 1985 yet another budget process. This was the so-called Gramm-Rudman-Hollings resolution, which combined deficit-reduction formulas with mandatory program cutbacks (exempting certain programs) and unprecedented delegations of authority to the President and even to staff agencies (Office of Management and Budget, Congressional Budget Office, and General Accounting Office). Committee stalemate was only one element in this dilemma (conflicts between the chambers, and between Congress and the President, were equally or more important), but the inability of congressional organization to consolidate consideration of pressing budgetary matters contributed to the conflict.

For an institution reputed to be slow and tradition-bound, Congress has attempted a surprisingly large number of major reorganization efforts in the past generation. It has undertaken two joint committee investigations (1945, 1965), four major committee reform efforts (1973–1974 and 1979–1980 in the House, 1976–1977 and 1984–1985 in the Senate), a "study committee" of former members (Senate, 1983), two administrative review bodies (one for each house), and two major budgetary revampings, not to mention numerous informal efforts. Still, the agenda of proposed innovations is lengthy, and pressures for further institutional innovation are going to persist. This is the most eloquent testimony to the continuing nature of Congress's crisis of adaptation.

Committee-system modernization is politically the roughest reorganization challenge. It severely upsets the institution's internal balance, for it threatens not only members' committee careers, but also their mutually supportive relationships with potent outside clientele groups.

CONGRESS AS A COLLECTION OF POLITICIANS

A second set of pressures for a change emanates from individual members of Congress, their careers, activities, and goals. Senators and representatives make their own claims upon the institution, claims that must be satisfied if Congress is to attract talented men and women, provide a work place where this talent can be utilized, and command loyalty from its members.

Individual legislators harbor a variety of goals. All members, or virtually all of them, want to be re-elected; a few members seem to have no other interest. But men and women—even politicians—do not live by re-election alone. They seek opportunities to contribute, to shape public policy, to see their ideas come to fruition, to influence others, and to work in dignity and sanity. In a body of 535 politicians (540, actually), this jostling of individual goals and careers inevitably causes friction. No less than the institution itself, these individual careers are beset by stresses and strains.

Of all the factors affecting today's politicians in the United States, the most conspicuous is the long-term ebbing of local political party organizations and loyalties. In only a minority of areas do party organizations still serve as sponsors and anchors for political careers. Nor do voters rely as heavily as they once did upon party labels to guide their choices. Hence, politicians are thrust into the role of individual entrepreneurs, building their own campaign organizations and scrabbling for PAC money to finance their careers. This yields an electoral politics resembling a series of cottage industries—a situation that parallels the fragmentation of interest groups, in which the traditional array of broad-purpose groups is dissolving into a fluid system of narrow-purpose groupings.

At the same time, rising constituency and campaign demands have inundated individual legislators and their staffs. The average House district includes more than half a million people. Education levels have risen; communications and transportation are easier. Public opinion surveys show unmistakably that voters expect legislators to "bring home the bacon" in terms of federal services and to communicate frequently with the home folks. In 1984, the House Post Office logged 200 million pieces of incoming mail, seven times the 1970 figure. Surveys suggest that future constituency demands will not diminish.

"The Incumbency Party"

At first glance, senators' and representatives' careers would seem to be thriving. Certainly incumbents generally do well at the polls. Since World War II, an average of 91 percent of all incumbent representatives and 75 percent of incumbent senators running for re-election have been successful. In 1984, 95 percent of the House members and 90 percent of the senators who contested in the general elections were returned to office.

Partisan swings are less pronounced than they once were. What is more, electoral competition has been relatively low, although recently there is a slight trend toward more competition, especially in Senate races. In any given election year, only about 15 percent of the congressional races are "marginal," that is, won by a margin of 55 percent or less. Little wonder, then, that political observers remark that Congress is not controlled by the Democrats or the Republicans, but by the "incumbency party."

In an era of weak political parties, incumbency itself, with its attendant visibility and opportunities for ombudsman service, is a potent factor (though not the only one) in the electoral picture. A 1977 survey found that 15 percent of all citizens (or members of their families) had requested help from a member of Congress. By better than a two-to-one margin (69 percent to 31 percent), the citizens were satisfied with the service they had received. No fewer than two-thirds of all respondents claimed to have received some communication from their members of Congress. Half could correctly identify his or her name. And, as we have noted, citizens see their own representatives in far rosier hues than they do the Congress as a whole.

American legislators, especially House members, have always been expected to run errands for constituents. Yet in an era of limited government, there were few errands to run. At the turn of the century, for example, constituency mail was pretty much confined to rural mail routes, Spanish War pensions, free seed, and very occasionally a legislative matter. A single clerk sufficed to handle correspondence.

As Capitol Hill observers whose memories go back to the early 1960s can attest, this constituency service role has grown quantitatively and qualitatively. Senators and representatives now head veritable cottage industries for communicating with voters—not merely responding to constituents' requests, but generating these requests through newsletters, targeted mailings, and free telephone access. Staff and office allowances have grown, district offices have proliferated, and recesses are now called "district" (House) or "nonlegislative" (Senate) work periods. This apparatus extends the legislators' ability to reach their constituents, and it provides badly needed ombudsman services for citizens who find coping with the federal bureaucracy a bewildering prospect.

Several years ago, the monetary value of this apparatus to the average representative was placed at $600,000 annually, all provided by taxpayers. This included $388,000 in staff salaries and office space, $143,000 in communication (mostly franked mail) and travel, and $36,000 in miscellaneous benefits. The biennial advantage for an incumbent would thus exceed $1.2 million, and the figure for a senator would be even higher over a single year. Not included in this accounting are such ancillary services as reduced rates for radio and television recording studios and use of such informational resources as the Congressional Research Service.

Role Conflicts

Which came first, the first congressional apparatus for performing constituency service functions or the public's expectation that such functions should be performed? I believe that legislators react to what they interpret as strongly held and legitimate voter expectations. There is no question that voters expect accessibility and material service, and that not a few legislators feel antipathy toward constituency chores, even while acknowledging they are essential aspects of the job, and ones that yield handsome dividends at the polls.

Indeed, legislative and constituency role conflicts are now at dangerously high levels because of heavy demands in both areas. Senators long ago relegated the bulk of their legislative work to staff aides; in the House the transition came later and, for many, not without a sense of loss. Even in the early 1960s, many representatives did their own research and preparation for committee meetings and floor debates. According to a 1965 study, the average House member devoted virtually one day a week to "legislative research and reading"; another 2.7 hours a week was spent writing speeches and articles.

Today's representatives probably spend as much time in the chamber and in committee as did their predecessors of two decades ago, given the burgeoning committee meetings and floor votes. Qualitatively, however, legislative duties are quite differently performed. According to a 1977 survey, the average representative reportedly spent 12 minutes a day preparing legislation or speeches and another 11 minutes reading. With such schedules, reliance upon staff aides is essential.

Legislators are beset by these conflicting

demands, and many of them want to spend more time on legislation than they do. In the 1977 survey, 154 House members were asked to identify the differences between what others expected them to do and what they thought they should be doing. The most frequently mentioned problem, mentioned by fully half of the members, was that "constituent demands detract from other functions." A second complaint, cited by 36 percent of the legislators, was that "scheduling problems and time pressures detract from the work of the House."

Role conflict is not the only factor impinging upon the congressional career. The seeming intractability of public problems and the difficulty of gaining credit for domestic policy achievements have tempered the rewards of public life. So has the post-Watergate antigovernment sentiment. The press and the public have adopted a moralistic stance toward government and its agents, who are often regarded as guilty until proven otherwise. Stung by criticism, Congress has enacted stricter rules over campaign finance, financial disclosure, and ethics. However desirable, the new codes have exacted a price in legislators' morale and self-regard.

Declining Careerism?

Whatever the reason, many senators and representatives evidence weariness and alienation from their jobs. In a survey of House members in the mid-1960s, a generally high level of satisfaction with the institution's performance was discovered—an attitude characterized as "a vote of aye—with reservations." A survey conducted a decade later yielded not even such measured optimism. That study, which focused on foreign policy, uncovered widespread discontent among members of both houses. Dissatisfaction was expressed by four-fifths of the legislators and extended to all groups and factions of Capitol Hill. In the 1977 survey of the House members, only 16 percent of the representatives thought the House was "very effective" in performing its principal functions.

Few observers in the 1980s would judge congressional careers to be attractive or rewarding. To the mounting stresses and strains of public life have been added the peculiar characteristics of this era: divided government, partisan stalemate, redistributive pressures, and preoccupation with fiscal matters. In the House, the pent-up frustration of Republicans, long in the minority, has flared up periodically into open warfare against the majority Democrats, the other body, and even President Reagan. In the Senate, with its greater freedom of action, the frustrations grow not out of partisan divisions, but out of the disarray of the chamber's rules, procedures, and structures. Deference to individual senators' needs and schedules has become such an inviolable principle that orderly scheduling and deliberation are virtually impossible to achieve. In 1985 the situation prompted a group of senators to hold a series of informal meetings on "quality of life," meaning the life of the Senate and its members (and their families). Some senators, like former Majority Leader Baker, advocated televising Senate sessions in the hope it would force the body to tighten up its procedures.

Congressional retirements are by no means a bad thing, of course, and there is always a long queue of would-be candidates. Indeed, turnover during the 1950s and 1960s was uncommonly low. And in the absence of meaningful competition in many states and a large majority of House districts, voluntary retirement is the chief avenue for achieving turnover. Nonetheless, the number of voluntary retirements, and the number of prominent citizens who have declined to become candidates, is cause for concern. With other careers becoming relatively more attractive, with leadership within Congress more easily and rapidly attained, with congressional life betraying new stresses and strains, tomorrow's critics could conceivably be talking about a problem no one would have taken seriously a few years ago: How to keep senators' or representatives' jobs attractive enough to draw talented individuals and command these individuals' loyalty once they are there.

The heightened demands thrust upon the two Congresses may well lie beyond the reach of normal men and women. Reflecting on the multiplicity of presidential duties, Woodrow Wilson once remarked that the United States might be forced to pick its leaders from among "wise and prudent athletes," a small class of people. The same might now be said of senators and representatives. And if the job specifications exceed reasonable dimensions, will reasonable human beings volunteer for the jobs?

CONCLUSIONS

Congress is essentially a reactive institution. For better or worse, it mirrors the nation's political life—its values, standards, and organizing principles. Today's Congress is little different: it is open, representative, egalitarian, and fragmented. It is short on consensus and leadership, and there is less ideological or partisan commitment than in earlier eras.

Critics of the post–World War II era worried about the representative character of Congress. Long careers and low turnover seemed to heighten the insular, small-town atmosphere of the Hill; newly active ethnic and racial groupings were ill represented; because of the seniority system, leaders were especially unrepresentative; decision making was all too often done in closed circles and behind closed doors. Few commentators would now fault Congress on these counts. Capitol Hill is a far more open, democratic place than it was a decade or so ago.

Today's members of Congress are by and large—and contrary to popular beliefs—a diligent, even harried, group of men and women. Although it has its share of *poseurs* and philanderers, Congress is populated mainly by earnest individuals who are so busy casting floor votes and keeping appointments that they have little time left for expertise or reflection. There pervades an atmosphere of frantic frustration: Members are busier than ever, but the complexity of their tasks and the fullness of their schedules militates against meaningful involvement in any given issue. Members are torn by conflicting expectations from the Washington community and the home communities that form their electoral bases.

Congress no doubt reflects the atomization of political life in the United States. This era is likely to prevail until the pressure of adaptive challenges becomes too strong to resist, or the galvanizing force of an issue or a political movement once again changes the face of the American political landscape.

Reading 10.4

Report of the Temporary Select Committee to Study the Senate Committee System

Agreement seems to be universal in Washington these days that the U. S. Senate is in a state of disarray and that, therefore, some major internal and procedural changes are in order. The following internal study, commonly known as the "Quayle Report" in honor of the Select Committee's chairman Senator Dan Quayle (R—Ind.), vividly illustrates the degree of dissatisfaction among U.S. senators and their desire for change. The proposals offered here indicate the likely issues and topics of debate concerning future congressional reform and change.

I. SUMMARY

The Temporary Select Committee to Study the Senate Committee System finds indications of substantial problems with the operation of the committee system and with the operation of the Senate as a whole.

To improve the operation of the committee system the Selection Committee makes the following recommendations:

1. Limit senators' committee assignments to 2 "A" committees and 1 "B" committee, without exceptions.
2. Reduce total slots on "A" committees to 200 and total slots on "B" committees to approximately 100.
3. Limit the number of subcommittees a committee may establish to 5 (except Appropriations).
4. Limit senators to 2 "A" and "B" committee and subcommittee chairmanships.
5. Limit senators to membership on 2 subcommittees of each committee on which they serve (except Appropriations).
6. Limit senators to a total of 9 "A" and "B" committees and subcommittees except for members of the Appropriations Committee who are limited to 11.
7. Require that the majority and minority leaders not be counted for the purpose of determining the size of a quorum on the committees on which they serve.
8. Provide for sequential referral of reported bills to committees with a jurisdictional interest.
9. Provide for referral of legislative provisions of reported appropriations bills to authorizing committees.
10. Encourage the utilization of the existing computerized scheduling system by requiring committee chairmen to announce a list of committee members with meeting conflicts.
11. Establish a joint House-Senate committee on intelligence.
12. Establish a temporary committee to study the 2-year budget process and propose revisions in the budget procedure.

In regard to the operation of the Senate the Committee makes the following recommendations:

1. Discourage the proliferation of non-germane amendments by providing for a "germaneness motion" requiring a super-majority under which non-germane amendments are prohibited, making non-debatable rulings of the chair that an amendment is non-germane and requiring a super majority to overrule the chair after the germaneness motion has been adopted.
2. Provide for a two-hour time limit on the motion to proceed.
3. Establish a more meaningful cloture procedure.

Source: Report of the Temporary Select Committee to Study the Senate Committee System, U.S. Senate, 98th Congress, 2d session (December 14, 1984), pp. 1–16.

II. INTRODUCTION

S. Res. 127, passed June 6, 1984, established the Temporary Select Committee to Study the Senate Committee System and instructed the Select Committee to ". . . conduct a thorough study of the Senate committee system, . . . and to make recommendations which promote the optimum utilization of Senators' time, (and) optimum effectiveness of committees . . ."

The committee's hearings on the problems of the Senate committee system produced a number of witnesses who saw major impediments to the effective operation of committees and who believed that these impediments hinder the operation of the Senate as a whole and adversely affect the optimum utilization of senators' time.

The Federalist papers provide a historical perspective on what the Senate was intended to be and how it was intended to operate. Alexander Hamilton described the need for a body with stability and continuity that will not be constantly swept by the whims of change, a body that can dispassionately review the actions of the more numerous branch. The Senate was designed to protect us, in his words, against the "effects of a mutable policy." Such a policy, he said, ". . . poisons the blessings of liberty itself. It will be of little avail to the people, that the laws are made by men of their own choice, if the laws be so voluminous that they cannot be read, or so incoherent that they cannot be understood; if they be repealed or revised before they are promulgated, or undergo such incessant changes that no man who knows what the law is today can guess what it will be tomorrow."

The tradition is clear—the Senate is not to be judged by how much it does, but rather by how well it does it. The early Senate fulfilled those expectations. Lord Bryce, the learned author of the *American Commonwealth*, writing at the beginning of this century, noted that "the Senate has expressed more adequately the judgment, as contrasted with the emotion, of the nation." He went on to say that ". . . the Senate has succeeded in making itself eminent and respected . . . and has furnished a vantage ground from which men of ability may speak with authority to their fellow citizens."

Based on the record of the hearings that the Committee held July 31 and August 2, 1984, the Senate may not be fulfilling its role adequately today. Fourteen Senators testified before the Committee and detailed their views on the modern Senate's trivialization and proliferation of processes and issues. Senator Howard Baker, the distinguished majority leader, put the problems and their causes this way: "Two factors interrelate—the loss of the status of a public forum in the Senate and the proliferation of bills and amendments and issues in the committee system. We focus too much on detail and too little on the broad general principles."

Senator Sam Nunn expressed a very similar point when he said, "Without some prudent, thoughtful changes in how the Senate and its committees conduct their business, we run the risk of becoming increasingly mired in duplication and details while we accomplish less and less. In essence, the Senate and the Congress as a whole is choking on its own processes."

Senator Ted Stevens underscored all of these points: "I think it is the redundancy of the process that has destroyed the confidence that the public used to have in the Senate because we never finish anything. (We) (n)ever make a decision. It is always a preliminary decision which may be addressed later at the whim of anybody."

If the evidence in the record of the committee hearings is not sufficiently persuasive to support the charge that the Senate is not fulfilling its historic mission and that both the committee system and the Senate as a whole trivialize and proliferate issues and processes, the committee suggests senators review the *Congressional Record* for the last few weeks of the 98th Congress, when criticism of the way in which the Senate conducts business reached a crescendo.

Senator Lloyd Bentsen said: "That's one of the deteriorations of this institution. You've got to have unanimous consent to get things done and I'm tired of it."

Senator Mark Hatfield said: "If the Senate cannot under its normal procedures finish the legislative calendar, then loading up appropriations bills is a poor excuse. We may enjoy certain political therapy by going through the motions and getting our little publicity out of the hometown newspapers, but this does violence to the institution. This does violence to the appropriations process, and to the Senate."

Senator Bob Packwood said: "We have managed from roughly 1970 or 1971 onward to so pervert and torture the processes of this body that we are approaching being inert."

From the most senior to the most junior, senators expressed similar concerns about the welfare of the Senate as an institution.

Senator John Stennis, number one on the seniority list, pointed out that ". . . the Senate has lost much in the way of ability to debate and be heard, transmit ideas to other leaders and thereby produce conclusions." We must find, he said, ". . . a way that will give us a chance to have real debate, real exposure of the facts, opinions, conclusions, judgments and recommendations, molded into law the best we can, for the general welfare of the people."

Senator Daniel Evans, number 100 on the seniority list, voiced his concerns during the last weeks of the 98th Congress: "I have watched with increasing dismay our performance as a Senate during the past week . . . (T)he experience of the last week has been dismal . . . represent(ing) a failure on the floor of the Senate."

The issue that faces us today—and more importantly, that will face the 99th Congress when it convenes—is not whether the need for some changes has been adequately demonstrated, but whether the Senate will demonstrate the wisdom and courage to adopt the proper remedies for these problems. Change or reform of any kind, because it alters the known to achieve the unknown, is difficult both to forge and to achieve. But useful and necessary change can be accomplished as long as we keep two principles in mind.

First, we must consider the welfare of the Senate as an institution as our first priority, rather than our parochial interests as individual senators.

Second, we must recognize that formal rules changes are only an indication of what we want to achieve. True changes will come only when all senators exercise collective self-restraint in the context of the committee system and within the greater context of the Senate.

S. Res. 127 does not direct the Select Committee to investigate or solve all of the problems of the Senate. The Resolution instructs the Committee to focus its attention on the committee system and the Committee has done so in the Resolutions it has reported.

The Committee believes that the Senate committee system should serve as a legislative filter and refiner. Bills should be referred to the committee of appropriate jurisdiction so that the committee members, a group of experts in their area, may carefully analyze, critique, and alter proposed legislation, then report it to their colleagues on the Senate floor after thorough consideration or not report at all, as they deem best. In this way not only would poorly-crafted or ill-considered legislation be filtered out and kept off the Senate Calendar, but a bill emerging from committee would be a refined product, technically sound, thoroughly understood by committee members and ready for consideration by the Senate. The committee report and minority and additional views would further crystallize the issues for floor consideration.

Clearly, this is an idealized picture of the committee system, but it is a useful yardstick against which to measure the current system. In order to illustrate the failure of the committee system to operate as intended in the last session, the Committee suggests senators reflect on the Senate's handling of two important issues: the Civil Rights Act of 1984 and the Foreign Aid authorization and appropriations.

The Civil Rights Act of 1984 was offered as an amendment to the Continuing Resolution. It was a highly technical bill, yet it was never marked up in committee. The result of this failure of the committee system was the consideration of an extremely complex bill on the floor without the benefit of a committee report. In addition, offering this bill as an amendment to the Continuing Resolution tied the Senate into such a tangle of procedural knots that the Senate failed to consider other needed legislation in a timely manner.

The Foreign Aid appropriations bill was also considered as part of the Continuing Resolution and was enacted without Senate debate or passage of a foreign aid authorization bill. The Continuing Resolution thus served as both the authorizing and appropriations bill. In theory, the authorization and appropriations processes are complementary; in considering authorization and appropriations bills, the Senate benefits from the expertise of both the authorizing and the Appropriations Committee. As in the case of the Civil Rights Act of 1984, not only was the authorizing committee unable to perform its proper function, but the Senate failed to benefit from the expertise of the committee it has established to enable it to fulfill its constitutional role in the development of foreign policy.

These examples show that the committee system is not acting as a legislative filter and refiner. It is not the intent of the Select Committee to criticize committee members or committee chairmen by noting these examples. The Committee only wishes to make clear that the problems of the committee system are serious enough to require corrective action. On the final Senate Calendar for the 98th Congress there remained more than four times the number of Senate bills than the calendar for the 89th Congress (20 years ago). Essential authorization bills die together with matters of lesser importance because the committee system is not assisting the Seante in establishing essential priorities.

In the second session of the 98th Congress, of the thirteen regular Appropriations bills, only four had been enacted by the deadline mandated by the Budget Act (seven days after Labor Day). The Committee is fully aware that the failure of the Senate to consider appropriations bills on the floor is not due to the negligence of the Appropriations Committee, but rather to many causes, including the confusion, duplication, and deadline problems generated by the annual budget process. The annual budget process has become an ongoing project, making it impossible to enact both authorizations and appropriations on time.

It is the belief of the Committee that if Senators will agree to reduce their committee assignments, our committees will be better able to perform their duties and the Senate as a whole will be taken more seriously as a reliable and informed national policymaker.

While the Select Committee's jurisdiction and the resolutions that we report are limited to the committee system, it is clear that the committee system operates in the context of the Senate and that neither the problems of the committee system nor the problems of the Senate can be adequately addressed unless the entire institution is examined. Every senator who testified before the Committee addressed problems beyond those of the committee system, and the Committee would be derelict in its duty if it did not address these broader issues and call the attention of the Senate to the fact that committee reform, while necessary, is only one of the steps that must be taken to restore the Senate to its historic role. Many senators suggested changes in the Senate's procedure on matters like cloture, germaneness, the motion to proceed, and others. Therefore, the Committee's report discusses not only committee system reform, but also proposes steps the committee believes essential to the improvement of the environment in which the committee system operates. These additional matters are discussed in Part IV, "Other Recommendations."

III. RECOMMENDATIONS RELATING TO THE COMMITTEE SYSTEM

Committee Assignment Limitations

Current Rules Rule XXV of the current *Standing Rules of the Senate* limits senators to service on no more than two "A" committees and no more than one "B" committee.

The "A" committees are Agriculture, Appropriations, Armed Services, Banking, Commerce, Energy, Environment, Finance, Foreign Relations, Governmental Affairs, Judiciary, and Labor.

The "B" Committees are Budget, Rules, Small Business, Veterans' Affairs, Joint Economic, Aging, and Intelligence.

Rule XXV also provides 55 exceptions to these assignment limitations covering additional committee assignments for 50 senators during the 98th Congress.

In addition, Rule XXV contains a provision allowing the Majority and Minority Leaders to increase the size of committees by up to 2 members in order to accord to the majority party a majority of seats on all standing committees. This provision also permits a senator to have an extra "A" or "B" committee assignment in order to fill the additional slots.

Committee Recommendation The Select Committee recommends the elimination of all 55 exceptions to the 2 "A", 1 "B" assignment limitations and across-the-board enforcement of those limitations.

The committee recommends the retention of the provision allowing the leadership to adjust the size of committees and authorize additional memberships when needed for party majority reasons.

In addition, in recognition of the fact that the Indian Affairs Committee has been made a permanent legislative committee, the Select Committee recommends that the Indian Affairs Committee be established as a "B" committee.

Background A recurring theme in the Select Committee hearings was the proliferation of committees, subcommittees and assignments and the resulting conflicting demands on senators' time and attention. Before the reform efforts of the Stevenson-Brock Committee (1976–1977), there were 240 slots on standing committees. For the 98th Congress there are 292 slots on standing committees, largely due to the numerous exceptions written into the *Rules*. In addition, when a senator acquires an extra committee, that senator also acquires additional subcommittees, further increasing the size and number of subcommittees.

When senators acquire additional committee and subcommittee commitments, it becomes increasingly difficult for them to attend all of the meetings scheduled for each of their panels. This situation frustrates not only each individual senator, but the chairmen of committees when they try to muster a quorum to conduct business.

In the opinion of the Select Committee, it is not practical or equitable to eliminate only some exceptions to the assignment limitations. Therefore the Committee recommends the repeal of all the exceptions.

The Committee sent out a letter to the 50 senators with exceptions and suggested this course of action as the most reasonable. Of the senators who responded to the Committee letter, over half expressed their willingness to give up their extra committees and abide by the assignment limitations as long as those limitations are applied to the entire Senate.

Table 10.4.1.
Committee membership levels.

	Present	Recommended
"A" committees:		
Agriculture	18	15
Appropriations	29	27
Armed Services	18	15
Banking	18	15
Commerce	17	17
Energy	21	17
Environment	18	15
Finance	20	19
Foreign Relations	18	15
Governmental Affairs	18	13
Judiciary	18	17
Labor	18	15
Total	231	200
"B" committees:		
Budget	22	21
Rules	12	11
Small Business	19	13
Veterans' Affairs	12	11
Intelligence	15	11
Aging	19	13
Joint Economic	10	10
Indian Affairs*	7	7
Total	109	97

*Not currently counted as a "B" committee

Committee Membership Levels

Current Rules Committee membership levels are set in the *Rules*. For the 98th Congress there are 231 "A" committee slots and 109 "B" committee slots.

Committee Recommendation The Select Committee recommends that the "A" slots be reduced to 200 and the "B" slots be reduced to 97. Table 10.4.1 shows recommended committee membership levels.

Background These reductions in committee membership levels are necessary with the enforcement of the 2 "A", 1 "B" assignment limitations. These levels would provide 2 "A" slots for each senator, in accordance with the rule allowing senators to serve on no more than 2 "A" committees, and approximately 1 "B" slot for each senator, in accordance with the rule allowing senators to serve on no more than 1 "B" committee.

The number of "B" slots in the above chart is 97 instead of 100 because of the current 53–47 party composition of the Senate. A six-member majority is not sufficient for the majority party to maintain a majority on all 8 "B" committees, especially since the Joint Economic Committee requires, by statute, a 2-member majority. The proposed "B" committee levels do not provide "B" committee slots for 3 senators, which is consistent with current practice because every senator does not serve on a "B" committee.

If all senators want "B" committee assignments, the total of "B" committee slots must be increased by 6. This increase can be accomplished by the leadership under Rule XXV, paragraph 4(c) and waivers provided for the 3 members who would be assigned to an additional "B" committee.

The levels shown in table 10.4.1 are recommended levels, but any alterations in those levels must be mathematically consistent, keeping the overall total of "A" slots at 200 and the overall total of "B" slots at 97 or a level which enables the majority party to maintain a majority on all "B" committees (up to 103).

The Committee notes that, in general, committee membership levels have tended to creep upwards over time. Table 10.4.2 illustrates this tendency.

Subcommittee Limitations

Current Rules There are currently no limitations on the number of subcommittees a committee may establish.

A senator may serve on a maximum of 3 subcommittees on each of his "A" committees (except for Appropriations, whose members may serve on any number of sub-

Table 10.4.2.
Changes in committee membership levels.

	1973–1974 93d Congress	1983–1984 98th Congress	Change
"A" committees:			
Agriculture	13	18	+5
Appropriations	26	29	+3
Armed Services	15	18	+3
Banking	15	18	+3
Commerce	18	17	−1
Energy	15	21	+6
Environment	14	16	+2
Finance	17	20	+3
Foreign Relations	17	17	—
Governmental Affairs	15	18	+3
Judiciary	16	18	+2
Labor	16	18	+2
"B" committees:			
Budget	15	22	+7
Rules	9	12	+3
Small Business	17	19	+2
Veterans' Affairs	9	12	+3
Intelligence	—	15	—
Aging	22	19	−3
Joint Economic	20	20	—

committees), and a maximum of 2 subcommittees on each of his "B" committees.

Committee Recommendation The committee recommends that committees be limited to establishing a maximum of 5 subcommittees, except for the Appropriations Committee, which may retain 13 subcommittees, and that a corresponding budget reduction for affected committees be ensured.

In addition, the Committee recommends that senators be limited to serving on 2 subcommittees on each of their "A" and "B" committees.

Background In the opinion of the Committee, limiting committees to a maximum of 5 subcommittees will help to control the tendency of subcommittees to proliferate. Table 10.4.3 shows the effect of the proposed limitation on the current number of subcommittees.

The Committee feels that senators should be limited to service on 2 subcommittees per committee in order to reduce the size of subcommittees as well as the number of panels to which senators are assigned. In addition, this measure will ensure, if committees are limited to 5 subcommittees, that senators are covering a reasonable share (two subcommittees out of five) of the committee's jurisdiction.

The elimination of 30 subcommittees would, in the opinion of the Congressional Budget Office, save an estimated $6.5 million on an annual basis.

Committee and Subcommittee Chairmanships

Current Rules Current rules allow a senator to chair one "A" or "B" committee. A chairman of an "A" committee may chair only one subcommittee of all of the "A"

Table 10.4.3.
Impact on subcommittees.

	"A"		"B"		Total	
	Committee	Subcommittee	Committee	Subcommittee	Committee	Subcommittee
Now	12	94	7	17	19	110
5 subcommittees per committee*	12	68	7	12	19	80

*Except Appropriations.

committees on which he serves. A chairman of a "B" committee may not chair any subcommittee of that committee.

Committee Recommendation The Committee recommends that senators who chair an "A" or "B" committee be limited to chairing one subcommittee of all such committees and that no senator be permitted to chair more than 2 subcommittees of all "A" and "B" committees of which he is a member.

Background This limitation is necessary to reflect the lower number of chairmanships available for majority senators when committees are limited to establishing a maximum of 5 subcommittees. The number of committees and the reduction in subcommittees shown in Table 10.4.3 also equal the reduction in the number of available chairmanships. In other words, total "A" and "B" committee and subcommittee chairmanships will be reduced from the current 110 to 80.

Nine-Unit Rule

Current Rules There is currently no limit on the total number of "A" and "B" committees and subcommittees (units) a senator may serve on.

Committee Recommendation Limit the total number of "A" and "B" committees and subcommittees (units) on which a senator may serve to 9 except for members of the Appropriations Committee who are limited to 11.

Background The 9 "units" rule would, in general, reflect serve on 2 "A" committees, 4 "A" subcommittees, 1 "B" committee and 2 "B" subcommittees. However, it has an additional purpose.

Since the committee recognizes that from time to time senators may acquire exemptions to the assignment limitations, the 9-unit and 11-unit limits would act as a ceiling on senators who do acquire waivers. Senators who acquire waivers for additional committee assignments would have to adjust their membership accordingly on other "A" and "B" units to remain under the unit ceilings.

Majority and Minority Leaders' Committee Assignments

Current Rules Rule XXVI requires that a committee may not report unless a majority of the committee is physically present. There is no special provision for committees on which the majority or minority leaders serve.

Committee Recommendation The committee recommends that when the majority or minority leaders are members of a committee, the requirement for a majority of members be applied as though the total committee membership consisted of the number of committee members exclusive of the leader or leaders on the committee.

Background It is the opinion of the Committee that the administrative duties of the majority and the minority leaders are so important and time-consuming that it is reasonable for chairmen of the committees on which they serve to be allowed to determine a majority of the membership without counting the majority and/or minority leaders as members of the committee.

For example, if the majority and minority leaders were both members of a 15-member committee, the committee's quorum requirement would drop from 8 members (necessary for a 15-member committee) to 7 members (necessary for a 13-member committee).

This provision would apply only to the determination of a majority for quorum purposes. The majority and minority leaders would continue to vote and participate in committee business like other members.

Bill Referrals

Current Rules Rule XVII currently provides that bills shall be referred to the committee with jurisdiction over the subject matter which predominates in the bill. The rule also provides for a joint, or a sequential, referral of bills upon joint motion of the majority and minority leaders. Sequential referrals are also regularly accompanied by unanimous consent.

Committee Recommendation The committee recommends adoption of a new rule that, if a committee reports a bill which contains matter in the jurisdiction of another committee, that bill shall, at the request of the chairman or ranking minority member, be referred to the other committee for a period not to exceed 30 calendar days (excluding days when the Senate is not in session) for consideration of those matters within the other committee's jurisdiction. The time period may be altered by the Senate.

Background The Select Committee does not believe that it is possible to draw such neat jurisdictional lines that all matters within a bill will always fall within the jurisdiction of a single committee. Subject areas inevitably overlap, and the tendency for bills to become longer and more complex increases the difficulty of vesting complete jurisdiction in one committee. Sequential referral seems to be the appropriate procedure for dealing with these jurisdictional overlaps. The proposed rule is based on a procedure already applicable to small business matters and the Small Business Committee to report general legislation if it is germane to subject matter contained in the House-passed bill.
is, of course, the possibility of delay, but the Select Committee believes that time problems can be worked out.

Bill Referral—Appropriation Bills

Current Rule Rule XVI authorizes the Appropriations Committee to report amendments which provide appropriations for purposes which are not authorized by existing law and that have not been previously authorized by the Senate. That rule also, in effect, authorizes the Appropriations Committee to report to report general legislation if it is germane to subject matter contained in the House-passed bill.

Committee Recommendation The Select Committee recommends that a similar system of sequential referral apply to bills reported from the Appropriations Committee as recommended for those reported from other committees. In other words, legislative provisions in Appropriations bills within the jurisdiction of an authorizing committee would be referred to that committee for a limited time period of five calendar days or a shorter period if agreed to by the majority and minority leaders.

In order to clarify the Committee's

intent, the phrase "legislative provision" is intended to include any change in substantive law, but does not include an appropriation for a program whose authorization has expired provided that the terms of the authorization are not changed. It is further the intent of the Committee that this referral provision apply to any legislation reported by the Appropriations Committee, whether it be an original bill or an amendment to a bill originating in the House of Representatives. On the other hand, the provision does not apply to amendments offered on the floor, even if offered by direction of a committee.

Background The Select Committee believes that the same principle of sequential referral applicable to regular bills under the authorizing bill referral recommendation above should also be applicable to appropriations bills when they carry legislation within the jurisdiction of the authorizing committees.

Recognizing the greater time pressure which often accompanies the enactment of appropriation bills, the Select Committee proposes that the referral period on such bills be limited to five days rather than the 30 days applicable to other bills. The committee also recommends a provision allowing the majority and minority leaders to shorten that time period at their discretion.

It is the opinion of the Select Committee that, without this kind of provision, the tendency for appropriation bills to become cluttered with authorizing and other legislation will continue to seriously undermine the jurisdiction of the authorizing committees. By providing for such a referral, the authorizing committees will be able to carry out their responsibilities.

Scheduling of Committee Meetings

Current Rules Rule XXVI requires committees to schedule meetings during one of two meeting periods, 9:00 A.M. to 11:00 A.M. or 11:00 A.M. to 2:00 P.M., but this requirement is routinely ignored.

Committee Recommendation The committee recommends that committee chairmen be required to announce a list of the committee members who have other mark-up meeting conflicts when the chairman announces a committee mark-up meeting.

Background During Select Committee hearings, senators repeatedly expressed their concern over the difficulty of attending conflicting committee meetings. In the opinion of the Committee this problem could be alleviated by the use of the existing computerized scheduling system, called LEGIS REPORTS, which is maintained by the Office of the Secretary of the Senate, the Daily Digest and the Senate Computer Center. Through this system schedules and meeting conflicts can be accessed for a particular member or for all members of a particular committee or subcommittee. A listing of mark-ups, executive sessions, hearings and conference meetings is updated as the staff of the Secretary of the Senate receives information.

The Committee feels that requiring a committee chairman to announce a list of committee members who have meeting conflicts when he announces a committee meeting will encourage chairmen to consult the computerized schedule before setting up committee meetings. The Committee hopes that this procedure will minimize the problem of committees with overlapping membership scheduling meetings at the same time.

Joint Intelligence Committee

Current Rules The Select Committee on Intelligence was established by S. Res. 400, 94th Congress "to oversee and make continuing studies of the intelligence activities and programs of the United States Government, and to submit to the Senate appropriate proposals for legislation."

No Senator may serve on the committee for more than eight years continuously.

Committee Recommendation The Committee recommends the establishment of a joint Senate-House Committee on Intelligence appointed by the leadership of the two Houses with a small professional staff. The Joint Committee on Intelligence would consist of five members from each body, three from the majority and two from the minority, and its rules would be modeled on those of the Joint Committee on Atomic Energy.

The Committee also recommends that the eight-year service limitation be extended to ten years so that there will be no disruption while the new Joint Committee is being established.

Background The oversight of intelligence activities is the most sensitive task entrusted to the Congress. Review of intelligence activities must be conducted on a non-partisan basis, yet in a manner which allows for effective congressional oversight of the activities of the Executive. Such a balance is most likely to be found in a bipartisan, bicameral committee, attuned to the views of the leadership of the two bodies and staffed by a professional core of experts. The Congress faced a similar need in the early days of atomic energy and met that need with the creation of the Joint Committee on Atomic Energy. That experience has provided the model for the Committee's recommendation.

Two-Year Budget Process

Current Rules The jurisdiction over the amendments to the Budget Act that would be required to establish a two-year budget process is divided among the Governmental Affairs, the Budget, and the Rules Committees.

Committee Recommendation The Committee recommends the appointment of a Select Committee to study the budget process with particular emphasis on the feasibility of a two-year budget process and with the authority to propose legislation to improve the congressional budget process including the feasible and desirable components of two-year budgeting. This committee would consist of twelve members, equally divided between majority and minority, including two members of the Committee on Governmental Affairs, two members of the Rules Committee, two members of the Budget Committee, two members of the Appropriations Committee and four members from the Senate at large. This committee would select its chairman from among its members. The committee would be instructed to report to the Senate within 180 days and would exist for the duration of the first session of the 99th Congress.

Background Testimony before the Select Committee on the need for a two-year budget process was overwhelming. The experience of the last two years shows clearly that there is not time in a single year to implement three separate legislative processes—the budget process as well as the authorization and the appropriation processes. The one-year cycle does not allow sufficient time for the fulfillment of mandated deadlines for all three processes, with the result that the authorizations are late and appropriations cannot be enacted in time. While support for a two-year budget process is extensive, the Committee recognizes that there are many difficult questions that must be resolved in order to move towards that goal. There is some diversity of opinion as to which process should be dealt with in which years of a Congress. These disagreements are heightened by the need to enable a newly elected president to achieve his program in the shortest possible period of time.

A two-year budget will, of course, entail legislation requiring action by the House as well as the Senate. The Committee is pleased that a House task force has already received much testimony on the two-year budget and is well aware that close cooperation will be needed between House and Senate to enact such legislation. However, the Committee believes that the two-year budget process can best be achieved through the normal legislative process rather than by establishing some special new mechanism.

The Select Committee notes that the need for a two-year process was recognized when the Budget Act was enacted. The Act called for the submission of advance authorizations. That provision has, however, not been followed by any administration. It appears that advance authorizations are not sufficient to accomplish the extension of the timetable that is required with the institution of a budget process. Therefore, the broader approach of the biennial budget would be a possible solution. The Select Committee is convinced that, with the expertise already residing in the Budget, Governmental Affairs, and Rules Committees, the new select committee will be able to produce recommendations within the 90-day time period.

IV. OTHER RECOMMENDATIONS

Nongermane Amendments

The Problem Under current rules, amendments must be germane in the following cases: after cloture is invoked, on general appropriations bills, and under certain statutory procedures, most importantly on budget resolutions and reconciliation bills. Germaneness is also regularly required under unanimous consent agreements.

The opportunity to offer non-germane amendments lies at the heart of Senate procedure. It is an essential component of the principle of the protection of the minority. With this opportunity, the majority cannot foreclose debate and votes on issues that a minority wants brought to national attention. In addition, the opportunity to offer such amendments enables Senators to bring to the floor issues on which the committee of jurisdiction has not acted.

Recommendation While non-germane amendments have a legitimate place in Senate procedure, they can also be used to divert the Senate from important policy debates and to impede action on essential legislation. One way to preserve the protection that non-germane amendments give, while protecting the ability of the Senate to conduct its business, is to provide for a special germaneness rule, invoked by 60% of those present and voting. To ensure that the rule can be effectively enforced, it would also be necessary to require a similar majority to overturn rulings of the chair holding an amendment non-germane. This proposal has a distinguished history, having been suggested by the present minority leader and majority leader.

Filibuster and Cloture

The Problem The tradition of unlimited debate prevailed in the Senate until 1917. A procedure to cut off debate was adopted only as a result of the blockage by a small group of Senators of the Wilson Administration's measure to authorize the arming of merchant ships immediately prior to World War I. The history of limitations on debate in the Senate is set forth in the Minority Leader's scholarly insertions in the *Congressional Record* of March 10, 1981, and no attempt to review that history will be made here. That history shows that this is another area in which the Senate has balanced the rights of the minority with the ultimate duty of the Senate to act on the important issues of the day.

It is also abundantly clear from that history that neither unlimited debate—nor the authority to cut if off—were intended to be used lightly. The principle of unlimited debate was designed to protect the minority exercising its right to delay, or even prevent, action on issues of fundamental principle. The authority to cut off debate enabled a strong majority to act after the minority had exercised its rights. Filibuster and cloture were meant for great issues, but they have become trivialized as recent history all too clearly demonstrates. In the last 6 weeks of the 98th Congress, more cloture votes took place than during the first 10 years of the existence of Rule 22. The Senate voted 7 times on cloture petitions; three of those votes were on the motion to proceed. Eight other cloture petitions were filed and later vitiated.

By comparison, from 1963 to 1965, when the Senate considered such controversial issues as amending Rule 22, the Civil Rights Act of 1964, legislative apportionment, and the Voting Rights Act of 1965, only 4 cloture votes took place.

Cloture is not only invoked too often, it is invoked too soon and it is invoked on procedural as well as substantive issues. Each of the cloture petitions at the end of the 98th Congress was filed on the same day that the matter came before the Senate as compared to the cloture petitions on the Treaty of Versailles and the Civil Rights Act of 1964 which were filed after these matters had been pending in the Senate for 51 and 57 days, respectively.

Recommendation To restore the historic balance between unlimited debate and the invocation of cloture, it is necessary to ensure that unlimited debate is permitted only on substantive issues by providing for a two-hour time limit on the motion to proceed and to make cloture no only more difficult to invoke, but more effective once invoked.

Illustration 10.A.

Excerpts from the Senate Study Group (Pearson-Ribicoff Committee) Report to the Senate Committee on Rules and Administration, 1983.

The following report by two former senators makes some very specific recommendations for tidying up the U.S. Senate. Although these recommendations are a bit more comprehensive than those of the preceding Quayle Committee, like the Quayle Report they point the way to the future concerns and considerations of congressional reformers. However, also like the Quayle Report, the Pearson-Ribicoff Report has been largely inconsequential in terms of concrete and specific changes. Four concluding questions to be addressed by students of Congress are: (1) Why haven't these proposals been put into effect? (2) Are these recommended changes desirable? (3) Is it likely that any of these reforms will be enacted in the near future? and (4) What would have to occur for these proposals to become reality?

This report to the Committee on Rules and Administration by The Senate Study Group is made in pursuance of S. Res. 392, submitted by Senator Mathias and agreeed to by the Senate on May 11, 1982. The resolution, in part, reads as follows:

Resolved, That the President of the Senate shall appoint a Study Group on Senate Practices and Procedures (hereinafter referred to as the "Study Group") which shall consist of two former United States Senators, one of whom shall be appointed upon the recommendation of the Majority Leader of the Senate and one of whom shall be appointed upon the recommendation of the Minority Leader of the Senate.

Sec. 2. It shall be the duty and function of the Study Group to make a full and complete study of the practices and procedures of the United States Senate with a view to recommending to the Senate such revisions thereof as may be necessary or appropriate to preserve and enhance the traditions, customs, functions, forms, and spirit of the United States Senate while enabling the Senate to conduct debate which is focused on major issues of national policy.

*****

Sec. 5. The Study Group shall conclude its study and submit a report thereon to the ommittee on Rules and Administration not later than June 1, 1983, which report shall set forth the results of such study together

Illustration 10.A (continued)

with the Study Group's findings and recommendations resulting from such study.

After adoption of the resolution, the President of the Senate, on the recommendations of the Majority and Minority Leaders, appointed former Senators James B. Pearson and Abraham Ribicoff as members of the Study Group. The Parliamentarian Emeritus, Dr. Floyd M. Riddick, and staff of the Rules and Administration Committee, were designated to assist the Senate Study Group in their deliberations and report.

After lengthy consideration by the Study Group, the following subjects were agreed upon to be discussed and further explored; after several meetings, the Study Group agreed that specific recommendations would center around the following outline.

Source: Senate Study Group Report, pp. 1–6.

SENATE STUDY GROUP

An Outline of Recommendations

I. *Senate Leadership Issues*
   A. Through agreement by both bodies to a concurrent resolution, establish an annual agenda of major legislative issues, in coordination with the House leadership, for each Congressional session. Require a premium vote (an absolute three-fifths majority) to change the agenda. Televise Senate debate on these major issues.
   B. Provide for a permanent Presiding Officer of the Senate who shall establish the presence of a quorum for purposes of legislative and executive business of the Senate. Require the Presiding Officer to enforce strictly rules regarding quorums and votes, and, with full support of the party caucuses, impose restraints on the exercise of each individual Senator's rights regarding:
      1. record votes;
      2. quorum calls; and, in addition,
      3. abolish the practice of individual holds on the consideration of matters before the Senate.
   C. Maintain a week in advance schedule for those weeks the Senate is in session. Allow these weekly schedules to be modified on motion by the leadership. Require premium votes to change the weekly schedule.
   D. Do not bring up new Senate bills on the same subject more than once during the same session (or, require a premium vote decided without debate to do such).
      Add to Rule V of the Standing Rules the following provision:
         When a bill or amendment has been passed, or has been rejected, no bill or amendment of the same substance shall be considered during that same session on objection by any member unless proposed by the Majority and Minority Leaders or on motion without debate by a two-thirds majority vote.
   E. Use recess periods during a daily session for the purpose of caucusing by the Majority and Minority Leaders in resolving differences during debate on legislative and executive matters.
   F. Reestablish the old procedure for the disposition of measures on the call of the calendar. This would require no change to the Rules.
   G. Restore the old practice of the Leaders' requesting unanimous consent for the absence of any Senators on official business or for other reasons. (All other Senators would be deemed in or around the Capitol and such presence could be established as a measure of diligence.)
   H. Adopt new procedures for each daily session of the Senate. These new practices would restore previous Senate traditions and would include:
      1. The Senate shall fix a time certain for its legislative and executive sessions. Eash session shall be for one calendar day, during which

time the Senate may recess for brief periods at the request of the Majority and Minority Leaders. At the beginning of each session, the Presiding Officer shall determine the presence of a quorum. If no quorum is present within thirty minutes of the time fixed for the session, the Presiding Officer shall adjourn the Senate to the next day's session, as set by previous order or Rule. (Differing quorums may be established for different types of sessions, but final action on any proposed legislation or executive business must be taken by quorums of full membership. The Presiding Officer shall strictly enforce rules regarding the presence of a quorum.)

2. Once the Presiding Officer has established the presence of a quorum, the session shall begin with the deliverance by the Chaplain of the customary prayer.
3. After recognition of the Majority and Minority Leaders, the Senate shall immediately proceed to the day's business, the call of the consent calendar, or other matters so established by motion, without debate, of the Majority and Minority Leaders.
4. Speeches or remarks not related to the day's session shall be delivered only at the end of that day's business, if time remains for such extraneous matters.
5. No speech shall be read in its entirety; rather, Senators shall speak extemporaneously using notes to refresh their memories, except for those matters of a complex or technical nature, or matters containing executive or judicial policy statements or proclamations, which may be read in their entirety.

II. *Floor Procedure and Practice*

A. Debate
   1. require debate to be relevant at all times during the discussion of legislation and executive business. The Pastore rule, requiring debate to be germane, has been ignored.
   2. amount of debate
      a. too much on all of the following:
         - motion to proceed to consideration (limit motions on legislative matters to one hour of debate.)
         - consideration of measure itself (leave as is.)
         - after cloture is invoked (tighten the existing time limits in Rule XXII.)
      b. not enough on amendments when time limits have expired as in the case of reconciliation measures (amendments called up and no time for debate), as well as when operating under unanimous consent agreements for time limits and amendments can be called up with no time for debate. Abolish the reconciliation process, and require that amendments not be acted on unless time is provided for debate.

B. Amending process
   1. require germaneness of amendments after a certain amount of debate by a premium vote. (The goal should be a germaneness requirement for not less than the last half of time for debate.)
   2. Require a statement of purpose on the face of the amendment as to:
      a. statue being amended
      b. agency or program affected
      c. subject matter of amendment
      Do this by standing order.
   3. Require that amendments, except for one-paragraph minor amendments no longer than ten lines, be printed a day in advance (or permit by a premium vote.)
   4. Require that modifications of amendments be made available to all Senators prior to the start of a vote.
   5. Do not consider any contested amendments on controversial subjects more than once during a session (or, require a premium vote decided without debate to do such).

C. Amend Rule XVI to correct abuses in the use of germaneness when a point of order is raised against an amendment as being legislation on a general appropriations bill.

D. After passage of a measure, require within five days a committee chairman's resume of differences between committee reported bill and the bill as passed by the Senate.

III. *Senate Committees*

A. Their actions should be in accordance with the Senate agenda and their committee jurisdictions (which does not prohibit hearings on any matters within committee jurisdictions).

B. Use subcommittees only for investigations and hearings; do not establish standing subcommittees or any separate staff groups for legislative purposes.

C. Make Congressional budgeting a simplified two-year process.

D. Consolidate standing, select, and special committees of the Senate. Further limit the number of committee assignments for each Senator.

E. Amend the Senate Standing Rules with the following provision:

> Any bill or resolution proposing Senate procedures different from the existing or established procedures, after having been reported by any other Senate committee, shall not be eligible for Senate consideration until that measure has been referred to the Committee on Rules and Administration for a period not in excess of sixty days for its review and report to the Senate with possible proposed amendments in such a measure dealing with Senate procedure.

Glossary: Learning Your Way Around

Congress, like any work environment, has its own vocabulary. The following glossary presents a lexicon of some commonly used congressional terms. Familiarity with them is essential for an appreciation of the congressional environment.

Act The term for legislation which has passed both houses of Congress and has been signed by the President or passed over his veto, thus becoming law. Also used technically for a bill that has been passed by one House and engrossed. (See Engrossed Bill.)

Adjournment Sine Die Adjournment without definitely fixing a day for reconvening; literally "adjournment without a day." Usually used to connote the final adjournment of a session of Congress. A new session usually begins on January 3 and can continue until noon, January 3, of the following year.

Adjournment to a Day Certain Adjournment under a motion or resolution which fixes the next time of meeting. Neither House can adjourn for more than three days without the concurrence of the other. A session of Congress is not ended by adjournment to a day certain.

Amendment Proposal of a member to alter the language or stipulations in a bill or act. It is usually printed, debated, and voted upon in the same manner as a bill.

Appeal A senator's challenge of a ruling or decision made by the presiding officer of the Senate. The senator appeals to members of the chamber to override the decision. If carried by a majority vote, the appeal nullifies the chair's ruling. Although rarely used, the same procedure is available in the House to appeal rulings made by the Speaker and the chairman of the Committee of the Whole.

Appropriation Bill Grants the actual moneys usually approved by authorization bills, but not necessarily the total amount permissible under the authorization bill. An appropriation bill originates in the House, and normally is not acted on until its authorization measure is enacted. General appropriations bills are supposed to be enacted by the seventh day after Labor Day before the start of the fiscal year in which they apply. (*See* Continuing Appropriations.) In addition to general appropriation bills, there are two specialized types.

Authorization Bill Authorizes a program, specifies its general aim and conduct, and, unless "open-ended," puts a ceiling on moneys that can be used to finance it. Usually enacted before appropriation bill is passed. (*See* Contract Authorizations.)

Bills Most legislative proposals before Congress are in the form of bills, and are designated as HR (House of Representatives) or S (Senate) according to the house in which they originate and by a number assigned in the order in which they were introduced, from the beginning of each two-year congressional term. *Public bills* deal with with general questions, and become *public laws* if approved by Congress and signed by the President. *Private bills* deal with individual matters such as claims against the government, immigration and naturalization cases, land title, etc., and become *private laws* if approved and signed.

The introduction of a bill, and its referral to an appropriate committee for action, follows the process given in "How Our Laws Are Made" (House Document No. 95–259). (*See also* Concurrent Resolution, Joint Resolution, Resolution.)

Bills Introduced Any number of members may join in introducing a single bill. Many bills in reality are committee bills and are introduced under the name of the chairman of the committee or subcommittee as a formality.

"Learning Your Way Around," *For New Employees of the United States House of Representatives*, 96th Congress, 2d session, pp. 71–88. Reprinted from the public domain.

All appropriation bills fall into this category, as do many other bills, particularly those dealing with complicated, technical subjects. A committee frequently holds hearings on a number of related bills, and may agree on one of them or an entirely new bill. (*See* Clean Bill *and* By Request.)

Budget The document sent to Congress by the President in January of each year estimating government revenue and expenditures for the ensuing fiscal year and recommending appropriations in detail. The President's budget message forms the basis for congressional hearings and legislation on the year's appropriations.

By Request A phrase used when a senator or representative introduces a bill at the request of an executive branch agency or private organization, but does not necessarily endorse the legislation.

Calendar An agenda or list of pending business before committees or either chamber. The House uses five legislative calendars. (*See* Consent, Discharge, House, Private, *and* Union Calendars.)

In the Senate, all legislative matters reported from committee are placed on a single calendar. They are listed in order, but may be called up irregularly by the majority leader either by motion, or by obtaining the unanimous consent of the Senate. Frequently the minority leader is consulted to assure unanimous consent. Only cloture can limit debate on bills thus called up. (*See* Call of the Calendar.)

The Senate also uses one nonlegislative calendar for treaties, etc. (*See* Executive Calendar.)

Calendar Wednesday In the House on Wednesdays, committees may be called in the order in which they appear in Rule X of the House Manual, for the purpose of bringing up any of their bills from the House or the Union Calendars, except bills which are privileged. General debate is limited to two hours. Bills called up from the Union Calendar are considered in Committee of the Whole. Calendar Wednesday is not observed during the last two weeks of a session, and may be dispensed with at other times by a two-thirds vote.

Call of the Calendar Senate bills which are not brought up for debate by a motion or a unanimous consent agreement are brought before the Senate for action when the calendar listing them in order is "called." Bills considered in this fashion are usually noncontroversial, and debate is limited to five minutes for each Senator on a bill or on amendments to it.

Caucus An organization of members of the House or Senate. The organizations may be officially recognized, as are the majority (Democratic) and minority (Republican) caucuses, or they may be unofficial groups of members having shared legislative interests.

Chamber Meeting place for the total membership of either the House or the Senate, as distinguished from the respective committee rooms.

Clean Bill Frequently after a committee has finished a major revision of a bill, one of the committee members, usually the chairman, will assemble the changes plus what is left of the original bill into a new measure and introduce it as a "clean bill." The new measure, which carries a new number, is then sent to the floor for consideration.

Clerk of the House Chief administrative officer of the House of Representatives. (*See* Secretary of the Senate.)

Cloture The process by which a filibuster can be ended in the Senate, other than by unanimous consent. A motion for cloture can apply to any measure before the Senate, including a proposal to change the chamber's rules. It requires 16 senators' signatures for introduction and the votes of three-fifths of the entire Senate membership (60 if there are no vacancies), except that to end a filibuster against a proposal to amend the Standing Rules of the Senate a two-thirds vote of senators present and voting is required. It is put to a roll-call vote one hour after the Senate meets on the second day following introduction of the motion. If voted, cloture limits each senator to one hour of debate.

Committee A subdivision of the House or Senate which prepares legislation for action by the respective house, or makes investigations as directed by the respective house. There are several types of committees. (*See* Standing *and* Select or Special Committee.) Most standing committees are divided into subcommittees, which study legislation, hold hearings, and report their recommendations to the full committee.

Only the full committee can report legislation for action by the House or Senate.

Committee of the Whole The working title of what is formally "The Committee of the Whole House [of Representatives] on the State of the Union." Unlike other committees, it has no fixed membership. It is comprised of any 100 or more House members who participate—on the floor of the chamber—in debating or altering legislation before the body. Such measures, however, must first have passed through the regular committees and be placed on the calendar.

Technically, the Committee of the Whole considers only bills directly or indirectly appropriating money, authorizing appropriations, or involving taxes or charges on the public. Actually, the Committee of the Whole often considers other types of legislation. Because the Committee of the Whole need number only 100 representatives, a quorum is more readily attained, and business is expedited.

When the full House resolves itself into the Committee of the Whole, it supplants the speaker with a "chairman." The measure is debated or amended, with votes on amendments as needed. When the committee completes its action on the measure, it dissolves itself by "rising." The Speaker returns, and the full House hears the chairman of the Committee of the Whole report that group's recommendations. The full House then acts upon the recommendations.

At this time members may demand a roll-call vote on any amendment adopted in the Committee of the Whole.

Concurrent Resolution A concurrent resolution, designated H. Con. Res. or S. Con. Res., must be passed by both houses but does not require the signature of the President and does not have the force of law. Concurrent resolutions generally are used to make or amend rules applicable to both houses or to express the sentiment of the two houses. A concurrent resolution, for example, is used to fix the time for adjournment of a Congress.

Conference A meeting between the representatives of the House and Senate to reconcile differences between the two houses over provisions of a bill. Members of the Conference Committee are appointed by the speaker and the President of the Senate and are called "managers" for their respective house. A majority of the managers for each house must reach agreement on the provisions of the bill (often a compromise between versions approved by the House and Senate) before it can be sent up for floor action in the form of a "conference report." There it cannot be amended and if not approved by both houses, the bill goes back to conference. Elaborate rules govern the conduct of the conferences. All bills which are passed by House and Senate in slightly different form need not be sent to conference; either chamber may "concur" in the other's amendments. (*See* Custody of the Papers.)

Congress This term refers to the legislative branch of our national government. The Congress is composed of the House of Representatives and the Senate. The term *Congress* may also refer to the two-year long cycle of legislative meetings beginning on January 3 of each odd-numbered year.

Congressional Record The daily, printed account of proceedings in both House and Senate chambers, with debate, statements, and the like reported verbatim. (Members of Congress may edit and revise remarks made on the floor.) Committee activities are not covered, except that their reports to the parent body are noted. Highlights of legislative and committee action are embodied in a Digest section of the *Record*, and members of Congress are entitled to include material on items of general interest in an appendix known as "Extension of Remarks."

Congressional Terms of Office Begin on January 3 of the year following the general election and terminate in two years for the House and six years for the Senate.

Consent Calendar Members of the House may place on the Consent Calendar any bill appearing on the Union or House Calendar which is considered to be noncontroversial. Bills on the Consent Calendar are normally called on the first and third Mondays of each month. On the first occasion when a bill is called in this manner, consideration may be blocked by the objection of any member. On the second time, if there are three objections, the bill is stricken from the Consent Calendar. If fewer than three members object, the bill is given immediate consideration.

A bill on the Consent Calendar may be postponed in another way. A member may ask that the measure be passed over "without prejudice." In that case, no objection is recorded against the bill, and its status on the Consent Calendar remains unchanged.

A bill stricken from the Consent Calendar remains on the Union or House Calendar.

Continuing Appropriations When a fiscal year begins and Congress has not yet enacted all the regular appropriation bills for that year, it passes a joint resolution "continuing appropriations" at rates generally based on the previous year's appropriations for government agencies not yet funded.

Contract Authorizations Found in both authorization and appropriation bills, these authorizations are stopgap provisions which permit the federal government to let contracts or obligate itself for future payments from funds not yet appropriated. The assumption is that funds will be available for payment when contracted debts come due.

Correcting the Record Rules prohibit members from changing their votes after the result has been announced. But frequently, hours, days, or months after a vote has been taken, a member announces that he was "incorrectly recorded." In the Senate, a request to change one's vote almost always receives unanimous consent. In the House, members are prohibited from changing their votes if tallied by the electronic voting system. If taken by roll call, a vote may be changed if consent is granted. Errors in the text of the *Record* may be corrected by unanimous consent.

Custody of the Papers To reconcile differences between the House and Senate versions of a bill, a conference may be arranged. The House with "custody of the paper"—the engrossed bill, engrossed amendments, messages of transmittal—is the only body empowered to request the conference. That body then has the advantage of acting last on the conference report when it is submitted.

Dilatory Motion A motion, usually made upon a technical point, for the purpose of killing time and preventing action on a bill. The rules outlaw dilatory motions, but enforcement is largely within the discretion of the presiding officer.

Discharge a Committee Relieve a committee from jurisdiction over a measure before it.

In the House, if a committee does not report a bill within 30 days after the bill was referred to it, any member may file a discharge motion. This motion, treated as a petition, needs the signatures of 218 members (a majority of the House).

If a resolution to consider a bill (*See* Rule) is held up in the Rules Committee for more than seven legislative days, any member may enter a motion to discharge the committee. The motion is handled like any other discharge petition in the House.

Occasionally, to expedite noncontroversial legislative business, a committee is discharged upon unanimous consent of the House, and a petition is not required. (For Senate procedure, *see* Discharge Resolution.)

Discharge Calendar The House calendar to which motions to discharge committees are referred when the necessary 218 signatures have been obtained.

Discharge Motion In the House, a motion to discharge a committee from considering a bill. If passed by a majority, the bill is brought to the floor for consideriation without being reported by the committee. Alternatively, a discharge petition requires signatures of 218 House members.

Discharge Resolution In the Senate, a special motion any senator may introduce to relieve a committee from consideration of a bill before it. The resolution can be called up on motion for approval or disapproval, in the same manner as other matters of Senate business. (For House procedure, *see* Discharge a Committee.)

Division Vote Same as standing vote. (*See below.*)

Enacting Clause Key phrase for bills saying, "Be it enacted by the Senate and House of Representatives. . . ." A successful motion to strike the enacting clause from legislation kills the measure.

Engrossed Bill The final copy of a bill as passed by one House, with the text as amended by floor action and certified to by the clerk of the House or the secretary of the Senate.

Enrolled Bill The final copy of a bill which has been passed in identical form by both houses. It is certified to by an officer of the house of origin (House clerk or Senate secretary) and then sent on for signatures of the House speaker, the Senate President, and the President of the United States. An enrolled bill is printed on parchment.

Executive Calendar An additional, nonlegislative calendar in the Senate, on which presidential documents such as treaties and nominations are listed.

Executive Document A document, usually a treaty, sent to the Senate by the President for consideration or approval. These are identified for each session of Congress as Executive A, 97th Congress, lst Session; Executive B, etc. They are referred to committee in the same manner as other measures. Unlike legislative documents, however, treaties do not die at the end of a Congress, but remain "live" proposals until acted on by the Senate or withdrawn by the President.

Executive Session Meeting of a Senate or a House committee (or, occasionally, of the entire membership) which only the group's members are privileged to attend. Frequently witnesses appear before committees meeting in executive session, and other members of Congress may be invited, but the public and press are not allowed to attend.

Expenditures The actual spending of money as distinguished from the appropriation of it. Expenditures are made by the disbursing officers of the administration; appropriations are made only by Congress. The two are rarely identical: in any fiscal year expenditures may represent money appropriated one, two, or more years previously.

Filibuster A time-delaying tactic used by a minority in an effort to prevent a vote on a bill. The most common method is unlimited debate, but other forms of parliamentary maneuvering may be used. The stricter rules in the House make filibusters more difficult, but they may be attempted through various delaying tactics.

Fiscal Year Financial operations of the government are carried out in a 12-month fiscal year, beginning on October 1 and ending on September 30. The fiscal year carries the date of the calendar year in which it ends.

Floor The chamber in which the House or the Senate meets.

Floor Manager A member, usually representing sponsors of a bill, who attempts to steer it through debate and revision to a final vote in the chamber. Floor managers are frequently chairmen or ranking members of the committee that reported the bill. Managers are responsible for apportioning the time granted supporters of the bill for debating it. The minority leader or the ranking minority member of the committee often apportions time for the opposition.

Frank The facsimile signature of a member of Congress used on envelopes in lieu of stamps for official outgoing mail.

Germane Pertaining to the subject matter of the measure at hand. All House amendments must be germane to the bill. The Senate requires that amendments be germane only when they are proposed to general appropriation bills, bills being considered under cloture, or, often, when proceeding under an agreement to limit debate.

Grants-in-Aid Payments by the federal government which aid the recipient state, local government or individual in administering specified programs, services, or activities.

Hearings Committee sessions for hearing witnesses. At hearings on legislation, witnesses usually include specialists, government officials and spokesmen for persons affected by the bills under study. Subpoena power may be used to summon reluctant witnesses. The public and press may attend "open" hearings but are barred from "closed" or "executive" hearings.

Hopper Box on House clerk's desk where bills are deposited on introduction.

House The House of Representatives, as distinct from the Senate, although each body is a "house" of Congress.

House Calendar Listing of public bills, other than appropriations or revenue measures, awaiting action by the House of Representatives.

Immunity Constitutional privilege protecting members of Congress from judicial actions concerning their legislative duties.

Joint Committee A committee composed of a specified number of members of both House and Senate. Usually a joint committee is investigative in nature. There are a few standing joint committees, such as the Joint Economic Committee and the Joint Committee on Taxation.

Joint Resolution A joint resolution, designated H. J. Res. or S.J. Res., requires the approval of both houses and the signature of the President, just as a bill does, and has the force of law if approved. There is no real difference between a bill and a joint resolution. The latter is generally used in dealing with limited matters, such as a single appropriation for a specific purpose.

Joint resolutions also are used to propose amendments to the Constitution. They do not require presidential signature, but become a part of the Constitution when three-fourths of the states have ratified them.

Journal The official record of the proceedings of the House and Senate. The Journal records the actions taken in each chamber, but unlike the *Congressional Record*, it does not include the verbatim report of speeches, debate, etc.

Law An act of Congress which has been signed by the President, or passed over his veto by the Congress. Laws are listed numerically by Congress; for example, the Civil Rights Act of 1964 (H.R. 7152) became Public Law 88—352 during the 88th Congress.

Legislative Day The "day" extending from the time either house meets after an adjournment until the time it next adjourns. Because the House normally adjourns from day to day, legislative days and calendar days usually coincide. But in the Senate, a legislative day may, and frequently does, extend over several calendar days. (*See* Recess.)

Lobby Any group seeking to influence the passage or defeat of legislation. Originally the term referred to persons frequenting the lobbies or corridors of legislative chambers in order to speak to lawmakers.

The right to attempt to influence legislation is based on the First Amendment to the Constitution which says Congress shall make no law abridging the right of the people "to petition the government for a redress of grievances."

Majority Leader Chief strategist and floor spokesman for the party in nominal control in either chamber. He is elected by his party colleagues.

Majority Whip In effect, the assistant majority leader, in the House or Senate. His job is to help marshal majority forces in support of party strategy.

Manual The official handbook in each house prescribing its organization, procedures, and operations in detail. The *House Manual* contains rules, orders, laws, and resolutions affecting House business; the *Senate Manual* is the equivalent for that chamber. Both volumes contain previous codes under which Congress functioned and from which it continues to derive precedents. Committee powers are outlined. The rules set forth in the manuals may be changed by elaborate chamber actions also specified by the manuals.

Marking up a Bill Going through a measure, usually in committee, taking it section by section, revising language, penciling in new phrases, etc. If the bill is extensively revised, the new version may be introduced as a separate bill, with a new number. (*See* Clean Bill.)

Memorial A request for congressional opposition or an objection from an organization or citizens' group to particular legislation or government practice under the purview of Congress. All communications, both supporting and opposing legislation, from state legislatures are embodied in memorials which are referred to appropriate committees.

Minority Leader Floor leader for the minority party. (*See* Majority Leader.)

Minority Whip Performs duties of whip for the minority party. (*See* Majority Whip.)

Morning Hour The time set aside at the beginning of each legislative day for the consideration of regular routine business. The *hour* is of indefinite duration in the House, where it is rarely used. In the Senate it is the first two hours of a session following an adjournment, but it can be terminated earlier if the morning business has been completed. This business includes such matters as messages from the President, communications from the heads of departments, messages from the House, the presentation of petitions and memorials, reports of standing and select committees, and the introduction of bills and resolutions.

During the first hour of the morning hour in the Senate, no motion to proceed to the consideration of any bill on the calendar is in order except by unanimous consent. During the second hour, motions can be made but must be decided without debate. Senate committees may meet while the Senate is in the morning hour.

Motion Request by a member of Congress for any one of a wide array of parliamentary actions. He *moves* for a certain procedure, or the consideration of a measure or a vote, etc. The precedence of motions, and whether they are debatable, is set forth in the House and Senate Manuals.

Nominations Appointments to office by the executive branch of the government, subject to Senate confirmation.

Notice Quorum Call In the Committee of the Whole House a notice quorum call may be made by the chairman when the point of order is made that a quorum is not present. If 100 members, which constitute a quorum in the Committee of the Whole House, appear within the specified time period, the notice quorum call is not recorded. If 100 members fail to appear, a regular quorum call, which is recorded, is made (*See* Quorum.)

Omnibus Claims Bill See Private Calendar.

One-Minute Speeches Addresses by House members at the beginning of a legislative day. The speeches may cover any subject, but are limited strictly to one minute's duration. By unanimous consent, members may also be recognized to address the House for longer periods after completion of all legislative business for the day. Senators, by unanimous consent, are permitted to make speeches of a predetermined length during "morning hour."

Override a Veto If the President disapproves a bill and sends it back to Congress with his objections, Congress may override his veto by a two-thirds vote in each chamber. The Constitution requires a yea-and-nay roll call. The question put to each house is: "Shall the bill pass, the objections of the President to the contrary notwithstanding?" (*See also* Pocket Veto *and* Veto.)

Pair Historically, a gentleman's agreement between two lawmakers on opposite sides to withhold their votes on roll calls so the absence of one from Congress will not affect the outcome of a recorded vote.

In the House, "live" and "general" pairs are used. When a vote is taken, the names of members paired are printed in the *Congressional Record* with a record of the vote. A "live" pair indicates how a member would have voted; a "general" pair gives no such indication.

Parliamentarian The officer charged with advising the presiding officer regarding questions of procedure.

Petition A request or plea sent to one or both chambers from an organization or private citizen's group asking support of particular legislation or favorable consideration of a matter not yet receiving congressional attention. Petitions are referred to appropriate committees for appropriate action. (*See* Memorial.)

Pocket Veto The act of the President in withholding his approval of a bill after Congress has adjourned—either for the year or for a specified period. However, the U. S. District Court of Appeals for the District of Columbia on August 14, 1974, upheld a congressional challenge to a pocket veto used by President Richard Nixon during a six-day congressional recess in 1970, declaring that it was an improper use of the pocket veto power. When Congress is in session, a bill becomes law without the President's signature if he does not act upon it within 10 days, excluding Sundays, from the time he gets it. But if Congress adjourns within that 10-day period, the bill is killed without the President's formal veto.

Point of Order An objection raised by a Member of Congress that the House is departing from rules governing its conduct of business. The objector cites the rule violated, the chair sustaining his objection if correctly made. Order is restored by the chair's suspending proceedings until it conforms to the prescribed "order of business." Members sometimes raise a "point of no order"—when there is noise and disorderly conduct in the chamber.

President of the Senate Presiding officer of the Senate, normally the Vice President of the United States. In his absence, a President *pro tempore* (president for the time being) presides.

President Pro Tempore The chief officer of the Senate in the absence of the Vice President. He is elected by his fellow senators. The recent practice has been to elect to the office the senator of the majority party with longest continuous service.

Previous Question In this sense, a "question" is an "issue" before the House for a vote and the issue is "previous" when some other topic has superseded it in the attention of the chamber. A motion for the previous question, when carried, has the effect of cutting off all debate and forcing a vote on the subject originally at hand. If, however, the previous question is moved and carried before there has been any debate on the subject at hand and the subject is debatable, then 40 minutes of debate is allowed before the vote. The previous question is sometimes moved in order to prevent amendments from being introduced and voted on. The motion for the previous question is a debate-limiting device and is not in order in the Senate.

Private Calendar Private House bills dealing with individual matters such as claims against the government, immigration, land titles, etc., are put on this calendar. Two members may block consideration of a private bill in the chamber. If blocked, it is then recommitted to committee. An "omnibus claims bill" is several private bills considered as one. As with any bill, no part of an omnibus claims bill may be deleted without a vote. When a private bill goes to the floor in this form, it can be defeated only by a majority of those present. The private calendar can be called on the first and third Tuesdays of each month.

Privilege Privilege relates to the rights of members of Congress and to the relative priority of the motions and actions they may make in their respective chambers. The two are distinct. "Privileged questions" concern legislative business. "Questions of privilege" concern legislators themselves. (*See below.*)

Privileged Questions The order in which bills, motions, and other legislative measures may be considered by Congress is governed by strict priorities. For instance, a motion to recommit can be superseded by a motion to table, and a vote would be forced on the latter motion only. A motion to adjourn, however, would take precedence over this one, and is thus considered of the "highest privilege."

Pro Forma Amendment *See* Strike out the Last Word.

Questions of Privilege These are matters affecting members of Congress individually or collectively.

Questions affecting the rights, safety, dignity, and integrity of proceedings of the

House or Senate as a whole are questions of privilege of the House or Senate, as the case may be.

Questions of "personal privilege" relate to individual members of Congress. A member's rising to a question of personal privilege is given precedence over almost all other proceedings. An annotation in the House rules points out that the privilege of the member rests primarily on the Constitution, which gives him a conditional immunity from arrest and an unconditional freedom to speak in the House.

Quorum The number of members whose presence is necessary for the transaction of business. In the Senate and House, it is a majority of the membership (when there are no vacancies, this is 51 in the Senate and 218 in the House). A quorum is 100 in the Committee of the Whole House. If a point of order is made that a quorum is not present, the only business in order is either a motion to adjourn or a motion to direct the Sergeant at Arms to request the attendance of absentees or a quorum call indicating the presence of a sufficient number of members.

Reading of Bills Traditional parliamentary law required bills to be read three times before they were passed. This custom is of little modern significance except in rare instances. Normally the bill is considered to have its first reading when it is introduced and printed, by title, in the *Congressional Record*. Its second reading comes when floor consideration begins and may be an actual reading of the bill. The third reading (usually by title) takes place when action has been completed on amendments.

Recess Distinguished from adjournment, a recess does not end a legislative day and therefore does not interfere with unfinished business. The rules in each house set forth certain matters to be taken up and disposed of at the beginning of each legislative day. The House usually adjourns from day to day. The Senate often recesses.

Recommit to Committee A simple motion, made on the floor after deliberation on a bill, to return it to the committee which reported it. If approved, recommittal usually is considered a death blow to the bill. A motion to recommit may include instructions to the committee to report the bill again with specific amendments or by a certain date. Or the instructions may be to make a particular study, with no definite deadline for final action.

Reconsider a Vote A motion to reconsider the vote by which an action was taken has, until it is disposed of, the effect of suspending the action. In the Senate the motion can be made only by a member who voted on the prevailing side of the original question, or by a member who did not vote at all. In the House it can be made only by a member on the prevailing side.

A common practice after close votes in the Senate is a motion to reconsider, followed by a motion to table the motion to reconsider. On this motion to table, Senators vote as they voted on the original question, to enable the motion to table to prevail. The matter is then finally closed and further motions to reconsider are not entertained. In the House, as a routine precaution, a motion to reconsider usually is made every time a measure is passed. Such a motion almost always is tabled immediately.

Motions to reconsider must be entered in the Senate within the next two days of actual session after the original vote has been taken. In the House, they must be entered either on the same day or on the next succeeding day the House is in session.

Recorded Vote A vote upon which each member's stand is individually made known. In the Senate, this is accomplished through a roll call of the entire membership, to which each senator on the floor must answer "yea," "nay," or, if he does not wish to vote, "present." Since January 1973, the House has used an electronic voting system both for yeas and nays and other recorded votes. (*See* Teller Vote.)

The Constitution requires yea-and-nay votes on the question of overriding a veto. In other cases, a recorded vote can be obtained by the demand of one-fifth of the members present.

Report Both a verb and a noun, as a congressional term. A committee which has been examining a bill referred to it "reports" its findings and recommendations to the whole body when the committee returns the measure. The process is called "reporting" a bill.

A "report" is the document setting forth the committee's explanation of its action. House and Senate reports are numbered separately and are designated S. Rept. or H. Rept. Conference reports are numbers and designated in the same way as regular committee reports.

Most reports favor a bill's passage. Adverse reports are occasionally submitted, but more often, when a committee disapproves a bill, it simply fails to report it at all. When a committee report is not unanimous, the dissenting committeemen may file a statement of their views, called miniority views and referred to as a minority report. Sometimes a bill is reported without recommendation.

Rescission An item in an appropriation bill rescinding, or cancelling, funds previously appropriated but not spent. Also, the repeal of a previous appropriation by the President to cut spending, if approved by Congress under procedures in the Budget and Impoundment Control Act of 1974.

Resolution A simple resolution, designated H. Res. or S. Res., deals with matters entirely within the prerogatives of one house or the other. It requires neither passage by the other chamber nor approval by the President, and does not have the force of law. Most resolutions deal with the rules of one house. They also are used to express the sentiments of a single house, as condolences to the family of a deceased member or to give "advice" on foreign policy or other executive branch business. (*See also* Concurrent *and* Joint Resolutions.)

Rider A provision, usually not germane, which its sponsor hopes to have approved more easily by tacking it on to other legislation. Riders become law if the bills in which they are included become law. Riders providing for legislation in appropriation bills are outstanding examples, though technically they are banned. The House, unlike the Senate, has a strict germaneness rule; thus riders are usually Senate devices.

Rule The term has two specific congressional meanings. A rule may be a standing order governing the conduct of House or Senate business and listed in the chamber's book of rules. The rules deal with duties of officers, order of business, admission to the floor, voting procedures, etc.

In the House, a rule also may be a decision made by its Rules Committee about the handling of a particular bill on the floor. The committee may determine under which standing rule a bill shall be considered, or it may provide a "specific rule" in the form of a resolution. If the resolution is adopted by the House, the temporary rule becomes as valid as any standing rule.

A special rule sets the time limit on general debate. It may also waive points of order against provisions of the bill in question or against specified amendments intended to be proposed to the bill. It may even forbid all amendments or all amendments except, in some cases, those proposed by the legislative committee which handled the bill. In this instance it is known as a "closed" or "gag" rule as opposed to an "open" rule which puts no limitation on floor amendments. (*See* Suspend the Rules.)

Secretary of the Senate Chief administrative office of the Senate, responsible for direction of duties of Senate employees, education of pages, administration of oaths, receipt of registration of lobbyists, and other activities necessary for the continuing operation of the Senate.

Select or Special Committee A committee set up for a special purpose and a limited time by resolution of either House or Senate. Most special committees are investigative in nature.

Senatorial Courtesy Sometimes referred to as "the courtesy of the Senate," it is a general practice without written rule applied to consideration of executive nominations. In practice, generally it means nominations from a state are not to be confirmed unless they have been approved by the senators of the President's party of that state, with other senators following their lead in the attitude they take toward such nominations.

Sergeant at Arms The officer charged with maintaining order in the chamber, under the direction of the speaker or presiding officer.

Session of Congress Each Congress is composed of two sessions. A new session of Congress begins each January 3 at noon and continues until adjourned "sine die." (*See* Adjournment Sine Die.)

Sine Die *See* Adjournment Sine Die.

Slip Laws The first official publication of a bill that has been enacted into law. Each is published separately in unbound, single-sheet, or pamphlet form. Slip laws usually become available two or three days after the date of presidential approval.

Speaker The presiding officer of the House of Representatives, elected by its members.

Special Session A session of Congress which takes place after Congress has adjourned sine die. Special sessions are convened by the President of the United States under his constitutional powers.

Stand A lawmaker's position, for or against, on a given issue or vote. He can make known his stand on a roll-call vote by answering "yea" or "nay," by "pairing" for or against, or by "announcing" his position to the House or Senate. (*See* Pair, *and* Recorded Vote *above. See also* Teller Vote *below.*)

Standing Committees A group permanently provided for by House and Senate rules. The standing committees of the House were last reorganized by the Committee Reorganization Act of 1974. Senate committees were reorganized in the Legislative Reorganization Act of 1946 and by a special resolution in 1977.

Standing Vote A nonrecorded vote used in both House and Senate. A standing vote, also called a division vote, is taken as follows: Members in favor of a proposal stand and are counted by the presiding officer; then members opposed stand are counted. There is no record of how individual members voted. In the House, the presiding officer announces the number for and against. In the Senate, usually only the result is announced.

Statutes-at-Large A chronological arrangement of the laws enacted in each session of Congress. Though indexed, the laws are not arranged by subject matter nor is there an indication of how they affect previous law. (*See* U.S. Code.)

Strike from the Record Remarks made on the House floor may offend some member, who moves that the offending words be "taken down" for the speaker's cognizance, and then expunged from the verbatim report carried in the *Congressional Record*.

Strike out the Last Word A motion by which House members are entitled to speak for a fixed time on a measure then being debated by the chamber. A member gains recognition from the chair by moving to strike out the last word of the amendment or section of the bill then under consideration. The motion is pro forma, and customarily requires no vote.

Substitute A motion, an amendment, or an entire bill introduced in place of pending business. Passage of a substitute measure kills the original measure by supplanting it. A substitute may be amended.

Supplemental Appropriations An appropriation to cover the difference between an agency's regular appropriation and the amount deemed necessary for it to operate for the full fiscal year.

Suspend the Rules Often a time-saving procedure for passing bills in the House. The wording of the motion, which may be made by any member recognized by the speaker, is: "I move to suspend the rules and pass the bill. . . ." A favorable vote by two-thirds of those present is required for passage. Debate is limited to 40 minutes and no amendments from the floor are permitted. If a two-thirds favorable vote is not attained, the bill may be considered later under regular procedures. The suspension procedure is in order on the first and third Mondays and Tuesdays of each month.

Table a Bill The motion to "lay on the table" is not debatable in either house, and is usually a method of making a final, adverse disposition of a matter. In the Senate, however, different language is sometimes used. The motion is worded to let a bill "lie on the table," perhaps for subsequent "picking up." This motion is more flexible, merely keeping the bill pending for later action, if desired.

Teller Vote In the House, members file past tellers and are counted as for or against a measure, but they are not recorded individually. The teller vote is not used in the Senate. In the House, tellers are ordered upon demand of one-fifth of a quorum. This is 44 in the House, 20 in the Committee of the Whole.

The House also has a recorded teller vote procedure, introduced in 1971 (now largely supplanted by electronic voting), under which the individual votes of members are made public just as they would be on a yea-and-nay vote. (*See* Recorded Vote.)

Treaties Executive branch proposals which must be submitted to the Senate for approval by two-thirds of the Senators present. Before acting on such foreign policy matters, senators usually send them to committee for scrutiny. Treaties are read three times and debated in the chamber much as are legislative proposals, but are rarely amended. After approval by the Senate, they are ratified by the President.

Unanimous Consent *See* Without Objection.

Union Calendar Bills that directly or indirectly appropriate money or raise revenue are placed on this House calendar chronologically according to the date reported from committee.

U. S. Code A consolidation and codification of the general and permanent laws of the United States arranged by subject under 50 titles, the first six dealing with general or political subjects, and the other 44 alphabetically arranged from "agriculture" to "war and national defense." The code is now revised every six years and a supplement is published after each session of Congress.

Veto Disapproval by the President of a bill or joint resolution, other than one proposing an amendment to the Constitution. When Congress is in session, the President must veto a bill within 10 days, excluding Sundays, after he has received it; otherwise it becomes law with or without his signature. When the President vetoes a bill, he returns it to the House of its origin with a message stating his objections. The veto then becomes a question of high privilege. (*See* Override a Veto.)

When Congress has adjourned, the President may pocket veto a bill by failing to sign it. (*See* Pocket Veto.)

Voice Vote In either House or Senate, members answer "aye" or "no" in chorus and the presiding officer decides the result. The term also is used loosely to indicate action by unanimous consent or without objection.

Whip *See* Majority Whip.

Without Objection Used in lieu of a vote on noncontroversial measures. If no member voices an objection, motions, amendments or bills are thus passed in either the House or the Senate.

Endnotes and References

Reading 1.1

1. Taken from James Madison's notes at the Constitutional Convention as recorded in Tansill, 1927:120. Emphasis was Madison's.
2. The quotations are taken from the Modern Library edition of *The Federalist*, in the following sequence: pp. 244, 313, 338, 323, 330, 338, 338, 337.
3. These categories benefit from the discussion in Davidson et al., 1966, Chapter 1. They propose three theories–literary ("a restatement of the constitutional formulation of blended and coordinate powers"), executive-force ("the executive initiates and implements; the legislature modifies and ratifies"), and party-government ("not a theory about Congress . . . but rather a proposal to reconstruct the American party system").
4. Quoted in de Tocqueville, 1945:270. This incredibly prescient statement was first brought to my attention in Schlesinger, 1973:377.
5. By 1900 Wilson had already expressed doubts that Congress was predominant. See the preface to the 15th edition of *Congressional Government.*
6. The voters have shown a propensity in recent years to split their tickets. Between 1947 and 1981, the Congress and the White House were controlled by different parties nearly half of the time (16 of 34 years). In the 1980 elections another variation was introduced: a Republican President and Senate, a Democratic House of Representatives.

References

American Political Science Association, Committee on Political Parties. 1950. "Toward a More Responsible Two-Party System." *American Political Science Review* 44:1–99.

Burnett, Edmund Cody. 1964. *The Continental Congress.* New York: W. W. Norton.

Bryce, James. 1915. *The American Commonwealth.* New York: Macmillan.

Dahl, Robert A. and Charles E. Lindblom. 1953. *Politics, Economics, and Welfare.* New York: Harper Torchbooks.

Hyneman, Charles S., and George W. Carey., eds. 1967. *A Second Federalist.* New York: Appleton-Century-Crofts.

Keefe, William J. 1980. *Congress and the American People.* Englewood Cliffs, N.J.: Prentice-Hall.

Kelly, Alfred H., and Winfred A. Harbison. 1948. *The American Constitution: Its Origins and Development.* New York: W. W. Norton.

King, Anthony, ed. 1978. *The New American Political System.* Washington, D.C.: American Enterprise Institute.

Schlesinger, Arthur Jr. 1973. *The Imperial Presidency.* Boston: Houghton Mifflin.

Tansill, Charles C., ed. 1927. *Formation of the Union of the American States.* Washington, D.C.: U.S. Government Printing Office.

de Tocqueville, Alexis. 1945. *Democracy in America.* New York: Alfred A. Knopf.

Wilson, Woodrow. 1913. *Congressional Government.* Boston: Houghton Mifflin.

Reading 1.2

1. U.S. Congress, Joint Committee on the Organization of the Congress, *Hearings,* part 3 (Washington, D.C.: Government Printing Office, 1945), pp. 670–71.
2. Two useful examples are Aaron Wildavsky, *The Politics of the Budgetary Process* (Boston: Little, Brown, 1964); and Samuel Huntington, *The Common Defense* (New York: Columbia University Press, 1961), esp. pp. 123–46.
3. Ralph K. Huitt, "What Can We Do about Congress?" *Milwaukee Journal,* part 5 (December 13, 1964), p. 1.
4. See Ralph K. Huitt, "Congressional Reorganization: The Next Chapter." Paper presented at the annual meeting of the American Political Science Association, Chicago, Illinois, September 8–12, 1964.

Reading 1.3

The author thanks Kenneth Janda and Judy Schneider for their comments and assistance.

1. See Burdett A. Loomis, "The 'Me Decade'

and the Changing Context of House Leadership," in Frank H. Mackaman, ed., *Understanding Congressional Leadership* (Washington, D.C.: CQ Press, 1981), pp. 168–69; William Greider and Barry Sussman, *Washington Post,* June 29, 1975; Daniel Rapoport, "Congress Report: It's Not a Happy Time for House, Senate Leadership," *National Journal,* vol. 8 (February 7, 1976), p. 171; Adam Clymer, "Leadership Gap in the Senate," *New York Times,* September 28, 1977; and Robert G. Kaiser, "Majority Leader Byrd Has Made Converts in 2 Years," *Washington Post,* October 28, 1978. On various leaders' views, see Mary Russell, *Washington Post,* March 31, 1974; Steven S. Smith and Christopher J. Deering, *Committees in Congress* (Washington, D.C.: CQ Press, 1984), p. 252; and Robert L. Peabody, "Senate Party Leadership: From the 1950s to the 1980s," in Mackaman, *Understanding Congressional Leadership,* pp. 71–72, 109.

2. Joseph Cooper, "The Origins of the Standing Committees and the Development of the Modern House," *Rice University Studies,* vol. 56 (Summer 1970), pp. 17–22; Ralph V. Harlow, *The History of Legislative Methods in the Period before 1825* (New Haven, Conn.: Yale University Press, 1917); and Lee Robinson, "The Development of the Senate Committee System" (Ph.D. dissertation, New York University, 1954).
3. The argument for this model of legislative decisionmaking was stated most recently by Arthur Maass, in *Congress and the Common Good* (New York: Basic Books, 1984).
4. Donald R. Matthews, *U. S. Senators and Their World* (Durham: University of North Carolina Press, 1960), Chap. 5.
5. See David J. Rothman, *Politics and Power: The United States Senate 1869–1901* (New York: Atheneum, 1969), Chaps. 1, 2.
6. See Richard F. Fenno, Jr., *The United States Senate: A Bicameral Perspective* (Washington, D.C.: American Enterprise Institute, 1982); and Lewis A. Froman, Jr., *The Congressional Process: Strategies, Rules, and Procedures* (Boston: Little, Brown, 1967), pp. 7–8.
7. See Norman J. Ornstein, "The House and the Senate in a New Congress," in Thomas E. Mann and Norman J. Ornstein, eds., *The New Congress* (Washington, D.C.: American Enterprise Institute, 1981), pp. 363–83; and Smith and Deering, *Committees in Congress,* Chap. 1.
8. Lawrence C. Dodd, "Congress and the Quest for Power," in Lawrence C. Dodd and Bruce I. Oppenheimer, eds., *Congress Reconsidered* (New York: Praeger, 1977), pp. 270–72; and Rochelle Jones and Peter Woll, *The Private World of Congress* (New York: Free Press, 1979), Chaps. 3, 6.
9. This is Fenno's conclusion about decisionmaking processes within congressional committees. See Richard F. Fenno, *Congressmen in Committees* (Boston: Little, Brown, 1973).
10. See Michael Foley, *The New Senate* (New Haven, Conn.: Yale University Press, 1980), especially Chap. 4.
11. Norman J. Ornstein, Robert L. Peabody, and David W. Rohde, "The Senate through the 1980s: Cycles of Change," in Lawrence C. Dodd and Bruce I. Oppenheimer, eds., *Congress Reconsidered,* 3d ed. (Washington, D.C.: CQ Press, 1985), p. 18.
12. Richard E. Cohen, "Strains Appear as 'New Breed' Democrats Move to Control Party in the House," *National Journal,* vol. 15 (June 25, 1983), p. 1328.
13. James L. Sundquist, *The Decline and Resurgence of Congress* (Washington, D.C.: Brookings, 1981), p. 371.
14. Randall B. Ripley and Grace A. Franklin, *Congress, the Bureaucracy and Public Policy,* 3d ed. (Homewood, Ill.: Dorsey, 1980), Chap. 8.
15. See Roger H. Davidson, "Two Avenues of Change: House and Senate Committee Reorganization," in Lawrence C. Dodd and Bruce I. Oppenheimer, eds., *Congress Reconsidered,* 2d ed. (Washington, D.C.: CQ Press, 1981), pp. 103–37; and Roger H. Davidson and Walter J. Oleszek, "Adaptation and Consolidation: Structural Innovation in the U.S. House of Representatives," *Legislative Studies Quarterly,* vol. 1 (February 1976), pp. 37–65.
16. Roger H. Davidson and Walter J. Oleszek, *Congress against Itself* (Bloomington: Indiana University Press, 1977), p. 263.
17. That overlapping jurisdictions continue to be a problem for the House was most evident in the House reaction to the 1983 scandals in the Environmental Protection Agency. Five separate subcommittees from four different committees stumbled over each other to investigate allegations of mismanagement and political manipulation of agency decisions, eventually forcing Speaker O'Neill to intervene. Despite appeals from the speaker, the subcommittee chairmen refused to coordinate their activities. See Jo-

seph A. Davis, "House Subcommittees Begin Reviewing EPA Documents: Two More Officials Are Fired," *Congressional Quarterly Weekly Report,* vol. 41 (February 26, 1983), pp. 411–13; and Howard Kurtz, "Levitas Pact on EPA Documents Faulted by Panel Chairman," *Washington Post,* February 20, 1983.

18. Academic observers have commented that there may be an ideal mix of centralization and decentralization, labeling the mix "integrated specialization" or "channeled expressiveness." See Charles O. Jones, "House Leadership in an Age of Reform," in Mackaman, *Understanding Congressional Leadership,* p. 122; and Allen Schick, "Complex Policymaking in the United States Senate," in *Policy Analysis on Major Issues,* prepared for the Commission on the Operation of the Senate, 94th Cong. 2d sess. (Washington, D.C.: U.S. Government Printing Office, 1977), p. 21.
19. Charles O. Jones comes to a similar conclusion, although Jones prefers to view the reforms as opportunities for expression rather than participation. See Jones, "House Leadership in an Age of Reform," p. 131.
20. It should also be noted that House Republicans rejuvenated their caucus in the mid-1960s. Gerald Ford promised a more active Republican conference when he became its chairman in 1963. The conference was not used as planned, however, although it established a staff and became more active after Melvin Laird took the chairmanship in 1965. See Charles O. Jones, *The Minority Party in Congress* (Boston: Little, Brown, 1970), p. 36; and Randall B. Ripley, *Party Leaders in the House of Representatives* (Washington, D.C.: Brookings, 1967), p. 46.
21. See Smith and Deering, *Committees in Congress,* Chap. 6.
22. Ibid., Chaps. 6, 7.
23. See Bruce F. Freed, "House Democrats Dispute over Caucus Role," *Congressional Quarterly Weekly Report,* vol. 33 (May 3, 1975), pp. 911–15.
24. On the use of the caucus, see Sundquist, *Decline and Resurgence of Congress,* pp. 383–87.
25. Ann Cooper, "Democrats Still Arguing over Party Caucus Role on Legislative Issues," *Congressional Quarterly Weekly Report,* vol. 36 (April 15, 1978), pp. 875–76.
26. Smith and Deering, *Committees in Congress,* p. 196.
27. See Peabody, "Senate Party Leadership." Also see John G. Stewart, "Two Strategies of Leadership: Johnson and Mansfield," in Nelson W. Polsby, ed., *Congressional Behavior* (New York: Random House, 1971), pp. 61–92; Randall B. Ripley, *Power in the Senate* (New York: St. Martin's Press, 1969), pp. 91–96; and Andrew J. Glass, "Mansfield Reforms Spark 'Quiet Revolution' in Senate," *National Journal,* vol. 3 (March 6, 1971), p. 500.
28. David W. Rohde, Norman J. Ornstein, and Robert L. Peabody, "Political Change and Legislative Norms in the U.S. Senate, 1957–1974," in Glenn R. Parker, ed., *Studies of Congress* (Washington, D.C.: CQ Press, 1985), pp. 175–79.
29. Fenno, *Congressmen in Committees,* p. 182.
30. The four committees are Appropriations, Armed Services, Finance, and Foreign Relations. This rule formalized the "Johnson rule" initiated by Democratic Majority Leader Lyndon Johnson in the 1950s and adopted by the Republicans soon thereafter.
31. See Ripley, *Power in the Senate,* pp. 91–96; Rohde, Ornstein, and Peabody, "Political Change and Legislative Norms," pp. 163–65; and Stewart, "Two Strategies of Leadership," p. 69.
32. On the significance of the scope of conflict, see E. E. Schattschneider, *The Semisovereign People* (Hinsdale, Ill.: Dryden Press, 1960), Chap. 1.
33. See, for example, Alan Ehrenhalt, "In the Senate of the '80s, Team Spirit Has Given Way to the Rule of Individuals," *Congressional Quarterly Weekly Report,* vol. 40 (September 4, 1982), pp. 2175–82; Burdett Loomis, "Congressional Caucuses and the Politics of Representation," in Dodd and Oppenheimer, *Congress Reconsidered,* 2d ed., pp. 204–20; Ornstein, "The House and Senate in a New Congress"; Norman J. Ornstein, Robert L. Peabody, and David W. Rohde, "The Contemporary Senate into the 1980s," in Dodd and Oppenheimer, *Congress Reconsidered,* 2d ed., pp. 13–30; Barbara Sinclair, *Majority Leadership in the U.S. House* (Baltimore: Johns Hopkins University Press, 1983), Chap. 1; and Tim Cook, "Marketing the Members: The Ascent of the Congressional Press Secretary," paper prepared for the 1985 annual meeting of the Midwest Political Science Association.
34. Bruce I. Oppenheimer has labeled this the "new obstructionism." See his "Congress and the New Obstructionism," in Dodd and

Oppenheimer, *Congress Reconsidered,* 2d ed., pp. 275–95.
35. See Smith and Deering, *Committees in Congress,* Chap. 5.
36. Sundquist, *Decline and Resurgence of Congress,* p. 395.
37. Sinclair emphasizes this theme in *Majority Leadership in the House.*
38. Two aides of Senate Majority Leader Howard Baker have provided an account of Baker's role. See James A. Miller and James D. Range, "Reconciling an Irreconcilable Budget: The New Politics of the Budget Process," *Harvard Journal on Legislation,* vol. 20 (Winter 1983), pp. 4–30.
39. See Norman J. Ornstein, "The Open Congress Meets the President," in Anthony King, ed., *Both Ends of the Avenue* (Washington, D.C.: American Enterprise Institute, 1983), pp. 204–10.
40. The term is Senator Quayle's. See Martin Tolchin, "The Changing Senate: Senators Assail Anarchy in New Chamber of Equals," *New York Times,* November 25, 1984.
41. Confidential interview with the author, December 6, 1984. The proposal was considered by the Committee on Organization, Study, and Review of the Democratic caucus in November 1984.
42. Diane Granat, "Junior Democrats Gain a Louder Voice; Leadership Panels Will Serve as Forum," *Congressional Quarterly Weekly Report,* vol. 42 (December 8, 1984), p. 3054.
43. Confidential interview with the author, January 31, 1985.
44. Cohen, "Strains Appear as 'New Breed' Democrats Move to Control Party," p. 1330.
45. Quoted in Diane Granat, "House Democrats Expand Leadership: Wright Claims Speaker's Job; Race On for Majority Leader," *Congressional Quarterly Weekly Report,* vol. 43 (February 9, 1985), p. 283.
46. The adopted rule reduced the number of slots on the twelve major committees and exempted eleven senators from the limit of two major committee assignments, primarily to satisfy the committee party ratios that party leaders had agreed to earlier. Jacqueline Calmes and Diane Granat, "Senate Cuts Committee Slots, Members Assigned to Panels," *Congressional Quarterly Weekly Report,* vol. 43 (February 23, 1985), pp. 348–64.
47. In 1982 the House Democratic caucus adopted a rule that provides that, except for Appropriations, standing committees are limited to eight subcommittees; committees with more than thirty-five members and fewer than six subcommittees may increase the number to six or, with the approval of the Steering and Policy Committee, may have seven. Two committees were forced to abolish subcommittees to meet the limit at that time.
48. Bruce I. Oppenheimer, "Changing Time Constraints on Congress: Historical Perspectives on the Use of Cloture," in Dodd and Oppenheimer, eds., *Congress Reconsidered,* 3d ed., p. 398.
49. See Walter J. Oleszek, *Congressional Procedures and the Policy Process,* 2d ed. (Washington, D.C.: CQ Press, 1984), pp. 186–93.
50. For Baker's announcement, see *Congressional Record,* daily edition (December 6, 1982), p. S13901.
51. Quoted in Steven V. Roberts, "Panel Proposes Sweeping Changes in Senate Rules," *New York Times,* November 30, 1984.
52. Quoted in "How Senators View the Senate: What Has Changed and What It Means," *New York Times,* November 25, 1984.

Reading 2.1

1. Note, too, that coattails were not the issue here. While Eisenhower's 1956 margin of victory exceeded Kennedy's 1960 margin, Eisenhower did not provide very long coattails in his win. Therefore, the difference between 1958 and 1962 cannot be passed off simply as a larger "surge" corresponding with a larger "decline."
2. Bloom and Price (1975) argue similarly that the President's party is punished during recessionary periods, but not rewarded for periods of prosperity.
3. Born argues that the measurement of coattails has been a major flaw of previous work and is the reason why he finds substantial effects where others have found insignificance.

References

Abramowitz, A. I. 1975. "Name Familiarity, Reputation, and the Incumbency Effect in a Congressional Election." *Western Political Quarterly* 28:668–84.

———. 1980. "A Comparison of Voting for U. S. Senator and Representative." *American Political Science Review* 74:633–40.

———. 1983. "Partisan Redistricting and the 1982 Congressional Elections." *Journal of Politics* 45:767–70.

_______. 1985. "Economic Conditions, Presidential Popularity, and Voting Behavior in Midterm Congressional Elections." *Journal of Politics* 47:31–43.

Abramowitz, A. I., A. Cover, and H. Norpoth 1985. "The President's Party in Midterm Elections: Going From Bad to Worse." *American Journal of Political Science.* Forthcoming.

Abramowitz, A. I. and J. A. Segal 1985. "Determinants of the Outcomes of U. S. Senate Elections." SUNY—Stony Brook. Unpublished manuscript.

Bloom, H. S. and H. D. Price 1975. "Voter Response to Short-Run Economic Conditions: The Asymmetric Effect of Prosperity and Recession." *American Political Science Review* 69:1240–54.

Bond, J. R., C. Covington, and R. Fleisher 1985. "Explaining Challenger Quality in Congressional Elections." *Journal of Politics* 47: 510–29.

Born, R. 1984. "Reassessing the Decline in Presidential Coattails: U.S. House Elections From 1952–1980." *Journal of Politics* 46:60–79.

_______. 1985. "Partisan Intentions and Election Day Realities in the Congressional Redistricting Process." *American Political Science Review* 79:305–19.

Cain, B. E. 1985. "Assessing the Partisan Effects of Redistricting." *American Political Science Review* 79:320–33.

Caldeira, G. A., S. C. Patterson, and G. A. Markho 1985. "The Mobilization of Voters in Congressional Elections." *Journal of Politics* 47:490–509.

Calvert, R. L. and J. A. Ferejohn 1983. "Coattail Voting in Recent Presidential Elections." *American Political Science Review* 77: 407–19.

Campbell, A. 1966. "Surge and Decline: A Study of Electoral Change" in *Elections and the Political Order,* eds. A. Campbell, P. E. Converse, W. E. Miller, and D. E. Stokes. New York: John Wiley & Sons.

Cover, A. 1977. "One Good Term Deserves Another: The Advantage of Incumbency in Congressional Elections." *American Journal of Political Science* 21:523–42.

Cover, A. and B. S. Brumberg 1982. "Baby Books and Ballots: The Impact of Congressional Mail on Constituent Opinion." *American Political Science Review* 76:347–59.

Cover, A. and D. Mayhew 1981. "Congressional Dynamics and the Decline of Competitive Congressional Elections," in *Congress Reconsidered.* eds. L. Dodd and B. Oppenheimer, 2d ed. Washington, D.C.: Congressional Quarterly Press.

Feldman, S. 1982. "Economic Self-Interest and Political Behavior." *American Journal of Political Science* 26:446–66.

Fenno, R. 1982. *The United States Senate: A Bicameral Perspective.* Washington, D.C.: American Enterprise Institute.

Fiorina, M. P. 1977. *Congress: Keystone of the Washington Establishment.* New Haven: Yale University Press.

_______. 1978. "Economic Retrospective Voting in American National Elections: A Micro Analysis." *American Journal of Political Science* 22:426–43.

Fishel, J. 1973. *Party and Opposition: Congressional Challengers in American Politics.* New York: David McKay.

Glantz, S., M. Burkart, and A. Abramowitz 1976. "Election Outcomes: Whose Money Matters." *Journal of Politics* 38:1033–41.

Goldenberg, E. N. and M. W. Traugott 1984. *Campaigning for Congress.* Washington, D.C.: Congressional Quarterly Press.

Gopoian, J. D. and D. M. West 1984. "Trading Security for Seats: Strategic Considerations in the Redistricting Process." *Journal of Politics* 46:1080–96.

Hibbing, J. R. and J. R. Alford 1981. "The Electoral Impact of Economic Conditions: Who Is Held Responsible?" *American Journal of Political Science* 25:423–39.

Hinckley, B. 1980. "The American Voter in Congressional Elections." *American Political Science Review* 74:641–50.

_______. 1981. *Congressional Elections.* Washington, D.C.: Congressional Quarterly Press.

Hunt, A. R. 1983. "National Politics and the 1982 Campaign," in *The American Elections of 1982.* eds. T. E. Mann and N. J. Ornstein. Washington, D.C.: American Enterprise Institute.

Hurley, P. A. and K. Q. Hill 1980. "The Prospects for Issue Voting in Contemporary Congressional Elections: An Assessment of Citizen Awareness and Representation." *American Politics Quarterly* 8:425–49.

Jacobson, G. C. 1978. "The Effects of Campaign Spending in Congressional Elections." *American Political Science Review* 72: 469–91.

———. 1983a. *The Politics of Congressional Elections.* Boston: Little, Brown.

———. 1983b. "Reagan, Reaganomics, and Strategic Politics in 1982: A Test of Alternative Theories of Midterm Congressional Elections." Paper presented at the 1983 meeting of the American Political Science Association, Chicago, Illinois.

Jacobson, G. C. and S. Kernell 1981. *Strategy and Choice in Congressional Elections.* New Haven: Yale University Press.

Kernell, S. 1977. "Presidential Popularity and Negative Voting: An Alternative Explanation of the Midterm Congressional Decline of the President's Party." *American Political Science Review* 71:44–66.

Kinder, D. R. and D. R. Kiewiet 1979. "Economic Grievances and Political Behavior: The Role of Personal Discontents and Collective Judgments in Congressional Voting." *American Journal of Political Science* 23:495–527.

Kramer, G. H. 1971. "Short-Term Fluctuations in U. S. Voting Behavior, 1896–1964." *American Political Science Review* 65:131–43.

Lanoue, D. J. 1985. "Modelling Presidential Popularity: Do Real Disposable Income Levels Matter?" Paper presented at the 1985 meeting of the Midwest Political Science Association, Chicago, Illinois.

Maisel, L. S. 1982. *From Obscurity to Oblivion: Congressional Primary Elections in 1978.* Knoxville, Tenn.: University of Tennessee Press.

Mann, T. E. 1978. *Unsafe at Any Margin.* Washington, D.C.: American Enterprise Institute.

Mann, T. E. and N. J. Ornstein. 1983. "Sending a Message: Voters and Congress in 1982." in *The American Elections of 1982.* eds. T. E. Mann and N. J. Ornstein. Washington, D.C.: American Enterprise Institute.

Mann, T. E. and R. E. Wolfinger 1980. "Candidates and Parties in Congressional Elections." *American Political Science Review* 74:617–32.

Mayhew, D. R. 1974. *Congress: The Electoral Connection.* New Haven: Yale University Press.

Miller, W. E., A. H. Miller, and E. J. Schneider. 1980. *American National Election Studies Data Sourcebook, 1952–1978.* Cambridge, Mass. and London: Harvard University Press.

Miller, W. E. and D. E. Stokes. 1963. "Constituency Influence in Congress." *American Political Science Review* 57:45–57.

Mueller, J. E. 1970. "Presidential Popularity from Truman to Johnson." *American Political Science Review* 64:18–34.

———. 1973. *War, Presidents, and Public Opinion.* New York: John Wiley & Sons.

Norpoth, H. 1984. "Economics, Politics, and the Cycle of Presidential Popularity." *Political Behavior* 6:253–73.

Owens, J. and E. Olson. 1980. "Economic Fluctuations and Congressional Elections." *American Journal of Political Science* 24:469–93.

Parker, G. R. 1980. "The Advantage of Incumbency in House Elections." *American Politics Quarterly* 8:449–64.

Polsby, N. 1968. "The Institutionalization of the U.S. House of Representatives." *American Political Science Review* 62:144–68.

Ragsdale, L. 1980. "The Fiction of Congressional Elections as Presidential Events." *American Politics Quarterly* 8:375–98.

Squire, P. 1985. "Results of Partisan Redistricting in Seven U. S. States during the 1970s." *Legislative Studies Quarterly* 10:259–66.

Tidmarch, C. M., L. J. Hyman, and J. E. Sorkin 1984. "Press Issue Agendas in the 1982 Congressional and Gubernatorial Election Campaigns." *Journal of Politics* 46:1226–42.

Tufte, E. R. 1975. "Determinants of the Outcomes of Midterm Congressional Elections." *American Political Science Review* 69: 812–26.

———. 1978. *Political Control of the Economy.* Princeton, N.J.: Princeton University Press.

Uslaner, E. and M. M. Conway. 1985. "The Responsible Congressional Electorate: Watergate, the Economy, and Vote Choice in 1974." *American Political Science Review* 79:788–803.

Wolfinger, R. E. and S. J. Rosenstone. 1980. *Who Votes?* New Haven: Yale University Press.

Wolfinger, R. E., S. J. Rosenstone, and R. A. McIntosh. 1981. "Presidential and Congressional Voters Compared." *American Politics Quarterly* 9:245–55.

Yiannakis, D. E. 1981. "The Grateful Electorate: Casework and Congressional Elections." *American Journal of Political Science* 25: 568–80.

Reading 2.2

1. Donald E. Stokes and Warren E. Miller, "Party Government and the Saliency of

Congress," Chapter 11 in Angus Campbell et al., *Elections and the Political Order* (New York: John Wiley & Sons, 1966), p. 205. The same may not be true among, say, mayors.

2. *Ibid.*, p. 204. The likelihood is that senators are also better known than their challengers, but that the gap is not so wide as it is on the House side. There is no hard evidence on the point.
3. In Clapp's interview study, "Conversations with more than 50 House members uncovered only one who seemed to place little emphasis on strategies designed to increase communications with the voter." The exception was an innocent freshman. Charles L. Clapp (see #4 for particulars).
4. A statement by one of Clapp's Congressmen: "The best speech is a nonpolitical speech. I think a commencement speech is the best of all. X says he has never lost a precinct in a town where he has made a commencement speech." See Charles L. Clapp, *The Congressman: His Work as He Sees It* (Washington, D.C.: Brookings Institution, 1963), p. 96.
5. These and the following figures on member activity are from Donald C. Tachenon and Morris K. Udall, *The Job of the Congressman* (Indianapolis: Bobbs Merrill, 1966), pp. 283–88.
6. Another Clapp Congressman: "I was looking at my TV film today—I have done one every week since I have been here—and who was behind me but Congressman X. I'll swear he had never done a TV show before in his life but he only won by a few hundred votes last time. Now he has a weekly television show. If he had done that before he wouldn't have had any trouble." Clapp, *The Congressman*, p. 92.
7. On questionnaires generally see Walter Wilcox, "The Congressional Poll—and Non-Poll," in eds. Edward C. Dreyer and Walter A. Rosenbaum, *Political Opinion and Electoral Behavior* (Belmont, Calif.: Wadsworth, 1966), pp. 390–400.
8. Ellen Szita, Ralph Nader Congress Project profile on George E. Shipley (D—Ill.) (Washington, D.C.: G. Rossman, 1972), p. 12. The Congressman is also a certified diver. "When Shipley is home in his district and a drowning occurs, he is sometimes asked to dive down for the body. 'It gets in the papers and actually, it's pretty good publicity for me,' he admitted." p. 3. Whether this should be classified under "casework" rather than "advertising" is difficult to say. (Congress Project profiles referred to in future footnotes will be called "Nader profiles" for short. For all of them the more complete citation is the one given here.)
9. Lenore Cooley, Nader profile on Diggs, p. 2.
10. Anne Zandman and Arthur Magida, Nader profile on Flood, p. 2.
11. Norman C. Miller, "Yes, You are Getting More Politico Mail. And It Will Get Worse," *The Wall Street Journal*, March 6, 1973, p. 1.
12. Monthly data compiled by Albert Cover.
13. After serving his two terms, the late President Eisenhower had this conclusion: "There is nothing a Congressman likes better than to get his name in the headlines and for it to be published all over the United States." From a 1961 speech quoted in *The New York Times*, June 20, 1971.
14. In practice the one might call out the Army and suspend the Constitution.
15. These have some of the properties of what Lowi calls "distributive" benefits. Theodore J. Lowi, "American Business, Public Policy, Case-Studies, and Political Theory," *World Politics* 16 (1964), p. 690.
16. On casework generally see Kenneth G. Olson, "The Service Function of the United States Congress," in American Enterprise Institute, *Congress: The First Branch of Government* (Washington, D.C.: American Enterprise Institute for Public Policy Research, 1966), pp. 337–74.
17. Sometimes without justification. Thus this comment by a Republican member of the House Public Works Committee: "The announcements for projects are an important part of this. . . . And the folks back home are funny about this—if your name is associated with it, you get all the credit whether you got it through or not." James T. Murphy, "Partisanship and the House Public Works Committee," Paper presented to the annual convention of the American Political Science Association, 1968, p. 10.
18. "They've got to *see* something; it's the bread and butter issues that count—the dams, the post offices and the other public buildings, the highways. They want to know what you've been doing." A comment by a Democratic member of the House Public Works Committee. *Ibid.*
19. The classic account is in E. E. Schattschneider, *Politics, Pressures, and the Tariff* (New York: Prentice-Hall, 1935).
20. "Israeli Schools and Hospitals Seek Funds in

Foreign-Aid Bill," *The New York Times,* October 4, 1971, p. 10.

21. Richard F. Fenno, Jr., *Congressmen in Committees* (Boston: Little, Brown, 1973), p. 40. Cf. this statement on initiative in the French Third Republic: "Most deputies ardently championed the cause of interest groups in their district without waiting to be asked." Bernard E. Brown, "Pressure Politics in France," *Journal of Politics* 18 (1956), p. 718.
22. For a discussion of the politics of tax loopholes, see Stanley S. Surrey, "The Congress and the Tax Lobbyist—How Special Tax Provisions Get Enacted," *Harvard Law Review* 70 (1957), pp. 1145–82.
23. A possible example of a transaction of this sort: During passage of the 1966 "Christmas tree" tax bill, Sen. Vance Hartke (D–Ind.) won inclusion of an amendment giving a tax credit to a California aluminum firm with a plant in the Virgin Islands. George Lardner, Jr., "The Day Congress Played Santa," *The Washington Post,* December 10, 1966, p. 10. Whether Hartke was getting campaign funds from the firm is not wholly clear, but Lardner's account allows the inference that he was.
24. Thus this comment of a Senate aide, "The world's greatest publicity organ is still the human mouth. . . . When you get somebody $25.00 from the Social Security Administration, he talks to his friends and neighbors about it. After a while the story grows until you've single-handedly obtained $2,500 for a constituent who was on the brink of starvation." Donald R. Matthews, *U.S. Senators and Their World* (Chapel Hill: University of North Carolina Press, 1960), p. 226.
25. For some examples of particularistically oriented Congressmen, see the Nader profiles by Sven Holmes on James A. Haley (D–Fla.), Newton Koltz on Joseph P. Addabbo (D–N.Y.), Alex Berlow on Kenneth J. Gray (D–Ill.), and Sarah Glazer on John Young (D–Tex.). For a fascinating picture of the things House members were expected to do half a century ago, see Joe Martin, *My First Fifty Years in Politics* (New York: McGraw-Hill, 1960), pp. 55–59.
26. Michael Barone, Grant Ujifusa, and Douglas Matthews, *The Almanac of American Politics* (Boston: Gambit, 1972), pp. 479–80.
27. Any teacher of American politics has had students ask about Senators running for the Presidency (Goldwater, McGovern, McCarthy, any of the Kennedys), "But what bills has he passed?" There is no unembarrassing answer.
28. Fenno, *Congressmen in Committees,* pp. 242–55.
29. In the terminology of Stokes, statements may be on either "position issues" or "valence issues." Donald E. Stokes, "Spatial Models of Party Competition," Chapter 9 in Campbell et al., *Elections and the Political Order,* pp. 170–74.
30. Clapp, *The Congressman,* p. 108. A difficult borderline question here is whether introduction of bills in Congress should be counted under position taking or credit claiming. On balance probably under the former. Yet another Clapp congressman addresses the point: "I introduce about sixty bills a year, about 120 a Congress. I try to introduce bills that illustrate, by and large, my ideas—legislative, economic, and social. I do like being able to say when I get cornered, 'Yes, boys, I introduced a bill to try to do that in 1954.' To me it is the perfect answer." *Ibid.,* p. 141. But voters probably give claims like this about the value they deserve.
31. On floor speeches generally see Matthews, *U.S. Senators,* p. 247. On statements celebrating holidays cherished by ethnic groups, Hearings on the Organization of Congress before the Joint Committee on the Organization of the Congress, 89th Congress, 1st session, 1965, p. 1127; and Arlen J. Large, "And Now Let's Toast Nicolaus Copernicus, the Famous German," *The Wall Street Journal,* March 12, 1973, p. 1.
32. Sometimes members of the Senate ostentatiously line up as "cosponsors" of measures—an activity that may attract more attention than roll-call voting itself. Thus in early 1973, seventy-six senators backed a provision to block trade concessions to the U.S.S.R. until the Soviet government allowed Jews to emigrate without paying high exit fees. "'Why did so many people sign the amendment?' a northern Senator asked rhetorically, 'Because there is no political advantage in not signing. If you do sign, you don't offend anyone. If you don't sign, you might offend some Jews in your state.'" David E. Rosenbaum, "Firm Congress Stand on Jews in Soviet Is Traced to Efforts by Those in U.S.," *The New York Times,* April 6, 1973, p. 14.
33. ". . . an utterly hopeless proposal and for that

reason an ideal campaign issue." V. O. Key, Jr., *Southern Politics* (New York: Alfred A. Knopf, 1949), p. 232.

34. Instructions on how to do this are given in Tacheron and Udall, *Job of the Congressman*, pp. 73–74.
35. William Lazarus, Nader profile on Edward R. Roybal (D–Cal.), p. 1.
36. On obfuscation in congressional position taking see Raymond A. Bauer, Ithiel de Sola Pool, and Lewis A. Dexter, *American Business and Public Policy* (New York: Atherton, 1964), pp. 431–32.
37. "Elaborate indexes of politicians and their records were kept at Washington and in most of the states, and professions of sympathy were matched with deeds. The voters were constantly apprised of the doings of their representatives." Peter H. Odegard, *Pressure Politics: The Story of the Anti-Saloon League* (New York: Columbia University Press, 1928), p. 21.
38. On Farm Bureau dealings with congressmen in the 1920s see Orville M. Kile, *The Farm Bureau through Three Decades* (Baltimore: Waverly Press, 1948), Chapter 7.
39. V. O. Key, Jr., "The Veterans and the House of Representatives: A Study of a Pressure Group and Electoral Mortality," *Journal of Politics* 5 (1943), pp. 27–40.
40. "The American Medical Association: Power, Purpose, and Politics in Organized Medicine," 63 *Yale Law Journal* (1954), pp. 1011–18. See also Richard Harris, *A Sacred Trust* (New York: New American Library, 1966).
41. On the NRA generally, see Stanford N. Sesser, "The Gun: Kingpin of 'Gun Lobby' Has a Million Members, Much Clout in Congress," *The Wall Street Journal*, May 24, 1972, p. 1. On the defeat of Sen. Joseph Tydings (D–Md.) in 1970: "Tydings himself tended to blame the gun lobby, which in turn was quite willing to take the credit. 'Nobody in his right mind is going to take on that issue again [i.e., gun control],' one Tydings strategist admitted." John F. Bibby and Roger H. Davidson, *On Capitol Hill: Studies in the Legislative Process* (Hinsdale, Ill.: Dryden Press, 1972), p. 50.
42. A cautious politician will not be sure of an issue until it has been tested in a campaign. Polling evidence is suggestive, but it can never be conclusive.
43. David Prios, *Who Makes the Laws?* (Cambridge, Mass.: Schenkman, 1972), p. 29. Magnuson was chairman of the Senate Commerce Committee. "Onto the old Magnuson, interested in fishing, shipping, and Boeing Aircraft, and running a rather sleepy committee, was grafted a new one: the champion of the consumer, the national legislative leader, and the patron of an energetic and innovative legislative staff." *Ibid.* p. 78.
44. Marjorie Hunter, "Hollings Fight on Hunger Is Stirring the South," *The New York Times*, March 8, 1969, p. 14. The local reaction was favorable. "Already Senator Herman E. Talmadge, Democrat of Georgia, has indicated he will begin a hunger crusade in his own state. Other senators have hinted that they may do the same."
45. Robert Griffith, *The Politics of Fear: Joseph R. McCarthy and the Senate* (New York: Hayden, 1970), p. 29. Richard Rovere's conclusion: "McCarthy took up the Communist menace in 1950 not with any expectation that it would make him a sovereign of the assemblies, but with the single hope that it would help him hold his job in 1952." Richard Rovere, *Senator Joe McCarthy* (Cleveland: World, 1961), p. 120.
46. Robert A. Schoenberger, "Campaign Strategy and Party Loyalty: The Electoral Relevance of Candidate Decision-Making in the 1964 Congressional Elections," *American Political Science Review* 63 (1969), pp. 515–20.
47. Robert S. Erikson, "The Electoral Impact of Congressional Roll Call Voting," *American Political Science Review* 65 (1971), p. 1023.
48. Griffith, *The Politics of Fear*, pp. 122–31. The defeat of Sen. Millard Tydings (D–Md.) was attributed to resources (money, endorsements, volunteer work) conferred or mobilized by McCarthy. "And if Tydings can be defeated, then who was safe? Even the most conservative and entrenched Democrats began to fear for their seats, and in the months that followed, the legend of McCarthy's political power grew." *Ibid.*, p. 123.
49. Paul H. Douglas, *In the Fullness of Time* (New York: Harcourt Brace Jovanovich, 1972).
50. Barone, et al., *Almanac of American Politics*, p. 53. Maillaird was given a safer district in the 1972 line drawing.
51. On member freedom, see Bauer et al., *American Business and Public Policy*, pp. 406–07.
52. Linda M. Kupferstein, Nader profile on William A. Barrett (D–Pa.), p. 1. This profile

gives a very useful account of a machine Congressman's activities.

53. One commentator on New York detects "a tendency for the media to promote what may be termed 'press release politicians.'" A result is that "younger members tend to gravitate towards House committees that have high rhetorical and perhaps symbolic importance, like Foreign Affairs and Government Operations, rather than those with bread-and-butter payoffs." Donald Haider, "The New York City Congressional Delegation," *City Almanac* (published bimonthly by the Center for New York City Affairs of the New School for Social Research), vol. 7, no. 6, April 1973, p. 11.
54. Leo M. Snowiss, "Congressional Recruitment and Representation," *American Political Science Review* 60 (1966), pp. 627–39.
55. The term is from Joseph A. Schlesinger, *Ambition and Politics: Political Careers in the United States* (Chicago: Rand McNally, 1966), p. 10.
56. *Ibid.*, p. 92; Matthews, *U.S. Senators*, p. 55. In the years 1953–1972 three House members were appointed to the Senate, and 85 gave up their seats to run for the Senate. Thirty-five of the latter made it, giving a success rate of 41 percent.
57. Thus upstate New York Republicans moving to the Senate commonly shift to the left. For a good example of the advertising and position-taking strategies that can go along with turning a House member into a senator, see the account on Sen. Robert P. Griffin (R–Mich.) in James M. Perry, *The New Politics* (New York: Clarkson N. Potter, 1968), Chapter 4.
58. Fenno, *Congressmen in Committees*, pp. 141–42.
59. "Thurmond Image Seen as Changing," *The New York Times*, October 17, 1971, p. 46.

Reading 2.3

1. It is a complicated concept. See Hannah Pitkin, *The Concept of Representation* (Berkeley: University of California Press, 1967).
2. For an account of this literature, see Walter J. Stone, "Measuring Constituency-Representative Linkages: Problems and Prospects," *Legislative Studies Quarterly* 4 (1979):624.
3. Ibid., pp. 624–26.
4. Compare Stone, "Linkages," with Gillian Dean, John Siegfried, and Leslie Ward, "Constituency Preference and Potential Economic Gain: Cues for Senate Voting on the Family Assistance Plan," *American Politics Quarterly* 9 (1981):341–56.
5. Stone, "Linkages," pp. 632–34.
6. Richard F. Fenno, Jr., *Home Style: House Members in their Districts* (Boston: Little, Brown, 1978), p. 233.
7. David R. Mayhew, *Congress: The Electoral Connection* (New Haven: Yale University Press, 1974), p. 140.
8. From a study by Everett C. Ladd, Jr., cited by George F. Will, "Slash 'Waste,' Cure Everything," *Hartford Courant*, December 14, 1978, p. 30.
9. Quoted in William J. Crotty and Gary C. Jacobson, *American Parties in Decline* (Boston: Little, Brown, 1980), p. 242.
10. Mayhew, *Electoral Connection*, pp. 174–77; Morris P. Fiorina, "The Decline of Collective Responsibility in American Politics," *Daedalus* 109 (Summer 1980):25–45.
11. Fiorina, "Decline of Collective Responsibility," pp. 26–27.
12. Ibid., pp. 39–44; see also the introduction to this book.

Reading 3.1

References

Aberbach, J. D., R. D. Putnam, and B. A. Rockman. *Bureaucrats and Politicians in Western Democracies.* Cambridge, Mass.: Harvard University Press, 1981.

Asher, H. B. "Committees and the Norm of Specialization." *Annals of the American Academy of Political and Social Science* 411 (January 1974):63–74.

Brady, D. W. "Personnel Management in the House." In *The House at Work.* Edited by J. Cooper and G. C. Mackenzie. Austin: University of Texas Press, 1981.

Corson, J. J., and R. S. Paul. *Men Near the Top.* Baltimore: Johns Hopkins University Press, 1966.

Davidson, R. H. "Congress and the Executive: The Race for Representation," in *Congress: The First Branch of Government.* Edited by A. De Grazia. Garden City, N.Y.: Doubleday. 1967.

Fenno, R. F., Jr. *The President's Cabinet.* New York: Vintage, 1959.

———. *Congressmen in Committees.* Boston: Little, Brown, 1973.

———. *Home Style: House Members in Their Districts.* Boston: Little, Brown, 1978.

Foss, P. O. *Politics and Grass.* Seattle: University of Washington Press, 1960.

Fox, H. W., Jr., and S. W. Hammond. *Congressional Staffs: The Invisible Force in American Lawmaking.* New York: Free Press, 1977.

Heclo, H. *A Government of Strangers: Executive Politics in Washington.* Washington, D.C.: Brookings Institution, 1977.

Huntington, S. P. "Congressional Responses to the Twentieth Century." In *Congress and America's Future.* 2d ed. Edited by D. B. Truman. Englewood Cliffs, N.J.: Prentice-Hall, 1973.

Kaufman, H. *The Administrative Behavior of Federal Bureau Chiefs.* Washington, D.C.: Brookings Institution, 1981.

Kilpatrick, F. P., M. C. Cummings, and M. K. Jennings. *The Image of the Federal Service.* Washington, D.C.: Brookings Institution, 1963.

Lowi, T. J. "How the Farmers Get What They Want." In *Legislative Politics U.S.A.* 3d ed. Edited by T. J. Lowi and R. B. Ripley. Boston: Little, Brown, 1973.

Mayhew, D. R. *Congress: The Electoral Connection.* New Haven, Conn.: Yale University Press, 1974.

Neustadt, R. E. "Politicians and Bureaucrats." In *Congress and America's Future.* 2d ed. Edited by D. B. Truman. Englewood Cliffs, N.J.: Prentice-Hall, 1973.

Ornstein, N. J., T. E. Mann, M. J. Malbin, and J. F. Bibby. *Vital Statistics on Congress, 1982.* Washington, D.C.: American Enterprise Institute, 1982.

Polsby, N. W. "Institutionalization in the House of Representatives." *American Political Science Review* 62 (March 1968): 144–68.

Price, H. D. "The Congressional Career—Then and Now." In *Congressional Behavior.* Edited by N. W. Polsby. New York: Random House, 1971.

Ripley, R. B. *Power in the Senate.* New York: St. Martin's Press, 1969.

Stanley, D. T. *The Higher Civil Service.* Washington, D.C.: Brookings Institution, 1964.

Stanley, D. T., D. E. Mann, and J. W. Doig. *Men Who Govern.* Washington, D.C.: Brookings Institution, 1967.

Wilensky, H. L. *Organizational Intelligence.* New York: Basic Books, 1967.

Witmer, T. R. "The Aging of the House." *Political Science Quarterly* 79 (December 1964): 526–41.

Yates, D. *Bureaucratic Democracy.* Cambridge, Mass.: Harvard University Press, 1982.

Reading 3.2

Disclaimer This paper was written for academic purposes and does not necessarily reflect the position of the Department of Defense, the National Defense University, or the National War College.

Thank You The author wishes to thank the American Political Science Association's Congressional Fellowship Program (particularly Executive Director Thomas Mann) under whose auspices much of this research was undertaken. Also, many thanks to the following senators and their appointment secretaries:

- Senator James Abdnor (R—South Dakota)
- Senator Mark Andrews (R—North Dakota)
- Senator William L. Armstrong (R—Colorado)
- Senator Max S. Baucus (D—Montana)
- Senator William S. Cohen (R—Maine)
- Senator Thad Cochran (R—Mississippi)
- Senator Christopher J. Dodd (D—Connecticut)
- Senator Charles E. Grassley (R—Iowa)
- Senator John Heinz (R—Pennsylvania)
- Senator Daniel K. Inouye (D—Hawaii)
- Senator Spark M. Matsunanga (D—Hawaii)
- Senator John Melchner (D—Montana)
- Senator Claude Pepper (D—Florida)
- Senator Dan Quayle (R—Indiana)
- Senator Steve Symms (R—Idaho)
- Senator Paul S. Trible, Jr. (R—Virginia)
- Senator Paul E. Tsongas (D—Massachusetts)

Also, thanks to Myra Evans and Sue O'Keefe who typed and edited the manuscript.

References

Abramowitz, Alan I. "A Comparision of Voting for U. S. Senator and Representative in 1978," *American Political Science Review* 74 (1980), pp. 633–40.

Cohen, William J. *Roll Call.* New York: Simon and Schuster, 1981.

Davidson, Roger H. and Walter T. Oleszek. *Congress and Its Members.* Washington, D.C.: CQ Press, 1981.

The Federalist Papers. Morton Books, 1961.

Fenno, Richard F., Jr. *Congressmen in Committees.* Boston: Little, Brown, 1973a.

Fenno, Richard F., Jr. "The United States Senate: A Bicameral Perspective." Paper presented at the 1981 meeting of the American Political Science Association, Washington, D.C.

Froman, Lewis A. *The Congressional Process: Strategies, Rules and Procedures.* Boston: Little, Brown, 1967.

Hinkley, Barbara. *Congressional Elections.* Washington, D.C.: CQ Press, 1981.

Huitt, Ralph K. "The Internal Distribution of Influence: the Senate," in *The Congress and America's Future.* 2d ed. ed. David B. Truman. Englewood Cliffs, N.J.: Prentice-Hall, 1973, pp. 91–117.

Jacobsen, Gary C. *The Politics of Congressional Elections.* Boston: Little, Brown, 1983.

Jewell, Malcolm and Samual C. Patterson. *The Legislative Process in the United States,* 3d ed. New York: Random House, 1977.

Jones, Charles O. "Will Reforms Change Congress?" in *Congress Reconsidered.* ed. Lawrence Dodd and Bruce I. Oppenheimer. New York: Praeger, 1977, pp. 247–60.

Jones, Charles O. *The United States Congress: People, Places and Policy.* Homewood, Ill.: Dorsey Press, 1981.

Keefe, William J. *Congress and the American People.* Englewood Cliffs, N.J.: Prentice-Hall, 1980.

Kozak, David C. *Contexts of Congressional Decision Behavior.* Lanham, Md.: University Press of America, 1984.

Mann, Thomas E. "Elections and Change in Congress" *The New Congress.* ed. Thomas E. Mann and Norman J. Ornstein. Washington, D.C.: American Enterprise Institute, 1981, pp. 32–54.

Oleszek, Walter T. *Congressional Procedures and the Policy Process,* 2d ed. Washington, D.C.: CQ Press, 1984.

Ornstein, Norman J. "The House and the Senate in a New Congress," in *The New Congress.* ed. Thomas E. Mann and Norman J. Ornstein. Washington, D.C.: American Enterprise Institute, 1981, pp. 363–86.

Polsby, Nelson W. "Strengthening Congress in National Policy-making." *Yale Review* (Summer 1970), pp. 481–97.

Polsby, Nelson W. *Congress and the Presidency.* 3d ed. Englewood Cliffs, N.J.: Prentice-Hall, 1975.

Vogler, David J. *The Third House: Conference Committees in the United States Congress.* Evanston, Ill.: Northwestern University Press, 1981.

Young, James S. *The Washington Community.* New York: Columbia University Press, 1966.

Reading 3.3

1. Michael J. Malbin, *Unelected Representatives: Congressional Staff and the Future of Representative Government* (New York: Basic Books, 1980, paperback edition, 1982), p. 10.

Reading 3.4

1. While the discussion here focuses on Congressional district offices, the study is based on research conducted during 1974 in Los Angeles County, California, and which included the district office operations of all 91 federal, state, and local office holders who were maintaining legislative field offices in Los Angeles County that year. Thus, the sample here includes 20 House offices plus two Senate offices, along with 69 state and local offices. In many ways the district office activities of, for example, Los Angeles City Councilmen or California State Assemblymen (both of whom have generous staff resources) are indistinguishable from those of L.A.-based congressmen. That is especially true when all share the same constituency. Accordingly, some of the data to be presented here as well as some of the discussion applies to legislative district offices in general, irrespective of level of government. During the research, some 130 political aides were interviewed. The interviews, which generally involved the aide in charge of each district operation, averaged 70 minutes in length and followed elaborate printed formats. In a few cases, incumbents were also interviewed. (These data were supplemented in 1976 by interviews with district aides to Colorado Congressmen.) All interviewees were promised anonymity; therefore, quotes, anecdotes, and data are attributed to office types rather than specific individuals.
2. There has been relatively little research done on Congressional activities outside of Washington, D.C. The major work, of course, is Richard F. Fenno, Jr., *Home Style: House Members in Their Districts* (Boston: Little, Brown, 1978). See also John D. Cra-

nor and Joseph W. Westphal, "Congressional District Offices, Federal Programs, and Electoral Benefits," paper presented at the 1978 Meeting of the Midwest Political Science Association, Chicago, April 20–22, 1978; Jamie R. Wolf, "A Congressman's Day at the District Office," *The Washington Monthly,* April 1974, pp. 45–57; "House Members Use District Offices in Increasing Number, Many Different Ways," *Staff* 8 (94th Congress); "Senate Use of State Offices Shows Highly Varied Pattern," *Staff* 4 (94th Congress), *Staff,* a publication very useful in these matters, was published until March 1979 by the now defunct House Commission on Information and Facilities. A number of the back issues of *Staff* are reproduced in the *Final Report of the House Commission on Information and Facilities,* 95th Congress, 1st Session, House Document No. 95–22, December 1976. See also the author's Ph.D. dissertation, from which this paper is drawn: "Political Staffing: A View from the District," UCLA, 1975.

3. Steven H. Schiff, "Congressional Office Management, with Emphasis on the Assignment of Staff to District Offices," Paper presented at the American Political Science Association Convention, Washington, D.C., September 2, 1979.
4. A number of district offices use part-time employees—typists who come in once a week, caseworkers who work one or two days a week, lawyers and PR specialists on call for when their expertise is needed. If these people were to be carried on the payroll they would count as one of the 18 allowable employees. The solution is to rotate part-timers on and off the payroll at irregular intervals but to utilize their services regularly as needed. In one House office I visited, a political science professor worked full-time during the summers and academic breaks and was available as a consultant year round. He was actually paid whenever "holes" in the payroll were available—regardless of whether or not they coincided with the periods he worked. In another congressional office the top aide that I interviewed, as well as the press aide, were off the payroll—for three months—in order to campaign. Their combined salaries of some $5,000 per month were being reallocated to various part-time workers to compensate them for work already done and work that would be expected in 1975. Of the 435 Representatives, 107 appeared to be using this payroll shuffle technique. They were culled from the House payroll reports as employing 21 or more clerks in a six-month period during fiscal year 1974 *and* having one or more persons who rotate on and off the payroll. The House payrolls (and other office expenditures) can be found in *Report of the Clerk of the House,* published twice annually. The practice of shuffling the payroll is perfectly legal, but it involves a serious complication. If a staffer were to be injured or taken ill or die while working in a Congressional office—but not carried on the payroll at that particular time—he or she would be ineligible for the various disability compensations, death gratuities, survivor premiums, and other benefits normally available. A lesser problem is the fact that the payroll shuffling itself can involve a considerable number of manhours—and becomes an added management burden for offices that follow the practice.
5. W. C. Love, Jr., "The Congressman as Educator," Unpublished master's thesis, MIT, August 1966. Also see John S. Saloma III, *Congress and the New Politics* (Boston: Little, Brown, 1969), pp. 174–77.
6. Saloma, *Congress and the New Politics,* p. 185.
7. For an excellent discussion of this matter and of Congressional casework in general, see John R. Johannes, "Congressional Caseworkers: Attitudes, Orientations, and Operations," Paper delivered at the 1978 annual meeting of the Midwest Political Science Association Meeting, Chicago, April 20–22, 1978, pp. 20–23.
8. John R. Johannes, "Casework as a Technique of Congressional Oversight of the Executive," paper presented at the 1978 Annual Meeting of the American Political Science Association, New York City, August 31–September 3, 1978.
9. Saloma, *Congress and the New Politics,* p. 192. Charles L. Clapp, *The Congressman: His Work as He Sees It* (Garden City, N.Y.: Anchor Books, 1963) pp. 74, 84, 94. Michael Walter advised in his political how-to-do-it book: "One last thing: the records kept in the office—mailing lists, financial reports, correspondence—are very important, necessary if political activity is to be sustained for any length of time or renewed after some temporary setback. Someone should look after them, and activists should insist that they are in fact looked after by people they know and trust." Michael Walters, *Political*

Action (Chicago: Quadrangle Books, 1971), p. 47.

10. David Mayhew, *Congress: The Electoral Connection* (New Haven, Conn.: Yale University Press, 1974), p. 5.
11. Larry Light, "Crack Outreach Programs No Longer Ensure Re-election," *Congressional Quarterly Weekly Report*, February 14, 1981, pp. 316–18.
12. U. S. Congress, Joint Committee on the Organization of Congress, Hearings Pursuant to S. Con. Res. 2, (May 24, 1965), p. 264.
13. Morris P. Fiorina, *Congress: Keystone of the Washington Establishment* (New Haven, Conn.: Yale University Press, 1977).

Reading 4.1

1. On the Rules Committee, which sets the House agenda, the majority party enjoys a two-to-one edge, while on the committees responsible for raising and spending federal revenues—Ways and Means, Appropriations, and Budget—the majority party holds at least 60 percent of the seats. Republicans were outraged in 1981 when Democrats continued to hold 65 percent of the Ways and Means seats.
2. The one exception is the Rules Committee, whose Democratic members are appointed by the Speaker. Also on Rules, unlike other committees, Democrats' tenure need not be respected by the Speaker.
3. Democrats call their full membership the Caucus, while Republicans refer to theirs as the Conference. House Republicans have an intermediate step, with the Executive Committee's work being reviewed by the full Committee on Committees before referral to the Conference.
4. The House Appropriations Committee is an exception to this practice. The Democratic Caucus approves nominees to chair the subcommittees of this one committee.

References

Bullock, Charles S., III. "Initial Committee Assignments of the 92d Congress." Paper presented at the annual meeting of the Southwest Political Science Association, Dallas, Texas, 1973.

———. "House Committee Assignments." In *The Congressional System*. 2d ed. ed. Leroy N. Rieselbach. North Scituate, Mass.: Duxbury, 1979, pp. 58–86.

Shepsle, Kenneth A. *The Giant Jigsaw Puzzle*. Chicago: University of Chicago Press, 1978.

Smith, Steven S. and Christopher J. Deering. *Committees in Congress*. Washington, D.C.: CQ Press, 1984.

Wolanin, Thomas R. "Committee Seniority and the Choice of House Subcommittee Chairmen: 80th–91st Congresses." *Journal of Politics* 36 (August 1974): 687–702.

Reading 4.2

1. Walter Bagehot discussed the dignified and efficient parts of English government in *The English Constitution* (World's Classics ed., London: Oxford University Press, 1928).

Reading 4.3

1. An excellent discussion of this problem will be found in Robert Samberg, "Conceptualization and Measurement of Political System Output," unpublished manuscript (Rochester, N.Y.: University of Rochester, 1971).

Reading 4.4

1. Roger H. Davidson, "Subcommittee Government: New Channels for Policy Making," in *The New Congress*, ed. Thomas E. Mann and Norman J. Ornstein (Washington, D.C.: American Enterprise Institute for Public Policy Research, 1981), pp. 99–133; Lawrence C. Dodd and Bruce I. Oppenheimer, "The House in Transition: Change and Consolidation," in *Congress Reconsidered*, 2d ed. ed. Lawrence C. Dodd and Bruce I. Oppenheimer (Washington, D.C.: CQ Press, 1981), pp. 31–61.
2. Dodd and Oppenheimer, "The House in Transition," 41.
3. See Lawrence C. Dodd and Richard L. Schott, *Congress and the Administrative State* (New York: John Wiley & Sons, 1979), p. 124. For example, Dodd and Schott argue that "by the mid-1970s, Congress had institutionalized subcommittee government."
4. David Maraniss, "Competing Interests Snarl Gas Debate," *Washington Post*, June 26, 1983, A1.
5. The term "institutionalization" has been applied to some of the processes of change we discuss in this and the next two chapters. We choose not to package the changes in structure and process we discuss under such

an umbrella concept. One reason is that the decade and a half examined here is an insufficient baseline for saying much about long-term processes like institutionalization. Second, there is a tendency to pile up indicators of such broad-based concepts without examining the relationship between the various features of committee operations. At this stage it is preferable not to obscure the separate features by putting a broad label on them. A third reason is that institutionalization is often associated with viability, a topic beyond the scope of this and the next two chapters. As the choice of concepts for the model suggests, we also do not believe it is particularly useful or necessary to adopt alternative packages of concepts, such as those that might be suggested by organization theorists or systems modellers. See Nelson W. Polsby, "Institutionalization in the U.S. House of Representatives," *American Political Science Review* 62 (1968), pp. 144–168; Steven Haeberle, "The Institutionalization of the Subcommittees in the U.S. House of Representatives," *Journal of Politics* 40 (1978), pp. 1054–65; Joseph Cooper and David W. Brady, "Toward a Diachronic Analysis of Congress," *American Political Science Review* 75 (1981), pp. 988–1006.

6. *Congressional Record* (bound), February 17, 1967, 3784. We thank Roger Davidson for bringing this story to our attention.
7. Ibid., pp. 3784–85.
8. Lawrence C. Dodd, "Congress and the Quest for Power," in *Congress Reconsidered,* 1st ed. ed. Lawrence C. Dodd and Bruce I. Oppenheimer (New York: Praeger Publishers, 1977), 272.
9. For example, see Richard F. Fenno, *Congressmen in Committees* (Boston: Little, Brown, 1973), pp. 94, 97–98, 105, 107, 110, 172, 175–177, 189; George Goodwin, Jr., *The Little Legislatures* (Amherst: University of Massachusetts Press, 1970), pp. 48–52; John F. Manley, *The Politics of Finance* (Boston: Little, Brown, 1970), pp. 73–74; Donald R. Matthews, *U.S. Senators and Their World* (New York: Vintage, 1960), pp. 161–63; Polsby, "Institutionalization," pp. 167–68; and Randall B. Ripley, *Power in the Senate* (New York: St. Martin's Press, 1969), pp. 142–43.
10. The reported correlation coefficient is Spearman's *r*.
11. Excludes Senate Budget, which was created in 1974.
12. Ideally, we could trace subcommittee recommendations to the full committee and to the floor to examine the role of subcommittees. Unfortunately, House and Senate policies for archiving committee records make this very difficult or impossible. The House and Senate now require committees to send their noncurrent records to the National Archives. House records are unavailable to the public for 50 years; Senate records are unavailable for 20 years, unless specific approval to see particular documents is gained from each committee chair.
13. Woodrow Wilson, *Congressional Government: A Study in American Politics* (1885; reprint, Baltimore: The Johns Hopkins University Press, 1981), p. 63. Wilson asserted that when a bill is referred to committee "it crosses a parliamentary bridge of sighs to dim dungeons of silence [whence] it will never return. The means and time of its death are unknown, but its friends never see it again."
14. Calculated from Thomas J. O'Donnell, "Controlling Legislative Time," in *The House at Work,* ed. Joseph Cooper and G. Calvin Mackenzie (Austin: University of Texas Press, 1981), Table 5.2, p. 131.
15. Cited in U.S. Congress, House Select Committee on Committees, *Final Report,* H. Rept. No. 96-866, 96th Congress, 2d sess., p. 198.

Reading 5.5

1. Senate Republican Conference Rules, February 9, 1971, p. 2.
2. As assistant to the floor leader, the party whip has responsibilities in several areas, including: (1) the scheduling and management of legislation; (2) keeping his party advised about proposed action on legislation; (3) securing party unity to insure that the legislative program is carried out; (4) remaining informed about national and international problems and the status of bills in standing committees; (5) dealing with all procedural questions on the floor; and (6) offering various technical motions relative to the organization of the Senate at the beginning of each new Congress. Since 1941, for example, the majority party whip has announced the hour of meeting for the Senate. See Floyd M. Riddick, "Majority and Minority Leaders of the Senate." Senate Document 95–24 (Washington, D.C.: U.S. Government Printing Office, 1977).

3. Personal interview, Mr. Cecil Holland, administrative assistant to Sen. Robert Griffin, Washington, D.C., April 1972.
4. Marvin E. Stromer, "The Making of a Political Leader," (1969), 49.
5. Personal interview, Senator Thomas Kuchel. April 1970. Washington, D.C.
6. Personal interview, Senator Robert Griffin, Washington, D.C., April 1972.
7. *Congressional Record* (May 12, 1936), p. 7046.
8. Stromer, "Political Leader," p. 46.
9. Personal Interview, Sen. Leverett Saltonstall. November 1969, Boston, Mass.
10. David B. Truman, *The Congressional Party*, N.Y.: Alfred A. Knopf, 1959, Chapter 8.
11. *The New York Times*, March 29, 1934, p. 22.
12. Personal interview, Sen. Robert Griffin. Washington, D.C., April 1972.
13. Press release (1–77), Office of U.S. Senator Alan Cranston, January 5, 1977, p. 1.
14. Personal interview. Sen. Ted Stevens. Washington, D.C., February 1977.
15. It was reported, for example, that "the choice of Senator Humphrey for Democratic whip was intended to give the party's advanced liberal wing a greater voice in the leadership councils." See *The New York Times*, December 2, 1960, p. 24. Geography, too, may play a role in the selection of party whips. In 1956, Sen. George Smathers (D–Fla.) thought of seeking the whip position but stated that since a southerner, Lyndon Johnson of Texas, already held the floor leader's post, a geographic division in the leadership was desirable. See *The New York Times*, November 13, 1956, p. 1. For further discussion of the geographic aspects of Whip selection see Rowland Evans and Robert Novak, *Lyndon B. Johnson: The Exercise of Power*, N.Y.: New American Library, 1966, pp. 41–44.

Reading 5.6

References

Davidson, R. H. "Congressional Committees: The Toughest Customers." *Policy Analysis* 2 (Spring 1976):299–323.

Dreyfus, D. A. "The Limitation of Policy Research in Congressional Decision-making." *Policy Studies Journal* 4 (Spring 1976): 269–274.

Fenno, R. F. *Congressmen in Committees*, Boston: Little, Brown, 1973.

Havemann, J. "Congress Tries to Break Ground Zero in Evaluating Federal Programs." *National Journal*, May 22, 1976, pp. 706–13.

Jones, C. O. "Why Congress Can't Do Policy Analysis (or words to that effect)." *Policy Analysis* 2 (Spring 1976):251–64.

———. "Somebody Must be Trusted: An Essay on Leadership of the U.S. Congress." In *Congress in Change: Evolution and Reform.* ed. N. J. Ornstein. New York: Praeger Publishers, 1975.

———. *Party and Policy-Making: The House Republican Policy Committee.* New Brunswick, N.J.: Rutgers University Press, 1964.

Ripley, R. B. "Congressional Party Leadership and the Impact of Congress on Foreign Policy," in vol. 5 of Appendices to Report of the Commission on the Organization of the Government for the Conduct of Foreign Policy. Washington, D.C.: Government Printing Office, 1975.

———. "Congressional Party Leaders and Standing Committees." *Review of Politics* 36 (July 1974):394–400.

Schick, A. "The Supply and Demand for Analysis on Capitol Hill." *Policy Analysis* 2 (Spring/1976):215–34.

Stewart, J. G. "Central Policy Organs in Congress." In *Congress against the President.* ed. H. C. Mansfield. New York: Academy of Political Science, 1975.

Reading 5.7

Reference

Cooper, Joseph, and David W. Brady. (1981) "Institutional Context and Leadership Style: The House from Cannon to Rayburn." *American Political Science Review* 75 (June): 411–25.

Reading 6.1

1. *Constitution, Jefferson's Manual, and Rules of the House of Representatives*, 94th Congress, 2d Session, House Document No. 94–663, pp. 121–22.
2. U.S. Congress, Senate, *Congressional Record*, January 26, 1977, 123, S 1538–S 1541. Majority Leader Robert C. Byrd requested and received the unanimous consent of the Senate to bypass the committee stage and place the measure directly on the calendar

for immediate floor consideration. For important bills, this is an unusual procedure.

3. The *Los Angeles Times,* February 7, 1977, p. 5.
4. U.S. Congress, House, *Congressional Record,* March 9, 1976, 122, H1779.
5. The formal rules of the House are contained in *Constitution, Jefferson's Manual, and Rules of the House of Representatives,* 94th Congress, 2d Sess., House Document No. 94–663. The Senate's formal rules are in *Senate Manual,* 95th Congress, 1st Session, Senate Document No. 95–1.
6. Lewis Deschler, *Deschler's Procedure, A Summary of the Modern Precedents and Practices of the U.S. House of Representatives, 86th–94th Congress* (Washington, D.C.: U.S. Government Printing Office, 1974); and Floyd M. Riddick, *Senate Procedure, Precedents and Practices* (Washington, D.C.: U.S. Government Printing Office, 1974).
7. Donald Matthews, *U.S. Senators and Their World* (Chapel Hill: University of North Carolina Press, 1960), Chapter 5. Several of the folkways described by Matthews have undergone considerable change. For example, the norm of "apprenticeship," specifying that new members should be seen and not heard, has all but disappeared in both chambers.

Reading 6.2

1. *Senate Journal,* April 23, 1789. The original rule provided: When a bill or other message shall be sent from the Senate to the House of Representatives, it shall be carried by the Secretary, who shall make one obeisance to the chair on entering the door of the House of Representatives, and another on delivering it at the table into the hands of the speaker. After he shall have delivered it, he shall make an obeisance to the Speaker, and repeat it as he retires from the House.
2. When the Speaker and/or the Vice President are unable to sign duly enrolled bills or joint resolutions, they may be signed by the authorized presiding officers of the two bodies.
3. Article 1, Section 7, provides that: "Every bill which shall have passed the House of Representatives and the Senate, shall, before it become a law, be presented to the President of the United States; if he approve he shall sign it, but if not he shall return it, with his objections to that house in which it shall have originated, who shall enter the objections at large on their Journal, and proceed to reconsider it. If after such reconsideration two thirds of that house shall agree to pass the bill, it shall be sent, together with the objections, to the other house, by which it shall likewise be reconsidered, and if approved by two thirds of that house, it shall become a law. But in all such cases the votes of both houses shall be determined by yeas and nays, and the names of the persons voting for and against the bill shall be entered on the Journal of each house respectively. If any bill shall not be returned by the President within ten days (Sundays excepted) after it shall have been presented to him, the Same shall be a law, in like manner as if he had signed it, unless the Congress by their adjournment prevent its return, in which case it shall not be a law."
4. In the computation of the 10 days, the day on which the bill is presented to the President, like Sundays, is excluded.

Reading 7.2

1. Julius Turner, *Party and Constituency: Pressures on Congress,* rev. ed., revised by Edward V. Schneider, Jr. (Baltimore: Johns Hopkins University Press, 1970), p. 34.
2. Donald R. Matthews and James A. Stimson, *Yeas and Nays: Normal Decision-Making in the U.S. House of Representatives* (New York: Wiley-Interscience, 1975).
3. Aage R. Clausen, *How Congressmen Decide: A Policy Focus* (New York: St. Martin's Press, 1973), p. 14.
4. John W. Kingdon, *Congressmen's Voting Decisions* (New York: Harper & Row, 1973), p. 230. Also see the second edition of this work, 1981.
5. Lewis Dexter, *The Sociology and Politics of Congress* (Chicago: Rand McNally, 1969), p. 159. Also see Lewis Anthony Dexter, "The Job of the Congressman," in *Readings on Congress,* ed. R. E. Wolfinger (Englewood Cliffs, N.J.: Prentice-Hall, 1971), p. 81.
6. Kingdon, *Congressmen's Voting,* p. 22.
7. Kovenock discovered that information inputs coming directly from members of the House were three times as great as from other sources. See Kovenock, as quoted in John S. Saloma, III, *Congress and the New Politics* (Boston: Little, Brown, 1969), p. 218. Bauer, Pool, and Dexter note that "Congressmen develop an implicit roster of fel-

low Congressmen whose judgement they respect, whose viewpoint they normally share, and to whom they can turn for guidance on particular topics of the colleague's competence." See Raymond A. Bauer, Ithiel de Sola Pool, and Lewis Anthony Dexter, *American Business and Public Policy* (New York: Atherton, 1963), p. 437.

8. Kingdon, *Congressmen's Voting*, p. 227.
9. Davidson, Kovenock, and O'Leary found that "the most frequently mentioned problems were associated with the complexity of decision-making: the lack of information." The problem of deficient information for decision-making was cited by 62 percent of their sample—the most frequently mentioned complaint. See Roger H. Davidson, David M. Kovenock, and Michael D. O'Leary, *Congress in Crisis: Politics and Congressional Reform* (Belmont, Calif.: Wadsworth, 1966), pp. 75–78.
10. Turner, *Party and Constituency*, p. 34.
11. Clausen, *How Congressmen Decide*, p. 14.
12. Roger H. Davidson, *The Role of the Congressman* (New York: Pegasus, 1969), p. 117.
13. See the following for historical and analytical reviews of legislative behavior research: Heinz Eulau and Katherine Hinckley, "Legislative Institutions and Processes," in *Political Science Annual, 1966* ed. J. A. Robinson (Indianapolis: Bobbs-Merrill, 1966), pp. 85–181; Norman Meller, "Legislative Behavior Research," *Western Political Quarterly* 13 (1960):131–53; Norman Meller, "Legislative Behavior Research Revisited: A Review of Five Years' Publications," *Western Political Quarterly* 18 (1965):776–93; Norman Meller, "Legislative Behavior Research," in *Approaches to the Study of Political Science*, ed. M. Haas and H. S. Kariel (Scranton, Pa.: Chandler, 1970), pp. 239–66; Robert L. Peabody, "Research on Congress: A Coming of Age," in *Congress: Two Decades of Analysis*, ed. R. K. Huitt and R. L. Peabody (New York: Harper & Row, 1969), pp. 3–73; and John C. Wahlke, "Behavioral Analyses of Representative Bodies," in *Essays on the Behavioral Study of Politics*, ed. A. Ranney (Urbana: University of Illinois Press, 1962), pp. 173–90.
14. Peabody, "Research on Congress," p. 70.
15. Meller, "Legislative Behavior," p. 251.
16. Theodore J. Lowi, "American Business, Public Policy, Case Studies, and Political Theory," *World Politics* 16 (1964):677–715; T. J. Lowi, "Distribution, Regulation, Redistribution: The Functions of Government," in *Public Policies and Their Politics*, ed. R. Ripley (New York: W. W. Norton, 1966), pp. 27–40; T. J. Lowi, "Four Systems of Policy, Politics, and Choice," *Public Administration Review* 32 (1972):298–301.
17. Randall B. Ripley and Grace A. Franklin, *Congress, the Bureaucracy, and Public Policy*, rev. ed. (Homewood, Ill.: Dorsey Press, 1980).
18. John M. Bacheller, "Lobbyists and the Legislative Process: The Impact of Environmental Constraints," *American Political Science Review* 71 (1977):252–63.
19. Michael T. Hayes, "The Semi-Sovereign Pressure Groups," *Journal of Politics* 37 (1978):136–61.
20. Charles O. Jones, "Speculative Augmentation in Federal Air Pollution Policy-Making," *Journal of Politics* 36 (1974):438–64.
21. David E. Price, "Policy-Making in Congressional Committees: The Impact of Environmental Factors," *American Political Science Review* 72 (1978):548–74.
22. James Q. Wilson, *Political Organizations* (New York: Basic Books, 1973), and *American Government: Institutions and Policies* (Lexington, Mass.: D.C. Heath, 1980).
23. For a complete report of the results of the research, see David C. Kozak, *Contexts of Congressional Decision Behavior*, unpublished Ph.D. dissertation, University of Pittsburgh, 1979.
24. Price, "Policy-Making," p. 572.
25. Kingdon, *Congressmen's Voting*, pp. 292–93.
26. James D. Thompson, *Organizations in Action* (New York: McGraw-Hill, 1967), p. 134.
27. Fredrick N. Cleaveland, "Legislating for Urban Areas: An Overview," in *Congress and Urban Problems*, ed. F. N. Cleaveland (Washington, D.C.: Brookings Institution, 1969), pp. 356–57.
28. *Ibid.*, p. 357.
29. The position that cue-taking is best viewed as an extension of ideological voting, or a means to it, is presented by John W. Kingdon, "Models of Legislative Voting," *Journal of Politics* 36 (1977):563–95; and Helmut Norpoth, "Explaining Party Cohesion in Congress: The Case of Shared Policy Attitudes," *American Political Science Review* 70 (1976), pp. 1156–71.
30. Roland Young, *The American Congress* (New York: Harper & Row, 1958), p. viii.
31. Louis A. Froman, *The Congressional Process: Strategies, Rules, and Procedures* (Boston: Little, Brown, 1967), Chapter 1.

32. Nelson W. Polsby, "Strengthening Congress in National Policymaking," *Yale Review* (Summer 1970): 481–97.
33. Norman J. Ornstein, "The House and the Senate in a New Congress," in *The New Congress*, ed. Thomas E. Mann and Norman J. Ornstein (Washington, D.C.: American Enterprise Institute, 1981), pp. 363–83.

Reading 7.3

References

———. 1976. "Congressional Politics and Urban Aid." *Political Science Quarterly* 91 (Spring):19–45.

Caraley, Demetrios. 1978. "Congressional Politics and Urban Aid: A 1978 Postscript." *Political Science Quarterly* 93 (Fall):411–19.

Clausen, Aage 1973. *How Congressmen Decide: A Policy Focus.* New York: Harper & Row.

Clausen, Aage and Richard Cheney 1970. "A Comparative Analysis of Senate-House Voting on Economic and Welfare Policy: 1953–1964." *American Political Science Review* 64 (March):138–52.

Cleaveland, Frederic, ed. 1969. *Congress and Urban Problems.* Washington, D.C.: Brookings Institution.

Collie, Melissa P. 1984. "Voting Behavior in Legislatures." *Legislative Studies Quarterly* 9 (February):3–50.

Dommel, Paul. 1974. *The Politics of Revenue Sharing.* Bloomington, Ind.: Indiana University Press.

Dye, Thomas R. and Thomas L. Hurley. 1978. "The Responsiveness of Federal and State Governments to Urban Problems." *Journal of Politics* 40 (February):196–207.

Edner, Sheldon. 1976. "Intergovernmental Policy Development: The Importance of Problem Definition." in Charles O. Jones and Robert D. Thomas, eds., *Public Policy Making in a Federal System.* Beverly Hills, Calif.: Sage, pp. 149–68.

———. 1981. "Is Federalism Compatible with Prefectorial Administration?" *Publius* 11 (Spring), pp. 3–22.

Elazar, Daniel. 1984. *American Federalism: A View from the States.* 3d ed. New York: Harper & Row.

Hale, George E. and Marian L. Palley. 1981. *The Politics of Federal Grants.* Washington, D.C.: Congressional Quarterly Press.

Hero, Rodney E. forthcoming, 1986. "Contemporary Perspectives on American Federalism: A Framework and an Application." *American Review of Public Administration.*

Kettl, Donald. 1983. *The Regulation of American Federalism.* Baton Rouge, La.: Louisiana State University Press.

Kingdon, John W. 1973. *Congressmen's Voting Decisions.* New York: Harper & Row.

Kozak, David C. 1984. *Contexts of Congressional Decision Behavior.* Lanham, MD: University Press of America.

Lowi, Theodore J. 1964. "American Business, Public Policy, Case Studies, and Political Theory." *World Politics* 16:677–715.

———. 1984. "Ronald Reagan—Revolutionary" in Lester M. Salamon and Michael E. Lund, eds., *The Reagan Presidency and the Governing of America.* Washington, D.C.: Urban Institute Press, pp. 29–56.

Madison, James 1961. *The Federalist.* Numbers 10, 51, and others. New York: Mentor Books.

Nathan, Richard P., Charles Adams, Jr., and associates. 1977. *Revenue Sharing: The Second Round.* Washington, D.C.: Brookings Institution.

Nathan, Richard P. and Mary M. Nathan. 1979. *America's Governments.* New York: John Wiley & Sons.

Ornstein, Norman J., Thomas E. Mann, Michael J. Malbin, and John F. Bibby. 1982. *Vital Statistics on Congress, 1982.* Washington, D.C.: American Enterprise Institute.

Patterson, Samuel C. and Gregory A. Caldeira. 1984. "The Etiology of Partisan Competition," *American Political Science Review* 78 (September):691–707.

Pressman, Jeffrey L. 1975. *Federal Programs and City Politics.* Berkeley, Calif.: University of California Press.

Riker, William H. 1955. "The Senate and American Federalism." *American Political Science Review* 49 (June):452–68.

Rothman, Rozann. 1978. "The Ambiguity of American Federal Theory," *Publius* 8 (Summer):103–22.

Schattschneider, E. E. 1975. *The Semi-Sovereign People.* Hinsdale, Ill.: Dryden Press.

———. 1981. "Federalism in the 96th Congress," *Publius* 11 (Summer):155–92.

Schechter, Stephen L. 1983. "Federalism in the 97th Congress," *Publius* 13 (Spring):97–128.

Stein, Robert M. 1981. "The Allocation of Federal Aid Monies: The Synthesis of Demand-Side and Supply-Side Explanations," *American Political Science Review* 75 (June):334–43.

Stephens, G. Ross. 1974. "State Centralization and the Erosion of Local Autonomy." *Journal of Politics* 36 (February):44–76.

Stewart, William H. 1982. "Metaphors, Models, and the Development of Federal Theory," *Publius* 12 (Spring):5–24.

Walker, David. 1981. *Toward a Functioning Federalism.* Cambridge, Mass.: Winthrop.

Weidner, Edward. 1967. "Decision Making in a Federal System." In Aaron Wildavsky, ed., *American Federalism in Perspective.* Boston: Little, Brown, pp. 223–38.

Wirt, Frederick M. 1980. "Does Control Follow the Dollar? School Policy, State-Local Linkages, and Political Culture," *Publius* 10 (Spring):69–88.

Wright, Deil S. 1982. *Understanding Intergovernmental Relations* (Monterey, Calif.: Brooks/Cole).

Reading 8.1

My I.O.U.'s lie scattered all over the United States among my friends in and out of academia. They are too numerous to list here, but Theodore Anagnoson, Viktor Hofstetter, John Kingdon, and Herbert McClosky deserve special thanks. So do the Russell Sage Foundation and the University of Rochester for their financial help. A slightly different version of this article was delivered under the title "Congressmen in Their Constituencies: An Exploration," at the American Political Science Association Convention in San Francisco, September 1975. It is a part of a larger study, *Home Style: U.S. House Members in their Constituencies* (Boston: Little, Brown, forthcoming).

1. Dexter's seminal article was "The Representative and His District," *Human Organization* 16 (Spring, 1957), pp. 2–14. It will be found, revised and reprinted, along with other of Dexter's works carrying the same perspective in: Lewis Dexter, *The Sociology and Politics of Congress* (Chicago: Rand McNally, 1969).
2. Political science studies conducted in congressional constituencies have been few and far between. The most helpful to me have been: *On Capitol Hill,* ed. John Bibby and Roger Davidson (New York: Holt, Rinehart and Winston, 1967); *On Capitol Hill,* ed. John Bibby and Roger Davidson (Hinsdale, Ill.: Dryden, 1972); John Donovan, *Congressional Campaign: Maine Elects a Democrat* (New York: Holt, Rinehart and Winston, 1957); Charles Jones, "The Role of the Campaign in Congressional Politics," in *The Electoral Process,* ed. Harmon Zeigler and Kent Jennings (New York: Prentice-Hall, 1966); John Kingdon, *Candidates for Office: Beliefs and Strategies* (New York: Random House, 1966); David Leuthold, *Electioneering in a Democracy* (New York: John Wiley & Sons, 1968). And no one interested in this subject should miss Richard Harris's superb "How's It Look?" *New Yorker,* April 8, 1967. The most recent study is: *The Making of Congressmen,* ed. Alan Clem (North Scituate, Mass.: Duxbury, 1976).
3. The group contains sixteen men and 1 woman. In the title of the paper and in the Introduction, I have deliberately employed the generic language "House member," "member of Congress," "representative," and "his or her" to make it clear that I am talking about men and women. And I have tried to use the same language wherever the plural form appears in the paper. That is, I have tried to stop using the word "congressmen." In the body of the paper, however, I shall frequently and deliberately use "congressman" and "his" as generic terms. Stylistically, I find this a less clumsy form of the third person singular than "congressperson," followed always by "his or her." This usage has the additional special benefit, here, of camouflaging the one woman in the group. Where necessary, I have used pseudonyms for these seventeen members in the text.
4. Additional evidence will be found in: Donald R. Matthews and James A. Stimson, *Years and Nays: Normal Decision Making in the U.S. House of Representatives* (New York: John Wiley & Sons, 1975), pp. 28–31.
5. Marginal districts probably tend to be heterogeneous. Safe districts probably are both heterogeneous and homogeneous. On the relationship of electoral conditions to homogeneity and heterogeneity, I owe a lot to my conversations with Morris Fiorina. See his *Representatives, Roll Calls and Constituencies* (Boston: Lexington, 1974).
6. On the usefulness of the distinction, see Donald Stokes and Warren Miller, "Party Government and the Saliency of Congress," *Public Opinion Quarterly* 26 (Winter 1962), pp. 531–46. In M. Barone, G. Ujifusa, and D. Matthews, *Almanac of American Politics*

(Boston: Gambit, 1974), the authors often describe congressional districts as artificial and containing no natural community of interest. See for example, pages 86, 133, 146, 162, 376, 402, 419, 373, 616.

7. See Donald B. Johnson and James R. Gibson, "The Divisive Primary Revisited: Party Activists in Iowa," *American Political Science Review* 68 (March, 1974), pp. 67–77.
8. The term is that of Leo Snowiss, "Congressional Recruitment and Representation," *American Political Science Review* 60 (September, 1966), pp. 627–39.
9. For example, Theodore H. White, *The Making of the President: 1960* (New York: Atheneum, 1961), pp. 276–78; Marshall Frady, *Wallace* (New York: New American Library, 1969), pp. 2–4, 38–39; Theodore H. White, *The Making of the President: 1972* (New York: Atheneum, 1973), pp. 147, 414–415, 456–57.
10. On recent trips, wherever possible, I have also asked each congressman at the end of my visit, to rank order the events of the visit in terms of their "political importance" to him and in terms of the degree to which he felt "at home" or "comfortable" in each situation.
11. Two of the best studies ever on the point are David Mayhew, *Congress: The Electoral Connection* (New Haven: Yale University Press, 1974), and John Kingdon, *Congressmen's Voting Decisions* (New York: Harper & Row, 1973).
12. The basic research was done by John Saloma, and is reported in his *Congress and the New Politics* (Boston: Little, Brown, 1969), Chapter 6; in Donald Tacheron and Morris Udall, *The Job of the Congressman* (Indianapolis: Bobbs Merrill, 1966), pp. 280–88; and in *Guide to the Congress of the United States* (Washington: Congressional Quarterly, 1971), pp. 532ff. But no one has expanded Saloma's work. A pioneer work, which would have given us a wider perspective, but which seems to have been neglected is Dorothy H. Cronheim, "Congressmen and Their Communication Practices" (Ph.D. dissertation, University of Michigan, Department of Political Science, 1957).
13. These surveys will be described in the next section of the paper. We shall not, however, again use the figures on total number of days spent in the district. They seem less reliable than the others, when checked against the few cases in which I have the complete record. Also, it should be noted that the number of cases for which the total number of days was collected was 401.
14. Other kinds of data were collected which might also be useful as an indication of district staff strength. Three of them correlated very highly with the indicator being used, so that it does not appear we are missing much by relying on one indicator. The measure we are using in the article—percent of staff expenditures allocated to district staff—showed a correlation of .861 with number of people on the district staff, of .907 with the percent of total staff members allocated to the district, and of .974 with the dollar amounts spent on district staff. Also recorded were the rank, in the total staff hierarchy, of the highest paid person on the district staff, as another indicator of district staff allocation practices. That indicator has not been used in the article, but it might be noted that the range is from first (*i.e.,* the highest paid district staffer is the highest paid of all the congressman's staffers) to more than ninth (anything above nine was not recorded).
15. See footnote 18.
16. The 1974 interviewers were Larry Fishkin, Nancy Hapeman, Bruce Pollock, Kenneth Sankin, Fred Schwartz, and Jacob Weinstein. The 1975 interviewers were Joel Beckman, Joanne Doroshow, Arthur Kreeger, and Susan Weiner. Sandra Bloch, Fishkin, Hapeman, and Schwartz helped with the analysis. During the later stages of the analysis, I have leaned particularly heavily on Viktor Hofstetter.
17. There were eleven members who went home every night—eight from Maryland, two from Virginia, and one from Pennsylvania. In computing averages, they were coded at ninety-eight trips (more than anyone else) rather than at 365, so as to minimize distortion. Also, so as to minimize distortion, caused by these cases, we have used the *median* number of trips in the analysis of this section rather than the average number of trips.
18. The most common replies were "every week," "once a month," "twice a month," "every other week," "between once and twice a month," "three or four times a month," etc. Congressmen placed in the "low" category were those whose staffers were unwilling to go as high as "twice a month." Congressmen whose trips were reported as "once a week" or more fell into the "high" category. But some respondents said

"every week except for a few" or "every week, but maybe he missed one or two here or there." So, we decided to try to capture that sense by including in the "high" category people who were reported to have made somewhat less than fifty-two trips. (Doubtless, those who said they went home every week missed a few too.) Since a sizeable group had forty trips and none had forty-one or forty-two, the cut was made at that point, which made 43+ the "high" category. The middle category were those who remained —people who went home at least twice a month (twenty-four trips) but not as often as forty-three times in 1973.

19. The frequency of 1973 home visits does not bear any relationship to whether the member's electoral margin declined, increased, or remained the same between 1972 and 1974.
20. See Fiorina, *Representatives, Roll Calls and Constituencies,* Chapter One. For an analysis of why House members ought to worry, see Robert Erickson, "A Reappraisal of Competition for Congressional Office: How Careers Begin and End," paper presented at Conference on Mathematical Models of Congress, Aspen, Colorado, 1974. The one piece of research which dovetails best with my research is Warren Miller, "Majority Rule and the Representative System of Government" in *Cleavages, Ideologies and Party Systems,* ed. Erik Allardt and Yrjo Littunen (Helsinki, 1964), Chapter 10. Miller uses subjective marginality as the measure of competitiveness and relates it to the policy attitudes of the congressman and his re-election constituency.
21. The number of cases is lower here than for the other parts of the analysis because the data were collected in 1975—after a number of the 1973 congressmen were no longer available for questioning.
22. An excellent study of district staff operations in California, containing many stimulating comments on the general subject is: John D. Macartney, "Political Staffing: A View From the District" (Ph.D. dissertation, University of California, Los Angeles, Department of Political Science, 1975).
23. For example, Aage Clausen, *How Congressmen Decide: A Policy Focus* (New York: St. Martin's, 1973); Barbara Deckard, "State Party Delegations in the U. S. House of Representatives: A Study in Group Cohesion," *Journal of Politics* 34 (February 1972), pp. 199–222; John Ferejohn, *Pork Barrel Politics* (Stanford, Calif.: Stanford University Press, 1974); John Kessel, "The Washington Congressional Delegation," *Midwest Journal of Political Science* 8 (February 1964), pp. 1–21; Matthews and Stimson, *Yeas and Nays.*
24. Fifty-six per cent, or 72 of 129.
25. Erving Goffman, *The Presentation of Self in Everyday Life* (New York: Doubleday, 1959). The language I have quoted appears in the Introduction.
26. Goffman, Chapter 3, especially p. 128. Often comments made in the "back regions" provide clues for "at homeness" estimates. "We're having breakfast tomorrow with a businessman's group. They're really a bunch of hoodlums."
27. The two styles are the most common among my group. They may be the most common among all representatives. In his study of representation, Paul Peterson uses two very similar analytical categories, "particularistic representation" (person-to-person) and "universalistic representation" (issue-oriented) Paul Peterson, "Forms of Representation: Participation of the Poor in the Community Action Program," *American Political Science Review* 64 (June 1970), 491–501. Other styles will be elaborated in a later, lengthier study, of which this paper is a part.
28. See Morris Fiorina, "Electoral Margins, Constituency Influence and Policy Moderation: A Critical Assessment," *American Politics Quarterly* 1 (October 1973), pp. 479–98.
29. See Stokes and Miller, "Party Government," p. 542; and Charles S. Bullock, III, "Candidate Perceptions of Causes of Election Outcome," paper delivered at American Political Science Association Convention, New Orleans, 1973, Tables 7, 8. In his analysis of ten congressional campaigns in 1962, David Leuthold found that "probably more than half the appeals (of the candidates) . . . were based on the qualities of the candidate or his opponent." Leuthold, *Electioneering in a Democracy,* p. 113. He believes that voters are looking for ability, concern, and similarity to themselves. That, in the somewhat different words, qualification, empathy, and identification, is what my representatives think the voters want. See Leuthold, pp. 23–24.
30. The first people to view congressional incumbency, in the light of SRC analyses, as a long-term force were Robert Arseneau and Raymond Wolfinger, "Voting Behavior in Congressional Elections," paper delivered at American Political Science Association Convention, New Orleans, 1973. Observations consistent with those here, made in

different contexts are David Mayhew's emphasis on "the expected incumbent differential" and Charles Jones's conclusion that House campaigns are less likely to be "issue-oriented" than "image-oriented" and "issue-involved." Home style contributes to the congressman's "incumbent differential" and to his "image." Mayhew, *The Electoral Connection;* Jones, "The Role of the Campaign in Congressional Politics." From an election analysis perspective Walter Dean Burnham has recently emphasized the "office specific" nature of elections and the need to develop ways of looking at congressional elections that are not simply imitative of what we have done for presidential elections. Walter Dean Burnham, "Insulation and Responsiveness in Congressional Elections," *Political Science Quarterly* 90 (Fall 1975), pp. 411–435.

31. Kingdon, *Congressmen's Voting Decisions,* pp. 46–53.
32. *Congressional Record,* Daily Edition, July 23, 1974, H6962–H6963.
33. *Congressional Record,* Daily Edition, August 1, 1974, E5209–E5210.
34. Kingdon's respondents told him that they could explain one vote that went contrary to constituent expectations, but not "a string of votes." Kingdon, pp. 41–42.
35. Goffman, *Presentation of Self in Everyday Life,* pp. 136ff. A possible pattern of explanation requiring further research is that members explain their activities in different policy areas to distinctive groups in the constituency. See Clausen, *How Congressmen Decide,* especially his discussion of a special foreign policy constituency on pp. 225–226.
36. See also, Richard F. Fenno, "If, as Ralph Nader Says, Congress is 'The Broken Branch,' How Come We Love Our Congressmen So Much?", paper presented to Time, Inc. Symposium, Boston, Massachusetts, December 1972, and reprinted in *Congress in Change,* ed. Norman Ornstein (New York: Praeger, 1975).
37. Kenneth Prewitt, "Political Ambitions, Volunteerism and Electoral Accountability," *American Political Science Review* 64 (March 1970), 5–17.
38. Hanna F. Pitkin, *The Concept of Representation* (Berkeley: University of California Press, 1972). Pitkin recognizes the complexity of constituencies—see p. 220 of her book—but she does not incorporate the idea into her analysis.
39. Alan Abramowitz, "Name Familiarity, Reputation and the Incumbency Effect in a Congressional Election," *The Western Political Science Quarterly* 28 (December 1975), pp. 668–84; Albert Cover, "One Good Term Deserves Another: The Advantage of Incumbency in Congressional Elections," paper delivered at American Political Science Association Convention, Chicago, September 1976; John Ferejohn, "On the Decline of Competition in Congressional Elections," *American Political Science Review* 71 (March 1977), pp. 166–76; Morris Fiorina, "The Case of the Vanishing Marginals: The Bureaucracy Did It," *American Political Science Review* 71 (March 1977), pp. 177–81; Raymond Wolfinger and Robert Arseneau, "Voting Behavior in Congressional Elections." See also Edward N. Muller, "The Representation of Citizens by Political Authorities: Consequences for Regime Support," *American Political Science Review* 64 (December 1970), pp. 1149–66, esp. p. 1157; Glenn R. Parker and Roger H. Davidson, "Bases of Public Assessments of Government Performance: The Content of Congressional Evaluations," unpublished paper, University of California at Santa Barbara.
40. Mayhew, *The Electoral Connection.*
41. See Stephen Frantzich, "Congressional De-Recruitment: A New Look at Turnover in House Membership," unpublished paper, Hamilton College, 1975.
42. The argument of the last paragraphs is more fully contained in Richard Fenno, "Strengthening a Congressional Strength," paper presented at a conference on "The Role of Congress" sponsored by Time, Inc., Washington, 1975, reprinted in *Congress Reconsidered,* ed. Lawrence Dodd and Bruce Oppenheimer (New York: Praeger, 1977).

Reading 8.2

1. Kay Lehman Schlozman and John T. Tierney, "More of the Same: Washington Pressure Group Activity in a Decade of Change" (Paper delivered at the annual meeting of the American Political Science Association, Denver, Colo., Sept. 2–5, 1982, pp. 21–22.)
2. Theodore Lowi, *The End of Liberalism,* 2d ed. (New York: W. W. Norton & Co., 1979); Mancur Olson, *The Rise and Decline of Nations* (New Haven, Conn.: Yale University Press, 1982).
3. Mancur Olson, *The Logic of Collective Action* (Cambridge, Mass.: Harvard University

Press, 1971); Robert Salisbury, "An Exchange Theory of Interest Groups," *Midwest Journal of Political Science* 13 (February 1969), pp. 1–32; Terry M. Moe, *The Organization of Interests* (Chicago: University of Chicago Press, 1980).

4. David Truman's widely used definition of interest groups is "any group that, on the basis of one or more shared attitudes, makes certain claims upon other groups in the society for the establishment, maintenance or enhancement of forms of behavior that are implied by the shared attitudes." Truman, *The Governmental Process,* 2d ed. (New York: Alfred A. Knopf, 1971).
5. James Madison, "Federalist 10," in *The Federalist Papers,* 2d ed., ed. Roy P. Fairfield (Baltimore: Johns Hopkins University Press, 1981), p. 16.
6. L. Harmon Ziegler and Wayne Peak, *Interest Groups in American Society,* 2d ed. (Englewood Cliffs, N.J.: Prentice-Hall, 1972), p. 35.
7. Common Cause, *The Government Subsidy Squeeze* (Washington, D.C.: Common Cause, 1980), 11.
8. Truman, *The Governmental Process,* 519.
9. Carole Greenwald, *Group Power* (New York: Praeger, 1977), 305.
10. Lowi, *The End of Liberalism,* 63.
11. Murray Edelman, *The Politics of Symbolic Action* (Chicago: Markham Press, 1971).
12. Theodore J. Lowi, *Incomplete Conquest Governing America* (New York: Holt, Rinehart and Winston, 1976), 47.
13. Gabriel Almond and Sidney Verba, *The Civic Culture* (Boston: Little, Brown, 1963), Chs. 8 and 10.
14. *Ibid.,* pp. 246–47.

Reading 8.4

A small portion of this paper was adapted from a presentation delivered at a conference on the presidency and Congress at the White Burkitt Miller Center for Public Affairs, University of Virginia, January 24–25, 1980. The author is grateful to Michael Malbin, John Kessel, Austin Ranney, Tom Mann, and Anthony King for helpful comments.

1. Ralph K. Huitt, "The Outsider in the Senate: An Alternative Role," *American Political Science Review* 55 (September 1961), pp. 566–75.
2. Michael J. Robinson, "Three Faces of Congressional Media," in Thomas E. Mann and Norman J. Ornstein, eds., *The New Congress* (Washington, D.C.: American Enterprise Institute, 1981), pp. 55–98.
3. Robert G. Baker with Larry L. King, *Wheeling and Dealing* (New York: W. W. Norton & Co., 1978), p. 67.
4. On the impact of the class of '58 on the Senate of the 1960s and early 1970s, see Michael Foley, *The New Senate: Liberal Influence on A Conservative Institution, 1959–1972* (New Haven, Conn.: Yale University Press, 1980).
5. See, as examples, Norman J. Ornstein, ed., *Congress in Change: Evolution and Reform* (New York: Praeger, 1975); Roger H. Davidson and Walter J. Oleszek, *Congress against Itself* (Bloomington: Indiana University Press, 1977); Lawrence Dodd and Bruce Oppenheimer, eds., *Congress Reconsidered,* 2d ed. (Washington, D.C.: Congressional Quarterly Press, 1981); and Mann and Ornstein, *New Congress.*
6. John F. Bibby, Thomas E. Mann, and Norman J. Ornstein, *Vital Statistics on Congress 1980* (Washington, D.C.: American Enterprise Institute, 1980), pp. 71–73.
7. Quoted in Norman J. Ornstein, ed., *The Role of the Legislature in Western Democracies* (Washington, D.C.: American Enterprise Institute, 1981), p. 163.
8. It should be noted that this definition of reciprocity is much broader than that used by Donald R. Matthews in *U.S. Senators and Their World* (New York: Vintage, 1960) in his discussion of folkways in Chapter 5.
9. Evidence gathered from appropriate *Congressional Directories.* See also Robinson, "Three Faces," p. 83.
10. On public interest groups, see Jeffrey Berry, *Lobbying for the People* (Princeton, N.J.: Princeton University Press, 1978) and Andrew MacFarland, *Public Interest Lobbies: Decision Making on Energy* (Washington, D.C.: American Enterprise Institute, 1976).
11. These figures come from Marc Kaufman, "Study Ties Growth to Lobbyists," *Washington Star,* October 6, 1980.
12. The incident was made even more embarrassing for the president when Mineta was asked by newsmen whether he was upset by the oversight. He responded that he was not unhappy at all: he thought that Prime Minister Ohira was the leader of Ireland!
13. *Congressional Insight* 5, no. 26 (June 26, 1981).
14. See Martin Schram, "Reagan the Tax Lobbyist: An Artist at Work," *Washington Post,* August 13, 1981, p. A3.

Reading 9.2

1. *Ashwander* v. *TVA,* 297 U.S. 288, 347 (1936) (Brandeis, J., concurring), quoting from *Liverpool, N.Y. & P.S.S. Co.* v. *Emigration Commissioners,* 113 U.S. 33 (1885).
2. *INS* v. *Chadha,* 462 U.S. 919, 952 (1983).
3. *Ibid.*, p. 958.
4. *Ibid.*, p. 959.
5. *Ibid.*, p. 951.
6. *Ibid.*, p. 967.
7. *Ibid.*, p. 968.
8. *Chadha* v. *INS,* 634 F.2d 408 (9th Cir. 1980); *Clark* v. *Valeo,* 559 F.2d 642, 650 n. 10 (D.C. Cir. 1977); and *Atkins* v. *United States,* 556 F.2d 1028, 1059 (Ct. Cl. 1977).
9. *AFGE* v. *Pierce,* 697 F.2d 303 (D.C. Cir. 1982); *Consumers Union, Inc.* v. *FTC,* 691 F.2d 575 (D.C. Cir. 1982); and *Consumer Energy Council of America* v. *FERC,* 673 F.2d 425 (D.C. Cir. 1982).
10. *AFGE* v. *Pierce,* 697 F.2d at 308.
11. *Ibid.*
12. Louis Fisher, *Constitutional Conflicts between Congress and the President* (Princeton, N.J.: Princeton University Press, 1985), pp. 164–166.
13. *Weekly Compilation of Presidential Documents,* vol. 20 (July 18, 1984), p. 1040.
14. H. Rept. No. 916, 98th Cong., 2d Sess. (1984), p. 48.
15. Louis Fisher, *Presidential Spending Power* (Princeton, N.J.: Princeton University Press, 1975), pp. 75–98.
16. *Sibbach* v. *Wilson & Co.,* 312 U.S. 1, 14–15 (1941); and *INS* v. *Chadha,* 462 U.S. at 935, n.9.
17. Military Construction Appropriation Act, Pub. L. No. 98-473, 98 Stat. 1881 (sec. 108), and 1882 (sec. 118).
18. 40 U.S.C. §484(e)(6); 41 C.F.R. §101-47.304-12(f).
19. *City of Alexandria* v. *United States,* 3 Ct. Cl. 667, 675–678 (1983).
20. *City of Alexandria* v. *United States,* 737 F.2d 1022, 1026 (C.A.F.C. 1984).
21. See 41 Op. Att'y Gen. 230 (1955) and 41 Op. Att'y Gen. 300 (1957).
22. *Congressional Record,* vol. 131, H137 (daily ed. January 24, 1985).
23. Trade and Tariff Act, Pub. L. No. 98-573, 98 Stat. 3014 (1984).
24. H. Rept. No. 1156, 98th Cong., 2d Sess. (1984), p. 151.
25. 19 U.S.C. §2191 (1982).
26. Reorganization Act Amendments, Pub. L. No. 98-614, §3(a)(1), 98 Stat. 3192 (1984).
27. Pub. L. No. 97-86, §203, 95 Stat. 1102 (1981).
28. Pub. L. No. 97-377, 96 Stat. 1846 (1982).
29. Pub. L. No. 98-473, 98 Stat. 1916–1918, 1935–1937 (1984).
30. "Legislative Veto after Chadha," *Hearings before the House Committee on Rules,* 98th Cong., 2d Sess. (1984), p. 11.
31. H.R. 3939, 98th Cong., 1st Sess. (1983).
32. *Congressional Record,* vol. 129, S17081-84 (daily ed. November 18, 1983) and 130 Cong. Rec. S926 (daily ed. February 3, 1984).
33. H.R. 5759, 98th Cong., 2d Sess. (1984).
34. D. C. Home Rule Act. Pub. L. No. 98-473, 98 Stat. 1974–75 (1984).

Reading 9.3

The author is indebted to the Marquette University Committee on Research and the Johnson Fund of the American Philosophical Society for the funding that made this research possible. He also wishes to thank the anonymous reviewers for their helpful suggestions.

1. Because data were collected in the context of another study, no effort was or can be made to separate cases and projects. Federal projects constituted about 10 percent of all incoming cases 1977–1978, with little variance across offices. For about one-third of the sample of senators and representatives, data were obtained from more than one of their offices, yielding more accurate estimates than would be had by, say, interviewing only in Washington. When conflicting estimates emerged between or among offices, follow-up phone calls or personal interviews were used, averages were computed, or the more credible estimate was relied upon, depending on the circumstance. Clearly, these procedures cannot yield flawless data, but they give the best data available.
2. Estimates come mainly from staff members. Overall, senators in 1977–1978 were reported to average about 3.7 hours weekly (a median of 2.9) on cases and projects; members of the House had a mean of 5.9 hours and a median of 3.0.
3. This variable was coded as "0," "1," "2," or "3 or more." In the Senate sample, 17 percent used three or more devices to solicit cases, 24 percent used two devices, 26 percent used one, and 26 percent claimed not to do anything. In the House comparable figures were 28, 26, 27, and 15 percent. Seven percent of the Senate sample and 4 percent

of the House sample merely answered affirmatively without indicating how many of these devices were used.

4. As a check on this variable, and to provide comparability with other studies, a separate analysis was done on the percentage of total casework- and projects-related staff located in state and district offices. The correlation between this staffing variable and the percentage of casework done at home was .67 for the House and .79 for the Senate. The results of the analysis were essentially the same as those reported in the text.
5. These regions were defined as follows: East: Connecticut, Maine, Massachusetts, New Hampshire, New Jersey, New York, Pennsylvania, Rhode Island, Vermont; South: Alabama, Arkansas, Florida, Georgia, Louisiana, Mississippi, North Carolina, South Carolina, Tennessee, Texas, Virginia; Border: Delaware, Kentucky, Maryland, Missouri, Oklahoma, West Virginia; Midwest: Illinois, Indiana, Iowa, Kansas, Michigan, Minnesota, Nebraska, North Dakota, Ohio, South Dakota, Wisconsin; West: Alaska, Arizona, California, Colorado, Hawaii, Idaho, Montana, Nevada, New Mexico, Oregon, Utah, Washington, Wyoming.
6. Representatives elected before 1964 were only half as active in stimulating casework requests as were those elected since. In the Senate, members elected before 1964 were only one-fourth as energetic. Once in office, members relax the rate of growth of constituency service activities (Born, 1982).
7. Using the 1976 results instead of the 1970–1976 electoral trend—as did Cain, Ferejohn, and Fiorina (1981), who with a smaller sample found a relationship—produces no noticeable difference except in terms of decentralization of casework to home offices and in the proportion of casework-related staff located away from Washington. The implication is that for some staffing decisions, *recent* electoral experience may be crucial. When districts have "always" or "on average" been marginal, perhaps members are less sanguine about "quick fix" solutions such as staff allocations.
8. One might, of course, argue that the size of staffs and case loads are simultaneously determined: that larger staffs generate more cases. That is possible, but not probable. Hustling cases might produce larger case loads, and so might moving staffs to district offices, but is doubtful that members would allocate staffs to handling large numbers of cases until and unless those cases actually developed. (Dropping the case load variable from the equations has no noticeable effect on the other coefficients. Nor does the coefficient for the size of staff have any effect in an equation modeling casework loads.)

References

Born, Richard. 1982. Perquisite employment in the U.S. House of Representatives, 1960–1976: The influence of generational change. *American Politics Quarterly* 10 (July): 347–362.

Breslin, Janet. 1977. Constituent service. In U.S. Congress, Senate, Commission on the Operation of the Senate. *Senators: offices, ethics, and pressures.* 94th Cong., 2d sess. Committee Print, pp. 19–36.

Brown, Stephen P., Beth C. Fuchs, and John P. Hoadley. 1979. Congressional perquisites and the vanishing marginals: The case of the class of '74. Paper presented at the Annual Meeting of the American Political Science Association, Washington, D.C., August 31–September 3, 1979.

Cain, Bruce E., John A. Ferejohn, and Morris P. Fiorina. 1981. The electoral connection in comparative perspective: Constituency service in Great Britain and the U.S. Paper presented at the Annual Meeting of the Midwest Political Science Association, Cincinnati, Ohio, April 16–18, 1981.

Cavanagh, Thomas E. 1979. Rational allocation of congressional resources: Member time and staff use in the House. In Douglas W. Rae and Theodore J. Eismeier, eds., *Public policy and public choice.* Beverly Hills, Calif.: Sage:209–47.

Clark, Harold D. 1978. Determinants of constituency service behavior in Canada: A multivariate analysis. Paper presented at the Annual Meeting of the Midwest Political Science Association, Chicago, April 22, 1978.

Clark, Harold D., Richard G. Price, and Robert Krause, 1975. Constituency service among Canadian provincial legislators: Basic findings and a test of three hypotheses. *Canadian Journal of Political Science,* 8 (December):520–42.

Cover, Albert D. 1980. Contacting congressional constituents: Some patterns of perquisite use. *American Journal of Political Science* 24 (February):125–35.

Cranor, John D., and Joseph W. Westphal. 1978. Congressional district offices, federal programs, and electoral benefits: Some observations on the passing of the marginal representatives, 1974–1976. Paper presented at the Annual Meeting of the Midwest Political Science Association, Chicago, April 20–22, 1978.

Davidson, Roger H. 1969. *The role of the congressman.* New York: Pegasus.

Dodd, Lawrence C. 1977. Congress and the quest for power. In Lawrence C. Dodd and Bruce I. Oppenheimer, eds., *Congress reconsidered.* New York: Praeger:269–307.

Dowse, R. E. 1972. The MP and his surgery. In Dick Leonard and Valentine Herman, eds., *The backbencher and Parliament: A reader.* London: Macmillan:46–60.

Elazar, Daniel J. 1972. *American federalism: A view from the states.* 2d ed. New York: Thomas Y. Crowell.

Elling, Richard C. 1979. The utility of state legislative casework as a means of oversight. *Legislative Studies Quarterly* 4 (August): 353–80.

_______. 1980. State legislative casework and state administrative performance. *Administration and Society* 12 (November): 327–56.

Eulau, Heinz, and Paul D. Karps. 1977. The puzzle of representation: Specifying components of responsiveness. *Legislative Studies Quarterly* 2 (August):233–54.

Fenno, Richard F. 1973. *Congressmen in committees.* Boston: Little, Brown.

_______. 1978. *Home style: House members in their districts.* Boston: Little, Brown.

Fiorina, Morris P. 1977. *Congress: The keystone of the Washington establishment.* New Haven, Conn.: Yale University Press.

_______. 1981. Some problems in studying the effects of resource allocation in congressional elections. *American Journal of Political Science* 25 (August), pp. 543–67.

Frantzich, Stephen. 1979. Who makes our laws? The legislative effectiveness of members of the U.S. Congress. *Legislative Studies Quarterly* 4 (August):409–28.

Hammond, Susan Webb. 1977. The operation of senators' offices. In U.S. Congress, Senate, Commission on the Operation of the Senate, *Senators: Offices, ethics, and pressures.* 94th Cong., 2d sess. Committee Print, pp. 4–18.

Jacobson, Gary C. 1981. Incumbents' advantages in the 1978 U.S. congressional elections. *Legislative Studies Quarterly,* 6 (May):183–200.

Jewell, Malcolm E. 1982. *Representation in state legislatures.* Lexington: University Press of Kentucky.

Johannes, John R. 1979. Casework as a technique of U.S. congressional oversight of the executive. *Legislative Studies Quarterly,* 4 (August):325–51.

_______. 1980. The distribution of casework in the U.S. Congress: An uneven burden. *Legislative Studies Quarterly* 5 (November):517–44.

Johannes, John R., and John C. McAdams. 1981. The congressional incumbency effect: Is it casework, policy compatibility, or something else? *American Journal of Political Science* 25 (August):512–42.

Kumbhat, M. C., and Y. M. Marican. 1976. Constituent orientation among Malaysian state legislators. *Legislative Studies Quarterly* 1 (August):389–404.

LeDuc, Lawrence, Jr., and Walter L. White. 1974. The role of opposition in a one-party dominant system: The case of Ontario. *Canadian Journal of Political Science* 7 (March):86–100.

McAdams, John C. 1981. Styles of representation in the U.S. House: 1977–1978. Paper presented at the Annual Meeting of the American Political Science Association, New York, September 3–6, 1981.

Macartney, John D. 1975. Political staffing: A view from the district. Ph.D. diss., University of California, Los Angeles.

Mayhew, David R. 1974. *Congress: The electoral connection.* New Haven, Conn.: Yale University Press.

Mohapatra, Manindra Kumar. 1976. The ombudsmanic role of legislators in an Indian state. *Legislative Studies Quarterly* 1 (August):295–314.

O'Donnell, Thomas J. 1982. The effects of electoral shifts and legislative responsibilities on the allocation of time by congressmen. Paper presented at the Annual Meeting of the Midwest Political Science Association, Milwaukee, Wis., April 29–May 1, 1982.

Parker, Glenn R. 1980. Sources of change in congressional district attentiveness. *American Journal of Political Science,* 24 (February): 115–24.

———. 1981. Interpreting candidate awareness in U.S. congressional elections. *Legislative Studies Quarterly* 6 (May):219–34.

Parker, Glenn R., and Suzanne L. Parker. 1982. The causes and consequences of congressional district attention. Paper presented at the Annual Meeting of the American Political Science Association, Denver, Colorado, September 2–5, 1982.

Peterson, Steven A., and William H. Dutton. 1981. Errand-boy behavior and local legislators. Paper presented at the Annual Meeting of the Midwest Political Science Association, Cincinnati, Ohio, April 16–18, 1981.

Powell, Linda W. 1982. Constituency service and electoral margin in the Congress. Paper presented at the Annual Meeting of the American Political Science Association, Denver, Colorado.

Rundquist, Barry S., and Lyman A. Kellstadt. 1982. Congressional interaction with constituents: A career perspective. Paper presented at the Annual Meeting of the American Political Science Association, Denver, Colorado.

Walker, Jack L. 1977. Setting the agenda in the U.S. Senate: A theory of problem selection. *British Journal of Political Science* 7 (October):423–45.

Yiannakis, Diana Evans. 1979. House members' communications styles: Newsletters and press releases. Paper presented at the Annual Meeting of the Midwest Political Science Association, Chicago, April 19–21, 1979.

———. 1981. The grateful electorate: Casework and congressional elections. *American Journal of Political Science* 25 (August):568–80.

Reading 9.4

1. James L. Sundquist, *The Decline and Resurgence of Congress* (Washington, D.C.: The Brookings Institution, 1981), p. 39.
2. The timetable for 1986 has different dates, as follows:

- January 10—The "snapshot" of the deficit for FY 1986 is taken.
- January 15—OMB and CBO report to GAO.
- January 20—GAO issues the report to the President, based on the findings of CBO and OMB.
- February 8—The President submits his FY '87 budget.
- March 1—The order takes effect.

Any cost of living allowance (COLA) scheduled to take effect on January 1 would be deferred beginning January 1, 1986, under this plan. If it is later determined that a sequestration order will not take effect, the COLAs would be restored retroactive to January 1.

Reading 9.5

1. For additional discussions of agenda setting, see Cobb and Elder (1972), Bachrach and Baratz (1970), and Schattschneider (1960).
2. Both quotes from the *New York Times*, June 17, 1980.

References

Arnold, R. Douglas. *Congress and the Bureaucracy.* New Haven, Conn.: Yale University Press, 1979.

Bailey, Stephen K. *Congress Makes a Law.* New York: Columbia University Press, 1950.

Berman, Daniel M. *A Bill Becomes a Law.* New York: Macmillan, 1966.

Eidenberg, Eugene, and Roy Morey. *An Act of Congress.* New York: W. W. Norton, 1969.

Ippolito, Dennis S. *The Budget and National Politics.* San Francisco: W. H. Freeman, 1978.

Jones, Charles O. *An Introduction to the Study of Public Policy,* 2nd ed. North Scituate, Mass.: Duxbury Press, 1981.

Jones, Charles O., and Dieter Matthes. "Policy Formation." *Encyclopedia of Policy Studies.* New York: Marcel Dekker, 1982.

LeLoup, Lance T. *The Fiscal Congress: Legislative Control of the Budget.* Westport, Conn.: Greenwood Press, 1980.

Mansfield, Harvey C., ed. *Congress Against the President.* New York: Praeger Publishers, 1975.

Neustadt, Richard E. *Presidential Power.* New York: John Wiley & Sons, 1960.

Peabody, Robert L., et al. *To Enact a Law: Congress and Campaign Financing.* New York: Praeger Publishers, 1972.

Price, David E. *Who Makes the Laws?* Cambridge, Mass.: Schenkman, 1972.

Ranney, Austin, ed. *Political Science and Public Policy.* Chicago: Markham, 1968.

Redman, Eric. *The Dance of Legislation.* New York: Simon and Schuster, 1973.

Ripley, Randall B., and Grace A. Franklin. *Congress, the Bureaucracy, and Public Policy* rev. ed. Homewood, Ill.: Dorsey Press, 1980.

Schick, Allen. *Congress and Money.* Washington, D.C.: The Urban Institute, 1980.

Sundquist, James L. *Politics and Policy: The Eisenhower, Kennedy, and Johnson Years.* Washington, D.C.: Brookings Institution, 1968.

Reading 9.6

References

Huntington, S. P. *The Common Defense.* New York: Columbia University Press, 1961.

Lowi, T. J. "Making Democracy Safe for the World: National Politics and Foreign Policy." In *Domestic Sources of Foreign Policy.* ed. J. N. Rosenau. New York: Free Press, 1967.

Reading 9.7

1. In recent years the study of policy effects has effloresced among analysts writing in a number of different scholarly traditions. The range of writings on policies substantially shaped by Congress includes the following: James T. Bonnen, "The Distribution of Benefits from Cotton Price Supports," in *Problems in Public Expenditure Analysis,* ed. Samuel B. Chase (Washington, D.C.: Brookings Institution, 1968); on urban renewal: Theodore J. Lowi, *The End of Liberalism* (New York: W. W. Norton, 1969), Chapter 9; Richard Urban and Richard Mancke, "Federal Regulation of Whisky Labelling: From the Repeal of Prohibition to the Present," *Journal of Law and Economics* 15 (1972): 411–26; Richard S. Smerne, Alvin Rabushka, and Helen A. Scott, "Serving the Elderly—An Illustration of the Niskanen Effect," *Public Choice* 13 (1972):81–90; A. Bruce Johnson, "Federal Aid and Area Redevelopment," *Journal of Law and Economics* 14 (1971):245–84; James W. Davis, Jr., and Kenneth M. Dolbeare, "Selective Service and Military Manpower: Induction and Deferment Policies in the 1960s" Chapter 5 in *Political Science and Public Policy,* ed. Austin Ranney (Chicago: Markham, 1968); Yale Brozen, "The Effect of Statutory Minimum Wage Increases on Teen-Age Employment," *Journal of Law and Economics* 12 (1969):109–22; on national policies generally: Charles L. Schultze et al., Setting National Priorities, the 1973 Budget (Washington, D.C.: Brookings, 1972), Chapter 15. There is an analysis of the attention (or rather the lack of it) that Congress gave to impact at the time it considered a policy decision in Aaron Wildavsky, "The Politics of ABM," *Commentary,* November 1969, pp. 55–63.
2. Thus, for example, this critique: "The people of this country . . . are, as it seems to me, thoroughly tired of the stagnation of business and the general inaction of Congress. They are disgusted to see year after year go by and great measures affecting the business and political interests of the country accumulation at the doors of Congress and never reach the stage of action." The author was Henry Cabot Lodge in 1889. Quoted in George B. Galloway, *History of the House of Representatives* (New York: Thomas Y. Crowell, 1961), p. 133.
3. Roger H. Davidson, David M. Kovenock, and Michael K. O'Leary, *Congress in Crisis* (Belmont, Calif.: Wadsworth, 1966), pp. 56–59.
4. See G. L. Bach, *Making Monetary and Fiscal Policy* (Washington, D.C.: Brookings Institution, 1971), pp. 118, 155.
5. The only theories of legislative logrolling that make any sense are the ones that impose information costs on observers. Thus Barry on the "pork barrel": "[I]t is perhaps easy to guess that logrolling under conditions of imperfect information will tend to produce over-investment in projects which yield specific benefits to determinate groups, because such benefits are highly visible to the beneficiaries whereas costs are not so visible to the general taxpayer." Brian Barry, *Political Argument,* (London: Routledge and Kegan Paul, 1965), p. 318.
6. John F. Manley, *The Politics of Finance: The House Committee on Ways and Means* (Boston: Little, Brown, 1970), p. 309. Coleman makes the relevant point that Keynesian macroeconomics is after all an "organic-type theory" not built by aggregating individual preferences. "The fact that Keynes' goal is a benevolent one, supposedly beneficial to the people, has often obscured the fact that its perspective is that of the state, and that there is no microeconomic substructure through which individual pursuit of their interests leads to a Keynesian policy." "Individual Interests and Collective Action," pp. 53–54.
7. Edward C. Banfield, "Revenue Sharing in Theory and Practice," *The Public Interest,* Spring 1971, pp. 41–42.
8. On struggles over the corps under Roosevelt and Truman, see Arthur Maass, *Muddy Waters: The Army Engineers and the Nation's Rivers* (Cambridge, Mass.: Harvard University Press, 1951), Chapters 3, 5. Par-

ticularism is no doubt universal. It is hard to top this example drawn from the experience of the Italian parliament of the late 19th century: "The deputies, in fact, look upon themselves as agents to procure favors for their constituents, and a striking illustration of the extent to which this is carried is furnished by the difficulty the government found when it managed the railroads in running fast express trains, on account of the interference of the members of the chamber, who insisted that all the trains passing through their districts should stop at way stations." A. L. Lowell, *Governments and Parties in Continental Europe* (Boston: Houghton Mifflin, 1896), I:220.

9. Sets of voters who are organized for political action should not be confused with sets of voters who have intense preferences. Whether the latter become the former depends upon whether there are incentives to organize and stay organized. One specific pattern is that producers have better incentives than consumers. On the general point, see Mancur Olson, Jr., *The Logic of Collective Action* (Cambridge, Mass.: Harvard University Press, 1965), pp. 125–31; and Barry, *Political Argument*, p. 273.
10. E. E. Schattschneider, *Party Government* (New York: Rinehart, 1959), p. 194. In the 1930s, 1931 and 1936 were the only years in which the fiscal effects of tax and spending activities of American governments (at all levels) were clearly countercyclical. In both cases the Keynesian instruments were apparently veterans' bonus bills passed over presidential vetoes (Hoover's and Roosevelt's). See E. Cary Brown, "Fiscal Policies in the Thirties: A Reappraisal," *American Economic Review* 46 (1956): 483.
11. "It is difficult to imagine any other issue on which Congress has been less responsive to public sentiment for a longer period of time." Hazel Erskine, "The Polls: Gun Control," *Public Opinion Quarterly* 36 (1972): 456.
12. There is an analysis of agricultural clientelism in Lowi, *The End of Liberalism*, pp. 102–15. A clientele system less developed in Congress than in some European parliaments is the one in education. With the nationalization of educational financing it seems likely that the two congressional houses will sooner or later create independent education committees (separate from labor) whose members will service education groups in bipartisan fashion.
13. The best analysis of the impact of Congressmen's electoral needs on the organization of the Executive Branch is in Harold Seidman, *Politics, Position, and Power: The Dynamics of Federal Organization* (New York: Oxford University Press, 1970): Chapters 2, 5.

Reading 10.1

1. For a concise analysis of the emergence of Congress as an institution, see Randall B. Ripley, *Congress: Process and Policy* (New York: W. W. Norton, 1975), pp. 27–57; and Malcolm E. Jewell and Samuel C. Patterson, *The Legislative Process in the United States*, 3d ed. (New York: Random House, 1977), pp. 30–59.
2. Samuel P. Huntington, *Political Order in Changing Societies* (New Haven: Yale University Press, 1968), pp. 93–139.
3. George B. Galloway, *Congress at the Crossroads* (New York: Thomas Y. Crowell, 1946), p. 334.

A Note on the Type

The text of this book was set in 10/12 Trump Medieval via computer-driven cathode-ray tube. Designed in 1950 by Georg Trump, this typeface is based on classical letterforms and is characterized by an incised, streamlined quality. The balanced weight of the letters, the large x-height, and squared curves enhance legibility. Trump was originally cut and cast by the C. E. Weber Type Foundry of Stuttgart, West Germany.

Composed by Eastern Graphics, Binghamton, New York

Printed and bound by Kingsport Press, Kingsport, Tennessee